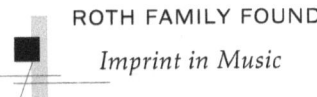

ROTH FAMILY FOUNDATION

Imprint in Music

Michael P. Roth
and Sukey Garcetti
have endowed this
imprint to honor the
memory of their parents,
Julia and Harry Roth,
whose deep love of music
they wish to share
with others.

The publisher and the University of California Press Foundation gratefully acknowledge the generous support of the Roth Family Foundation Imprint in Music, established by a major gift from Sukey and Gil Garcetti and Michael P. Roth.

Cursed Questions

Cursed Questions

On Music and Its Social Practices

Richard Taruskin

UNIVERSITY OF CALIFORNIA PRESS

University of California Press
Oakland, California

© 2020 by Richard Taruskin
Music examples prepared by Bryce Cannell

Library of Congress Cataloging-in-Publication Data

Names: Taruskin, Richard, author.
Title: Cursed questions : on music and its social practices /
   Richard Taruskin.
Description: Oakland : University of California Press, [2020] |
   Includes bibliographical references and index.
Identifiers: LCCN 2019032946 (print) | LCCN 2019032947 (ebook) |
   ISBN 9780520344280 (cloth) | ISBN 9780520344297 (paperback) |
   ISBN 9780520975453 (ebook)
Subjects: LCSH: Music—Historiography. | Musicology. | Music—Social
   aspects. | Music—Philosophy and aesthetics.
Classification: LCC ML3797 .T37 2020 (print) | LCC ML3797 (ebook) |
   DDC 780.72—dc23
LC record available at https://lccn.loc.gov/2019032946
LC ebook record available at https://lccn.loc.gov/2019032947

Manufactured in the United States of America

29 28 27 26 25 24 23 22 21 20
10 9 8 7 6 5 4 3 2 1

In Memory of Joseph Kerman
1924–2013

CONTENTS

Introduction	1
1. The History of What?	30
2. Did Somebody Say Censorship?	41
3. Haydn and the Enlightenment?	72
4. Is There a Baby in the Bathwater? *On aesthetic autonomy*	99
5. Shall We Change the Subject? A Music Historian Reflects	147
6. "Alte Musik" or "Early Music"? *On pseudohistory*	180
7. Nicht blutbefleckt?	208
8. What Else? *On musical representation*	226
9. Unanalyzable, Is It?	252
10. Essence *or* Context? *On musical ontology*	282
11. But Aren't They All Invented? *On tradition*	306
12. Which Way Is Up? *On the sociology of taste*	340
13. A Walking Translation? *On musicology east and west*	400
Index	*437*

Introduction

> *The patience to ask and to keep asking questions, without the assurance of agreement or the availability of methods apt to elicit it, is the philosopher's gift. It is an expression of intellectual hope, and the repudiation of philosophy is a counsel of despair.*
> —KIERAN SETIYA[1]

I

Laß die heil'gen Parabolen,
Laß die frommen Hypothesen—
Suche die verdammten Fragen
Ohne Umschweif uns zu lösen.
—HEINRICH HEINE, ZUM LAZARUS, I (1853)

Брось свои иносказанья	Bros' svoí inoskazan'ya
И гипотезы пустые!	I gipotezï pustïye!
На проклятые вопросы	Na proklyatïye voprosï
Дай ответы нам прямые!	Dai otvetï nam pryamïye!

—HEINE, *K LAZARYU*, AS LOOSELY TRANSLATED BY
M. L. MIKHAILOV, *SOVREMENNIK*, 1858, NO. 3: 125

MIKHAILOV'S VERSION IN ENGLISH:
Give up your allegories
And empty hypotheses!
To cursed questions
Give us straight answers!

Heine's ironic quatrain, in the instantly famous translation by the poet and underground revolutionary Mikhaíl Larionovich Mikhailov, bequeathed a meme to the Russian language. Since the middle of the nineteenth century, the words "cursed

---

1. Kieran Setiya, "Monk Justice," *London Review of Books*, 30 August 2018, 42.

questions" (*proklyatïye voprosï*) have stood in Russian for all the relentless imponderables, be they social, political, aesthetic or eschatological, that, as Mikhail Epstein puts it, "baffle the mind and torment the heart."² They are unanswerable, and yet, as Allen Tate once said, they are "perpetually necessary and . . . perpetually impossible," and their very intolerability "has its own glory."³ They are ineluctable. They are vital. They are addictive. This is the book of an addict.

Mikhailov's translation, you may have noticed, is not quite accurate. Besides the liberties of diction and syntax one will find in any poetic translation, there is an apparent howler in the second line. In place of Heine's "pious hypotheses" (*frommen Hypothesen*), Mikhailov has "empty" ones (*gipotezï pustïye*), and he also leaves out the adjective *heil'gen* (holy) in the first line without replacing it. That was because, in addition to all the usual necessities and impossibilities, Russian writers faced the most stringent censorship in post-Napoleonic Europe.⁴ They had to disguise all discussion of social, moral, or political issues as innocent hypotheses and allegories about historiography or philosophy or the arts. Cursed questions were all they had.

And that is why Russians, and we who study them, are such inveterate readers between the lines and so perpetually conscious of limits to what may be said out loud, and not just in Russia. And that is why, although it touches little on the Russian subject matter I habitually address, I have given this book a title out of Russian intellectual history. When the University of California Press invited me to compile a set of essays to complement those in *The Danger of Music*, the volume they brought out in 2010, I surveyed the titles of my unpublished or uncollected texts and saw, not exactly to my surprise, how many were cast as rhetorical questions, like so many Russian titles of old, such as Alexander Herzen's *Kto vinovat?* (Who Is to Blame?) of 1846, or Nikolai Chernyshevsky's *Chto delat'?* (What Is to Be Done?) of 1863 (both appropriated by Lenin), or Tolstoy's "Tak chto zhe nam delat'?" (roughly, "OK, So What Should We Do Once and for All?") of 1886, or, in a less enigmatic and riskier vein, Nikolai Nekrasov's *Komu na Rusi zhit' khorosho?* (Who Can Live Happily in Russia?) of 1862. Interrogative titles became my principle of selection.

It was more than just a titling conceit. My education, upbringing, and cultural heritage have predisposed me to share in some measure the restless outlook of the

---

2. Mikhail Epstein (Mikhaíl Naumovich Epshteyn), *Slovo i molchaniye: Metafizika russkoy literaturï* (Moscow: Vïsshaya shkola, 2006), 9 ("неразрешимы для ума и мучительны для сердца").

3. Allen Tate, "Is Literary Criticism Possible?" (1950), in Tate, *The Man of Letters in the Modern World* (New York: Meridian Books, 1955), 174.

4. Sure enough, the text Mikhailov had submitted had *svyatïye* (sacred, holy) in place of *pustïye*, unacceptable because of the ironic way Heine linked the words *pious* and *holy*, which must connote truth, with *Umschweif* (mealy-mouthed circumlocution) in the last line. See Vadim Serov, *Entsiklopedicheskiy slovar' krïlatïkh slov i vïrazheniy* (Encyclopedic dictionary of winged words and expressions), s.v. проклятые вопросы: http://bibliotekar.ru/encSlov/15/230.htm (accessed 4 April 2018).

old Russian *intelligentsia*—a word that went into Yiddish, too, and thus into my parents' vocabulary so that I have known it since childhood. I am, perhaps as a result, inclined to what may look like a catechistical expository manner. In fact it is anything but that. The difference between a catechism and the tradition of the cursed question is that the answers in a catechism (or in any pseudo-dialogue, whether between Socrates and Glaucon or between Igor Stravinsky and Robert Craft) were in place before any questions were asked. The questions in such writings are merely pretexts or eliciting devices, whereas in the realm of the truly accursed the questions come first, the answers never.

Indeed, addicts of the cursed questions have often implied that any question that can be answered is not worth asking. Eternal pondering and wondering were both necessary and sufficient. The greatest virtuoso of the cursed question at its most cosmic, perhaps, was the religious philosopher Nikolai Berdyayev (1874–1948), who, in a famous essay on the parable of the Grand Inquisitor from Dostoyevsky's last novel, wrote that "the 'cursed questions' that tormented some nobody named Ivan Karamazov, entailing God, immortality, freedom, suffering, and universal salvation, accord better with the heights and depths of real moral problems than all the commandments and prohibitions of petty, worldly morality, which seek merely to train people for polite society."[5] "Petty, worldly morality" was Berdyayev's definition of what most of us would call matters of life and death. Dostoyevsky's great achievement was to devise a parable that was as inconclusive as it was compelling.

Is that really a strength? The fear that an endlessly deferred answer is a failure or a weakness was what gave rise to the concept of the cursed question to begin with, and it is still with us, still potent, still doing harm. It is at the root of science envy, that great bane of the humanities. Science makes progress; shouldn't we do the same? The mark of scientific progress, according to a philosopher, David J. Chalmers, who studies it, is "collective convergence to the truth"—something his own field seems never to achieve.[6] The lack of collective convergence, the fact that "philosophical arguments seem not to lead to agreement but to sophisticated disagreement" (15), is the curse to which this introduction, and indeed this whole book, is devoted. It has been known to scare people off. The Harvard logician Harry Sheffer gave Isaiah Berlin a temporary fright at a crossroads in his career, when he was returning to Oxford from his wartime duty as a diplomat in the USA, remarking

---

5. N. A. Berdyayev, *Sub specie aeternitatis: Opïtï filosofskiye, sotsial'nïye i literaturnnïye (1900–1906 g.)* (St. Petersburg: Pirozhkov, 1907), 106 (rearranged for concision).

6. "Why Isn't There More Progress in Philosophy?," the 2013 Annual Lecture to the Royal Institute of Philosophy, available at www.youtube.com/watch?v=uUfz6oahp2Q. A revised text is published at http://consc.net/papers/progress.pdf. The quoted phrase is on p. 2. Further page references will be made in the main text.

that in philosophy the same old questions kept on being raised. One had no hope of increasing permanent knowledge. All night long, sleepless on the flight back to England, Berlin considered what Sheffer had said and concluded that he was right. He wanted to study something which might change people's understanding of life, to know more at the end of his life than he did at the beginning.[7]

He got over it, realizing that the "hope of increasing permanent knowledge" was a form of utopian thinking. This book is dedicated to that Heinian disillusion. It is a book intent, as Samuel Beckett instructs us, on failing better.[8]

To be sure, Chalmers admits, "sophistication is itself a kind of progress," and yet he confesses that the practice of philosophy leads inevitably to "a lowering of expectations." But this, I'd say, is also a kind of progress: progress away from utopian thinking. Should that not suffice? Is the kind of solution that drives convergence necessarily the outcome we should seek?

Its superiority may be challenged, I think, on at least two grounds. The first would dispute the notion that collective convergence of opinion is a valid measure of truth. Even the hard sciences abound in counterexamples, discarded theories (phlogiston, geocentrism, bodily humors) that once commanded consensus. We can define knowledge as "justified true belief"[9] and yet acknowledge that justification, hence our notion of truth, can only be provisional. The "fallibilist" principle, part and parcel of what is now considered basic scientific method, asserts as its fundamental premise that we can have certainty not of truth but only of falsehood, and that to hold something true is only to say that it has not yet been proven false. That thesis has made a different sort of progress as it moved from natural science (where it was prominently associated with Karl Popper)[10] into moral philosophy (where it has been associated with names like Isaiah Berlin and Bernard Williams). Big philosophical problems like my cursed questions may not be soluble, but they can be whittled down, just as objective reality may not be directly or completely known, but it can be approached through the exposure and elimination of error.

The second argument against the assumed superiority of science would question the process through which convergence is obtained. In the three cases just cited (phlogiston, geocentrism, humors), new theories proved persuasive on the basis of experiment, observation, and inference—that is, empirical demonstration.

---

7. As recounted in Noel Annan, *The Dons: Mentors, Eccentrics, and Geniuses* (Chicago: University of Chicago Press, 1999), 216.

8. "Ever tried. Ever failed. No matter. Try again. Fail again. Fail better." Samuel Beckett, "Worstward Ho," in *Nohow On* (New York: Grove Press, 1996), 77.

9. That is the definition given in the *Stanford Encyclopedia of Philosophy*, s.v. "The Analysis of Knowledge" (https://plato.stanford.edu/entries/knowledge-analysis/#KnowJustTrueBeli; accessed 11 April 2018). I agree that "true" is superfluous and misleading.

10. See his "Truth, Rationality, and the Growth of Scientific Knowledge," in Karl R. Popper, *Conjectures and Refutations* (New York: Basic Books, 1962), 215–50.

According to Chalmers (13), this method has a power "to compel agreement" that has not been, and perhaps cannot be, matched in philosophy. Philosophical arguments, unlike scientific demonstrations, rely, he says, on "premises that opponents can deny without too much cost." Can we increase the cost? Stalin had ways, of course. And the fact that Stalin can be (and certainly used to be) located on a time line with the old Russian intelligentsia, whose quasi-catechistical manner his own writing style took to the point of caricature, only shows yet again the ease with which the tradition of the question, shading into the tradition of the answer, is perverted by power. It is only when one insists both on posing questions and on keeping them open that one can avoid slippage into dogma and authoritarian coercion, the *bêtes noires* with which the essays in this book constantly engage. As William James in his wisdom once put it, the object of inquiries such as the ones found here ought not to be that "of forcing a conclusion or of coercing assent, but of deepening our sense of what the issue . . . really is."[11]

II

The cursed questions addressed in this book are of both types as inherited from the nineteenth-century Russian tradition—the existential on the one hand, and the practical-programmatic or action-oriented on the other. The usually forlorn hope is to find ways of resolving the former into the latter—that is, to find ways of doing that improve being. Both types of question have been posed in the musicological literature from the very beginning—or at least from the beginning of my exposure to it. When deciding on the contents of this volume, I recalled an exemplary cursed question from the past: an article that appeared in the maiden issue of *Current Musicology*, the graduate-student-run journal produced at the Columbia University music department since the spring of 1965. I entered the Columbia graduate program in the fall of that very year, so I very nearly witnessed the journal's birth (indeed, did witness it from afar as a senior undergraduate), and received my copy of the first and (then) only issue as part of a pitch (by Gordana Lazarevich, a member of the first editorial staff, who visited our "Bibliography and Methodology" class at its first meeting) to join the team. (I did join, as the first "corresponding editor" from the home institution—an absurd position that did not last long on the masthead.)

The article's title was paradigmatic to the point of parody: "What Should Musicology Be?" Its author was Prof. Edward A. Lippman, who was both our Bibliography and Methodology teacher and the "Faculty Advisor" on the journal's

---

11. William James, "The Dilemma of Determinism" (1884), in James, *The Will to Believe and Other Essays in Popular Philosophy*, ed. F. H. Burkhardt, F. Bowers, and I. K. Skrupskelis (Cambridge, MA: Harvard University Press, 1979), 55.

masthead. It belies the common assumption that musicology only became self-reflective in the 1980s, following the publication of Joseph Kerman's purposely provocative *Contemplating Music,* which (according to legend) single-handedly spawned the "new musicology" of the 1990s.[12] In fact, the connection between Kerman's book and its presumed progeny is a canard. The book actually gives little premonition of the dramatic turn within the discipline that was just around the corner. Reading it now, one is struck by the conventionality and obsolescence of its positions, which even at the time of writing represented no more than a *gemäßigte Moderne* for all that it was advertised and widely taken as *le dernier cri,* and also by its obliviousness to what was imminent: namely, the "post-structuralism, deconstruction and serious feminism" which, Kerman wrote in 1985, "have yet to make their debuts in musicology or music theory."[13]

Meanwhile, Lippman's article, way back in the antediluvian sixties, was already broaching what, as I write in 2018, is among the hot-button issues in today's musicology: the social turn (explicitly rejected by Kerman, it should be recalled) whereby the practices and assumptions of ethnomusicology and its older, unprefixed sibling have been converging—a turn which the older "new musicology," with its "low hermeneutics," only served to postpone.[14] Lippman's precocious consideration of that possibility was a response to a provocation that was then regarded, as Kerman's would be two decades later, as the strongest challenge to date to the musicological status quo: the designated volume *Musicology* in the series "Humanistic Scholarship in America," commissioned by the Council of Humanities at Princeton. It was authored by a team of three, consisting of Claude Palisca (1921–2001), an unprefixed musicologist who asserted that "musicologist" meant "music historian" *tout court;* an ethnomusicologist, Mantle Hood (1918–2005), who asserted that a music scholar must also be a performer; and a rare hybrid, Frank Ll. Harrison (1905–87), an Irish scholar whose work was located on the cusp between the two subdisciplines, and who made a strong pitch for the

---

12. Joseph Kerman, *Contemplating Music: Challenges to Musicology* (Cambridge, MA: Harvard University Press, 1985). The book had first been issued in Great Britain, in a series of "masterguides," under the general editorship of Frank Kermode, to the various humanistic disciplines. Its original title, quite simply, was *Musicology* (London: Fontana, 1985). For the acrid flavor of early "new musicology" one may sample the exchange between Lawrence Kramer and Gary Tomlinson, each vying for recognition as Kerman's truest votary: Kramer, "The Musicology of the Future," *repercussions* 1, no. 1 (1992): 5–18; Tomlinson, "Musical Pasts and Postmodern Musicologies: A Response to Lawrence Kramer," *Current Musicology* 53 (1993): 18–24; Kramer, "Music Criticism and the Postmodernist Turn: In Contrary Motion with Gary Tomlinson, ibid., 25–35; Tomlinson, "Tomlinson Responds," ibid., 36–40.
13. Kerman, *Contemplating Music,* 17.
14. For "low hermeneutics," see Carolyn Abbate, "Music—Drastic or Gnostic?," *Critical Inquiry* 30 (2004): 505–36.

purview that his own work exemplified long ahead of schedule, the convergence that is only now, more than half a century later, becoming prevalent.[15]

Lippman recognized Harrison's "great discernment" in diagnosing "our dilemma," as he called it, thanks to "the objectivity naturally possessed by an outsider," more a reference to Harrison's nationality than to the type of musicology he practiced. As testament to Harrison's discernment, Lippman noted that he

> finds that we have erred in neglecting the less pretentious varieties of music such as jazz and folk music, and indeed in neglecting the history of American music in general. Most of all have we overlooked the larger social connections of music. We must broaden our concern, he counsels, and turn from style, taken as an autonomous phenomenon, to man and culture.[16]

If only! But no, Lippman did not endorse Harrison's prescription any more than Kerman did in the almost exactly contemporaneous manifesto from which *Contemplating Music* eventually grew, and which was also a response to the Palisca-Hood-Harrison book.[17] In fact, Lippman endorsed no prescription and offered no proposals. He passed the buck, complaining that "any course that may be advocated by theoretical considerations must depend for its implementation upon capable and talented students," and yet

> we cannot expect to attract undergraduates to a field neither they nor their teachers have any knowledge of, especially if its values and achievements are in fact not worth

---

15. Frank Ll. Harrison, Mantle Hood, and Claude V. Palisca, *Musicology* (Englewood Cliffs, NJ: Prentice-Hall, 1963). For an example of Harrison's ahead-of-the-game convergent practice, see Frank Llewellyn Harrison, *Music in Medieval Britain* (London: Routledge & Paul, 1959). His evident model was Ernst Hermann Meyer's Marxist study *Early English Chamber Music: The History of a Great Art from the Middle Ages to Purcell* (London: Lawrence & Wishart, 1946). Meyer, a refugee from Nazi Germany with two strikes against him as a Jewish Communist, was primarily a composer. After the war he went home from Britain to what had become the Soviet zone of occupation, later the German Democratic Republic.

16. Edward A. Lippman, "What Should Musicology Be?," *Current Musicology*, no. 1 (Spring 1965): 55. Further page references will be made in the main text.

17. Joseph Kerman, "A Profile for American Musicology" (delivered as a plenary address at the national meeting of the American Musicological Society in December 1964), *JAMS* 18 (1965): 61–69. When reprinting this piece a third of a century later, Kerman explicitly recanted and apologized for having categorically dismissed Harrison's prescriptions ("European observers have a very simple recipe for national integrity: study your own American music, they say, as we have built our musicology around *Stamm* and *Liederbuch*, *Risorgimento* opera and Elizabethan madrigal, Bulgar folksong, and the like. The critically-inclined scholar has a very simple answer: unfortunately, American music has not been interesting enough, artistically, to merit from us that commitment") and for waffling the question of genres fit for research ("About jazz, Harrison has a real point, but such an extremely complex one that I ask leave to pass over it in the present discussion"); "A Profile for American Musicology," 67–68, and Joseph Kerman, *Write All These Down: Essays on Music* (Berkeley: University of California Press, 1998), 11n6.

their attention. If musicology cannot enhance musical experience and understanding, it can hardly call for notice either from musicians or from scholars, but only from those of routine intelligence and little imagination, and we should not be surprised if students of superior mentality seem to wander into the field more by accident than design, or in default of any other pursuit more appropriate for them. (58)

I wonder now that, as a new graduate student in the field, I did not feel demeaned or insulted on reading these words. But Lippman was quick to point out, Herzen-like, that I was not to blame. Rather,

> Our major complaint must then be addressed, as it so often turns out, to earlier education, and even more correctly, to the whole temper and attitude of the society in which this education has its place. . . . The average American is peculiarly unable to grasp music as a cultural-historical expression in the way in which he understands painting and literature. As a result, while these latter arts take on a certain measure of significance and dignity, musical works are essentially gross stimuli without specific stylistic quality. In the response to music, historical awareness is absent, and the listener takes the indulgence of his feelings as the sole source of meaning. (58–59)

An argument so limitlessly opened out is an argument of despair. One watches, fascinated, as fatalism overtakes it:

> We can make natural science part of musicology or exclude it. We can undertake interpretive studies or confine ourselves to the cataloguing of facts. We can produce more and more editions of music and even secure a wider influence through the medium of newspapers and record companies, or radio and television. Whatever course we adopt will be of relatively little effect on the ultimate place of musicology in the United States; it will not in itself provide respect or jobs or an audience for musicologists, nor will it make possible the publication and sale of serious books on music. Even the enlightened revision of the curricula of primary and secondary schools and of colleges, and the encouragement of actual playing and singing will not make us experience music as a significant expression of culture in the face of public attitudes and educational ideals that are deaf or hostile to musical values. The underlying social determinants of the place of music and musicology resist change with a discouraging stubbornness; we can guess only that music and musicology have a common fate. (59–60)

And finally, "what musicology should be is less important than what American culture should be if musicology is to exist" (60). Not even Nikolai Berdyayev at his most pessimistic was ever quite that passive—and this was the (supposedly) tumultuous sixties! Not for scholars, though. It was because the academy was the proverbial refuge from the world's turbulence—and was the literal refuge of many (including me) who found protection there from the threat of conscription into an unpopular war—that when, so soon thereafter, political upheavals reached America's campuses they created such a sense of disorientation and disruption, quickly followed by the relief of a resumed complacency. No wonder musicology remained as stagnant as it did until the disciplinary turmoil of the 1980s. By then many of us were indeed restless and impatient. And that is when cursed questions began invading our literature with a vengeance.

I never expected to take so active a part in advancing them, but circumstances I have recounted in the introductions to some previous books gave me access to much wider audiences than musicologists usually address.[18] The need for topical hooks when writing for general readerships was a large inducement to attach musical discussions to much broader social and cultural issues such as have traditionally invited cursed questions. By the time I retired from classroom teaching at the end of 2014, I had become used to hearing myself referred to as "America's public musicologist." With that reputation came invitations, many to keynote disciplinary conferences of various kinds, and once I'd published *The Oxford History of Western Music*, I found I had become a "generalist," liable to be invited to the most unpredictable venues. That accounts in part for the range of issues these essays address. The retirement, moreover, of the editors with whom I worked closely during my stint as a public intellectual—Leon Wieseltier at the *New Republic* and James Oestreich at the *New York Times*—has delivered me back, so to speak, to less public, more insularly disciplinary turf, and most of the pieces here were prepared for audiences of professional listeners and, now, readers.

My present and recurrent questions are now the cursed questions of the discipline; but this a welcome development for me, since throughout my career, first at Columbia and later at Berkeley, I taught the introductory seminar required of all incoming students, where we did nothing at all but pose and luxuriate in the cursed questions this book addresses. The book is in this sense the product of that long and, for me, formative pedagogical experience. It is a fair indication of the steep rise in our disciplinary self-consciousness and self-reflection over the many years of my career that when I took over the teaching of these proseminars (at Columbia from 1977, at Berkeley from 1988), they were, at both institutions, the courses no one else wanted to teach, whereas the assignment is in most departments now regarded as a plum.

So these are essays that collectively pose the question Ed Lippman raised half a century ago—"What Should Musicology Be?"—though I hope to avoid his fatalism and passivity as emphatically as I reject both of the Russian "classical" relationships to cursed questions, whether Berdyayev's eschatological snobbery or Chernyshevsky's dogmatic prescriptions (to say nothing of Lenin's). My aim in posing and worrying the questions after which my essays are named is the same as

---

18. See in particular the introduction ("Last Thoughts First") to R. Taruskin, *Text and Act: Essays on Music and Performance* (New York: Oxford University Press, 1995), 3–47; and the preface ("Against Utopia") to R. Taruskin, *The Danger of Music and Other Anti-Utopian Essays* (Berkeley: University of California Press, 2010), ix–xvi.

when I taught my novices: to encourage the regulation of practice in accordance with ethics, seeing such regulation in terms of what in mathematics is called an asymptote: a line that a curve perpetually approaches but never reaches as it heads toward infinity. The asymptote symbolizes the perfect practice that we will never achieve. The curve of our actual practice must nevertheless be seen in relation to the unreachable goal, and must be seen to approach it.

III

A few words in advance about each of the essays and how they assay this task will serve, I hope, to furnish this disparate assortment, if not with a common theme, then at least with a common objective. I offer them up front, rather than in the form of postscripts to the individual chapters as in some of my other books, because of this overriding purpose. The exception is "Nicht blutbefleckt?" (chapter 7), which elicited a retort from the late Charles Rosen that demanded a sustained and content-specific response from me. My belated rejoinder has taken the form of a postscript because there can, alas, be no further exchanges between us.

"The History of What?" (chapter 1) is the introduction to *The Oxford History of Western Music*, printed as part of the front matter to the first volume of the original hardcover sequence of six, and reprinted in each volume of the paperback edition, which was slightly revised so as to permit issuance in the form of five *separata*. There have been many reviews of The Ox (as I habitually call it), and I do not mean to answer them; but one sentence has been so consistently (and, I will venture to add, disingenuously) pounced upon that I do see a need for amplification. That sentence is this one:

This set of books is an attempt at a true history.

In context, I would insist, the meaning of this sentence, hence the character of my claim, is clear enough. I had been discussing the difference between a history and a survey; I had observed that most books that call themselves general histories of music were actually surveys; and I promised the reader a history, in the true sense of the word as just defined, *viz.*, as an "effort truly to explain why and how things happened as they did." Reviewers pretended that I was claiming a monopoly on truth, implying that other historians wrote falsehoods. (Charles Rosen went so far as to accuse me of "maintain[ing] that this is the first history of music which not only relates what was done but how and why,"[19] which misses the point altogether: mine is hardly the first book to do what any history does, but surveys, as opposed

---

19. Charles Rosen, "From the Troubadours to Frank Sinatra" (review of *The Oxford History of Western Music*), part 1, *New York Review of Books*, 23 February 2006 (www.nybooks.com/articles/2006/02/23/from-the-troubadours-to-frank-sinatra).

to histories, do not even relate what was done, let alone how or why, contenting themselves with the description of what was produced.) I doubt whether any reader unmotivated by whatever it was that motivated reviewers to misread me had so misread me, but I want to call renewed attention to the point in the new context that the present discussion provides.

One of the main explanatory features distinguishing "a true history" from a survey, I emphasized in my introduction, was attention to *discourse,* a word that has had a vastly enhanced currency and range of application in the humanistic disciplines in the wake of Michel Foucault and his theories of knowledge and power. In The Ox I define discourse as "social contention as embodied in words and deeds." That contest is what establishes the ground rules within which people think—that is, establishes the limits of the thinkable. Cursed questions, as I think of them, are the levers with which one tries to destabilize the discourse (or what Foucault called the episteme). That is one of the things that the essays in this book attempt. It is one of the things that The Ox itself has been credited with doing, as when one sympathetic reader—in an essay that, as it happens, had a question for a title—described the last two volumes as having "overturned the master narrative of twentieth-century music history as a story of inexorable innovation, instead placing their emphasis on political and social matters."[20]

That is a gratifying, indeed a fortifying, thought. Would that it were true. Yet there is an important difference between the place cursed questions occupy in polemics, on the one hand, and in historiography on the other, and I work hard to respect that difference in my work. Polemics work the levers directly, while all that historiography can properly do is show how they have been worked. If showing achieves something it is because the thing shown had been hidden. That is what the chapters in the fifth volume of The Ox that have become controversial sought to accomplish, above all the chapter on Elliott Carter's reception, which emphasized patronage and vocational strategizing, for discussing which I was accused of maliciously exposing, or even fabricating, dirty secrets.[21] The destabilizing effect came about not through an explicit negation of the composer's autonomous agency but by giving an elaborate illustration of interaction between the agent in question and the enabling and constraining environment within which the agent acted—an exemplification, in other words, of the theory of affordances broached in several of the chapters that follow, most broadly in "What Else?" (chapter 8). In polemics you can render your value judgments directly; in historiography you

---

20. Marina Frolova-Walker, "An Inclusive History for a Divided World?," *Journal of the Royal Musical Association* 143 (2018): 1–20, at 3.

21. Many have been carrying on in this now quite normal endeavor in the wake of The Ox; particularly pertinent to the instance at hand is Rachel S. Vandagriff, "An Old Story in a New World: Paul Fromm, the Fromm Music Foundation, and Elliott Carter," *Journal of Musicology* 35 (2018): 535–66.

submit pertinent examples for the reader to judge. As I say again and again in The Ox, it is no business of mine as a historian to take sides; my business is to show the sides (and measures) taken, by whom, and with what result.

This proviso is not unrelated to the old writer's-workshop bromide "Show it, don't say it," and points yet again to the stylistic and methodological parallels between historiography and imaginative fiction that Hayden White expounded some forty years ago.[22] But though at times a fine one, the line between the genres remains real—realer than White wished his readers to believe—and still worthy of respect. Between the covers of a book like this one I can take sides, and just watch me. But doing so in a work of historiography turns historiography into propaganda.

Many are those who have challenged this distinction, declaring that observing it is impossible: to which I answer that calling a task impossible is too often just a way out of attempting one that is difficult. Those who wish to avoid the difficulty of respecting the fine line in question often claim that the discourse itself has taken sides before the historian has even sat down to write. One can only choose which side to take—or in blunter language, one's choice is only between harder and softer propaganda. The proof of that, reviewer after reviewer observed but none more emphatically than Rosen, was how easy it was to deduce my convictions and preferences—in one word, my prejudices—from my performance. "He claims not to have followed his own taste on what to include," Rosen wrote, and quoted my "hope [that] readers will agree that I have sought neither to advocate nor to denigrate what I did include." And then, triumphantly: "His hope has been thwarted. In writing about art, a pretense of objectivity never succeeds: clearly, Taruskin writes much better about music he likes than about music to which he is indifferent. His prejudices loom large throughout the volumes."[23]

All I can say to that, and I am happy to say it, is that his surmises as to my likes and my indifference were as often as not wildly incorrect, as were those of all the other reviewers who amused themselves identifying my goats and sheep. Such attempts were not serious critiques but rather defensive endeavors to reduce my arguments to matters proverbially beyond dispute, whereas I had worked hard to insure that any sentence that went into The Ox was, as we say in the lab, falsifiable—that being one criterion that distinguishes what J.L. Austin called "constative" utterances from "performative" ones; or, as I put it to my pupils, the difference between a responsible scholarly hypothesis and a loose and therefore negligible assertion.[24] That, I believe, is the distinction that counts between

---

22. See his *Metahistory* (Baltimore: Johns Hopkins University Press, 1973) and *Tropics of Discourse* (Baltimore: Johns Hopkins University Press, 1978).

23. Rosen, "From the Troubadours to Frank Sinatra," part 1.

24. On constative vs. performative "speech acts" (or illocution) see J(ohn) L(angshaw) Austin, *How to Do Things with Words,* 2nd ed. (Cambridge, MA: Harvard University Press, 1962); compare Popper on hypotheses and falsification in the essay referenced in n. 10.

scholarly writing in the strong or narrow sense and the other sorts of writing that a scholar may do, and I have struggled to put that belief into practice.

Marina Frolova-Walker, whose words I quoted a few paragraphs back, made an analogous distinction in the course of correcting what she took to be a small misstatement in "Nicht blutbefleckt?" (chapter 7). Comparing the careers of Elliott Carter and Tikhon Khrennikov, I wrote that both were placed *hors de concours* by their respective musical establishments, with the result that "both enjoyed major careers and achieved true historical significance . . . without having any real audience for their work." "We could make one small correction to this comparison," Prof. Frolova-Walker noted,

> because Khrennikov's light music, such as his popular songs and operettas, actually did enjoy a large audience, which is only somewhat reduced in present-day Russia. Taruskin is no doubt aware of this, but preferred not to blunt his rhetorical purpose in what was not, after all, a scholarly article. Still, if we restrict the comparison to Khrennikov's more earnest works, the parallel does indeed hold.[25]

To answer quibble with quibble, that restriction was, I thought, implied (as did my reader, evidently). But, no longer quibbling, I courteously reject the cover my critic is offering me. Any constative assertion must be falsifiable, wherever it is made, even in polemics. No rhetorical purpose justifies a lie. The difference between the scholarly and the nonscholarly that I try to heed, and have exhorted my pupils to observe, is that polemics do admit, alongside the falsifiable and constative, categories of utterance that are not subject to empirical or logical falsification. Advocacy (or praise) and denigration are examples of such utterances. Having been vigilant in weeding such things out of The Ox, I am left sensitive to reading a statement such as Frolova-Walker's that "Taruskin praises *The Love for Three Oranges* for breaking down the fourth wall and drawing its alienating devices from the eighteenth century, declaring that it thus becomes 'an indispensable link in the history of twentieth-century opera.'"[26]

I am sure that last-quoted phrase would have pleased Prokofieff, but does that reduce it to "praise"? I reached anxiously for volume 4 of The Ox to find the paragraph from which it came. Here it is, part of a discussion of Prokofieff's opera in relation to its literary antecedents, among which the most proximate was a treatment by the Russian theatrical director Vsevolod Meyerhold of a *fiaba* or theatricalized fable by Carlo Gozzi:

> Meyerhold's *Love for Three Oranges*, then, was perhaps the earliest application, at least in such an overwhelming dose, of the illusion-destroying "art as art" gimmickry that would within a couple of decades become a modernist cliché. What makes it

25. Frolova-Walker, "An Inclusive History for a Divided World?," 4.
26. Ibid.

historically so significant is the clarity of its descent from an eighteenth-century aristocratic model, thus connecting two important strands in what would become the heritage of postwar "neoclassicism." Even if Prokofieff had never set it, Meyerhold's response to Gozzi would have been a prime document of the nascent modernist manner and its sources. But since Prokofieff did set it, it becomes an indispensable link in the history of twentieth-century opera as well.[27]

Rather than praise, the paragraph offers justification for inclusion. I insist upon this distinction, and insist that it is not a quibble, because the besetting sin of the modernist master narrative, the very thing I sought most deliberately to overturn in my own work, was the casual equation of historical significance with aesthetic value. What I sought to convey in the paragraph just quoted was not my admiration for the opera but the reason why I was including it in my narrative, rather than others that I might admire more. I have written repeatedly, both in The Ox itself and in its defense, that my principle of selection was at all times pragmatic rather than aesthetic. I included what my story needed rather than what I liked. That is why it was beside the point for Rosen to complain of the "curious misjudgment" whereby I chose "to give more space to Lili Boulanger than to Ruth Crawford Seeger: of the latter, one of the most interesting composers of the twentieth century, he treats only very minor pieces, neglecting the important string quartet and violin sonata for which she is most admired."[28] I agree with Rosen's high evaluation of Ruth Crawford Seeger and her two excellent chamber works. But what my story needed, in the second chapter of volume 4, was an account of the misogynist prejudice that kept Nadia Boulanger out of the running for the Prix de Rome and enabled Lili Boulanger, by virtue of a superior understanding of the stakes, to compete successfully.[29] Once again, as so often, it was not "the music itself" but the affordance that, in my judgment, needed to be remarked. And when I did write about Crawford Seeger, what seemed in context to be of moment was the renunciation of her composing career, not its highlights.

Perhaps needless to say, the misascription of value judgment works more commonly the other way. I have become well used to being charged with denigrating what I have neglected to praise—or more accurately, what I have neglected to instruct my readers to praise. Thus David Blake has read me as "castigating Princeton—and academic music departments by extension—as 'a closed enclave, a hothouse growth, [the] cultivators [of academic composition] standing with backs resolutely turned to their counterparts in other walks of American musical

---

27. R. Taruskin, *Music in the Early Twentieth Century*, The Oxford History of Western Music, vol. 4 (New York: Oxford University Press, 2010), 499.

28. Rosen, "From the Troubadours to Frank Sinatra," part 1.

29. Here, of course, I was following Annegret Fauser's splendid article "*La Guerre en dentelles:* Women and the *Prix de Rome* in French Cultural Politcs," *Journal of the American Musicological Society* 51 (1998): 83–129.

life.'" Hostile and misleading accounts like mine, he adds, "imagine a locked, ivied, and gothic-arched gate dividing art music written by dead white men—and studied by old white men—from the diverse musical forms and composers outside."[30]

I had not remembered castigating Princeton—or anything else—that way, so once again I reached anxiously for The Ox, and found to my renewed relief that the pronoun *it*, standing as the subject of the partially quoted sentence, had stood not for Princeton or any other university, but for "postwar serialism in America," and that my description—enclave, hothouse, turned backs, and all—was a paraphrase of Milton Babbitt's famous call, in that immortally mistitled Tanglewood address of 1957, for a "total, resolute and voluntary withdrawal from this public world to one of private performance and electronic media," whereby American composers would do themselves "an immediate and eventual service" and thus ensure (according to the even more famous jeremiad at the end of the screed) that "music" would *not* "cease to evolve, and, in that important sense, . . . cease to live."[31]

It has long been Babbitt's fate to serve as synecdoche—whether for postwar American serialism (*chez moi*) or, far less accurately, for Princeton (*chez Blake*)—but unless it was Babbitt's intent to castigate the thing for which he stood, neither was it mine in paraphrasing him. As written, rather than as quoted, my description of midcentury attitudes among academic composers of serial music seems accurate enough. To point out that it mischaracterizes "twenty-first-century musicological inclusivity" is an impertinence; and to complain that it endangers the discipline of musicology in the face of "neoliberalist logics assailing the contemporary university" is to engage in precisely the sort of "paranoid reading" against which the author fancies himself a crusader.[32]

IV

As I used to enjoy telling audiences who heard it as a copiously illustrated talk, "Did Somebody Say Censorship?" (chapter 2) was written by someone who had actually been accused of practicing censorship ("and can anyone else in the room make that statement?"). Thus the question it embodies was for me actual, not hypothetical—and one especially cursed. And to the exasperation of those who expected to hear an unqualified condemnation of censorship, it is precisely as a

---

30. David Blake, "Musicological Omnivory in the Neoliberal University," *Journal of Musicology* 34 (2017): 321, purporting to quote *The Oxford History of Western Music* 5:164 (the square brackets and the words they enclose are Blake's). Later (p. 324), the author misquotes his own misquotation, attributing to me the phrase "hothouse oven," which, had I used it, would indeed have been a "polemical caricature" of the American university, about which I was not writing.

31. Milton Babbitt, "The Composer as Specialist," better known, after its first publication (*High Fidelity*, February 1958), as "Who Cares If You Listen?"

32. Blake, "Musicological Omnivory," 321, 350.

cursed question that I treat the issue. Like the questions the Russians could never get to the bottom of, this one shows itself to be ambiguous and ambivalent as soon as one begins probing, and unresolvable into a simple, categorical, or "absolutist" opposition to an act that the United States Constitution specifically (though not in fact absolutely) enjoins the United States government from performing through legislation. For many that aspect of our constitutional history, involving as it does the Bill of Rights, perhaps the most sacred of our foundational documents, has reduced all discussion of censorship to a simple matter of applying or invoking the First Amendment, and condemning all censorious acts that would, as government action, be forbidden under its terms. But I have yet to meet anyone who actually opposes all acts of censorship. We all have limits. Can they be rationalized, or are they irreducibly subjective and impervious to argument? That is the question I took it as my task to answer. And that is why I felt the need to survey so many examples before attempting generalization.

My generalization, as finally stated, is often found to imply a surprising and unsatisfactory conclusion—namely, that the act of censorship, whether as prohibition or as alteration ("bowdlerization"), is not what demands to be judged, but rather the purpose that the act is seen to embody or serve. That is what is known as situational ethics or reflective morality. It is applied more often to life-and-death issues such as euthanasia and abortion, but the issue of arts censorship offers another arena in which to assert the superiority of a moral view that admits the possibility of competing rights rather than insisting that the only choice is the bald and blatant, inevitably prejudiced, and therefore far easier adjudication of right and wrong.

As classically defined by John Dewey, reflective morality "demands observation of particular situations, rather than fixed adherence to a priori principles."[33] It is not the same, however, as relativism, because motivating purposes, once defined, do remain susceptible to a priori judgment. I contrived my consideration of censorship to culminate in the crispest possible demonstration that "in practice what in some times and places we call right is in other times and places wrong."[34] The fact that the example involved the sensitivities of Jews, a group to which I belong, aroused, to my sorrow but not surprise, additional resistance. Those bent on dismissal have all too predictably tried to reduce the point to one of self-interest.[35]

---

33. John Dewey, *Ethics* (1932), in *The Collected Works of John Dewey*, vol. 7 (Carbondale: Southern Illinois University Press, 2008), 329.

34. Joseph Fletcher, "Naturalism, Situation Ethics, and Value Theory," in *Normative Ethics and Objective Reason*, Ethics at the Crossroads, vol. 1, ed. George F. McLean (Washington, DC: Council for Research in Values and Philosophy, 1996), 28.

35. "I know, I know—Taruskin playing the anti-Semitic card? Shocking" (Matthew Guerrieri, "The Censures of the Carping World," in *Soho the Dog: Classical Music and Other Entertainments* [weblog], 26 October 2007: https://sohothedog.blogspot.com/2007/10/censures-of-carping-world.html; accessed 9 April 2018).

There is also the pitfall that Leo Strauss dubbed *reductio ad Hitlerum*, sometimes called Godwin's Law and paraphrased as "the first one to mention the Nazis loses the argument," since my very last example did just that.[36] Hitler and his party will curse any question. But they loom so large in the history of the twentieth century, and their presence in our consciousness has by now become so ramified, that the danger cannot serve as an alibi.

They come up again, more tangentially, in "Haydn and the Enlightenment?" (chapter 3), which is an expanded version of a short essay written on commission for the booklet accompanying a commercial recording. The topic was assigned, but I insisted on adding the question mark to the title (and not merely to make the essay eligible for inclusion in this book). Periodization, and the attendant nomenclature, has always been one of the cursed questions of arts historiography. It is, most agree, a necessary evil. Periodization usefully limits frames of reference; but it also admits all sorts of useless baggage, especially when, as in the case of Enlightenment, the nomenclature is both anachronistic and value-laden. So the essay begins with a critique of the term and its applicability, as well as an account of its changing connotations, which suffered a crisis in the wake of the totalitarian movements of the twentieth century. One cannot consider the Enlightenment today without considering as well the Romantic backlash, to which so many thinkers of unquestioned academic prestige have contributed. Thus the essay on Haydn and the Enlightenment had to morph, in part, into a defense of Haydn against that "postmodern" backlash—to give it its now-outdated yet still relevant name—and the problems it has created for scholars of eighteenth-century music. That side of things had no place in a booklet essay, yet it was the part I felt needed to be written. My vindication of Haydn's "Enlightened" credentials in terms not of immanent musical content but of social transaction sounds a theme that will resound in the later chapters of this book. The transactions, however, linked back in unforeseen ways to the immanent content, regardless of how that may be defined.

"Is There a Baby in the Bathwater?" (chapter 4), probably the prickliest essay in the book (and for that reason the one most laced with jokes), tackles the issue of immanent content head-on, because the cursed question it addresses, that of aesthetic autonomy, is the most intractable of all when it comes to music. It was written at the invitation of Prof. Albrecht Riethmüller of the Freie Universität Berlin for a university-wide "seminar" (or what we would call a lecture series) held during the

---

36. See Leo Strauss, *Natural Right and History* (Chicago: University of Chicago Press, 1953), 42–43 ("In following this movement towards its end we shall inevitably reach a point beyond which the scene is darkened by the shadow of Hitler. Unfortunately, it does not go without saying that in our examination we must avoid the fallacy that in the last decades has frequently been used as a substitute for the *reductio ad absurdum*: the *reductio ad Hitlerum*. A view is not refuted by the fact that it happens to have been shared by Hitler"). On the Godwin version, see www.independent.co.uk/voices/comment/invoke-the-nazis-and-you-ve-lost-the-argument-8209712.html (accessed 9 April 2018).

2005–6 academic year under the rubric *Ästhetische Autonomie?* The question mark, of course, was what attracted me, as did the propaedeutic, which as of this writing is still available online and which reads, in part (and in my translation):

> Since the late eighteenth century, the idea of aesthetic autonomy has been a guiding concept of artistic evolution. It has guaranteed the special nature of modern Western art in comparison both to what is premodern and to what is non-Western. Over the past two decades the concept of aesthetic autonomy has been subjected to critical questioning. Through what Rüdiger Bubner calls "the aestheticizing of the everyday world," the boundaries between art and non-art have grown increasingly blurry. The politicization of works of art no longer seems taboo. Globalization, increasingly noticeable in the arts, has led to a less specific notion of what constitutes Western art. Against the background of these developments, these university lectures will put the concept of "Aesthetic Autonomy" and its relevance to today's artistic and art-theoretical situation to the question.[37]

The list of speakers included some prominent names in literary and cultural theory and art history (Stephen Greenblatt, Michael Fried, Boris Groys, Barbara Stafford) and the titles promised a wide-ranging treatment of the theme. I was surprised to find myself the only musicologist on the agenda, since music has always been by common consent, at least since the Romantics, the paradigmatic autonomous art, the one toward the condition of which (in a maxim that will be quoted more than once within the covers of this book) all the other arts aspired. I was more than surprised, moreover, I was downright amazed to learn when I got to Berlin on the eve of my talk, which was scheduled last, that mine would be the only contribution to the "seminar" that would do what the propaedeutic promised (and that I had taken as not only a promise but a behest), namely put aesthetic autonomy to the question. The other speakers, I was told, had applied the concept without reservations. Prof. Riethmüller told me this with a certain displeasure, and also told me that the series had been a letdown, with a dwindling attendance, and that I should not take a low turnout too personally.

---

37. "Seit dem späten 18. Jahrhundert ist der Gedanke ästhetischer Autonomie zu einem Leitkonzept der Evolution der Künste geworden. Er begründet die Spezifik der modernen okzidentalen Kunst sowohl im Vergleich zur vormodernen Kunst des Westens als auch zur Gesamtheit der nicht-westlichen Kunst. Es ist ein Phänomen der letzten zwei Jahrzehnte, daß das Konzept ästhetischer Autonomie zum Gegenstand einer kritischen Befragung wird. Durch die 'Ästhetisierung der Lebenswelt' (R. Bubner) verwischen sich zunehmend die Grenzen zwischen Kunst und Nicht-Kunst. Die Politisierung von Kunstwerken scheint nicht länger mit einem Tabu belegt. Schließlich bedeutet die auch im Bereich der Künste immer stärker spürbare Globalisierung eine Zurücknahme der Spezifitätsmerkmale der westlichen Kunst. Vor dem Hintergrund dieser Entwicklungen beabsichtigt die Universitätsvorlesung, das Konzept der 'Ästhetischen Autonomie' auf seine Relevanz für die heutige Situation der Künste und der Kunsttheorie hin zu befragen" (www.geschkult.fu-berlin.de/e/sfb626/veranstaltungen/veranstaltungsarchiv/veranstaltungsreihen/veranstaltungsreihen_programme/sfb626_aesthetische_autonomie_karte.pdf; accessed 9 April 2018).

In the event, I thought the turnout quite satisfactory, even if it was to a degree an assemblage of familiar musicological faces. I knew, at least, that I would not disappoint those who wanted a fight: as I noted in the talk, its critique of the stipulated concept became increasingly intense, even heated, as the matter approached my own areas of professional concern. Since I was already known for my skepticism of aesthetic autonomy, I thought I had nothing to lose by giving that skepticism free rein. In particular, I half-relished, half-dreaded the prospect of expounding at full strength my negative evaluation of T. W. Adorno's defense of aesthetic autonomy right there in, as I fancied it, the belly of the beast.

But when I had finished and it was time for questions, I was perplexed by the friendly equanimity with which my polemics had been received. I put it down to politeness—the diplomatic politeness that had been shown me the whole evening by all present, who had spoken only English, even in calling the seminar to order and announcing housekeeping details, out of consideration for their speaker, who could read German, more or less, but could not speak it. I didn't know whether to interpret it as deference to the guest of honor or as sympathy for a handicapped person, but I was a little let down at having apparently failed to provoke. At dinner afterward I asked Thomas Schmidt (or Schmidt-Beste, as he was then known), my neighbor on the left, why no one had batted an eyelash when I said all those terrible things about Adorno. I will never forget what he told me, in his wonderfully cultivated Oxford English: "Ah, my dear," he said, "Adorno is your problem now."

V

I had not yet noticed that, but it should have been obvious. Adorno's musical spokespersons, exegetes, and defenders have for decades been well-nigh exclusively Anglophone: Max Paddison, Lydia Goehr, Richard Leppert, Susan McClary, Ian Pace, James Currie, Seth Brodsky, Mark Berry, J. P. E. Harper-Scott—and the list goes on.[38] The most conspicuous German-language publication on Adorno to

---

38. For example, Max Paddison, *Adorno's Aesthetics of Music* (Cambridge: Cambridge University Press, 1993); Lydia Goehr, "Adorno, Schoenberg, and the *Totentanz der Prinzipien*—in Thirteen Steps," *Journal of the American Musicological Society* 56 (2003): 595–636; Richard Leppert, "Introduction," in T. W. Adorno, *Essays on Music*, ed. with commentary by Richard Leppert (Berkeley: University of California Press, 2002), 1–83; Susan McClary and Richard Leppert, eds., *Music and Society: The Politics of Composition, Performance, and Reception* (Cambridge: Cambridge University Press, 1989); Ian Pace, "Notation, Time, and the Performer's Relationship to the Score in Contemporary Music," in *Unfolding Time: Studies in Temporality in Twentieth-Century Music*, ed. Darla Crispin and Mark Delaere (Leuven: Leuven University Press, 2009); James R. Currie, *Music and the Politics of Negation* (Bloomington: Indiana University Press, 2012); Seth Brodsky, *From 1989; or, European Music and the Modernist Unconscious* (Oakland: University of California Press, 2017); J. P. E. Harper-Scott, *The Quilting Points of Musical Modernism: Revolution, Reaction, and William Walton* (Cambridge: Cambridge University Press, 2012).

appear since the last turn of the century is the official centennial biography by Stefan Müller-Doohm, published by Adorno's publisher, which has been translated into English.[39] In his home country, where Adorno is still regarded as a major moral philosopher, his musical writings now attract little attention, and by now that attention, in sharp contrast to Anglophone adulation, is generally critical. The most recent German publications that I have been able to identify as concerning Adorno as a musical thinker all emphasize his outdatedness. One is an edited collection of conference papers that consider, under the rubric "Society within the Work," Adorno's signal contention (and one that still receives strong endorsement from Anglophone musicologists), seeing it strictly as a historical phenomenon of the mid-twentieth century.[40] Another, on Adorno's jazz criticism, acknowledges the divergence of opinion between those who see it as justified critique and those who see it as mere intolerant *Verriss* (hatchet work).[41] Yet another, on Adorno's treatment of Wagner in relation to Nietzsche, juxtaposes his essays with highly critical responses by continental European writers who now attract the same uncritical welcome from Anglophone scholars of the humanities as does (or did) Adorno.[42]

The reason why Anglophone scholars have been such suckers for Adorno has something to do with the long and now embarrassing neglect that not only he, but all sociologically or philosophically oriented thinkers about music suffered for far too long a time, until Rose Rosengard Subotnik, at first in the face of furious and career-damaging opposition, forced her colleagues to pay attention.[43] It was also

39. Stefan Müller-Doohm, *Adorno: Eine Biographie* (Frankfurt am Main: Suhrkamp, 2003); translated by Rodney Livingstone as *Adorno: A Biography* (Cambridge: Polity Press, 2009).

40. Richard Klein, ed., *Gesellschaft im Werk: Musikphilosophie nach Adorno* (Freiburg: Karl Alber, 2015), 9: "Speculation, scholarly research, musical practice and sociopolitical critique come together in Adorno in a manner that is inspiring even where the philosopher errs or exaggerates. Adorno takes the discourse of 'society within the work' seriously, precisely where it differs most from the aesthetics of our day" (Bei Adorno treffen spekulatives Denken, wissenschaftliche Forschung, musikalische Praxis und politisch-soziale Kritik auf eine Weise zusammen, die noch da inspirierend ist, wo der Philosoph irrt oder übertreibt. Die Rede von der 'Gesellschaft im Werk' nimmt Adorno dort ernst, wo er sich von der Ästhetik unserer Tage am meisten unterscheidet). Compare Robert Walser: "We should have learned long ago from Adorno that social relations and struggles are enacted within music itself" (*Running with the Devil: Power, Gender, and Madness in Heavy Metal Music* [Middletown, CT: Wesleyan University Press, 1993], 104).

41. Franz-Joseph Kemper, *"Mit den Ohren denken": Adorno über Jazz—Verriss oder berechtigte Kritik?* (Munich: Grin, 2016); compare Richard Leppert: "Some scholars have read Adorno's comments on blacks and jazz as racist, a charge that is, frankly, absurd, and not least the result of careless reading" ("Commentary," in Adorno, *Essays on Music*, ed. Leppert, 351.

42. Erik M. Vogt, *Ästhetisch-politische Lektüren zum "Fall Wagner": Adorno—Lacoue-Labarthe—Žižek—Badiou* (Vienna: Turia + Kant, 2015).

43. The articles through which she accomplished this feat were "Adorno's Diagnosis of Beethoven's Late Style: Early Symptom of a Fatal Condition," *Journal of the American Musicological Society*

she who best answered the nagging, nearly cursed question of why it should have been scholars of popular music, a new field within the musicology of the 1970s and 80s, who were the first to make a fetish of him despite the fact that he treated their subject with such unmitigated derision. In another important early article, "The Role of Ideology in the Study of Western Music," which was even more obviously written against the disciplinary grain of the profession in which she had been trained, Subotnik distinguished what she called "Continentalist" scholarship from the Anglo-American variety.[44] Although few were using the term in the early 1980s, she was clearly describing what today would be called two "discourses," two frames that defined and delimited the range of theoretical reference and the habits of thought that determined practice within their respective milieux.

The Anglo-American was the one within which all of us who came up in musicology in the 1960s were educated. It was epitomized by Philip Gossett, a University of Chicago colleague who goes unnamed within Subotnik's article, when he told her that she "approached the study of music with a philosophical orientation and was therefore bound to falsify music and music history" (1). Subotnik's article was the first to imply, by means of this distressing anecdote, that the very pretense of value-freedom or philosophical nonalignment was an expression of a priori values and a philosophical alignment. For those who were able to read it with an open mind, it was one of the prime consciousness-raisers on the way toward transcending the dichotomy Subotnik was expounding.

The great novelty in Subotnik's argument was the defense of Continentalist thinking, the discourse of which Adorno was the model exponent. To quote her definition of it, therefore, is to quote a historic document: the first such definition to appear in the Anglophone musicological literature. In answer to Subotnik's then-cursed question—to wit, "Are all human utterances based on a philosophical orientation?"—she notes that Continentalists will "tend to answer ... in the affirmative."

> Continentalists tend to approach their studies with the idea that all men, including themselves, operate with a comprehensive, though not necessarily conscious, immutable, or irrefutable view of how things are. Continentalists are thus often prone to treat the study of musical utterance as a kind of meta-study in which various levels of ideological orientation are to be distinguished and taken into account in any work of interpretation or evaluation. These orientations include those of the composer, of the historian or critic, and of any who develop theories about either or both. Moreover, the Continentalist's point of departure is more likely to be an awareness of his own ideological framework than the musical artifact, the so-called object of study, itself.

---

29 (1976): 242–75; and "The Historical Structure: Adorno's 'French' Model for the Criticism of Nineteenth-Century Music," *19th-Century Music* 2 (1978–79): 36–60.

44. Rose R. Subotnik, "The Role of Ideology in the Study of Western Music," *Journal of Musicology* 2 (1983): 1–12. Page references to this source will be made in the main text.

> But Continentalists are also generally forced into considering the possibility of distinguishing within any artifact between two levels of structure to which meaning and value can be assigned: first, the internal or autonomous structure of the artifact itself; and, second, the structure of cultural, philosophical, and ideological premises underlying or surrounding the artifact and, ultimately, the study of the artifact. (2)

I call the question of philosophical orientation, as Subotnik posed it in this essay, her "then-cursed" question because it has since, I think, been answered. No one whose eyes are open would hesitate today before agreeing with this particular plank in what Subotnik calls the Continentalist platform. Not to acknowledge that we all approach the act of observing the world with preconceptions seems to us all by now to be "patently naive," as Subotnik wrote of Gossett's implicit claim of freedom from all bias (a claim already belied by his intolerance toward her work). No one today would claim to be able to see things not from a particular point of view but exactly as they are. If our eyes are open now, it is she whom we should thank first for opening them. But the fact that we have all become to this extent Continentalists by Subotnik's definition does not imply general assent to the specifics of Continentalist arguments, as my own rejection of Adorno's strain of ideological critique will suffice to testify, even as I acknowledge the enormous service that Subotnik performed in bringing it to general attention.

Her crucial—indeed, transformative—point, prior to any consideration of specifics, concerned the need to engage with alternative views as a preventative measure against complacency at best, dogma at worst, these being the besetting sins of the Anglo-American (or, as she overbluntly put it, empiricist) persuasion. She took the issue of aesthetic autonomy as the test case. "The Continentalist's method of approach," she wrote,

> is likely to require some attention to the problem of musical autonomy, even if only to reject the notion, whereas the empiricist may work a lifetime without giving a single thought to ideological context, which lies beyond his own scientifically defined domain of study. The Continentalist may consciously suppress what differs from his ideology, whereas the Anglo-American may never even recognize the possibility of valid differences from his way of looking at things because he is unconscious of having an ideology. And the empiricist would vigorously deny the Continentalist assertion that his own anti-ideology is itself simply another ideology, a principle of conceptual selection with no privileged access to the truth. (3–4)

She likens the difference to that between rival Christian sects. One does not have to accept her particular description of Catholics and Protestants to appreciate the aptness of a comparison between scholarly positions and confessional ones, given the overriding purpose of demonstrating that scholarly positions and preferences are, as the existentialist cliché would have it, always-already ideological. "In Catholic fashion," she wrote, the Continentalist viewpoint is more likely to allow for some awareness of the ideologies it rejects and to encompass a place, however lowly, despised, or even hellish, for those ideologies in its world view; whereas the Anglo-American mode of thought, in traditional Protestant fashion, allows for freedom and equality of thought but only within a very narrow range of the Elect, and simply disregards the human remainder. (9–10)

As a practice informed by the more exclusionary view, moreover, and "despite its assertions to the contrary," Subotnik argued that

> mainstream American musicology today, no less than its Continentalist counterparts, makes its judgments and selections very largely on ideological grounds, but that in contrast to the work of a first-rate Continentalist such as Adorno, empiricist musicology does not make its own ideological biases explicit, that it seldom gives serious attention to constructs which it ultimately rejects, and that it tends to narrow rather than broaden its field of study wherever possible, thereby excluding considerations of meaning and denying itself a specifically humanistic value. (9)

These are no longer controversial assertions within "mainstream American musicology." To insist on them as passionately as Subotnik insisted when publishing the article in 1983 (having first delivered it three years earlier as a plenary address before a safer audience at the national meeting of the Society for Ethnomusicology) would now be to beat a dead horse. But let us not forget the matador who killed it.

And now I think we can see what made Adorno so popular with students of popular music, who until the 1980s could be found mainly in departments of sociology rather than musicology. His *Verriss*, which assigned to popular music exactly that lowly, despised, and hellish place that Catholics and Continentalists reserved for alien bodies and modes of thought, was something they could engage with. Engagement with the silence of disregard can be all too easily silenced as impertinence. Adorno's strictures opened the door. That is why the usual answer to those expressing the bemusement I am affecting here at the way popular music scholars seem to kiss the hand that slaps them was always to praise Adorno for "asking the right questions." (To which I could only reply, "Have you ever seen his answers?")

Rose Subotnik reappears in "Shall We Change the Subject?" (chapter 5); so do Adorno and even Gossett. That circling is in the nature of cursed questions and their bearers. Another who circles back is Joseph Kerman, that peerless spur not only to my thinking but to that of so many of my contemporaries, who returns so often in these ruminations that I have dedicated the book to his memory despite the frequency with which we differ in these pages, as we used to do face to face. But if recurrence is inevitable, so are its ever-changing and therefore renewing contexts. In chapter 5, the topic that reconfigures the question is freedom: of thought, expression, and action. It provides a nexus between an issue, censorship, that a previous essay had addressed, and the issue of disciplinary constraint. As my interests as a historian became ever more focused on the Cold War as a historiographical period, it became ever more important to me to identify and expose the constraints within which musicians in the so-called West, and we music scholars in particular, performed their functions, since the Cold War cliché postulated a stark contrast between freedom on one side of the Iron Curtain and constraint on the other. Like all radical binaries, when accepted as a framing premise it stifled thought and worked as a consciousness-lowering restriction. If we in the West were to reap the sort of benefit we now patronizingly assumed our counterparts were enjoying on the other side, now that constraints had been lifted, we needed to know under what constraints we ourselves had been operating. These are the matters that the concluding essay of this book, lucky chapter 13 (which directly and historically compares East and West), will address head-on. Nothing, I have found, is more difficult than to propose freedom to those who already think themselves free.

It is because I have tried to do that that I have been called a censor. Hence chapter 5 is the one in which I report most fully on that experience, following my defense of the Boston Symphony's free and yet costly decision to postpone performance of choruses from the opera *The Death of Klinghoffer* in the aftermath of September 11, 2001—not just on the press skirmishes, on which I have reported before,[45] but on the academic controversies, both within musicology and, across departmental lines, with our confrères in neighboring disciplines.

"'Alte Musik' or 'Early Music'?" (chapter 6) was another foray into a beast's belly—a different (though related) beast this time, in Vienna rather than Berlin—the cursed questions it broaches being the relationship between histor(iograph)y and fiction and the role of pseudohistorical fiction in history. I resort to what used to be the common "postmodernist" play of parentheses, nesting historiography within history, because that typographical affectation raises yet another cursed question, the relationship between what happened (history) and the stories that we tell about it (historiography). The pseudohistorical fictions the chapter considers include those perpetrated by performers as well as by scholars and composers. The chapter thus bridges two of my preoccupations as a critic of music(ologic)al practice.

"Nicht blutbefleckt?" (chapter 7), one of the few essays herein composed for print rather than oral delivery, concerns the triple nexus between (a) the importance of conceptualizing the Cold War as a historiographical period, (b) the responsibility of the historian always to contextualize, and (c) the necessary dis-

---

45. In the postscript to the title essay in R. Taruskin, *The Danger of Music and Other Anti-Utopian Essays*, 174–78.

tinction between historiography and advocacy. Charles Rosen, who denied that last-named necessity (or even the possibility of observing it) was my most determined antagonist on this score, and wrote an answer to the piece that achieved a much wider circulation than the original. Thus this shortest item in the book left the longest wake, and required the single postscript on reprinting to bring the discussion up to its present state (a function otherwise discharged by this introduction).

The issue addressed in "What Else?" (chapter 8) is that of representation, a question that has burgeoned in music studies as the Romantic models of aesthetic autonomy and absolute music have receded—or rather, as they have been properly contextualized and historicized. What remains a cursed question is the relationship among the various levels on which the act or concept of representation can be applied to music. Music can represent the world. Must it? The mind can represent music. Must it? How do such terms as expression, evocation, stimulation, or arousal relate to musical representation? It is when considering these questions that Kant's exhortation *Sapere aude!* still seems a necessary appeal. Musicians are still inclined to answer such questions by invoking authorities—Hanslick, Stravinsky, their teachers—whose precepts contradict experience.

VI

The lingering hold of unquestioned authority is the curse addressed as well in "Unanalyzable, Is It?" (chapter 9). I especially appreciated being asked to prepare this essay for delivery as a keynote address to a conference of music theorists and analysts, two populations that are often represented as antagonistic toward historical musicology and its occasional envoys such as I was that night. I hasten to add that I was accorded a warm reception by an audience that seemed to appreciate the forthrightness with which I seized my opportunity to question old verities and their spokespersons. The convergence of historical musicology and ethnomusicology is widely recognized and applauded. I have not lately seen much resistance to it from either side. The situation in the case of music theory is different. Here one sees massive protectionism. Steven Rings, a prominent music theorist (and one, moreover, whom I name in chapter 9 as friendly), has entered a protectionist plea in an essay posted online by the Society for Music Theory (SMT) only days ago as I write:

> Disenchantment in various forms arguably pervades the postmodern humanities, as both diagnosis and method: the critical theorist disenchants, unmasks, demystifies. Most music theorists, it need hardly be said, do something quite different. As the SMT celebrates its 40th year, music theory—with its wide-eyed enthusiasms and unapologetic close readings, its loving attention to the sonic and the aesthetic, its

frequent aloofness from the social and political—remains a discipline apart, a sort of blissed-out, sylvan glade within the Left-melancholic academy.

Depending on one's intellectual commitments, this may be cause of celebration or withering critique.[46]

As one whose mood tends to be sanguine rather than melancholic, and who is often outflanked on the left, I am not sure I qualify as a spokesman for what Prof. Rings thinks of as the academy, but if his description of music theory is accurate, you can put me down for withering critique. I do think that our business as scholars is disenchantment, nor need that define us all as critical theorists. As I hope the essays in this book will show, critical theorists can vie with music theorists as enchanters, and enchanters do not lack for opportunities in nonacademic walks of life. If I must choose, I'll choose enlightenment. But as I hope chapter 9 will show, we do not face so bald a choice, and if the asperity with which music theory defends its bliss is any indication, it may not be quite so idyllic a glade as its champions contend. The Society for Ethnomusicology (SEM) originated, like the SMT, as a secession from the American Musicological Society (AMS), but its members no longer eye the parent organization with so much suspicion. In its behavior, the SMT often exhibits not bliss but malaise. The conclusion of Rings's eclogue seems to bear this out, in its insistence that "enchantment can provide the somatic and affective fuel for interpersonal generosity and real-world political action." Or not. There are more direct means for achieving these things, if you truly think they are your assignment in life.

But there is no need for bad conscience. Musical analysis well executed is as efficacious a mode of achieving justified true belief as any other, as long as one begins with an adequately open mind and is willing to apply adequate tests. One can engage with the aesthetic without committing aestheticist fallacies and without submitting to comforting authorities. As Carl Dahlhaus, with characteristic insistence, asserted:

> Adherents of the socio-historical school have been tireless in their campaign against the autonomy principle, but their arguments generally fall short of the mark. To begin with, it is quite defensible in methodological terms for us to isolate an object so long as we do not question the reality of the connections from which it has been extracted. (It is a cheap rhetorical trick to talk about "false abstractions" without at the same time pointing out—in addition to the indubitable fact that they are abstract—precisely why they happen to be false.) We can always leave the social context of musical works out of consideration without belittling its importance;

---

46. Steven Rings, "Music's Stubborn Enchantments (and Music Theory's)," paper delivered at the plenary session of the fortieth national meeting of the SMT (2017), *Music Theory Online* 24, no. 1 (March 2018), http://mtosmt.org/issues/mto.18.24.1/mto.18.24.1.rings.html (accessed 12 April 2018).

doing so only means that we consider social context irrelevant to the particular end we have in view, i.e. understanding those inner workings of a piece of music that make it art.[47]

I suppose I am one of those tireless adherents against whom Dahlhaus here inveighs. (After chapter 4, about the baby and the bathwater, I could hardly deny it.) But I see no reason to return intransigence for intransigence. I have always liked the paragraph I have just quoted, because it comes in the midst of the chapter in Dahlhaus's book whose title—"The Significance of Art: Historical or Aesthetic?"—is held up in chapter 1 of this book ("The History of What?") as an egregious false binary, and yet Dahlhaus seems to be arguing here for a both/and rather than an either/or. Our recognition that both the object and its context are real does not oblige us to discuss them both together at all times. Dahlhaus's caveat, that omission does not imply disparagement, applies in both directions. It seconds the warning that Rings issued from music-theoretical terrain, and it is one to which adherents of the sociohistorical school can appeal with equal profit. If there is to be questioning or belittling, let it be explicit rather than tacit. That acknowledgment is the least we can ask of each other as an earnest of good faith.

Yet I do have a problem after all with Dahlhaus's ostensibly conciliatory paragraph, and it is not a small one. The "particular end" he asserts as justification for neglect of context rings false to me, and I am indeed prepared to say why. To say that the inner workings of a piece are what "make it art" is impermissibly to essentialize and naturalize the category "art," which as a product of culture does not have an essential nature. What is it, then? With that cursed question we have crossed into the domain of ontology, the most purely philosophical (or as Dahlhaus would say, abstract) of the domains abutting the arts, and the one to which chapter 10 ("Essence *or* Context?"), with its binarizing—but (say I) not falsely binarizing—title, pertains.

To lay the cards on the table straight off, I reject the notion that art has an essence because, while it does have products susceptible to physical or phenomenological description, art as such is the social practice that gives rise to those products. Like all practices, it takes place in an ever-changing environment that renders it mutable both in its processes and in the values that shape its products. To say, moreover, that only products of a certain kind (i.e., those with the right "inner workings") are definable as art is to legislate covertly social distinctions. Thus, what Dahlhaus always characterized as the "strong" view of art (entailing "relative autonomy") has always seemed to me a weakness in his position: spurious as a definition of art and regressive as social theory. And I suspect that many more

---

47. Carl Dahlhaus, *Foundations of Music History*, trans. Bradford Robinson (Cambridge: Cambridge University Press, 1983), 27.

agree with me than would admit to doing so. What else would account for the bad conscience detectable not only in the protestations of music theorists but also in Dahlhaus's aggressive, preemptively judgmental style of argumentation (well demonstrated in the cited paragraph, which I cited in full for the sake of the demonstration).

I too have been accused of aggressive behavior, Lord knows, but in chapter 10, in which I engage more closely with a particular (and proudly essentialist) philosopher than in anything else I have written, I tried to keep things light and airy—partly out of affection for Nick Zangwill, my nonce opponent, who is a man of great charm and good humor; partly because I engage in this essay in a very questionable practice, viz., quoting from my opponent's superseded drafts (albeit with his permission); and partly because the proxy in our debate was the long-dead and oft-misunderstood Eduard Hanslick, whose writings, even when mistaken, were of such excellence in concept and expression as to make engagement a pleasure. Not only that, but the prospect of settling a matter of such great importance to me, who have always regarded essentialism the way any member of a minority regards it (i.e., with the greatest apprehension and antipathy), was beyond exhilarating.

I had another chance at essentialism in "But Aren't They All Invented?" (chapter 11), in which I was asked as conference keynoter to consider the nature of tradition; and again I was able and eager to conclude with the proviso that tradition, while it can have definitions, does not and cannot have a nature. Here I was arguing against a fashionable theory put forth by Eric Hobsbawm and Terence Ranger, in their edited volume *The Invention of Tradition,* that the thing their title names is a spurious version of something that (thus implicitly) has a genuine version as well. My title, "But Aren't They All Invented?," telegraphed my conclusion: that invented traditions are indeed "real"; that there can be no other kind; and that tradition, like art (but even more obviously), is to be regarded as a mutable social practice rather than a static condition, let alone a thing; and that it is the representation of tradition as static that is the political enemy, the thing to be unmasked. As so often happens when I am preoccupied by a cursed question, my best evidence fell into my lap in the form of two essays that I discovered in the course of work but not because I was looking for them. This kind of serendipity is so frequent in my experience that I have long since given it a name, "clippings from God," to whom thanks are, as always, due. But I am also grateful to Daniel Leech-Wilkinson and Sean Williams for such crisp examples of the supervention of tradition, that is to say of unsanctioned social practice, over the asociality that is still, thanks to the lingering reverberations of the big Romantic bang, the consciously adopted "strong" ideal of artists who regard their art as "high."

The pitched battle between the high and the low—overt as aesthetics, often covert as social politics—that was the history of twentieth-century art is the explicit subject of "Which Way Is Up?" (chapter 12), the longest and most complex chapter in the book (and for that very reason a bit recalcitrant when it comes to summarizing in advance), which originated as a keynote to a conference on music and middlebrow culture. Every theme seems to find a recapitulation within it, on the way to a head-on confrontation with what I see as the cursed question of all our cursed questions: the relationship between art (or "the aesthetic") and morality. All I can say here, up front, is how grateful I was (and am) for the chance to formulate it—as I was grateful for the chance, afforded by the invitation to attend and address a conference on East-West translations at the University of Chicago, to draft chapter 13 ("A Walking Translation?"), the apparent lagniappe to fill out a baker's dozen, but in fact the most intensely personal of all the essays in this volume (I myself being the titular ambulant) and the one that finally returns me to my wonted Russian terrain.

Professional life after retirement has been full of surprises, and its best moments have usually come to me, as here, via the kindness of strangers (and a few friends as well). So let me conclude these introductory remarks with thanks to those who have extended the invitations to which the contents of this book have been the responses, and to those who have helped me refine them: Heloisa Amaral, Jack Balkin, Karol Berger, Chistopher Chowrimootoo, Caryl Clark, Georgia Cowart, Sarah Day-O'Connell, Mark Delaere, Caryl Emerson, Peter Franklin, Kate Guthrie, Stephen Hinton, David Josephson, Sanford Levinson, Melanie Lowe, Nicholas Mathew, Maribeth Payne, Albrecht Riethmüller, Marina Ritzarev, Peter Schmelz, Elaine Sisman, Rūta Stanevičiūtė, Cornelia Szabo-Knotik, Hugo Ticciati, Miriam Tripaldi, László Vikarius, Joshua Walden, and Nick Zangwill.

1

The History of What?

> *The argument is no other than to inquire and collect out of the records of all time what particular kinds of learning and arts have flourished in what ages and regions of the world, their antiquities, their progresses, their migrations (for sciences migrate like nations) over the different parts of the globe; and again their decays, disappearances, and revivals; [and also] an account of the principal authors, books, schools, successions, academies, societies, colleges, orders—in a word, everything which relates to the state of learning. Above all things, I wish events to be coupled with their causes. All this I would have handled in a historical way, not wasting time, after the manner of critics, in praise and blame, but simply narrating the fact historically, with but slight intermixture of private judgment. For the manner of compiling such a history I particularly advise that the matter and provision of it be not drawn from histories and commentaries alone; but that the principal books written in each century, or perhaps in shorter periods, proceeding in regular order from the earliest ages, be themselves taken into consultation; that so (I do not say by a complete perusal, for that would be an endless labour, but) by tasting them here and there, and observing their argument, style, and method, the Literary Spirit of each age may be charmed as it were from the dead.*
> —FRANCIS BACON, DE DIGNITATE ET AUGMENTIS SCIENTIARUM, LIBRI IX (1623)[1]

Mutatis mutandis, Bacon's task was mine. He never lived to complete it; I have—but only by dint of a drastic narrowing of scope. My *mutanda* are stated in my title (one not chosen but granted; and for that honor I extend my thanks to the Delegates of Oxford University Press). For "learning and the arts" substitute music. For "the different parts of the globe" substitute Europe, joined in volume 3 by America.

Originally published as the introduction to *The Oxford History of Western Music* (New York: Oxford University Press, 2005), 1:xxi–xxx.

1. Francis Bacon, *Of the Dignity and Advancement of Learning,* trans. James Spedding, in *The Works of Francis Bacon,* 15 vols., ed. James Spedding, Robert Leslie Ellis, and Douglas Denon Heath (Boston: Houghton, Mifflin, 1857–82), 8:419–20.

(That is what we still casually mean by "the West," although the concept is undergoing sometimes curious change: a Soviet music magazine I once subscribed to gave news of the pianist Yevgeny Kissin's "Western debut"—in Tokyo.) And as for antiquities, they hardly exist for music. (Jacques Chailley's magnificently titled conspectus, *40,000 ans de musique,* got through the first 39,000 years—I exaggerate only slightly—on its first page.)[2]

Still, as the sheer bulk of this offering attests, a lot was left, because I took seriously Bacon's stipulations that causes be investigated, that original documents be not only cited but analyzed (for their "argument, style, and method"), and that the approach should be catholic and as near exhaustive as possible, based not on my preferences but on my estimation of what needed to be included in order to satisfy the dual requirement of causal explanation and technical explication. Most books that call themselves histories of Western music, or of any of its traditional "style periods," are in fact surveys, which cover—and celebrate—the relevant repertoire but make little effort truly to explain why and how things happened as they did. This set of books is an attempt at a true history.

Paradoxically, that means it does not take "coverage" as its primary task ("for that," as Bacon says, "would be an endless labour"). A lot of famous music goes unmentioned in these pages, and even some famous composers. Inclusion and omission imply no judgment of value here. I never asked myself whether this or that composition or musician was "worth mentioning," and I hope readers will agree that I have sought neither to advocate nor to denigrate what I did include.

But there is something more fundamental yet to explain, given my claim of catholicity. Coverage of all the musics that have been made in Europe and America is obviously neither the aim of this book nor its achievement. A glance at the table of contents will instantly confirm, to the inevitable disappointment and perhaps consternation of some, that "Western music" here means what it has always meant in general academic histories: it means what is usually called "art music" or "classical music," and looks suspiciously like the traditional canon that has come under so much justified fire for its long-unquestioned dominance of the academic curriculum (a dominance that is now in irreversible process of decline). A very challenging example of that fire is a fusillade by Robert Walser, a scholar of popular music, who characterizes the repertoire treated here in terms borrowed from the writings of the Marxist historian Eric Hobsbawm. "Classical music," writes Walser,

> is the sort of thing Eric Hobsbawm calls an "invented tradition," whereby present interests construct a cohesive past to establish or legitimize present-day institutions or social relations. The hodgepodge of the classical canon—aristocratic and

---

2. Jacques Chailley, *40,000 ans de musique: L'homme à la découverte de la musique* (Paris: Plon, 1961), translated by Rollo Myers as *40,000 Years of Music: Man in Search of Music* (New York: Farrar, Straus & Giroux, 1964).

bourgeois music; academic, sacred and secular; music for public concerts, private soirées and dancing—achieves its coherence through its function as the most prestigious musical culture of the twentieth century.[3]

Why in the world would one want to continue propagating such a hodgepodge in the twenty-first century?

The heterogeneity of the classical canon is undeniable. Indeed, that is one of its main attractions. And while I reject Walser's conspiracy-theorizing ("present interests construct" indeed), I definitely sympathize with the social and political implications of his argument, as will be evident (for some—a different some—all too evident) in the many pages that follow. But that very sympathy is what impelled me to subject that impossibly heterogeneous body of music to one more (perhaps the last) comprehensive examination—under a revised definition that supplies the coherence that Walser impugns. All of the genres he mentions, and all of the genres that are treated in this book, are literate genres. That is, they are genres that have been disseminated primarily through the medium of writing. The sheer abundance and the generic heterogeneity of the music so disseminated in "the West" is a truly distinguishing feature—perhaps the West's signal musical distinction. It is deserving of critical study.

By critical study I mean a study that does not take literacy for granted, or simply tout it as a unique Western achievement, but rather "interrogates" it (as our hermeneutics of suspicion now demands) for its consequences. The first chapter of the *Oxford History* makes a fairly detailed attempt to assess the specific consequences for music of a literate culture, and that theme remains a constant factor—always implicit, often explicit—in every chapter that follows, right up to (and especially) the concluding ones. For it is the basic claim of this multivolumed narrative—its number-one postulate—that the literate tradition of Western music is coherent at least insofar as it has a completed shape. Its beginnings are known and explicable, and its end is now foreseeable (and also explicable).

And just as the early chapters are dominated by the interplay of literate and preliterate modes of thinking and transmission (and the middle chapters try to cite enough examples to keep the interplay of literate and nonliterate alive in the reader's consciousness), so the concluding chapters are dominated by the interplay of literate and postliterate modes, which have been discernible at least since the middle of the twentieth century, and which sent the literate tradition (in the form of a backlash) into its culminating phase.

---

3. Robert Walser, "Eruptions: Heavy Metal Appropriations of Classical Virtuosity," *Popular Music* 2 (1992): 265. The authority to which Walser appeals is Eric Hobsbawm and Terence Ranger, eds., *The Invention of Tradition* (Cambridge: Cambridge University Press, 1983). For a more thorough discussion of Hobsbawm and Ranger, see "But Aren't They All Invented?," chapter 11 in this volume.

This is by no means to imply that everything within the covers of these volumes constitutes a single story. I am as suspicious as the next scholar of what we now call metanarratives (or worse, "master narratives"). Indeed, one of the main tasks of this telling will be to account for the rise of our reigning narratives and show that they too have histories with beginnings and (implicitly) with ends. The main ones, for music, have been, first, an aesthetic narrative—recounting the achievement of "art for art's sake" or (in the present instance) of "absolute music"—that asserts the autonomy of artworks (often tautologically insulated by adding "insofar as they are artworks") as an indispensable and retroactive criterion of value; and second, a historical narrative—call it "neo-Hegelian"—that celebrates progressive (or "revolutionary") emancipation and values artworks according to their contribution to that project. Both are shopworn heirlooms of German romanticism.

These romantic tales are "historicized" in volume 3, the key volume of the set for it furnishes our intellectual present with a past. This is done in the fervent belief that no claim of universality can survive situation in intellectual history. Each of the genres that Walser names has its own history, moreover, as do the many that he does not name, and it will be evident to all readers that this narrative devotes as much attention to a congeries of "petits récits"—individual accounts of this and that—as it does to the epic sketched in the foregoing paragraphs. But the overarching trajectory of musical literacy is nevertheless a part of all the stories, and a particularly revealing one.

The first thing that it reveals is that the history narrated within these covers is the history of elite genres. For until very recent times, and in some ways even up to the present, literacy and its fruits have been the possession—the closely guarded and privileging (even life-saving) possession—of social elites: ecclesiastical, political, military, hereditary, meritocratic, professional, economic, educational, academic, fashionable, even criminal. What else, after all, makes high art high? The casting of the story as the story of the literate culture of music turns it willy-nilly into a social history—a contradictory social history in which progressive broadening of access to literacy and its attendant cultural perquisites (the history, as it has sometimes been called, of the democratization of taste) is accompanied at every turn by a counterthrust that seeks to redefine elite status (and its attendant genres) ever upward. As most comprehensively documented by Pierre Bourdieu, consumption of cultural goods (and music, on Bourdieu's showing, above all) is one of the primary means of social classification (including self-classification)—hence, social division—and (familiar proverbs notwithstanding) one of the liveliest sites of dispute in Western culture.[4]

---

4. Most relevantly for our present purposes in his *Distinction: A Social Critique of the Judgement of Taste*, trans. Richard Nice (Cambridge, MA: Harvard University Press, 1987).

Most broadly, contestations of taste occur across lines of class division, and are easiest to discern between proponents of literate genres and nonliterate ones; but within and among elites they are no less potent, no less heated, and no less decisively influential on the course of events. Taste is one of the sites of contention to which this book gives extensive and, I would claim, unprecedented coverage, beginning with chapter 4 in the first volume and lasting to the bitter end. Indeed, if one had to be nominated, I would single out social contention as embodied in words and deeds—what cultural theorists call "discourse" (and others call "buzz" or "spin")—as the paramount force driving this narrative.

It has many arenas. Perhaps the most conspicuous is that of meaning, an area that was for a long time considered virtually off-limits to professional scholarly investigation, since it was naively assumed to be a nonfactual domain inasmuch as music lacks the semantic (or "propositional") specificity of literature or even painting. But musical meaning is no more confinable to matters of simple semantic paraphrase than any other sort of meaning. Utterances are deemed meaningful (or not) insofar as they trigger associations, and in the absence of association no utterance is intelligible. Meaning in this book is taken to represent the full range of associations encompassed by locutions such as "If that is true, it means that . . . ," or "that's what M-O-T-H-E-R means to me," or, simply, "know what I mean?" It covers implications, consequences, metaphors, emotional attachments, social attitudes, proprietary interests, suggested possibilities, motives, significance (as distinguished from signification) . . . and simple semantic paraphrase, too, when that is relevant.

And while it is perfectly true that semantic paraphrases of music are never "factual," their assertion is indeed a social fact—one that belongs to a category of historical fact of the most vital importance, since such facts are among the clearest connectors of musical history to the history of everything else. Take for example the current impassioned debate over the meaning of Dmitry Shostakovich's music, with all of its insistent claims and counterclaims. The assertion that Shostakovich's music reveals him to be a political dissident is only an opinion, as is the opposite claim, that his music shows him to have been a "loyal musical son of the Soviet Union"—as, for that matter, is the alternative claim that his music has no light to shed on the question of his personal political allegiances. And yet the fact that such assertions are advanced with passion is a powerful testimony to the social and political role Shostakovich's music has played in the world, both during his lifetime and (especially) after his death, when the Cold War was playing itself out. Espousing a particular position in the debate is no business of the historian. (Some readers may know that I have espoused one as a critic; I would like to think that readers who do not know my position will not discover it here.) But to report the debate in its full range, and draw relevant implications from it, is the historian's ineluctable duty. That report includes the designation of what elements within the sounding composition have triggered the associations—a properly historical sort of analysis that is particularly abundant in the present narrative. Call it semiotics if you will.

But of course semiotics has been much abused. It is an old vice of criticism, and lately of scholarship, to assume that the meaning of artworks is fully vested in them by their creators, and is simply "there" to be decoded by a specially gifted interpreter. That assumption can lead to gross errors. It is what vitiated the preposterously overrated work of Theodor Wiesengrund Adorno, and what has caused the work of the "new musicologists" of the 1980s and 1990s—Adornians to a man and woman—to age with such stunning rapidity. It is, all pretenses aside, still an authoritarian discourse and an asocial one. It still grants oracular privilege to the creative genius and his prophets, the gifted interpreters. It is altogether unacceptable as a historical method, although it is part of history and, like everything else, deserving of report. The historian's trick is to shift the question from "What does it mean?" to "What has it meant?" That move is what transforms futile speculation and dogmatic polemic into historical illumination. What it illuminates, in a word, are the stakes, both "theirs" and "ours."

Not that all meaningful discourse about music is semiotic. Much of it is evaluative. And value judgments, too, have a place of honor in historical narratives, so long as they are not merely the historian's judgment (as Francis Bacon was already presciently aware). Beethoven's greatness is an excellent case in point because it will come in for so much discussion in the later volumes of this book. As such, the notion of Beethoven's greatness is "only" an opinion. To assert it as a fact would be the sort of historians' transgression on which master narratives are built. (And because historians' transgressions so often make history, they will be given a lot of attention in the pages that follow.) But to say this much is already to observe that such assertions, precisely insofar as they are not factual, often have enormous performative import. Statements and actions predicated on Beethoven's perceived greatness are what constitute Beethoven's authority, which certainly *is* a historical fact—one that practically determined the course of late-nineteenth-century music history. Without taking it into account one can explain little of what went on in the world of literate music-making during that time—and even up to the present. Whether the historian agrees with the perception on which Beethoven's authority has been based is of no consequence to the tale, and has no bearing on the historian's obligation to report it. That report constitutes "reception history"—a relatively new thing in musicology, but (many scholars now agree) of equal importance to the production history that used to count as the whole story. I have made a great effort to give the two equal time, since both are necessary ingredients of any account that claims fairly to represent history.

Statements and actions in response to real or perceived conditions: these are the essential facts of human history. The discourse, so often slighted in the past, is in fact the story. It creates new social and intellectual conditions to which more statements and actions will respond, in an endless chain of agency. The historian needs to be on guard against the tendency, or the temptation, to simplify the story by neglecting this most basic fact of all. No historical event or change can be meaningfully asserted unless its agents can be specified; and *agents can only be people*. Attributions of agency unmediated by human action are, in effect, lies—or at the very least, evasions. They occur inadvertently in careless historiography (or historiography that has submitted unawares to a master narrative), and are invoked deliberately in propaganda (i.e., historiography that consciously colludes with a master narrative).

I adduce what I consider to be an example of each (and leave it to the reader to decide which, if any, is the honorable blunder and which the propaganda). The first comes from Pieter C. van den Toorn's *Music, Politics, and the Academy*, a rebuttal of the so-called New Musicology of the 1980s.

> The question of an engaging context is an aesthetic as well as an historical and analytic-theoretical one. And once individual works begin to prevail for what they are in and of themselves and not for what they represent, then context itself, as a reflection of this transcendence, becomes less dependent on matters of historical placement. A great variety of contexts can suggest themselves as attention is focused on the works, on the nature of both their immediacy and the relationship that is struck with the contemporary listener.[5]

The second is from the most recent narrative history of music published in America as of this writing, Mark Evan Bonds's *A History of Music in Western Culture*.

> By the early 16th century, the rondeau, the last of the surviving *formes fixes* from the medieval era, had largely disappeared, replaced by more freely structured chansons based on the principle of pervading imitation. What emerged during the 1520s and 1530s were new approaches to setting vernacular texts: the Parisian chanson in France and the madrigal in Italy.
>
> During the 1520s, a new genre of song, now known as the Parisian chanson, emerged in the French capital. Among its most notable composers were Claudin de Sermisy (ca. 1490–1562) and Clément Jannequin (ca. 1485–ca. 1560), whose works were widely disseminated by the Parisian music publisher Pierre Attaingnant. Reflecting the influence of the Italian *frottola*, the Parisian chanson is lighter and more chordally oriented than earlier chansons.[6]

---

5. Pieter C. van den Toorn, *Music, Politics, and the Academy* (Berkeley: University of California Press, 1995), 196.

6. Mark Evan Bonds, *A History of Music in Western Culture* (Upper Saddle River, NJ: Prentice Hall, 2003), 142–43.

This sort of writing gives everybody an alibi. All the active verbs have ideas or inanimate objects as subjects, and all human acts are described in the passive voice. Nobody is seen as doing (or deciding) anything. Even the composers in the second extract are not described in the act, but only as an impersonal medium or passive vehicle of "emergence." Because nobody (except the publisher Attaingnant) is doing anything, the authors never have to deal with motives or values, with choices or responsibilities, and that is their alibi. The second extract is a kind of shorthand historiography that inevitably devolves into inert survey, since it does nothing more than describe objects, thinking, perhaps, that is how one safeguards "objectivity." The first extract commits a far more serious transgression, for it is ideologically committed to its impersonality. Its elimination of human agency is calculated to protect the autonomy of the work-object and actually prevent historical thinking, which the author evidently regards as a threat to the universality (in his thinking, the validity) of the values he upholds. It is an attempt, caught as it were in the act, to enforce what I call the Great Either/Or, the great bane of contemporary musicology.

The Great Either/Or is the seemingly inescapable debate, familiar to all academically trained musicologists (who have had to endure it in their fledgling proseminars), epitomized in the question made famous by Carl Dahlhaus (1928–89), the most prestigious German music scholar of his generation:

Is art history the *history* of art, or is it the history of *art*?

What a senseless distinction! What seemed to make it necessary was the pseudo-dialectical "method" that cast all thought in rigidly—and artificially—binarized terms: "Does music mirror the reality surrounding a composer, OR does it propose an alternative reality? Does it have common roots with political events and philosophical ideas, OR is music written simply because music has always been written and not, or only incidentally, because a composer is seeking to respond with music to the world he lives in?" These questions all come from the second chapter of Dahlhaus's *Foundations of Music History*, the title of which—"The Significance of Art: Historical or Aesthetic?"—is yet another forced dichotomy. The whole chapter, which has achieved in its way the status of a classic, consists, throughout, of a veritable salad of empty binarisms.[7]

This sort of thinking has long been seen through—except, it seems, by musicologists. A scurrilous little tract—David Hackett Fischer's *Historians' Fallacies*—that graduate students of my generation liked to read (often aloud, to one another) behind our professors' backs includes it under the rubric "Fallacies of Question-Framing," and gives an unforgettable example: "Basil of Byzantium: Rat or Fink?"

---

7. Carl Dahlhaus, *Foundations of Music History*, trans. J. Bradford Robinson (Cambridge: Cambridge University Press, 1983), 19.

("Maybe," the author comments, "Basil was the very model of a modern ratfink.")[8] There is nothing a priori to rule out both/and rather than either/or. Indeed, if it is true that production and reception history are of equal and interdependent importance to an understanding of cultural products, then it must follow that types of analysis usually conceived in mutually exclusive "internal" and "external" categories can and must function symbiotically. That is the assumption on which this book has been written, reflecting its author's refusal to choose between this and that, but rather to embrace this, that, and the other.

Reasons for the long if lately embattled dominance of internalist models for music history in the West (a dominance that in large part accounts for Dahlhaus's otherwise inexplicable prestige) have more than two centuries of intellectual history behind them, and I shall try to illuminate them at appropriate points. But a comment is required up front about the special reasons for their dominance in the recent history of the discipline—reasons having to do with the Cold War, when the general intellectual atmosphere was excessively polarized (hence binarized) around a pair of seemingly exhaustive and totalized alternatives. The only alternative to strict internalist thinking, it then seemed, was a discourse that was utterly corrupted by totalitarian co-option. Admit a social purview, it then seemed, and you were part of the totalitarian threat to the integrity (and the freedom) of the creative individual.

In Germany, Dahlhaus was cast as the dialectical antithesis to Georg Knepler, his equally magisterial East German counterpart.[9] Within his own geographical and political milieu, then, his ideological commitments were acknowledged.[10] In the English-speaking countries, where Knepler was practically unknown, Dahlhaus's influence was more pernicious because he was assimilated, quite erroneously, to an indigenous scholarly pragmatism that thought itself ideologically uncommitted, free of theoretical preconceptions, and therefore capable of seeing things as they actually are. That, too, was of course a fallacy (Fischer calls it, perhaps unfairly, the "Baconian fallacy"). We all acknowledge now that our methods are grounded in and guided by theory, even if our theories are not consciously preformulated or explicitly enunciated.

And so this narrative has been guided. Its theoretical assumptions and consequent methodology—the cards I am in the process of laying on the table—were, as it happens, not preformulated; but that did not make them any less real, or lessen their potency as enablers and constraints. By the end of writing I was sufficiently self-aware

---

8. David Hackett Fischer, *Historians' Fallacies: Toward a Logic of Historical Thought* (New York: Harper Torchbooks, 1970), 10.

9. See Anne C. Shreffler, "Berlin Walls: Dahlhaus, Knepler, and Ideologies of Music History," *Journal of Musicology* 20 (2003): 498–525.

10. See James M. Hepokoski, "The Dahlhaus Project and Its Extra-Musicological Sources," *Nineteenth Century Music* 14 (1990–91): 221–46.

THE HISTORY OF WHAT? 39

to recognize the kinship between the methods I had arrived at and those advocated in *Art Worlds*, a methodological conspectus by Howard Becker, a sociologist of art. Celebrated among sociologists, the book has not been widely read by musicologists, and I discovered it after my own work was finished in first draft.[11] But a short description of its tenets will round out the picture I am attempting to draw of the premises on which this book rests, and a reading of Becker's book will, I think, be of conceptual benefit not only to the readers of this book but also to the writers of others.

An "art world," as Becker conceives it, is the ensemble of agents and social relations that it takes to produce works of art (or maintain artistic activity) in various media. To study art worlds is to study processes of collective action and mediation, the very things that are most often missing in conventional musical historiography. Such a study tries to answer in all their complexity questions like "What did it take to produce Beethoven's Fifth?" Anyone who thinks that the answer to that question can be given in one word—"Beethoven"—needs to read Becker (or, if one has the time, this book). But of course no one who has reflected on the matter at all would give the one-word answer. Bartók gave a valuable clue to the kind of account that truly explains when he commented dryly that Kodály's *Psalmus Hungaricus* "could not have been written without Hungarian peasant music. (Neither, of course, could it have been written without Kodály.)"[12]

An explanatory account describes the dynamic (and, in the true sense, dialectical) relationship that obtains between powerful agents and mediating factors: institutions and their gatekeepers, ideologies, patterns of consumption and dissemination involving patrons, audiences, publishers and publicists, critics, chroniclers, commentators, and so on practically indefinitely until one chooses to draw the line. Where shall it be drawn? Becker begins his book with a piquant epigraph that engages the question head-on, leading him directly to his first, most crucial theoretical point: namely, that "all artistic work, like all human activity, involves the joint activity of a number, often a large number, of people, through whose cooperation the art work we eventually see or hear comes to be and continues to be." The epigraph comes from the autobiography of Anthony Trollope:

> It was my practice to be at my table every morning at 5:30 a.m.; and it was also my practice to allow myself no mercy. An old groom, whose business it was to call me, and to whom I paid £5 a year extra for the duty, allowed himself no mercy. During all those years at Waltham Cross he was never once late with the coffee which it was his

---

11. It was a timely book review by the British sociologist Peter Martin that luckily put me on to Becker's work: "Over the Rainbow? On the Quest for 'the Social' in Musical Analysis," *Journal of the Royal Musical Association* 127 (2002): 130–46.

12. Béla Bartók, "The Influence of Peasant Music on Modern Music," in Piero Weiss and Richard Taruskin, ed., *Music in the Western World: A History in Documents*, 2nd ed. (Belmont, CA: Thomson-Schirmer, 2008), 381.

duty to bring me. I do not know that I ought not to feel that I owe more to him than to any one else for the success I have had. By beginning at that hour I could complete my literary work before I dressed for breakfast.[13]

Quite a few coffee porters, so to speak, will figure in the pages that follow, as will agents who enforce conventions (and, occasionally, the law), mobilize resources, disseminate products (often altering them in the process), and create reputations. All of them are at once potential enablers and potential constrainers, and create the conditions within which creative agents act. Composers will inevitably loom largest in the discussion despite all caveats, because theirs are the names on the artifacts that will be most closely analyzed. But the act of naming is itself an instrument of power, and a propagator of master narratives (now in a second, more literal, meaning), and it too must receive its meed of interrogation. The very first chapter in volume 1 can stand as a model, in a sense, for the more realistic assessment of the place composers and compositions occupy in the general historical scheme: first, because it names no composers at all; and second, because before any musical artifacts are discussed, the story of their enabling is told at considerable length—a story whose cast of characters includes kings, popes, teachers, painters, scribes, and chroniclers, the latter furnishing a Rashomon choir of contradiction, disagreement, and contention.

Another advantage of focusing on discourse and contention is that such a view prevents the lazy depiction of monoliths. The familiar "Frankfurt School" paradigm that casts the history of twentieth-century music as a simple two-sided battle between an avant-garde of heroic resisters and the homogenizing commercial juggernaut known as the Culture Industry is one of the most conspicuous and deserving victims of the kind of close observation encouraged here of the actual statements and actions of human agents ("real people"). Historians of popular music have shown over and over again that the Culture Industry has never been a monolith, and all it takes is the reading of a couple of memoirs—as witnesses, never as oracles—to make it obvious that neither was the avant-garde. Both imagined entities were in themselves sites of sometimes furious social contention, their discord breeding diversity; and paying due attention to their intramural dissensions will vastly complicate the depiction of their mutual relations.

If nothing else, this brief account of premises and methods, with its insistence on an eclectic multiplicity of approaches to observed phenomena and on greatly expanding the purview of what is observed, should help account for the extravagant length of this submission. As justification, I can offer only my conviction that the same factors that have increased its length have also, and in equal measure, increased its interest and its usefulness.

13. Howard Becker, *Art Worlds* (Berkeley: University of California Press, 1982), 1.

2

Did Somebody Say Censorship?

I

This essay is the product of four brouhahas and an invitation. The invitation was to a conference held in February 2002 at the Law School of the University of Texas at Austin under the rubric "Law, Music, and Other Performing Arts." The conveners, Professors Sanford Levinson of UT and Jack Balkin of Yale, were familiar with the brouhahas in which I had become involved, thanks to my occasional role as critic or gadfly in the public media. They wanted me, among other things, to comment on them collectively.[1] I prepared a little tape of recorded excerpts from musical works that have given offense over the years, and that have been altered—sometimes by the composers or librettists, sometimes by performers, still other times by legally constituted authorities—on the basis (or in anticipation) of their reception by various audiences. In this expanded version I have broadened the range of reference, increasing both the number of individual examples and the variety of types and genres surveyed, and now encompassing a couple of examples in which it was not the verbal texts that gave offense but the actual musical sounds.

Originally presented at Case Western Reserve University, Music and Culture Lecture Series, 22 March 2004.

1. See S. Levinson and J. Balkin, "Law, Music, and Other Performing Arts," *University of Pennsylvania Law Review* 139 (1991): 1597–1658 (the omnibus review article from which the conference took its name); Levinson and Balkin, review of R. Taruskin's *Text and Act*, *MLA Notes* 53 (1996), 419–23. My main contribution to their 2002 conference in Austin was "Setting Limits," the keynote address, published subsequently in R. Taruskin, *The Danger of Music and Other Anti-Utopian Essays* (Berkeley: University of California Press, 2008), 447–65.

Prepare to be bombarded as I attempt to raise questions about the nature of censorship as applied to the arts. The questions are of two basic types: first, when is it really censorship? and second, is it necessarily a bad thing?

So let's plunge right in, with an item that did not figure in my Texas presentation (ex. 2.1).

That is the beginning of J. S. Bach's setting of a notorious verse from the Gospel according to St. Matthew (27:25): "His blood be upon us, and on our children," or in Luther's German, *Sein Blut komme über uns und unsre Kinder*. The line was in the news in 2004, two years after the Texas conference, when Mel Gibson was prevailed upon to remove it, not from the soundtrack but from the vernacular subtitles in his movie *The Passion of the Christ*.[2]

No one ever asked Bach to remove it. His setting of the Passion was meant to be performed before an audience of Lutheran believers in church, where no one who could possibly take offense at it, or be frightened of its import, was likely to set foot. Most members of Bach's congregation had probably never seen a member of the community on whom the curse of shedding Christ's blood was being called down, except perhaps at trade fairs. Jews had been banished from Saxony during the Reformation and were only just being let back as tradesmen during Bach's period of residency in Leipzig.[3] And surely neither Bach nor any other eighteenth-century Lutheran musician ever foresaw the day when their works, under what would have been to them incomprehensible historical and social conditions, not to mention incomprehensible doctrines of pure aesthetics and autonomous art, would be detached from their religious surroundings and performed under secular auspices before audiences of mixed faiths, nationalities, and even races.

But now Bach's Passion settings are routinely performed that way, and Jews not only listen to them but participate in performances as well. And social problems inevitably arise. When a chorus of Swarthmore College students began rehearsing Bach's other surviving Passion setting, based on the Gospel of John, members were appalled to find themselves called upon, repeatedly, to sing, "Die, Jews!" Of course, they thought that because they didn't know that in German *die Juden* simply means "the Jews." But they were not altogether wrong to be appalled, since the St. John Passion is the one that explicitly ascribes the murder of Christ not to *das Volk*, "the people," and their *Hohenpriester*, their High Priests, but to *die Juden* alone. It was to settle the controversy engendered by the refusal of some members of the chorus to participate that Michael Marissen, a Bach specialist who then taught at Swarthmore, was called into the fray. The result, this time, was ideal: a

---

2. See, for example, Sharon Waxman, "Gibson to Delete a Scene in 'Passion,'" *New York Times*, 4 February 2004.

3. Joseph Jacobs and Schulim Ochser, "Saxony," in *Jewish Encyclopedia: The Unedited Full-Text of the 1906 Jewish Encyclopedia*, www.jewishencyclopedia.com/articles/13241-saxony.

EXAMPLE 2.1. St. Matthew Passion, Coro: Sein Blut komme über uns.

marvelous book that seeks to address the issues through frank discussion and education.[4]

What I particularly admire about Marissen's book is that, even though he ends up advancing an interpretation of the Gospel that exonerates the Jews from guilt (they being but the instrument, at worst, of a fore-ordained outcome brought about through the sins of all mankind), he took seriously the concerns of non-Christian singers and listeners. He specifically rejected the notion that exonerating Bach, Luther, or John of anti-Semitism in the modern sense of the word would solve the problem. Even if doctrinal anti-Judaism is properly distinguished from racial anti-Semitism, even if it be conclusively demonstrated that Bach's purposes in setting the text were unrelated to malice or persecution, the problem is not one of vindicating the work within its makers' horizon of understanding (to speak hermeneutically), but rather that of reconciling the work to our own contemporary horizon, and to its potential contemporary impact.

Marissen is particularly contemptuous of the tendency to dismiss out of hand any ethical evaluation of the content of artworks deemed to have unassailable aesthetic value. "The whole point of great music is that it transcends anything you can put into words" is his paraphrase of remarks he has frequently encountered from musicians defending the Bach Passions; but he regards such a defense as not only inadequate but actually counterproductive.[5] He also allows that contemporary listeners may actually learn the "fact" that the Jews killed Christ directly from Bach, to admit which is to admit that a great work of art can actually have an evil impact on its beholders. There are many who continue to resist such an admission, and it is to them that my words here are particularly addressed.[6]

So I intend not only to raise difficult questions but also to risk answering them. I am hiding behind Michael Marissen at the moment because his expertise outranks mine where Bach is concerned, but I have not hesitated to make similar interventions. Indeed, I have felt obliged to do so. These were the brouhahas to which I referred at the outset. And the reason why there have been brouhahas is

---

4. Michael Marissen, *Lutheranism, Anti-Judaism, and Bach's "St. John Passion"* (New York: Oxford University Press, 1998).

5. Ibid. ix.

6. Among them was Charles Rosen, who reacted witheringly to my broaching this question in my *Oxford History of Western Music:* "Taruskin asks if we have the right to listen to the chorus in Bach's St. John's Passion where the Jews demand the death of Jesus: he hastens to say that he is only posing the question, not giving an answer, but some questions are too foolish to be asked" (Charles Rosen, "From the Troubadours to Frank Sinatra," *New York Review of Books,* 9 March 2006, 45). But of course, Rosen's version was not my question, as this essay will elaborate. Deflecting the question onto the matter of rights is a tactic designed to make things easy for the complacent by stigmatizing ethical concerns as already constituting a form of censorship. See R. Taruskin, *The Oxford History of Western Music* (New York: Oxford University Press, 2005), 2:389.

that I have espoused the view that Marissen affirms when he writes that although the proper way to address the problem of Bach's Passions is by way of education, nevertheless, "if the *St. John Passion* for some reason has to be performed without providing an educational context, I suggest that any passages easily running the risk of giving serious offense might be carefully excised or altered but acknowledged as such in the program in order to avoid accusations of censorship."[7]

Of course, if there is a program note, then the performance does have an educational context. I think excisions and alterations can be justified even without acknowledgment, and I don't think that censorship is necessarily the proper name for them.

I know of only one case in which the St. John Passion has actually been altered along lines such as Marissen or I have envisaged. Lukas Foss (né Fuchs, 1922–2009), an American composer and conductor who first came to the United States as a refugee from Nazi Germany, conducted a German-language performance with the New York Philharmonic in 1966 in which the phrase *die Leute*, "the people," was consistently interpolated in place of *die Juden*, "the Jews." The orchestra's archives preserve correspondence about the proposed alteration, specifically mentioning the anti-Semitism of the biblical account; but the program contains no discussion of the issue, or even an acknowledgment that the text had been altered.[8] Apart from Foss I know of no other performer of the St. John Passion who has had sufficient courage—or, if you prefer, sufficient disrespect for art—to duplicate his act. Both of the English-language recordings of the work that are known to me—an old one under Robert Shaw and a somewhat less old one under Benjamin Britten—keep the Jews in their place of dishonor.[9]

It is not surprising that this should be so. To commit such a textual substitution, or to espouse such a view as Marissen or I have voiced, means favoring, in case of conflict, the interests of the contemporary audience above those of the ancient hallowed dead. Ultimately it means rejecting what elsewhere I have called the "poietic fallacy," meaning the belief that what matters most (or more strongly, that all that matters) in evaluating a work of art is the quality of the maker's input, not its effect on an audience. For at least a century and a half, the poietic fallacy has been one of the main props to the whole concept of art as opposed to entertainment, its great Other.[10] Hence the brouhahas.

---

7. Marissen, *Lutheranism*, 6.

8. For the correspondence, see http://archives.nyphil.org/index.php/artifact/b43a520f-f010-42d9-b4ea-bdae80f0ba58; for the program, see http://archives.nyphil.org/index.php/artifact/d50ca831-0bc0-457b-9961-97ea01a8cadc/fullview#page/6/mode/2up .

9. The Shaw recording was issued by RCA Victor (LM 6103) in 1950; the Britten was issued in Great Britain by Decca in 1972 and has been reissued in the United States on CD (London 443 859-2).

10. See R. Taruskin, "The Poietic Fallacy," *Musical Times* 145, no. 1886 (Spring 2004): 7–34; reprinted in *The Danger of Music*, 301–30.

One of them concerned Stravinsky, a composer to whom I have devoted many "disinterested" scholarly investigations. In 1952, not centuries before the Holocaust but seven years after it, Stravinsky set to music, as part of his *Cantata on Old English Texts*, an anonymous fifteenth-century English carol that repeats the blood libel against the Jews:

> The Jews on me they made great suit
> And with me made great variance
> Because they lov'd darkness rather than light.

When Stravinsky made his second, stereophonic, recording of the *Cantata* in 1965, according to the authoritative if not infallible Robert Craft, the tenor, Alexander Young, was invited to alter the phrase "The Jews on me" to "My enemies," but Young refused, as he put it, "to tamper with a classic," even with the composer's consent.[11] I have doubts about the story, which Craft told at second hand (saying he had only "heard" that this had happened at a recording session he had not attended) in polemical rebuttal to my claim that Stravinsky's setting the line when he did showed that "his artistic sensibilities were more acute than his moral ones."[12] I also expressed doubt as to the truth of a letter from Lillian Libman, Stravinsky's personal manager, claiming (in reply to a protest by Jacob Drachler, a painter) that "Mr. Stravinsky . . . got quite a jolt from the lines himself when he first heard the piece, and he had changed the text, substituting, I think, 'my foes' or 'my enemies' (we can't remember which)." I called the letter "an offhand attempt to dispose of a nuisance."[13] Others have sought and found in Libman's letter vindication against any suggestion that Stravinsky entertained any personal prejudice against Jews.[14]

My view, that Stravinsky set the text not necessarily with malice but in an aesthetically justified indifference to the fate of the Jews, received some unexpected confirmation when Robert Craft published a volume of memoirs—his own, not Stravinsky's—in 2002. There he revealed that after Stravinsky conducted the première performance of the *Cantata* at a Los Angeles Chamber Symphony concert in November 1952,

---

11. Robert Craft, in "Jews and Geniuses: An Exchange" (with R. Taruskin), *New York Review of Books*, 16 February 1989; available online at www.nybooks.com/articles/1989/06/15/jews-and-geniuses-an-exchange.

12. R. Taruskin, in "Jews and Geniuses: An Exchange" (with Robert Craft), cited in previous note. See also R. Taruskin, "Stravinsky and Us," in *Cambridge Companion to Stravinsky*, ed. Jonathan Cross (Cambridge: Cambridge University Press, 2003), 260–84, at 279; reprinted in Taruskin, *The Danger of Music*, 429–47.

13. *The Danger of Music*, 440.

14. E.g., Pieter van den Toorn, "Will Stravinsky Survive Postmodernism?" *Music Theory Spectrum* 22 (2000): 121.

the piece was savaged by Mildred Norton, a Los Angeles reviewer, because of the line.... Stravinsky contended that the offending line amounted to dogma at the time it was written, and that the poem was an untouchable classic.... Lawrence [Morton] wished to program the Cantata in one of his 1953 concerts [called Evenings on the Roof at the time] and asked me to discuss with him the possibility of changing the line and of convincing Stravinsky to accept it. After much thought and a slight adjustment of the musical rhythm, we agreed to substitute the phrase "My enemies on me made great suit." I took him to see Stravinsky, whom he did not know, and who said that he had not intended to hurt or affront anyone and that the reaction had surprised him. By this time he had received a letter from Alexander [*recte* Alexandre] Tansman, his biographer in the early California years, then living in Paris, criticizing him for having set such a text only seven years after the opening of the death camps. Stravinsky did not answer and never spoke to Tansman again.[15]

Indeed, Craft reports that four years later, on coming unexpectedly face to face with Tansman, "his close friend in Hollywood during the war years, ... Stravinsky cut him dead, ignored his outstretched hand, and did not utter a word in response to his welcome," so resentful was he over Tansman's disapproval of his choice of texts to set. Nevertheless, Craft continued, Stravinsky "consented to my Evenings on the Roof performance with the emended text. It is not printed in the score, and the only recorded performance that uses it is mine."[16]

By the time he made that record, Craft and I had clashed in print over the matter in the *New York Review*,[17] and I had drawn further attention to it in a review published in the *New York Times* in 1992.[18] Later I made the *Cantata* the culminating exhibit in "Stravinsky and Us," my 1996 Proms inaugural lecture, which I repeated on many platforms before publishing it in 2003.[19] I feel entitled, perhaps, to some of the credit or the blame for Robert Craft's decision finally to record the textual substitution he claimed to have proposed in 1952. Because the recording was not accompanied by any announcement or discussion of the substitution, it counts as a bowdlerization if not a case of actual censorship.

This brouhaha went on for a while. In March 2004 you could have gone to your local newsstand and bought the current issues of both of the main British music magazines, in either of which you would have found a denunciation of my Proms lecture in its published version. In *BBC Music Magazine,* Bayan Northcott found it "depressing" that anyone would publish my "much-pedalled [*sic!*] thesis ... that Stravinsky managed to impose his formalist values so totally on modernism that

---

15. Robert Craft, *An Improbable Life* (Nashville: Vanderbilt University Press, 2002), 137–38.
16. Ibid., 180. The recording to which Craft here refers is "Stravinsky the Composer, vol. VIII: In New Directions" (Music Masters 67158 [1995]). The tenor soloist is Thomas Bogdan.
17. See the exchange referenced in notes 11 and 12 above.
18. "Stravinsky's Darkness and Light," *New York Times,* Arts and Leisure, 9 August 1992, 25.
19. See note 12.

when he set a line of anti-Semitic medieval verse six [*sic*] years after the Holocaust, nobody protested or even noticed. He entitles this tissue of tendentious generalizations and tricky logic 'Stravinsky and Us.' Speak for yourself, Professor Taruskin."

That I do. But at least Northcott, even if he—trickily? tendentiously?—exaggerated it, got my thesis right. In *The Gramophone*, Stephen Walsh, Stravinsky's biographer, deplored my attempt "to get us to close our ears to the anti-Semitic line in Stravinsky's *Cantata*." How obtuse is that? I adduce these topsy-turvy responses to my efforts to get listeners to open their ears as proof that I am not arguing with straw men. We remain conditioned by the formalist values to which Northcott obliquely called attention, to the point where my reviewers—and they were far from alone—simply could not cope intellectually with an argument that called for the ethical or political evaluation of an admired work of art. Instead we are, many of us, merely repelled viscerally, or phobically.

II

Perhaps that is because we still associate such calls with once powerful, now discredited totalitarian viewpoints. They remind us uncomfortably, perhaps, of old Soviet habits. True enough, the history of Soviet music teems with examples of textual substitutions like the ones practiced by Foss on Bach or Craft on Stravinsky. And because they were demanded not by a critic or a musicologist but by a government that had a monopoly on political power, and one that was fully prepared to repress both works and their creators, these examples count, even on the strictest construction, as censorship in that they constituted what is known in American law as prior restraint: interference in advance to prevent publication or performance, or to demand alteration as the price of dissemination.

The best-known instance, and the exemplary one, was the refurbishing of the libretto to Glinka's patriotic opera *A Life for the Tsar* so as to remove the Tsar for whom the titular life is laid down. It was the only way to preserve for the Soviet performing repertory, and return to active duty, the foundation stone of the Russian musical canon at a time (1939: the year of the Hitler-Stalin pact and the rape of Poland) when Russia was in need of an infusion of old-fashioned patriotism to supplement the internationalist revolutionary message of Marxism-Leninism. (Nor did it hurt that the opera features a built-in, highly invidious contrast of Russian and Polish musical idioms.) The absence of the foundation stone from the performable repertoire was an embarrassing anomaly. Earlier Glinka's opera had been the obligatory season opener for the Russian Imperial Theaters. But that was just the trouble: the foundation stone had been laid in the name of what was known in Tsarist times as Official Nationalism, a doctrine that located the integrity of the nation in the integrity of dynastic rulership, that identified the legitimacy of the nation in the divine right of its sovereign, and that thus implicitly supported every institution that supported the Tsarist hierarchy, right down to, and especially, the institution of serfdom. The culminating "Hymn-march," as Glinka called it, a rousing anthem (to a text by the poet Vasiliy Zhukovsky) with a melody that had been skillfully foreshadowed throughout the four acts that preceded it, proclaimed the civic and religious unity—in the person of the Tsar—that the opera was written to sanctify:

> Slav'sya, slav'sya nash russkiy tsar'! Glory, glory to thee, our Russian Caesar!
> Gospodom dannïy nam tsar'-gosudar! Our sovereign, granted us by God!
> Da budet bessmerten tvoy tsarskiy rod! May thy royal line be immortal!
> Da im blagodenstvuyet russkiy narod! May the Russian people prosper
>   through it!

Its replacement, the culmination of the new libretto by Sergey Gorodetsky, transferred the object of the titular sacrifice to the people's militia, organized against the marauding Poles by a peasant named Minin (who is named in the new text) and a nobleman named Pozharsky (who is not), and made *Rus'*—ancient, holy Russia—the object of veneration at the end:

> Slav'sya, slav'sya tï, Rus' moya! Glory, glory to thee, O Russia mine!
> Slav'sya tï russkaya nasha zemlya! Glory to thee, our Russian land!
> Da budet vo veki vekov sil'na May for all eternity mighty be
> Lyubimaya nasha rodnaya strana! Our beloved native country!

What the Soviets did in 1939 had innumerable precedents in the nineteenth century, when state censorship of theaters was considered normal everywhere in Europe, but was particularly stringent in Tsarist Russia, where practically no opera was performed with its original libretto. (Rossini's *Guillaume Tell*, for example, was performed in London and Berlin as *Andreas Hofer*, set in the Austrian Tyrol, and at the St. Petersburg Italian Opera as *Carlo il Temerario*, set in fifteenth-century Burgundy.)[20]

Nevertheless, the reinstatement of the original Tsarist text by the Moscow Bolshoy Theater in 1989 was a thrill—to be followed two years later by the re-adoption of the Tsarist Russian tricolor flag and the Imperial double-headed eagle as state seal. Glinka's restored opera signaled the beginning of the end for Soviet power. You didn't have to be a monarchist to applaud it.

But here is its funhouse mirror reflection. The same year that Gorodetsky revised the libretto to Glinka's opera, Stalin celebrated his sixtieth birthday (on December 21, as if by design the shortest day—and longest night—of the year). Sergey Prokofieff, only lately back in the USSR after eighteen years in emigration,

---

20. See Abram A. Gozenpud, *Russkiy opernïy teatr XIX veka (1857–1872)* (Leningrad: Muzïka, 1971), 78.

honored what seem to have been the terms of an implicit contract and greeted the event with his *Zdravitsa*, or "Toast to Stalin," a beautiful choral-orchestral composition that glorified, as a sort of Jascha Appleseed, one of the great twentieth-century butchers. Prokofieff actually did a lot of the work on this piece in the United States, during his last foreign tour in 1938, some of it, evidently, sitting poolside in a luxury California hotel.[21] Here is the culmination, replete with high Cs for the choral sopranos on the final word:

Nashey kreposti vïsokoy—znamya tï!	Thou art the banner on our fortress high!
Mïsley nashikh, krovi nashey—	Thou art the fire in our thoughts,
plamya tï, STALIN!	our blood, O STALIN!

To ask the sopranos to sing that high on the final vowel of Stalin's name was, one might argue, already an example of Soviet oppression. But then, seventeen years later, came Khrushchev's famous "secret speech," and Stalin's name went the way of the Tsar's. Prokofieff's *Zdravitsa* continued in repertory, but the text was changed to register the new political situation. As the Tsar had been replaced by Rus' at the end of Glinka's opera, so Stalin was now replaced by the Party as recipient of Prokofieff's toast. Supplanting Stalin's name, fortunately, was easy. The ever trusty "Slava!," Russian for "Hooray," stood ready.

I siyayet solntse nashe nad stranoy	And our sun shines over the country
I poyom mï slavu partiyi rodnoy!	And we sing the praises of our beloved
SLAVA!	Party! HOORAY!

As in the case of Glinka's opera, when it comes to illustrating this change with recordings, one finds, as if paradoxically, that recorded performances of *Zdravitsa* with the original text are likely to be more recent than those of the bowdlerized versions. That is because, in the wake of the Soviet collapse, it became fashionable to perform not only the *Zdravitsa* but other musical artifacts as well of what, since Khrushchev's speech, has been known as the "cult of the personality" (*kul't lichnosti*—more accurately the cult of [Stalin's] person) with their original texts intact. Going back to Stalinist originals is a harder thing to explain than going back to Tsarist ones, and my attempts to account for it have amounted to my brouhaha No. 2. My best guess is that it is cathartic for Russian musicians now to perform, as an assertion of political liberty, anything that had ever been banned under the

---

21. On the improbable story of *Zdravitsa*, and also Prokofieff's other Stalinist potboiler, the "October Cantata," see Simon Morrison and Nelly Kravetz, "The Cantata for the Twentieth Anniversary of October, or How the Specter of Communism Haunted Prokofiev," *Journal of Musicology* 23 (2006): 227–62; on its text, see Vladimir Orlov, "Prokofiev and the Myth of the Father of Nations: The Cantata *Zdravitsa*," *Journal of Musicology* 30 (2013): 577–620.

Soviets; and under Vladimir Putin a mini-cult of Stalin's person has sprung up among those who would like to Make Russia Great Again.

And yet, when it comes to glorifying Stalin, I would like to see them draw the line. Unlike the tsars, Stalin still has living victims, and I would much prefer that works glorifying him remained unplayed for now, or perhaps relegated, like the statuary monuments of Soviet rule, to a special playground—and I've said so. And I have been met by a huge blast of indignant protest at my apparent wish to censor works of "intrinsic musical worth," to quote John Rockwell of the *New York Times*.[22] Vladimir Ashkenazy, who has made quite a specialty of cult-of-personality fare, lumps *Zdravitsa* with the propitiatory offerings Prokofieff and Shostakovich made after the Communist Party's "Resolution on Music" of 1948, which had accused them of "formalism." His account, put forward in the *New York Times* to promote or justify a Carnegie Hall performance of *Zdravitsa* (as well as Shostakovich's music for the film *The Fall of Berlin*, in which Stalin descends godlike from the sky to proclaim the restoration of peace after World War II), rehearses a familiar litany of distortion:

> *Zdravitsa* ("A Toast"), written in 1939 for Stalin's 60th birthday, was one of several pieces in which Prokofiev demonstrated his new loyalties. He was stunned when, despite these efforts, he was denounced in 1948.... Shostakovich was immediately dismissed from his posts at the Moscow and Leningrad conservatories. In addition, performances of most of his and Prokofiev's major pieces were banned. Since this fiat was printed in all the major Soviet newspapers, either composer could have been arrested by the MGB (a predecessor of the KGB).... Shostakovich was warned to protect himself as much as he could. The only thing left to him was to accept without hesitation commissions from the authorities for an oratorio, "Song of the Forests," and music for the films "The Fall of Berlin" and "The Unforgettable Year 1919." Similarly, Prokofiev had to write his "On Guard for Peace." All these pieces offered obsequious glorifications of Stalin. No doubt the dictator was delighted; both composers received Stalin prizes, and danger was averted for the moment. Whatever criticism one may make of this often unadventurous and simplistic music, it is not hard to speculate what turn the composers' lives would have taken if these compromises had not been made.[23]

His performance of *Zdravitsa*, Ashkenazy implies, amounted to a symbolic plea on behalf of the suffering composer: Look what they made him do. But *Zdravitsa* was composed on Prokofieff's own initiative as part of a Faustian bargain with the Soviet regime, which wooed him in the thirties with promises, kept at first, of

---

22. The phrase comes from Rockwell's introductory essay in the program book for the Lincoln Center Festival, of which he was the curator, in 1996. He was replying to my centennial article "Prokofiev, Hail... and Farewell?" *New York Times*, Arts and Leisure, 21 April 1991, 25.

23. Vladimir Ashkenazy, "Making Music in the Shadow of Stalin," *New York Times*, 16 February 2003.

unique privileges and lavish compensation. Nor is the work unadventurous or simplistic. In fact, judged by its music alone, it is arguably among Prokofieff's finest creations. Many excellent musicians were bowled over by it at the time of its première. In a memoir published in 1961, Sviatoslav Richter recalled "the unforgettable impression" he had received "from one of [Prokofieff's] best works, the little *Zdravitsa*: it was not a composition but some kind of blinding flash [*eto ozareniye kakoye-to, a ne sochineniye . . .*]."[24] As late as 1997, the year of his death, in a post-Soviet filmed interview, Richter allowed that although its subject matter rendered it no longer playable, nevertheless it was "an absolute work of genius" (*eto absolyutno genial'noye proizvedeniye*).[25] That more or less sums up my opinion as well.

My resistance to performing it despite my admiration for its music stems not from a wish to exercise censorship. Coercion is wrong from any quarter. I would hope, rather, to persuade the likes of Rockwell and Ashkenazy to get beyond their need to defend the worshipped figure of the composer and recognize the need for some discretion in the name of Stalin's victims. Is it really an insult to Prokofieff or to his memory to be nauseated at the sight of well-fed and carefree people lustily cheering works that glorify a mass murderer because they like the tunes?

It could never happen with Hitler. The whole premise of Mel Brooks's *The Producers*—film and musical alike—is that glorifications of Hitler are absolutely taboo, whatever the occasion or the medium, and that the taboo can be overcome only through the broadest, most unsubtle satire that, in the movie or show, is obvious and knowing on the part of all concerned—author, actors, and audience alike (although, according to the ridiculous plot, inadvertent). Corroboration of the absolute taboo on Nazi language in respectable places is ubiquitous and nothing if not fastidious. One example I found quite by accident, listening to a Bayreuther Festspiele recording of Wagner's *Lohengrin*, preserving the Wieland Wagner production first mounted in 1958,[26] is the alteration of the title character's last words on stage, immediately before his departure after restoring Gottfried von Brabant to his human form. According to the original score, he sings:

Seht da den Herzog von Brabant!	Behold the Duke of Brabant!
Zum Führer sei er euch ernannt!	Let him be proclaimed your leader!

But in the recorded live performance, the tainted word *Führer,* on which of course Lohengrin reaches his loudest and longest high A, is changed to *Schützer* (protector or custodian), lest an unwelcome (or at least impolitic) association impinge on

---

24. "O Prokof'yeve," in Semyon Isaakovich Shlifshteyn, ed., *S. S. Prokof'yev: Materialï, dokumentï, vospominaniya*, 2nd ed. (Moscow: Muzgiz, 1961), 455–70, at 470.
25. Bruno Monsaingeon, *Richter: L'Insoumis/The Enigma/Der Unbeugsame* (1998).
26. Cond. Wolfgang Sawallisch, Philips 6747 241 (4 LPs, 1966).

listeners' consciousness.²⁷ That squeamishness no longer attaches to the memory of Stalin, and perhaps it never did, whether inside or outside former Soviet territory. For Americans, Hitler was the wartime enemy, Stalin the wartime ally. Political murder does not inspire as much revulsion, it seems, as racial genocide. In Russia, Stalin has been a political football, and an ambiguous emblem. Even during my stay there in the 1970s as an exchange student, it was possible, though officially frowned on, to praise Stalin as an emblem of pertinacity and strong leadership. For some, he was a macho idol. I was told that truck drivers liked to display little Stalin icons on their dashboards, and I witnessed myself a spontaneous cheer when Stalin appeared fleetingly in a war documentary that was released during my time there. Now he is undergoing a more ominous rehabilitation in Putin's Russia, which only makes it seem the more urgent that his victims, who were just as dead or ruined as Hitler's, and comparably numerous, be shown respect, which to my mind includes the same exercise in discretion that is routinely performed in the case of the Nazi dictator.

These matters are debatable, of course; but debatable matters need to be debated openly, not silenced on spurious grounds of aesthetic propriety. The difficulty I have had in getting many of my readers to see the difference between discretion and censorship seems to me sadly symptomatic of the attitudes that have been instilled in classical musicians and music lovers. A pitiful sign of the times, it is—I would suggest—a clue as to why the prestige of classical music now seems to be in an irreversible decline.

III

Before moving on to other examples of easily derided Soviet censorship, I'd like to remind you of a similar case involving Beethoven—or is it a similar case? The largest and most ambitious composition Beethoven completed during what Lewis Lockwood has termed "the fallow years," the six years separating the Eighth Sym-

---

27. My curiosity aroused, I took a little census on YouTube and found an additional substitution: *Herrscher* (sovereign, ruler) in a 2012 La Scala performance under Daniel Barenboim (www.youtube.com/watch?v=H6MWyCP-r8o, at 1:01:12). *Schützer* appears to have been introduced by Wieland Wagner. Its status as the official postwar Bayreuth version is corroborated by a 1960 recording under Maazel (www.youtube.com/watch?v=g1w2Pz-AWAY, at 1:00:12), but an earlier Bayreuth clip, from 1953, under Joseph Kielberth, featuring Wolfgang Windgassen, keeps *Führer* in its place (www.youtube.com/watch?v=seK-2qH_PZw, at 7:09). The F-word can also of course be heard in prewar broadcast clips from the Metropolitan Opera (1935) under Artur Bodanzky, featuring Lauritz Melchior (www.youtube.com/watch?v=IEczOsot4wM at 12:37), and Bayreuth (1936) under Furtwängler, featuring Franz Völker (www.youtube.com/watch?v=GKmQjiVxwg8, at 7:28), as well as in an old Vienna recording under Rudolf Kempe (www.youtube.com/watch?v=9VCxrJQ4oxY, at 2:56) and, much more recently, the 2009 Naxos recording under Semyon Bychkov (www.youtube.com/watch?v=Jthu-8oLU2s, at 6:57), where it might even have been a "principled" restoration in the name of "authenticity."

phony (op. 93) and the *Hammerklavier* Sonata (op. 106),[28] was a cantata called *Der glorreiche Augenblick,* op. 136. The anomaly in the opus numbers tells us that the cantata was not published during Beethoven's lifetime. It was, in fact, his first *opus posthumum*. And it is possible that you have never heard of it, let alone heard it, since from the beginning the cantata—a bombastic political potboiler performed before the assembled crowned heads of Europe gathered for the Congress of Vienna in 1815 to celebrate "the glorious moment" of imperial restoration following the final defeat and exile of Napoleon—has been the dirty secret of the Beethoven catalogue. Its first recording was not issued until 1997.[29]

So utterly does this reactionary harangue fail to fit the heroic Beethoven myth that when it was finally published, in 1837, its text was replaced by a more "aesthetic" sort of celebration, *Preis der Tonkunst* (In Praise of Music) by Friedrich Rochlitz, who as editor of the *Allgemeine musikalische Zeitung* was the most influential critic of his time. Rochlitz did for Beethoven exactly what Gorodetsky would later do for Glinka. And though it may seem that the cases are not analogous, since one was evidently self-motivated, or perhaps requested by the publisher, as an antipolitical intervention, while the other was a notorious instance of political intervention by a one-party state, they both had the same purpose: namely, to make what was deemed a desirable piece kosher for performance and publication.

There is a move afoot in Beethoven scholarship to upgrade *Der glorreiche Augenblick*. Three scholars thus far—Nicholas Mathew, William Kinderman, and (especially) Stephen Rumph—have declared it an indispensable document for understanding the composer's fugue-happy late period, since it furnishes a cultural and, yes, political correlate for his unexpected stylistic turn toward religious—or perhaps better, religiose—archaism.[30] That scholarly move has met predictable opposition from traditionalist scholars like Lockwood, who refuses to see in the cantata anything more than "patriotic sycophantry," a "plodding fabrication," a "casual simulation" of Beethoven's "serious style, . . . toss[ed] off . . . to capitalize on current national feeling, and [worst of all?] to make money."[31] Do we care if such a work is altered or eradicated by others? Should we? Lockwood seems to call for its suppression when he writes that works like *Wellington's Victory* and *Der glorreiche Augenblick* "should be set aside as negligible byproducts, not as works in

---

28. Lewis Lockwood, *Beethoven: The Music and the Life* (New York: W. W. Norton, 2002), ch. 16 ("The 'Fallow' Years"), 333–48.

29. Koch International Classics 7737 (Collegiate Chorale and Orchestra of St. Lukes under Robert Bass).

30. Nicholas Mathew, *Political Beethoven* (Cambridge: Cambridge University Press, 2013); William Kinderman, *Beethoven* (New York: Oxford University Press, 2001; 2nd ed., 2010); Stephen Rumph, *Beethoven after Napoleon: Political Romanticism in the Late Works* (Berkeley: University of California Press, 2004).

31. Lockwood, *Beethoven*, 339–40.

FIGURE 2.1. *Bozhe, Tsarya khrani!* (Russian Imperial hymn), words by Vasiliy Andreyevich Zhukovsky, music by Alexey Fyodorovich Lvov. Composer's autograph.

the main line."[32] Is his position, with which I am not in sympathy, any different from my own stance with respect to Prokofieff's *Zdravitsa*? Am I being arbitrary or inconsistent? I'll leave that one unanswered for now, with a promise to return to the question of consistency in conclusion.

Another work that is reliably denigrated as a potboiler is Chaikovsky's irrepressible *1812* Overture, and here we can return to the Soviet scene and witness some unusual instances of politically motivated suppression or alteration of textless music. Or is it untexted? Chaikovsky's overture may be not have words underlaid to its notes, but it quotes a number of texted pieces, one of which—the Tsarist hymn *Bozhe, tsarya khrani!* (God Save the Tsar), to a melody by Alexey Lvov that was adopted in 1833—was of course forbidden in Soviet Russia (fig. 2.1).

Like many of the passages that have already figured in this discussion, the quotation of the forbidden melody comes at the most conspicuous place possible, the peroration, replete with obbligato cannonades.[33] And yet even in Soviet times, the *1812* Overture was an indispensable warhorse. The solution was to commission the Soviet composer Vissarion Shebalin (1902–63) to splice Glinka's newly sanitized "Hymn-march" into Chaikovsky's climax. Fortunately for us, we can still hear this relic from the *ancien régime soviétique* on YouTube. See if you can keep a straight face when you hear it: www.youtube.com/watch?v=kOEAtiBNMvc, at 14:00. If you laughed, as almost everyone does to whom I've played this surrogate climax,

---

32. Ibid., 347.
33. In case you need a reminder, YouTube can supply it: www.youtube.com/watch?v=VbxgYlcNxE8, at 13:59.

it is probably not only because the seams show (though they do, egregiously), but because, as we know now, the Hymn-march was just as tainted by Tsarism as the official hymn. Both their texts were composed by the same great poet, Vasiliy Zhukovsky, who in his day was an enthusiastically reactionary censor on behalf of the Tsar's regime. Indeed, Glinka's march was often used as an alternate national anthem in the nineteenth century, especially before Lvov's melody was composed as an alternative setting of words that Zhukovsky had originally written to fit the tune of "God Save the King."

Politics was not the only grounds for censorship in the USSR. Prudery, common to all authoritarian regimes, was another dependable motive. Here the locus classicus was Shostakovich's opera *The Lady Macbeth of the Mtsensk District*, with its sensational rape scene, which prompted W. J. Henderson, a New York critic of the old guard, to declare Shostakovich "without a doubt the foremost composer of pornographic music in the history of the art."[34] Unlike Glinka's or Prokofieff's or Chaikovsky's pieces, Shostakovich's opera was not doctored after it had been unexpectedly denounced in the historic unsigned *Pravda* editorial "Muddle Instead of Music" in 1936.[35] The state had no interest in salvaging it, so it was simply repressed, not to return to the Soviet stage until 1962. By then Shostakovich had subjected the score to a revision so thorough as to require a new opus number, creating a problem of versions as acute as that of Musorgsky's *Boris Godunov*.[36] One of the things that went, predictably, was the so-called pornophony.

Perhaps needless to say, Shostakovich's opera is now performed only in its original version, and returning to the original in this case might seem a particularly virtuous act of restoration. The story of the original opera's suppression is one of the most blatant and brutal in the annals of totalitarianism as it affected the arts, and its restitution is therefore seen as a particularly significant vindication of the composer's integrity. But just as in the case of *Boris Godunov*, the matter is not as simple as it may look. Many purported restorers of Shostakovich's opera, or Musorgsky's, actually conflate the versions tacitly. In the case of Shostakovich, the

---

34. *New York Sun*, 9 February 1935. He went on, "The whole scene is little better than a glorification of the sort of stuff that filthy pencils write on lavatory walls." See Nicolas Slonimsky, *Lexicon of Musical Invective: Critical Assaults on Composers since Beethoven's Time*, 2nd ed. (Seattle: University of Washington Press, 1969), 176. In some of my earlier writings I erroneously traced to Henderson the coinage "pornophony," long associated with Shostakovich's opera; its origins remain (to me) obscure.

35. "Sumbur vmesto muzïki," *Pravda*, 28 January 1936 (now known to have been the work of David Iosifovich Zaslavsky, a staff writer); both a facsimile of the Russian text and a translation may be found in Piero Weiss and Richard Taruskin, ed., *Music in the Western World: A History in Documents*, 2nd ed. (Belmont, CA: Thomson/Schirmer, 2007), 422–24.

36. On *Boris*, see R. Taruskin, "Musorgsky vs. Musorgsky: The Versions of *Boris Godunov*," *19th-Century Music* 8 (1983–84): 91–118, 245–72; reprinted in Taruskin, *Musorgsky: Eight Essays and an Epilogue* (Princeton: Princeton University Press, 1993), 201–99.

revised version of the final scene, which depicts a convoy of prisoners en route to Siberia, is often retained. Shostakovich expanded that scene when he revised the opera, and in particular expanded the role of an "old convict" whose manly bass voice has seemed to many listeners and commentators to be the conscience of the play. Indeed, the expanded last scene is easily read as the composer's oblique reference to his own plight as a creative spirit imprisoned within a totalitarian environment, and so its interpolation into the version of the opera that was suppressed seems like an apt internal comment on that suppression.

And yet, since the publication in 1993 of Shostakovich's letters to his friend Isaak Glikman, we have had strong evidence that Shostakovich sincerely meant to remove much of what had offended the Soviet leadership in 1936, and the pornophony in particular. In March 1955 he sent to Glikman a list of the changes he proposed to make in the libretto before submitting the opera for rehabilitation.[37] All of them were motivated, he now said, by a civil solicitude, altogether at variance with the composer's brash and somewhat cynical younger self, for the sensibilities of the audience. The text that had been suppressed now embarrassed him, he said; there is reason to believe that the graphic sexual imagery of the music did likewise. We do know that he made efforts after 1960, when the new version was well on its way, to discourage performances of the old (for example, at La Scala and at the Deutsche Oper am Rhein in Düsseldorf).[38] Thus it is not at all clear that those who restore the pornophony in *Lady Macbeth* are truly vindicating the composer. They may with equal justice be viewed as overriding the composer's wishes—is that censorship?—and pandering to the tastes of the contemporary audience. In any case, audiences today sooner react to the pornophonic scene not with shock but with amusement. Could that possibly be what the composer intended? Does that matter?

There is one case where I think it definitely does matter that we restore the composer's original version: namely, Prokofieff's Seventh Symphony, his last, composed in 1952 after his body had been weakened by a severe brain concussion and a whole series of heart attacks, and his spirit had been crushed by the so-called *Zhdanovshchina*, the postwar clampdown on the arts administered by Andrey

---

37. Letter of 21 March 1955, in Dmitriy Shostakovich–Isaak Glikman, *Pis'ma k drugu* (Moscow: DSCH; St. Petersburg: Kompozitor, 1993), 109–10; translated in *Story of a Friendship: The Letters of Dmitry Shostakovich to Isaak Glikman 1941–1975*, trans. Anthony Phillips (London: Faber & Faber, 2001), 55–57.

38. Laurel E. Fay, *Shostakovich: A Life* (New York: Oxford University Press, 2000), 237. The Düsseldorf production in 1959, actually the German staged première, was advertised as "the last time the work would be shown in its original version." That was the production Elliott Carter attended and later excoriated in an oft-cited review ("Current Chronicle: Germany, 1960," *Musical Quarterly* 46 [1960]: 367–71; reprinted in *The Writings of Elliott Carter*, ed. Else Stone and Kurt Stone [Bloomington: Indiana University Press, 1977], 212–16).

Zhdanov, Stalin's culture czar. Like the other members of the so-called Big Four of Soviet music—Shostakovich, Khachaturyan, Myaskovsky—who had been censured along with him at the January 1948 hearings that Zhdanov convened at the headquarters of the Central Committee of the Soviet Communist Party, Prokofieff made efforts to conform, and the Seventh Symphony, dedicated to Soviet youth, was one of these. Dmitry Kabalevsky, Prokofieff's minder in those terrible years, has recalled Prokofieff's concern that he might have overfulfilled the norm, so to speak, simplifying his music to the point of childishness.[39]

In the end, the symphony was given a posthumous Lenin Prize, redeeming Prokofieff's reputation as a Soviet composer—but not before a final revision was exacted. The symphony ended with a slow, refulgent coda, easily enough read, I should think, as nostalgic. Word came back to Prokofieff after the symphony's *pokaz* ("showing," i.e. audition) at the Union of Composers that the ending was not deemed optimistic enough, in the spirit of socialist realism. So for the sake of the dangled prize (something he could not ignore in view of the straitened circumstances to which the Zhdanovshchina had reduced him) Prokofieff tacked on a coda to the coda, which reprised the zippy first theme of the finale. It was almost the last music he wrote.[40] Like so much music composed during the five years between the Zhdanovshchina and the death of Stalin, the revised ending of Prokofieff's Seventh Symphony is attractively tuneful, enormously skilled, and altogether unendurable to anyone who knows its history.

IV

Far less well known than the Soviet Zhdanovshchina was the American one, which actually preceded its Soviet counterpart by several months. Calling it a Zhdanovshchina is of course a heavy, possibly clubfooted, irony. Its ostensible aim seemed diametrically opposed to the Soviet one, since it sought to purge American art and entertainment of communist values rather than enforce them. But it was similar in its early–Cold War zeal to repudiate the wartime alliance that united the USA and the USSR in opposition to the now vanquished threat of fascism, and to redefine national values in opposition to a new adversary. The earliest victim was Hanns Eisler, a German Jewish Communist who had sought refuge in the United States, and who was deported to the Soviet zone of occupied Germany for being "the Karl Marx of Communism in the musical field," to quote the chief counsel of the House

---

39. Dmitry Kabalevsky, "A Vivid Personality," in *Sergei Prokofiev: Autobiography, Articles, Reminiscences*, ed. S. Shlifstein, trans. Rose Prokofeva (Honolulu: University Press of the Pacific, 2001), 219.

40. For the full story, see Simon Morrison, *The People's Artist: Prokofiev's Soviet Years* (New York: Oxford University Press, 2009), 373; and Marina Frolova-Walker, *Stalin's Music Prize: Soviet Culture and Politics* (New Haven, CT: Yale University Press, 2016), 81–88. Frolova-Walker attributes the idea of the alternative ending to Samuil Samosud, who conducted the première.

of Representatives Committee on Un-American Activities, before which Eisler was interrogated in September 1947 by freshman congressman Richard M. Nixon, among others.[41] The most famous victim was Aaron Copland, whose music had come, during the depression and the war, virtually to define America to classical music audiences worldwide. He was summoned to testify before Senator Joseph McCarthy's Permanent Subcommittee on Investigations in the spring of 1953.

A few weeks earlier, one of Copland's most overtly patriotic works, *A Lincoln Portrait,* composed in 1942 (the first full year of America's involvement in the war), became an object of political controversy when it was selected by the Republican National Committee (Lincoln having been the first Republican president) for performance at a concert to celebrate the inauguration of Dwight David Eisenhower, the Supreme Allied Commander of the war in Europe, as president on January 20, 1953. It seemed an irreproachable choice as inauguration fare, its closing pages rehearsing the stirring conclusion of the Gettysburg Address. But Fred Busbey, a Republican congressman from Illinois, Lincoln's state, took vociferous exception. Copland had taken part in the notorious Cultural and Scientific Conference for World Peace, held at New York's Waldorf-Astoria Hotel in 1949. That identified him, in the words of *Life* magazine, which gave the event a lot of unfriendly publicity, as among the "dupes and fellow travelers" of the world communist movement.[42] Busbey complained, on the floor of the House of Representatives, that "there are many patriotic composers available without the long record of questionable affiliations of Copland. The Republican Party would have been ridiculed from one end of the United States to the other if Copland's music had been played at the inaugural of a President elected to fight communism, along with other things."[43] Copland's work was stricken from the program, which, now devoid of any American music at all, could be fairly called an un-American activity.

A Lincoln Portrait, like Copland's reputation, has survived the invidious leftist taint: one of its most prominent recordings featured, as the voice of Lincoln, the actor Charlton Heston, already famous as the voice of Moses, who later achieved a second renown as the voice of the National Rifle Association. More recent performers of the part have included Senator Alan K. Simpson, Republican of Wyoming, and even the Baroness Margaret Thatcher. But when you hear the first recording of the piece, made in February 1946, in which the Lincoln part is read—in a vociferous manner, quite the opposite of the suave pastoral delivery now standard—by Melvyn

---

41. "Hearings Regarding Hanns Eisler/Committee on Un-American Activities/House of Rrepresentatives/Washington, D.C./24, 25 and 26 September 1947," in *Music since 1900,* ed. Nicolas Slonimsky, 4th ed. (New York: Charles Scribner's Sons, 1971), 1396. Eisler's response: "I would be flattered" (quoted in Albrecht Betz, *Hanns Eisler: Political Musician,* trans. Bill Hopkins [Cambridge: Cambridge University Press, 2006], 200).

42. *Life,* 4 April 1949, 42.

43. Quoted in Slonimsky (ed.), *Music since 1900,* 951.

FIGURE 2.2. Communist campaign poster, 1936: note Abraham Lincoln, delivering the Gettysburg Address, in the middle of the panel at bottom.

Douglas, another famous Hollywood actor, whose wife, Senator Helen Gahagan Douglas, would be one of the early victims of Nixon's electoral red-baiting, and in which the Boston Symphony Orchestra is conducted by Serge Koussevitzky, who at the time was the chairman of the Music Committee of the National Council of American-Soviet friendship, a committee of which Aaron Copland was vice-chair, you cannot help being reminded of *agitprop*—Soviet agitational propaganda ("of the people, by the PEOPLE, for THE PEOPLE!!").[44]

Congressman Busbey, by his lights, was not wrong. *A Lincoln Portrait* was a product of the Popular Front, the project decreed by the Comintern in 1935 to couch antifascist propaganda not in the image of communist internationalism but in the image of popular nationalism. The Popular Front chimed easily enough with the revolutionary founding myth of the United States, which is why the American Communist Party (for which Aaron Copland had actively campaigned in 1936) could make so much headway with its slogan "Communism is Americanism of the 20th century" (fig. 2.2).[45]

Abraham Lincoln, the Great Emancipator, was another conspicuous point of intersection between Americanist and Communist mythology. The Communist-dominated American contingent that fought on the side of the Loyalists in the Spanish Civil War was called the Abraham Lincoln Brigade. In *The Lonesome Train,* a cantata composed the same year as *A Lincoln Portrait,* Earl Robinson, a composer far more explicitly identified with the Communist Party and its various fronts than Copland, managed to put a paraphrase of the concluding slogan from *The Communist Manifesto* into the mouth of our sixteenth president: "Well, I'll tell ya, ma'am," Robinson's Lincoln drawls (in words by Millard Lampell of the

---

44. It has been reissued on CD: Buddulph Records B000009N73 ("Serge Koussevitzky Plays American Music").

45. See Maurice Isserman, *Which Side Were You On? The American Communist Party during the Second World War* (Middletown, CT: Wesleyan University Press, 1982), 9. On Copland's Communist activities, see Howard Pollack, *Aaron Copland: The Life and Work of an Uncommon Man* (New York: Henry Holt, 1999), 280.

Almanac Singers), "it seems to me the strongest bond of human sympathy, outside your family, of course, should be the one uniting all working people of all nations, tongues, and kindreds."[46]

The year 1942, to repeat, was the first year of America's involvement in the Second World War; and although great efforts have been made to erase the fact from the American memory, the Soviet Union was our ally in that conflict. A decade later those amnesiac efforts were underway, and it is altogether understandable that a Republican politician would have been made squeamish, at the onset of the Cold War, which was just then reaching a critical hot point in Korea, by the prospect of an inadvertent recollection of what had become a highly equivocal fact of American history.

But was removing Copland's *Lincoln Portrait* from the program of a Republican Party gala in fact an act of censorship? Or was it an exercise of discretion, of a kind I myself have advocated in the case of Prokofieff's *Zdravitsa?* It depends, of course, and literally, on where one is coming from—or more precisely, on which among conflicting legitimate interests one chooses to endorse. A closely related recent case was the Boston Symphony Orchestra's cancellation, two months after the terrorist attacks of September 11, 2001, of a scheduled performance of choruses from *The Death of Klinghoffer,* one of the operas masterminded by the director Peter Sellars, which drew upon the talents of poet Alice Goodman and composer John Adams.

The orchestra management decided that performing excerpts from a work that depicts, in a spirit of *tout comprendre c'est tout pardonner,* the killing of a disabled American Jew by Palestinian nationalists would have been inappropriate given the national mood of mourning for the victims of an act perpetrated by a comparable group of Muslim extremists. The decision was widely, and passionately, denounced for what was perceived by many to be an act of censorship. A protest by the arts editor of the *San Francisco Chronicle* vividly conveys the passions, even the hysteria, that the BSO's policy aroused. "There is something deeply wrong," he wrote, "when a nation galvanizes its forces, its men and women, its determination and its resolve, to preserve the right of the yahoos at the Boston Symphony Orchestra to decide to spare its listeners something that might challenge them or make them think."[47]

No nation had done that. And here we come to my brouhaha No. 3, because one of the stronger endorsements the BSO management received at the time was an article I wrote for the *New York Times,* in which I gave reasons for agreeing that the

---

46. The 1944 Decca recording, featuring Burl Ives, is available on YouTube: www.youtube.com/watch?v=F7v4LRrM2B0 (the quoted sentence is at 21:34).

47. David Wiegand, "Boston Symphony Missed the Point on Art and Grieving," *San Francisco Chronicle,* 7 November 2001, available at www.sfgate.com/entertainment/article/Boston-Symphony-missed-the-point-on-art-and-2860361.php.

canceled performance would have inflicted pain on members of the audience, and asked, "Why should we want to hear this music now?"[48] While agreeing that censorship is deplorable, I argued that forbearance can be noble. Can we not distinguish between them? Ought we not?

One of my reasons for intervening was indignation that the composer had joined in the chorus casting him as a victim. That was crybaby behavior, I thought, and deserved a rebuke. And I was rebuked in turn when Mr. Adams told a London reporter that I had "argue[d] that *Klinghoffer* is so virulent and so twisted a work of art that it should be banned forever."[49] I had done no such thing, although I did express a view that those who regard *The Death of Klinghoffer* as biased in favor of the Palestinians despite its claim of "evenhandedness" were correct.

That was not then, nor is it now, the relevant issue. That issue, as I conceive it, is the false sighting of censorship to squelch free debate. Here John Adams is in the company of Oliver Stone, who responded to a critic far more famous and influential than I, who had lodged a complaint about one of his movies. "And who is John McCain to tell us what's right or wrong, what's culturally correct or not?" Stone wanted to know. "Who the hell is he? Just because he served his country and went to prison [in a Vietnamese POW camp]? This is a form of tyranny. It really is censorship, and it's working."[50]

It may be working, but it's not censorship, just criticism. Stone and Adams are in the company of the distinguished musicologist Reinhold Brinkmann, who responded angrily to an article in which I harshly criticized some of the music and some of the pronouncements of his Harvard colleague Donald Martino, by comparing my words with Nazi criticism of Schoenberg.[51] But you know what? The Nazis had every right to criticize, as do we. It is not for their criticism that we revile the Nazis. Adams, Stone, and Brinkmann were all practicing intimidation—which is also distinguishable from censorship, albeit less defensible than discretion.

V

After all that unpleasantness, it may be time for something light and amusing. Here's the middle stanza of a cute little comic song by W. S. Gilbert that many of us can still sing to the tune to which it was set by Arthur Sullivan:

---

48. R. Taruskin, "Music's Dangers and the Case for Control," *New York Times*, 7 December 2001; reprinted with an update as "The Danger of Music and the Case for Control" in Taruskin, *The Danger of Music*, 168–80, at 173.

49. "Making Musical History," formerly at www.london.sinfonietta.org.uk/interact/ask_adams.html; quoted in Taruskin, *The Danger of Music*, 174.

50. "Dialouge [sic]: Oliver Stone and Daniel Aronofsky," at http://aronofksy.tripod.com/interview18.html.

51. Quoted in Paul Mitchinson, "Settling Scores," *Lingua Franca*, July/August 2001.

There's the nigger serenader, and the others of his race,
And the piano-organist—I've got him on the list!
And the people who eat peppermint and puff it in your face,
They never would be missed—they never would be missed!
Then the idiot who praises, with enthusiastic tone,
All centuries but this, and every country but his own;
And the lady from the provinces, who dresses like a guy,
And who "doesn't think she waltzes, but would rather like to try";
And that singular anomaly, the lady novelist—
I don't think she'd be missed—I'm sure she'd not be missed!

That was Ko-ko, the Lord High Executioner in *The Mikado*, first performed in 1885, telling us of the list he's keeping, "if one day it should happen that a victim must be found," of "society offenders who might well be underground, and who never would be missed."[52] Needless to say, the words have been changed since then—many times. Even by the time the song was first recorded, by the comic baritone Walter Passmore in 1907, with what looks to us all like a horrible racial slur in the first line nonchalantly still in place, "the lady novelist" had already become "the lady motorist."[53] The substitution had been made by Gilbert himself, not because anyone found the original reference offensive, but (presumably) because it was no longer sufficiently topical. In other Edwardian revivals he made more substitutions at that point: "the critic dramatist" (probably a knowing self-reference) and "the scorching bicyclist."[54] The nigger serenader, though, was never removed from the list of desirable victims, at least not by Gilbert.

But mores and meanings change. "Dresses like a guy," for example, had in 1885 nothing to do with what we would call cross-dressing or with lesbianism. The lady from the provinces, ignorant of urban fashion, dresses so bizarrely by London standards that she looks as if she is celebrating Guy Fawkes Day, when the gunpowder plot was celebrated annually with burnt effigies clothed in rags. So "dresses like a guy" sounded to London audiences in 1885 the way "dresses like a scarecrow" might sound to us. As for "nigger," it was considered a neutral designation for dark-skinned foreigners until the early twentieth century, when it became the term of obloquy that we know it to be today.[55] In 1907 it was unlikely to have been

---

52. W. S. Gilbert and Sir Arthur Seymour Sullivan, *The Mikado; or, The Town of Titipu*, in *The Complete Plays of Gilbert and Sullivan* (Garden City, NY: Garden City Publishing Co., 1941), 305–6.

53. Available on YouTube at www.youtube.com/watch?v=NsG_x_NgBqc.

54. These and others are recorded in Ian Bradley, ed., *The Annotated Gilbert and Sullivan* (Harmondsworth, UK: Penguin Books, 1982).

55. Even as late as 1926, Henry Watson Fowler, the most authoritative arbiter of British usage, judged the word offensive only if applied to "others than full or partial negroes" (*A Dictionary of Modern English Usage* [Oxford: Clarendon Press, 1926], 378). The full definition: "*Nigger*, applied to others than full or partial negroes, is felt as an insult by the person described, & betrays in the speaker, if not deliberate insolence, at least a very arrogant inhumanity."

considered offensive by any likely member of the Gilbert and Sullivan audience. The British were slow to react to its changing meaning, if recordings of Ko-ko's song are any indication. We can trace the second stanza's vicissitudes after Gilbert's death in 1911 through the recorded legacy of the D'Oyly Carte Opera Company's Martyn Green, the greatest of all Ko-kos, a series of preserved performances spanning almost a quarter century. His recording from 1936 put "Prohibitionist" in place of "lady novelist."[56] (A 1942—i.e. wartime—recording by Sir Henry Lytton inserted "the clothing rationist" at this point.)[57] But the nigger serenader, like a national monument, stood firm.

The earliest recording I know that did away with the N-word was issued in 1950, reflecting changes made by A. P. Herbert of the D'Oyly Carte Opera Company for a tour of the United States in 1948. God Bless America![58] Not that "the banjo serenader" is much of an improvement, given that "his race" is still the reason for his presence on the list. In 1952 Martyn Green performed the song on American television one Sunday afternoon, on *Omnibus*, the upper-middlebrow variety show curated by Alistair Cooke, and dropped the first four lines altogether, beginning the second verse with "the idiot who praises . . . "[59] That version also preserves what I would nominate as the silliest and most unfathomable emendation of all to replace the lady novelist: "the girl who's never kissed." Whether it is supposed to mean "who *is* never kissed" or "who *has* never kissed," it lasted long enough to be recorded commercially in 1960.[60]

What should we do with this verse now? In 1992 Sir Charles Mackerras gave an answer when he recorded *The Mikado* post–D'Oyly Carte and simply removed Ko-ko's second verse wholesale. I'm sure it's not been missed. I, at least, have heard no protests at its omission; indeed, the 1996 edition of *The Penguin Guide to Compact Discs and Cassettes* actually praised Mackerras for cutting what it called the song's "unpalatable" lines.[61]

Often enough, lines later deemed unpalatable are actually introduced into theater songs in the name of topicality. "You're the Top," from Cole Porter's 1934 hit *Anything Goes,* contains this stanza:

---

56. HMV Album 260; reissued many times on LP and CD.
57. Bradley, *Annotated Gilbert and Sullivan,* 274.
58. Available on YouTube at www.youtube.com/watch?v=14WKZ62g33c (at 24:47).
59. On Youtube at www.youtube.com/watch?v=Th4c3TPPYwA, at 2:17.
60. *Martyn Green in Famous Gilbert and Sullivan Songs,* Columbia CL 832.
61. Quoted in J. M. Balkin and Sanford Levinson, "Interpreting Law and Music: Performance Notes on 'The Banjo Serenader' and 'The Lying Crowd of Jews,'" *Cardozo Law Review* 20 (1999): 1513; also at Yale Law School Legal Scholarship Repository, http://digitalcommons.law.yale.edu/cgi/viewcontent.cgi?article=1251&context=fss_papers, p. 2.

You're the top!
You're an Arrow collar.
You're the top!
You're a Coolidge dollar.
You're the nimble tread of the feet of Fred Astaire.
You're an O'Neill drama,
You're Whistler's mama,
You're Camembert!

And here is the version heard the next year by London audiences, who couldn't be counted on to know what a Coolidge dollar, an Arrow collar, an O'Neill drama, or even Whistler's mama might be:

You're the top!
You're a dress by Patou.
You're the top!
You're an Epstein statue.
You're the nimble tread of the feet of Fred Astaire.
You're Mussolini,
You're Mrs. Sweeney,
You're Camembert!

Now it is we Americans who need a glossary. Jean Patou (1880–1936) was the most sought after Paris couturier and parfumier. Jacob Epstein (1880–1959) was an American-born British sculptor of then-scandalous reputation. Mrs. Sweeney, better known as the Duchess of Argyll, was the racy lady (or in contemporaneous parlance, the nymphomaniac) about whom Thomas Adès and Philip Hensher wrote their opera, *Powder Her Face*. But we all know who Mussolini was, and we may be incredulous that he could have been invoked so enthusiastically in 1935. At that point he still had plenty of respectable admirers, but the line naming him could not have lasted long on the British stage: Mussolini started behaving like a bad boy that very year, when he invaded Ethiopia.

Other instances of line substitutions in musicals and theatrical revues are too numerous to even try listing, or even wholesale deletions before the fact, like "I'm an Indian Too," the number with which Ethel Merman brought down the house in the first production of Irving Berlin's *Annie Get Your Gun* in 1946, but which was thought unpresentable when the show was revived in 1999. That may indeed have been censorship, but nobody seriously complained.[62] Nor did anyone complain when the part of Jeff, the black boy, in Aaron Copland's school opera *The Second*

---

62. See, for example, Steve Cohen's archly titled but ultimately approving "Annie Get Your Sensitivity Training" (2006), at TotalTheater.com, www.totaltheater.com/?q=node/280.

Hurricane was bowdlerized for a performance and recording under Leonard Bernstein in 1960. The original words, written by Edwin Denby in 1937, are these:

> You was all mighty mean when you first come;
> I'se mighty scared of you all
> Now you'se mighty nice and I'se not scared at all.
> I'se not scared with you aroun',
> I'se not scared that we can drown,
> Come on, river, show what you can do.
> Jefferson Brown ain't scared of you.[63]

And this is what listeners to the recording heard:

> You were all mighty mean when you first came;
> I sure was scared of you all.
> Now you're mighty nice and I'm not scared at all.
> I'm not scared with you aroun',
> I'm not scared that we can drown,
> Come on, river, show what you can do.
> Jefferson Brown's not scared of you.[64]

I don't think I need to explain what was done here or why; nor (although I might be wrong) do I expect anyone to object in the name of authenticity.

But Copland's friend and colleague Virgil Thomson did object when the 1952 Columbia recording of his *Five Songs from William Blake* was reissued in 1979 by Composers Recordings Inc. as *Four Songs from William Blake*. This is the one that was suppressed:

> My mother bore me in the southern wild,
> And I am black, but O! my soul is white;
> White as an angel is the English child:
> But I am black as if bereav'd of light.
> ...
> Thus did my mother say and kissed me,
> And thus I say to little English boy.
> When I from black and he from white cloud free,
> And round the tent of God like lambs we joy:
>
> I'll shade him from the heat till he can bear,
> To lean in joy upon our fathers knee.
> And then I'll stand and stroke his silver hair,
> And be like him and he will then love me.

---

63. *The Second Hurricane: A Play Opera in Two Acts* (Boston: C. C. Birchard, 1937).
64. New York Philharmonic, soloists and chorus from the High School of Music and Art (New York), Columbia Records MS 6181 (1960).

Thomson circulated a letter to various friends in the music world in which he conceded that "once or twice there have been objections on the part of the black community to this being performed," but wanted to know their "view of the matter," perhaps with an eye toward exerting pressure on the record folks.[65] Earlier he had written, to a singer who wanted to program the piece but had misgivings, "If you are timid about our colored friends, simply omit 'The Little Black Boy.'"[66] That, of course, was an ironic proposal, couched in terms both racist and macho. Virgil Thomson, who also cast aspersions on Gershwin's *Porgy and Bess* for what he called its "gefilte fish orchestration," was no paragon of charity.[67]

But the question Thomson's response to censorship raises goes beyond personal racism and machismo. Why should there be reservations about, or resistance to, the suppression of an art song that offends African Americans (even if Blake, the author of the text, can easily be exonerated from blame by those who read his poem carefully) when no such reservations are expressed when a theater song is suppressed or altered for similar reasons?

An answer is suggested by another example, involving what is by a long way the oldest musical setting to enter into the present discussion: a motet by the Burgundian court musician Antoine Busnoys, who died the same year Columbus sailed the ocean blue. It is a setting of the Easter sequence, *Victimae paschali laudes,* the text of which is credited to Wipo of Burgundy (ca. 995–ca. 1048), who served as chaplain to the Holy Roman Emperor Conrad II:

1. *Victimae paschali laudes immolent Christiani.*	To the Paschal victim sing in praises, O Christians.
2. *Agnus redemit oves: Christus innocens Patri Reconciliavit peccatores*	The lamb redeems the sheep, the sinless Christ reconciles sinners to the Father.
3. *Mors et vita duello confixere mirando: Dux vitae mortuus regnat vivus.*	Life and death engage in wondrous struggle, The prince of life though dead reigns living.
4. *Dic nobis Maria, quid vidisti in via? Sepulcrum Christi viventis Et gloriam vidi resurgentis:*	Tell us, Mary, what didst though, passing, see? The empty tomb from which the living Christ arose in glory.

65. 25 September 1978; Tim Page and Vanessa Weeks Page, eds., *Selected Letters of Virgil Thomson* (New York: Summit Books, 1988), 368.

66. To William Parker, 17 May 1976; *Selected Letters,* 350.

67. See Virgil Thomson, "George Gershwin," *Modern Music* (November–December 1935), 13–19; in various reprintings Thomson changed "gefilte fish" to "plum pudding," thus obliquely acknowledging the original formulation to have been a gratuitous slur.

5. Angelicos testes, sudarium, et vestes. Surrexit Christus spes mea: praecedet suos in Galilaeam.	I saw angels in splendor, shroud and vestments cast aside; Christ, my hope, has risen and he has gone before you to Galilee.
6. Credendum est magis soli Mariae veraci Quam Judaeorum turbe fallaci.	Honest Mary is more to be believed than the lying crowd of Jews.
7. Scimus Christum surexisse a mortuis vere: Tu nobis, victor Rex, miserere.	We know that Christ has truly risen from death. Victorious King, have mercy on us.

If you look up this hymn in the *Liber usualis,* the book of Gregorian chants in common use before Vatican II, you will find verse 7, about Christ's ascension, but not its melodic twin, about the lying crowd of Jews. That is because the Council of Trent, the legislature convened by Pope Paul III in 1545 to initiate the Counter-Reformation, deleted verse 6 as a gesture of reconciliation with the Jews, even though removing it left the sequence musically as well as textually deformed. To retain it now in liturgy would be literally more Catholic than the Pope.

The situation facing modern performers, in other words, is exactly that of the Bach Passions, seemingly made easier by the fact that the line in question is no longer canonical, nor even in accord with present-day Catholic doctrine. I don't mean to suggest that performing the line today is unjustifiable; I have even done it myself, trusting that all those sixteenth-century bishops were right about the unintelligibility of texts when sung in artful polyphonic settings.[68] But I was nevertheless taken aback when I read, in the notes accompanying a recent recording of Busnoys's motet, the actual justification provided by the choir's director. "This verse has long been abolished from the Catholic liturgy," he wrote, "but to excise it here would render the piece unperformable. Despite misgivings, we have left the text intact."[69]

That is simply not true. As I pointed out in a review of the recording, there are all kinds of ways one could perform the piece without the offending verse. One can vocalize. One can bowdlerize. I even suggested a couple of euphemisms for *Judaeorum,* including *peccatorum* ("of sinners"), *populorum* ("of civilian citizens"), and so on. One can repeat line 7 in place of line 6 or else simply stretch it over the music assigned to both verses. One might even call attention to one's expurgation, thereby at once raising the problem explicitly and publicly (and therefore educa-

---

68. For their complaints, see Weiss and Taruskin, *Music in the Western World,* 2nd ed., 113–14.
69. Alexander Blachly, notes accompanying Dorian Records CD DOR-90184 (Antoine Busnoys: *In Hydraulis* and other works) performed by Pomerium, Alexander Blachly director (1993).

tionally) and also avoiding the charge of bowdlerization, which is by definition "silent" and therefore underhanded.[70]

Mind you, I did not advocate or prescribe any of these practices in the given case; I merely challenged what I saw as an equivocation. The last alternative I proposed, substituting another text altogether, was so widespread in Busnoys's time that it has a name—*contrafactum*—which all musicologists learn. Why is it, I asked, that we do not think that is a proper way to treat a Busnoys motet today, when there is no reason to suppose that the composer himself would have batted an eyelash?

And this became brouhaha No. 4, as email lists and early music chat rooms began filling up with familiar denunciations of my move to censor Busnoys, or censor Blachly, or censor *somebody*. And of course I was lectured to think and do exactly as I do think and do: "The idea of tampering with musical masterpieces is preposterous," Remo Mazzetti Jr. wrote in to the *Times*. "Censorship is never the answer; only the education of the closed-minded and ignorant can help correct this age-old problem."[71] Yes indeed to the part after the semicolon; but as I am in the process of arguing, the idea of tampering with musical masterpieces is not always preposterous. The question is, when is it or is it not? How does one decide?

VI

So let us broaden the purview of the question as it applies to Busnoys: why is it deemed unthinkable by many today to alter the text of a Renaissance motet in a fashion that was entirely acceptable in the Renaissance? It can only be, I think, because we have learned to treat all classical music texts, whether sacred or secular, as holy writ; and composers, now thought of as creators rather than as craftsmen, are accorded the deference due to the original Creator. Broadway or operetta songs belong to a genre that is regarded as temporal and provisional, and therefore freely negotiable. Changing their texts and tunes is expected when times change. It is the price, willingly paid, of extending their appeal to audiences—that is, extending their life. Motets and art songs by Busnoys or Thomson, by contrast, are regarded, at times quite anachronistically, as timeless and inviolate, and beyond negotiation, least of all for the sake of audiences. Since the advent of Romanticism, more than two long centuries ago, treating the audience with contempt has virtually amounted to the definition of a "serious" attitude toward art.

---

70. See R. Taruskin, "The Trouble with Classics—They Are Only Human," *New York Times*, 14 August 1994; reprinted, under the title "Text and Act," in Taruskin, *Text and Act: Essays on Music and Performance* (New York: Oxford University Press, 1995), 353–59.

71. "Music Censorship: On Revising Classics," letter to the Arts and Leisure editor, *New York Times*, 28 August 1994.

At the risk of fomenting brouhaha No. 5 right here and now, I put it to you that it is time to stop doing these things. They don't do art any good at all. Rather, they contribute to the decline in the respect accorded art in contemporary society and culture. Audiences are no longer cowed by contempt. On the contrary: the process through which, over the course of the twentieth century, aesthetic disinterestedness has shaded into moral indifference, and artistic autonomy into social irrelevance, has become obvious to all who haven't buried their heads in the sand; nor do most of us accept any longer the pretense that art is in and of itself a transcendent good that outweighs all potential harms. Those of us who love it still will need to defend it, in the words of our own Dr. Strangelove, against its devotees.[72] And that will require that we make some fundamental admissions.

Art can be harmful; indeed, it can be lethal, as when a collapsing outdoor installation by Christo actually killed a spectator in California as recently as 1991. "Yes, art can be very dangerous," was the smugly admiring comment of one critic for whom artistic value was still to be measured in terms of *l'audace, toujours de l'audace*.[73] Many of us were shocked and disgusted, but was anyone really surprised when Karlheinz Stockhausen pronounced the destruction of the World Trade Center by terrorists the greatest artwork in history?[74] While a work of music might never equal Christo's feat, to say nothing of Al-Qaeda's, the same perverse admiration surfaces whenever its asociality is offered as proof of art's authenticity. Better accept social and ethical negotiation of aesthetic value as the most necessary evidence—indeed, the price—of art's continuing relevance.

To illustrate this last point, I offer one last example: a recording of Mozart's Requiem Mass (K. 626) made in Germany in 1941 under the direction of Bruno Kittel (1870–1948), one of the country's leading choral conductors and the director, from 1935 to 1945, of the Stern Conservatory in Berlin. All references in the liturgical text to the Jewish heritage of Christianity were purged from this performance. *Te decet hymnus, Deus, in Sion; et tibi reddetur votum in Jerusalem* ("A hymn, O God, becometh Thee in Zion; and a vow shall be paid to Thee in Jerusalem") in the Introit became *Te decet hymnus, Deus, in coelis; et tibi reddetur votum hic in terra* ("A hymn, O God, becometh Thee in heaven; and a vow shall be paid to thee here on earth"). *Quam olim Abrahae promisisti* ("As once Thou didst promise Abra-

---

72. Cf. Theodor Wiesengrund Adorno, "Bach gegen seine Liebhaber verteidigt," *Merkur: Deutsche Zeitschrift für europäisches Denken* (June 1951); translated by Samuel Weber and Shierry Weber Nicholsen as "Bach Defended against His Devotees," in Adorno, *Prisms: Cultural Criticism and Society* (London: Neville Spearman, 1967), 135–46.

73. Quoted in T. E. Krieger, *The Portable Pundit* (New York: Warner Books, 2000), 8–9.

74. For an especially lucid commentary, see Terry Castle, "Karlheinz Stockhausen: The Unsettling Question of the Sublime," *New York*, 5 September 2011 ("The Encyclopedia of 9/11"), available at http://nymag.com/news/9-11/10th-anniversary/karlheinz-stockhausen.

ham") in the Offertory became *Quam olim homini promisisti* ("As once Thou didst promise mankind").⁷⁵

A review that greeted the recording on its original release accounted for the textual discrepancies by observing that "Mozart's Requiem is the most profound and deeply moving of all Masses for the Dead that are dedicated to the memory of the dear departed, and it should not be allowed to languish in obscurity simply because a handful of passages in the text are unsuited to our time."⁷⁶ In other words, the elimination of all references to the Jews is justified on precisely the same grounds that others (including me) have used to justify the removal of references to the Jews from the St. John Passion, or Stravinsky's *Cantata*, or Busnoys's *Victimae paschali*. In any and all of these cases the proposed modification is equally interpretable as a constraint on performance ("bad") or an enabler of performance ("good"). The act itself—call it censorship or discretion, call it bowdlerization or sanitation, call it expurgation or liberation—is morally and ethically neutral. Its evaluation depends entirely upon our reading of historical conditions and motives—that is, on the values and purposes the act is seen to embody or serve.

A wonderful old story from the New York art world may help clarify this point. The members of the Eighth Street Artists Club were arguing, one evening in 1952, about whether or not it was vain to sign your paintings. Fairfield Porter shut the debate down by observing, "If you are vain it is vain to sign your pictures and vain not to sign them. If you are not vain it is not vain to sign them and not vain not to sign them."⁷⁷ Again, the act itself is neutral. The motivating values are what count, and they cannot be inferred from the act itself, only from our knowledge of the circumstances and our evaluation of them. For such knowledge and evaluation we ourselves are individually answerable. Not the act but the values are what deserve praise or censure. Issuing a blanket condemnation of censorship—or of signing one's pictures—to cover all cases in advance only postpones consideration of values, evades thought, and threatens art with irrelevance.

---

75. This recording, with its Nazified text, is reissued on CD in the *Deutsche Grammophon Centenary Collection*, vol. 1 (The Early Years): DG 459004 (1998), disc 5.

76. "Mozart's Requiem, die tiefste und erschütterndste aller dem Andenken teurer Toten gewidmeten Trauermessen, sollte nicht um einzelner unzeitgemässer Textstellen willen in den Schatten der Musikpflege zurücktreten" (Hermann Steffani in *Zeitschrift für Musik;* quoted in the notes accompanying the Deutsche Grammophon reissue referenced in the preceding footnote).

77. Rackstraw Downes, "Introduction," in Fairfield Porter, *Art in Its Own Terms: Selected Criticism 1935–1975* (New York: Taplinger, 1979), 5.

3

Haydn and the Enlightenment?

I

Immanuel Kant's cursed question, "What is Enlightenment?" was part of the title to his famous essay of 1784, "Beantwortung der Frage: Was ist Aufklärung?" The rest of the title promised an answer, and sure enough, a "short answer" came in the very first paragraph:

> Enlightenment is man's emergence from his self-imposed nonage (*Unmündigkeit*). Nonage is the inability to use one's own understanding without another's guidance. This nonage is self-imposed if its cause lies not in lack of understanding but in indecision and lack of courage to use one's own mind without another's guidance. *Dare to know!* (*Sapere aude.*) "Have the courage to use your own understanding," is therefore the motto of the Enlightenment.[1]

So: asked and answered. But if Joseph Haydn had been the one asking, he would have simply wanted to know what words like *Aufklärung* or *Unmündigkeit* might possibly mean. Like much innovative philosophy, Kant's ideas required a new vocabulary. The philosopher's strategy was to invest existing words with new meanings that put them in a new relationship, and to use that first paragraph to

---

Originally published in part as a booklet note for Haydn, Symphonies 31, 70, 101 (Scottish Chamber Orchestra, Robin Ticciati conducting), Linn Records 11615 (2015).

1. "An Answer to the Question 'What Is Enlightenment?'" (1784), trans. John Richardson, in Immanuel Kant, *Essays and Treatises on Moral, Political, Religious, and Various Philosophical Subjects* (London: William Richardson, 1798–99), 1.

FIGURE 3.1. Daniel Chodowiecki, "Aufklärung" (Göttinger Taschen Calender für das Jahr 1792).

define them. If, like most readers, Haydn had known the word *Aufklärung* at all without reading Kant's essay (and there is no evidence that he ever did read it), he would have known it as a technical military term, German for what in English, borrowing from French, we call *reconnaissance*. It stems, in German, not from the word *light* (*Leucht,* whence *Erleuchtung,* "illumination"), but from *clear,* that is, not cloudy or indistinct (*klar,* whence *Klärung,* "clarification"). Literally, then, *Aufklärung* means "up-clearing" or "out-figuring"—deciding what's what. Unlike *enlightenment,* its original and by now traditional English translation, *Aufklärung* is not a metaphor. The resonance with illumination or elucidation (possibly stemming from the echo *klär-/[é]clair*) has made the awesome moment of radiance in Haydn's oratorio *Creation* ("where God says 'Let there be light!' and the audience must cover its ears")[2] an emblem of his newly Enlightened times, as one can see from Daniel Chodowiecki's famous copper-plate engraving of 1791 (fig. 3.1). Nevertheless, that resonance would more likely have occurred to an Anglophone or Francophone (like Mme de Staël, who spread the sally about *Creation*) than it would have to Haydn.

Mündig, in German, derived from *Mund*, "mouth," is also a technical term—a legal one. It means "of age," as in "coming of age," when you can act on your own behalf (that is, speak with your own mouth). So *Unmündigkeit*, translated into its English equivalent, would be "minority," the state of being underage, legally a child. John Richardson, Kant's eighteenth-century translator, a Scottish philosophy tutor living in Germany, resorted to the fancy Latinate *nonage*, literally "not of age," which now itself requires translation.[3] He probably did so deliberately, to create the momentary confusion that *Unmündigkeit* was no doubt meant to provoke. As a reader noted in exasperation as early as 1789, "*Aufklärung* is a word that no one understands anymore without commentary."[4] Since then, things have only gotten worse.

What could all of this have meant to an eighteenth-century musician? That is the question with which all who have sought to apply the term *Aufklärung* or its English equivalent to the work of such persons, and to the exemplary Haydn in particular, have struggled. "One must be clear," we are punningly warned at the outset of the one full-length attempt to do so, "in defining what the Enlightenment may have meant to a late eighteenth-century Austrian composer."[5] Not much, one is wise to concede, in terms of his professional practice. To look for intimations of Enlightenment in Haydn's actual scores, as the example of *Creation* already warns us, is likely to lead us astray. In English, the term *Enlightenment*, in its philosophical application, is surprisingly recent, and hopelessly anachronistic to the period it now describes. The *Oxford English Dictionary* records no use of it in intellectual history before 1865—and then only as a pejorative: "shallow and pretentious intel-

---

2. Anne Louise Germaine de Staël-Holstein (Madame de Staël), *De l'Allemagne*, trans. John Murray (London, 1813); quoted in Peter Le Huray and John Day, *Music and Aesthetics in the Eighteenth and Early-Nineteenth Centuries* (Cambridge: Cambridge University Press, 1981), 302. While the quip is often attributed to Mme de Staël, she reports it as an overheard "witty remark."

3. James Schmidt, a professor of political philosophy at Boston University, has compiled a chronological survey of translations of "*selbstverschuldeten Unmündigkeit*, the great train wreck of syllables standing at the close of the first sentence of Kant's answer to the question 'What is enlightenment?'" Among them: "self-imposed pupilage" (1841), "voluntary immaturity" (1890), "self-incurred tutelage" (1963), "self-imposed dependence" (1995), "self-incurred minority" (1996). See https://persistentenlightenment.com/2013/06/17/voluntary-nonage-translating-kant-on-enlightenment-part-4.

4. "Aufklärung ist ein Wort, das eigentlich nun ohne Commentar kein Mensch mehr versteht" (*Annalen der neuesten theologischen Litteratur und Kirchengeschichte*, Jhrg. 1 [Leipzig: Johann Ambrosius Barth, 1789], 468).

5. David P. Schroeder, *Haydn and the Enlightenment* (Oxford: Clarendon Press, 1990), 9.

lectualism, unreasonable contempt for tradition and authority, etc."—in other words, French.

This derision shows at least some perspicacity in deriving the term not from Kant's German but from the French of the *philosophes,* for whom by the 1780s it was already a cliché to call their time the *siècle des Lumières.* As a period label, the term Enlightenment did not take root in English until the 1930s at the earliest. Until then, the standard English epithet for the eighteenth century as a cultural period was "The Age of Reason," after the title of Thomas Paine's famous tract of 1794, and Paine's titular phrase retains its currency even now alongside the E-word, since the most basic definition of Enlightenment is the assertion of reason as the source of legitimacy and authority. It is worth mentioning that Paine's two earnest, urgent volumes found no room for any discussion of music, which has never been any literary man's or political activist's idea of a rational domain. Although he never said as much (since no one thought to ask him), it was not likely to have been Haydn's idea of one either.

So we will only be led further astray if we expect Haydn to share our present-day view of his time. Donald Jay Grout, in the first edition of his famous *History of Western Music,* used the term Enlightenment just where one might have expected it to appear, to introduce the chapter on "Classical style," musicological code for the latter half of the eighteenth century. He broached the issue by juxtaposing two quotes: one by Andreas Werckmeister, the theorist of tuning and temperament (hence a musical scientist in the narrowest sense of the term), dating from 1691, identifying music as "a gift of God, to be used only in His honor"; and the other by Charles Burney, the music historian, from 1776: "Music is an innocent luxury, unnecessary, indeed, to our existence, but a great improvement and gratification of the sense of hearing."[6] The difference between them illustrates Grout's characterization of "the temper of the Enlightenment" as "secular, skeptical, empirical, practical, liberal, equalitarian, and progressive."[7] But which definition should we expect Haydn to have preferred—Haydn, who headed the scores of each of his perfectly secular and famously progressive symphonies with the Latin invocation *In nomine Domini* ("In the name of the Lord") and followed the last double bar with the words *Laus Deo* ("Praise to God")? He would likely have regarded Burney's definition as an example of French frivolity.

Those secular symphonies have of course undergone a tacit and quite revolutionary revaluation since Haydn's day. They are now his emblematic genre, which

---

6. Andreas Werckmeister, *Der Edlen Music-Kunst, Würde, Gebrauch und Mißbrauch* (Frankfurt, 1691), preface; Charles Burney, *A General History of Music* (1776), 2nd ed. (London: for the author, 1789), xvii (s.v. "Definitions"); both quoted in Donald Jay Grout, *A History of Western Music* (New York: W. W. Norton, 1960), 411.

7. Grout, *A History,* 412.

has made them the emblematic genre of the Classical style, which in turn has made them the emblematic musical manifestation of the Enlightenment. The subtitle of David Schroeder's *Haydn and the Enlightenment* identifies the book as a study of "The Late Symphonies." And yet, as Schroeder himself was forced to recognize, Haydn never altered his view—now firmly defined as pre-Enlightened—that vocal genres stood higher than instrumental ones on a scale of value defined by the power of edification. Quite rightly, the author sees Haydn's signal achievement as that of achieving "intelligibility" in purely instrumental genres;[8] and yet he acknowledges it to have been "universally acknowledged" in the eighteenth century "that intelligibility was not possible without a text."[9] Indeed, André Ernest Modeste Grétry, the French specialist in *opéras comiques*, described Haydn's instrumental works as a sort of quarry, "a vast dictionary from which a dramatic composer can draw material at will, but which he must then use to accompany the warm expression of words." A composer of instrumental music, even one with Haydn's genius, is in effect only half a composer, "like a botanist who discovers a plant but must wait for a doctor to discover its use."[10]

"Grétry's suggestion that Haydn's symphonies would benefit from the addition of words does him no favours," writes Julia Prest ("him" being Grétry, it seems, though it could also be Haydn), as if just to show how thoroughly conventional thinking about musical genres has been revolutionized since the eighteenth century.[11] But there is no reason to think that Haydn ever dissented from the traditional assignment of values. In an autobiographical sketch of 1776, by which time he had already composed more than sixty symphonies, Haydn listed three operas, an oratorio, and a setting of the *Stabat Mater* as his most important works, by which he meant those that had received the highest approbation from audiences. In a letter of 1784, by which time he had published the string quartets, op. 33, now regarded as the earliest works to show his fully mature "classical" style (and which he himself had advertised as being written in a "new and special manner"), he named the opera *Armida* (first performed in February of that year) as his "best work up to now."[12] He even told his

---

8. Schroeder, *Haydn and the Enlightenment*, 142: "Largely through Haydn's brilliant contrivance, an intelligibility of the highest order was achieved in instrumental music."

9. Ibid., 68.

10. "Il me semble que le compositeur dramatique peut regarder les œuvres innombrables de Haydn comme un vaste dictionnaire où il peut sans scrupule puiser des matériaux, qu'il ne doit reproduire cependant qu'accompagnés de l'expression intime des paroles. Le compositeur de la symphonie est, dans ce cas, comme le botaniste qui fait la découverte d'une plante en attendant que le médecin en découvre la propriété" (*Mémoires ou essai sur la musique par M. Grétry* [Paris: chez l'auteur, 1789], 287–88).

11. Review of *Grétry's Operas and the French Public* by R. J. Arnold (Aldershot: Ashgate, 2016) in the *Times Literary Supplement* (13 July 2016).

12. Quoted in Schroeder, *Haydn and the Enlightenment*, 66.

biographer Griesinger that "instead of the many quartets, sonatas, and symphonies, he should have written more vocal music," regretting that he did not become, as Mozart had, "one of the foremost opera composers."[13]

Schroeder calls the chapter in which he takes note of these apparent discrepancies "Theory versus Practice," implying that in Haydn's case they might not have jibed. "Curiously," he writes, "his own comments about his works do not necessarily reflect what would appear to be his priorities in terms of actual composition."[14] Circling back to this curiosity after reviewing the stats, he leaves the matter unresolved:

> The view of Haydn held during the first half of the twentieth century, that his only serious achievements were his instrumental works, is no doubt still in need of further realignment. However, it is difficult to imagine, in the light of his output, advocating the opposite extreme, as Haydn himself appears to be doing. How could he seriously argue that all his finest achievements are in the area of vocal music, and that he should not have expended so much time and energy on instrumental works?[15]

Schroeder even asserts that "it seems more probable that he moved away from opera for his own artistic reasons rather than external circumstances or impositions."[16] But if we take into account the conditions that determined Haydn's activities, and particularly the conditions of his employment, there will no longer seem to be anything curious in his remarks, nor will we continue to entertain the vain assumption that we can deduce his or any eighteenth-century creator's priorities merely by surveying his output. That assumption is a misapprehension born precisely of an anachronistic application of "Enlightenment" ideals—in this case the ideal of autonomous agency, which turns all external forces into "impositions." To wonder why Haydn did not write more operas or fewer symphonies is to forget that "the most intensively cultivated genre of Haydn's earlier career"[17] was one he never would have dreamt of cultivating on his own—namely the baryton trio, of which he composed 126 specimens (as against 107 symphonies, 68 string quartets, and 45 piano trios). These reflected the priorities of Prince Nikolaus Eszterházy, the employer, not the employee; and those, in the eighteenth century, were the priorities that counted. Even in his ripest period, that of the London symphonies, Haydn was composing according to the terms of a contract, with J. P. Salomon, not according to the untrammeled dictates of his muse.

---

13. Vernon Gotwals, ed. and trans., *Haydn: Two Contemporary Portraits* (Madison: University of Wisconsin Press, 1968), 63.
14. Schroeder, *Haydn and the Enlightenment*, 66.
15. Ibid., 67.
16. Ibid., 5.
17. Elaine R. Sisman, *Haydn and the Classical Variation* (Cambridge, MA: Harvard University Press, 1993), 128.

Rather than impositions or predilections, the proper model to apply, if one is looking to explain such choices as Haydn exercised in pursuance of his career, is that of affordances. The term is recent, but what it names—*environmental properties that offer action possibilities*, to boil it down to the smallest possible number of words—defines the relationship between agents and actions in a manner that allows a dynamic and dialectical account of what are too often presented as dichotomies (such as predilections vs. impositions).[18] Affordances both enable and constrain. Consider in this light the oft-noted fact that after his return from his second stint in London, in 1795, Haydn stopped composing symphonies and, but for the opp. 76 and 77 quartets, turned his attention entirely to vocal genres: his two English oratorios (*The Creation*, 1798; *The Seasons*, 1801) and no fewer than six settings of the Roman Mass, composed between 1796 and 1802. In view of his stated (and, to some writers, paradoxical) apportionment of value, this might seem a reversion to predilection upon the cessation of impositions. But not so fast: some of the Masses were composed to mark the name day of Princess Maria Hermenegild, wife of Prince Nikolaus II Eszterházy, the grandson of the baryton-playing Nikolaus I, and Haydn's last patron.[19] They were thus the composer's last contracted labors, and what is a contract but an accepted (and in that sense self-imposed) obligation? So one can argue either that the late Masses finally represented Haydn's predilections, or that they constituted the Eszterházy family's final imposition upon him.

Or one can argue, more realistically, that they were the final fruits of Haydn's unprecedentedly fertile response to his life's affordances. Those affordances—the possibilities for action presented at various times by Count Morzin, the Princes Eszterházy, the publishing house of Artaria, the Loge Olympique de Paris, and J. P. Salomon—were what enabled a wheelwright's son to become the great musician of his age. And they were what constrained him from becoming the sort of opera composer that the (arguably) less well adapted Mozart became—Mozart, who never found a Haydnesque aristocratic niche until it was almost too late,[20] and therefore had to act more frequently, and riskily, on his own initiative, i.e., accord-

---

18. The term as such was coined by the ecological psychologist James Gibson in a study of animal behavior: "The affordances of the environment are what it offers the animal, what it provides or furnishes, either for good or ill." He justifies the coinage by observing that the term "refers to both the environment and the animal in a way that no existing term does," thus implying "the complementarity of the animal and the environment" (J. Gibson, *The Ecological Approach to Visual Perception* [Boston: Houghton Mifflin, 1979], 127). The term and concept are now widely applied to humans as well as animals and to social as well as natural environments. This may be its first application to Haydn.

19. See Jeremiah McGrann, "Of Saints, Name Days, and Turks: Some Background on Haydn's Masses Written for Prince Nikolaus II Esterházy," *Journal of Musicological Research* 17 (1998): 195–210.

20. See Christoph Wolff, *Mozart at the Gateway to His Fortune: Serving the Emperor, 1788–1791* (New York: W. W. Norton, 2012).

ing to predilection. Even if, taking account of his post-London independent wealth and the de facto freedom it gave him, we prefer to regard Haydn's late Masses as voluntary rather than enforceable submissions to the terms of an ancient contract, they still testify, in their religiosity, to values quite at variance with those associated with the Enlightenment.

II

Further ironic testimony to a poor fit between the man, his times, and the term as commonly applied was the seventh volume of the ten-volume *New Oxford History of Music*, which came out in 1973 with the title *The Age of Enlightenment: 1745–1790*. There is no entry for "Enlightenment" in the book's index, however; and it is discussed at length only in the volume's introduction (by Gerald Abraham, the actual editor—as opposed to the nominal ones, but that's another story) and in the peroration, a concluding chapter by Frederick Sternfeld called "Instrumental Masterworks and Aspects of Formal Design," which seems to have been commissioned to serve as the other bookend. Abraham cheerfully admitted of the music treated in between that "by no means all the changes it underwent in passing from the age of Bach and Handel to that of Haydn and Mozart can be linked with the ideas of Enlightenment,"[21] but Sternfeld made a game effort to turn the so-called sonata form, especially as found in the first movements of Haydn symphonies, into such a link, specifically with the idea of individual, independent comprehension or "understanding," so highly valued by Kant. Comparing the final ritornello in a Baroque concerto with the ending of a Classical symphonic movement, Sternfeld wrote that

> to relate such unchanging ritornelli to the codas of Haydn, not to mention Beethoven, would be false, for the very essence of these codas is thematic mutation.... To recognize in the recapitulation the return of the primary group as well as the secondary and closing groups produced the kind of delight cherished by the age of Enlightenment, for by this reprise one might understand more thoroughly the significance of the opening section.[22]

This would seem to suggest that the values and virtues of the Age of Reason were somehow encoded in Haydn's actual musical sounds and their vicissitudes in a way that was lacking, say, in Bach's. The temptation to debunk this or any such

---

21. *The New Oxford History of Music*, vol. 7: *The Age of Enlightenment: 1745–1790*, ed. Egon Wellesz and Frederick Sternfeld (London: Oxford University Press, 1973), xvi. Not the least dated aspect of this formulation was the assumption, already convincingly refuted, that a single stylistic evolution linked "the age of Bach and Handel to that of Haydn and Mozart"; see Daniel Heartz, "Approaching a History of 18th-Century Music," *Current Musicology* 4 (1969): 92–95.

22. *New Oxford History* 7:612.

immanent claim is hard to resist. But it takes just a little tweak to make it ring true—and in a way that finally justifies the pairing of Haydn's name with our E-word after all. Abraham's essay makes that tweak when he writes about the most measurable change that took place in the eighteenth-century world of music, the change not in the musical product but in its consumers, the audience:

> The popularity of the "concert symphony," leading to the diffusion throughout Europe of printed sets of parts and consequently to the standardization of the orchestra, was the result of social change: the emergence of considerable middle-class audiences.... The same audiences, when they made music instead of passively listening to it, provided the principal market for the quantities of easy keyboard music, the keyboard sonatas with flute or violin accompaniment, the Lieder of the Berlin school, and the host of simple songs and romances with keyboard or harp accompaniment which came from the presses of London and Paris.[23]

To speak of "emergence" makes the process sound a bit magical, and to attempt a real explanation would require a book.[24] But the social change that Abraham sketches here was the real eighteenth-century story, and it continued apace throughout the nineteenth. As any composer knows (and as Aaron Copland actually said), "when the audience changes, music changes."[25] Anyone who knows anything about Haydn's Horatio-Alger biography knows he was the great musical protagonist of this change within the eighteenth century: starting life a virtual peasant, elevated through lucky circumstances to a life of incredibly productive servitude to aristocratic patrons; lucky again to live long enough to be pensioned just as those middle-class audiences (first—where else?—in England) began clamoring for his wares; and ending his days a wealthy celebrity, the very image of the self-made man, who told his biographer Albert Christoph Dies (and he was the first composer to know that he had biographers) that "young people can see from my example that something still may come from nothing."[26] The social transformations of the eighteenth century delivered Haydn's paramount affordance. Having begun by furnishing music on demand to a noble coterie, Haydn ended by purveying his wares to throngs of *honnêtes hommes* in big concert rooms and to even

---

23. Ibid., xvi.
24. That book, or rather that series of books, has been the principal contribution of the historian William Weber: see his *Music and the Middle Class: The Social Structure of Concert Life in London, Paris, and Vienna between 1830 and 1848* (London: Croom Helm, 1975); *The Rise of Musical Classics in Eighteenth-Century England: A Study in Canon, Ritual, and Ideology* (Oxford: Clarendon Press, 1992); *The Great Transformation of Musical Taste: Concert Programming from Haydn to Brahms* (Cambridge: Cambridge University Press, 2008).
25. Aaron Copland, *Music and the Imagination* (Cambridge, MA: Harvard University Press, 1952), 107.
26. Gotwals (ed. and trans.), *Haydn: Two Contemporary Portraits,* 80–81 (transcribed from an interview on 15 April 1805).

larger, unseen throngs of potential purchasers (of string quartets and piano trios, to be sure, but also of "simple songs and romances with keyboard or harp accompaniment," genres he had hardly touched until, through J. P. Salomon, London beckoned).

The aristocratic genres were reevaluated by a new audience of skilled listeners, which had its *Kenner* as well as *Liebhaber*—its connoisseurs as well as amateurs. Goethe said of the string quartet, one of the genres that Haydn sired, that in it one heard "vier vernünftige Leute sich untereinander unterhalten"—four people conversing. And however we choose to translate the untranslatable term *vernünftige*— whether as "reasonable" or "rational" or "intelligent"—we sooner see them conversing in one of the public or semipublic spaces of the imagined Enlightenment (coffeehouse, drawing room) than in a palace chamber (where the conversation would have been described as *galant*). Goethe even said of his four vernünftigers that "man glaubt ihren Diskursen etwas abzugewinnen"—one believes one might learn something from their discourse.[27]

It is this discourse that David Schroeder's *Haydn and the Enlightenment*, of which the full subtitle is "The Late Symphonies *and Their Audience*,"[28] seeks to elucidate. It is in this sense that his thesis—"that Haydn was thoroughly committed to the goals of the Enlightenment, and like his literary compatriots, used his works to serve these goals"—finally fits.[29] "The heightened sense of intelligibility found in the late symphonies," he continues (and, it goes without saying, in the quartets as well), "in effect involves the building of a kind of lesson in listening directly into the work, thereby placing the audience in a position of being walked through the process of discovery."[30] Schroeder correlates this insight with actual technical features in the music that even an *honnête homme* might readily perceive, thus redeeming what might have seemed the excessively immanent way in which Frederick Sternfeld had associated the content of Haydn's music with the precepts and delights of Enlightenment.

Having dramatized the form of his musical movements with greater contrasts than earlier composers employed, Haydn often gives the listener "a special opportunity to contemplate the relationship of the foregoing conflicting forces in a direct way, [for example] after a fermata or some other attention-arresting device, such as the return of the drum-roll along with part of the slow introduction in Symphony No. 103."[31] Any teacher of music appreciation has learned to appreciate the

---

27. Johann Wolfgang von Goethe, letter to Carl Friedrich Zelter, 9 November 1829; Max Hecker, ed., *Briefwechsel zwischen Goethe und Zelter 1799–1832* (Leipzig: Insel-Verlag, 1915), 3:233.
28. Italics added.
29. Schroeder, *Haydn and the Enlightenment*, 1.
30. Ibid., 20.
31. Ibid. Haydn apparently stole this idea from his former pupil Ignace Pleyel. See Arthur Searle, "Pleyel's 'London' Symphonies," *Early Music* 36 (2008): 231–244.

usefulness of Haydn's instrumental music in teaching a class of *honnêtes naïfs* to perceive the overall shape of a harmonically articulated movement. We direct their listening to just that sort of signal, which often produces a reaction in students that, we hope (and sometimes observe), epiphanically combines amusement with illumination. Such a teacher is only doing in a more openly and verbally didactic way what Haydn has already contrived his music to accomplish wordlessly—to create, in Schroeder's words, an audience of "critical" listeners, both "reflective" and "alert."[32]

It is thus, Schroeder claims, that "Haydn's idea of the symphony was shaped by the Enlightenment." Not only shaped by it, but also, literally, defined (that is, limited) by it, for "his goal was to achieve, not supersede intelligibility," as Romantics would later strive to do. The Romantic mystique discouraged critical or reflective listening. It sought to affect listeners unawares, leaving them in a state of wonder. Wagner was perfectly explicit about this: he meant his music to appeal not to the mediating, cogitating mind but to the dumb immediacy of the *Gefühlsverständnis*, the "feelings' understanding" or empathy, "the only organ," he tells us, "at which I aimed."[33] Wagner's heirs, the late, late romantics of the twentieth century known as modernists, also preferred to keep their tricks secret, and the loss to listeners' self-confidence has been great. Listeners no longer dare to know, it seems, and they have been lost to classical music in numbers that by now everyone recognizes as catastrophic. An attempt to stanch this mass defection recently appeared on the Op-Ed page of the *New York Times*, one of the few newspapers that still employs a (shrinking) stable of classical music reviewers. It was written by a professional violist and radio commentator, and it contained this story, actually meant to give encouragement:

> Years ago I was rehearsing a piece for flute, viola and piano by the composer Seymour Barab. Mr. Barab was attending the rehearsal, and the pianist asked him at one point if it was important to "bring out," or highlight, a certain clever rhythmic pattern. Mr. Barab's instant reaction was to shout: "No! It's none of your business!"
>
> Mr. Barab's position, expressed in his inimitable fashion, was that it was not the performer's job to try to *teach* the audience, nor was it the audience's responsibility to try to pass some sort of test in rhythm recognition. If he, the composer, had done his job well, and had organized and manipulated his musical materials in a compelling fashion, the music would "work," and the audience would enjoy it.[34]

Haydn would have disagreed. He wanted more from his audience, and didn't mind teaching them. In this he differed even from Mozart, who in a famous letter to his father wrote that his recent piano concertos contained "passages here and

---

32. Ibid., 169, 41, 173, respectively.
33. Richard Wagner, "A Communication to My Friends," trans. William Ashton Ellis, in *Richard Wagner's Prose Works*, vol. 1 (London: Kegan Paul, Trench, Trübner, 1892), 389.
34. Miles Hoffman, "Don't Fear Classical Music," *New York Times*, 19 April 2018.

there that only connoisseurs can fully appreciate—yet the common listener will find them satisfying as well, although *without knowing why.*"[35] Mozart was making the usual distinction between *Kenner* and *Liebhaber,* between connoisseurs of music and those who merely loved it. Haydn wanted to open up his workshop to the *Liebhaber* and make *Kenner* out of them. Perhaps he knew, as we are now finding out, that ignoring the *Liebhaber* means losing them—and the *Kenner* too, who were once *Liebhaber,* after all. We who strove to make the actual processes of musical development intelligible to our classes—and not only intelligible, but meaningful, moving, and at times even hilarious—were in our way Haydn's henchmen, in smaller measure maintaining his project and turning our students, as he turned the Londoners, into enlightened—that is, Enlightened—listeners.

This time the term is surely right. It is fair to call the listeners we were trying to train "enlightened," because one of Haydn's contemporaries actually did so, in a small but revealing press skirmish that arose in the wake of Haydn's early London appearances. One of the few—the *very* few—detractors to comment negatively on Haydn's Salomon concerts was William Jackson (1730–1803), a provincial organist, in a 35-page pamphlet called *Observations on the Present State of Music, in London,* which came out during the summer following Haydn's first season there. Without naming names, he complains of gross decline since the time of Franz Xaver Richter and Carl Friedrich Abel, owing to the folly of "later composers," who,

> to be grand and original, have poured in such floods of nonsense, under the sublime idea of *being inspired,* that the present Symphony bears the same relation to good music as the ravings of a Bedlamite do to sober sense. Sometimes the Key is perfectly lost by wandering so far from it that there is no road to return—but extremes meet at last of themselves. The measure is so perplexed by arbitrary divisions of notes, that it seems as if the composer intended to exhibit a table of twos, threes, and fours. And, when discords get so entangled that it is past the art of men to untie the knot, something in the place of Alexander's sword does the business at once. All these paltry shifts to conceal the want of Air, can never be admitted to supply its place. Where there is *really* Air it will exist under all disadvantages of performance. But, what would become of our sublimities, if it were not for the short cut of a *Pianissimo* so delicate as almost to escape the ear, and then a sudden change into all the *Fortissimo* that Fiddling, Fluting, Trumpeting, and Drumming can bestow.[36]

It may not be easy for us to recognize Haydn in this description of wild avant-gardism, but to contemporary readers the final complaint, about excessive

---

35. W. A. Mozart to Leopold Mozart, 28 December 1782, trans. Robert Spaethling, in *Mozart's Letters, Mozart's Life* (New York: W. W. Norton, 2000), 336 (italics added).

36. William Jackson, *Observations on the Present State of Music, in London* (London: Harrison & Co., 1791), 15; cited from Carol MacClintock, ed., *Readings in the History of Music in Performance* (Bloomington: Indiana University Press, 1979), 406–7.

contrast, gave his identity away. Jackson's screed is chiefly remembered today for the indignant reply it elicited from Dr. Burney himself, who leapt in to defend the unnamed but unmistakable objects of libel. "Mr. Jackson boasts a claim to *candour*, for 'not mentioning the name of any living professor,'" he taunted, but it "will hardly be granted by intelligent musical readers, who can no more help thinking of HAYDN when *symphonies* are mentioned, than of HANDEL when *oratorio choruses* are in question."[37] Later he adds the names "VANHALL, PLEYEL, and MOZART" to the list of defendants (102). He argues not against the prosecutor's conservatism as such, still less against the fastidiousness of his taste, but against his want of tolerance. "He sees but one angle of the art of music; and to that all his opinions are referred" (103).

Here is where the E-word comes into play. "A liberal and enlightened musician, and hearer of music," Burney declares, "receives pleasure from various styles and effects, even when melody is not so vulgarly familiar as to be carried home from once hearing [it]; or even when there is no predominant melody, if a compensation be made by harmony, contrivance, and the interesting combination of the whole" (101). Needless to say, the author of *Haydn and the Enlightenment* did not miss this important testimony to a contemporary linkage of his titular terms, made all the more attractive and noteworthy because of the further linkage between enlightenment and liberality that has always been one of the Enlightenment's best vibrations. It gave encouragement to the claim that the values of tolerance and liberality were actually coded into the musical substance of Haydn's compositions (first quartets, later symphonies) owing precisely to the complex textures and heightened contrasts—the "meeting of extremes," the "paltry shifts"—at which William Jackson issued his harshest rebukes. David Schroeder connects this, first, with Goethe's *vernünftige Leute*, observing that, beginning with the "new and special" Op. 33,

> the music places four intelligent people in a "harmonious" setting, sharing both intellectual and heartfelt experience. The ability to share and exchange the important material offers a strong sense of unified purpose, one in which the player is both aware of his individual importance and the role he plays in creating the whole. *In a very real way, then,* the quartet became a realization of one of the highest goals of the Enlightenment. With accompaniments that can be transformed to melodies and vice versa, there is an apparent recognition of a higher social truth which is that differences do not preclude equality.[38]

And later, with regard to the major orchestral works and *their* audience:

---

37. Charles Burney, review of Jackson, *Observations on the Present State of Music, Monthly Review*, October 1791, 196–202; reprinted in H. C. Robbins Landon, *Haydn: Chronicle and Works*, vol. 3 (Bloomington: Indiana University Press, 1976), 100–104, at 100. Further citations from this source will be made in the main text.

38. Schroeder, *Haydn and the Enlightenment*, 62 (italics added).

Haydn *can be seen* to be demonstrating a very fundamental yet difficult truth: opposition is inevitable, and the highest form of unity is not the one which eliminates conflict. On the contrary, it is one in which opposing forces can coexist. The best minds of Haydn's age aspired to tolerance, not dogmatism. It is precisely this message that *can be heard* in many of Haydn's late symphonies.[39]

These are bold claims in their implication that the thematic, harmonic, and textural variety within Haydn's works (this being, by critical consensus, his "new and special manner") actually symbolizes a pluralistic worldview, and that the subsumption of this kaleidoscopic surface within the shapely and well-directed thematic and harmonic argument one observes in Haydn's mature sonata forms actually symbolizes the harmonization of diverse opinion and mobilization of action to achieve the common good. Schroeder comes closest to claiming that these readings represent Haydn's actual intent when contending that the "sonata form as Haydn conceived it was not the natural outcome of evolutionary process or stylistic development," but a "brilliant contrivance" specifically designed to make intelligible the cultural and social messages the music embodied and conveyed.[40]

Vibrations as good as these are literally too good to be true, and Schroeder seems, semitacitly, to concede the weakness of his case for immanent representation by resorting to the overly protesting locutions I put into italics in the foregoing extracts. One never calls "very real" something one thinks is real, and to say that something *can be seen* or *can be heard* is to acknowledge that it is not likely to be so seen or heard without the special pleading.

III

Despite his being a member of a Masonic lodge, moreover, there is little reason to think that Haydn entertained the egalitarian sentiments that writers such as Schroeder find immanently communicated by the facture of his quartets. What little expression he gave to his social attitudes shows him to have been profoundly ambivalent, as people who live through social upheavals tend to be. He often expressed his delight at the good fortune that made his music ever more valuable to ever more listeners as his career went on, and he was aware of the new freedoms that his lucky survival amid propitious social changes had earned him. But he was also aware of the paradoxes that attended the new, socially supported independence that came to him late in life. Was he the beneficiary of social emancipation, as we who look back on history in a triumphant mood might be quick to assume, or was he just the flukily successful weatherer of social abandonment? "How sweet is some degree of liberty!" he wrote home to Marianne von Genzinger, his confi-

39. Ibid., 88 (italics added).
40. Ibid., 142.

dante (and, by many, presumed lover) after eight months of wild success in London:

> I had a kind prince, but was obliged at times to depend on base souls. I often sighed for release and now I have it in some measure. I appreciate the good sides of all this, too, though my mind is burdened with far more work. The realization that I am no longer a bond servant sweetens all my toil.[41]

That is where quotation from this letter often ends.[42] But the very next sentence reads, "Yet, dear though this liberty is to me, I should like to enter Prince Esterházy's service again when I return, if only for the sake of my family."[43] Haydn knew that freedom and security varied inversely, and that the Enlightenment—whatever it was—brought danger along with opportunity. Some, quoting the letter as far as we have now taken it, have concluded (in the words of Peter Gay, the author of a monumental three-volume study—or, as he prefers, interpretation—of the Enlightenment) that Haydn, used to being "handed from one princely Esterhazy to another almost as if he had been a favorite horse," found "the habit of submission" hard to break, and "returned to his masters."[44] But no, the end of this fascinating letter actually tells a different story: he decided to face the danger. His prince, he reports, had sent him a letter in which he

> strongly objects to my staying away for so long, and absolutely demands my speedy return; but I can't comply with this, owing to a new contract which I have just made here. And now, unfortunately, I expect my dismissal, whereby I hope that God will give me the strength to make up for this loss, at least partly, by my industry.[45]

But even this is not the end of the story because, as we know, Haydn continued to fulfill contracted work for the Eszterházy heirs until, with the *Harmonie-Messe* of 1802, he (but for a single unfinished quartet that finally drained him dry) laid down his pen at last. So it would be better to stick with Burney and seek Haydn's Enlightenment affinities in the public sphere, and in the illumination his work imparted to his audiences.

Illumination is of course a synonym for our titular word; and if anything may fairly be called Haydn's contribution to Enlightenment, this would be it. Schroeder aptly compares Haydn's relationship to the London audience with the model advo-

---

41. Letter of 17 September 1791; in James Cuthbert Hadden, *Haydn*, The Master Musicians (London: J. M. Dent, 1902), 220.

42. E.g., in Karl Geiringer's *Haydn: A Creative Life in Music*, 3rd ed. with Irene Geiringer (Berkeley: University of California Press, 1982), 115.

43. Hadden, *Haydn*, 220.

44. Peter Gay, *The Enlightenment*, vol. 2: *The Science of Freedom*, rev. ed. (New York: W. W. Norton, 1996), 226.

45. Hadden, *Haydn*, 220.

cated by Anthony Ashley Cooper, the Third Earl of Shaftesbury (1671–1713), in his celebrated and very idealistic treatise *Characteristics of Men, Manners, Opinions, Times*, a book that Haydn had in his library at the time of his death.[46] Shaftesbury, the first writer (nearly a century before Kant) to use the Kantian term *disinterested* with reference to art appreciation, had held up as an example of that *sine qua non* the relationship between artist and audience that had obtained, he fancied, in ancient times, when authors "formed their audience, polished the age, refined the public ear and framed it right, that in return they might be rightly and lastingly applauded," whereas "our modern authors, on the contrary, are turned and modelled (as themselves confess) by the public relish and current humour of the times."[47]

Haydn, the darling of the London public, but an artist formed in the exacting crucible of aristocratic connoisseurship, was the type of artist of whom Shaftesbury approved: "The more they courted the public," he advised, "the more they instructed it." Shaftesbury was particularly keen to exhort poets to "recommend wisdom and virtue (if possibly they can) in a way of pleasantry and mirth."[48] This, of course, was Haydn's particular strength, nurtured in interaction with his knowing prince and brought to its pinnacle before the London throngs. Even during his lifetime, Haydn's music was compared with the wit (*vis comica*) of Laurence Sterne,[49] and in our day whole books have been written about his humorous rhetoric.[50] And the best proof of its relationship to the values of the Enlightenment is the trouble it made for Haydn once the romantic backlash set in, beginning with E. T. A. Hoffmann and extending to the antihumanist writers of our own time, who recognize that the optimistic and unintransigent comic style

---

46. Ibid., 12. Schroeder emphasizes that Haydn had the English-language edition of 1790 (obviously acquired in London) rather than the German translation published in the 1770s, and wonders whether he could actually have read it. Even if it had been a gift or an impulse purchase, he writes (probably basing his assertion on an introspection that many of us can confirm), "owning a book may very well have been a type of concrete or tangible endorsement of ideas and theories with which he had been familiarized in conversation with friends or at a literary salon."

47. "Advice to an Author," in Antony Earl of Shaftesbury, *Characteristics of Men, Manners, Opinions, Times*, vol. 1 (Basil: Tourneisen & Legrand, 1790), 228; quoted in Schroeder, *Haydn and the Enlightenment*, 16 (corrected by comparison with the original edition).

48. Ibid., 206; quoted in Schroeder, *Haydn and the Enlightenment*, 17.

49. The reference to Sterne comes from Johann Karl Friedrich Triest, "Bemerkungen über die Ausbildung der Tonkunst in Deutschland im achtzehnten Jahrhundert," *Allgemeine Musikalische Zeitung* (1801), quoted by Dies (Gotwals [ed. and trans.], *Haydn: Two Contemporary Portraits*, 199). A full translation, by Susan Gillespie, of Triest's long essay can be found in Elaine Sisman, ed., *Haydn and His World* (Princeton, NJ: Princeton University Press, 1997), 321–94.

50. See especially Gretchen A. Wheelock, *Haydn's Ingenious Jesting with Art: Contexts of Musical Wit and Humor* (New York: Schirmer Books, 1992); and Mark Evan Bonds, "Haydn, Laurence Sterne, and the Origins of Musical Irony," *Journal of the American Musicological Society* 44 (1991): 57–91.

endorses the here-and-now over imagined perfection, and social harmony over disruption.[51]

This subtext emerges with particular clarity in the final paragraph of David Schroeder's book, published in 1990, in that dawn following the fall of the Berlin wall, when bliss it was for many of us to be alive. It seems to echo Francis Fukuyama's "The End of History?"—that nearly contemporaneous and famously premature victory lap on behalf of the Enlightenment and its universal truths[52]—in the way it links Haydn reception history to a gladsome narrative of moral triumph. Recalling that in 1877, when interest in Papa Haydn was decidedly the province of antiquarians, one such (the English organist and bibliophile Edward Francis Rimbault) had declared him "a name to be honoured, both in music and in morals,"[53] Schroeder continues, in decorous *crescendo*:

> While Haydn was never completely lost from public view, it was nevertheless necessary for a revival of his works to take place in the twentieth century. If one considers the relationship of popularity and challenge which applied to the original reception, it is much less the popular aspect than the challenge which has guaranteed Haydn's durability and place in the current repertoire. Concerning the latter, the composer was not only writing for his contemporary audience but also for posterity. The values which the artist could share with his own audience can, of course, be shared with other generations as well. While Haydn, like other artists and writers of the Enlightenment, was attempting to inculcate a certain view of morality, that sense of values has a more universalized aspect which the twentieth century has by no means entirely abandoned. In fact, this century is able to look to the Enlightenment as the source of those values which we continue to hold as being important concerning social structure, education, political organization, and all the various freedoms and liberties which are now taken entirely for granted (although in all too few countries). It should come as no surprise that the composer who devised musical means for imparting these values and who directly or indirectly set the standard for all subsequent symphonists should continue to engage the imagination of the present age.[54]

One reads these brave words now with a wince or a cringe, at the very least with a twinge of embarrassed nostalgia for those days, not as many decades ago as per-

---

51. For E. T. A. Hofmann, Haydn merely "grasps romantically the human in human life; he is more accommodating, more comprehensible for the common man," and therefore not to be compared with Mozart, who "laid claim to the superhuman, to the marvelous that dwells in the inner spirit," let alone Beethoven, whose music "wields the lever of fear, awe, horror, and pain, and it awakens that eternal longing that is the essence of the romantic" ("Beethoven's Instrumental Music" [1813], trans. Oliver Strunk, in Strunk, ed., *Source Readings in Music History* [New York: W. W. Norton, 1950], 777). For contemporary anti-Enlightenment polemic, see below.
52. Francis Fukuyama, "The End of History?" *The National Interest* 16 (Summer 1989): 3–18.
53. *The Leisure Hour* 26 (1877): 572; quoted in Schroeder, *Haydn and the Enlightenment*, 200.
54. Schroeder, *Haydn and the Enlightenment*, 200–1.

haps it feels, when such talk seemed to express not complacency but justified elation. Even at the time of Schroeder's writing, though, universalist rhetoric was under strong attack from those who saw it less as benign observation than normative prescription, according to which a standard was set that gave its promulgators leave to proclaim dominion over those who failed to measure up to it. We are now well acquainted with the links that have been asserted between the "universalized aspect" of moral value that Haydn is said to have inculcated and what Edward Rimbault's contemporaries and compatriots had called the White Man's Burden; and we are also familiar with the lines drawn—first in Frankfurt, now throughout the academic world—between the Age of Reason and the rationalized administrative efficiency with which the twentieth century dispensed death and destruction in the name of empire or eugenics. Now it is the proponents of Enlightenment, those who still celebrate common values and look for likeness, who have grown defensive in the face of a new Romanticism that looks for difference and celebrates distinction.[55] There is no less fashionable idea now than that of ageless human nature.[56] So it will not surprise anyone to learn that views of Haydn such as that exemplified by Schroeder's study have fallen under something of a cloud, dismissed as "optimistic—emancipatory, even—readings that betray a reductive and uncritical conception of the Enlightenment."[57]

Not only the discourse around Haydn's music, but the music—forgive me— "itself," has come under fire at times of agonizing reappraisal. Writing the same year as Fukuyama but in a very different mood, Leo Treitler looked back two decades to the very different turbulence of the Vietnam War, no blissful dawn, and his (as he now confessed it) blind adherence to reductive, uncritical Enlightenment thinking. "It is no wonder," he wrote,

> that the historiographic mold inherited from the age of Enlightenment that cast history as a story of transformation toward the perfection of reason in man and society gave way to apocalyptic forms, or that accomplished American humanists would have come to question the very possibility of an authentic and morally legitimate humanistic study, to question the presumption of humanists to be the privileged purveyors of humane values. If Lyndon Johnson was at large, asked one, why were we

---

55. As I write, Steven Pinker's *Enlightenment Now!*—an especially embattled restatement of the old universals (New York: Viking, 2018)—is polarizing critical opinion.

56. And for an embattled defense of *that*, see the (as I write) latest book by Roger Scruton, the most dependable upholder of traditional wisdom: *On Human Nature* (Princeton, NJ: Princeton University Press, 2018).

57. Melanie Lowe, "Difference and Enlightenment in Haydn's Instrumental Music," in *Rethinking Difference in Music Scholarship*, ed. Olivia Bloechl, Melanie Lowe, and Jeffrey Kallberg (Cambridge: Cambridge University Press, 2015), 133–69, at 134. Several pages later (142–43), Lowe specifically addresses Schroeder's "uncritical optimism about the late [Haydn] symphonies' participation in and furthering of enlightened thought," adducing some of the same interpretations I have also cited, above.

not in jail? And if the executioners of Auschwitz were lovers of Goethe, asked another, how would our humanistic values protect us from the possibility of our own barbarism? Better not to think about it. To be sure there was a whiff of self-serving demagoguery about such slogans; it was an opportune time for opportunism. But there was no escaping the dilemma posed by students who could not easily integrate lectures on the forms of Haydn symphonies with their forced awareness that their presence in the lecture hall was a privilege granted them in a society that was just then making such a display of its barbarity.[58]

Inevitably (for those days), it was periwigged, liveried Haydn who was most easily pressed into service as paradigm for academic escapism and "irrelevance." The words hurt, because what Treitler derided was precisely the sort of teaching by which we who taught those Haydn symphonies sought to maintain Enlightenment in our own benighted (or re-nighted) times. One way of dealing with bad conscience of this kind is to find what seemed to be missing in the place one had been missing it, or, failing that, to allow deconstruction to have its way with texts and thus reassuringly reveal the simultaneous presence of hegemonic discourse and its emancipatory antithesis. Susan McClary's reading of what she actually called "A Musical Dialectic from [sic] the [sic] Enlightenment" is perhaps the best-known case in point. She interpreted the improbably quick retransition from the harmonic far-out point (G-sharp major!) reached by the soloist in the slow movement of Mozart's Piano Concerto no. 17 in G, K. 453, to the orchestra's tonic reprise in C major not as an example of what Wye J. Allanbrook would call "comic closure," thus an embodiment of the Enlightenment's optimistic (and socially conservative) spirit, but rather (à la Frankfurt) as enacting a repressive subjugation of the protagonist by a dominating collectivity.[59] Yet by the same token, the soloist's subjective transgressions against "pure order" give implicit encouragement to "previously disenfranchised producers (ethnic minorities, members of the working class, women) and forms of culture."[60]

More recently, Melanie Lowe has sought and found similar double codings in two late works of Haydn. In the first movement of the *Oxford* Symphony (no. 92), the reprise of the first theme in the secondary key at the end of the recapitulation enacts a hegemonic "bracketing of difference," but also, and simultaneously, it evokes what Ruth Solie has called "resistance against subsumption into an undif-

---

58. Leo Treitler, *Music and the Historical Imagination* (Cambridge, MA: Harvard University Press, 1989), 5–6.

59. Susan McClary, "A Musical Dialectic from the Enlightenment: Mozart's 'Piano Concerto in G Major, K. 453,' Movement 2," *Cultural Critique*, no. 4 (Autumn 1986): 129–69. Cf. Wye J. Allanbrook, *The Secular Commedia: Comic Mimesis in Late Eighteenth-Century Music* (Berkeley: University of California Press, 2014), chap. 4 ("Comic Finitude and Comic Closure").

60. McClary, "A Musical Dialectic," 164.

ferentiated universal subject" represented by the tonic.[61] In the final movement of the Piano Trio in G, Hob. XV:25, the famous "Rondo all'ongorese," Lowe finds aporia where straightforward (and, nowadays, often disapproving) exoticist reading has been the rule: "the expressive assimilation and structural containment of such 'exotic' elements [as *verbunkos* and *alla turca*], the democratic spirit of the finale's governing contredanse topic, and the political projection of a single will in the textural relations among the three instruments, [all] interact and contradict one another."[62]

Lowe is somewhat uncomfortably aware that her two readings occupy differing levels of engagement with the text. "My political reading of the . . . 'Oxford' Symphony depends on structural and tonal details that may—or may not—be immediately audible or apparent, particularly to a lay listener," she confesses, whereas in the "Gypsy" rondo "the politics of difference reside saliently at the musical surface."[63] Given the audience to which the *Oxford* was addressed, and the importance of that social fact to the interpretation of music in relation to the Enlightenment, this inconsistency seems rather worrying, and indicates to me that if one expects to read the Enlightenment within a musical text as a coded representation, one will *reprendre son bien où on le trouve*, as Molière might say, that is, pounce on what one needs, wherever one may find it.[64] Opportunistic readings such as these do not lend much support to the connection between Haydn's musical work and any particular philosophical orientation, which usually defines the interpreter more accurately than the object interpreted. Better, it seems to me, to stick to social transactions rather than embodied meanings as the locus of Haydn's connection with the culture of Enlightenment, and to the manner of address and engagement that had such a profound impact on that "liberal and enlightened hearer of music" we read about in Burney. Haydn deeply affected with his example the way people listened to music, especially instrumental music, and what they expected to find therein.

IV

This change in listeners, which I strove to elicit (with Haydn's help) as a music appreciation instructor back in the day, can be found described on high philo-

---

61. Lowe, "Difference and Enlightenment in Haydn," 157, quoting Solie, "Introduction," in Ruth Solie, ed., *Musicology and Difference: Gender and Sexuality in Music Scholarship* (Berkeley: University of California Press, 1993), 6.

62. Ibid., 167.

63. Ibid., 157–58.

64. The paraphrased remark is attributed to Molière (who is said to have offered it as a defense against a charge of plagiarism) by Jean D'Alembert in his *Éloge de Boileau-Despréaux* (*Oeuvres complètes de D'Alembert*, vol. 2, part 1 [Paris: Belin, 1821], 437.

sophical terms and in the most elegant English in a book issued back many more days, during the time of Haydn's second London visit, though not by a member of his actual London audience (although he might almost have made it to that scene). Adam Smith, the great economist, spent his mature years living in Edinburgh and Glasgow, and the book, *Essays on Philosophical Subjects,* was a posthumous collection of his unpublished writings issued in 1795, five years after the author's death, by a committee of his friends and disciples. In the spirit of British antiquarianism, Smith mentions no composer alive at his time of writing: Corelli and Handel are his *loci classici*. I would nevertheless suggest that Smith's discussion of music in the long essay "Of the Nature of that Imitation which takes place in what are called the Imitative Arts" reflects his experience listening to the kind of music that David Schroeder dissects in his treatise linking Haydn with the philosophy of the Enlightenment. As Smith's discussion makes especially clear, it is not a matter of homology, analogy, or direct representation of Enlightenment morals or principles that Smith discerned in the instrumental music that engaged his interest as a philosopher, or anything else that can be called, in the original Platonic or Aristotelian sense, an imitation (*mimesis*).

In fact, Smith's discussion of music is one of the earliest to disassociate music from the imitative arts altogether—and it happens by degrees, the ontogeny of his own argument recapitulating the phylogeny of musical philosophizing as it evolved over the course of the eighteenth century. "It is Instrumental Music which can best subsist apart, and separate from both Poetry and Dancing," Smith writes, and because it is unattached to words and cannot be directly correlated with verbal meaning, it becomes questionable whether such music can be said to exemplify "the merits of imitation," through which "a thing of one kind" is made to "resemble another thing of a very different kind."[65] The question then becomes whether there is anything "of a different kind" that instrumental music does imitate. If not, the delineation of its peculiar content and effect becomes a pressing issue.

At first it seems that Smith is heading for an arousal theory such as had been previously offered to Anglophone readers by Charles Avison, whereby music acts as an emotional stimulus that elicits a corresponding response, "raising" the passions of engaged listeners without necessarily reminding them of emotionally exciting objects or experiences.[66] Although it does elicit emotional responses as strong as those experienced when contemplating painting, dancing, or poetry, instrumental music does not achieve this by way of sympathy. Rather,

---

65. *Essays on Philosophical Subjects by the Late Adam Smith, LL.D., Fellow of the Royal Societies of London and Edinburgh* (London: T. Cadell & W. Davies, 1795), 152, 154. Further references to this source will be made in the main text.

66. Charles Avison, *An Essay on Musical Expression* (London: C. Davis, 1753); relevant excerpts in Piero Weiss and Richard Taruskin, eds., *Music in the Western World: A History in Documents,* 2nd ed. (Belmont, CA: Thomson/Schirmer, 2008), 244–47.

it becomes itself a gay, a sedate, or a melancholy object; and the mind naturally assumes the mood or disposition which at the time corresponds to the object which engages its attention. Whatever we feel from instrumental Music is an original, and not a sympathetic feeling: it is our own gaiety, sedateness, or melancholy; not the reflected disposition of another person. (164)

Smith acknowledges, however, that the chief emotion that instrumental music elicits is the sheer pleasure of hearing it, and that the arousal theory assigns to instrumental music a much weaker power of emotional stimulation, and consequently a lesser aesthetic value, than vocal. Since this assignment contradicts his own experience, Smith is impelled to seek the intrinsic value of instrumental music in some other, as yet uncharted sphere, and here is where his theory becomes original, and momentous.

Even if we concede that "its powers over the heart and affections are, no doubt, much inferior to those of vocal Music," Smith insists, "it has, however, considerable powers." Their route to the affections, however, runs through the mind (or what Smith calls the "attention"), not the heart. He describes a cognitive process, proceeding by way of fully conscious memory and expectation, rather than an emotional contagion; and that process involves the apperception of just such "structural and tonal details" as Melanie Lowe feared might be beyond the ken of "lay listeners." Smith was one lay listener who could and did perceive and react to such musical stimuli, even if he does not follow through with the sort of political interpretation that Lowe's idea of Enlightenment values might require. That is why I would offer what now follows as an "Enlightened" theory of musical response, genuinely so called and contemporaneous with the music we now seek to interpret in that light. "By the sweetness of its sounds," Smith writes, instrumental music

> awakens agreeably, and calls upon the attention; by their connection and affinity it naturally detains that attention, which follows easily a series of agreeable sounds, which have all a certain relation both to a common, fundamental, or leading note, called the key note; and to a certain succession or combination of notes, called the song or composition. By means of this relation each foregoing sound seems to introduce, and as it were prepare the mind for the following: by its rythmus, by its time and measure, it disposes that succession of sounds into a certain arrangement, which renders the whole more easy to be comprehended and remembered. Time and measure are to instrumental Music what order and method are to discourse; they break it into proper parts and divisions, by which we are enabled both to remember better what is gone before, and frequently to foresee somewhat of what is to come after: we frequently foresee the return of a period which we know must correspond to another which we remember to have gone before; and, according to the saying of an ancient philosopher and musician, the enjoyment of Music arises partly from memory and partly from foresight. When the measure, after having been continued so long as to satisfy us, changes to another, that variety, which thus disappoints, becomes more

agreeable to us than the uniformity which would have gratified our expectation: but without this order and method we could remember very little of what had gone before, and we could foresee still less of what was to come after; and the whole enjoyment of Music would be equal to little more than the effect of the particular sounds which rung in our ears at every particular instant. By means of this order and method it is, during the progress of the entertainment, equal to the effect of all that we remember, and of all that we foresee; and at the conclusion, to the combined and accumulated effect of all the different parts of which the whole was composed. (171–72)

No Music Humanities instructor ever put it better. But Smith's peroration goes even further in the direction of musical absolutism (not to say "absolute music"). Ever since I first encountered Smith's text,[67] I have relied on the paragraphs that follow (and particularly the big, fat first one, which Piero Weiss and I ensconced prominently in our school anthology *Music in the Western World*)[68] to answer the most basic questions—the *cursed questions*—which not only I but, surely, those of my readers who have served alongside me as musical missionaries will have had to field over the course of their (our) careers:

A well-composed concerto of instrumental Music, by the number and variety of the instruments, by the variety of the parts which are performed by them, and the perfect concord or correspondence of all these different parts; by the exact harmony or coincidence of all the different sounds which are heard at the same time, and by that happy variety of measure which regulates the succession of those which are heard at different times, presents an object so agreeable, so great, so various, and so interesting, that alone, and without suggesting any other object, either by imitation or otherwise, it can occupy, and as it were fill up, completely the whole capacity of the mind, so as to leave no part of its attention vacant for thinking of anything else. In the contemplation of that immense variety of agreeable and melodious sounds, arranged and digested, both in their coincidence and in their succession, into so complete and regular a system, the mind in reality enjoys not only a very great sensual, but a very high intellectual, pleasure, not unlike that which it derives from the contemplation of a great system in any other science. A full concerto of such instrumental Music, not only does not require, but it does not admit of any accompaniment. A song or a dance, by demanding an attention which we have not to spare, would disturb, instead of heightening, the effect of the Music; they may often very properly succeed, but they cannot accompany it. That music seldom means to tell any particular story, or to imitate any particular event, or in general to suggest any particular object, distinct

---

67. And let me express my gratitude to the late Alan Lessem, in whose short article "Imitation and Expression: Opposing French and British Views in the Late 18th Century" (*Journal of the American Musicological Society* 27 [1974]: 325–30) I first encountered not only Smith but also several other texts that went into the group of readings that appeared in *Music in the Western World* under the rubric "A Side Trip into Aesthetics" (243–52).

68. Weiss and Taruskin (eds.), *Music in the Western World*, 250–51.

from that combination of sounds of which itself is composed. Its meaning, therefore, may be said to be complete in itself, and to require no interpreters to explain it. What is called the subject of such Music is merely, as has already been said, a certain leading combination of notes, to which it frequently returns, and to which all its digressions and variations bear a certain affinity. It is altogether different from what is called the subject of a poem or a picture, which is always something which is not either in the poem or in the picture, or something quite distinct from that combination, either of words on the one hand, or of colours on the other, of which they are respectively composed. The subject of a composition of instrumental Music is a part of that composition: the subject of a poem or picture is no part of either.

The effect of instrumental Music upon the mind has been called its expression. In the feeling it is frequently not unlike the effect of what is called the expression of Painting, and is sometimes equally interesting. But the effect of the expression of Painting arises always from the thought of something which, though distinctly and clearly suggested by the drawing and colouring of the picture, is altogether different from that drawing and colouring. It arises sometimes from sympathy with, sometimes from antipathy and aversion to, the sentiments, emotions, and passions which the countenance, the action, the air and attitude of the persons represented suggest. The melody and harmony of instrumental Music, on the contrary, do not distinctly and clearly suggest any thing that is different from that melody and harmony. Whatever effect it produces is the immediate effect of that melody and harmony, and not of something else which is signified and suggested by them: *they in fact signify and suggest nothing.* . . .

Instrumental Music, therefore, though it may, no doubt, be considered in some respects as an imitative art, is certainly less so than any other which merits that appellation; it can imitate but a few objects, and even these so imperfectly, that without the accompaniment of some other art, its imitation is scarce ever intelligible: imitation is by no means essential to it, and the principal effects which it is capable of producing arises from powers altogether different from those of imitation. (172–75)

I will not claim that Adam Smith needed Haydn or his music in order to learn these lessons; he has given ample proof of his capacity to live up to Kant's demand for original and independent, not to mention brilliant, thought. I will claim, however, that Haydn's music and the experience of listening to it served to instill—and this very much by design—the listening habits and skills that Adam Smith here describes, which David Schroeder declares to be constitutive of "reflective," "alert," and "critical" listening, and which Burney actually called "enlightened." Many would now see Smith's case as overstated (and I have italicized in quoting it one phrase that definitely seems to me to be a potentially mischievous exaggeration); but if so, I will concede that corrective efforts are seldom free of a tendency toward enthusiastic—and in my view, allowable—hyperbole. Anyone concerned that Smith has overplayed his hand when claiming that melody and harmony *in fact signify and suggest nothing* will find ample qualification elsewhere in this book.

Indeed, Smith provides the necessary qualifications himself, right in the passages I have quoted, when he quite explicitly allows (as Hanslick would also do, two generations later) that music is perfectly capable of imitation if desired (although not so effortlessly capable as the arts with more obvious models in nature) and that the high intellectual pleasure he describes does not replace but joins (and, implicitly, enhances) the sensual pleasure that (everyone will agree) music delivers as well as or better than any other art. That was the point I loved making to my cherished nonmajors as well. Listen hard, and you'll enjoy it more. Haydn, who deliberately filled his music with so much absorbing and engaging detail, provided cognitive fodder precisely to enhance the emotional payoff. "Once I had seized upon an idea," he told Griesinger, "my whole endeavor was to develop and sustain it in keeping with the rules of art," and this, he admonished, was "what so many of our new composers lack: they string one little bit after another, they break off when they have hardly begun, and nothing remains in the heart when one has listened to it."[69] Mind and heart thus work in synergy. Their opposition was a Romantic prejudice. The age of reason was also the age of sympathy. Without taking account of the latter, the former will not suffice to characterize Enlightenment, at least for music.

So do we need the term at all? Like all labels, it coarsens and reduces, especially when it comes with the definite article. To say "the" Enlightenment sends us looking for a thing, or even a place (as when we say, for example, that a musical dialectic comes "from" it); and then we are especially prone to apply the word normatively. The problem with reduction, moreover, is that it covers up contradiction, the very thing that keeps philosophers in business; and we may locate the basic contradiction of the term Enlightenment within the work of Kant, the very one whose famous definition started us on our way. That definition emphasized independence—hence originality—of thought. It is to Kant, indeed, that we owe the paradoxical definition of artistic genius that still reigns among us today. "The talent (or natural gift) which gives the rule to art," he wrote, is nevertheless "a *talent for producing that for which no definite rule can be given*."[70]

Whether or not he ever read Kant, or even heard of him, Haydn certainly agreed with both of these incompatible principles. When, according to Griesinger,

---

69. Gotwals (ed. and trans.), *Haydn: Two Contemporary Portraits*, 61. Translation adjusted by comparison with the original text: "Hatte ich eine Idee erhascht, so ging mein ganzes Bestreben dahin, sie den Regeln der Kunst gemäß auszuführen und zu soutenieren. So suchte ich mir zu helfen, und das ist es, was so vielen unserer neuen Componisten fehlt, sie reihen ein Stückchen an das andere, sie brechen ab, wenn sie kaum angefangen haben: aber es bleibt auch nichts im Herzen sitzen, wenn man es angehört hat" (Georg August Griesinger, *Biographische Notizen über Joseph Haydn* [Leipzig: Breitkopf & Härtel, 1810], 124).

70. Immanuel Kant, *Critique of Judgment*, trans. J.H. Bernard (New York: Hafner Press, 1951), 135.

he heard that Johann Georg Albrechtsberger had decreed that one cannot use fourths in "pure style" (*reinsten Satze*), he scoffed, "What does that mean? Art is free and should not be limited by mere craftsmanship."[71] And just as surely he agreed that he had genius according to Kant's definition. Out in the sticks at the Eszterházy estate, he told the same biographer, "I could, as head of an orchestra, make experiments, observe what enhanced an effect and what weakened it, thus improving, adding to, cutting away, and running risks; I was set apart from the world, there was nobody in my vicinity to confuse and annoy me in my course, and so I had to become original [*und so mußte ich original werden*]."[72]

At the same time, however, it was Kant who expounded the principle that our natural rights stem from our common humanity, the chief evidence for which is our basic similarity to one another—that is, our common human nature, the basis of that much-abused notion "common sense" (*sensus communis*), "the mere healthy (not yet cultivated) understanding [that] we regard as the least to be expected from any one claiming the name of man," and that forms our judgments, including our aesthetic judgments.[73] Aesthetic judgments are only sound, according to Kant, when they are widely shared. Can art appeal to the *sensus communis* and at the same time display rule-flouting original genius? This is a narrowly couched and seemingly benign version of the question that has tormented Enlightened political thought ever since the eighteenth century: Can equality coexist with excellence?

Haydn's contemporaries were aware of this problem, and accorded him (along with Shakespeare) the rare accolade of ascribing to his art the power of transcending it. His biographer Griesinger actually invoked Kant himself in proclaiming Haydn a genius the novelty of whose ideas baffled even himself, but whose finished work was universal in its appeal.[74] And while there were those who complained that his works were "too flighty, trifling, and wild, . . . introducing a species of sounds totally unknown," time had vindicated them by actually altering the *sensus communis,* so that the new species had come to seem "original, masterly, and beautiful."[75] Haydn's excellence had raised the standard, allowing humans, accordingly, to improve in their equality.

---

71. "Was heißt das? . . . die Kunst ist frey, und soll durch keine Handwerks fesseln beschränkt werden" (Griesinger, *Biographische Notizen,* 114).

72. Gotwals (ed. and trans.), *Haydn: Two Contemporary Portraits,* 17; cf. Griesinger, *Biographische Notizen,* 24–25.

73. Kant, *Critique of Judgment,* 135.

74. Gotwals (ed. and trans.), *Haydn: Two Contemporary Portraits,* 60; cf. Griesinger, *Biographische Notizen,* 113.

75. "An Account of Joseph Haydn, a Celebrated Composer of Music," *European Magazine and London Review,* October 1784; quoted in Elaine Sisman, "Haydn, Shakespeare, and the Rules of Originality," in *Haydn and His World,* ed. E. Sisman (Princeton, NJ: Princeton University Press, 1997), 21.

And beyond original, masterly and beautiful, in his last works Haydn achieved the sublime. This is another link with Kant, who had taken from the writings of Edmund Burke the notion that at its most intense, the aesthetic can offer us inklings of the great as well as the pleasing, and that in this it could assume the place in the lives of enlightened humans that dogmatic religion had occupied in the world of their benighted ancestors. Haydn's oratorios *The Creation* and *The Seasons*, works written under the direct impact of the Handel oratorios that had bowled him over in England, exemplify the natural religion of enlightened thinkers—including the Masons, Haydn having joined a Vienna lodge in 1785. The God depicted in Haydn's oratorios is the God of the Deists, the benign creator God who, in *The Creation*, puts exultant man in charge of His creation; and that happy pantheism achieves its apotheosis in *The Seasons*. There is no more exultant moment in all of music than the moment when, out of the mysterious sonic mists of the initial "Representation of Chaos" (Haydn's one deliberate attempt to, in Schroeder's words, "supersede intelligibility") the blinding flash (transformed into the deafening blast of C major that Mme de Staël found so remarkable) announces the primeval dawn; and thereafter the story of creation, and of Adam and Eve, is all sweetness and light: no fall, no expulsion, no need, therefore, for redemption.

Some actually felt that the unclouded optimism of Haydn's oratorios was impious. Haydn's answer to them, expressed in a letter he sent, in July 1801, to a Bohemian schoolmaster named Karl Ockl, are words Kant would have approved. "I am simply astonished," Haydn wrote.

> The creation has always been considered the most sublime and inspiring image to contemplate. To accompany it with suitable music could surely have no other effect than to enhance these sacred feelings in the hearts of men, and confirm their belief in the goodness and omnipotence of the Creator. How can it be a sacrilege to arouse such holy feelings?[76]

In a beautiful act of synthesis, Elaine Sisman sees this celebration of natural religion as Haydn's alpha and omega, linking up his early *Tageszeiten* symphonies, his maiden offering to the Eszterházys, with the culminating oratorios to subsume his whole career under the sign of those mighty "aesthetic ideas" inspired by nature that, according to Kant, "quicken the mind into imaginative response."[77] It is in the specific processes by which Haydn contrived to perform this quickening of his listeners' minds that we find his truest relationship to what we now call The Enlightenment.

---

76. H.C. Robbins Landon, *Haydn: Chronicle and Works*, vol. 5 (Bloomington: Indiana University Press, 1978), 70–71.

77. Elaine Sisman, "Haydn's Solar Poetics: The *Tageszeiten* Symphonies and Enlightenment Knowledge," *Journal of the American Musicological Society* 66 (2013): 5–102, at 91.

4

Is There a Baby in the Bathwater?
On aesthetic autonomy

Art should be independent of all clap-trap—should stand alone, and appeal to the artistic sense of eye or ear, without confounding this with emotions entirely foreign to it, as devotion, pity, love, patriotism, and the like. All these have no kind of concern with it, and that is why I insist on calling my works "arrangements" and "harmonies." Take the picture of my mother, exhibited at the Royal Academy as an "Arrangement in Grey and Black." Now that is what it is. To me it is interesting as a picture of my mother; but what can or ought the public to care about the identity of the portrait?
—JAMES MCNEILL WHISTLER (1890)[1]

We, too, have mothers.
—RICHARD TARUSKIN (2018)

As my patient respondent Prof. Riethmüller can attest, it took me a very long time to gain a purchase on the topic of this seminar and this talk. Not that it was in any way new to me: like many musicologists, I have been thinking and writing about aesthetic autonomy for many years. As your propaedeutic states, aesthetic autonomy has undergone a serious interrogation in the past two or three decades among historians of the arts, and among music historians I am one of the more notorious interrogators—obviously, else why would you have invited me to address you?

But aesthetic autonomy is not merely something historians know historically. It has been the dominant regulative concept of art-theory and art-practice for more than two centuries, and has so many aspects and ramifications that it has

---

Originally presented at Freie Universität Berlin, Kunsthistoriches Institut, 13 February 2006 (Lecture series, "Aesthetische Autonomie?") and published in *Archiv für Musikwissenschaft* 63 (2006): 163–85, 309–27.

1. "The Red Rag," *The World*, 22 May 1878, 4–5; reprinted in Whistler, *The Gentle Art of Making Enemies* (New York: G. P. Putnam & Sons, 1892), 127–28.

become nebular. Trying to isolate and capture it for purposes of discussion—or dissection—is like trying to put a cloud in a box. So I have been spending months in search of a strategy for this talk, and I feel the need, at the outset, for some rigorous definitions, since experience has taught me that one cannot take it for granted that we all mean the same thing by our titular term, or that in this period of shifting paradigms one can count on consensus.

I. FOUR TYPES OF AUTONOMY

There are at least four ways in which the phrase "aesthetic autonomy" can be construed, corresponding to four moments in its history. They are of course mutually implicated, but here is how I would artificially disengage them and lay them out on the laboratory table:

First, and most broadly, the term can mean the autonomy of aesthetics within philosophy. That was the implicit view of the earliest writers on the subject, including Alexander Baumgarten, who coined the term in his pioneering treatise *Aesthetica*, of 1750. This foundational document was not a treatise about art, but rather sought to provide a rationale for including knowledge gained through sensory perception—Baumgarten called it *scientia cognitionis sensitivae*, "the science of sensory cognition"—within a formal epistemology that had up until then been confined to the so-called higher faculties of cognition, namely conceptual reason and logic.[2] Baumgarten was making a bid on behalf of full rights for nonlinguistic or prelinguistic modes of perception, and that is also the premise of the so-called resurgence or rehabilitation of autonomy after its years in the interrogation chamber that may be observed in several humanistic disciplines today, in a fully declared alliance with cognitive psychology.[3] This broadest interpretation of aesthetic autonomy is the one most faithful to its etymology. Baumgarten's ersatz Latin title was adapted directly from the Greek word for "sensation" or "perception" in the most general sense. It was the transfer of aesthetics to the realm of art, beginning with *Briefe über die Empfindungen* (1755) by Moses Mendelssohn (whose grandson rather distinguished himself in my field), that brought the notion of autonomy, in *its* literal, etymological sense—that of following its own laws (again from the Greek: *auto*/self + *nomos*/law)—out into the open.

Thus the second meaning of "aesthetic autonomy" that I would propose is the one that refers to the autonomy of art within the range of human activities and

---

2. See Alexander Gottlieb Baumgarten, *Theoretische Aesthetik: Die grundlegenden Abschnitte aus der "Aesthetica,"* ed. Hans Rudolf Schweizer (Hamburg: Meiner, 1983), 3.

3. See especially *Artful Science: Enlightenment Entertainment and the Eclipse of Visual Education* (Cambridge, MA: MIT Press, 1994) and *Good Looking: Essays on the Virtues of Images* (Cambridge, MA: MIT Press, 1996) by Barbara Maria Stafford, my immediate predecessor as lecturer in the Freie Universität seminar.

achievements, requiring independent criteria of evaluation. That was what Kant tried to supply in his *Kritik der Urteilskraft* of 1790, and Kant's categories are still the ones normally invoked when artworks are defined or ranked as autonomous. You know the drill: they must be disinterested both in their motivation and in the mode of their contemplation, they must have the appearance of purposiveness (*Zweckmässigkeit*) without having an actual purpose (*Zweck*) or socially sanctioned function.[4] These are the criteria that have come under heaviest attack for the way in which they have seemed to divorce art from social concerns. But it should at the same time be obvious that these very criteria were particularly valuable in gaining recognition, and respect, for musical works as autonomous entities on a par with the products of the other artistic media, and had an enormous impact, first, on music criticism and, a little later, on musical practice in the nineteenth century, the "music century," when music came into its own as a fine art.

There is irony in this, since Kant himself had a notorious tin ear and thought of music as by far the lowest of the fine arts. "If," he wrote, "we estimate the worth of the beautiful arts by the culture they supply to the mind and take as a standard the expansion of the faculties which must concur in the judgment for cognition, music will have the lowest place among them (as it has perhaps the highest among those arts which are valued for their pleasantness), because it merely plays with sensations."[5] Indeed, Kant found music to be basically a nuisance:

> The case of music is almost like that of the delight derived from a smell that diffuses itself widely. The man who pulls his perfumed handkerchief out of his pocket attracts the attention of all around him, even against their will, and he forces them, if they are to breathe at all, to enjoy the scent; hence this habit has gone out of fashion. Those who recommend the singing of spiritual songs at family prayers do not consider that they inflict a great hardship upon the public by such *noisy* (and therefore in general pharisaical) devotions, for they force the neighbors either to sing with them or to abandon their meditations.[6]

And yet Kant, for whom music was more to be compared with perfume as a sense experience than with philosophy as a cognitive one, nevertheless provided willy-nilly the means for the elevation of music to the status of philosophical model for all the other arts—the art, to recall Walter Pater's famous remark, to

---

4. Matthew Pritchard interestingly complicates the drill by reference to Kant's distinction, elsewhere in the *Critique of Judgment*, between "free" and "dependent" beauty, the former being *Zwecklos* and autonomous, the latter of potential moral relevance ("Music in Balance: The Aesthetics of Music after Kant, 1790–1810," *Journal of Musicology* 36 [2019]: 39–67, esp. 46–49). But since Kant assigns music only to the first category, this distinction makes no real difference to the present argument.

5. Immanuel Kant, *Critique of Judgment*, trans. J. H. Bernard (New York: Hafner Press, 1951), 174.

6. Ibid., including an author's note.

whose condition all the other arts aspire.[7] And this is because if the arts are to be ranked in order of their autonomy—that is, their freedom from worldly function—then that art will come out best which specifies its content least, for in that lack of specificity—that abstraction—lies its freedom from limitation and possible constraint. If autonomy means withdrawal from the social, then—again according to etymology, this time from the Latin—abstraction is implied, for *abstractus* means, literally, "drawn away," withdrawn. Adding the tenets of Romanticism to those of Kant's critique produced the exaltation of music as "the most Romantic of all the arts," to quote E. T. A. Hoffmann's immortal essay "Beethoven's Instrumental Music."[8] The high status Hoffmann thus conferred on music is one that it has continued to enjoy (at least among philosophers and other academic humanists) to this day. And that is surely one of the reasons why, among the academic disciplines, musicology is the domain in which aesthetic autonomy has undergone the least interrogation; why musicologists who have questioned its status as a regulative concept still enjoy the reputation (which they would not deserve in any other campus department) of a contentious avant-garde; and why, I suppose, I am standing before you today.

In the same essay, which expanded on a review of Beethoven's Fifth Symphony that Hoffmann had published in 1810, the great critic asserted, in a revolutionary transvaluation of values, that instrumental music stood higher than vocal. One can see how textless music would stand higher within an aesthetic that valued abstraction, but Hoffmann's emphasis on wholeness—or unity—in conjunction with autonomy shows his inheritance from Kant's principle of *Zweckmässigkeit* in its improbable (and, strictly speaking, logically untenable) tandem with *Zwecklosigkeit*.[9] Art can be autonomous only if the maker shapes it with sufficient mastery and control. The most significant and influential aspect of Hoffmann's critique of Beethoven (giving rise, as it did, to the whole field of music analysis) was that, where everyone else marveled or scoffed at Beethoven's seeming wildness and abandon, Hoffmann demonstrated the master's sovereign control over his material and the economy with which Beethoven constructed huge movements out of min-

---

7. Walter Pater, *The Renaissance: Studies in Art and Poetry* (1893), ed. Donald L. Hill (Berkeley: University of California Press, 1980), 106.

8. E. T. A. Hoffmann, "Beethoven's Instrumental Music," *Zeitung für die elegante Welt*, December 1813, reprinted in *Kreisleriana*, part I (1814); translated by Martyn Clarke in *E. T. A. Hoffmann's Musical Writings*, ed. David Charlton (Cambridge: Cambridge University Press, 1989), 96.

9. Ibid., 96: "When music is spoken of as an independent art, does not the term properly apply only to instrumental music?"; 98: "Our aesthetic overseers have often complained of a total lack of inner unity and inner coherence in Shakespeare, when profounder contemplation shows the splendid tree, leaves, blossom, and fruit as springing from the same seed; in the same way only the most penetrating study of Beethoven's instrumental music can reveal its high level of rational awareness, which is inseparable from true genius and nourished by study of the art."

imal motivic ideas. Without that economy of structure and perfection of form, art could not rank as autonomous.

Also significant is the fact that Mozart's symphonies, rather than Haydn's, were the earliest ones that, in Hoffmann's view, merited the epithet "Romantic" (implying fully autonomous) in the strongest sense, for whereas Haydn's art "romantically apprehends the humanity in human life," it was Mozart who "leads us deep into the realm of spirits."[10] Hoffmann offers a certain amount of direct description of the sounding music as evidence for this distinction, but I suspect that it owed as much if not more to the well-known facts of Mozart's and Haydn's biographies. Haydn spent the bulk of his career in the secure embrace of aristocratic patronage, and afterwards made his strongest impression in Great Britain, the nation of shopkeepers, in a pair of almost inconceivably lucrative concert tours arranged by J. P. Salomon, the Diaghilev of his day. Mozart, after years of fruitless endeavors to find secure employment, spent his last decade as a financially vulnerable "free artist" in Vienna, earning his living by teaching and by giving "academies," concerts at which his own keyboard performances were the chief draw, and for which he composed his numerous piano concertos.

It was not the concertos that Hoffmann placed at the Mozartean pinnacle, however (for they had an obvious *Zweck*); rather, it was the final trio of symphonies, Nos. 39, 40, and 41, which Mozart composed during the summer of 1788. The first of them, which in Hoffmann's day was called "The Swan Song," is specifically cited and described by Hoffmann in relation to "the realm of spirit," and all three have retained their aura in music history as the earliest symphonies that were unmotivated by any specific, or at least known, prospect of performance. In the case of every one of Haydn's symphonies, we know why he composed it and when and where it was first performed, and this is true of all of Mozart's earlier symphonies as well. We do not know why he composed the last three, and we do not know when or where they were first performed. Our ignorance has allowed speculation that the symphonies were composed "for their own sake," as *ars gratia artis*, thus becoming the earliest musical masterworks that truly exemplify *Zweckmässigkeit ohne Zweck*; and the fact that they are by common consent Mozart's greatest achievements in the realm of orchestral music makes it easy to posit a connection between their aesthetic value and their "disinterested" status. It is altogether possible, indeed likely, that their status as disinterested is merely the result of a documentary lacuna. But the example of Beethoven's career, already underway in 1788, in which none of his symphonies (save, ironically enough, the last, but never mind) were called forth by any external social demand, has made it both easy and very desirable to assimilate Mozart's last symphonic works to the Beethovenian standard of autonomy.

10. Ibid., pp. 97–98.

Hoffmann's further insistence that the musician's (and, preeminently, Beethoven's) "kingdom," like Christ's, "is not of this world"—"for where in nature do we find the prototypes for our art, as painters and sculptors do?"—sounds the third note on my agenda, declaring musicians to be first among the artists whom the concept of aesthetic autonomy has liberated from social constraint.[11] This notion, that it is the artist as well as the art that achieves autonomy under the Romantic dispensation, was a response to a sudden change in the fortunes of artists, who found themselves socially emancipated—or perhaps it would be more accurate to say socially abandoned—with the collapse of the patronage system. It received another terrific if fortuitous boost from the accident of Beethoven's deafness, which not only turned the composer's biography into a drama of struggle and victory, but effectively removed him from this world—that is, the world of daily musical business in which composers functioned visibly as performers—and turned him into a commanding unseen presence. Beethoven's unsought social isolation became an emblem of the artist's new station, one that all artists now had to emulate.

Hoffmann's view of the artist's role—or lack of one—in society was taken further by Schopenhauer, surely the philosopher who had the profoundest direct impact on artists from his time all the way down to ours—and why not? What philosopher has ever flattered artists more than he did? For many, the prestige that Schopenhauer's philosophy has granted artists has more than made up for their catastrophic loss of economic and social security. I can attest that more than one composer has confided to me personally that they have taken as their highest inspiration the famous dictum from Schopenhauer's *Parerga und Paralipomena* of 1851, to wit—

> Intellectual life floats ethereally, like a fragrant cloud rising from fermentation, above the reality of the worldly activities which make up the lives of the peoples, governed by the will; alongside world history there goes, guiltless and not stained with blood, the history of philosophy, science, and the arts

—that Hans Pfitzner, before them, had copied lovingly into the score of his opera *Palestrina* as epigraph in the very midst of the First World War, while Europe was enduring the greatest bloodbath in its history, and the dictum that Thomas Mann would cite in *Betrachtungen eines Unpolitischen* (1918), his rueful memoir of the war years, as the motto of a passive conservatism that now had a lot to answer for.[12]

---

11. E. T. A. Hoffmann, "Johannes Kreisler's Certificate of Apprenticeship," in *Kreisleriana*, part II (1814); Charlton (ed.), *E. T. A. Hoffmann's Musical Writings*, 163.

12. The original German, transcribed directly from Pfitzner's vocal score (Berlin: Fürstner, 1916): "Dieses intellektuelle Leben schwebt, wie eine ätherische Zugabe, ein sich aus der Gärung entwickelnder wohlriechender Duft über dem weltlichen Treiben, dem eigentlich realen, vom Willen geführten Leben der Völker, und neben der Weltgeschichte geht schuldlos, und nicht blutbefleckt die Geschichte der Philosophie, der Wissenschaft, und der Künste." Mann's gloss on Schopenhauer's pronouncement

Here I might add parenthetically that musicology, the discipline I practice, and which I have already characterized as somewhat backward among the humanistic disciplines at least in its relationship to the paradigm of aesthetic autonomy, was actually founded on the model of Schopenhauer's tenet of aesthetic autonomy. In his "Umfang, Methode und Ziel der Musikwissenschaft" of 1885, commonly regarded as modern musicology's founding document,[13] Guido Adler defined (and, implicitly, restricted) the fledgling science, like the more established art history of the day, as a classificatory exercise à la Linnaeus. Like the art historians he called it *Stilkritik*, or style criticism. Style criticism, which attended only to the internal organization of the artwork, never to external circumstances, was still pretty much the exclusive preoccupation of the discipline when I had my initiation into it in the 1960s. It may well be still the dominant one if dominance is measured not by debates in the journals but by a census of practitioners; and every attempt to widen horizons has been met with a resistance that may be diminishing with time, and that may have lost some of its institutional support, but which can still compensate for any loss in conviction with renewed invective. (Charles Rosen's review of my *Oxford History of Western Music* in the *New York Review of Books*, which appeared shortly after I drafted this talk, can serve as an ideal, and very lengthy, illustration.)[14]

Belief in the personal autonomy of artists leads paradoxically to a very impersonal treatment of art history, in which, to quote J. Peter Burkholder, who like me has recently completed a general history of music (in his case a thorough revision of the venerable textbook of Donald J. Grout), "often enough it seemed like

---

takes the form of a wonderful seventeen-page excursus on Pfitzner's opera (brand new at the time of his writing). Writing of the second act, dominated by Palestrina and his tormentor, Cardinal Borromeo, Mann sees their relationship as that between "pessimism and humor," and marvels, "I have never perceived their correlation more strongly and never more sympathetically than [here]. The optimist, the reformer, in a word, the politician [i.e., Borromeo], is never a humorist; he is lofty-rhetorical. The pessimistic moral philosopher, however, whom one likes to call today quite figuratively the 'esthete' [i.e., Palestrina (= Schopenhauer)], will behave toward the world of will, reality, guilt and practical affairs with a natural preference for humor; as an artist he sees them as picturesque and amusing, in sharp contrast to the quiet dignity of intellectual life" (Thomas Mann, *Reflections of a Nonpolitical Man*, trans. Walter D. Morris [New York: Frederick Ungar, 1983], 301). And this is the conclusion: "If one has broad shoulders and strong teeth, if one is called Zola, Bjørnstjerne Bjørnson, or [Theodore] Roosevelt, then a harmonious effect may result. But if one entered the world a little noble and old, with a natural calling to skepticism, to irony, and to melancholy; if the blush of life that one displays for effect is hectic or cosmetic, if it is basically—estheticism, then the matter has its ethical offensiveness. I cannot overlook this" (314).

13. Originally published in *Vierteljahrschrift für Musikwissenschaft* 1 (1885): 5–20; translated and annotated in Erica Mugglestone, "Guido Adler's 'The Scope, Method, and Aim of Musicology' (1885): An English Translation with an Historico-Analytical Commentary," *Yearbook for Traditional Music* 13 (1981): 1–21.

14. "From the Troubadours to Frank Sinatra," *New York Review of Books* 53, no. 3 (26 February 2006): 41–45; and 53, no. 4 (9 March 2006): 44–48.

musical styles developed without the intervention of human beings"—except for those human beings, especially plentiful in the nineteenth and twentieth centuries, who perpetrated revolutionary technical innovations.[15] They are lauded as musicians, of course, but their innovations seem to be valued only, and precisely, as such—that is, as innovation. Innovation was presented as an intrinsic good and portrayed as the engine that drove the stylistic evolution that furnished the content of the historical narrative. At best, innovation was seen as tantamount to a breakthrough, in terms borrowed at fourth or fifth hand from Hegel, to a new stage in the consciousness and exercise of freedom. Any attempt at contextualization, or even the suggestion that contextualization had value as explanation, was—and is—resisted with great passion, since it is seen as limiting that exercise.

The passionate invective and the continued resistance testify to a very high personal and moral stake in the autonomy principle, observing which takes us to the fourth, most general, and (loosely but meaningfully speaking) "highest" stage in the construal of aesthetic autonomy. In fact it takes us right back to Kant, who justified the aesthetic as a means—indeed, the sole means—through which humans can think about the superhuman. "By an aesthetical idea," he wrote, "I understand that representation of the imagination which occasions much thought, without however any definite thought, i.e., any *concept*, being capable of being adequate to it; it consequently cannot be completely compassed and made intelligible by language."[16] As my friend and colleague Karol Berger interprets this passage, "It is one of the functions of art to embody such ideas, to represent that which cannot be represented, to provide hints of the transcendent realm." As such, the contemplation of art provides the only available access to an intuition of the *noumenon*, the underlying unknowable reality of things, our belief in which gives us "our moral experience of freedom."[17] Our sense of ourselves, not merely as artists but in the most crucial sense as human beings, endowed by our creator with free will—which means not merely the absence of constraint but the freedom to choose to act *autonomously*, voluntarily accountable to our in-dwelling moral *law* (or, as Berger summarizes it, our "power to do our duty even when it conflicts with our desire")[18]—comes to us through the disinterested contemplation of art.

---

15. J. Peter Burkholder, "Rewriting *A History of Western Music*," Keynote Address for Teaching Music History Day, Bowling Green State University, 15 October 2005 (typescript courtesy of the author), 2. In place of "a story whose central character is an abstraction and is constantly changing," Burkholder has, he says, "tried instead to focus on people making choices within a range of options determined by musical and cultural traditions and by innovations in both music and culture" (3).

16. Kant, *Critique of Judgment*, 157.

17. Karol Berger, *Bach's Cycle, Mozart's Arrow: An Essay on the Origins of Musical Modernity* (Berkeley: University of California Press, 2007), 337.

18. Ibid., 336.

I take it that this interpretation of aesthetic autonomy, in conjunction with the peculiarly abstract nature of music, underlies Schopenhauer's famous assertion that music transcends representation, embodying the Will directly (his version of the *noumenon*), and echoes through the whole history of musical aesthetics, right down to my own favorite formulation, by the American composer Roger Sessions (my favorite because it dispenses with transcendental terms while, as I see it, holding on to the essential insight):

> What music conveys to us—and let it be emphasized, this is the *nature of the medium* itself, not the consciously formulated purpose of the composer—is the nature of our existence, as embodied in the movement that constitutes our innermost life: those inner gestures that lie behind not only our emotions, but our every impulse and action, which are in turn set in motion by these, and which in turn determine the ultimate character of life itself.[19]

And it takes us forward to Adorno's contention that the music that best exemplifies aesthetic autonomy is also the music that represents the last, forlorn moral hope of humanity in the face of modernity, a contention that he put into a typically paradoxical nutshell (meanwhile reconciling it with Schopenhauer's romanticism) when he alleged that the more an artwork stands aloof from the social and political world, the more socially and politically implicated (and potent) it is.[20]

These are all beautiful thoughts—and not just beautiful in the aesthetically autonomous sense. At all of its levels of construal, the doctrine or discourse of aesthetic autonomy is an attempt to answer a question—the big cursed question—that none of us can really answer fully, even those of us who have devoted our whole lives to answering it: namely, why it is that people sit still and enraptured in concert halls, intently watching and listening while people on stage zealously hit skins with sticks, blow into brass tubes or cane reeds, and scrape horsehair over sheep gut. Anybody who does this will know what *Zweckmässigkeit ohne Zweck* is all about without elaborate explanations, and the skin-hitters, tube-blowers, and gut-scrapers know best of all. We know that art is valuable for its own sake, worth our time even if it does not give us new or useful knowledge. We know that this value does lie in wholeness and unity—and we know it not in the spirit of academic formalism, but in the spirit of E. T. A. Hoffmann, and even before

---

19. Roger Sessions, *Questions about Music* (New York: W. W. Norton, 1971), 45 (italics original)

20. The nutshell is mine, actually. (Adorno was not one for nutshells.) It paraphrases any number of typically diffuse formulations, like the following: "Windowless—that is to say, without being conscious of society, and in any event without being constantly and necessarily accompanied by this consciousness—the works of art, and notably of music, which is far removed from concepts, represent society. Music, one might think, does this the more deeply the less it blinks in the direction of society" (Theodor W. Adorno, *Introduction to the Sociology of Music*, trans. E. B. Ashton [New York: Seabury Press, 1976), 211.

Hoffmann, in the spirit of Joseph Haydn, whose works became ever more economical with musical material over the course of his career even as they became more tonally complex, and who, according to his biographer Griesinger, complained of another composer's work that he flitted from idea to idea, made nothing of his themes, and so one was left "with nothing in one's heart."[21] There is our baby, splashing happily in the bathwater; the question is, how has Baby been faring since Hoffmann and Haydn first observed him there?

II. KANT IRONICALLY ANTICIPATED

And, by way of parenthesis, just how old is our baby? It is often assumed that all of this Germanic theorizing about art arose at the same time as did the repertoire of highly developed textless instrumental music that provides its best, or acutest, illustration—the music we now call "absolute music" (after Wagner, who actually intended the term not as praise but as derogation).[22] And it is true that as regulative concepts, both aesthetic autonomy and absolute music date from the around the turn of the nineteenth century. But there is earlier music—far earlier music—that fits the description "highly developed textless instrumental music," and considering it for a moment will serve to disengage the theorizing from the repertoire to what I consider a necessary extent: that is, the extent sufficient to demonstrate that aesthetic autonomy is not a property of artworks, even the most abstract or transcendent of artworks, but rather a term that designates a way of apprehending, describing, and valuing artworks.

In a way, what I want to do is to create (and then solve) a problem for the theory of aesthetic autonomy similar to the problem that Lydia Goehr faced (and failed to solve), in her marvelous and influential book *The Imaginary Museum of Musical Works*, when it came to defending her assertion of a related hypothesis, namely "that 1800, or thereabouts, should be the point at which the work-concept became regulative."[23] The work-concept, the idea that music does not exist merely as a prac-

---

21. Georg August Griesinger, *Biographische Notizen über Joseph Haydn* (Leipzig: Breitkopf & Härtel, 1810), 60.

22. Wagner coined the term in 1846 in a "program" for Beethoven's Ninth Symphony, where he wrote of the instrumental recitative in the finale that, "already almost breaking the bounds of absolute music, it stems the tumult of the other instruments with its virile eloquence ... " See Carl Dahlhaus, *The Idea of Absolute Music*, trans. Roger Lustig (Chicago: University of Chicago Press, 1989), 18. The most recent attempts at contextualizing the term and comprehending the range of its applications are Sanna Pederson, "Defining the Term 'Absolute Music' Historically," *Music and Letters* 90 (2009): 240–62; and Mark Evan Bonds, *Absolute Music: The History of an Idea* (New York: Oxford University Press, 2014).

23. Lydia Goehr, *The Imaginary Museum of Musical Works: An Essay in the Philosophy of Music* (Oxford: Clarendon Press, 1992), 115.

tice or activity but also (indeed preeminently) consists of a body of discrete conceptual entities known as works, is closely bound up with the idea of music as a fine art, and with that of the fine arts as aesthetically autonomous. Without such entities or objects, there would be nothing to store in Goehr's titular "imaginary museum."

The main counterexample that Goehr was forced to confront was the treatise *Rudimenta musicae* by Nikolaus Listenius (1533, revised as *Musica* in 1537), a primer that was very popular in the Lutheran singing-schools of the sixteenth century. Over the course of fifty years it appeared in more than forty editions. It is celebrated by music historians because, in addition to the traditional categories of *musica theoretica* and *musica practica*, Listenius posited a third category, *musica poetica*, which he described as follows:

> [*Musica*] *poetica* is that which is not content with either an understanding of the subject [like *musica theoretica*] or with the practice alone, but rather leaves some work [*opus*] behind after the labor, as when music or a musical song is written by someone, whose goal is a complete and accomplished work. For it consists in making or constructing, that is, in such labor that even after itself, when the artificer is dead, leaves behind a perfect and absolute work (*opus perfectum et absolutum*).[24]

Goehr, who is careful to leave the word *opus* in Listenius's definition untranslated so as to reserve the word *work* for her chosen period, ascribes Listenius's formulation to a blind copying of Aristotle's tripartition *episteme/energeia/ergon*, with *opus* standing for *ergon* ("making"), which is a synonym for *poetica*, and dismisses Listenius with a general caution against infinite regress and with many specific quibbles.[25] The dismissal is forced and unconvincing—and also unnecessary. Goehr could have admitted that Listenius had anticipated the notion of a discrete and finished work without harm to her "central claim" that the work-concept became a regulative concept around 1800. A regulative concept is one that controls action because it confers value. Goehr defines the guiding force of regulative concepts as deriving from *phronesis*, or practical wisdom, "rather than dictation by explicit or formalized rules abstracted from practice." One follows it voluntarily for the sake of its perceived advantages.[26] What conferred this sort of value on the work-concept after 1800 was precisely its congruence with the exalted discourse of aesthetic autonomy that was taking shape around the same time. It was the whole ideological cluster that was unique and distinctive, and provided the philosophical underpinning for the past two centuries of musical theory and practice.

---

24. Adapted from Goehr's translation in ibid., 116.
25. Ibid., 116–18.
26. Ibid., 103.

The earliest body of textless instrumental music that seems to have been used (if you will excuse an oxymoron that I intend to redeem) as an object of disinterested contemplation (albeit with no great conferral of value) is a small repertoire of what in the sixteenth century were known in Italy as *canti,* were known in Germany by the humanistic Latin term *carmina* (sing. *carmen*), and have been known since the late nineteenth century in musicologese (a dialect of German) as *Chansonbearbeitungen.* As the last term suggests, they are instrumental arrangements or reworkings of French songs in international circulation. Such pieces, which probably reflect an earlier nonliterate practice comparable to today's jazz improvisations on standard tunes, began to appear in manuscripts during the last third of the fifteenth century. They exist in two-part, three-part, and four-part textures (very occasionally with even more parts), in which at least one part (usually the melody part or *superius* [whence "soprano"], but sometimes the tenor, and very occasionally both) is taken over directly from a preexisting polyphonic art song. The very earliest extant examples are duos in which the superius of a phenomenally popular rondeau called *J'ay pris amours* (I have chosen love: ex. 4.1a) is accompanied by a virtuoso counterpoint. These earliest examples appear in treatises on advanced notation, and they were evidently devised as test pieces.[27]

But from duos that test and display virtuoso reading skills it is but a step to untexted chanson arrangements that test and display virtuoso composing skills. About thirty such pieces survive based on *J'ay pris amours,* mostly anonymous but including works attributed to almost all the leading composers of the day: Josquin des Prez, Jacob Obrecht, Henricus Isaac, Johannes Martini, Antoine Busnoys, Jean Japart, and Johannes Ghiselin, among others. Many of them are spectacular tours de force, like one by Martini that puts two voices in strict and very close imitation against both the superius and the tenor of the original chanson, in effect writing a canon against two concurrent cantus firmi. In another, Isaac replaces the original tenor with a part that is confined to repetitions and transpositions of the five-note *devise* or motif to which the famous title words are sung. Busnoys's setting is based on the original tenor with all the intervals inverted. Japart puts the original melody part in the bass and runs it backwards. Obrecht's setting—in effect four settings laid end to end—is by far the longest *carmen* in existence and must have boggled its listeners' minds. There is even an anonymous arrangement in which the melody part of *J'ay pris amours* is shoehorned into counterpoint with the tenor of Hayne van Ghizeghem's *De tous biens playne* (Full of all good things), another very popular chanson on which dozens of *Bearbeitungen* were composed.

---

27. The whole body of *J'ay pris amours* pieces from which the examples described here are drawn is given, together with a much fuller commentary, in R. Taruskin, *J'ay pris amours,* Renaissance Standards 5 (Miami: Ogni Sorte Editions, 1982).

What motivated all of this beguiling ingenuity? Amusement for the composers? Yes, to be sure, but not only for the composers. There was an audience to sustain it, a public audience that was soon to become, in the classic economic sense, a "market." The existence of that audience is attested by a new kind of musical text-source called a partbook: a volume, or rather a set of volumes, each of which contains a single part—superius, tenor, contratenor, bassus, etc.—from a polyphonic texture. The earliest complete set of partbooks now extant is the so-called *Glogauer Liederbuch*, a set of three books now thought to have been compiled and copied in the late 1470s by Martin Rinkenberg, the abbot of the monastery of Canons Regular in the Silesian town of Żagań (Sagan in German).[28] The partbooks now belong to the old Royal (Jagiellonian) Library in Kraków.

The *Glogauer Liederbuch* is a huge miscellany of Latin-texted, German-texted, and textless compositions, which evolved over the period of its compilation from a predominantly devotional collection into a more secular and recreational one, with which, evidently, the canons and brothers amused themselves in convivial singing and playing.[29] That has been the chief use of partbooks ever since. Nowadays we associate partbooks with chamber music—string quartets and the like—a genre that, while by now thoroughly professionalized, began as a convivial one. The music in the *Glogauer Liederbuch*, especially the textless pieces, can be regarded as being among the earliest extant chamber music.

Significantly, the *Glogauer Liederbuch* contains no fewer than three textless arrangements of *J'ay pris amours*. They are not found elsewhere and are thus probably the work of local composers. They are identified not by the original French title but by a German one, *Gross senen* (Great longing). The first consists of the original superius and tenor plus a new contratenor, placed, very unusually, in the topmost position. The other two are based on the original tenor only, accompanied by two new voices. One of them (ex. 4.1b) places the tenor in the traditional tenor position, in the middle range. The other (ex. 4.1c) replaces the *contratenor bassus* of its companion, below the tenor, with a *contratenor altus* above it. There is even a fourth *Gross senen* setting in the *Glogauer Liederbuch*, based on the superius of the preceding pair of arrangements (ex. 4.1d). It thus contains no original *J'ay pris amours* material at all, but is still demonstrably a part of the famous song's

---

28. See Pawel Gancarczyk, "Abbot Martin Rinkenberg and the origins of the 'Glogauer Liederbuch,'" *Early Music* 37 (2009): 27–36.

29. See Pawel Gancarczyk, "The Former 'Glogauer Liederbuch' and Early Partbooks: On the Origin and Function of a New Type of Musical Codex," *Tijdschrift van de Koninklijke Vereniging voor Nederlandse Muziekgeschiedenis* 64 (2014): 30–46. The earliest, partially surviving partbook sets seem to have been copied for use in processional singing, for which large-format choirbooks, which show all the parts on a single opening, would not have been practical; see Susan Rankin, "Shrewsbury School, Manuscript VI: A Medieval Part Book?," *Proceedings of the Royal Musical Association* 102 (1975–76): 129–44.

EXAMPLE 4.1A. Anonymous rondeau, *J'ay pris amours*, Ms. Nivelle de la Chausée, f. lxxi'–lxxii.

EXAMPLE 4.1B. Anonymous, *Gross senen* (II), Kraków, Biblioteka Jagiellońska, olim Berlin, Öffentliche wissenschaftliche Bibliothek, Mus. ms. 40098 (*Glogauer Liederbuch*), no. 277.

EXAMPLE 4.1C. Anonymous, *Gross senen* (III), *Glogauer Liederbuch*, no. 278.

EXAMPLE 4.1D. Anonymous, *Gross senen* (IV), *Glogauer Liederbuch*, no. 279.

tradition. It is not the musical child of *J'ay pris amours* but its grandchild. The family resemblance can be discerned only by those who are familiar with the middle generation.

Another, equally popular type of textless instrumental piece or *carmen* that was cultivated at the time consisted of little sections extracted from Masses and motets, the high liturgical genres of the day. These extracts are sometimes identified as such, but more often not. It was always a particular type of Mass or motet section that was chosen for this purpose: the so-called *tenor tacet* sections that formed the middles of motets or of the constituent items (Kyrie, Gloria, etc.) that formed the Mass Ordinary. Most fifteenth-century Masses, and many fifteenth-century motets, carried familiar tunes in their tenors, from which they usually took their names. A *Missa L'homme armé* (there were dozens of them) had a tenor based on a famous song associated with the Burgundian Order of the Golden Fleece; a *Missa Alma Redemptoris Mater* had a tenor based on one of the Gregorian chants called antiphons to the Blessed Virgin Mary, sung in convents and monasteries at the conclusion of the liturgical day; a *Missa J'ay pris amours* had a tenor based on the tenor of the famous chanson we have already been considering. The middle sections of constituent units, for contrast, gave the tenor a rest and used a different texture. That texture was the kind called "pervading imitation," in which the various parts (usually three, since the tenor was resting) enter one by one, all singing the same material. It is the texture best known from the fugues of the seventeenth and eighteenth centuries, and the *tenor tacet* sections from fifteenth-century Masses and motets were its hotbed.

Imitation was "purely musical" patterning *par excellence;* it could therefore sustain a "purely musical" listener's interest. So these little Mass sections, too, became popular as abstract chamber music for instruments. One famous example, found in many sources including the *Glogauer Liederbuch,* was a Benedictus by Isaac. It was the middle section of the Sanctus from a Mass by Isaac based on the tenor of a chanson by Antoine Busnoys called *Quant j'ay au cuer* (Since I hold in my heart). Like most Masses based on the tenors of love songs, Isaac's Mass was probably meant for feasts of the Virgin Mary or for "Lady Masses," votive Masses in which Mary was called upon to intercede on behalf of a petitioner. The tenorless Benedictus contains no hint of Busnoys's tenor, however. Its emphasis on pure patterning pleasure, as well as its floridity, entailing a great proliferation of quick notes, often in melodic sequences, made it appear a very paradigm of "instrumental style" in the opinion of modern scholars—until, that is, the Mass from which it was extracted was discovered and notions of "instrumental" vs. "vocal" style had to be radically revised.

The final stage in the evolution of the *carmen* consisted, predictably enough, of specially composed songs-without-words in a style adapted from those of *Chansonbearbeitungen* or *tenor tacet* sections, but without any preexisting material.

Such pieces amounted to the earliest "abstractly" conceived chamber music, intended for an audience of playing and listening connoisseurs. Lorenzo the Magnificent of Florence must have been particularly fond of them, because his court composer, none other than Henricus Isaac, wrote more *carmina* than anyone else, and many of them are preserved in Florentine manuscripts. One especially piquant example of the, so to speak, "independent" instrumental *carmen* is a little three-part piece called *La Alfonsina*, composed by Johannes Ghiselin, a northern French composer who worked in Italy at the court of Ferrara. The title translates as "Alfonso's little piece," after the composer's patron, Alfonso I d'Este, duke of Ferrara, the husband of Lucrezia Borgia. It seems to be a knowing emulation of Isaac's *Benedictus*. Its opening point of imitation is a veritable rewrite of Isaac's, disguised (or rather, displayed) by reversing the order of its constituent phrases.

A similar piece by Josquin des Prez is called *La Bernardina* (Bernardo's little piece), and one of Johannes Martini's most widely disseminated pieces, found in the *Glogauer Liederbuch* among many other sources, was called *La Martinella* (Martini's little piece). Somewhat later, a Swiss-German pupil of Isaac's named Ludwig Sennfl identified a few of his *carmina* by naming their final notes: *Carmen in la* (Song in A), *Carmen in re* (Song in D), and the like, anticipating by centuries the practice of identifying abstract or "functionless" instrumental music by naming its key (Sonata in A major, Symphony in D minor).

All in all, the *carmen* or *Chansonbearbeitung* emerges as a very important genre historically. A few scattered predecessors apart (dating back as far as the thirteenth century), it was the earliest form of composed (rather than improvised) instrumental chamber music, in effect the earliest form of "functionless" (*Zwecklos*) or "autonomous" instrumental music that forms a distinct *corpus* or body of work in the Western literate tradition of music. Of course the word *functionless* should not be misunderstood: obviously, everything that is used has its use. If the Glogauer chanson arrangements were played for recreation and enjoyed, then recreation and enjoyment were their function. If Beethoven string quartets are played at concerts, then providing the content of concert programs is their function. But providing the occasion for active (players') or passive (listeners') enjoyment of sound patterns is a very different, far less utilitarian sort of function than marching or dancing or worship. It emphasizes leisure, contemplation, pleasure in sensuous diversion and abstract design—in a word, it implies "aesthetics," almost three centuries before Baumgarten.

We are contemplating, in short, the earliest manifestation of the condition of "absolute" art or art-for-art's-sake as defined by the German thinkers whose lofty ideas about art are the subject of our seminar, and of this talk. Does that mean that the repertoire of *carmina* or *Chansonbearbeitungen* should be regarded as a counterexample that annuls the special distinction German philosophy has enjoyed in the domain of aesthetics? Not at all—any more than Listenius's reference to *opus perfectum et absolutum* annuls the significance of the musical work-concept as defined by Goehr, which emerged around the same time as the German philosophy. What is relevant and distinctive is not the thing or the concept itself, but the value placed on it, and its status as a regulative ideal. Our modern concept of "absolute music" is not completely or even accurately defined if we do not emphasize the supreme value placed on it as an art-experience, since the nineteenth century, by musicians who have inherited the German Romantic aesthetic. By contrast, the fifteenth-century forerunner genre, compared with the supremely valued genres of its day like the cyclic Mass Ordinary or the motet, or even with a texted courtly song like the original *J'ay pris amours,* was the lowest and lightest of genres, mere fluff. And yet the leisured clerical senior citizens who sat around amusing themselves with the *Glogauer Liederbuch* in the last decades of the fifteenth century could nevertheless be described as the earliest literate "music lovers" in the modern, aesthetic sense.

But now here is the kicker. It was the growth and spread of that kind of "disinterested" music-loving that supported the earliest music business: written music as a commodity possessing monetary exchange value. It is no accident, as Marxists used to say, that the partbook format was very quickly adopted as standard by the earliest music publishers, who sprang up once a method was found for printing polyphonic mensural music from movable type. The very earliest such publication, Ottaviano Petrucci's *Harmonice musices odhecaton* (One hundred polyphonic pieces, 1501), containing mostly textless chanson arrangements including some of those *J'ay pris amours* that we have been considering, along with Isaac's famous *Benedictus,* Ghiselin's *La Alfonsina,* and other pieces that used pervading imitation, retained the traditional choirbook format, with all the parts printed in a single opening (superius and tenor on the left, the two contratenors on the right); and so were its two sequels, *Canti B numero cinquanta* (Songs, vol. II, numbering fifty, 1502), and *Canti C numero cento cinquanta* (Songs, vol. III, numbering one hundred and fifty, 1504), equal in size to the other two collections combined—proof positive that this new genre of instrumental chamber music had a reliable market. The same year as *Canti C,* however, Petrucci shifted over to the more convenient and economical partbook format, not only for subsequent books of chamber music but for sacred vocal music as well—his first partbooks were a set called *Motetti C,* or Motets, Book 3—and his commercial competitors quickly followed suit. Partbooks, many containing *carmina,* became the commercial format *par excellence*. The earliest absolute music was also the first commodified music.

The name Petrucci does not appear in Lydia Goehr's index, but it should have been there, for the production of printed music books, and the new music-economy thus ushered in, was a crucial stage in the conceptualizing of a "piece" or "work" of music as an objectively existing thing—a tangible, concrete entity that can be placed in one's hands in exchange for money; that can be handled and transported; that can be seen as well as heard; that can be, as it were, gazed upon by the ear and eventually stored in an imaginary museum. This "thingifying" or reification of music—leading to its commercialization and the rise of middlemen for its dissemination—was the long-range result of musical literacy, and allowed the literate genres to triumph in the age of printing. The genre that midwifed the debut of the commercial music-thing was the textless instrumental *Chansonbearbeitung*, the earliest genre of "absolute music."

From this point on, music would be defined, at least for the urban and the educated, as something that was *primarily* written: a text. Fluff though it may have been, then, the instrumental *Chansonbearbeitung*—the commercialized, middle-class by-product of the high-purpose, high-class genres of the day, amounting to the bastard offspring of Mass, motet, and chanson—was indirectly of decisive importance to the future of literate music and music-making in the West.

III. KANT IRONICALLY DISTORTED

Let us pause to savor, if not the contradiction, then at least the piquant irony of the situation: the very same body of music that was the first to achieve aesthetic autonomy as it would later be defined and canonized by German philosophers was also the first to achieve commodification and commercial exploitation. Granted, it is only by convention that these aspects should be regarded as contradictory, but it is that convention that brings us together today, the convention whose recent interrogations have produced such anxieties in the theory and practice of art. Most people now concede that the convention had always implied, or rather mandated, a certain amount of false consciousness, not to say hypocrisy.

Here is a striking example of that false consciousness—one that I witnessed at a festival and conference organized around the music of Dmitry Shostakovich in the summer of 2004. The very mention of the name of Shostakovich in a talk about aesthetic autonomy might seem bizarre. As a representative of Soviet music, Shostakovich would seem to inhabit a domain where aesthetic autonomy was at the very least an incongruous and suspect notion, at worst an illicit one. The recent, strident debates over the significance of Shostakovich's legacy, exactly insofar as they were debates over the meaning of his music and its social role, would seem all the more decisively to detach him from all consideration of aesthetic autonomy, which depends on abstraction.

The Shostakovich debate has not been a debate between proponents of autonomy and proponents of functionality, but rather a debate about two social functions: political mouthpiece vs. political resister. Was the composer complicit in his government's attempt to turn the arts, through the doctrine of socialist realism, into a delivery mechanism for political propaganda, or was he a clever and courageous propagandist for a dissident political agenda? It was easy enough to see through the surface debate to an underlying Cold War–stipulated contest between two rival exploitations. Both were violations of the composer's (and by extension, any composer's) integrity and his right to self-determination. Many were moved to declare a plague on both houses and uphold the right of Shostakovich—standing now as representative not of Soviet music but of artists as free individuals—to an impartial hearing that respected his personal as well as aesthetic autonomy and demanded of his music nothing more (or less) than the traditional satisfaction of aesthetic requirements like mastery, economy, and unity, and the concomitant value such music has to an audience of art-loving (or artistry-loving) connoisseurs.

"Listen to Shostakovich as if he were Haydn" became a mantra for this ad hoc formalist faction. People who wanted to do this were often heard citing tin-eared Kant as an ironclad authority, as if Kant's inability to hear in music anything beyond the "play of sensations" imposed an obligation on us all not to overstep that implied limit, or as if Kant had not also written that "Enlightenment" implied the ability "to make use of one's own understanding without the guidance of another" (perhaps the best possible definition, after all, of autonomy);[30] or as if they themselves even listened to Haydn in so drastically limited a fashion. As evidence that they did not I need merely cite their attendance at the Shostakovich conference; but the story I am about to tell is even better evidence.

As proof of the sufficiency of sensation as aesthetic gratification, or of the sufficiency (as he put it) of "the notes" as animators of the high aesthetic satisfaction that others were mistakenly seeking in "ideas," one of the unauthorized Kantians at the Shostakovich conference cited the enormous emotional rush he experienced whenever he heard the moment, near the end of the fugal finale from Schumann's Piano Quintet in E-flat Major, op. 44 (1843), when the main theme of the first movement, as he put it, "unexpectedly returns." It produced as great an emotional yield as any novel, he claimed, but without any hint of "extramusical" content.

Everyone in the room, or at least those who knew the moment and had felt the rush, nodded eagerly in pleasurable agreement with his musical perception, as did I. But Kant would not have nodded; for the way in which the speaker described the cathartic moment in Schumann's quintet undermined his purported philosophical point even as it confirmed his "musicality." He might have described it as the moment when the main theme of the first movement is juxtaposed as a countersubject with the main fugue subject of the finale, and in that case I would have had to allow that he was speaking as a formalist, and was describing a patterned play of sensations. But he used the word *return*; and "return" is not a sensation but a met-

---

30. Immanuel Kant, "An Answer to the Question: What Is Enlightenment?" (*Beantwortung der Frage: Was ist Aufklärung?*, 1784), trans. James Schmidt, in *What Is Enlightenment? Eighteenth-Century Answers and Twentieth-Century Questions*, ed. J. Schmidt (Berkeley: University of California Press, 1996), 58.

aphor: one so apt and powerful, indeed, that it has become a *topos*—and not just one of many such *topoi*, but one of the most emotionally fraught, archetypal *topoi* in all of Western culture. Once we speak of "return," Schumann's quintet is in the tradition of the *Odyssey* and the Prodigal Son and the Apocalypse, along with operas by Monteverdi and Dallapiccola, novels by Thomas Hardy and Joseph Conrad, paintings by Rembrandt and Pinturicchio, ballets by Prokofieff, poems by Yeats, and so on in an endless stream (to allude only to works that actually have the word *return* or one of its synonyms in their titles).

And if it be objected that my unauthorized Kantian was somehow using the word in a nonmetaphorical sense, exempt from all the baggage I've been weighing up, I must counter by pointing out that what prompted his claim was a memory not of sounds alone, but of an emotional rush, and that the sounds he described in making his point were not simply the sounds Schumann notated but the sounds his memory had mediated through topical association.

Must such an association always be present? Is not the effect of "return" so common in classical music, so ubiquitous, as to have long since become an inert convention devoid of any necessary association? Doesn't every piece in "sonata form" have a "recapitulation"? Yes, of course; but why is it called that? And why did it become so conventional as to be virtually mandatory? It will not do merely to say that it creates a satisfying shape. Whence the satisfaction? Significant restatement— that is, restatement after an intervening absence—is so established a part of musically significant form that it would hardly be an exaggeration to say that perception of musical form is tantamount to the perception of recurrences, and that musical analysis is essentially an accounting of recurrences. Calling recurrences recapitulations or returns means that the metaphor is part of the convention, so habitual a part of our musical response that it has become naturalized and transparent.[31]

But what else could have prompted responses such as those that Roger Sessions groped toward naming in the wonderful passage cited above? They were the responses that motivated his life's vocation, and Sessions's attempt to name them, tantalizingly hampered by music's ostensible want of semantics, led him, as it had led Schopenhauer a century before, into granting primacy to musical gestures like "returns," regarding them as the truest of all musical perceptions precisely because they were the least indebted to definite objects. They directly represented the structure of experience—a perception W. H. Auden seconded when he described music as "a virtual image of our experience of living as temporal, with its double

---

31. I hope it is clear that I mean to critique as a pretense, rather than endorse as an ideal, the notion that one can listen to music like Schumann's abstractly, rather than through a field of tropes and topics. Somehow, Edmund Goehring managed to read me as endorsing it, in his very interesting book *Coming to Terms with Our Musical Past: An Essay on Mozart and Modernist Aesthetics* (Rochester, NY: University of Rochester Press, 2018), 140–42.

aspect of recurrence and becoming."[32] These are introspective versions of Schopenhauer's cosmic pronouncement that music in its virtual motions directly embodies the Will—the primal desire, anterior to any object or representation—giving knowledge of a reality that could be inwardly intuited through feeling but outwardly expressed only indirectly, through metaphors.[33]

Wagner, who cast himself consciously (as Sessions and Auden perhaps did tacitly) as a follower of Schopenhauer, would later try to encapsulate the same intuition in his outwardly counterintuitive definition of "music drama" as *deeds of music made visible* (*Ersichtlich gewordene Thaten der Musik*).[34] Reversing the usual perspective, according to which the music is described rather casually as a metaphor for the action, Wagner conceived the action as a defining metaphor for the music. Nietzsche, who understood this first and best, thanked Wagner for putting it so. Without the story to channel and delimit its force, Nietzsche thought, the inchoate power of the music at the end of *Tristan und Isolde* might well have turned lethal.[35]

And to think that all of this was implicit in the observation of my unauthorized Kantian at the Bard festival in 2004, who thought he was merely describing vibrations in the air. "My God!" Charles Ives once exclaimed. "What has sound got to do with music!"[36] Clearly sounds are not dispensable, and not even Ives was seriously implying that they were. But unless the sounds we hear are mediated by a consciousness that is equipped to invest them with meaning, they do not register as music. Such a consciousness not only assigned some of the heard sounds in Schumann's quintet to a category labeled "return" that had been learned from life-experience; it also (to remind you) apprehended the return as "unexpected," signaling yet another way in which the receiver was collaborating with the sender of the meaningful message. Without such collaboration, involving manipulative

---

32. W. H. Auden, "Music in Shakespeare: Its Dramatic Use in His Plays," *Encounter*, December 1957, 31–44, at 33: "When we now speak of music as an art, we mean that the elements of tone and rhythm are used to create a structure of sounds which are to be listened to for their own sake. If it be asked what such music is 'about,' I do not think it too controversial to say that it presents a virtual image of our experience of living as temporal, with its double aspect of recurrence and becoming."

33. Or, in Schopenhauer's actual words: "Music gives the innermost kernel preceding all form, the heart of things" (*The World as Will and Representation*, vol. 1 [1819], trans. E. F. J. Payne [New York: Dover, 1969], 263).

34. "On the Term Music Drama" (1872), in *Richard Wagner's Prose Works*, vol. 5, trans. W. Ashton Ellis (London: Kegan Paul, Trench, Trübner, 1896), 303.

35. "To genuine musicians I direct the question whether they can imagine a human being who would be able to perceive the third act of *Tristan and Isolde*, without any aid of word and image, purely as a tremendous symphonic movement, without expiring in a spasmodic unharnessing of all the wings of the soul?" (Friedrich Nietzsche, *"The Birth of Tragedy" and "The Case of Wagner,"* trans. Walter Kaufmann (New York: Vintage Books, 1967), 127.

36. Charles Ives, *Essays before a Sonata*, in *Three Classics in the Aesthetics of Music* (New York: Dover, 1962), 168.

skills on the part of the sender that come under the heading of rhetoric, and of interpretive skills on the part of the receiver that come under the heading of analysis, there can be no experience deserving of the name aesthetic.

The necessary cooperation of the receiver—that is, the necessity of a cooperating and competent intelligence in the endeavor—seriously compromises, if it does not altogether vitiate, the claim that Schumann's notes were autonomously efficacious. The aesthetic effect was produced through multiple intentions and interventions, and it is only an act of forgetfulness, or an act of will, that allows us to imagine that our response is merely to sound patterns, when they leave us (to quote Haydn, the very man whose "purely musical" appeal was contrasted with the spuriously adulterated sort of listening associated with Shostakovich) with so much in our hearts.

To call false consciousness by such names as forgetfulness or willfulness or fantasy is morally less severe than calling it hypocrisy. Euphemisms may be indulged in a good cause. As long as the fantasy claim of musical understanding unmediated by metaphors or other sorts of "ideas" could help maintain a high standard of art production, and help maintain support for it, and especially as long as it might seem to protect artists—say, Shostakovich—from political threat, hypocrisy could be overlooked. What many of us came to feel, as the twentieth century approached its end, was that the innocuous hypocrisy was no longer innocuous. It had started doing harm. The affectation of disinterestedness and the assertion of autonomy that sustained art in the nineteenth century had metamorphosed counterproductively into a social irrelevance and a social indifference that threatened it in the twentieth.

I see these regrettable metamorphoses with particular clarity, I think, because I came to music historiography from practical activity, having been trained in composition and having spent some years as a professional performer, and also because I have engaged in music criticism as well as "disinterested" scholarship. In the remainder of this talk, therefore, I will try to outline some specific ways in which, as I see it, the doctrine of aesthetic autonomy, so necessary and beneficial to the establishment of the fine art of music in the nineteenth century, has damaged the twentieth-century practice of music in all four of these domains—composition, performance, criticism, and historiography. The domains are by no means as discrete as my discussion will presuppose: once again, this will be a laboratory dissection, not a life drawing. Still, the schematic approach may serve to project the issues in high relief.

IV. HARM TO COMPOSERS

A turning point for composition was indicated as early as 1848, when Franz Brendel, the editor of the *Neue Zeitschrift für Musik,* wrote in an editorial that "one must have scientific and critical insight about the whole undertaking before any kind of musical creation can proceed," and that "criticism and composition go hand in hand, and what we speak of theoretically will at the same time be aspired to by our best composers of the age."[37] It was his definition of musical progress, to be echoed more forcefully in the fourth edition of Brendel's famous history of music, where he declared that "the essence of today's art" can no longer be realized in "the old naturalistic way"—that is, instinctively or intuitively by musicians out to please their patrons or their listeners (for that would taint art with *Zweck*)—but only with "the intervention of theory and criticism," and by "art's presupposing theory and criticism within itself."[38]

The theory in question was an amalgam of Kantian autonomy and Hegelian auto-emancipation, and it led creative artists to find their self-validation not in their contribution to society, but in their contribution to the history of their art. One could even say that artists were viewed—by others, to be sure, but even by themselves—as belonging to two distinct and differently valued groups: those who lived in society, and those who lived in history. We all know which group enjoyed—and still enjoys—the greater prestige. To be pleasing, even on the high terms implied by Haydn's criteria, would henceforth carry a stigma—one that stemmed, it could be argued, from the ancient Aristotelian distinction between activity worthy of a free man and that worthy only of a slave, but additionally mediated by the German idealist philosophy of the nineteenth century, and then by the unique social horrors of the twentieth. From a race to the employment office, the herd of artists now turned toward the patent office, to which they have been racing ever since—or at least (to be hopeful) until very recently.

The implied snobbery of aesthetic autonomy also played a part in establishing the defining modernist dictum that (as I choose to couch it) *the customer is always wrong*. I use the word *modernist* here in the spirit of Leonard B. Meyer, for whom modernism was "late, late Romanticism."[39] There is a direct line connecting E. T. A. Hoffmann's assertion that "Romantic sensibility is rare, and romantic talent even rarer"; his comparison between Haydn, who is "comprehensible to the majority," and the far greater Beethoven, whose "mighty genius intimidates the musical rabble";[40] and Arnold Schoenberg's maxim that "if it is art it is not for everybody;

---

37. "Fragen der Zeit. IV. Der Fortschritt," *Neue Zeitschrift für Musik* 29 (1848): 215. My thanks to Sanna Pederson for bringing this passage to my attention.

38. Franz Brendel, *Geschichte der Musik in Italien, Deutschland und Frankreich von den ersten christlichen Zeiten bis auf die Gegenwart*, quoted in Carl Dahlhaus, *Esthetics of Music*, trans. William Austin (Cambridge: Cambridge University Press, 1982), 63.

39. Leonard B. Meyer, "A Pride of Prejudices; or, Delight in Diversity," *Music Theory Spectrum* 13 (1991): 241.

40. "Beethoven's Instrumental Music," in Charlton (ed.), *E. T. A. Hoffmann's Musical Writings*, p. 98.

if it is for everybody it is not art."⁴¹ On the way from Hoffmann to Schoenberg new aesthetic categories—entertainment and kitsch—had to be put forward to accommodate new castes of *refusés*. So much critical energy now goes into legislating class distinctions, and artists, having (as Brendel foretold) folded the roles of theorist and critic into their own newly self-conscious identities, have internalized the new class consciousness.

But in so doing, have they not—wittingly or unwittingly—allowed a new strain of *Zweck* to contaminate the autonomy of their endeavor? Artists who renounce the public and its blandishments are paid in a new coin, that of prestige. (Nor are they without patronage: from governments or publishers in Europe, from academic institutions or corporate foundations in America.) It is the sort of thing demystifying sociologists of taste like Pierre Bourdieu have investigated empirically (and which moralizing philosophers like Lev Tolstoy knew all about a century before Bourdieu), and it often rests on the assumption of false converses, like "if (as Schoenberg says) art is not for everyone, then what is not for everyone (and ideally, not for anyone) is *ipso facto* art."⁴²

It is for discussing and documenting such aspects of artistic behavior that I have earned the enmity of many composers, most conspicuously those who have with various degrees of acrimony been reviewing *The Oxford History of Western Music*. It is perhaps odd to ask composers to review historical works in academic or quasi-academic journals. To adapt a famous sally by Roman Jakobson, one might as well ask an elephant to review a treatise on zoology. And to continue with zoological analogies, it probably looked to the editors who made the assignments like a potential source of amusement to let the mongoose have a go at the cobra. But I actually think it appropriate and revealing, given the post-Brendelian "theoretical" preoccupations of modernist musicians, to have composers pronounce their anathema on work like mine. Why composers and historians (or at least this historian) should be regarded as natural enemies is indeed an interesting question.

The trouble lay in my explicit rejection of Schopenhauer's dictum about the separateness of the reality of life and strife, "governed by the will," from the spotless, pacific history of the arts. For composers it's been a lovely alibi, starting with Hans Pfitzner himself, who three years after copying it into the score of *Palestrina* came forth with his notorious pamphlet *Die neue Aesthetik der musikalischen Impotenz*, in which he again invoked Schopenhauer's idyllic picture of blameless and bloodless purity, but this time in order to assign blame and call for blood. My

---

41. "New Music, Outmoded Music, Style and Idea" (1946), trans. Dika Newlin, in Arnold Schoenberg, *Style and Idea: Selected Writings*, ed. Leonard Stein (Berkeley: University of California Press, 1984), 124.

42. See especially Pierre Bourdieu, *La distinction: Critique sociale du jugement* (Paris: Éditions de minuit, 1979); translated by Richard Nice as *Distinction: A Social Critique of the Judgment of Taste* (Cambridge, MA: Harvard University Press, 2002).

critics had no such agenda where Jews or cultural Bolsheviks were concerned, perhaps, but they were infuriated all the same by my refusal to grant composers the insulation they demanded from the wider world or to credit the "disinterestedness" of their profession. It wasn't even that I depicted composers as engaged with moral, political, or social issues. Some composers, after all, openly admit to that much. My chief sins were, first, to depict composers in the act of managing their careers, and second, to place emphasis on the impact of fraught political environments such as the Cold War not only on the world of government and diplomacy, but also on the world of art, and in particular on their crucial role in maintaining the doctrine of aesthetic autonomy.

Thus a composer reviewing my five-volume history for *Tempo*—originally the house organ of Boosey & Hawkes, now a new-music newsletter published by Cambridge University Press—contrasts the "genial, colloquial, and avuncular tone" of volumes 1–3, which cover everything up to the nineteenth century, with the "ever harsher, more forceful, and stridently moralistic" tone of the last two volumes, which divide the twentieth century.[43] I don't think my tone changed; nor, I suspect, do most of my readers. What I think changed was my reviewer's sense of the stakes, and the implied challenge to his alibi.

My method throughout the book, not just in the twentieth-century volumes, required the flouting of what I like to call the "poietic fallacy," whereby only the freely acting composer can be viewed as a true historical agent.[44] That is the assumption on which virtually all music history has been written (except by authors easily written off as "vulgar Marxists" or "vulgar sociologists") since Brendel's day, and composers have learned to expect it and regard it as their due. Thus another composer, reviewing the fifth volume for the *Musical Times,* was nonplussed and annoyed to find me discussing Elliott Carter's Third Quartet and *Symphony for Three Orchestras* "tangentially, through a review of their critical reception, and not through any sort of musical analysis."[45] But the beginnings of Carter's preeminence among American composers can be located in a review by William Glock, in the British magazine *Encounter,* of Carter's First Quartet following its European première at a festival of contemporary music in Rome. Both the festival and the magazine were sponsored by the Congress for Cultural Freedom. That Cold War connection is as historically significant as the connection between neoclassicism and the disillusioned aftermath of World War I, to cite another point at which

---

43. Rodney Lister, review of *The Cambridge History of Twentieth-Century Music* and *The Oxford History of Western Music, Tempo,* no. 235 (January 2006): 54.

44. See R. Taruskin, "The Poietic Fallacy," *Musical Times* 145, no. 1886 (Spring 2004): 7–34; reprinted in Taruskin, *The Danger of Music and Other Anti-Utopian Essays* (Berkeley: University of California Press, 2009), 301–29.

45. Christopher Fox, review of *The Oxford History of Western Music,* vol. 5, *Musical Times* 146, no. 1893 (Winter 2005): 106.

composers have seen fit to balk when reviewing my work, and (as we shall see) not only composers.[46]

Cold War contextualization was seen by many reviewers as a mark of retaliation against composers of whom I disapproved or whose success I resented. But at the time of writing I personally regarded György Ligeti, for whom my respect bordered on reverence, and for many of whose works I had (and have) great affection, as the greatest composer alive—which did not protect him in the least from my contextualizing efforts. I considered it just as necessary and appropriate to emphasize the ways in which the Cold War shaped Ligeti's career and reception as it was in the case of Carter, and I do not think that such a view diminishes his achievement (or, for that matter, Carter's) in the least.

Particularly significant as a historical fact is the way Ligeti was promoted as a poster boy after his defection from Hungary following the insurrection of 1956. I mean this quite literally. After he was "acquired" by the publishing house of Schott, the firm commissioned from a technician named Rainer Wehinger what it was pleased to call a "Hörpartitur" or "aural score" of Ligeti's electronic composition *Artikulation*. This score was a paradoxical thing indeed. It was, to begin with, misnamed, since it was not needed for hearing anything. Nor was it needed for performance, because electronic pieces are (to use the art historian's word) autographic, fully realized by the maker, and require no mediation by performers.

The score, in short, was utterly useless—but (to recall Kant) it was not at all *Zwecklos*. Purpose it certainly had. It was visually attractive, formed of fanciful shapes intended both as analogies to the sounds that the music contained and as a sort of homage to the visual world of Joan Miró, the Spanish surrealist artist, whom Ligeti had mentioned as a favorite and, in some sense, as an influence on his work. Having thus been turned into a pretty visual object, *Artikulation* was issued both as a conventional score in black and white and as a vividly colored poster that has no musical application at all but cries out for hanging on a wall (it's on mine!) and serves as an effective advertisement of the publisher's investment in the composer.[47] It both beautifully and very concretely exemplified the hard currency of the economy of prestige.

Schott's promotion of Ligeti was reminiscent of the way in which Stockhausen's famous *Klavierstück XI* was promoted—and commodified—by Universal Edition. *Klavierstück XI* was the early "aleatory" piece in which the pianist is oxymoronically directed to decide spontaneously the order of presentation of nineteen precisely notated fragments, which had to be printed on a single page. Not only did

---

46. See *The Oxford History of Western Music* (New York: Oxford University Press, 2005), 5:280–95. The chapter about which Fox complained actually contains a great deal of analysis of Carter's music (especially of the First Quartet).

47. See the *Oxford History* 5:49–54.

Universal have the music beautifully engraved on an outsized sheet of specially manufactured heavy paper that came rolled in a cylinder; the firm also supplied a custom-designed wooden music stand with clips that could hold the thing open on the piano. It must have been staggeringly expensive to produce, with little chance (at first, anyway) of earning the investment back: the very definition of a loss-leader, a high-prestige item. But it was no selfless or "disinterested" act.

Nor was it a selfless act for the American army of occupation to set up the Darmstadt Ferienkurse für Neue Musik in 1946.[48] What was at first an act of *ex post facto* antifascist propaganda metamorphosed—one could almost say "naturally"—into anticommunist propaganda as postwar shaded into cold war. And it was precisely that advent and that metamorphosis that turned the Darmstadt enterprise by 1949 into a "total-serialist" redoubt. Autonomous art thus answered the *Zhdanovshchina*, the 1948 Soviet clampdown on music that epitomized totalitarian control by enforcing conformity with the canons of socialist realism. But total serialism, within its own—admittedly much smaller—domain, was as much an imposed style as the other; and its domain has been tendentiously magnified in Cold War historiography. It was a perfect example, as if designed by Rousseau himself, of enforced freedom.

The ideal of aesthetic autonomy at its pinnacle of purity, by fostering a now-discredited and hopelessly academicized avant-garde, has contributed heavily to the social and cultural marginalization of music as a serious fine art. A tragicomic example of that marginalization comes by way of the Pulitzer Prize, one of the most prestigious awards an artist or scholar can earn in America. (And it is also a stunning example of the independence of cultural capital from monetary, because the Pulitzer purse is negligible.) The annual prize recipients in fiction, history, biography, and drama, even (sometimes) poetry, are almost always figures of interest to the public at large. Those awards are publicly debated; sides are taken; approval and disapproval are vehemently aired. The prize in music, until very recently, traditionally went to somebody the general music public had never heard of (often enough to somebody *I'd* never heard of), and nobody ever cared who won it, except jealous fellow-professionals.

And then even the professionals began to despise it. When the composer John Adams won it in 2003 for his 9/11 memorial *On the Transmigration of Souls*, he expressed what one critic called "ambivalence bordering on contempt."[49] To another he wrote, as if paraphrasing my own judgment, that "among musicians that I know, the Pulitzer has over the years lost much of the prestige it still carries in other fields like literature and journalism," for "anyone perusing the list of past winners cannot

---

48. See Amy Beal, "Negotiating Cultural Allies: American Music in Darmstadt, 1946–1956," *Journal of the American Musicological Society* 53 (2000): 105–40.

49. Gary Giddins, "The Academy's Pulitzer," *Village Voice*, 29 April 2003, www.villagevoice.com/2003/04/29/the-academys-pulitzer.

help noticing that many if not most of the country's greatest musical minds are conspicuously missing, . . . passed over year after year, often in favor of academy composers who have won a disproportionate number of prizes."⁵⁰ With the award of the prize in 2018 to the rapper Kendrick Lamar, about whom a large public certainly does care, the Pulitzer judges have come around to recognizing the meaninglessness of their habitual public recognition of artists without a public. The decision was widely viewed as an attempt to make amends. Can the prize now ever go again to composers of contemporary "classical" music? Or has their marginalization been effectively pronounced hopeless?⁵¹

If so, the doctrine of aesthetic autonomy has claimed a large class of victims. One of them, Charles Wuorinen (who won the prize in 1970), cried out in pain that awarding it to Kendrick Lamar signaled "the final disappearance of any societal interest in high culture."⁵² His bitterness is understandable, but he has forgotten whose back was turned first. Half a century ago the musical press was full of proudly defiant calls like Milton Babbitt's for "total, resolute, and voluntary withdrawal" into the ivory tower, through which, Babbitt promised, "the composer would do himself and his music an immediate and eventual service."⁵³ The actual consequence of defection and disaffection in the name of aesthetic autonomy has been public indifference and professional demoralization. What the Germans call "serious music" (*ernste Musik*) has simply stopped mattering to the art-consuming public in America, and I am skeptical as to whether the situation is really so different in Europe, where lingering state support has masked the immediate effects of what in America has been a catastrophic fall. As Pieter van der Merwe, a South African music historian, puts it with particularly strong but certainly not mis-

---

50. Quoted in Anne Midgette, "Dissonant Thoughts on the Music Pulitzers," *New York Times*, 9 April 2003, www.nytimes.com/2003/04/09/arts/dissonant-thoughts-on-the-music-pulitzers.html.

51. The 2019 prize, awarded after these thoughts had been set down, was evidently an attempt to find a middle path between the autonomous and the *engagé*. It went to Ellen Reid, an academically trained but academically unaffiliated composer, for a stylistically eclectic opera called p r i s m, which according to the citation "uses sophisticated vocal writing and striking instrumental timbres to confront difficult subject matter: the effects of sexual and emotional abuse" (www.pulitzer.org/winners/ellen-reid). The composer's website identifies her as cofounder of Luna Composition Lab, "a mentorship program for young self-identified female, non-binary, and gender non-conforming composers" (https://ellenreidmusic.com/_update/wp-content/uploads/2019/04/EllenReid_Bio_2019.pdf). It is worth noting that in this work the composer has modified the avant-garde idiom of some of her earlier compositions in a recognizably demotic direction.

52. Quoted in Will Robin, "Embodying High Culture, Crankily," *New York Times*, 27 May 2018, Arts and Leisure, 8.

53. Milton Babbitt, "The Composer as Specialist" (first published under the title "Who Cares If You Listen?" *High Fidelity* 8, no. 2 [February 1958]: 38–40, 126–27), reprinted in Piero Weiss and Richard Taruskin, eds., *Music in the Western World: A History in Documents*, 2nd ed. (Belmont CA: Thomson/Schirmer, 2008), 481–82, at 482.

placed emphasis, "for the general public, 'classical music' belongs mainly to the eighteenth and nineteenth centuries, carries on with rapidly diminishing vigor into the first few decades of the twentieth, and has ceased to exist by 1950."[54]

The public in question is, after all, the one that, all legends and old wives' tales notwithstanding, supported the eighteenth- and nineteenth-century repertoires when they were new, and ensured their survival into the twentieth—a survival vouchsafed by the principle of aesthetic autonomy in its robust early days. From what point of view could the alienation of this public be seen as a normal or healthy development, let alone an "inevitable" one? Only from a point of view comfortably insulated—whether within the walls of an academic music department, or by grace of a philanthropic foundation, or by cooperation with an organization (like—while it lasted—the Union of Soviet Composers) that dependably commissioned work that no one wanted to hear but that served its ideological agenda. All these institutions promised protection from the "tyranny" of demand. The shift that has taken place over the course of the twentieth century from a vital consumer economy to a lifeless, command-driven producer's economy—shockingly reminiscent, for anyone with the wit to observe it, of the Soviet economy in its decrepit final days—is usually blamed, complacently or irately, on the consumers. It is better regarded as an unsought and unwanted by-product of aesthetic autonomy, too long and too literally believed in by the producers.

V. HARM TO PERFORMANCE

Overcommitment to aesthetic autonomy has had a heavy and equally dubious impact on musical performance, promoting (again, to be hopeful, until recently) an ever more exacting division between the creative and re-creative functions, and establishing an authoritarian hierarchy between them that effectively sterilized twentieth-century performance of all literate (or "classical") repertoires, as one may easily verify through recordings.

My own most conspicuous, or notorious, contribution to the historical study and critique of performance practice was the thesis, now generally accepted, that the so-called historical performance movement that originated in the 1920s and reached its peak of influence in the 1980s was in fact an assertion not of historical but of modernist standards.[55] Again there was a certain false consciousness to expose. It was easy to show that both the performances and the stated desiderata of "early music" artists who claimed that their work was "historical" were in fact

---

54. Pieter van der Merwe, *Roots of the Classical: The Popular Origins of Western Music* (Oxford: Oxford University Press, 2004), 466.

55. See R. Taruskin, *Text and Act: Essays on Music and Performance* (New York: Oxford University Press, 1995).

far closer to the norms articulated by such modernist spokesmen as Ezra Pound or Stravinsky than those advanced by any writer on performance who was contemporaneous with the "early music" repertoires that were being revived or modified by the use of period instruments, et cetera. More germane to the movement than the revival of period timbres was the extreme literalism with which the musical texts were interpreted, and it was very easy to show that such literalism was altogether anachronistic to the performance practice of any period earlier than the modernist one. Once that anachronism was widely acknowledged, moreover, performances started loosening up.

Paradoxically enough, however, I contended that this anachronism enhanced, rather than diminished, the claim that historical performers made to "authenticity," since their literalism made them an authentic voice of their own time rather than a spurious voice of the past. This assurance did not console performers who equated authenticity with historical verisimilitude. Nor did it really console me, because twentieth-century literalism produced musical results in earlier repertories that were, I thought, displeasing and harmful to audience appeal. The fact that "historical" performers often expressed hostility to audience appeal was the best evidence I could cite of their modernist affinities, which, like those of composers, originated in a false construal or deterioration of the old ideal of aesthetic autonomy. It was another way in which our baby was being drowned in the bathwater.

In the "Sixth Lesson" of *Poétique musicale,* his Harvard lectures of 1939–40, Stravinsky distinguished categorically between *execution,* which he defined as "the strict putting into effect of an explicit will that contains nothing beyond what it specifically commands," and *interpretation,* in which he saw "the root of all the errors, all the sins, all the misunderstandings that interpose themselves between the musical work and the listener and prevent a faithful transmission of its message."[56] Stravinsky's moralistically charged language was derived directly from the discourse of aesthetic autonomy, because the essential sin of "interpreters" was that of saddling the autonomous artwork with an external *Zweck*—namely, the self-seeking expression or interposition of the performer's ego between the composer and the listener. Compare Stravinsky's praise of Pierre Monteux, the original conductor of *Le sacre du printemps:* "Monteux, almost alone amongst conductors, has never cheapened 'Le Sacre' or looked for his own glory in it."[57] Strangely equivocal words, these, from the man who found his own greatest glory in the piece; but that sort of puritanical praise (which has antecedents as far back as Hoffmann) finds innumerable echoes in twentieth-century music criticism.

---

56. Igor Stravinsky, *Poetics of Music in the Form of Six Lessons,* trans. Arthur Knodel and Ingolf Dahl (bilingual edition) (Cambridge, MA: Harvard University Press, 1970), 163.

57. Igor Stravinsky and Robert Craft, *Expositions and Developments* (1961) (Berkeley: University of California Press, 1981), 144.

How often, for example, do we hear virtuosos decried or derided for distracting audiences from "the music" (or "the music itself")? Since the complaint is commonly found not only in reviews of concerts, but also in reviews of recordings, the offending distractions must be not merely visual (up-thrown limbs, tossing manes, whatever) but aural, too. Yet what can it mean to say that the sounds of the performance distract from the music? Aren't those sounds the music? (We have already heard Charles Ives's answer.) Or consider a quite recent review in which Paul Griffiths, a British critic then working for the *New York Times*, warmly praised the British tenor Ian Bostridge for his "self-elimination" from a performance of Schumann's *Dichterliebe*.[58] I don't know how it sounds to you, but to speakers of American English the phrase "self-elimination" has a foul ring.

To me it had a weirdly incongruous ring as well, since if there is a masterpiece of Western art music that is all about the Self, then surely it is *Dichterliebe*. But whose self? The singer's (as the occasion would suggest)? The poet's (as the title would suggest)? The composer's (as our habitual, casual attribution of the piece to Schumann would suggest)? Apparently none of them, as Griffiths's review seems to suggest, but rather a wholly idealized "self" that is identified with the text of the work rather than with the act of composing or performing it, a notional (or notational) self with which the performer's own personality must not compete and from which the performer's presence must not distract the audience. Only such a view can guarantee the autonomy of *Dichterliebe* from the great clamor of competing *Zwecke* that threaten its status as a timeless work of art rather than an ephemeral entertainment event.

Griffiths's criterion of impersonality in defense of art would seem to derive most immediately from the aesthetic of T. S. Eliot.[59] It represents what would seem the most refined position among critics. More common is a somewhat rougher version of the policing role, according to which the critic must always be on the lookout for divergences between the performance and the score and cry them down in the name of the composer's supremacy—the "explicit will" asserted by Stravinsky. Not surprisingly, the strongest recent exponent of this view in America was Gunther Schuller, a composer, who thundered, in a book on conducting, that "if an interpretation, no matter how compelling, how exciting, no matter how sublime at certain moments, is achieved from outside the score's basic information, to the extent that it ignores this core, it is to that extent invalid."[60]

One has to wonder who benefits from a view of performing that places correctness above excitement, inspiration, or conviction, just as one has to wonder who

---

58. "A Mysterious Presence, and Absence," *New York Times*, 18 March 1998.

59. Cf. "Tradition and the Individual Talent" (1919), in *Selected Prose of T. S. Eliot*, ed. Frank Kermode (New York: Harcourt Brace Jovanovich; Farrar Straus & Giroux, 1975), 36–44.

60. Gunther Schuller, *The Compleat Conductor* (New York: Oxford University Press, 1997), 106.

benefits when musicologists like Neal Zaslaw or Christoph Wolff, or a performer-critic like Charles Rosen—or even a self-described "historical" performer like the pianist Malcolm Bilson, who performs only on eighteenth-century instruments or their replicas—anachronistically decry and impugn the application, in modern performances of Mozart's concertos, of the sort of florid embellishment that Mozart is known to have practiced and to have expected from others. Why impose plainness and uniformity—that is, sameness and monotony—on the work of a composer who, from all indications, thought that variety was the spice of life? Is it not obvious that the doctrine of aesthetic autonomy, in a strong form that Mozart would not have understood, is at work here, and that our poor baby is drowning?[61]

It is not the anachronism as such (it is never that) but rather the hypocrisy, and the boredom thus enforced, that I oppose. And yet, while indignant, I would regard the issues raised thus far as falling safely within the purview of aesthetics. I do not—yet—necessarily see a moral issue. But recall the fourth of the "brouhahas" around which the discussion of censorship in chapter 2 was structured, the one concerning a choral director's decision that without its anti-Semitic verse Antoine Busnoys's setting of the Easter sequence *Victimae paschali laudes* would have been "unperformable," so that "despite misgivings, we are including it,"[62] when in fact there are endless ways, including some that were widely practiced in Busnoys's own day, in which one may alter the words of vocal works in performance. Once again, the doctrine of aesthetic autonomy imposes an anachronistically purist obligation on a modern performer of old music, forcing a choice that performers in earlier days never had to face between aesthetic and ethical values. To give preference to the aesthetic over the ethical amounts in this case to what Karol Berger calls "refined barbarism."[63] It characterizes (and regulates) not only the behavior of performers in our modern musical culture, but also, and especially, the behavior of critics.

VI. HARM TO CRITICS

Berger coined the phrase "refined barbarism" in a discussion of Bach's St. Matthew Passion, defending the relevance of theological issues to an aesthetic evaluation of a work more often treated "merely as an object of aesthetic delectation."[64] The issue arises more dependably in connection with the St. John Passion, the text of which attributes the crime of deicide explicitly to *die Juden* rather than *das Volk*. Again,

---

61. For a detailed discussion of this point, see R. Taruskin, "A Mozart Wholly Ours," in *Text and Act*, 273–91.
62. Alexander Blachly, notes to Dorian Records DOR-90184 (1993), *Antoine Busnoys: "In Hydraulis" and Other Works*.
63. Berger, *Bach's Cycle, Mozart's Arrow*, 111.
64. Ibid.

as in the case just considered, the issue I am about to raise involves anti-Semitism, an issue that arises as an artistic concern most often today in the United States, the country that has the most numerous and most culturally active Jewish minority in today's world—a subpopulation of which I am a member. I ask, though, that you summon up your powers of empathy and try to understand that I am bringing the matter to your attention not as a Jew, but as an American. My experience is that Europeans often find it hard to understand why the matter looms so large in the American artistic consciousness, and often regard the concern as evidence either of American provincialism or of the disproportionate influence of Jews on American cultural life. As an American, of course, I regard this attitude as yet another abuse of the autonomy principle.

Troubled by the readiness of so many of my colleagues among academics and musicians to ignore matters of mere life and death when they come into possible conflict with their aesthetic commitments, I have made a point of raising ethical concerns both in my journalistic activities and in my scholarship, including my most widely read publication, *The Oxford History of Western Music*. These efforts have always been met with strong resistance from all cohorts among my readers, and many of my reviewers. Invincible belief in aesthetic autonomy is by no means confined to the ill-informed or unreflectively hedonistic segment of the music-loving population that consumes music at concerts or in broadcasts. Nor is it a casual assumption.

On the contrary, it is a passionately professed article of misplaced faith for many influential critics—none more passionate than Charles Rosen, who objected vehemently to the discussion of the social issues attendant on modern performances of Bach's Passions that I felt called upon to include in my treatment of those centrally canonical works in the *Oxford History*. Since the issues do not admit, in a pluralistic society, of any definitive settlement, I cast the discussion as a series of rhetorical questions:

> Bach is long dead, but the St. John Passion lives on. Jews not only hear it nowadays, they often participate in performances of it, and are sometimes shocked to learn what it is that they are singing. Are they wrong? Does Bach's music redeem the text? Would it impair Bach's work from the standpoint of its present social use if the text were emended to exclude the blood libel? And if people disagree about the answers to these difficult questions, on what basis can they be adjudicated?
>
> It is no part of the purpose of this book to provide answers to these questions. But it is integral to its purpose to raise them, for they crystallize important historical problems—problems of appropriation, universalization, recontextualization—that have arisen along with the practice of historiography itself, and that historiography not only poses but in large part creates.[65]

---

65. *Oxford History of Western Music* 2:389.

In his review, Rosen replaced all these cursed questions with one I never posed—"Taruskin asks if we have the right to listen to the chorus in Bach's *St. John Passion* where the Jews demand the death of Jesus"—so that he might laugh the whole issue out of court with the remark that "some questions are too foolish to be asked."[66] Complacency on such a scale might seem risible, did it not so chillingly confirm Berger's diagnosis of "refined barbarism." What Berger has diagnosed, and (it turns out) not at all hyperbolically, is a deadly threat that blind fealty to aesthetic autonomy now poses to the art it once sustained.

Not that aesthetic autonomy was ever supposed to cover cases like the Bach Passions, which in their day were works of functional worship music. But as we see from Rosen's example, the concept has undergone a malignant growth and now is—or can be—invoked to defend anything at all. On the face of it, nothing could seem further removed from the concept of aesthetic autonomy than a work like Prokofieff's *Zdravitsa*, his "Toast to Stalin," composed to a servile set of fake folk texts greeting the Soviet dictator on his sixtieth birthday in 1939. And yet when I wrote of my disgust at seeing well-fed, carefree concertgoers cheering this ode to a mass murderer because they liked Prokofieff's pretty tunes, the result was another brouhaha (as per chapter 2) in which I was rebuked by several fellow critics for seeming to advocate the suppression of a composition that possessed "abstract musical worth."[67]

Although the unimportant work that inspired it may seem to render the matter trivial, there is a weighty philosophical issue at stake. If "abstract musical worth" can provide so ready an alibi as this, then the principle of autonomy has undergone a fundamental mutation: it has moved from one to the other of the "Two Concepts of Liberty" famously contrasted by Isaiah Berlin, amplifying on and critiquing an insight of John Stuart Mill, in his Oxford Inaugural Lecture of 1958.[68] From a "positive freedom," the voluntary rational assumption of an indwelling code of ethical behavior as celebrated by Kant, it has become a "negative freedom," merely the absence of external constraint, which if unaccompanied by ethical standards can swiftly degenerate into a state of amoral irresponsibility.

Connoisseurs of liberalism will recall that in this lecture, Berlin ultimately came down in favor of negative freedom, whereas I seem to be comparing it invidiously with its more exigent and obliging positive counterpart. But that is because Berlin was speaking in the context of political philosophy rather than aesthetics. His concern was with law and government. He saw the guarantee of negative free-

---

66. "From the Troubadours to Frank Sinatra," part 2, 45. See chapter 2, note 6, for a more patient reply to Rosen.

67. R. Taruskin, "Stalin Lives on in the Concert Hall—but Why?" *New York Times*, 25 August 1996; John Rockwell's rebuke, from which the quoted phrase is extracted, appeared in the program of the Lincoln Center Festival, which sponsored the performances my article deplored.

68. Reprinted in Isaiah Berlin, *Four Essays on Liberty* (London: Oxford University Press, 1969).

dom, within well-defined limits, as a legitimate and desirable function of government, while positive freedom means nothing—or worse, can mean the very opposite of freedom—if it is not self-imposed. When enforced by political authority rather than freely accepted by the individual, the idea of positive freedom becomes an Orwellian oxymoron. Transferred to the realm of aesthetics, this application of the two-concepts theory means that governments have done enough for the arts when they have renounced censorship. If a government presumes to enforce a code of beneficial artistic behavior, however benevolently, and regardless of whether it is done through a system of rewards or a system of punishments, all it has accomplished is the infringement of negative freedom, not the promotion of positive freedom.

But if all that aesthetic autonomy entails is the negative freedom of artists, all it has accomplished is the turning of art into the last redoubt of social irresponsibility. If in the name of aesthetic autonomy art criticism becomes a sanction for moral blindness, it will provide a poor justification for art in the face of encroaching philistinism. I believe that that is exactly what has happened. The brouhahas described in chapter 2 illustrate this most unhappy consequence and suggest my reasons for becoming, in our current intellectual atmosphere, so scandalously hostile to the idea of aesthetic autonomy in its present-day iteration, debased beyond hope of redemption.

Stravinsky's *Cantata* of 1952 remains paradigmatic. As the first composition in which he used constructive techniques identifiable with Arnold Schoenberg's twelve-tone system, it has been among the most revered of the great composer's late works, and an especially propitious signpost within the historical narrative that aesthetic autonomy has marked out for the historiography of music, according to which, free of all connection with the history of everything else, the history of music is reported as a spontaneous generation, style succeeding style in an inevitable and internally mandated progression toward ever greater abstraction—a development that "Marxists explain as a problem of social pressures when in fact it was an irresistible pull within the art," according to Stravinsky's own nervously emphatic avowal.[69]

No biography of Stravinsky or critical account of his composing career can ever do without a more or less detailed technical description of the *Cantata*'s second *ricercar*, the section in which Stravinsky, in the grip of that irresistible pull, derived the whole musical substance from transpositions, inversions, retrogrades, and retrograde inversions of an eleven-tone row (just one away from a full Schoenbergian complement). The amazing thing is that these technical descriptions—and there have been literally dozens of them—never so much as mention the text to which

---

69. Igor Stravinsky and Robert Craft, *Conversations with Igor Stravinsky* (Garden City, NY: Doubleday, 1959), 126.

the second ricercar is sung, or even mention, as a rule, that it *has* a text. That text, as we already know from chapter 2, was a fifteenth-century carol, "To-morrow Shall Be My Dancing Day," that narrates the life of Christ, including a verse that repeats the ancient guilt libel against the Jews, the very matter of which Bach's Passion settings also treat. It has always struck me as nothing less than extraordinary that this fact should never have been thought relevant to a description or analysis of the *Cantata* in the half-century since its publication, just as it is extraordinary that no one should ever have commented on the fact that Stravinsky selected such a text to set and publish seven years after the Nazi holocaust. This seems a remarkable blindness, to say the least.

But I have exaggerated slightly. There have actually been two published accounts of the *Cantata* since 1952 that have referred to the problem of its text. The first, in 1971, was by a painter and literary anthologist named Jacob Drachler, who in an article in the Jewish-interest magazine *Midstream* told how he had sent the composer a letter of protest and received a very offhand answer from Lillian Libman, Stravinsky's press agent, in which she allowed that it was unfortunate that Mr. Drachler had taken offense but insisted that the matter was irrelevant to the conception of the ricercar as a work of art and had no bearing on Stravinsky's attitudes toward the Jews. (Ms. Libman later incorporated the substance of her letter into a footnote in her memoir of the composer, *And Music at the Close*.)[70] The other account was by me, in a lecture called *Stravinsky and Us*, originally delivered as the first Proms Inaugural Lecture at the London Proms in 1996, and published six years later in *The Cambridge Companion to Stravinsky*.[71]

Need I even tell you that my article as published was vilified for its disrespect to the composer and his achievements? The most disheartening reaction of all was the response of a fellow musicologist, who quoted Ms. Libman's dismissive footnote in rebuttal to my discussion and declared the case closed.[72] I know of no other instance in which a scholar, writing in a refereed scholarly journal, relied on the words of a press agent to settle an aesthetic debate. That is the sort of work that the doctrine of aesthetic autonomy does in today's world of art and scholarship. In this case, moreover, unlike that of the Bach Passions, the issue is joined without anachronism. Stravinsky did indeed count upon, and explicitly seek, the cover of aesthetic autonomy, a concept of which he was one of the chief twentieth-century spokesmen. And so once again a concept that had been formulated in the context

---

70. Jacob Drachler, "The Case of the Stravinsky Cantata," *Midstream*, August/September 1971, 31–40; Lillian Libman, *And Music at the Close: Stravinsky's Last Years* (New York: W. W. Norton, 1972), 304n.

71. R. Taruskin, "Stravinsky and Us," in *The Cambridge Companion to Stravinsky*, ed. Jonathan Cross (Cambridge: Cambridge University Press, 2003), 260–84.

72. Pieter C. van den Toorn, "Will Stravinsky Survive Postmodernism?" *Music Theory Spectrum* 22 (2000): 121.

of instrumental music, which has always been its chief exhibit and highest exemplar, has been stretched to cover cases undreamt of in the original philosophy, which has by that act of transgression been discredited.

The saddest case to which I have been a party was the one that arose in the wake of the terrorist attacks of 11 September 2001, in conjunction with the Boston Symphony Orchestra's cancellation of a scheduled and advertised performance of choruses from *The Death of Klinghoffer*, one of the operas masterminded by the director Peter Sellars, with a libretto by the poet Alice Goodman and music by the composer John Adams. The facts of this case and aspects of its aftermath are discussed in detail elsewhere in this volume.[73] Here I will only add that my defense of the Boston Symphony's exercise of positive freedom was another intervention in what I took to be the classically liberal tradition of Isaiah Berlin and his updating of John Stuart Mill. Those who attempted to stigmatize and silence that time-honored position by equating it with censorship were illustrating the final consequence of allowing aesthetic autonomy to devolve from a positive into a negative freedom.

Like so many preventive measures taken in misguided preemptive defense of art, this one has been woefully counterproductive. The declaration of a *cordon sanitaire*, a sterile quarantine, around artworks in the name of aesthetic autonomy produces an unintended sort of sterilization—the kind of sterilization that renders art uninteresting to intellectually engaged people, reducing it rather to the level of fine consumer goods like expensive food or clothes. It is an abuse comparable to foreclosing responsible academic debate of politically volatile issues in the name of academic freedom, which only protects the irresponsible.

VII. HARM TO HISTORIANS

You see my temperature rising as the discussion homes in on my most vital areas of professional concern. Now for the hottest part, where I see misplaced notions of aesthetic autonomy—misplaced Romanticism—impeding the writing of history. I will focus this phase of the discussion around a pair of books I was recently given for review: *The Cambridge History of Nineteenth-Century Music*, edited by Jim Samson, published in 2001, and *The Cambridge History of Twentieth-Century Music*, edited by Nicholas Cook and Anthony Pople, which appeared in 2004. These volumes were published in Great Britain, but they are collaborative efforts that between them drew upon the expertise of forty-six authors from a wide variety of English- and German-speaking countries. They fairly represent the state of

---

73. In chapters 2, "Did Somebody Say Censorship?"; and 5, "Shall We Change the Subject? A Music Historian Reflects."

the music-historiographical discipline today, and to the extent that they are representative they show our discipline to be in depressing shape.

What continues most accursedly to impede it is Schopenhauer's halcyon vision of intellectual life, still floating ethereally, like a fragrant cloud, above the reality of worldly activities, and his tenacious belief, which becomes more a lie with every passing year, in the guiltless and bloodless history of philosophy, science, and the arts. At the dawn of the third millennium, with the guilty, bloodstained twentieth century at last behind us, it seems incredible that historians could still subscribe to such a view. By now it should be clear to one and all that the Schopenhauerian dogma frustrates—and was in part designed to frustrate—historical inquiry. It was precisely the exclusion of "the reality of worldly activities" from Romantic historiography that led to the rise of those weird notions of spontaneous generation— "inevitable" internally motivated technical progress—that composers so love to embrace and invoke, as we have seen Stravinsky doing (though it has done them few favors in return), and that in conventional music histories still substitute for explanations of style change.

The terms of the autonomist narrative were set for recent music historiography by Carl Dahlhaus, especially in his postulate distinguishing between general history and art history according to the terms of what in chapter 1 I called the Great Either/Or and characterized as a stale binarism left over from the Cold War, in which portraying art history as interactive or responsive to general history, or portraying works of art in relation to the historical conditions in which they were created, was taken as a "Marxist" concession to determinist rather than properly autonomist modes of historical explanation. The paradoxical result of such an exclusion in defense of human freedom was a historiography devoid of human agency. It was as if describing actual persons acting, reacting, and making choices within an actual social environment compromised their autonomy by specifying, and therefore limiting, their field of action. And the only way of not circumscribing their field of action, it then seemed, was not to describe it at all. But now that the Cold War in Europe has joined Bach, Beethoven, and Brahms in history, we should be able to recognize that the essential task of the art historian is not to choose between mutually exclusive alternatives, but to attempt their integration within a narrative that describes the mutually influential and mutually accommodating—in short, the truly dialectical—interaction of powerful agents and the mediating factors that specify their affordances.

The influence of Dahlhaus's insistence on choosing between the *history* of art and the history of *art* continues to hamper contemporary historiography, as the two Cambridge Histories attest, even where the contributors are most obviously struggling to transcend it. An example from each book will suffice to illustrate the encumbrance. Jim Samson, the distinguished editor of the nineteenth-century volume, is also one of its most prolific contributors, with three chapters to his credit, including the keynote chapter at the start. And right from the start he has a problem with mediation, which he displaces from the social sphere and casts instead as an internal dialogue within the mind of the historian through which he hopes to transcend the Dahlhausian Either/Or and give both "aesthetic value" and "social function" their due. "If our principal concern is with musical works" in their full autonomy, he writes,

> we will tend to value their atemporal quality, their presence and greatness (qualities that may be easier to recognize than to demonstrate), their capacity to endure what is often called the "test of time." ... Thus there is a sense in which ... this book present[s] a kind of syllabus of masterworks. This position will be mediated, however, by our knowledge that a powerful ideological element participated in the formation of this syllabus. ... If, on the other hand, our interest lies primarily in musical life, we will focus initially on the role that music plays in people's lives, on the nature and immediacy of its functions rather than on its quality *qua* music. The mediating factor here will be our realization that social responses to art are in considerable measure shaped, and may even be controlled, by the character and quality of the cultural artifacts themselves.[74]

This is what, in America, we call waffling. And as usual, it is agency—human action—that is being waffled. What shapes and controls response to works of art is the discourse about art—something carried on by people, not by "cultural artifacts themselves" acting on their own behalf. The discourse is what accounts for the "ideological element" in canon-formation to which Samson refers. Presence and greatness, the aura of autonomous artworks, are established by discourse, mediated by ... well, *media*, especially those media that educate, socialize, and acculturate us. Presence and greatness, in short, are perceptions, not historical facts; and a historiography that posits their facticity is just Romantic propaganda. But *authority* (that is, what perceived and argued presence and greatness confer), being the product of mediation and acculturation, is one of the most important historical facts a historian can—and must—interpret. By locating mediation within himself, rather than in the wider social world, Samson indulges in a Romantic fantasy that accords composers and works the power to "speak for themselves." By allowing himself to become the medium (in a dual sense), he frustrates the benefit of studying mediation on a par with production and reception.

That must be why, in a chapter entitled "The Great Composer," Samson suddenly puts the brakes on his account of ideology and its propagation of "(constructed) history" and "the weight of the (invented) past" and shifts into fullblown Romantic mode: "Yet this is not the whole story," he warns. "To demonstrate the contingency of the canon is not to devalue it, nor to diminish our wonder at the

---

74. Jim Samson, "The Musical Work and Nineteenth-Century History," in *The Cambridge History of Nineteenth-Century Music*, ed. J. Samson (Cambridge: Cambridge University Press, 2001), 10.

ineffable greatness of a Schubert quintet, a Brahms concerto." There follows a burst of truly astonishing assertions:

> First, that it is only within the traditions of West European art music that a sense of the canonic has been built centrally and formally into an unfolding history of music. And secondly, that the newly privileged status of art within European middle-class culture, however socially and politically contingent, resulted in ideal conditions for a unique flowering of creative genius, promoting those very qualities that refuse to yield to contingent explanation—the atemporal and disinterested, as against the temporal and functional. In the end we cannot quite explain away, though we may seek to explain, the presence and greatness of the Western canon.[75]

These remarks are not only Romantic; they are downright sentimental. Samson cites the influence of George Steiner's *Real Presences* on his thinking, and its insistence "that aesthetic value can only be understood in an essentialist way." But Steiner wrote as a critic and an advocate of his canonical artifacts—an interested party. Historians should resist the kind of paralyzing bad conscience Steiner's protective advocacy seeks to instill, if for no other reason than that historians should be able to see through the pretense that knowledge of contingencies precludes a personal investment in (or, as here, belief in the greatness of) what is accounted for. We may indeed believe, and yet maintain our consciousness that what we believe in is not an observed attribute but a value to which we have been acculturated.

Samson might have gotten over his susceptibility to Steiner had he read the same author's *In Bluebeard's Castle*, which begins with a pretense of contrition at "the failure of the humanities to humanize" the art-loving perpetrators of the Holocaust, only to recover a fanatically hypocritical complacency when Steiner takes his own expressions of remorse as evidence of the supremacy not only of Western culture but of Western morality as well. "What other races have turned in penitence to those whom they once enslaved?" he asks, in a dreadful parody of Samson's paean to the unique flowering of Western genius. "What other civilizations have morally indicted the brilliance of their own past?"[76] Contemplation of the depths of moral obtuseness to which our refined barbarism, the worship of autonomous art, can descend may dissuade us from thinking we need to carry such a thing into our scholarly work. I certainly hope it will.

When we reach the twentieth century, notions of aesthetic autonomy are most insistently raised in defense of Schoenberg and his pupils. And not groundlessly: whatever you may think of them or their activities, the composers of the Second Viennese School were clearly not in it for the money. The matter was made sensa-

---

75. Jim Samson, "The Great Composer," ibid., 266.
76. George Steiner, *In Bluebeard's Castle: Some Notes towards the Redefinition of Culture* (New Haven, CT: Yale University Press, 1971), 65.

tional by their rejection and persecution at the hands of the Nazis, which seemed a veritable enactment of the Schopenhauerian scenario whereby the most authentic art of the time was actively excluded from the bloodstained history that surrounded it. But when the rejection was entered into evidence on behalf of that authenticity, the circularity of the judgment became a problem. And that problem was compounded when a moral equivalency was asserted between, say, Hans Pfitzner's rejection of Schoenberg and his embrace of Hitler. What makes Pfitzner interesting, Paul Griffiths has observed, "is not the music alone, but the interpenetration of music and life, for he had the deficiency of luck, character or judgment to go wholeheartedly for the wrong side, and not just once but twice. He became a vituperative opponent of Schoenberg and Berg. And then he lent his name, his music and his actions to the Nazi cause."[77]

Were these really two sides of the same coin? Evidence that they were not—evidence, indeed, that poses an even graver problem for autnonomist historians—comes from the knowledge that has emerged over the last three or four decades about the political leanings of Anton Webern, the third member of the Viennese trinity. These, it turns out, were not so very different from Pfitzner's. And that may be why historians have tended to react to all attempts to integrate discussion of politics into discussion of this particular brand of twentieth-century music with such horror. Consider this passage from *The Cambridge History of Twentieth-Century Music*. It comes at the end of the chapter, by Hermann Danuser, on neoclassicism. In transcribing it I have italicized the words that, in my view, unfairly prejudge the issue:

> Can the music of Schoenberg, Webern or Stravinsky really be evaluated *only* when these composers' political attitudes are borne in mind? Do not critics in this post-Marxist period who *necessarily* link Webern's later work with his enthusiasm for Hitler short-circuit the methodological problem? Issues of the weight to be attached to contextualization require more serious consideration: it ought not to be given such prominence *on ideological grounds* that a critical evaluation of musical objectives is no longer viable. If historians interpret modernist classicism *too readily* in terms of the propaganda slogans of the day, such as Jean Cocteau's cry for a "rappel à l'ordre," then other, *deeper* artistic impulses will not be recognized. Only those critics who step back from an *all-embracing and deterministic* political interpretation of this phenomenon in cultural history will be able to achieve an evaluation that respects its aesthetic presuppositions.[78]

---

77. Paul Griffiths, "Gifted but Obtuse: Pfitzner's Odd Lot," *New York Times*, 25 July 1997, B16.
78. Hermann Danuser, "Rewriting the Past: Classicisms of the Inter-War Period," in *The Cambridge History of Twentieth-Century Music*, ed. Nicholas Cook and Anthony People (Cambridge: Cambridge University Press, 2004), 282–83.

What provoked this outburst was a piece I published a quarter-century ago in the American journal *Nineteenth-Century Music*.[79] Anyone who wishes can read it and evaluate the accuracy of Danuser's accusation that I hold the political views of composers to be the indispensable and sufficient key to the interpretation of their works, or that I insist on discussing them on ideological rather than methodological grounds. Those who read it may judge whether my political interpretations are all-embracing and deterministic, or whether impulses arising out of "aesthetic presuppositions" are necessarily deeper than ones arising out of the immediate historical environment. As to the somewhat softer charge that I too readily interpret music in light of political slogans, the obvious question is, How readily is too readily? There is nothing in Danuser's chapter to suggest any tolerance at all for such an interpretation. For him, to engage at all in political interpretation is to engage too readily. His phobic reaction testifies, I think, to the way in which assumptions of aesthetic autonomy have led to idealizations unworthy of historians.

But I do welcome the opportunity to explain why I think it desirable to inform my readers about Webern's—and Schoenberg's, and Stravinsky's, and everyone else's—political ideas. Doing so at the very least serves to counter and discredit base insinuations like those of Paul Griffiths, quoted above. The fact that fascism is still conjured up by critics and historians alike to smear artistic "conservatives" like Pfitzner is sufficient reason to call attention to its embrace by more than a few "radicals" like Webern. The standard ploy now with regard to Webern is to relieve him of responsibility for his political sympathies (and relieve the latter, in turn, of significance) by claiming that they were all, yes, "inevitable." As Anne Shreffler has written, "Given his fanatic reverence for authority, his extreme pan-German nationalism, and his conviction that the music of the Second Viennese School was the culmination of the great German musical tradition, it was perhaps predictable that he would share in the delusion of a great German Reich."[80]

Who, may I ask, predicted it? Not the scandalized Hartmann, not the mortified Schoenberg. Before the revelations of Hans and Rosaleen Moldenhauer in 1979 and Louis Krasner in 1987, the assumption among onlookers with respect to Webern had been the exact opposite of what turned out to be the case; and the news was greeted at first with dismay, denial, and denunciation, so terrifyingly did it threaten the props of the idealizing autonomist narrative.[81]

---

79. R. Taruskin, "Back to Whom? Neoclassicism as Ideology," *Nineteenth-Century Music* 16 (1992–93): 286–302; reprinted in Taruskin, *The Danger of Music*, 382–405.

80. Anne C. Shreffler, "Anton Webern," in *Schoenberg, Berg, Webern: A Companion to the Second Viennese School*, ed. Bryan Simms (Westport, CT: Greenwood Press, 1999), 287.

81. See Hans and Rosaleen Moldenhauer, *Anton Webern: A Chronicle of His Life and Works* (New York: Alfred A. Knopf, 1979), chap. 30; Louis Krasner, "Some Memories of Anton Webern, the Berg Concerto, and Vienna in the 1930s" (as told to Don C. Siebert), *Fanfare* 11 (1987): 335–47.

Finally, and most seriously, political considerations, alongside other matters arising in "the reality of worldly activities," help answer the main question that the autonomist narrative cannot answer: namely, why things happened when they did. If the post–World War I mood—the mood that produced both Cocteau's "call to order" and the rise of fascism—is to be discounted in principle as an explanation for musical changes, how can one then explain why, after a century of valuing spontaneity, expressivity, transcendence, and "formlessness" (or content-determined form), musicians should just then have suddenly become so obsessed with pattern and precision (Ezra Pound's words) and so leery of pathos?[82]

VIII. ULTIMATE HARM

Finally, I would like to turn very briefly to the most extreme manifestation of the autonomy principle in twentieth-century music and philosophy, namely T. W. Adorno's assertion of the autonomy principle as resistance. It will not surprise you that I consider this seemingly most redemptive turn to be the ultimate hypocrisy, and the ultimate, lethal pollution of our poor baby's bathwater.

Like the rest of the autonomy paradigm, the idea of freedom as resistance goes back to Kant, who recognized that we cannot control—or effectively alter—the laws of nature, but since we know nature through our powers of cognition (i.e., since nature is to us a concept mediated by the categories of reason), we can at least conceptualize alternatives to nature and avoid the hopelessness of passive resignation. That sentiment of resistance, of dissatisfaction with a status quo to which we have not been reconciled, however ineffectual it may prove to be, is nevertheless our most palpable and precious evidence of our autonomy. That is what Adorno valued most highly in Schoenberg, whose music violated every musical norm that was assumed to represent or embody the "nature" of sound, and thus in its very arbitrariness represented or embodied a subjectivity that had been liberated from dogma—that had "dared to know."

The music of Schoenberg and his Viennese pupils was in this sense the most autonomous and resistant music of its time, and therein lay the reason for Adorno's unquenchable faith in it, despite—nay, precisely because of—the microscopic extent of its presence within modernity's commercialized and commodified cultural scene. However ineffectual its social impact, such music did at least give evidence that better alternatives existed. Hence, too, Adorno's assignment of the highest ethical value to what seems the most insularly professional aspect of a music whose appeal has notoriously been chiefly, if not entirely, to professionals: that is, its technical structure rather than its emotional appeal or its overt or

---

82. For pattern and precision, see Ezra Pound, "Arnold Dolmetsch," in *Literary Essays of Ezra Pound* (New York: New Directions, 1968), 431–36, at 431.

implicit social messages, whatever they might be. Even—or especially—in his analysis of musical consumption, in the opening chapter of his *Introduction to the Sociology of Music,* Adorno privileges the "structural" listener over the "emotional" listener, precisely because the latter is more susceptible to manipulation by the culture industry.[83] The fashioning of a forbiddingly (if not altogether hermetically) complex structure, in this view, becomes an act of political and moral heroism. It is what Adorno explicitly called "autonomous composition."[84]

But are we not dealing again with false converses? Recall the passage in Adorno's little book on Berg in which he describes having to "console" Berg over the fantastic success of *Wozzeck* at its Berlin première. "That a work ... satisfying Berg's own standards could please a first-night audience was incomprehensible to him and struck him as an argument against the opera."[85] In *Introduction to the Sociology of Music,* Adorno still felt the need to rationalize that defiling taint of success, reminding the reader that, however vividly *Wozzeck* conveyed its social message, and however dramatically effective were its scenes of sex and violence, in the end "neither the details nor their structural connection were fully understood," and that residual incomprehensibility was what ultimately redeemed the work.[86] This passage, I think, is the best explanation for the substratum of hidden neoclassical structures in *Wozzeck* that has occasioned so much puzzled commentary. They are often explained as a scaffolding device to help the composer, but it is equally possible that they are there precisely not to be noticed or understood, so that the composer and his friends may retain their sense that they have after all resisted the public and not courted it, and thus maintain, behind a humanistic façade, a self-congratulating sense of superiority.

In the light of this anecdote, let us return briefly to Isaiah Berlin's essay "Two Concepts of Liberty," where he signals an important danger (one previously signaled by many Christian writers). "In seeking a sentiment of autonomy," Berlin warns,

> I may be seeking not ... security from coercion, arbitrary arrest, [or] tyranny.... Equally, I may not be seeking for a rational plan of social life, or the self-perfection of a dispassionate sage. What I may seek to avoid is simply being ignored, or patronized, or despised, or being taken too much for granted—in short, not being treated as an individual, having my uniqueness insufficiently recognized.... This is a hankering after status and recognition.[87]

---

83. Adorno, *Introduction to the Sociology of Music,* 5–10.
84. Theodor W. Adorno, *Mahler: A Musical Physiognomy,* trans. Edmund Jephcott (Chicago: University of Chicago Press, 1991), 19.
85. Theodor W. Adorno, *Alban Berg: Master of the Smallest Link,* trans. Juliane Brand and Christopher Hailey (Cambridge: Cambridge University Press, 1991), 10.
86. Adorno, *Introduction to the Sociology of Music,* 74.
87. Berlin, *Four Essays on Liberty,* 129.

And if it is that, it is merely vainglory. Is the gratuitous complication of musical structure anything other than that? Or Adorno's habit of camouflaging commonplace ideas behind maximally convoluted syntax, or his equally notorious refusal to organize his essays beyond the most primitive parataxis? Discussions of Adorno inevitably devolve into disputes as to what it was that he was really saying. Was that implied alibi possibly among the author's intentions? That is why I refuse to play along. Instead, I will close by adducing two quotes that have an immediate bearing on Adorno's assertion of a redemptive function (to put it as oxymoronically as the case warrants) for aesthetic autonomy.

The first is a favorite episode of Adorno's that I have encountered in three separate places when reading him. I'll quote the version of it that appears in an essay of 1945, "What National Socialism Has Done to the Arts," which was actually written in English, so as to circumvent any ambiguities of translation:

> Humanistic philosophy permeates Beethoven's whole work and determines even the most subtle details of his musicianship. The lack of experience of this humanistic spirit—and here I mean experience in a deeper sense than the listening over the air to some standard performance of a standard work—reflects, viewed in broad social terms, a vacuum ready to absorb the arbitrarily superimposed doctrines of totalitarianism. The German boy of our age who has no longer heard, as his father might have, the *Kreutzer* Sonata played by friends of his parents, and who never listened passionately and surreptitiously when he was supposed to go to bed, does not merely miss a piece of information or something which might be recognized as being educational. The fact that he has never been swept away emotionally by the tragic forces of this music bereaves him somehow of the very life phenomenon of the humane. It is this lack of experience of the imagery of real art, partly substituted and parodied by the readymade stereotypes of the amusement industry, which is at least one of the formative elements of that cynicism that has finally transformed the Germans, Beethoven's own people, into Hitler's own people.[88]

Need I spell out all the points that make this passage so deeply offensive? The ethnocentrism, the class prejudice, the making of himself—for surely this is a nostalgic memoir of little Teddie in his beddie—the measure of all things?[89] Or, above all, the traditional German nationalism—German art being the bearer of the universal "life phenomenon of the humane"—that jars so against the author's fancied opposition to another, less traditional, outcropping of German nationalism? Are we not tired of hearing that only those who respond to Beethoven are fully human?

---

88. Theodor W. Adorno, "What National Socialism Has Done to the Arts," in Adorno, *Essays on Music,* ed. Richard Leppert (Berkeley: University of California Press, 2002), 378.

89. For biographical confirmation, see Stefan Müller-Doohm, *Adorno: A Biography,* trans. Rodney Livingstone (Cambridge: Polity, 2005), 28 (quoting Adorno, *Erziehung zur Mündigkeit: Vorträge und Gespräche mit Hellmut Becker 1959–1969* [Frankfurt am Main: Suhrkamp, 1970]).

Do we still believe that no Nazi could have responded to Beethoven that way? Did Karajan stop being "musical" the day he joined the Nazi party? Did Karl Böhm lose his feeling for Beethoven on the day he accepted the offer of slave labor?

But of course Beethoven was not the culminating avatar of autonomous art for Adorno. That distinction was again reserved for Schoenberg, and for the *neue Musik* that followed in his wake. And so we find Adorno making the same claim, but now for a music even less within the reach of the readers he was addressing (and in some ways, as cognitive psychology has been strongly hinting, beyond the cognitive reach of anyone). In an essay of 1957, "Neue Musik, Interpretation, Publikum," that was reprinted two years later in the collection *Klangfiguren,* Adorno appeals to the German government to sponsor a public radio that "alone can provide a shelter for new music, separate as it is from the market, and can take up its cause, which is that of human beings."[90] At the end of this essay Adorno imagines the radio programming of utopia, disseminating new music in a way that might make it

> possible to overcome the apathy of the listening masses toward new music, and to put a stop to people slipping into the primitive sects formed by those who are no longer satisfied by traditional musical life yet have no grasp of the new. For this, however, it would be necessary to strengthen the autonomy of the radio so as to fend off the organized pressure exerted by the very same popular taste that it must change if it is to fulfill its obligations toward the public. For the public at large is always better, even nowadays, than those few who appeal to popular taste with the intention of thwarting the emergence of music worthy of human beings.[91]

The most dated aspects of this essay, of course, are its self-satisfied paternalism and the quaint, crude dichotomy between a monolithic culture industry and a heroic, equally monolithic avant-garde of resisters. We all know better now—don't we?—than to cast musical life in such radically simplified, dichotomized, black-and-white (which is to say, undialectical) terms. But as long as we still cling to the mythology of aesthetic autonomy, we have not put the revolting snobbery of Adorno's conclusion behind us. To single out as "music worthy of human beings" a music that is inaccessible to all but an infinitesimal, self-congratulating, and possibly mendacious fraction of actual humans seems to me no different from claiming that only the tiny fraction that possess the right bloodlines, or the right class affiliation, or the right racial or religious heritage, are fully human. If this is the use to which the doctrine of aesthetic autonomy is to be put, then the baby has drowned and it might as well be thrown out with the bathwater.

---

90. Theodor W. Adorno, *Sound Figures,* trans. Rodney Livingstone (Stanford, CA: Stanford University Press, 1999), 37.

91. Ibid., 38–39.

For if the grim history of the twentieth century has not discredited the idea of redemptive high culture and undermined the authority of its adherents, then there is no hope at all for art. George Steiner, one such adherent, after a lifetime devoted (in his words) to "the worship—the word is hardly exaggerated—of the classic" and to the propagation of the faith, found himself baffled by the example of the culture-loving Germans of the mid-twentieth century, "who sang Schubert in the evening and tortured in the morning." "I'm going to the end of my life," he confessed unhappily, "haunted more and more by the question 'Why did the humanities not humanize?' I don't have an answer."[92] But that is because the question—being the product of naive idealism and the cult of aesthetic autonomy—was the wrong question. It is all too obvious by now that teaching people that their love of Schubert makes them better people teaches them nothing more than self-regard, and inspires attitudes that are the very opposite of humane. Can't we find better reasons to cherish art?

---

92. Peter Applebome, "A Humanist and Elitist? Perhaps," *New York Times*, 18 April 1998, A15.

5

Shall We Change the Subject?
A Music Historian Reflects

I. GIVING THE PRESENT A PAST

The question I am most frequently asked since the appearance of my six-volume monster, *The Oxford History of Western Music*, is "What will you do *now?*," the emphasis suggesting that there may not be anything left to do, now that I've set down a narrative encompassing the whole thousand-year panoply from Gregorian chant to the chaos of postmodernism, and especially since, as those who had actually read the book knew, I had ventured to predict the end of the tradition of which I had written the history. Every so often, while working on it, I had to admit a superstitious little pang that I was putting myself out of business, though never (the suspicions of some reviewers notwithstanding) the hubristic thought that I might be putting my colleagues out of business, too.

By the time I finished writing I knew better, to my combined relief and horror. The relief was similar to the relief Steve Martin describes in *Born Standing Up*, when he writes of his "short-lived but troublesome worry" that writing comedy might be "a dead end because one day everything would have been done and we writers would just run out of stuff.... I assuaged myself," he goes on, "with my own homegrown homily: Comedy is a distortion of what is happening, and there will always be something happening."[1] That's just as true of historiography, which could be described as a distortion of what has happened. The very attempt at

---

Originally presented at Stanford University, Presidential Lecture, 3 March 2008.
  1. Steve Martin, *Born Standing Up: A Comic's Life* (New York: Charles Scribner's Sons, 2007), 104.

capturing it shows up the extent of the distortion, so nobody knows better than we historians how distorted our tale becomes in the telling.

I set out on my task of narration full of ideas about what was wrong with the scholarly tradition in which I had been trained, and set myself in conscious, fully disclosed opposition to some of its practices, with the result that my work has become controversial within the discipline. But as many of you will have realized by the time I finish this talk, in no other discipline than musicology would work like mine be thought of as radical, or even especially advanced. Why has music history been such a "laggard, insular subject," as Joseph Kerman, a perennial gadfly, complained in print? Kerman attributed the lag to musicology's "traditional paradigm," which he characterized as "Whiggish or Hegelian," and noted that "for many reasons, some of them obvious enough, this paradigm stopped working."[2] My perception is less optimistic. The old paradigm has not stopped working its iniquities; it goes deeper than Whiggishness, even deeper than Hegel's influence; and its consequences have affected not only the historiography of music, but the history and practice of music as well.

After writing the *Oxford History* I was far better aware of its shortcomings than my critics, who mainly complained about missing persons (a complaint that I regard as at once insignificant and telling). I knew better than they how I might have done it differently. That was the horror. What gave me that troubling perspective on my own work was my concurrent activity as a music journalist. A journalist is by definition concerned with the present, not the past, and, in the case of an arts journalist like me, with artifacts of the past only insofar as they exist in, and continue to affect, the present. I found that I was able as a critic to confront head-on issues that I could confront only askance as a historian. It was not a question of academic propriety or scholarly circumspection, because I regarded my journalistic arguments as altogether proper and as fully responsible, in their way, as my academic work. One of my main purposes in writing the *Oxford History* was to expose the historical contingency of our default assumptions, the truths we hold to be self-evident. And yet I found myself unable to shake these limiting assumptions when writing history to the extent I was able to do when writing journalism. It was not that I was helpless. Part of it was calculation, knowing, as Cocteau would say, *jusqu'où on peut aller trop loin*—how far one can go too far and still retain credibility with those whom one would persuade.[3] But when I think back on what I've written, I see how much further I might have gone, and I wish I had.

---

2. Joseph Kerman, "Sound and Vision" (review of *The Rest Is Noise* by Alex Ross), *New Republic*, 30 December 2007, https://newrepublic.com/article/63054/sound-and-vision.

3. Jean Cocteau, *Le coq et l'arlequin* (Paris: Éditions de la Sirène, 1918), 11 (defining "Le tact dans l'audace").

For the stakes are high. The "Western music" in my title, of course, is "Western classical music," or "art music," or—to put it as precisely as I tried to do in formally framing my topic—"music in the European literate tradition." And that music, as everybody knows who thinks or cares about it, is in trouble. It does not matter the way it once did. Some maintain, with varying degrees of equanimity, that the situation is inevitable, given the historical realities, and even in a way appropriate.[4] But I oppose that sort of fatalism. Historical realities are made, not given, and responses to them are chosen, not mandated. And the situation we are in cannot be considered healthy.

Think of it: at your institution, and of course at mine as well, composers are being trained every year to contribute to a tradition for which, as Peter van der Merwe has rightly observed, a "general public" has been lacking for more than half a century.[5] With almost negligible exceptions, although those exceptions are well known, contemporary classical music exists only within the academy. That is not true of any other contemporary fine art—not even of poetry. What troubles me is the thought that music historiography has contributed, and still contributes, to the creation of the historical realities that we now deplore, when it might have ameliorated them. In the time left to me as a historian I mean to try. Think of this talk as a down payment. To put it in a preliminary nutshell: just as Forster said, "Only connect," I say (somewhat aversely paraphrasing Frederic Jameson), "Only historicize."[6] Situating our present moment in history—seeing how we arrived at our present situation, and how we might have avoided it—is the first step toward leaving it behind.

II. THERE CAN BE NO DOUBT

My awareness of the problem—at first a dim and inarticulate awareness—goes back to the very beginning of my professional career. My original academic

---

4. The most conspicuous such voice was that of Charles Rosen, who was given to bland and incurious assertions such as this: "Boulez is more difficult than Rossini. There are historical reasons for this." See "The Irrelevance of Serious Music," in Charles Rosen, *Critical Entertainments: Music Old and New* (Cambridge, MA: Harvard University Press, 2000), 216; the quoted words first appeared in "Who's Afraid of the Avant-Garde?" *New York Review of Books*, 14 May 1998.

5. As already quoted in chapter 4 from his book *Roots of the Classical: The Popular Origins of Western Music* (Oxford: Oxford University Press, 2004), 466: "For the general public, 'classical music' belongs mainly to the eighteenth and nineteenth centuries, carries on with rapidly diminishing vigor into the first few decades of the twentieth, and has ceased to exist by 1950."

6. E. M. Forster, *Howards End*, chap. 22: "Only connect! That was the whole of her sermon. Only connect the prose and the passion, and both will be exalted, and human love will be seen at its height. Live in fragments no longer. Only connect, and the beast and the monk, robbed of the isolation that is life to either, will die"; Frederic Jameson, *The Political Unconscious: Narrative as a Socially Symbolic Act* (Ithaca, NY: Cornell University Press, 1981), 9: "Always historicize! This slogan—the one absolute and we may even say 'transhistorical' imperative of all dialectical thought—will unsurprisingly turn out to be the moral" (opening sentences of the preface).

specialty was Russian music in the nineteenth century. After defending a dissertation on Russian opera in the 1860s, I was assigned my first graduate seminar, at Columbia University in the fall of 1975. It was on Modest Músorgsky (and the first session was devoted to teaching the class how to pronounce his name, since everyone in America says Musórgsky). One reason why Musorgsky was an appropriate subject for a seminar, even for students who did not know any Russian, was that his works gave rise to several standard-issue musicological problems. One of these was the problem of "versions." Because Musorgsky grew up in a country that had no institutions of higher instruction in European classical music, and where musicians, let alone composers, had no social standing as such, Musorgsky took his place in a long line of gentry dilettante composers (the leisure class being the only one that could possibly cultivate a taste for such music or devote working time to its pursuit). He matured slowly as a composer and died young (shortly after his forty-second birthday), so he never gained what most musicians would consider an adequate professional grounding or a reliable composing technique.

As a result, he hardly ever finished any of his large-scale compositions, with the exception of the opera *Borís Godunóv* (and the second session of the seminar was devoted to pronouncing that name, in preference to "Bóris Goodenough"). *Boris Godunov* got finished not once but twice. Even up to the time of my seminar, however, that opera was rarely given in either of Musorgsky's own redactions. Usually it was Rimsky-Korsakov's edition of Musorgsky's second version, made after Musorgsky's death, that was actually performed in the theater—or if not Rimsky-Korsakov's then Shostakovich's, or if not Shostakovich's then Karol Rathaus's, or else one of several others. So comparison of these versions was an inescapable part of studying Musorgsky's legacy, and sure enough, one of the students in the seminar chose to compare the two authorial versions of the opera's second act with the other published redactions of the score.

I still remember the conclusion of the paper he wrote, foreshadowed at the end of the first paragraph: "There can be no doubt that Musorgsky himself was the best editor of his own music." What bothered me, at first vaguely, but stubbornly, was my impression, which grew to utter certainty, that this conclusion was not a conclusion but a premise: that my student could have reached no other conclusion—or at least, that he could have expressed no other opinion as the conclusion to a musicological research paper. It was not that I disputed the point. I thought I agreed with it at the time. I may still do. What bothered me was my consciousness even then that the foregone conclusion was mandated by the discipline, and that the discipline in some sense existed for the purpose of ratifying it.

It was one of a number of standard-issue research problems that gave rise to standard-issue conclusions. Another was the sort of sketch study that found, invariably (and inevitably), that, say, "Beethoven started with this, then he did that, then he did the other thing, and the piece got better and better," until it achieved the perfection we expected of Beethoven—or rather, until it achieved the perfection that Beethoven defined. Like the superiority not only of Musorgsky's conceptions but also of his realizations to those of his later (and better-trained) redactors, the perfection of Beethoven's work was an axiom—a fact assumed, not observed. Observation had to be tailored to the assumption. What we thought of as empirical research really amounted to a vast project of circular judgment and decree.

Again, it was not that I necessarily disagreed with the conclusion. I used to joke with my friends, though, as these ideas crystallized, that I was waiting for the study of versions that would uphold the hack over the genius or the sketch study that would conclude that Beethoven had made a botch of it. Even if one rejected the finding, its advancement would testify to a certain freedom of thought. But to suggest that Rimsky-Korsakov, let alone Rathaus, might have known or done better than Musorgsky, or that a rejected sketch might be preferable to the one that Beethoven ended up choosing, was simply unthinkable within the terms of my discipline. To advance such ideas would discredit the advancer. There was no freedom of thought. And if it seems any different now, it is mostly a matter of lip service. Just last month, Philip Gossett, the dean of Italian opera scholars, published an article on some newly discovered drafts for Verdi's opera *Un ballo in maschera*, in which the final paragraph contained these words: "While I do not believe that every compositional decision made by a composer during the course of his work on an opera is—almost by definition—an improvement, in this case there can be little doubt that [it] was an act of genius."[7] Need I add that virtually every case Prof. Gossett has considered in the course of a long career has turned out to be *such* a case?

How literally musicology bound its votaries to praise famous men one learns from a story that Rose Rosengard Subotnik, a cherished colleague who has preceded me in complaint, tells in the introduction to *Developing Variations,* her first collection of essays.[8] Her first teaching job after earning her doctorate in 1973 was at the University of Chicago, where the senior musicologist was the very eminent Edward Lowinsky, one of the German émigrés who, fleeing Hitler, established the discipline of musicology, very much on the German model, in the United States.[9] Subotnik had written an article, eventually published in 1976, which is now a historic document within our profession, since it was the first essay by an Anglophone music scholar to take seriously the contribution of the Frankfurt School,

---

7. Philip Gossett, "The Skeleton Score of Verdi's *Una Vendetta in Domino*: Two Surviving Fragments," *MLA Notes* 64 (2007–8): 417–34, at 432.

8. Rose Rosengard Subotnik, *Developing Variations: Style and Ideology in Western Music* (Minneapolis: University of Minnesota Press, 1991).

9. For this story, see David Josephson, "The German Musical Exile and the Course of American Musicology," *Current Musicology,* nos. 79 and 80 (2005): 9–53.

and in particular the music criticism of T. W. Adorno, as a part of the reception history of the European musical canon.[10]

She had taken Adorno's critique of Beethoven's *Missa solemnis*—in which the philosopher saw a retreat from the assertive musical rhetoric of Beethoven's middle-period instrumental music, which implied social protest and, well, the audacity of hope, into an "imploring" spiritual solipsism and an implied social impotence—and she extended this critique to the Ninth Symphony as well. She juxtaposed the introduction of words into the symphony's finale in the form of Schiller's rapturous "Ode to Joy" with some less optimistic, less affirmative words of Schiller's—"Wenn die Seele *spricht,* / spricht, ach, *die Seele* nicht mehr" (If the soul speaks aloud, alas, it is no longer the soul that speaks)—and she suggested that "Beethoven not only failed to communicate the content of his last symphony but actually came very near to violating that content in the attempt to communicate it."[11] Having read this essay, Prof. Lowinsky warned his younger colleague that "if [she] did not delete [this] particular reference to Beethoven, [she] would bitterly regret it in the future," so unthinkable was an ascription of any sort of failure to Beethoven. Subotnik interpreted the gesture as less a threat than an expression of genuine concern for her future peace of mind, for, as Lowinsky put it, "a scholar must be able to stand by his or her work throughout an entire career."[12] He could not imagine that upon mature reflection, or after longer experience, she would not come to her senses.

Prof. Lowinsky was right to be concerned about Rose Subotnik's future. As adumbrated in the introduction to this book, she was denied tenure at Chicago effectively because, as another colleague told her, she "approached the study of music with a philosophical orientation and was therefore bound to falsify music and music history."[13] What Subotnik in 1980 called the "patent naiveté" of that view will be obvious today, I trust, to one and all, and that in itself is testimony to an improvement in the American scholarly weather, even in musicology, over the last two or three decades. But the evolution has not gone all that far. We all may be inclined now to regard our positions as philosophically oriented, even ideologically oriented. We may even accept our philosophical orientations as historical, hence as contingent and therefore provisional. Yet as someone

---

10. Rose Rosengard Subotnik, "Adorno's Diagnosis of Beethoven's Late Style: Early Symptom of a Fatal Condition," *Journal of the American Musicological Society* 29 (1976): 242–75; reprinted in Subotnik, *Developing Variations*, 15–41.

11. Subotnik, *Developing Variations*, 34.

12. Ibid., xv.

13. Rose Rosengard Subotnik, "The Role of Ideology in the Study of Western Music," *Journal of Musicology* 2 (1983): 1. This article was based on a talk presented to the Society for Ethnomusicology at its annual meeting in November 1980.

once observed, accurate description is fine but what we need is change. (Yes, Marx.)[14]

Knowing that our consciousness is historical and philosophically, even politically, oriented is no insurance against error. Adorno may have been taken well on board by now (even Subotnik's former critics now read him and teach him), but he has joined Beethoven as another worshipped personality, another infallible authority. He has been accepted uncritically, at the price of almost total distortion, as is apparent from the fact that the first uncritical appropriators were scholars of popular music, a field that Adorno only deprecated. Undaunted, popular music scholars have co-opted him to the project of idealization, and we may now read Adornian studies of Madonna or Beyoncé that describe them the way Adorno described Schoenberg, or as my old pupil described Musorgsky.[15] The construction and preservation of an authentic and resilient subjectivity is now the reigning cliché of popular music studies, a stance even more utopian, and even more oblivious of historical realities, than studies of Beethoven or Musorgsky ever were. Today, no less than in the bad old 1970s, musicology and music historiography, whatever their ostensible subject matter, are still all about defending autonomous art—and autonomous artists—against social mediation, and justifying their ways to man.

III. PROHIBITING MY PREFERENCES

Let me return to Musorgsky now and offer as a parable an account of the social mediation of *Boris Godunov* that relates it from a different perspective to the question of artistic quality—a perspective that does pay attention, I think, to social, cultural, political, and economic realities alongside aesthetic desiderata. The most moving version of the opera I know—hence, according to at least one defensible (or, at least, one frequently defended) aesthetic criterion, the best version of the opera—is the version that I first came to know, long before I had embarked on close study of Musorgsky or of his works, as a movie. It was produced in Moscow in 1954, and its soundtrack was based on a recording made by artists from the Bolshoy Theater. The version of the score that it preserved and cinematographically "opened up," therefore, was the one performed at the Bolshoy as the official

---

14. Karl Marx, *Theses on Feuerbach* (1845), no. XI: "The philosophers have only *interpreted* the world, in various ways; the point is to *change* it" (Die Philosophen haben die Welt nur verschieden *interpretiert*; es kommt aber darauf an, sie zu *verändern*).

15. The best known is Susan McClary, "Living to Tell: Madonna's Resurrection of the Fleshly," *Genders*, no. 7 (Spring 1990); reprinted in McClary, *Feminine Endings: Music, Gender, and Sexuality* (Minneapolis: University of Minnesota Press, 1991), 148–68.

Soviet canonical version since 1939, when it was first staged in honor of the composer's birth centennial. It was very much a Soviet, even a Stalinist, product.[16]

This version was basically the standard Rimsky-Korsakov redaction of Musorgsky's second version, with the scoring thoroughly redone and with the many changes in harmonization (and, occasionally, the vocal tessitura) for the sake of conventional effectiveness, which had given rise to so many derisive attacks from purists and modernists beginning in 1908, when it was first shown abroad by Sergei Diaghilev. The one unconventional aspect of the Bolshoy production was the inclusion, from the first authorial version, of the then little-known scene that takes place on Red Square, before the multicolored chapel of the Blessed Vasiliy (known popularly in the West as St. Basil's Cathedral), in which the Holy Fool or *yurodivïy* directly confronts the title character with his crime. This scene, originally the opera's penultimate one (followed only by the death of Boris), was drawn, like the rest of the first version, directly from the opera's source-text, a play by Pushkin. When he revised the opera, Musorgsky replaced this scene with a new one that was to follow the death of Boris and provide the new version with its finale. This is the so-called Kromy Forest Scene, which has no counterpart in Pushkin's play.

The two scenes are mutually exclusive. They portray the crowd in contradictory ways, following differing historiographical traditions. Pushkin, hence Musorgsky's first version, followed the tradition of Ivan Karamzin, the Romanov dynasty's handpicked Official Historiographer, which portrayed the crowd as submissive and suppliant to the Tsar. The replacement scene, following a more recent—in fact then-contemporary—interpretation of the events of the so-called Time of Troubles by the populist historiographer Nikolai Kostomarov, portrayed the crowd as openly rebellious and seditious, and enthusiastic in its support of the False Dmitri, Boris's rival and nemesis. Not only that, but Musorgsky had made conflation impossible by transferring a big chunk of music, encompassing the Holy Fool's song and the episode in which a gang of boys steal his kopeck, from the one scene to the other.

But that manifest impossibility did not deter the Bolshoy Theater from commissioning a Rimsky-style reorchestration of the St. Basil's scene from the veteran composer Mikhaíl Ippolitov-Ivanov and incorporating both scenes, redundancy and contradiction be damned, into the new production, using them to flank the scene of Boris's death. One cannot make a coherent logical case for such a conflation, and there is good reason to think it was motivated in the first place by a Stalinist view of the opera's potential as a commentary on the illegitimacy of Tsarist

---

16. Dir. Vera Stroyeva. For a more detailed consideration of this version and the attendant historiographical issues, see R. Taruskin, "Crowd, Mob, and Nation in Boris Godunov: What Did Musorgsky Think, and Does It Matter?" *Journal of Musicology* 28 (2011): 143–165; reprinted in Taruskin, *Russian Music at Home and Abroad* (Oakland: University of California Press, 2016), 58–77.

rule, hence as a justification for the Russian Revolution, each scene contributing its mite to that propagandistic task. And yet both scenes are searingly effective musical and dramatic achievements. Both bring tears to the eyes of the audience, and the reprise of the Holy Fool's lament (which is not a reprise unless the two scenes are both included) is perhaps the opera's crowning stroke of musical and dramatic genius. No wonder the version of the opera concocted in Moscow possibly for political purposes became canonical in the Soviet Union, and is still often performed in post-Soviet Russia and abroad. Although unforeseen and seemingly disallowed by the author (even though it uses only material he composed), it is, I believe, a greater work than either of the two authorial versions.

It took me a long time to find the courage to say this. In fact, I once wrote a long article on the versions of *Boris Godunov* that ended with an explicit repudiation of conflation on grounds of dramaturgical and historiographical consistency and musical integrity.[17] Even when I wrote this I knew perfectly well that when it came to satisfying my own pleasure in the opera, the version I was disallowing was the one I preferred. And I also knew that the reason why I preferred it was not, as I at one time tried to convince myself that it was, because the role of the Holy Fool was so wonderfully performed in the movie by the great tenor Ivan Kozlovsky. I had seen the same version performed live at the Bolshoy during my year as an exchange student in Moscow in 1971–72. Indeed, I saw it that year as often as possible, so moving did I find it, despite the fact that the performances, by artists vastly inferior to the ones whose voices were preserved twenty years earlier in the film, were mostly pretty bad.

One of the things that most thrilled me, as an American abroad, was leaving the theater and taking a ten-minute stroll to the very place where the action of the scene at St. Basil's occurred. But that was not my reason for wanting the scene included despite its dramaturgical and musical inadmissibility. I already knew the scene and loved it before going to Russia to study it. The reason for my wanting it included was simply my goosebumps and tears. Why do goosebumps and tears fall so far outside the purview of professional musicology that when acting in the capacity of a professional musicologist I felt I had to ignore and even disavow them—or worse, disavowed them without even posing to myself the question I am now posing to you? And why might I myself still be inclined to offer Lowinskian warnings against self-marginalization to a younger colleague who posed them publicly before reaching the safe haven of tenure?

The reason, as I diagnose it now, is that the discipline of musicology is still in thrall to an unhistoricized historical legacy: a legacy of German romanticism that

---

17. R. Taruskin, "Musorgsky vs. Musorgsky: The Versions of *Boris Godunov*," *Nineteenth-Century Music* 8 (1984–85): 91–118, 245–72; reprinted in Taruskin, *Musorgsky: Eight Essays and an Epilogue* (Princeton, NJ: Princeton University Press, 1993), 201–99.

travels incognito as general aesthetic principles. If, as I believe, the resilience of this ancient heritage within musicology is greater than in other humanistic disciplines, it may be as a result of musicology's relative youth and its specific history in the Anglophone world as I have already described it when speaking of Lowinsky. In the United States, as well as Great Britain and its other former colonies, musicology has been basically a German import dating from the forced emigration of the cream of German musicology, which took place beginning in the run-up to World War II, and has been an established and productive discipline here only since that war. (The first American PhD in musicology was awarded as recently as 1945, at Columbia University. The recipient was Dika Newlin, for a dissertation, later published as a book, called *Bruckner, Mahler, Schoenberg*.[18] Her dissertation sponsor was Paul Henry Lang, a somewhat exceptional member of the founding generation in that he was Hungarian, non-Jewish, and an immigrant somewhat in advance of the tide, but intellectually he was altogether typical of the cohort. I was one of his last students, so I speak from first-hand observation.)

The authority within the Anglophone sphere of German musicology in the romantic tradition has been questioned from time to time, but it continues relatively unabated.[19] Persistent questioners have been marginalized within the discipline. Those who, like me, prudently waited until their professional status was safe before opening fire have attracted ferocious counterfire. Since the growth period of American musicology coincided with the Cold War, the German romantic heritage was rather improbably attached to a long-standing American pragmatism and became a truly impregnable position. The writings of the German musicologist Carl Dahlhaus were willy-nilly assimilated to it and became fetishes, sacred texts, as did Adorno's. One need only take a peek at the indexes in two recent authoritative compendia, *The Cambridge History of Nineteenth-Century Music*, published in 2001, and *The Cambridge History of Twentieth-Century Music*, published in 2004 (both of them the collaborative work of British and American scholars under British editors, albeit with a few continental contributions),[20] to

---

18. Morningside Heights, New York: King's Crown Press, 1947; revised ed., New York: W. W. Norton, 1952, rpt. 1978.

19. For an early, dramatic, but ultimately ineffectual flare-up, see Joseph Kerman, "A Profile for American Musicology," *Journal of the American Musicological Society* 18 (1965): 61–69 (reprinted in Kerman, *Write All These Down* [Berkeley: University of California Press, 1994], 3–11); Edward E. Lowinsky, "The Character and Purpose of American Musicology: A Reply to Joseph Kerman," *JAMS* 18 (1965): 222–34 (reprinted in Lowinsky, *Music in the Culture of the Renaissance and Other Essays* [Chicago: University of Chicago Press, 1989], 2:958–64); and Kerman, "Rebuttal to 'Reply' by Lowinsky," *JAMS* 18 (1965): 426–27.

20. *The Cambridge History of Nineteenth-Century Music*, ed. Jim Samson (Cambridge: Cambridge University Press, 2001); *The Cambridge History of Twentieth-Century Music*, ed. Nicholas Cook and Anthony Pople (Cambridge: Cambridge University Press, 2004). For a comprehensive review of both, see R. Taruskin, "Speed Bumps," *Nineteenth-Century Music* 29 (2005–6): 185–207.

confirm the extreme dependency of English-speaking musicology on these two preceptors (despite Adorno's many warnings against such a reception of his own writings)—but that is because both Germans have been read selectively, in support of what I have taken to calling the poietic fallacy.[21]

IV. TRIPARTITION

The term *poietic*, derived from the Greek *poiein* ("to make"), is borrowed from the so-called semiotic tripartition devised by the Swiss linguist Jean Molino and popularized within musicology by his pupil Jean-Jacques Nattiez.[22] According to this model, musical utterances have makers and receivers. Information and observations related to the making constitute poietic data. Information and observations related to the receiving are called *esthesic* data, from the Greek *aisthesis* ("perception"). The reason for the fancy terminology is merely to avoid confusion with the more ordinary but obviously related terms *poetic* and *aesthetic*. Molino called what lies between the poietic and esthesic poles, namely "the work itself," the *niveau neutre*, the "neutral level." It is clearly chimerical, since any act of describing it, or even observing it, must be within the realm of the esthesic. Even an act that describes or observes the poietic function is willy-nilly an esthesic act. To recognize that much is to render the whole tripartition chimerical, and it seems by now to have been discarded everywhere but French Canada. There is one aspect of Nattiez's adaptation, however, that was not chimerical, and that was his assignment of roles within musicology. The poietic is the perspective, in Nattiez's description, of historical musicology (the region I inhabit); the neutral level is what musical theorists and analysts think they are studying; and the esthesic is the province of criticism, or "critical musicology." Nattiez's account, therefore, is a realistic account of the chimeras of contemporary musical scholarship. As practice they are all inadequate and incoherent, but Nattiez observed them accurately.

The poietic fallacy, then, is the limitation of the purview of traditional music historiography to the history of composition. Only the maker's input is studied by historical musicologists; only composers are regarded as authentic historical agents. Newlin's *Bruckner, Mahler, Schoenberg* already set the tone, because its objective was the establishment of a creative or poietic dynasty, viewed and defended from an entirely internalist perspective. The overwhelming majority of

---

21. See R. Taruskin, "The Poietic Fallacy," *Musical Times* 145, no. 1886 (Spring 2004): 7–34; reprinted in R. Taruskin, *The Danger of Music and Other Anti-Utopian Essays* (Berkeley: University of California Press, 2008), 301–29.

22. See Jean Molino, "Fait musical et sémiologie de la musique," *Musique en jeu* 17 (1975): 37–62; translated by J. A. Underwood as "Musical Fact and the Semiology of Music," *Music Analysis* 9 (1990): 133–156; and Jean-Jacques Nattiez, *Music and Discourse: Toward a Semiology of Music*, trans. Carolyn Abbate (Princeton, NJ: Princeton University Press, 1990).

music-historical writings have had a similar mission, including the studies of versions and sketches at which I have been grousing. And that mission has even invaded criticism, which was supposed to be the bastion of the esthesic.

A representative example of poietic aggrandizement cropped up on the very morning I first drafted this paragraph, 2 February 2008. Writing in the London newspaper the *Independent,* where he was a regular editorial page columnist, Dominic Lawson, the son of Britain's premier global-warming scoffer, scoffed at impending commemorations of Herbert von Karajan's birth centenary this year by observing that "the cult of the conductor is often tiresome and meretricious; it is the composers themselves whom we should always celebrate."[23] Always and only celebrate, I would add. A few days later, on 6 February, Bernard Holland of the *New York Times* published a scathing if predictable column called "When Histrionics Undermine the Music and the Pianist," in which he chided performers—like Lang Lang, whose picture graced the piece—who by their body language call attention to themselves rather than to "the music" when performing.[24] (He was roundly answered in the letters column on 8 February by Tim Chadwick, an actor from Santa Monica, who wrote in to say that "if Mr. Holland wishes to attract more young people to classical music, I suggest he lighten up. Telling them that they must sit still and be good little musicians is not going to get their attention." Amen to that.)[25] The limitation that Jean-Jacques Nattiez has diagnosed in music history now applies to pretentious music criticism as well. But to account for it we have to leave semiotics and return to German romantic philosophy and its postulate of aesthetic autonomy.

Although it had predecessors, Immanuel Kant's *Critique of Judgment,* which appeared in 1790, looms in retrospect as the foundation of this tradition and its new criterion of value, epitomized in the slogan *Zweckmässigkeit ohne Zweck,* "purposiveness without purpose," plucked from his famous characterization of the object made by artists.[26] Artists, who produced objects for pure contemplation, were now defined

---

23. Dominic Lawson, "The Lesson of Karajan: There Is No Connection between Great Art and Good Character," available online at www.scribd.com/document/56098834/The-Lesson-of-K-There-is-No-Connection-Between-Great-Art-and-Good-Character.

24. www.nytimes.com/2008/02/06/arts/music/06look.html.

25. "Letters: Oh, Let Those Musicians Groove to the Beat!" www.nytimes.com/2008/02/08/opinion/lweb08pianist.html.

26. Immanuel Kant, *Kritik der Urteilskraft,* chap. 15: "Die objektive Zweckmäßigkeit kann nur vermittelst der Beziehung des Mannigfaltigen auf einen bestimmten Zweck, also nur durch einen Begriff erkannt werden. Hieraus allein schon erhellet: daß das Schöne, dessen Beurteilung eine bloß formale Zweckmäßigkeit, d. i. eine Zweckmäßigkeit ohne Zweck, zum Grunde hat, von der Vorstellung des Guten ganz unabhängig sei, weil das letztere eine objektive Zweckmäßigkeit, d. i. die Beziehung des Gegenstandes auf einen bestimmten Zweck, voraussetzt" (Objective purposefulness can be recognized only by means of an intuitive [i.e. manifold] relation to a definite purpose, that is, only through a concept. From this alone it is evident that the beautiful, whose judgment has a purely formal [as opposed to objective] purposefulness, that is, a purposefulness without purpose, is completely independent of

in contradistinction to craftsmen, who produced objects for use. Purposeless but purposive art could serve as the symbolic embodiment of human freedom and the vehicle of transcendent metaphysical experience. My language is of course ironic, since verbs like *serve* and nouns like *vehicle* imply purpose after all; and that is the kernel of my critique. But let me finish with description before elaborating the critique.

Kant himself had little appreciation for music as a fine art, and probably never thought of music (a mere "play of sensations") as exemplary of his aesthetics. Nevertheless, Kant's aesthetics eventually provided the means by which music could be elevated to the status of philosophical model for all the other arts—the art, to recall Walter Pater's famous remark, to whose condition all the other arts aspire.[27] The very absence of propositional content freed music from intrusion, limitation, and possible constraint. It could not be "made tongue-tied by authority" because (according to the theory) it had no tongue.[28] Thus was a concept of aesthetic autonomy, when expanded to encompass all of the arts, dialectically tied to politics. Artists, responsible to themselves alone, provide a model of human self-realization. All social demands on the artist—whether made by state, by church, or by paying public—and all social or commercial mediation were to be regarded as inimical to the authenticity of the creative product.

It goes without saying, but I'd better say it anyway, that this is the most asocial definition of artistic value ever promulgated. And the activity of art historians, and especially music historians as their practices have evolved, has been designed to protect and defend its asociality. In the twentieth century, such a theory of art could be seen as a bulwark against totalitarianism, which only intensified the pressure on musicology to adhere to the poietic fallacy. Adorno held up the German romantic aesthetic as a counterforce, as well, to the instrumentalizing and rationalizing tendencies of "administered" capitalist society, which turns human subjects into objects of economic exploitation. Since Adorno, alone among twentieth-century philosophers and sociologists, was trained in musical composition, he unsurprisingly held up classical music in its least "compromised" form (epitomized in the resolutely esoteric and unsellable work of Arnold Schoenberg) as the chief example of "truth-bearing" art, as opposed to the dehumanizing popular music churned out by the culture industry for mass dissemination.[29] That explains, per-

---

the idea of the good, because the latter is an objective purposefulness, that is manifested in the relation of the object to a definite purpose).

27. Walter Pater, *The Renaissance: Studies in Art and Poetry*, 3rd ed. (London: Macmillan, 1888), 140: "*All art constantly aspires towards the condition of music*" (italics original).

28. The phrase in quotes ("[art] made tongue-tied by authority") is among the litany of ills in Shakespeare's Sonnet LXVI ("Tired with all these, for restful death I cry").

29. For its most concentrated expression, see Adorno, *Philosophie der neuen Musik* (Tübingen: J. C. B. Mohr [Paul Siebeck], 1949; translated by Robert Hullot-Kentor as *Philosophy of New Music* (Minneapolis: University of Minnesota Press, 2006).

haps, why Adorno's writings have been so fetishized by music historians—and also why his appropriation against the grain by popular music scholars, eager to prove that the music they promote is also valuable (which, necessarily, means also autonomous), has been at once so unsurprising and so absurd.[30]

Of course Hegel, too, has played a part, to recall Joseph Kerman's diagnosis. The neo-Hegelian strain was first self-consciously advanced by Franz Brendel, whose *History of Music in Italy, Germany, and France from the Earliest Christian Times up to the Present*, first published in 1852, remained the most widely read general history of music until the first decades of the twentieth century. The book was an application to music of Hegel's ruling dictum that "the History of the world is none other than the progress of the consciousness of Freedom,"[31] and must therefore take the form of an ineluctable sequence of emancipations, with the great composers from Palestrina to Liszt and Wagner cast in the role of progressive liberators. This is the source of the stubborn "Whiggishness" that Kerman cites as the reason for musicology's laggard state. But as long as this political model found support in the wider world, its status as musicological orthodoxy was virtually unquestionable. The good political vibes were irresistible.

V. TRANSGRESSION

And yet outweighing even Hegel and his good vibrations was another strand, a far less attractive one, that also fed the poietic fallacy. It was related to the happy Whig version, but what it celebrated was an even more asocial tendency, this one getting closer to the frankly antisocial. This predisposition on the part of artists and their spokesmen has been most recently historicized by Anthony Julius, the celebrated British lawyer, who identifies it as the postulate of transgression, which Julius places at the heart of the modernist esthetic. "There have always been transgressive artworks," he writes. "Transgressions are as old—almost as old—as the rules they violate or the proprieties they offend." But, he adds, "it is only from the middle of the 19th century that the making of such works itself contributed to the definition of the project of art-making."[32]

---

30. See particularly Robert Walser's study of heavy metal rock, *Running with the Devil: Power, Gender, and Madness in Heavy Metal Music* (Middletown, CT: Wesleyan University Press/Hanover, NH: University Press of New England, 1993), with its explicit exhortation (based on the fallacious premise that Adorno's writings "challenge[d] . . . the Kantian orthodoxy that has ruled musicology") to "those working in the area of popular music" that they needed to get over their indignation at his "vague, vitriolic and transparently racist" attacks on it and instead seek "possibilities of adapting his methods to other ends," particularly that of "understand[ing] musical details as socially significant" (35).

31. Introduction to *Vorlesungen über die Philosophie der Geschichte* (1822), trans. John Sibree, in G. W. F. Hegel, *The Philosophy of History* (Mineola, NY: Dover, 1956), 19.

32. Anthony Julius, *Transgressions: The Offences of Art* (Chicago: University of Chicago Press, 2003), 53.

For a twentieth-century artist, not to transgress—against the norms of taste, or against the rules of traditional practice, or against social taboos, or against the peace—was tantamount to renouncing the vocation of artist. If a work of art did not transgress in one of these ways it was no longer art but kitsch, or (perhaps worse) entertainment. It is Julius's very interesting thesis that modernist art—which (as I would define it) means art created in the twentieth century according to the canons of nineteenth-century philosophy—must both embody transgression and disavow it when challenged by appealing to various "defenses," as Julius lawyerishly puts it—or alibis, as I would put it—invoking such higher principles as the raising of public consciousness (which Julius calls the "estrangement defense") or the quality of its execution (the "formalist defense") or its place in the sanctified history of its medium (the "canonic defense").[33]

This typology provides a framework into which a host of examples can be advantageously sorted. To the dozens of illustrations from the visual arts that Julius adduces one can easily supply musical counterparts. There is Arnold Schoenberg, the twentieth century's premier transgressor against the rules of traditional compositional practice, protesting that he is not a revolutionary but a faithful follower of Wagner and Brahms, whom he has uniquely succeeded in synthesizing.[34] (There's the canonic defense.) There is Igor Stravinsky, protesting that his ballet *The Rite of Spring,* which shocked its early audiences into legendary outrage with its transgressions against the norms of taste, was "un oeuvre architectonique et non anecdotique"—an architectural, not an anecdotal, work.[35] (There's the formalist defense.) And there have been any number of composers who—foolishly, in my view—justify their avant-gardism by confusing the transgressive with the progressive, insisting on the capacity of stylistically radical art to inspire radical social action, according to the idealistic terms of the estrangement defense. One of the most conspicuous was the Italian composer Luigi Nono, Schoenberg's son-in-law, who used his father-in-law's advanced compositional techniques to promote a political program that, when successful, invariably resulted in the suppression, as socially parasitical, of audience-alienating art like his own.[36]

---

33. Ibid., 26 (estrangement), 27 (formalist, canonic).

34. See Arnold Schoenberg, "Brahms the Progressive," in Schoenberg, *Style and Idea* (New York: Philosophical Library, 1950), 52–101.

35. Michel Georges-Michel, "Les deux Sacres du printemps," *Comoedia,* 11 December 1920, quoted in Truman C. Bullard, "The First Performance of Igor Stravinsky's *Sacre du printemps*" (PhD diss., University of Rochester, 1971), 1:2–3.

36. Nono addressed this question directly in an article of 1963, "Luigi Nono candidato del Pci con i lavoratori" (Candidate Luigi Nono of the Italian Communist Party with the Workers), justifying his candidacy for elected office. "Come mai un compositore di origine dodecafonica in una lista elettorale del Pci?" he asked, and answered, simply, "E perché no?" (How does a twelve-tone composer come to be on a Communist electoral slate? . . . And why not?); in Luigi Nono, *La nostalgia del futuro: Scritti scelti 1948–1986,* ed. Angela Ida De Benedictis and Veniero Rizzardi (Milan: Il Saggiatore, 2007), 155.

As the case of Nono makes especially clear, these utopian defenses are damaging to the cause of art in the real world. Writing of one of the fountainheads of the transgressive tradition, Edouard Manet's painting *Olympia* (a work, as it happens, that has been much commented on in recent musicological and metamusicological literature),[37] Julius first acknowledges that Manet's portrait of a prostitute meeting the viewer's gaze with a knowing look effectively countered the old hypocrisy of "pandering to, while affecting to deny, the erotic interest of the male viewer in the female nude," but notes, nevertheless, that it did not cease pandering. In Manet's work, and even more in Matisse's, Julius alleges, the artist "delivered nudes possessing a considerable erotic charge while rendering them in a certain sense unintelligible."[38] I am tempted to say that all of musicology is indicted in this sentence, for it unmasks the power of formalism to deflect attention from moral issues.

I am reminded first of all of Stravinsky's *Cantata* of 1952, which set a poem maligning the Jews, but at the same time employed—for the first time in Stravinsky's work—the serial technique pioneered by Schoenberg. The mountainous scholarly and critical literature about it analyzes the transgressive structure to a fare-thee-well but never once mentions the text, which belongs to a category that the Holocaust rendered inescapably (and impermissibly) transgressive. The formalist defense provided it with an alibi.[39] Ultimately we are led into the topsy-turvy realm of false converses, where if art is by nature transgressive then any transgression may be dignified in the name of art—as Karlheinz Stockhausen proved the morning after 9/11, when he called the destruction of the World Trade Center "the greatest work of art imaginable for the whole cosmos."[40]

So Anthony Julius's legalistic typology is more than tidy. It is wickedly strategic, because it exposes the contradiction at the heart of the modernist enterprise. The nonconformism of the modernist artist is regulated by a virtually irresistible conformist pressure. The transgressive artist works within constraints he dare not transgress. And, as Julius adds, it contributes to the impasse in which high art now

---

37. E.g., Mary Ann Smart, "The Silencing of Lucia," *Cambridge Opera Journal* 4 (1992): 119–141, at 127; Lawrence Kramer, *Music as Cultural Practice, 1800–1900* (Berkeley: University of California Press, 1993), 98–100; Karol Berger, "Diegesis and Mimesis: The Poetic Modes and the Matter of Artistic Presentation," *Journal of Musicology* 12 (1994), 407–33, at 427–28; Susan McClary, *Conventional Wisdom: The Content of Musical Form* (Berkeley: University of California Press, 2001), 172n3; Therese Dolan, *Manet, Wagner, and the Musical Culture of Their Time* (Aldershot: Ashgate, 2013), 66–67.

38. Julius, *Transgressions*, 70. For an example of the musicological commentary, see Kramer, *Music as Cultural Practice*, 98–100, 110.

39. See R. Taruskin, "Stravinsky and Us," in *Cambridge Companion to Stravinsky*, ed. Jonathan Cross (Cambridge: Cambridge University Press, 2003), 260–84; reprinted in Taruskin, *The Danger of Music*, 420–46.

40. Of the huge literature this remark generated, I am especially partial to Terry Castle's "Stockhausen, Karlheinz: The Unsettling Question of the Sublime," *New York*, 27 August 2011, http://nymag.com/news/9-11/10th-anniversary/karlheinz-stockhausen.

finds itself, for "to the extent that the transgressive continues to animate artists' understanding of art, it tends to be a constraint on the emergence of genuinely new art."[41] His conclusion is beautifully paradoxical: "The transgressive inhibits; it represents a boundary that today's artists must transgress."[42] To the demoralization of audiences by relentless transgression, Julius suggests, must now be added the demoralization of artists themselves as their self-created dilemma continues to resist solution.

Julius's analysis, which first appeared in 2002, reflected the post–Cold War order in which, for the moment at least, so-called Western values were perceived to have triumphed everywhere, and that made it possible for him to represent his case as universal. Had he been writing a couple of decades earlier, he would have had to acknowledge the persistence of pre-romantic aesthetics in large parts of the world, even a world viewed through Eurocentric spectacles. In those parts of the world it was the nontransgressive artist who received honors, and the value system that rewarded conformity was supported by an educational and socializing machine every bit as efficacious as the one that valorized transgression in the West. In the East, or non-West, of course, conformity went by other names, like service and cooperation, names that to Westerners could only sound like euphemisms. But Western values like creative freedom and originality (which protected the transgressive aesthetic) could also be construed as euphemisms—for self-indulgence, immaturity, vainglory—and certainly were so construed at the time. *That*, to quote Stravinsky after a morning spent listening to tapes of recent compositions at the Union of Soviet Composers in 1962, "was the real iron curtain."[43]

I was privileged to observe it during my year as an exchange student in Moscow. The biennial congress of the International Music Council, a suborganization of UNESCO, was held there that year. I managed, by staying close to Soviet friends in the crowd swarming at the door of the Hall of Columns, to crash its meetings. The violinist Yehudi Menuhin, the council's president, delivered a keynote address that was widely reported in Western media, because in it he named the then unmentionable Solzhenitsyn, alongside the sanctified Shostakovich, "as present-day illustrations of the vision and profundity of Russian art," as he reported it in his autobiography. Here is how that retrospective account continued:

> At that rejected name, the ice age descended upon the hall, and nothing I said subsequently served to lift it. Normally, I gather, a speech by a foreign dignitary, a guest of the Soviet Union, would have been noticed in the press, but neither *Pravda* nor *Izvestia* nor any other newspaper, nor television, nor radio, carried so much as a word. But

41. Julius, *Transgressions*, 53.
42. Ibid.
43. Igor Stravinsky and Robert Craft, *Dialogues and a Diary* (Garden City, NY: Doubleday, 1963), 254. Stravinsky used the French equivalent, *fer rideau*.

the channels of contraband information were in good repair, it seemed, and by that evening and throughout the following days I was enjoying lightning encounters with anonymous Muscovites who knew all about it. In the street, in theatre cloakrooms after concerts, I would feel a hand touch me, or a gift slipped into my pocket, and hear a whispered congratulation.[44]

Menuhin's recollections strike me as somewhat wishful. I was there, and looked around at the mention of the unmentionable name. I saw many ironic grins. The next day, at a panel, Alan Lomax, the American folklorist, departed from his prepared remarks to observe, rather tritely, that artists such as Solzhenitsyn, who challenge authority, should be neither condemned nor feared, because "they're just doing their job." I immediately switched on my simultaneous translation receiver to hear whether the remark was conveyed to the Russian speakers in the room, and it was. But it made no obvious impression. The hall, buzzing with an undertone of casual conversation like every Russian scholarly meeting I've ever observed, continued to buzz. Anyone looking for a shocked reaction would have been disappointed. At yet another panel, the American musicologist Barry Brook remarked that "it was best for all concerned" if artists were allowed to experiment, "even though it creates problems," because "that is what artists do." This time there were chuckles, and a patronizing reply from the dais by Georg Knepler, the East German musicologist.

I made a point of asking Soviet friends and acquaintances who had heard these remarks what they thought of them. My friends included students like me, no less congenitally irreverent than students everywhere, and my acquaintances included conservatory professors who, like professors everywhere, tended in their politics toward the liberal fringe. I think that by October, three months into my Moscow stay, I had become sufficiently de-exoticized in their eyes that they were not unduly inhibited in what they told me. The universal reaction that I elicited was respect for Menuhin but a tolerant shrug or an amused shake of the head, as if at a naughty child, with regard to Lomax and Brook. Those who bothered to continue invariably spoke of naiveté—both the naiveté of expecting that such words would accomplish anything, and the naiveté of misplaced faith in a discredited aesthetic.

Most Soviet artists, however they may have chafed—and chafe they certainly did—at bureaucratic meddling and restriction, particularly on travel, sincerely believed that their aesthetic views were more evolved and advanced than those of the West. Solzhenitsyn's courage inspired awe, but he was regarded primarily not as an artist—and certainly not as an artistic experimenter—but as a political dissident. The behavior of artistic experimenters was regarded as frivolous. Expressing particular contempt for Lomax, one of my Soviet acquaintances observed that if artistic challenges to authority were merely a matter of role-playing, then the

---

44. Yehudi Menuhin, *Unfinished Journey* (London: Futura, 1976), 368.

artist was in effect nothing other (hence no more) than the court jester, self-important, self-deluded, and impotent. This was, in essence, Marcuse's notion of "repressive tolerance," expressed far more convincingly than Marcuse managed to do, because my friend knew how to apportion the blame.[45]

VI. AFTER SERRA

The romantic aesthetic, both in its relatively benign autonomous phase and in its crueler transgressive one, envisions artist pitted against audience in deadly embrace. It is a self-fulfilling mandate that often produces spectacular collisions, like the one between Richard Serra and the denizens of the federal office building in lower Manhattan that he "decorated" with his abstract sculpture *Tilted Arc* in 1981. It came about through a miscalculation on the part of the General Services Administration, which commissioned the work and appointed a selection jury drawn entirely from the art world, which applied transgressive assumptions unanticipated by the commissioners, making the collision inevitable. The matter ended in heated public hearings and a lawsuit in 1985, and a court order to remove the work from view in 1989 amid a din of recriminations, bad feeling, and mutual suspicion that still reverberates.[46]

This regrettable episode in the recent history of public art set an ambiguous example. Different parties and interest groups drew different lessons from it. On the one hand, it induced the National Park Service, which oversaw the commissioning of the Vietnam Memorial in the year of *Tilted Arc*'s stormy unveiling, first to solicit blind submissions and then to appoint a selection committee comprising representatives both of the art world and of veterans' organizations, in hopes of a consensus that might avoid the polarization of interests that brought about the Serra fiasco. On the other hand, it provided those eager to exploit that polarization with an equally valuable precedent, as in the case of the Brooklyn Museum's "Sensation" show in the year 2000, in which Mayor Rudolph Giuliani was easily induced to play the part written for him while the museum administrators, in collusion with Charles Saatchi, the advertising tycoon who owned the works on display, and who stood like them to profit from the controversy, cynically insisted that the confrontation was unsought.[47] It is hard to identify a good guy in this tale

---

45. See Herbert Marcuse, "Repressive Tolerance," in Robert Paul Wolff, Barrington Moore Jr., and Herbert Marcuse, *A Critique of Pure Tolerance* (Boston: Beacon Press, 1969), 95–137.

46. The *Tilted Arc* affair has spawned a large literature. For Serra's own take on it, see his essay "Art and Censorship," in *Art and the Public Sphere*, ed. W. J. T. Mitchell (Chicago: University of Chicago Press, 1992), 226–33.

47. Indeed, profit they did. Ofili's dung-decorated painting went for $4.6 million (proceeds, of course, to Saatchi, not the painter) in a 2015 auction (covered in the Quartz *Daily Brief* newsblog as "Dung Deal": https://qz.com/441976/chris-ofilis-controversial-dung-decorated-virgin-mary-painting-sold-for-4-6-million/).

of mutual exploitation, with the possible exception of the much vilified painter Chris Ofili, whose *Holy Virgin Mary*, ritually decorated with elephant dung, provided the spark to set off the conflagration, and whose involvement in the proceedings was passive. Nor are there any good guys in the sorry saga of the cartoons lampooning the prophet Muhammad in the Danish newspaper *Jyllands-Posten*, wherein reckless provocation begat bloody reprisal.

A musical counterpart to these spectacles was the temporary cancellation of a revival of Mozart's *Idomeneo* at the Deutsche Oper in Berlin in 2006, in a production by Hans Neuenfels that included a transgression against religious piety (namely the decapitation of effigies of Poseidon, Jesus, Buddha, and Muhammad), unforeseen by Mozart, which elicited an anonymous bomb threat on Muhammad's behalf. Upon consultation, the police warned the intendant, Kirsten Harms, that the threat presented an "incalculable risk" and they would not be able to guarantee safety. Her consequent decision to call off the production roused the politicians into action. A spokesman for the chancellor, Angela Merkel, accused the Deutsche Oper of "falling on its knees before the terrorists," and pressured Harms to join the international War on Terror by reinstating the cancelled performances.[48]

In the end the threat was not carried out, but suppose for a moment that it had been, and that people had been injured or killed for the sake not even of Mozart but merely of the right of the director, Herr Neuenfels, to perpetrate a gratuitous and, frankly, juvenile provocation. Was it correct to value the right of artistic transgression over public safety? It was this sort of misevaluation, amounting to an ethical lapse, that Anthony Julius had in mind when writing that "the unreflective esteeming of the transgressive has had several unhappy consequences," among them "the impoverishing of our moral consciousness by its contempt for pieties."[49]

I don't mean to suggest that Mr. Julius regards public safety as a mere piety. He did not have the *Idomeneo* example in mind. But that example poses, perhaps even more pointedly than the ones he did cite, the problem to which he calls attention, namely that "the experience of contemplating taboo-breaking artworks [is] so often the very opposite of exhilarating."[50] If this is the situation we now face, of mutually disaffected and equally demoralized camps of art producers and art consumers, then scholarship and historiography have as much to answer for as anyone. Thanks to the poietic fallacy, scholarship and historiography have allowed themselves to be co-opted as spokesmen and advocates for art practices that arose concurrently with art scholarship and historiography themselves, and whose results now threaten the fine arts with moral indifference and social irrelevance.

48. See Judy Dempsey and Mark Landler, "Opera Cancelled over a Depiction of Muhammad," *New York Times*, 27 September 2006, www.nytimes.com/2006/09/27/world/europe/27germany.html.
49. Julius, *Transgressions*, 186.
50. Ibid., 188.

And yet, though he casts it as pessimistic, Anthony Julius's conclusion seems to me far too rosy a take on things. From my perch in the music wing of the American academy, I do not see that artists have become demoralized along with audiences in the way that Julius describes, but demoralized in a different way, as described by Julian Bell at the end of *Mirror of the World,* his new single-volume history of world art. "When did the Western avant-garde tradition breathe its last?" he asks. "On the night of 15 March 1989," he answers, "when contractors tore down Richard Serra's sculpture *Tilted Arc* in Federal Plaza, New York City." As it was dismantled and carried away for reassembly at a new site (not destroyed, as Bell seems to think), there was, he writes, "a widespread feeling that the old avant-garde impulse—to deliver a salutary aesthetic shock, to clear a space for critical reflection—was ceding to the free-flow of consumers and information in a world of unchecked capitalism."[51]

Capitalism? It was not capitalists who removed the sculpture but the national government ("the feds," in US parlance)—the same force that often intervenes in the affairs of art in noncapitalist societies—and only after public hearings and a lengthy lawsuit in which a court decided in favor of the office workers who had found the work oppressive in precisely the manner the artist intended. Bell's invoking what he must have thought the most surefire label of opprobrium seems less an expression of leftist opposition to capitalism than an expression of an older aristocratic disdain for ordinary people (tradesmen!) seeking redress against elites.

As for more informal evidence of smug and unreflective adherence to once-challenging but now outworn ideals, when we interview prospective additions to our composition faculty at the University of California, you may be sure that transgression—the delivery of "a salutary aesthetic shock"—is among the virtues habitually claimed by candidates and their supporters. We have a search going on right now [i.e., spring 2008], and of the four candidates interviewed so far, two have actually applied the word *transgressive* to their work, and a third, while he did not use that word, presented one composition called *Trespass,* and another called *After Serra,* which he introduced by telling what seems to be the art world's folktale version of the *Tilted Arc* affair, in which nameless "bureaucrats . . . came in the middle of the night with blow torches and destroyed it, . . . ripped it down without permission."[52] The story elicited a gasp from the audience, but not the piece. The

---

51. Julian Bell, *Mirror of the World: A New History of Art* (London: Thames & Hudson, 2007), 451–52. *Tilted Arc* is now in Alexandria, Virginia, partially reassembled in three sections described by a spokesman for the General Services Administration as "artifacts of what was formerly known as Tilted Arc" (quoted in Deborah Solomon, "Richard Serra Is Still the Man of Steel," *New York Times,* Arts and Leisure, 1 September 2019, 6).

52. *After Serra* (for flute, clarinet, violin, cello, and piano) is available on a CD by Ensemble 21 that samples its composer's works: Jason Eckardt, *Out of Chaos,* Mode Records 137 (2004). A photograph of *Tilted Arc* graces the cover. Eckardt's *Trespass* is recorded by the Oberlin Contemporary Music Ensemble in CD format on Tzadik Records 9006, issued in 2015.

piece delivered no shock, nor could it have done, since it was expressing an institutional orthodoxy. Artists who now speak of transgression are promising that they know what is expected of them, that they will obediently play their part, and that they will not transgress. The affirmation of transgression ensures that their assentingly strident and complaisantly jarring work will be received with equanimity. Thus the art world, at least the part of the art world that shares its lodgings with me, has holed up in its sanctuary, where it is nurturing its young in a spirit of complacency. It may be a misguided position, but it is not a demoralized one. It gives strength to its devotees and for the moment guarantees that the moral indifference and social irrelevance of serious art music will continue.

VII. AFTER 9/11

I make these judgments in a retrospect colored, inevitably, by the response to "nine-eleven," which had a most unfortunate musical repercussion. I'm not talking about Stockhausen, whose buffoonery was actually something of a comic relief in those scary days. And yet the buffoonery, according to Steve Martin's formula, was a distortion of what was happening, and what was happening was an alarming replay of the romantic glamour that had attached four years earlier to the Unabomber, identified as Theodore Kaczynski and captured in 1997. The aura of romanticism attached as always to the transgressor, and, to the helpless rage of his surviving victims, Kaczynski became a sort of folk hero, hailed by many as a "mad genius" and by *People* magazine as "one of the most fascinating people of the year."[53] The enormously enhanced body count achieved by the terrorists of 2001 inhibited the public expression of such celebrity adulation, except on the part of a fringe of artists and intellectuals, most memorably in a now much-regretted edition of the *London Review of Books,* prized by collectors, which appeared on 4 October.

The next month came the cancellation, by the Boston Symphony Orchestra, of its scheduled performances of choruses from John Adams's opera *The Death of Klinghoffer* because its portrayal, in a spirit of *tout comprendre c'est tout pardonner,* of the murder of an American Jew by Palestinian terrorists, and its implied plea that the cause that drove them to extreme measures be seriously pondered, seemed ill-timed to the national mood of mourning. In announcing the postponement, the orchestra's management explained that it preferred "to err on the side of being sensitive,"[54] and Robert Spano, the scheduled conductor, was quoted as agreeing:

---

53. For the reaction of a victim to the Unabomber's lionization, see David Gelernter, *Drawing Life: Surviving the Unabomber* (New York: Free Press, 1997).

54. "Boston Symphony Cancels Performances of Adams/Goodman *Death of Klinghoffer* Choruses," www.artscope.net/NEWS/new11272001-3.shtml.

"Before you pick the scab," he told Alex Ross, the *New Yorker*'s music critic, "you have to let it heal."⁵⁵

Maestro Spano's diplomatic remark was understandable, torn as he must have been between professional and personal loyalties. One of the members of the Tanglewood Festival Chorus, which was to have participated in the performance, had lost her husband on September 11, and several members of the chorus expressed their misgivings about singing Adams's "Chorus of Exiled Palestinians," with its violent expressions of hatred, so soon after singing in the memorial service for their colleague's loved one. The reaction to the orchestra's decision from the art world at large, however, uncomplicated by personal involvement, was nearly unanimous in its outrage, which bordered at times on hysteria. David Wiegand, the arts editor of the *San Francisco Chronicle*, enraged at what he perceived as a slight to Mr. Adams (who is, after all, a Bay Area luminary), wrote, "There is something deeply wrong when a nation galvanizes its forces, its men and women, its determination and its resolve, to preserve the right of the yahoos at the Boston Symphony Orchestra to decide to spare its listeners something that might challenge them or make them think."⁵⁶

It was Wiegand's reckless rant that moved me to intervene. What nation, after all, had done what he described? A government ban would indeed have been an intolerable intervention, but it was a decision by a private or corporate gatekeeper that Wiegand was protesting—one, moreover, that seemed motivated not by politics or ideology (the sort of "determination and resolve" at which Wiegand seemed to be railing) but by what seemed to me ordinary, quite human sympathy for victims, something that had been so conspicuously missing from many of the reactions to the event, including the reaction of Mark Swed, the music critic of the *Los Angeles Times*, who boasted, in a column titled "Seeking Answers in an Opera," that

> on September 12, preferring answers and understanding to comfort, I put on the CD of *The Death of Klinghoffer*, John Adams's opera about terrorists and their victims.... Opera is often called the most irrational art form. It places us directly inside its characters' minds and hearts through compelling music, often causing us to enjoy the company of characters we might normally dislike. Adams's opera requires that we think the unthinkable.⁵⁷

---

55. Alex Ross, "Hijack Opera Scuttled," *New Yorker*, 19 November 2001, www.newyorker.com /magazine/2001/11/19/hijack-opera-scuttled.

56. David Wiegand, "Boston Symphony Missed the Point on Art and Grieving," *San Francisco Chronicle*, 7 November 2001, www.sfgate.com/entertainment/article/Boston-Symphony-missed-the-point-on-art-and-2860361.php.

57. Mark Swed, "Seeking Answers in an Opera," *Los Angeles Times*, 7 October 2001, http://articles .latimes.com/2001/oct/07/entertainment/ca-54304.

Mr. Swed's decision to look for answers in what he himself described as an irrational source left me speechless at its misdirected sentimentality, particularly the implication that the opera's most praiseworthy property was its capacity to make us "enjoy the company of characters we might normally dislike." The assumption that the opera had lessons to teach rather than goosebumps and tears to impart was a comment both on the state of criticism and on the opera's qualities as a work of art. (No one, so far as I am aware, thinks of *The Death of Klinghoffer* as one of John Adams's better works; its reputation seems to be founded primarily, if not entirely, on its usefulness in political debate.) Marc Swed's eagerness to embrace the opera sounded to me like the old romantic worship of the transgressor once again escaping the bounds of art and invading real-world morality; and so did its echo in the *New York Times,* where Anthony Tommasini, Mr. Swed's counterpart, wrote that *The Death of Klinghoffer* offered mourners "the sad solace of truth."[58]

What these critics saw as truth was just the old habit of idealizing transgressors, so ingrained as to have become transparent to them. The same habit seemed to me to be guiding both Daniel Barenboim in his persistent efforts to breach the taboo on Wagner performances in Israel, and the reliable support he was given in the press.[59] Those who defended Maestro Barenboim's provocations, I thought, often failed to distinguish between voluntary abstinence out of consideration for people's feelings and a mandated imposition on people's rights. It was only a social contract that Barenboim defied, but he seemed to want credit for defying a ban. His acts seemed to regard transgression as an intrinsic value, implying that continuing to honor the sensibilities of Holocaust survivors was both an intolerable infringement on his career and an insult to Wagner's artistic greatness. To agree with him, one had to stretch the definition of censorship into moral terrain usually associated with forbearance or discretion or mutual respect.

Now the issue had been joined again, even more pointedly and painfully, in the aftermath of the September 11 attacks, and I felt a compelling impulse to register my dissent from the habitual responses of my cohort, because I felt so strongly that the automatic privileging of the autonomy of the artist over the claims of the larger community (as if artists did not belong to it), which in the nineteenth century constituted a moral investment that enabled art to thrive, was by the twenty-first century fatally degrading art in the eyes not only of the community, but of many

---

58. Anthony Tommasini, "John Adams, Banned in Boston," *New York Times,* 25 November 2001, www.nytimes.com/2001/11/25/arts/music-john-adams-banned-in-boston.html.

59. See, inter alia, Ewen MacAskill, "Barenboim Stirs Up Israeli Storm by Playing Wagner," *Guardian,* 9 July 2001, www.theguardian.com/world/2001/jul/09/ewenmacaskill; also see "Classical Music: Wagner, Nazis, and the Israeli Soul," ed. James Oestreich, *New York Times,* 12 January 1992, a compilation of solicited opinions from Leon Botstein, Edward Said, Shlomo Mintz, Robert Jay Lifton, Mimi Stern-Wolfe, Elie Wiesel, Joza Karas, and Joseph Horowitz, www.nytimes.com/1992/01/12/arts/classical-music-wagner-nazis-and-the-israeli-soul.html.

artists as well. To prejudge collisions between the interests of producers and those of consumers as collisions between right and wrong rather than as collisions of rights was destructive of moral as well as aesthetic discrimination. I was in the somewhat ticklish position of the philosopher Arthur Danto, another academic who like me moonlighted as a critic, who found himself on the unpopular—that is, populist—side of the controversy engendered by Serra's *Tilted Arc*. It was, he reminded his readers,

> a rusted slope of curved steel, twelve feet high and 112 feet long. It sticks up out of Federal Plaza in lower Manhattan like a sullen blade, and its presence there has divided the art world into philistines like myself, who think it should be removed, and esthetes, who want it to remain forever. The controversy is not over taste, since many philistines, myself included, admire it as sculpture, but over the relevance of the hostility it has aroused on the part of office workers, whose use of the plaza it severely curtails.[60]

Like Prof. Danto, I was on the side of the yahoos. I approved of the Boston Symphony's decision, which seemed to resist the romanticizing impulse in the name of ordinary unheroic civility. I felt the need to protest the protest at the orchestra's unglamorously decent behavior. Fortunately, also like Prof. Danto I had an outlet in which to express my unrespectable minority opinion, and a powerful one. In a long and fairly strongly worded front-page, above-the-fold article in the Arts and Leisure section of the Sunday *New York Times*, where thanks to fortunate friendships I had been a fairly regular stringer for more than a decade, I asked, simply, even simplemindedly, why people shouldn't be spared reminders of recent personal pain when they attend a concert. I asked why Mark Swed so despised comfort, and why he sought answers and understanding in an opera peopled by wholly fictional terrorists and semifictionalized victims, rather than in more relevant sources of information. I ventured the thought that when it came to acts of random slaughter, deterrence was more urgently needed than understanding, and I cautioned against the impulse to romanticize them. In conclusion, I quoted Jonathan Dollimore, a British literary critic and queer theorist, who wrote, in a brilliant article titled "Those Who Love Art the Most Also Censor It the Most," that "to take art seriously—to recognize its potential—must be to recognize that there might be reasonable grounds for wanting to control it."[61] That control, I argued, must in a liberal democratic society be exercised from within, as self-control, and I concluded that the Boston Symphony Orchestra, though it acted publicly and though its actions affected many who might have disagreed, had displayed some admirable courage in its voluntary decision—one that brought it plenty of adverse

---

60. Arthur C. Danto, *The Wake of Art* (New York: Routledge, 1998), 147.
61. Jonathan Dollimore, *Sex, Literature, and Censorship* (London: Polity Press, 2001), 97.

publicity and, so far as I know, sold no extra tickets—not to perform the choruses from *The Death of Klinghoffer*.[62]

Need I add that this article brought me more disparagement than any other piece I have ever published? In interviews with British journalists John Adams compared me with Joseph Goebbels, Hitler's minister of propaganda, and (seemingly worse) with John Ashcroft, then the US attorney general. Because I had questioned the wisdom of seeking answers to the dilemmas posed by this particular act of terrorism in this particular opera, I was accused by a fellow musicologist, Peter Tregear, of denying that "we should ever seek understanding in a work of art."[63] The very worst comment came from a British music critic named Tom Sutcliffe, who claimed that I had called for a general legal ban on the opera, as if such a thing could simply be declared, and asked "whether some forms of terrorism may not be a necessary and inevitable response to aspects of historic injustice (and not only in the Israel-Palestine context)."[64] This was chilling: it recalled Orwell's and Auden's altercation over the idea of "necessary murder" in what Auden called the "low dishonest decade" of the 1930s.[65] Were we in for another one? In any case, I had clearly transgressed—and I promise this will be the last time I rehearse this easy and tedious irony. But the disproportionate level of hysteria that followed the Boston Symphony Orchestra's decision to cancel a single scheduled set of performances seemed to redouble when a voice from within the academic community was raised in its defense, and that deserves, as we say, some interrogation.

VIII. MUSICOLOGICAL MORALS

The composer's distress was clearly self-interested; nothing much to investigate there. That he was provoked by journalists into reckless statements was also understandable; as Bill Clinton liked to say, that's what they live for. Ditto the irrespon-

---

62. R. Taruskin, "Music's Dangers and the Case for Control," *New York Times*, Arts and Leisure, 9 December 2001; reprinted with an update in Taruskin, *The Danger of Music*, 168–78. The update contains references to several of the responses described in the text above.

63. Peter Tregear, "For *alle Menschen*? Classical Music and Remembrance after 9/11," in *Music in the Post-9/11 World*, ed. Jonathan Ritter and J. Martin Daughtry (New York: Routledge, 2007), 168.

64. Tom Sutcliffe, "The Gospel according to Sellars: A Life in Full," *Independent*, 25 May 2003.

65. Auden: "To-day the deliberate increase in the chances of death, / The conscious acceptance of guilt in the necessary murder" ("Spain," 1937); Orwell: "Personally I would not speak so lightly of murder. To me, murder is something to be avoided. So it is to any ordinary person. The Hitlers and Stalins find murder necessary, but they don't advertise their callousness, and they don't speak of it as murder; it is 'liquidation,' 'elimination,' or some other soothing phrase. . . . Mr. Auden's brand of amoralism is only possible if you are the kind of person who is always somewhere else when the trigger is pulled" ("Inside the Whale," in Orwell, *An Age Like This: 1920–1940*, ed. Sonia Orwell and Ian Angus [Boston: Nonpareil Books/David R. Godine, 2000], 493–526, at 521). "Low dishonest decade" is from Auden's poem "September 1, 1939," on the start of World War II.

sible interventions by the journalists themselves. But what not only troubles me but also attracts my academic interest, and leads us back into the main matter of this talk, is the sort of interventions that have come from my academic colleagues, especially the musicologists among them. These have been of two kinds. The first, and less significant in my view, were the attempts to show that the work that had caused the Boston Symphony Orchestra's squeamish act was in fact blameless and innocuous, or else actually virtuous.

This was a kneejerk reaction that follows on the idealizing assumption that what is aesthetically good is also morally good. If a work considered to have aesthetic merit is charged with moral defect, there are on this view only two alternatives: to deny either the aesthetic merit or the moral defect and thus preserve the idealization. A relatively well known example is the philosopher Curtis Brown's argument, in response to feminist attacks on the principle of aesthetic autonomy, that "some moral views are not just false but ugly" and constitute an aesthetic blemish as well as a moral one; hence a work of art subjected to a convincing feminist critique must be no work of art.[66] Almost as fatuous was the defense of *The Death of Klinghoffer* by Robert Fink, a musicologist at UCLA, which tried to show that the opera was actually philo-Semitic, hence not only without moral blemish but actually just the opposite of what those who feared it imagined it to be.[67] His case depends on a highly selective reading of the libretto, based on suppositions as to the authors' intentions. It was a typical by-product of the poietic fallacy, and it nicely exposed the relationship between that fallacy and the venerable Intentional Fallacy. For that reason it may be worth discussing in methodology seminars, but it seems to me in the end as innocuous as it would have us think the opera.

Much more serious is the critique of my position by Martin Scherzinger, a musicologist then teaching at the Eastman School of Music. He engages with the moral issues head-on and shows, better than any other writer I could cite, just what is at stake in the matter of the poietic fallacy. Purporting to defend what he calls "the pure liberal position," namely "the unqualified embrace of free speech," he challenges me to "show, first, that the Boston Symphony Orchestra acted in the real interests of the community [in accordance with their claim] and, second, that the harms flowing from a performance of *Klinghoffer* outweigh whatever benefits may be claimed for it." Purporting to undermine what he (I think) invidiously calls my "act of moral vigilance" (meaning, as I take it, my act of vigilante-ism), he accuses me of inventing in the guise of identifying "both the interests promoted by

---

66. Curtis Brown, "Art, Oppression, and the Autonomy of Aesthetics," in *Arguing about Art: Contemporary Philosophical Debates*, ed. Aaron Ridley and Alex Neill, 2nd ed. (London: Routledge, 2002), 399–422, at 409.

67. Robert W. Fink, "Klinghoffer in Brooklyn Heights," *Cambridge Opera Journal* 17 (2005): 173–213.

the removal of the work and the community that is deemed too vulnerable to experience the opera."[68]

I am reminded of a delightful passage in one of the old viola da gamba manuals from which I studied during the period in my life when my main interest was in performing early music. It concerned stringing the instrument, and the first step was to tune the top string as high as it would go before breaking. How, I wondered, could that point be determined? Scherzinger is making a similarly unreasonable demand. The only way to show what he wants shown is actually to administer the harm. I assume he is similarly skeptical of preventive medicine. I am perfectly willing to admit that had the Boston Symphony not cancelled the performances, they might well have made no news at all. Some might have grumbled, a reviewer might have chided, a subscriber or two might have stayed home. The harm, if any, would likely have been small. But that, too, is only a guess; and that is precisely why the Boston Symphony management spoke of *erring* on the side of being sensitive. To presume on behalf of the author's rights against the claims of the community is, in that sense, also to err. Adopting the kind of experimental approach Scherzinger seems to endorse is in fact exactly what the jury of art experts did who selected Serra's *Tilted Arc* for installation in Federal Plaza. According to the work's eventual defenders, its purpose was precisely to raise consciousness of oppression. When it succeeded all too well, that success was touted as evidence of the value that mandated its retention. Scherzinger's point is similar: what he is really saying, and pretty flatly at that, is that the interests of the author outweigh the interests of the community, and the truest evidence of the value of his work, hence of the need to protect it, is precisely its potential for social harm.

I base this assessment on another, far more critical, moral objection Scherzinger makes against my defense of the Boston Symphony. He quotes a paragraph from my article that I have already paraphrased, in which I rejected the condoning of terrorism out of sympathy for its goals—and perhaps, begging your pardon, I'd better quote it in full. I wrote:

> If terrorism—specifically, the commission or advocacy of deliberate acts of deadly violence directed randomly at the innocent—is to be defeated, world public opinion must turn decisively against it. The only way to achieve that is to focus resolutely on the acts rather than their claimed (or conjectured) motivations, and to characterize all such acts, whatever their motivation, as crimes. This means no longer romanticizing terrorists as Robin Hoods and no longer idealizing their deeds as rough poetic justice. If we indulge such notions when we happen to agree or sympathize with the

---

68. Martin Scherzinger, "Double Voices of Musical Censorship after 9/11," in Ritter and Daughtry (eds.), *Music in the Post-9/11 World*, 109, 111.

aims, then we have forfeited the moral ground from which any such acts can be convincingly condemned.[69]

This passage had been singled out for hostile critique before. George Kateb of the New School for Social Research, a liberal political philosopher for whom I have a very high regard, put me in perhaps even more flattering company than did John Adams, lumping me with William Kristol and Dick Cheney in my "refusal to try to understand the adversary," and he exclaimed, "How bizarre for a scholar, of all people, to disown an interest in causes, even the causes of crime."[70] But that is hardly a fair characterization of what I wrote. I am as interested in causes as the next shocked liberal, and for the same reason, I should think: understanding the causes of terrorism can help reduce the incidence of its occurrences. But I do not see that understanding the cause is tantamount to justifying the act, and the refusal to justify the act is also, in my view, a way of reducing the incidence of occurrences. Martin Scherzinger's objection is different, and, I think, more pernicious. He accuses me of a moral inconsistency amounting to cowardice. Again, asking your indulgence, I quote a longish passage, this time from my accuser:

> The advantage of this moral mindset lies in not doubting itself; the disadvantage lies in not being able to afford to doubt itself. Thus Taruskin must freeze the dichotomy between *act* and *motivation* when it comes to terrorism (the defeat of which can be achieved only via resolute focus on the former and absolute negation of the latter). When it comes to acts of self-imposed censorship, in contrast, Taruskin's frozen dichotomy reverses itself; here the focus is resolutely on the motivations of the censoring community and concomitantly all consideration of the resulting acts is suspended.... It is noteworthy, for an argument that is doubtlessly confident that certain acts transcend all possible motivating ideas (as in the case of terrorism), that certain motivating ideas (such as sensitivity and forbearance) can sufficiently transcend their resulting acts. As a result, Taruskin cannot register complexity in either case; he can neither afford to entertain a motivation, however appalling and misguided, behind the terrorist attacks in New York City, nor can he afford to register an affront, however slight, on another fundamental value held by liberal Western democracy as a result of the Boston Symphony Orchestra's censorious act.[71]

But just look at the equations Scherzinger is making. Has he no sense of proportion? Must the same moral standards be applied to an act that results in the death of thousands as to an act that results in the cancellation of four musical per-

---

69. Taruskin, "Music's Dangers and the Case for Control" (see note 62 above), quoted in Scherzinger, "Double Voices," 109.

70. George Kateb, "A Life of Fear" (2003), *Social Research* 71 (2004): 887–926, at 890; reprinted in Kateb, *Patriotism and Other Mistakes* (New Haven, CT: Yale University Press, 2006), 60–93, at 62.

71. Scherzinger, "Double Voices," 110.

formances? If one of the acts is evaluated casuistically (in the true meaning of the term), that is, according to the merits of the individual case, wherein (*pace* Scherzinger) both act *and* motivation are taken into account, does that mean that both must be so evaluated?

In a more extended talk on censorship that I have given in recent years, I take note of a seeming paradox.[72] Out of sensitivity toward Jewish performers as well as members of their audiences, some conductors of Bach's St. John Passion have removed references to *die Juden* from the biblical text that accuses them of responsibility for the murder of Christ, replacing the phrase, for example, with *die Leute* ("the people"). I juxtapose this occasional alteration with a recording of Mozart's Requiem made in Germany in 1941, in which all references to the Jewish heritage of Christianity (in particular, the words *Zion, Jerusalem,* and *Abraham*) are replaced so that, in the words of a reviewer, the work "should not be allowed to languish in obscurity simply because a handful of passages in the text are unsuited to our time." Can one approve of the one substitution and condemn the other, given that the motivation in both cases is similar: making the piece performable within a given cultural (or social, or political) environment?

My answer, of course, is yes, because the act of modification per se is morally and ethically neutral. Its valuation depends entirely upon historical conditions and motives, which is to say, the values and purposes the act is seen to embody or serve, which cannot be inferred from the act alone. My question now, if you think my position reasonable, is whether it is equally reasonable to regard an act of terrorism—that is, of murder—as being morally and ethically neutral, its evaluation depending entirely on our reading of the historical context. I think not, which means I consider the applicability of situational ethics to be itself a matter of situational ethics.

But my real reason for bringing all of this up in the present context, and my more urgent objection to Martin Scherzinger's critique, is the other implicit moral equivalency he is proposing—namely, that between the perpetrators of 9/11 and the perpetrators of an opera called *The Death of Klinghoffer,* to be judged by identical standards or not at all. That is monstrous. Seen from one angle, it is a monstrous trivialization of 9/11. Seen from another, it is an equally monstrous, Stockhausenesque hyperbole with respect to the social and moral value of art. And the fundamental misjudgment behind it is the same slippage between artistic and criminal transgressions, and the tendency to conflate them imaginatively, that morbidly infests academic aesthetics. As I have already suggested, we music historians bear our share of guilt for this mindless magnification of the individual over the mass—here, John Adams over those whose sufferings he might have exacerbated—even on the part of self-describing Marxists who, following Adorno, continue to celebrate

---

72. See "Did Somebody Say Censorship?," chapter 2 in this volume.

the antisocial behavior of artists as if it were resistance to a worse peril, such as the hegemony of global capitalism and its threat to human agency.

IX. IF THIS BE...

Dissent on behalf of the audience amounts in the eyes of such writers to treason. Because I oppose the extent to which the score-fetishizing impulse grounded in aesthetic autonomy has invaded and impoverished the field of musical performance, I have been denounced as one who trusts "the 'logic' of the market" to ensure "a functioning social plurality." (My denouncer, James Robert Currie, prescribes "two minutes spent scanning the pages of Naomi Klein [or] Noam Chomsky" so that I may learn the "deeply irresponsible" error of my ways.)[73] Given the worry I expressed earlier about the self-censorship I feared I was imposing on myself when composing the *Oxford History*, finding myself willy-nilly soft-pedaling some of the ideas I have advanced more boldly in this essay, I was actually consoled to read an even less temperate condemnation—a real calumny—of my "pathological xenophobia, arrogance and neo-conservatism," as well as my "aggressive advocacy of the free market," in a blog maintained by Ian Pace, a British pianist and writer who specializes, both as researcher and as advocate, in the especially transgressive discourse of the mid-twentieth-century avant-garde. So something does seem to be getting through after all, at least to those who feel their interests threatened by the changes I would like to encourage. Their opposition is billed as leftist, but if so it is an echo of a very, very old left indeed, a left left behind, no longer in touch with either musical or political realities.

And so my prescription for the historiography of music turns out to be very close to that of one of my severest critics, Gary Tomlinson. The difference is that I see this prescription as implicit in my existing work, and he sees it as contradicting my existing work. That is unimportant. Our agreement is what counts. It is epitomized in Tomlinson's call for "a kind of history" he thinks I have failed to provide: one "that escapes the control and even the cognizance of those who have enacted it, that eludes their plotting of its networks and tracing of its transformations."[74] If Tomlinson, following Foucault, is unrealistically sanguine about the prospects of actually realizing such a thing (for he, like me, like you, like Foucault, and like everyone else, is among the enactors, plotters, and tracers), he nevertheless identifies the direction in which I think we need to go, away from the poietic fallacy and toward a fuller social analysis. I have indeed been trying.

---

73. James Robert Currie, "Impossible Reconciliations (Barely Heard)," *Music & Letters* 88 (2007): 121–33, at 129.

74. Gary Tomlinson, "Review Article: Monumental Musicology," *Journal of the Royal Musical Association* 132 (2007): 349–74, at 372.

At a Seattle conference on contemporary Baltic music some years ago, I called attention to what I assumed no one could have missed: namely, that virtually without exception, the music of every Baltic composer in attendance—young or old, Slavic or Scandinavian, male or female, left or right, post-Soviet or pre-NATO—followed the same trajectory: the more recent the work, the more consonant (or to put it more contentiously, the less dissonant and transgressive). That response to an evident but unacknowledged need, and not the hoary binaries (national vs. cosmopolitan, progressive vs. reactionary) that continued to dominate discussion in Seattle, was what I thought demanded acknowledgment and attention.[75] And yet when I brought it up, the fact was acknowledged but not the trend. Everybody claimed to be following a spontaneous creative mandate and seemed to resent the implied insult to their creative autonomy. But when everybody's spontaneous creative mandate mandates the same spontaneous creative act, you know that larger forces must be at work. It will be the task of tomorrow's historians to improve on the efforts of today's historians, like me, to identify them.

As long as the poietic fallacy holds sway, they will never be identified—and neither will the reasons for the earlier, "historical" style changes in which traditional music history has always dealt. At the very least we are back to my goosebumps and tears, and the challenge of finding a place for them in the historical account—a place prefigured in blurry but stirring fashion by Carolyn Abbate in "Music—Drastic or Gnostic?," a plea that we replace what she calls hermeneutics, the study of musical meaning as contained in scores, with the study of actual musical experience as encountered in live performance.[76] Since that, too, seems to me to be a hermeneutic project insofar as it is verbalized and transmitted, and since I cannot conceive of useful knowledge of human artifacts that is not historical knowledge, I would like to see this project historicized as well, along lines I proposed in the introduction to the *Oxford History*, where I recommended turning the question "What does it mean?" into the question "What has it meant?"[77] Studying the way in which not only composers but performers, listeners, and all who come in between have sought their goosebumps and tears—or their dollars and cents—will mean dealing dialectically with the relationship between producers and consumers, and identifying the mediating factors that control that dialectic—a dialectic with which those who now proclaim their allegiance to the old dialectic of hegemony and resistance seem unable or at least unwilling to cope. If the music

---

75. See R. Taruskin, "North (Europe) by Northwest (America)," *New York Times*, 18 April 2004; reprinted with an update in Taruskin, *On Russian Music* (Berkeley: University of California Press, 2008), 386–92.

76. Carolyn Abbate, "Music—Drastic or Gnostic?" *Critical Inquiry* 30 (2004): 505–36.

77. R. Taruskin, "The History of What?," chapter 1 in this volume.

historians of tomorrow turn out to be a little less impressed by claims of autonomy, and a little less in awe of transgression, and if my work will have contributed to that change, I will die a happy man. And if it should rub off on social attitudes as well, that will be a musicological blow against some of the real evils we now face.

6

"Alte Musik" or "Early Music"?
On pseudohistory

I

This essay was drafted as a keynote address for a symposium at the Arnold Schönberg Center in Vienna titled "Die Wiener Schule und die Alte Musik." The bilingual program, and the preliminary announcements, translated the title of the symposium as "The Second Viennese School and Early Music." My sense that the translation was tellingly inexact set me on the course of investigation and deduction that produced what follows.

    I was of course flattered to receive an invitation to address a conference at this distinguished venue, but also troubled, because I have acquired a dubious reputation where *die Wiener Schule* is concerned. A recent review of my *Oxford History of Western Music* notes quite matter-of-factly that "Schoenberg," in my telling, "seems to be the object of a personal vendetta."[1] Nor was I surprised to read it. Many other reviewers have found in my treatment of twentieth-century music a tone that "becomes ever harsher, more forceful, and stridently moralistic, . . . particularly as it pertains to Schoenberg and his immediate followers."[2] With respect

---

Originally presented as keynote address at conference "Die neue Wiener Schule und die alte Musik," Arnold Schoenberg Center, Vienna, 8 October 2009; published in *Twentieth-Century Music* 8 (2012): 3–28; reprinted in *Journal of the Arnold Schönberg Center* 11 (2015), Special issue, "Wiener Schule und Alte Musik/Viennese School and Early Music: Bericht zum Symposium," ed. Markus Grassel and Reinhard Kapp, 75–102.

    1. "A Feast for Musicians, Students, and Casual Concert-Goers," *Economist*, 13 August 2009.
    2. Rodney Lister, review of *The Cambridge History of Twentieth-Century Music* and *The Oxford History of Western Music*, *Tempo*, no. 235 (2006): 54, 51.

to something I will discuss below, namely Webern's orchestral transcription of the six-part ricercar from Bach's *Musikalisches Opfer,* the same reviewer accused me of coming, like Shakespeare's Marc Antony, "to bury Webern, not to praise him," the point of my analysis being that "Webern, in highlighting through his orchestration of the Ricercar a certain motivic coherence which he finds in the work, is distorting Bach, offering not 'a revelation, but a revision of Bach's priorities,' and committing a 'pseudohistorical fiction.'"[3]

Guilty as charged, your honor; I did say all those things. But the accusation of harboring a moral animus could only come from someone who regards the role of historian to be that of an advocate or at least an exegete, and who in the absence of advocacy can only see hostility. I would rather think that we all recognize the pursuit of understanding to be our common purpose, and that in seeking understanding we come neither to bury nor to praise. Maybe we can all agree that the primary weapon in pursuit of understanding is skepticism toward all claims; that the process of advancing understanding involves the testing of all claims against evidence; that the best outcome is m*ehr Licht;* that in order to let the light in one must dispel obstructions; that the primary obstruction in the way of scholarly light is unexamined myth; and that myths arise when the words of historical actors are taken to be the words of oracles rather than witnesses, and when their intentions are equated with their achievements.

Having said all that, I feel I can now frankly admit that "pseudohistorical fiction" is indeed my subject today, and that pseudohistorical fiction can serve a perfectly legitimate purpose for composers, performers, and listeners—perhaps even for critics. It is only historians who are pledged to expose what they take to be pseudohistory. But in the case of Schoenberg, Berg, and Webern the pseudohistory is now part of history and needs to be understood in the light of the legitimate purposes that it once served for these great musicians, and what it enabled them to achieve.

In constructing their idiosyncratic view of the past, the *Wiener Schule* was not unique, nor was it even unusual. I was momentarily surprised to find, in a book I was recently given for review, the following comment about the article, "Chromaticism," that Pierre Boulez contributed in 1961 to the Fasquelle *Encyclopédie de la musique,* in which he wrote with great enthusiasm about the madrigals of Cipriano de Rore and Carlo Gesualdo: "It appears as nothing short of amazing," the commentator, Glenn Watkins, exclaims (no doubt thinking of *Schoenberg est mort*), "that a leader of the radical avant-garde could simultaneously be making a call for an awareness of the musical past."[4] But of course it only appears so. As Watkins goes right on to show, nothing could have been less amazing. What else have avant-gardists ever done, throughout the history of music? The self-conscious

---

3. Ibid., 52.
4. Glenn Watkins, *The Gesualdo Hex* (New York: W. W. Norton, 2010), 123.

avant-garde stance necessarily implies a high awareness of history. Without it, the avant-garde could have no consciousness of itself as such. Historical awareness is something all composers have been cursed with since the middle of the nineteenth century, thanks in the first place to the neo-Hegelian historians of that time (with Franz Brendel at their head), and thanks in the second place to their antagonists, headed by Eduard Hanslick, the first professor of music history at the University of Vienna. Brendel's historiography underwrote the propaganda of the *neudeutsche Schule* (christened by Brendel himself); and the historiographical notions of the *neue Wiener Schule*, as most authoritatively enunciated by Webern, who earned his doctorate in musicology under Guido Adler, Hanslick's successor at the same university, were adapted directly from Brendel's precepts.

But appeals to ancient precedents to justify stylistic, technical, and aesthetic innovations in music have a much longer pedigree than that. The radical Florentine humanists who first theorized and then midwifed the birth of opera at the end of the sixteenth century claimed to be reviving the drama of ancient Greece, just as Wagner would claim 250 years later. Caccini's *Nuove musiche* were founded on the example of a vividly imagined *vecchia musica*, an invented *musica antica*. Monteverdi justified his *seconda prattica* by claiming that, whereas the musicians of the *ars perfecta* could claim a distinguished heritage going back to "the first to write down music for more than one voice, later followed and improved upon by Ockeghem, Josquin des Prez, Pierre de la Rue, Jean Mouton, Crequillon, Clemens non Papa, Gombert, and others of those times," he, that is Monteverdi, could claim a heritage that began with Plato.[5] And Plato surely beats Ockeghem.

Nor did such appeals end with the *neue Wiener Schule*. It has long been a commonplace that organizations specializing in the performance of very new music also perform very old music. The first concert given by Boulez's Domaine musical in January 1954 began with Bach's *Musikalisches Opfer* (not in Webern's orchestration, yet anything but a fortuitous choice nonetheless) and continued with Nono, Stockhausen, Webern, and Stravinsky. The second concert, in February, began with isorhythmic motets by Du Fay and ended with madrigals by Monteverdi and Gesualdo—works that, by Boulez's explicit stipulation, had "a particular relevance for our time."[6] The Los Angeles Evenings on the Roof concerts, begun by Peter Yates and continued by Lawrence Morton as the Monday Evening Concerts, featured a similar mixture. Stravinsky heard a lot of early music at these events, beginning in 1944, and immediately began imitating it in such works as his Mass (1944–48), the *Cantata* of 1952, and *In Memoriam Dylan Thomas* (1955). When

---

5. Giulio Cesare Monteverdi, "Dichiarazione," *Scherzi musicali* (1607); Piero Weiss and Richard Taruskin, ed., *Music in the Western World: A History in Documents*, 2nd ed. (Belmont, CA: Thomson/Schirmer, 2007), 146.

6. Quoted in Watkins, *Gesualdo Hex*, 122.

Robert Craft joined Stravinsky's ménage in 1948, he immediately began conducting for Morton, and the pieces he rehearsed and performed at the Monday Evening concerts were the ones he immediately began recording for Columbia records—the legendary Webern set, Stockhausen's *Zeitmasse* and Boulez's *Marteau sans maître,* quantities of Schoenberg, Berg, and Stravinsky, but also Gesualdo, Schütz, Monteverdi, and Bach.[7]

An example from my own lived and formative experience is the Group for Contemporary Music, the first university-based new-music ensemble (the first of countless such American groups), formed by the composers Charles Wuorinen and Harvey Sollberger at Columbia University when I was an undergraduate there and an avid attender at their concerts. The first program, on October 22, 1962, began with *Christes Crosse,* a formidable demonstration of metric proportions from Thomas Morley's *Plaine and Easie Introduction to Practicall Musick* of 1597. Thereafter the opening slot was always reserved for old music with "a particular relevance for our time." At the second concert it was "Music from the Mensural Codex of Nikolaus Apel (late 15th century)" (the title taken directly from the modern edition in the series *Das Erbe deutscher Musik*); at the third it was Wuorinen's *Bearbeitungen über das Glogauer Liederbuch,* after another volume of *Das Erbe deutscher Musik,* titled in German for some obscure but nevertheless characteristic reason. At the fourth and fifth concerts the opening pieces were what we would now call *ars subtilior* chansons, by "Matheus de Perusio" and Anthonello de Caserta (their names taken again directly from the modern editions in which the directors found them), including Matteo's *Le greygnour bien,* the redoubtable opening selection in Willi Apel's *French Secular Music of the Late Fourteenth Century,* published in 1950 by the Medieval Academy of America with a preface by Paul Hindemith, a book that was a veritable bible—all right, a pony—for generations of graduate students learning medieval notation. It was an inevitable choice at a time when academic composition in the United States and Western Europe was itself an *ars subtilior,* obsessed like its fourteenth-century predecessor with rhythmic complication.

II

Mentioning Hindemith is a reminder that the *Wiener Schule*'s appeals to historical precedents were matched—indeed, more than matched—by those of their antagonists, in the first place by the composer whom Schoenberg derided as *der kleine Modernsky* with his "echt falsches Haar wie eine Perücke ... ganz der Papa Bach."[8]

---

7. See Dorothy Lamb Crawford, *Evenings on and off the Roof: Pioneering Concerts in Los Angeles, 1939–1971* (Berkeley: University of California Press, 1995).

8. Schoenberg, *Drei Satiren,* op. 28 (Vienna: Universal-Edition, 1926), no. 2, "Vielseitigkeit."

So I turn to Stravinsky, and with some trepidation, because Stravinsky can so easily take over any essay of mine. I'll try to keep him in perspective. And the first thing I would point out about Stravinsky is that, like the *Wiener Schule,* he justified his work by appealing to old music at all phases of his career, not just the one we now call "neoclassical."

In fact, during his earliest period, the so-called Russian period, he appealed to the earliest music—the music of Russian, or ur-Slavic, prehistory. Before Stravinsky, most Russian composers who quoted folk songs quoted the long, lyrical songs known in Russian as *protyazhnïye pesni* ("drawn out" songs)—the beautiful tunes we remember from the work of Chaikovsky and the group the *Wiener Schule* would have called *das mächtige Häuflein,* either quoted directly from the singing of peasants (as particularly in the work of Balakirev) or from published transcriptions (as particularly in the work of Rimsky-Korsakov) or expertly imitated (especially by Borodin). Stravinsky quoted and imitated lyrical songs too, especially in *The Firebird,* his first ballet. But in *The Rite of Spring* he turned (very likely at the suggestion of his collaborator, the painter and archeologist Nikolai Roerich) to what was considered the much older repertory of *kalendarnïye pesni* or calendar songs, work and holiday songs that ritualized and memorialized the ancient pagan agrarian calendar.[9]

He mined them particularly from a book of Lithuanian wedding songs collected by a priest named Anton Juszkiewicz, Roerich probably having told him that sacrificial rituals had lasted longest in White Russian and Baltic territories on the western fringe of the Russian Empire. Stravinsky probably did not know that they were wedding songs, since the Polish and German title pages did not identify them as such, but it made no difference to the style of his ballet, since many wedding songs were fashioned like calendar songs out of tiny repetitive modules of restricted ambitus. The fantastically influential ostinato-driven style of *The Rite of Spring* was founded on a repertoire of folk songs chosen for their antiquity. Their presumed status as authentic remnants of pagan culture lent Stravinsky's music an irresistible aura of authenticity that certainly abetted its–and his—rise to eminence, and eventual dominance, in the world of modern music.

Another ostensibly ancient vein on which Stravinsky consciously drew was that of children's songs, in several opuses from his so-called Swiss years, corresponding to the duration of the First World War. These are the sort of homely two- or three-note chants children seemingly spontaneously adopt—or transmit to one another—in every culture. These chants are often thought of as a sort of *ur-Musik.* As one recent researcher, Pieter van der Merwe, has put it, "The best place to

---

9. See R. Taruskin, "Russian Folk Melodies in *The Rite of Spring,*" *Journal of the American Musicological Society* 33, no. 3 (Autumn 1980): 501–43; also R. Taruskin, *Stravinsky and the Russian Traditions: A Biography of the Works through "Mavra"* (Berkeley: University of California Press, 1996), chap. 12.

reconstruct the evolution of melody is the nursery."[10] That is of course a preposterous claim, being just an inversion of the old biologist's bromide about ontogeny recapitulating phylogeny, in which the scholar presumes to deduce phylogeny from ontogeny, as if the first music produced by infants represents, in actual historical terms, the infancy of music. There is no evidence at all to substantiate such a purely conceptual assumption. A broad range of music, from children's chant all the way to Brian Ferneyhough and Helmut Lachenmann, can be observed at the present moment. A comparable range could have been observed during the infancies of Ferneyhough and Lachenmann, when those worthies were themselves presumably confined to children's chanting. As early as there are written records of music, there is evidence of an ample stylistic range.

And the same caveat applies to the assumption that the simple, melodically restricted and rhythmically repetitive *kalendarnïye pesni* on which Stravinsky drew to evoke primitive humanity in *The Rite of Spring* are ipso facto older than the far more elaborate and "artistic" *protyazhnïye* on which the nineteenth-century Russians liked to draw. The equation of simpler with older—or, for an assumption that has also influenced a lot of modern music, the supposition that pentatonic is more ancient than diatonic—amounts to no more than arbitrarily turning an observed (and interpreted) horizontal axis of simple-to-complex ninety degrees to produce an imaginary vertical axis of early-to-late. As many readers will recall, the earliest actual document of musical notation known to history, the "Hurrian" (Sumero-Babylonian) hymn transcribed from a cuneiform tablet by Anne Draffkorn Kilmer and Richard L. Crocker in 1974 and dated somewhere between 1225 and 1400 BCE, in no way conforms to these conjectural models of musical prehistory. It is polyphonic, for one thing, and fully diatonic (i.e., with semitones).[11]

In fashioning the music of *The Rite of Spring*, then, Stravinsky was relying on a pseudohistorical fiction. And he was altogether correct to do so, since what he was after was not historical accuracy but historical verisimilitude—"truthiness," as we call it now in the States, after a popular fake-news comedian named Stephen Colbert. A subjective ring of truth was all he wanted or needed, and when we listen, that's all we need as well.

During Stravinsky's neoclassical period he competed for truthiness with Schoenberg, and their battle over it is a well-known story. But Stravinsky's latest phase, the so-called serial one, was just as strongly bolstered by alliances with ancient prototypes—far more ancient than the ones his so-called neoclassicism invoked. In December 1952, asked by a reporter from the *New York Herald-Tribune* to name

---

10. Pieter van der Merwe, *The Roots of the Classical* (Oxford: Oxford University Press, 2004), 27.

11. See Anne Draffkorn Kilmer, with Richard L. Crocker and Robert R. Brown, *Sounds from Silence: Recent Discoveries in Ancient Near Eastern Music* (Berkeley: Bit Enki Publications, 1976); includes an LP record, Bit Enki Records BTNK 101, reissued (s.d.) as CD.

his favorite composer, Stravinsky took his interviewer by surprise, the way he loved to do, and started rhapsodizing about the music of Heinrich Isaac: "He is my hobby, my daily bread. I love him. I study him constantly. And between his musical thinking and writing and my own there is a very close connection. . . . Here is the newly published volume of his 'Choralis Constantinus,' Book III: A great work. Not a home should be without it."[12]

The volume in question, edited as a doctoral exercise by Louise Cuyler, had been published in 1950 by the University of Michigan Press. Stravinsky had been playing it over, usually in tandem with Robert Craft at the keyboard, for about a year by the time he made this declaration of love; in fact, he was playing it in January 1952 at the same time that he was attending Robert Craft's rehearsals of Schoenberg's Septet-Suite, op. 29, and composing the *Cantata*, the first work in which he employed serial, if not yet twelve-tone, techniques.[13] Mention of Isaac of course brings Webern to mind, since Webern had also edited a volume (the second) of Isaac's mammoth collection of polyphonic Mass propers as *his* doctoral dissertation under Adler in 1908. It was published a year later in Adler's series of monuments, *Denkmäler der Tonkunst in Oesterreich.*[14] In 1956, Universal-Edition sent Stravinsky a photocopy of this volume, which Stravinsky had requested (according to his biographer, Stephen Walsh), "in order to study its elaborate canonic settings of the Mass liturgy."[15] But Stravinsky's acquaintance with a wide variety of medieval and Renaissance music, and his creative appropriations from it, go back a good bit further, probably to the year he spent at Harvard University in the Charles Eliot Norton Chair of Poetry (1939–40), during which he delivered the lectures that were subsequently published as *Poétique musicale*. While at Harvard he met Archibald T. Davison, then professor of choral music, who, together with Willi Apel, an émigré from Nazi Germany then employed at Harvard as a lecturer, was in the process of compiling the *Historical Anthology of Music*, a two-volume compendium of examples for use in music his-

---

12. Jay S. Harrison, "Talk with Stravinsky: Composer Discusses His Music," *New York Herald-Tribune*, December 21, 1952; quoted in Charles M. Joseph, *Stravinsky Inside Out* (New Haven, CT: Yale University Press, 2001), 252.

13. Robert Craft, Stravinsky: *Chronicle of a Friendship*, rev. and exp. ed. (Nashville, TN: Vanderbilt University Press, 1994), 72. See also R. Taruskin, "Stravinsky and Us," in *The Cambridge Companion to Stravinsky*, ed. Jonathan Cross (Cambridge: Cambridge University Press, 2003), 260–84; reprinted in R. Taruskin, *The Danger of Music and Other Anti-Utopian Essays* (Berkeley: University of California Press, 2009), 420–46.

14. Jahrgang 16, no. 1 (vol. 32) (Vienna: Artaria, 1909).

15. Stephen Walsh, *Stravinsky: The Second Exile—France and America, 1934–71* (New York: Alfred A. Knopf, 2006), 361. No source is given for the information quoted. The photocopy is listed as no. 426 in "A Catalogue of Some Books and Music Inscribed to and/or Autographed and Annotated by Igor Stravinsky, and of Private Recordings and Test-Pressings Labelled by Him in the Estate of Vera Stravinsky" (typescript, 1983), prepared by Robert Craft with the assistance of Brett Shapiro to facilitate the sale of Stravinsky's library.

tory classes, along the lines of Arnold Schering's *Geschichte der Musik in Beispielen* and other German textbooks of that type.

"*HAM*" served as a trusty *vade mecum* to generations of American college music majors from the time of its publication in 1946. That Stravinsky had it, read it, and used it is evident to anyone else who ever had it, read it, and used it, because so many of the examples of early music to which he made archly knowing reference in his books of conversation with Robert Craft can be found in this lowly source or others equally lowly. They include some very esoteric items, like "Par le deffaut," a chanson by Baude Cordier; or the "beautiful *seconda Stravaganza*" by Giovanni de Macque; or "that marvelous second Agnus Dei (the three-voice one) in [Josquin's] *Missa l'Homme armé*," which reflected Apel's special interest in the sort of musical oddities that would appeal to a modernist, who would have regarded them as pioneering or prescient—even prophetic inasmuch as they seemed to forecast his own coming.[16] And they also included the first Gesualdo madrigal Stravinsky ever copied out, according to Craft, namely "Io pur respiro" from the sixth book.

During his American years, Stravinsky collected pretty much the whole corpus of standard textbooks on early music. When I was working in his archive, during the temporary custodianship of the New York Public Library in 1983, I came across a letter from Faber and Faber to Stravinsky, dated 18 November 1960, confirming shipment of Carl Parrish's *A Treasury of Early Music*, another anthology that anyone who studied music in college or university in the 1950s or 60s would have used. In the very first piece of writing Robert Craft ever published on Stravinsky, an essay on the Mass published in 1949, he raised what he called "the problem of assimilation" of appropriate models for a work intended for actual Catholic devotional use. "The Credo," he wrote, "is redolent of plainsong, has a canonic Amen and a Plagal cadence. There is an exquisite use of Organum in the Gloria and an

---

16. Igor Stravinsky and Robert Craft, *Memories and Commentaries* (Garden City, NY: Doubleday, 1960), 100–101, 111. The most notorious example of "prophecy" in *HAM* was *Der Juden Tanz* (The Jews' Dance) by Hans Neusiedler (1508–63), a lute solo that, in Willi Apel's transcription, looks like a specimen of "bitonality" ca. 1920. As Apel notes in his commentary, "Shrill dissonances, otherwise unheard of before the adventurous experiments of twentieth-century music, result from the daring use of two conflicting tonal realms, D-sharp in the melody against E-natural in the harmony. They produce an extremely realistic picture [!!!], not lacking a touch of satire." See Archibald T. Davison and Willi Apel, eds., *Historical Anthology of Music* (1946), vol. 1: *Oriental, Medieval, and Renaissance Music*, rev. ed. (Cambridge, MA: Harvard University Press, 1966), 108 (score), 227 (commentary). Three years before the revised edition of *HAM* appeared, the lutenist Michel Podolski had shown that Apel had mistranscribed the piece from Neusiedler's tablature, which was based on a nonstandard tuning of the lute. Correctly transcribed, the piece is altogether conventional in harmony. See Michel Podolski, "Le *Juden Tantz*: Analyse et transcription," *Revue belge de musicologie* 17 (1963): 29–38. Perhaps needless to add, the transcription remained uncorrected in the revised edition of *HAM*. Truthiness often resists truth.

amazing revival of Gregorian Neumes in the Sanctus. The latter, for instance, contains a Climacus Resupinus Flexus, in modern notational cognates, of course."[17]

That bit of pseudomusicological nonsense had to be something Stravinsky himself imparted to Craft, I thought, and, recalling my own scholarly training, I had a hunch that the delightfully abstruse Latin term must have come from the chart, adapted from Dom Gregory Suñol's *Introduction à la Paléographie musicale gregorienne*, that Gustave Reese had printed in his *Music in the Middle Ages* of 1940, a somewhat more advanced textbook used by graduate students.[18] (I had already suspected that the opening of Stravinsky's ballet *Orpheus* [1946–47] was inspired by Reese's table of Greek scales.)[19] I wrote to Craft, with whom I was then in frequent correspondence, and he wrote back confirming that "Stravinsky did own Reese, Apel and Davison, Parrish and Ohl [*Masterpieces of Music before 1750*], . . . and in fact every anthology of 'old' music that he could find. Also every recording, from Anthologie Sonore down or up and including private ones."[20]

Almost every piece Stravinsky composed in America, beginning with *Orpheus* and the Mass, both completed in 1948, bears some resonance from early music—that is to say, from "pre-Bach" or pre-Baroque repertoires. Sometimes the connection does indeed seem to be a pseudohistorical validator of Stravinsky's stylistic departures, the most obvious case being that of the *Canticum sacrum ad honorem Sancti Marci Nominis* of 1955, the first piece of Stravinsky's to use—albeit intermittently—a full Schoenbergian twelve-tone row. It was composed for performance in the Venetian Basilica of San Marco, and the nonserial sections of the piece are obviously patterned on earlier music for that great church. At its first performance, at San Marco on 13 September 1956, it shared the program not with other religious works by Stravinsky, as originally requested by Alessandro Piovesan, the impresario of the Venice Biennale, but rather by a group of compositions that, in Stravinsky's words, would "effectively situate" his new piece: a ricercar by Andrea Gabrieli performed on four trombones, a Latin psalm setting by Schütz (a pupil of Giovanni Gabrieli's), a motet by Gesualdo, and the setting of *Lauda Jerusalem* from Monteverdi's Vespers collection of 1610. (The Gesualdo piece was jettisoned at Piovesan's request in favor of Giovanni Gabrieli's impressive concertato motet *In ecclesiis*. Piovesan argued that the substitution would produce a program that was "much more organic, more stylistically perfect," but Craft surmised that the real reason was that "Venice would not hear of a Neapolitan in the precincts of San Marco.")[21]

---

17. Robert Craft, "Stravinsky's Mass: A Notebook," in *Stravinsky: A Merle Armitage Book*, ed. Edwin Corle (New York: Duell, Sloan & Pearce, 1949), 203.
18. Gustave Reese, *Music in the Middle Ages* (New York: W. W. Norton, 1940), 131.
19. Ibid., 30.
20. Robert Craft to Richard Taruskin, personal communication, 7 November 1984.
21. Robert Craft, preface to Gesualdo-Stravinsky, *Tres Sacrae Cantiones* (New York: Boosey & Hawkes, 1960); quoted in Watkins, *Gesualdo Hex*, 336n30.

Whether the static pseudocounterpoint of quick repeated brass chords in the *Canticum sacrum* should be regarded as an obeisance to Monteverdi's *stile concitato* or to the Gabrielis' spatially oriented *chori spezzati,* or more simply and practically as an accommodation to the extremely live acoustics in San Marco (measurable on recordings as a six-second reverb), Stravinsky's work is indeed emblematic of our theme. In Glenn Watkins's well-chosen words, it is "rich with history and mirrors the lengthy and polyglot architectural record of the basilica itself: medieval, late-Renaissance, and early-Baroque musical elements flourish in tandem with Stravinsky's inaugural invocation of a dodecaphonic series, the avant-garde's testing ground of the day. The composer's recently declared notice of 'the past upon which the present is founded' had found an updated response."[22]

III

Stravinsky's response to the past was worth a fairly detailed look because it provides us not only with an embodiment of our theme, but also with an appropriate foil against which to examine the very different response of the *neue Wiener Schule*. And that examination, I hope, will justify my title. For "alte Musik" as envisioned by the Austro-German musicians of the *Wiener Schule*'s generation is quite different from "early music" as we use the term today, especially (but not only) in the Anglo-American cultural sphere. Indeed, the two terms imply opposite perspectives. To speak of "old music" is to look back upon it from the actual or conceptual present, the period we inhabit. Early music means "young music," not old, and to speak of it is to look forward to the present from an imagined past, or even to attempt inhabiting that imagined past without reference to the present.

A practical example of that difference can be observed by recalling the career of the lutenist Thomas Binkley (1931–95), one of the great early music performers of the twentieth century. He was an American midwesterner, born in Cleveland, Ohio, who graduated in 1954 from the University of Illinois, where he was introduced to early music by George Hunter (1918–2011), a great unsung pioneer of the movement, who ran the campus Collegium Musicum. Binkley then went to Munich to study musicology, and, together with another alumnus of Hunter's Collegium, the string player Sterling Jones, founded a performing group that, following normal German usage, he called the *Studio für alte Musik*. By the time the group issued its first recording, however (the first of about fifty), featuring Binkley, Jones, the British tenor Nigel Rogers, and the singer Andrea von Ramm (1928–99; a native German speaker, but not a native German, having been born and raised in then-independent Estonia), Binkley had rechristened it the *Studio der frühen Musik,* which at the time was not idiomatic in German.

22. Watkins, *Gesualdo Hex,* 159.

Why the change? I wish I could have interviewed Binkley on this score, but I never thought to do so while I knew him. It seems to me a virtual certainty, however, that it had to do with his perception of the differences to which I am calling attention. Even before so-called early-music performers began challenging so-called mainstream performers in the standard concert repertory, the term "early music" implied not only a repertoire (increasingly broad and ultimately impossible to define) but also a performance practice (much easier to define). And that performance practice went back to Stravinsky, in stark opposition to the performance practice to which the composers of the *Wiener Schule* remained faithful to the end of their lives.

It is true, of course, that Stravinsky was far longer lived than the composers of the *Wiener Schule,* and that even Schoenberg, the longest-lived of the three, did not live into the period when the early-music performance style became well enough defined to describe as such, or into the period defined by Stravinsky's so-called serial phase. But Stravinsky's ideas on performance were given a particularly forceful, conspicuous, and influential formulation in his *Poétique musicale.* (Indeed, the sixth lecture in that ghostwritten series, on performance, is, I am confident, the only one that reflected Stravinsky's own personal convictions.)[23] That lecture was delivered at Harvard in 1940 and first published in 1942. Schoenberg gave it a forceful if indirect rebuttal a few years later, which shows that Stravinsky's ideas and Schoenberg's did coexist in time and in active contention, and that comparing them is no anachronism.

Here is Schoenberg's, first. It comes from a three-page typescript, composed in English in 1948, titled "Today's Manner of Performing Classical Music." It was tidied up by Dika Newlin in 1950 and published for the first time in 1975 in the expanded edition of *Style and Idea,* edited by Leonard Stein. It is a vociferous protest, and it begins with a fusillade of startling assertions:

> Today's manner of performing classical music of the so-called "romantic" type, suppressing all emotional qualities and all unnotated change of tempo and expression, derives from the style of playing primitive dance music. This style came to Europe by way of America, where no old culture regulated presentation, but where a certain frigidity of feeling reduced all musical expression. Thus almost everywhere in Europe music is played in a stiff, inflexible meter—not in a tempo, i.e. according to a yardstick of freely measured quantities. Astonishingly enough, almost all European conductors and instrumentalists bowed to this dictate without resistance. All were suddenly afraid to be called romantic, ashamed of being called sentimental. No one

---

23. For a discussion, see R. Taruskin, "Stravinsky Lite, Even *The Rite,*" in Taruskin, *Text and Act* (New York: Oxford University Press, 1995), 360–66. On the authorship of *La poétique musicale,* see Valerie Dufour, *Stravinski et ses exégètes (1910–1940)* (Brussels: Éditions de l'Université de Bruxelles, 2006).

recognized the origin of this tendency; all tried rapidly to satisfy the market—which had become American. One cannot expect a dancer who is inspired by his body and narcotized by his partner to change tempo, to express musical feelings, to make a ritardando or *Luftpause*.[24]

Although this screed was composed in America in 1948, it reflects a view more accurately associated with the Germany of 1928 or so, when *Amerikanismus*, which meant commercialization and mechanization as well as modernization, took a lot of credit as well as blame for changes that were taking place in all of the arts. Those who favored it called it not *Amerikanismus* but *neue Sachlichkeit* (another term that Schoenberg hated with a passion). The remarks about the body and about drugs, of course, as well as Schoenberg's use of the word *primitive*, added a hint of racial revulsion, which can be read in its natural habitat, so to speak, in the responses to Krenek's *Jonny spielt auf* and other *Zeitopern* by Hindemith, Weill, Max Brand, and the transplanted American George Antheil.[25] The opposition to *Amerikanismus* remained alive—anachronistically alive, I would say—not only in Schoenberg's thinking and writing, but also in the now-fetishized writings of T. W. Adorno, and has therefore survived as a sort of fossil into the discourse of our own time.

Having seen how Schoenberg accounted for what he despised in the performance practice of his later years, let us now see how he accounted for the practice it had supplanted. "Music should be measured," he conceded

> —there is no doubt. As an expression of man it is at least subject to such change of speed as are dictated by our blood. Our pulse beats faster or slower, often without our recognizing it—certainly, however, in accommodation to our emotions. Let the most frigid person be asked a price much higher than she expected and feel her pulse thereafter! And what would become of the lie-detecting machine if we were not afflicted by such emotions? Who is able to say convincingly "I love you," or "I hate you," without his pulse registering? . . . Why is music written at all? Is it not a romantic feeling which makes you listen to it? Why do you play the piano when you could show the same skill on a typewriter? . . . Change of speed in pulse-beats corresponds exactly with changes of tempo.[26]

Schoenberg's reference to blood is surely an allusion to Brahms, who is said to have said that he provided metronome marks only when "good friends have talked me into putting them there, for I myself have never believed that my blood and a

---

24. Arnold Schoenberg, *Style and Idea*, ed. Leonard Stein (Berkeley: University of California Press, 1984), 320–21.
25. On the genre, see Susan C. Cook, *Opera for a New Republic: The Zeitopern of Krenek, Weill, and Hindemith* (Rochester, NY: University of Rochester Press, 1987); on *Jonny spielt auf* and its reception, see R. Taruskin, "The Golden Age of Kitsch," in *The Danger of Music*, 241–60.
26. Schoenberg, *Style and Idea*, 321.

mechanical instrument go well together."[27] It may seem paradoxical that Schoenberg should endorse the notion that tempo should be dictated by the pulse rate while so bitterly denouncing the musical impulses of "a dancer inspired by his body"—but that dancer has been narcotized by the music of a dance band and can no longer respond spontaneously to emotional stimuli. Schoenberg's allegiance is clearly to what Wilhelm Worringer called vitalism, the notion that art expresses the life force, the source both of our pulse and of our emotions.[28] In his transcription of Bach's *Saint Anne* Prelude and Fugue, Schoenberg imposes his blood pulse on the music with a bilingual multitude of tempo variations:

> *Allegro (poco moderato)—poco allargando—poco rit.—etwas breit—Tempo I—pesante—Tempo I—Etwas rascher—poco calando (ma poco!!!)—pesante—Etwas rascher als Tempo I—poco rit.—Etwas langsamer—poco allargando—poco rit.—Etwas breiter (aber nur sehr wenig)—L'istesso tempo—Sehr ruhig—poco allargando—L'istesso tempo (etwas schwerer)*

There is every reason to suppose that, in adding all of these obviously nonauthorial directions, Schoenberg meant not to supersede Bach's own performance practice but to restore it. The main reason for supposing this, of course, is that Bach was for Schoenberg the fountainhead of the German musical spirit, and that spirit was the very embodiment of vitalism.

The impulse Wilhelm Worringer opposed to the vital is what he called the geometrical. He associated it primarily with the art of early Christianity, but also with the modern art of his day. In a long essay that I published some thirty years ago,[29] I associated that geometrical impulse with the early theorists of post–World War I antiromantic modernism, especially Ezra Pound and T. E. Hulme, thence with the musical practices of Toscanini and then Stravinsky, and finally with those of "early music" as exemplified in the performances of the 1960s through the 1980s, the ideal to which Thomas Binkley seemed to pay tribute when he changed the name of his performing group from *Studio für alte Musik* to *Studio der frühen Musik*. (This seems especially evident when you consider that the group's specialty, particularly at the outset, was the music of the very periods that furnished Worringer with his chief examples of geometrical art.) I won't rehearse the whole argument again here, but that vital/geometrical distinction—rather than *Amerikanismus* or the music of dance bands—is where I would locate the source of the performing style that Schoenberg deplored. Regardless of its source, it is the philosophy of

---

27. Quoted in Bernard D. Sherman, "Metronome Marks, Timings, and Other Period Evidence Regarding Tempo in Brahms," in *Performing Brahms: Early Evidence of Performing Style*, ed. Michael Musgrave and Bernard D. Sherman (Cambridge: Cambridge University Press, 2003), 99.

28. On Worringer, see R. Taruskin, "The Pastness of the Present and the Presence of the Past," in *Authenticity and Early Music*, ed. Nicholas Kenyon (Oxford: Oxford University Press, 1988), 137–213; reprinted in Taruskin, *Text and Act*, 90–155, esp. 108–10.

29. This is the article referenced in the preceding note.

performance that Stravinsky espoused in the *Poétique musicale*, where one can find in abundance explicit endorsements of the same performance practice that Schoenberg excoriates, and many references to old music (and, in particular, to Bach) as exemplifying the geometrical in contradistinction to the vital.

Stravinsky, you will recall, subdivided "performance" into two subcategories, namely *execution* and *interpretation*. In one especially notorious sentence, Stravinsky defined "the idea of execution" as "the strict putting into effect of an explicit will that contains nothing beyond what it specifically commands."[30] This jibes, of course, with the Toscaninian injunction to play "com'è scritto," which means precisely the suppression, exactly as Schoenberg complained, of "all unnotated change of tempo and expression." Stravinsky made it entirely explicit when he wrote that

> the sin against the spirit of the work always begins with a sin against its letter and leads to the endless follies which an ever-flourishing literature in the worst taste does its best to sanction. Thus it follows that a *crescendo*, as we all know, is always accompanied by a speeding up of movement, while a slowing down never fails to accompany a *diminuendo*. . . . Great pride is taken in perfecting useless nuances—a concern that usually goes hand in hand with inaccurate rhythm.[31]

When one listens to his recordings, especially the recordings he made of music by other composers (for example, his incredibly dry and unyielding performance, with his son Soulima, of Mozart's Fugue in C minor for two pianos, K. 426, recorded in 1938), one sees that Stravinsky meant what he said. And that Schoenberg, speaking for his "school," also meant what he said is evident from his performance of the second movement of Mahler's Second Symphony, recorded in Los Angeles in 1934, or from Webern's recorded performance of his own arrangement of Schubert's *Deutsche Tänze*, D. 820.[32]

Here too the context in which Stravinsky's earliest twelve-tone compositions were performed becomes pertinent. When *Movements for Piano and Orchestra* had its première at Town Hall in New York on 10 January 1960, it was accompanied

---

30. Igor Stravinsky, *Poetics of Music in the Form of Six Lessons*, trans. Arthur Knodel and Ingolf Dahl (bilingual edition; Cambridge, MA: Harvard University Press, 1970), 163.

31. Ibid., 165.

32. Stravinsky's recording of the Mozart fugue, made for French Columbia in Paris, has intermittently appeared on CD (never on LP) and YouTube: e.g., *Stravinsky: Composer and Performer*, vol. 2 (Andante RE A 1100, 3 CDs, 2003). Schoenberg's recording of Mahler, with the Cadillac Symphony, can be found at the website of the Arnold Schoenberg Center or on YouTube (www.youtube.com/watch?v=F9KGqRoKGiY). Webern's recording of his Schubert arrangement is included in the comprehensive set of Webern's works under the direction of Pierre Boulez, first issued on LP in 1970 and reissued in 1991 as a set of three CDs (Sony Classical SM 3K 45 845); Boulez made his own recording of the German Dances with the Berlin Philharmonic in 1996 (Deutsche Grammophon Sterio 447 099-2), imitating Webern's supernuanced style half-heartedly, and very unconvincingly. Comparing the two is telling.

by works of Bach, Monteverdi, Schütz, and Gesualdo—almost precisely the same company the *Canticum sacrum* had kept in Venice in 1956—all conducted by Craft. Paul Henry Lang, reviewing the concert in the *New York Herald-Tribune*, criticized these performances almost exactly as one might have imagined Schoenberg criticizing them. It was vitalism vs. geometry redux, with the pulse once again the main point of contention. "So detached and bare" were Craft's performances, Lang wrote, "that a stethoscope could not have picked up a heartbeat in Schütz or Monteverdi."[33] But it was the performance of Gesualdo's chromatic motet *Aestimatus sum* that really provoked the critic:

> What is extremely peculiar about the choice of these unlikely bedfellows is the presence of Gesualdo among them. This exciting Italian composer was a psychopath possessed by an all-pervading eroticism, self-devouring masochism, and boundless egotism. His music is the most passionate expression of self-denunciation, here startlingly romantic, there hopelessly enmeshed in chromatic experiments. Surely, if any composer requires ardent interpretation it is this feverish freak of a genius of the late Renaissance.
>
> What on earth could have attracted these lovers of the arctic to the tropics? Gesualdo is all emotion and little logic, all impulse and little calculation. His magnificent inspirations either catch fire or become choked in a tangled maze. What do these unemotional Puritans seek in Gesualdo? Is it the warmth of life and emotional fervor they themselves are unable to experience? But if so, why do they perform him so coldly as to extinguish his essential qualities?[34]

Clearly, Robert Craft was a bit ahead of the game in so modernizing his approach to early music. Understandably stung by Lang's harsh words, he defended himself in a letter to a friend against the accusation that his performances were "cold, cold, cold" by claiming that "they are, I think, quite 'cool' (which means very hot)"—in the sense, that is, of sophisticated, up-to-date, "with it."[35] Love his performances or hate them, one has to agree that Craft was correct by the lights of his time.

But the vagaries of performance fashion were only an epiphenomenon, a surface ripple atop the real gulf that divided and distinguished the attitude of Stravinsky from that of the *Wiener Schule*, and this is the real distinction between "alte Musik" and "early music." The difference between the two terms represents an even more profound rift in the esthetics of the twentieth century—namely, that between familiarization and what, in the twentieth century, became known as defamiliarization (from the Russian *ostraneniye*, as coined by the Russian Formalists; compare the German *Entfremdung*). That is why "early music" is so heavily

---

33. *New York Herald-Tribune*, 24 January 1960; quoted in Watkins, *Gesualdo Hex*, 174.
34. Ibid., 174–75.
35. Quoted in Watkins, *Gesualdo Hex*, 176.

invested in what Hans Ferdinand Redlich so unforgettably derided as *musealer Klangmaterialismus*.[36] Its proponents never called it that, of course. They called it "authenticity." But the sense of authenticity promoted by "early music" derives its aura from a sense of difference—and distance—from what is standard and, by implication, unconsidered.

"Alte Musik," as understood at the time of the *Wiener Schule*, wished to hear Bach performed on the same instruments as Brahms, with the same nuances and the same articulations, because the sense of authenticity that "alte Musik" values derives its aura from a very considered sense of kinship. *Klangmaterialismus* is interested in the sounding surface. Timbre, texture, articulation, all matter as much as pitch or rhythm. At its most extreme, as enunciated, say, by Malcolm Bilson, "early music" puts the hardware front and center.[37] That was *Klangmaterialismus* at its very limit (and, as devotees of early music know very well, there has been retrenchment since). "Alte Musik," like the *Wiener Schule*, is idealistic, not materialistic. What matters is what lies below the surface—what Schoenberg, once he had learned the word in English, loved to call the "subcutaneous" level, where motives lurk.

IV

When Stravinsky turned to the past he looked for difference. He looked for "early music." When the *neue Wiener Schule* turned to the past they looked for sameness. They looked for "alte Musik." For Stravinsky the past was a tasting menu. He rummaged and browsed—often quite literally, as I've been relating, in standard reference sources—in search of *frissons*. And when he found them he did not proclaim a direct historical line from, say, Gesualdo to himself. He was open to everything, invested in nothing. What he was looking for in his eclectic and voracious way was in fact an escape from his immediate heritage, of which he had grown ashamed.

Not so Schoenberg. A moment of unintentional hilarity in Schoenberg's writings—alongside the many moments of intentional hilarity for which I cherish

---

36. Redlich coined the term in his edition of Monteverdi's *Orfeo* (Zürich, 1936); in his monograph on Monteverdi, he defines it as denoting "the tendency of some modern arrangers of old music to restore it according to the letter rather than to the spirit, by using obsolete and historical instruments (Cornetti, Viols, Portative, Chalumeau, etc.) but without simultaneously endeavouring to solve the problems either of 'Musica ficta,' Basso Continuo or of the many special types of ornamentation. The belief that the employment of ancient instruments alone ensures a historically faithful reading of old compositions shows an exaggerated appraisal of the purely *material* side of old music" (Hans F. Redlich, *Claudio Monteverdi* [London: Oxford University Press, 1952], 196).

37. "Perhaps it is wrong to put the instrument before the artist, but I have begun to feel that it must be done" (Malcolm Bilson, "The Viennese Fortepiano of the Late 18th Century," *Early Music* 8 [1980]: 161).

them—comes in "Nationale Musik," an essay in two parts dating from 1931, in which he asserted with truly frightening aggressiveness the hegemony of German music, and his own position at its head. "Remarkably," he wrote, "nobody has yet appreciated that my music, produced on German soil, without foreign influences, is a living example of an art able most effectively to oppose Latin and Slav hopes of hegemony and derived through and through from the traditions of German music." That's not the funny part. That's the scary part, Schoenberg at his least lovable. The funny part is when he lists his teachers: "primarily Bach and Mozart, and secondarily Beethoven, Brahms and Wagner." After listing the technical devices he learned from each of them, he adds, "I also learned much from Schubert and Mahler, Strauss and Reger too." And then the sentence that always makes me laugh: "I shut myself off from no one."[38]

There is your German universalism; and I only dare raise the point here in Vienna because that kind of parochialism seems rife now mainly in our Anglo-American academy, which is the reason I have been fighting it so hard. But it certainly characterized the view of the *Wiener Schule* toward *alte Musik* when it came to making appropriations. Consider: Schoenberg made arrangements of Bach, Handel, Monn, and Brahms (all right, Johann Strauss, too); Webern of Bach and Schubert (and Johann Strauss, too); Berg also did his Strauss arrangements for the Verein für Musikalische Privataufführungen, in his Violin Concerto he quoted Bach, and in his *Lyric Suite* he quoted Wagner. These composers cut themselves off from many, indeed from most, reminding me of the old Jewish saying, attributed to Reb Eliyahu ben Shlomo Zalman, the so-called Vilner Gaon (the Bible prodigy from Vilna), that the best way for a man to preserve his purity is never to leave his house.[39]

One can easily multiply quotations from Schoenberg, Berg, and Webern testifying to their insularity. Memoirs by Webern's pupils abound especially in exasperating anecdotes. To one he says, "If we want to understand philosophy we must turn to the ancient Greeks, and if we want to understand music we must turn to Mozart, Haydn, Beethoven, and the other great masters of the Austro-German tradition." To another pupil he says that "leading composers of other lands are but pale reflections of Germanic masters: Berlioz a French Beethoven, Tchaikovsky a Russian Schumann, Elgar an English Mendelssohn." To a third, Humphrey Searle, whom I name in order to identify him as English, he said, looking up from the score of Bruckner's Seventh Symphony, "Could your Elgar write an arch of melody

---

38. Arnold Schoenberg, "National Music," in *Style and Idea*, 173–74. I heard Ludwig Finscher say almost exactly the same thing in his keynote address at a Berkeley conference on Bach in April 1996. Speaking on modern appropriations of Bach, he referred to arrangements by Brahms, Reger, Busoni, Schoenberg, and Webern and then said, "Now that we have mentioned everyone . . . " With effort, I restrained my impulse to walk out.

39. Quoted by Leon Wieseltier in "Because They Believe," *New York Times Book Review*, 8 September 2009.

like that?"⁴⁰ The pupils were by turns shocked and amused, but always tolerant of the great musician's foibles, and I understand that perfectly well. From me it will touch off no vendetta. As one of the pupils wrote, "One may look upon this as a most confining attitude on Webern's part—not a single reference to Berlioz, to Verdi, to Mussorgsky, or even to the Liszt-Strauss vein in German music. But Webern's horizon was wholly filled by the music from Bach, through the Viennese classics to Wagner, Brahms and Mahler; he found his complete personal affirmation as composer therein."⁴¹ Whatever attitudes produced his music were the right attitudes for that purpose, and are in that sense immune from critique.

But we have a different purpose. We want to understand Webern's, Berg's, and Schoenberg's relationship to the past in its cultural context, and in its contribution to musical discourse. And that does require critique, especially insofar as their actual compositions—as opposed to their commentary—participate in the discourse. I have in mind the references one finds to the BACH cipher in such works as Schoenberg's Variations, op. 31, where it sounds forth as a proclamation, or his Suite for Piano, op. 25, a work that deserves to be compared with Stravinsky's contemporaneous "back to Bach" exercises, where it is built into the tone row (at the end, in reverse, so that it will be quoted literally in untransposed retrogrades); or in Webern's String Quartet, op. 28, where it wholly pervades the writing because the entire row consists of two transpositions of the cipher surrounding a retrograde inversion of it (though, as Webern boasted in the analysis that he prepared for Erwin Stein, "only *secretly* because . . . the original form never occurs in this brazen transposition," which is to say, *without* transposition).⁴²

These are all proprietary references. They celebrate heirship, ownership, a sense of belonging, not exotic discovery, and that sense of direct heirship, of being in a line of succession, is founded, as any musicologist today will tell you, on a pseudo-historical fiction. The idea of a straight evolutionary line "from Bach, through the Viennese classics to Wagner, Brahms and Mahler," to recall the words of Webern's pupil Arnold Elston, has been roundly refuted by modern scholarship, most pointedly by Daniel Heartz, who in an explosive four-page article of 1969, "Approaching a History of 18th-Century Music," showed succinctly but conclusively that the German tradition that supported Bach and Handel ended with them, whatever the Italianate admixtures, and the tradition that fed the Viennese classics actually originated in Italy, in comic opera.⁴³ The line asserted by proponents of German

---

40. Hans Moldenhauer, in collaboration with Rosaleen Moldenhauer, *Anton von Webern: A Chronicle of His Life and Work* (New York: Alfred A. Knopf, 1979), 507–8, 510, 512.

41. Arnold Elston, quoted in Moldenhauer, *Webern*, 508.

42. Translated by Zoltan Roman in Moldenhauer, *Webern*, app. 2, p. 756 ("brazen" substituted for "ostentatious").

43. Daniel Heartz, "Approaching a History of 18th-Century Music," *Current Musicology*, no. 9 (Fall 1969): 92–95.

universalism as pure and unbroken was in fact an arbitrarily spliced product of hybridization. We all know that now. No serious scholar would today endorse the ideas that sustained the historical self-image of the *Wiener Schule,* as promulgated, for example, in Webern's *Der Weg zur neuen Musik.*

But what of that? Neither Schoenberg nor Webern invented the pseudohistorical fictions to which they subscribed. As far as they were concerned, their fiction was unquestioned historical fact, as well as an article of devout belief. That belief is what shaped their approach to *alte Musik,* and therefore we have got to understand it, if we are to do justice to our theme. Who did invent it, then? Who did the splicing? Was it Beethoven, with all the Bachian fugues and Handelian pastiches of his post-Napoleonic phase? Was it Mendelssohn, who in 1829 brought the vocal works of Bach back into the public sphere and made Bach, through the new genre of German festival oratorio, a national emblem for all German speakers, not just Lutherans? Was it Franz Brendel, who in 1859 decreed that all who served the progressive ideals of German art (even if, like Berlioz and Liszt, they had allowed themselves to be born elsewhere) were members in spirit of the universal *neudeutsche Schule*? Actually, I would name as chief author of the myth of unbroken continuity the *neudeutsche Schule*'s bitterest enemy, Johannes Brahms, because Brahms performed the act of hybridization not just in words or in pastiche but in actual creative deed. In his Variations on a Theme by Haydn (1873), and later in the finale of his First Symphony (1876), Brahms adapted Bachian compositional techniques to Viennese classical forms.

In the last of the Haydn variations (and the fact that the theme may not actually have been by Haydn has no bearing on this argument) Brahms fashioned the first phrase of the theme into a ground bass. In so doing he did something that (as Brahms surely knew) Haydn never thought to do in any variation set. In fact, I think it is pretty clear that Brahms was explicitly invoking Bach's famous organ Passacaglia in C minor, because like Bach in that piece, Brahms suddenly and quite unorthodoxly transposed the ground bass to the soprano voice in preparation for the climax. By thus making Haydn shake hands with Bach, Brahms closed the historical gap to which Heartz drew such forceful if belated attention, and provided the precedent that made the pseudohistorical fiction true for his successors.

Schoenberg recognized this, of course: both in "Brahms the Progressive" and in his radio talk on the Cello Sonata, op. 99, he educed what I like to call his technique of micromanaging motives (or Developing Variation, to use his term) out of themes by Brahms.[44] And then, in his arrangement of the six-part ricercar from *Das musikalisches Opfer,* Webern used his trademark pointillistic instrumentation not merely for coloristic purposes, as is often assumed, but analytically, to extract hid-

---

44. Schoenberg, *Style and Idea,* 429–41; for a discussion, see R. Taruskin, *The Oxford History of Western Music,* rev. ed. (New York: Oxford University Press, 2010), 4:353–61.

den motives that in effect turn Bach into a Brahms—or a Schoenberg—in training.[45] What might, on the kaleidoscopic surface of Webern's transcriptions, appear to be a very orgy of *Klangmaterialismus* is in fact at the opposite extreme, dredging up the most arcane and abstract relationships that testify to the music's ideal structure, the occult level at which lay the true kinship between Bach and Webern himself. Webern in effect put the two ends of the invented tradition in contact, thus conclusively unifying and concretizing it. Although he would of course have claimed—and believed—that he was only making more explicit that which was already fully implicit in Bach's own writing, Webern's arrangement counts—in my view, anyway—as a *Verbesserung,* an improvement, to use the word Schoenberg applied to his Concerto for String Quartet with respect to its model, Handel's Concerto Grosso, op. 6, no. 7, exactly in the sense Schoenberg intended it: Webern's orchestration realized qualities in Bach's work that were latent, but fell short of full expression. Bach in Webern's hands became like Haydn in Brahms's hands: fully in touch at last with the implications of the tradition in which they participated.

V

Of course, one did not use a word like *Verbesserung* about Bach. As his biographer reports, Schoenberg "was furious if one mentioned Handel in the same breath as Bach."[46] In a letter to Berg, he wrote of his Quartet Concerto that "it will be a very good piece and that won't be Handel's doing."[47] And in the preface to the published score he wrote of Handel's "insufficiency with respect to thematic invention and development [that] could satisfy no sincere contemporary of ours." (What a contrast with every attitude implied by the term "early music," whereby it is assumed, however untenably, that modern taste should be set aside for the sake of historical authenticity.) He added in conclusion that he had achieved a "solidity of form and intensification of motivic development" that rendered Handel worthy of compari-

---

45. For pertinent discussions, see Joseph N. Straus, "The 'Anxiety of Influence' in Twentieth-Century Music," *Journal of Musicology* 9 (1991): 430–47; and R. Taruskin, *Oxford History of Western Music* 4:361–63.

46. H. H. Stuckenschmidt, *Arnold Schoenberg: His Life, World, and Work,* trans. Humphrey Searle (New York: Schirmer Books, 1978), 365.

47. Juliane Brand, Christopher Hailey, and Donald Harris, eds., *The Berg-Schoenberg Correspondence: Selected Letters* (New York: W. W. Norton, 1987), 444. Schoenberg's essay "New Music, Outmoded Music, Style and Idea" of 1946 contains a sustained and highly invidious comparison of Handel and Bach. A sample: "If . . . one compares [Bach's] counterpoint with Handel's, the latter's seems bare and simple, and his subordinate voices are really inferior. Also in other respects Bach's art is higher than Handel's. As a composer for the theatre Handel always had the power of beginning with a characteristic and often excellent theme. But, thereafter, with the exception of the repetitions of the theme, there follows a decline, bringing only what the editor of Grove's *Dictionary* would call 'trash'—empty, meaningless, etude-like broken chord figures" (*Style and Idea,* 117).

son with Mozart or Brahms.[48] Webern could have said as much about his Bach orchestration, but didn't. Why? Because unlike Handel, Bach had never been contaminated by loose Italian or theatrical ways—had never, so to speak, left his house—and had retained his purity, and his density.

Interestingly enough, one can find an altogether comparable assessment of Handel and Bach in the writings of Stravinsky. In *Expositions and Developments*, the third so-called conversation book with Craft, there is a sustained sacrifice of Handel on the altar of Bach, ending with the withering observation that "Handel's inventions are exterior; he can draw from inexhaustible reservoirs of allegros and largos, but he cannot pursue a musical idea through an intensifying degree of development."[49] Coming from one who in the very same book of memoirs said of the "Pergolesi" he was given to arrange for *Pulcinella* that "I looked, and I fell in love,"[50] the derogation of Handel must be another symptom of *der alte Modernsky*'s need to forge a retrospective solidarity with the *neue Wiener Schule*—a need that also found expression in Stravinsky's orchestration of the *Choral-Variationen über das Weihnachtslied "Vom Himmel hoch da komm' ich her*," quite clearly an emulation, in its intensification of the already very dense counterpoint of the original, of Schoenberg's and Webern's Bach arrangements.

The issue of *Klangmaterialismus*—an issue that is crucial, as I am claiming, to the distinction between "early music" and "alte Musik"—is curiously relevant to Schoenberg's arranging process. It provided him with a critical tool. Schoenberg's Bach transcriptions—the chorale preludes "Komm, Gott, Schöpfer, heiliger Geist" and "Schmücke dich, O liebe Seele," and the *St. Anne* Prelude and Fugue, all done between 1922 and 1928—use a slightly updated Wagner orchestra (updated by the addition of two pitched percussion instruments—celesta and xylophone—that were unavailable in Wagner's day) and employ quite conventional techniques of sumptuous scoring. The idea, as Schoenberg put it in a letter to the conductor Fritz Stiedry, was not "any 'full flavor' that comes of varied color; rather colors help to clarify the movements of the parts, and, in a contrapuntal texture, that is very important!" Schoenberg, who rarely let an opportunity go by to take a shot at performers (excepting those in his own coterie), added that he felt it was his duty toward Bach to transcend the limitations of Bach's instrument. "Whether the Bach organ was capable of [clarifying the movement of the parts] we do not know. Present-day organists are not; that I do know (and it is one of my starting points)."[51]

---

48. Joseph Auner, ed., *A Schoenberg Reader: Documents of a Life* (New Haven, CT: Yale University Press, 2003), 241.

49. Igor Stravinsky and Robert Craft, *Expositions and Developments* (Garden City, NY: Doubleday, 1962), 92.

50. Ibid., 127.

51. Auner (ed.), *A Schoenberg Reader*, 164.

And yet Schoenberg's transcriptions employ massive octave doublings—at times as much as quadruple doublings—such as might have seemed called for as a way of evoking the serried ranks of pipes that might be coupled when performing Bach's originals on a late-model nineteenth-century organ. These transcriptions have therefore seemed to me to be a protest or a polemic against the exactly contemporaneous *Orgelbewegung* or *Orgel-Erneuerungsbewegung,* which sought to defamiliarize the music of Bach—or at least to alienate it from what was viewed as "romantic" performance practice—by restoring it to its original timbres by restoring or copying the instruments on which it was originally played. Such an effort could only diminish Bach in the eyes of his self-proclaimed heirs. In the words of Adorno, it turned Bach into "a composer for organ festivals in well-preserved Baroque towns," rather than the fountainhead of contemporary music.[52] The *Orgelbewegung,* in short, was one of the earliest harbingers of the twentieth-century "early music" boom, and one of the most egregious early manifestations of *musealer Klangmaterialismus.* Schoenberg's opposition to it is altogether understandable in this light, since it sought precisely to dismantle the sense of direct inheritance of Bach in which Schoenberg and his pupils so fervently believed. So, big and lush as they are, Schoenberg's Bach transcriptions are not "klangmaterialistic." The Bach they presented to their beholders was a familiar Bach. The defamiliarizers of the *Orgelbewegung* were the klangmaterialists, since they were relying on a novel sound to accomplish a revisionary task.

But now compare Schoenberg's free transcriptions of concertos by Handel and Monn. They are riots of color, and riots of laughter, too—so obviously send-ups that only the forbidding name of the composer (and also, possibly, the ferocious difficulty of the solo parts) has prevented their becoming pop-concert favorites. Their gaudy scoring really amounts to graffiti—something that can be easily illustrated, I think, by looking at the orchestral percussion parts, and particularly at the use of the xylophone. The transcription of the *St. Anne* Prelude and Fugue employs a huge orchestra: thirty-one wind and brass parts that must be balanced by a massive complement of strings, but only six percussion instruments are called for besides timpani. In the String Quartet Concerto after Handel, the orchestra is much smaller, with only fourteen wind and brass parts, implying a correspondingly smaller complement of strings. But there are eight percussion parts besides the timpani, including piano instead of celesta. In the Cello Concerto after Monn, the wind and brass contingent is smaller yet—only thirteen parts to balance against the strings. But the percussion (besides timpani) has grown to ten instruments, including both piano and celesta. One can say that the weight of the per-

---

52. T. W. Adorno, "Bach gegen seine Liebhaber verteidigt," in Adorno, *Gesammelte Schriften* (Munich: Suhrkamp, 1970–86), 10:139; quoted in Mark Berry, "Romantic Modernism: Bach, Furtwängler, and Adorno," *New German Critique* 35 (2008): 82.

cussion writing varies inversely with the respect Schoenberg had for the original composer.

As for the xylophone, it is the most garish color in Schoenberg's palette, one traditionally associated with cartoon caricature (as in Saint-Saëns's *Danse macabre* or his "Fossils," along with other skeletons I could name) or expressionistic horror (recall the third act of *Wozzeck*, or Schoenberg's own *Begleitungsmusik zu einer Lichtspielszene*). In the *St. Anne* fugue the xylophone gets to double the huge unison run at the very end, and is otherwise confined to a grand total of four notes to reinforce sforzandos. In the Handel concerto it has a few notable solos, predictably including the answer to the notorious fugue subject—itself a joke—that consists of nothing but diminutions of a repeated note. In the Monn concerto, especially the outer movements, it never shuts up, and gets many solos. I am particularly conscious of them because of the peculiar circumstances under which I came to know the Monn transcription. I have heard the existing recordings—two under Robert Craft, an amazing performance by Yo-Yo Ma, and a new one by Mark Drobinsky, recorded in Yekaterinburg, Russia. But this is a piece one really has to experience live, which I have had the good fortune to do only once. That was in Russia, too, during my student year there in 1971–72. The Schoenberg-Monn concerto was given its Soviet première that season at the Small Hall of the Moscow Conservatory, with a wonderful cellist named Natalia Gutman—then a young but already famous "laureate of international competitions," as the standard poster phrase went, now known as an outstanding exponent of the late-Soviet modernists Shnitke, Denisov, and Gubaidulina. I knew Natasha Gutman through mutual friends I had made at the conservatory, and went to the concert as the guest of the percussionist Mark Pekarsky, who was playing the xylophone in the orchestra. I don't think I stopped laughing from one end of the piece to the other, not only as a result of the antics Schoenberg had composed into the cello part—if you've seen it you know that there is no other piece in which the cellist's left arm has to do so much leaping up and down—but also, and mainly, from the nonstop activity in the kitchen (to use the term Russian percussionists used). I was not the only one laughing. The whole audience was responding to the piece as if they were at a comedy club. And it was not the unfriendly laughter of the shocked bourgeoisie; it was the especially hip or knowing laughter of conservatory students who knew their music from the inside. After the concert I went backstage to offer congratulations and told Mark how funny it had been. "*Yeshcho by!*" he shouted in reply (the Russian for what in English would now be "Duhhh!"). He told me that it was he who had talked Natasha into performing the piece, precisely because he knew he would be the center of attention.

Was this the reaction Schoenberg would have wanted? *Yeshcho by!* Schoenberg's glorious sense—dare I say, his Jewish sense—of humor must be the best-kept secret in all of Western music. The fact that it usually goes completely unrecognized speaks many volumes about the culture of modernism—or what it became in the later twentieth century, when my generation was growing up. I am always especially amazed to witness the long serious faces all around me at performances of *Pierrot lunaire*, and I would like to close with an example from *Pierrot*, because it relates equally to Schoenberg's humor and to his attitude toward *alte Musik*, and ties together all the themes I have been broaching.

VI

When considering the relationship between the composers of the *neue Wiener Schule* and *alte Musik*, scholars often speak, at times in awe, of the prevalence of canons and other contrapuntal tours de force in their compositions. One of the densest of these constructions is "Der Mondfleck," the eighteenth melodrama in the *Pierrot* cycle. It is the one in which Schoenberg piles a strict canon for the violin and cello on top of a freer canon for the clarinet and piccolo plus a fugue for the piano (and piles the *Sprechstimme* part on top of all of that), and in which the two instrumental canons reverse direction halfway through and reproduce themselves in retrograde. I do love to quote all the solemn, awestruck commentary this piece has elicited, my favorite perhaps being Charles Rosen's exclamation that "Der Mondfleck" is "one of the most elaborate canons worked out since the end of the fifteenth century."[53]

But how elaborately "worked out" is a canon or a fugue that is written in an idiom that recognizes no distinction between consonance and dissonance, so that, harmonically speaking, literally anything can go? The essence of counterpoint has always been its "dissonance treatment." That, and that alone, is where skill is required and displayed. What makes Bach's *Musikalisches Opfer* or *Die Kunst der Fuge* such astonishing tours de force is not just the complexity of the texture, but the fact that that complexity is achieved within such exacting harmonic constraints. Take away the constraints, and you have rendered the tour de force entirely pointless. If he had had enough instruments at his disposal, Schoenberg could have piled six more canons on top of the texture as written, and it would have been no harder to calculate.

I have already made this point in print, both in *The Oxford History of Western Music* and in an article entitled "The Poietic Fallacy" that was published in the *Musical Times* in 2004.[54] And of course I have been roundly rebuked for my insolence. The pianist Ian Pace, who thinks himself a very loyal Schoenbergian, protested my "crude formulation":

---

53. Charles Rosen, *Arnold Schoenberg* (New York: Viking, 1975), 55.
54. See R. Taruskin, *Oxford History of Western Music* 4:462–66; R. Taruskin, "The Poietic Fallacy," *Musical Times* 145, no. 1886 (Spring 2004): 7–34.

In no sense is there "no distinction between consonance and dissonance" in "Der Mondfleck" (let alone "anything goes")—every pitch is as carefully worked out as in any piece of tonal music. Consonance and dissonance are not objects but loosely-defined areas within a spectrum: Schoenberg's harmonies (those resulting from the counterpoint) tend towards the more dissonant end of the spectrum compared to traditional tonal music and are not organised around a singular tonal hierarchy, but there is still much differentiation between different levels of dissonance (for example in terms of predominance of harmonies made up from whole- or semi-tones at different moments). Taruskin's sentence would make it seem as if the harmonic result is essentially arbitrary; it's far from that, at least as I hear it. . . . Taruskin is playing his conventional populist card as an attempt to marginalise all atonal music. [It] places him firmly within the middlebrow, as a cynical populist whilst still upholding middle-class taste.[55]

These strictures are familiar enough. Adornian high dudgeon is as conventional a playing card as any other. But if my observations on atonal canonic or fugal writing give evidence of a middlebrow attempt to marginalize all atonal music, then Arnold Schoenberg must share the dock with me. In the shorter of two essays titled "Composition with Twelve Tones" (1947), he wrote that "even the writing of whole fugues is a little too easy under these circumstances"—that is, circumstances of emancipated dissonance—and he recognized "no merit in writing canons of two or more voices." Instead, he maintained, "composing of these forms should only be undertaken for some special reason."[56]

That certainly applies to "Der Mondfleck," where the special reasons, as in most vocal music, are to be sought in the text. Kathryn Puffett has analyzed what Schoenberg called *das Verhältnis zum Text*[57] in that piece and determined that the retrograde occurs "at the exact moment Pierrot notices a white fleck of moonlight on the back of his coat." She interprets the combination of wind and string parts moving backward while the piano and voice parts continue to move forward as representing Pierrot "walking forwards while looking back over his shoulder" as he tries in vain to rub out what he thinks is a spot of plaster.[58] So far so good, and so far so droll; but why all the contrapuntal complication? I think it is part of the joke: an even better part, in fact. The text is all about Pierrot's efforts to rub out the spot of

---

55. http://mas.nfshost.com/index.php?topic=115.15 (accessed 18 September 2009; no longer active).

56. Schoenberg, *Style and Idea*, 248; also see P. Murray Dineen, "The Contrapuntal Combination: Schoenberg's Old Hat," in *Music Theory and the Exploration of the Past*, ed. Christopher Hatch and David W. Bernstein (Chicago: University of Chicago Press, 1993), p435–47.

57. Cf. "Das Verhältnis zum Text," in *Der blaue Reiter*, ed. Wassily Kandinsky and Franz Marc (Munich: Piper Verlag, 1912); translated by Dika Newlin as "The Relationship to the Text" in *Style and Idea*, 141–44.

58. Kathryn Puffett, "Structural Imagery: 'Pierrot lunaire' Revisited," *Tempo* 60, no. 237 (July 2006); 14–15.

moonlight—all frenzied but pointless activity. That is a perfect description of an elaborate contrapuntal texture with emancipated dissonance. Or to put it the other way around, an elaborate contrapuntal texture with emancipated dissonance is a perfect metaphor for the urgent but ineffectual efforts that Pierrot is making. From a bogus masterpiece of counterpoint, "Der Mondfleck" suddenly becomes a genuine masterpiece of self-mocking irony.

That self-mocking irony is one of Schoenberg's most attractive traits, and it is rarely given sufficient acknowledgment in our pompous and ponderous literature. In an especially unbuttoned mood, Schoenberg is reputed to have told a pupil one day, "Now that I have emancipated dissonance, anyone can be a composer." Do I believe that to be literally true? No more than I believe literally that "anything goes," harmonically, in atonal or twelve-tone music. A composer as craftsmanly as Schoenberg creates ad hoc harmonic norms, and they are easily discoverable in "Der Mondfleck," the augmented triads at the beginning of the piano fugue being especially telling in this regard, and Ian Pace is quite right to assert that even without a traditional criterion of consonance in "Der Mondfleck," "there is still much differentiation between different levels of dissonance (for example in terms of predominance of harmonies made up from whole- or semi-tones at different moments)." Analysis is still fruitful, and can uncover the consistent harmonic relations that produce the syntactical coherence and the well-sounding surface that listeners intuitively sense and admire in *Pierrot*. In twelve-tone music, of course, there are other, perhaps more objective criteria to judge the correctness of the writing.

But there are still problems of perception that cannot be willed away by critical fiat, and they bedevil analysis as well as naive listening. It is time to acknowledge them. I once hazarded the claim that any analytical method worthy of the name should offer a reliable tool for textual criticism.[59] I made that claim in a polemical context, as part of an ongoing exchange with Allen Forte over what I saw as the sterility of his "set-theoretical" analytical method and, in particular, its pitfalls as applied to Stravinsky's *Rite of Spring*. I still think my claim is valid, and by now I can cite examples. Knowledge of Stravinsky's octatonic usages, the reality of which were questioned long ago by Forte and even fairly recently in a bewilderingly impertinent article by Dmitri Tymoczko,[60] enabled me to conjecture a textual correction at the end of the first of Stravinsky's *Pribaoutki* of 1914, which subsequent inspection of the sketches confirmed.[61] But there are notorious places in the music of Schoenberg where misprints have remained uncorrected for many decades,

---

59. See R. Taruskin, "Forum: Reply to van den Toorn," *In Theory Only* 10, no. 3 (October 1987): 47–57.

60. Dmitri Tymoczko, "Stravinsky and the Octatonic: A Reconsideration" *Music Theory Spectrum* 25 (2002): 185–202.

61. Taruskin, *Stravinsky and the Russian Traditions*, 1171; see also Taruskin, "The Poietic Fallacy."

because no one is in possession of a reliable analytical criterion. The most famous one is the one toward the end of the first piano piece in opus 11, where analysts relying on what they have regarded as internal evidence (but which was really the pseudo-internal evidence of their own theoretical prejudices) have invariably proposed the wrong correction.[62]

There are similar long-standing misprints in "Der Mondfleck," too. Some of them can be putatively corrected on the basis of the canonic writing. Kathryn Puffett reports, and a mere glance at the score will confirm (after more than a century and countless printings!), that "there are several discrepancies in the canons, . . . in both pitch and rhythm, mostly in the retrograde half of the piece." She further reports that "in 1977, when the Schoenberg Archive was still in Los Angeles, Leonard Stein wrote to me describing Schoenberg's conducting score, on which most of the discrepant notes had been corrected in pencil."[63] I think it worth emphasizing that, according to what Stein reportedly told Puffett, Schoenberg corrected *most* of the discrepant notes. Why not all? Is that evidence of intention or of inattention? If we cannot tell (or if, as seems at least possible, Schoenberg could not tell), then how important, after all, are the details of pitch content in this music?

Charles Rosen raised the point years ago in his little Schoenberg monograph when he wrote that the "new eminence of color, texture, and dynamics entails, as a consequence, something that most respectable musicians have been reluctant to admit because it is conceived as something disreputable: the downgrading of the importance of pitch."[64] We are still reluctant, and music theorists, being perhaps the most respectable of all musicians, have been most reluctant of all; indeed, we still tend in our theoretical literature to fetishize pitch relations, and this has led, in the case of the music of the *neue Wiener Schule*, to many errors, unnecessary denials, and false claims.

So here is where we have the most to learn, perhaps, from studying the *neue Wieners* in conjunction with *alte Musik*. Rosen made the very sensible suggestion that Schoenberg relied as much as he did on canons, despite his own recognition that they were no longer the compositional achievement that they once had been, because during his pre-serial atonal period they provided a guide to writing in the absence of conventional norms, similar to the guide that the series would eventually provide in twelve-tone music.[65] (And this jibes, by the way, with the original rise of pervading imitation in Franco-Flemish polyphony in the fifteenth century; it mainly occurred at first in the *tenor tacet* sections of Masses and motets, where

---

62. See, e.g., Edward T. Cone, "Editorial Responsibility and Schoenberg's Troublesome 'Misprints,'" *Perspectives of New Music* 11 (1972): 65–75.
63. Puffett, "Structural Imagery," 20.
64. Charles Rosen, *Arnold Schoenberg* (New York: Viking, 1975), 49.
65. Ibid., 54–55.

it provided a scaffolding that elsewhere the cantus firmus had supplied.) Canonic writing also provided a criterion of correctness that reassured the composer, however arcane or even specious the criteria of harmonic correctness might be under conditions of emancipated dissonance.

Therefore I think we might extend Rosen's point as a way of understanding why Webern continued to rely heavily on canonic writing, and even touted it as a compositional achievement, when writing twelve-tone music, where there was once again a built-in criterion of correctness on which both analysts and performers could rely (though not infallibly) in critiquing the text.[66] Webern's boast, at the end of *Der Weg zur neuen Musik,* that the second movement of his Symphonie, op. 21, has a unity that "even the Netherlanders" could not have managed, is often regarded as naive, at least when compared with Schoenberg's wily urbanity.[67] In twelve-tone music, canons don't even have whatever merit they might possess in "Der Mondfleck." And Webern could never be accused of self-mocking irony. But if you count moral probity as a musical merit, then Webern's insistence on multiple or even redundant criteria of correctness makes not only aesthetic but also ethical sense, adding yet another dimension to his musical utopia.

---

66. For a sensible caveat with respect to Stravinsky, see Joseph N. Straus, "Stravinsky's Serial 'Mistakes,'" *Journal of Musicology* 18 (1999): 231–71.

67. Anton Webern, *The Path to New Music,* ed. Willi Reich, trans. Leo Black (Vienna: Universal Edition, 1960), 56.

7

Nicht blutbefleckt?

"Good heavens, I've never thought of it," Milton Babbitt exclaimed when a Canadian journalist asked him about the possible influence of the Cold War on his thinking about—hence his writing of—his music. "It certainly didn't have any influence on me in any musical way," he insisted, even while admitting that the politics of earlier decades had "profoundly influenced his politics and philosophy," according to the interviewer, Paul Mitchinson[1]—and even after Martin Brody had broken the ground for musical studies of "Cold War culture" with a study precisely of Babbitt,[2] conducted not by (let's say) an unsympathetic West Coast music historian, but by a member of the clan of academic serialists, albeit one who could be described, in words he had used to describe another, as "a staunch and impassioned, if progressively more disenchanted, partisan."[3] Babbitt had sat for interviews on the way to the Cold War article, and Brody thanks him for this "cooperation in editing them."[4] Had Babbitt forgotten? Did he suddenly disagree with what he had told his earlier interviewer?

Would that it were so simple. The seeming contradiction arose out of Babbitt's widely shared conviction that politics-and-philosophy was one thing, composing

---

Originally published as "Afterword: *Nicht blutbefleckt?*" *Journal of Musicology* 26, no. 2 (2009) (special issue: "Music and the Cold War"): 274–84.

1. Paul Mitchinson, "The Sound of Political Dissonance," *National Post,* 21 July 2001.
2. Martin Brody, "'Music for the Masses': Milton Babbitt's Cold War Music Theory," *Musical Quarterly* 77 (1993): 161–92.
3. Martin Brody, Review of *To Boulez and Beyond: Music in Europe since "The Rite of Spring"* by Joan Peyser, *Notes* 57 (2000–2001): 151–53, at 153.
4. Brody, "'Music for the Masses,'" 186.

another. But that conviction was an aspect of his politics and philosophy; and Brody had very effectively shown how Cold War (and prewar) anticommunism had furnished Babbitt with the incentive to develop his intransigent brand of music theory as well as the music that the theory justified, and that, in turn, gave the theory a *raison d'être*. Babbitt's composing and theorizing have always been symbiotic—famously and influentially so. The music and the heady combination of visionary speculation and rigorous analysis that accompanied it were mutually validating, and for a while that symbiosis of music and analysis was powerfully institutionalized in the pioneering Princeton PhD program in composition and in its clones, the countless other degree programs that Princeton's made not only possible but also necessary.

That Princeton degree program, inaugurated in 1962, was a major trophy of the Cold War. The call for it had come in 1958, the year after Sputnik, in Babbitt's celebrated if generally misunderstood manifesto "Who Cares If You Listen?"[5] What is misunderstood is its purpose, which was not to mock the "lay" audience or the composers it applauded so much as to convince the academic community (and his own university's administration in particular) that the most advanced music composition had reached the point where it deserved recognition as a type of scholarly or scientific research. That "immediate and eventual" purpose required an ever more resolute and vigilant restriction of "serious" musical discourse to a logical-positivist purview—or what Babbitt (in an article that Brody subjects to a useful gloss) more simply and loosely called "'scientific' language and 'scientific' method"—as well as an ever more abstract and technical conception of musical content and value.[6] The retreat into the ivory tower that Babbitt here advocated has

---

5. Based on a transcript of an improvised lecture, originally titled "Off the Cuff," which Babbitt had delivered at Tanglewood in the summer of 1957 (thus a couple of months before Sputnik). At the invitation of Roland Gelatt, the editor of *High Fidelity* magazine, Babbitt submitted it for publication under the title "The Composer as Specialist"; Gelatt ran it in the February 1958 issue under the now legendarily confrontational title that has ensured its lasting fame and its inclusion in innumerable anthologies. Babbitt registered his regrets in his own inimitable way in a memoir he delivered as a lecture at the request of the American Council of Learned Societies: "The talk was overheard by the editor of a magazine impredicatively entitled *High Fidelity*. He asked me to write it for publication; I resisted, he insisted, I capitulated, coward that I was and still am. My title for the article was 'The Composer as Specialist,' not thereby identifying that role of the composer in which he necessarily revelled, but in which, necessarily, he found himself. The editor, without my knowledge and—therefore—my consent or assent, replaced my title by the more 'provocative' one: 'Who Cares if You Listen?' a title which reflects little of the letter and nothing of the spirit of the article" (Milton Babbitt, "A Life of Learning," Charles Homer Haskins Lecture, ACLS Occasional Paper No. 17 [online at http://w.acls.org/uploadedFiles/Publications/OP/Haskins/1991_MiltonBabbitt.pdf], 15).

6. The article is "Past and Present Concepts of the Nature and Limits of Music," delivered, significantly enough, at a musicological congress and published in its proceedings: *International Musicological Society, Report of the Eighth Congress, New York 1961*, vol. 1 (Kassel: Bärenreiter, 1961), 398–403; reprinted as the lead essay in *Perspectives on Contemporary Music Theory*, ed. B. Boretz and E. Cone (New York: W. W. Norton, 1972), 3–9 (the quoted phrase is on page 3).

been compared to Schoenberg's *Verein für musikalische Privataufführungen* of 1918,[7] but a more apposite comparison would be to Guido Adler's "Umfang, Methode und Ziel der Musikwissenschaft" of 1885, another disciplinary blueprint that sought academic acceptance for a formerly excluded branch of musical learning by casting it in rigorously scientific terms, Adler's borrowed chiefly from the biological sciences as Babbitt's were borrowed from the philosophy of science.[8] The "science envy" of the Cold War period had a lengthy prehistory.

But the Cold War changed it, or at least intensified it, significantly. The logical positivism Babbitt so admired, preeminently represented on the Princeton campus by Carl Gustav Hempel, formerly of the Vienna Circle, was (among many other things) an instrument for the critique of politics and resistance to political or religious propaganda.[9] Given the geographical origin of the school, and the fate of its members, it was at first fascist propaganda that strict empirical verificationism was seen to resist. For Babbitt, veteran of the political skirmishes of the New York intellectual scene of the thirties, the chief resistance would always be to Soviet-style communism. Rivalry with the Soviet Union in the era of the superpowers, and after science had vouchsafed the decisive Allied victory in World War II, was what gave science the measure of glamour in the late 1950s and 60s that it took to (among many other things) persuade Princeton to authorize a research degree for musical composition. That the music recognized by that degree would be twelve-tone music went at first without saying. Twelve-tone music was the only music sufficiently abstract, autonomous, consistent, and self-referential to withstand a logical-positivist critique.[10]

The status of twelve-tone music as a no-spin zone, a haven of political nonalignment and implicit resistance in the postwar world, was widely touted and accepted from the start, both in Europe, where it could be seen to embody the "neither/nor" option within the territories formerly held or occupied by the fascists, now being wheedled by the two formerly allied, now opposing Cold War

---

7. E.g., in Piero Weiss and Richard Taruskin, ed., *Music in the Western World: A History in Documents*, 2nd ed. (Belmont, CA: Thomson/Schirmer, 2007), p. 481.

8. On Adler's aims and achievement, see Kevin Karnes, *Music, Criticism, and the Challenge of History: Shaping Modern Musical Thought in Late Nineteenth Century Vienna* (New York: Oxford University Press, 2008). The document itself is available in English translation, with a useful gloss, in Erica Mugglestone, "Guido Adler's 'The Scope, Method, and Aim of Musicology' (1885): An English Translation with an Historico-Analytical Commentary," *Yearbook for Traditional Music* 13 (1981): 1–21.

9. See Babbitt's essay "'My Vienna Triangle in Washington Square,' Revisited and Dilated" (1999), in *The Collected Essays of Milton Babbitt*, ed. Stephen Peles et al. (Princeton: Princeton University Press, 2003), 466–87.

10. Or so its advocates argued: see Benjamin Boretz, *Meta-Variations: Studies in the Foundations of Musical Thought* (Red Hook, NY: Open Space Publications, 1994). This long essay is actually Boretz's 1970 Princeton dissertation, completed under Babbitt's supervision, first published in *Perspectives of New Music* 7, no. 1 (1969–70), 1–74; 8, no. 2 (1969–70): 49–111; and 9, no. 1 (1970–71): 23–42.

powers,[11] and in America, where Aaron Copland, for one, sought refuge in it when called to account for his erstwhile political engagements.[12] These were among the factors determining serialism's seeming natural selection—in a development no one had predicted before the war—as a musical lingua franca, or even as the basis for a new era of common practice, with a prestige that not even Stravinsky could resist. And they were what ultimately made the utopian extension into "total serialism"—the use of neutral, culturally unburdened algorithms to control an ever greater number of musical parameters, in addition to pitch—so compelling. These postwar concerns were even projected backwards—with an assist from Babbitt's tendentious claim, in the article referenced in note 9, that Schoenberg, Schenker, and the Vienna Circle of logical positivists were the three points of a triangle within which he located his own turf—onto the work of the original Viennese trinity.

This was of course a serious historical error: Schoenberg's intensely subjective and metaphysical conceptions could scarcely have had any less to do with the philosophy of logical positivism, but for Babbitt—and, following Babbitt, many others—it became an article of faith as they traced the ancestry of the highly rationalized American academic serialism of the Cold War era back to the origins of Schoenbergian atonality in *fin de siècle* Vienna, and then yet further back to the universal, canon-defining figures to whom Schoenberg himself had appealed for validation. That patrimony—unrecognized and unclaimed in the Europe of "Schoenberg est mort"—gave the American serial ascendency its biggest push. The Cold War was one of its essential preconditions.

Babbitt's seemingly disingenuous disavowal of Cold War influence was typical of its beneficiaries. The politics of the apolitical stance fosters compartmentalization, and this too is something that goes much further back than the Cold War. Our German romantic heritage has conditioned us to imagine, in the words of Schopenhauer, that "alongside world history there goes, guiltless and unstained by blood [*schuldlos und nicht blutbefleckt*], the history of philosophy, science, and the arts."[13] The thought is undeniably attractive for the alibis it makes available. Defenders of aesthetic autonomy habitually ward off the threat of political or social contextualization with nervous sarcasm: "an unsuspecting public is led astray," according to a typically forced parody by Pieter van den Toorn, "by the formalist, specialist 'talk' of 'cold-war' meanies such as Milton Babbitt, Igor Stravinsky, Robert Craft and Allen Forte." But never fear, he teases; "the same public is nursed

---

11. See Mark Carroll, *Music and Ideology in Cold War Europe* (Cambridge: Cambridge University Press, 2006).

12. See Jennifer L. DeLapp, "Copland in the Fifties: Music and Ideology in the McCarthy Era" (PhD diss., University of Michigan, 1997).

13. Arthur Schopenhauer, *Parerga und paralipomena* (1851), best known by musicians as the epigraph to the score of Pfitzner's opera *Palestrina* (1917).

back to musical health and well-being, . . . to an appreciation of its own best interests, by the sympathetic intervention of its friendly neighborhood historical musicologist."[14]

Equally squeamish—and equally strategic—is Charles Rosen's phobic reaction to reception studies, by now the most widely practiced and uncontroversial aspect of contextualization.[15] It leads him to regard any contextualized study, even my *Oxford History of Western Music*, as an implicit "claim that the history of any art is the concern only of the receivers and not the creators." This, he warns, "is unwisely reductionist," as indeed it would be, were it my claim.[16] What I do claim is that stories are the creation of tellers, not doers, that they are thus distanced from the events that they portray, and that they are rhetorical constructions that respond to many intellectual currents and have political and social, as well as aesthetic, objectives. That late-twentieth-century reception was in large part molded by the Cold War is by now the uncontroversial consensus among professional historians, as a long list of scholars and publications attests,[17]—a consensus that has received an effective popularization at the hands of Alex Ross.[18]

But Rosen is enraged by the suggestion, hence his attempt to discredit my account of twentieth-century music history and historiography with slyly calculated praise. "Volumes 4 and 5 of *The Oxford History*," he wrote,

> are devoted to the twentieth century, and are the result of formidable research, presented in the liveliest way. The movements in the history of the last century are laid out at length: neoclassicism, expressionism, atonality, futurism, symphonic jazz, minimalism, electronic music—all there, with all the gossip, the factional struggles,

---

14. Pieter C. van den Toorn, "Review-Essay: Will Stravinsky Survive Postmodernism?" *Music Theory Spectrum* 22 (2000): 104.

15. This reaction is most vividly viewed in "Did Beethoven Have All the Luck?," Rosen's review of Tia DeNora's *Beethoven and the Construction of Genius: Musical Politics in Vienna, 1792–1803*, in the *New York Review of Books* (43, no. 18 [14 November 1996]), and the ensuing exchange with the author (44, no. 6 [10 April 1997]). In Rosen's later collection, *Critical Entertainments* (Cambridge, MA: Harvard University Press, 2000), he reprinted both his original review and his answer to DeNora, but not her rebuttal.

16. Charles Rosen, "From the Troubadours to Frank Sinatra," part 2, *New York Review of Books* 53, no. 4 (9 March 9 2006).

17. A short list would include Amy C. Beal, *New Music, New Allies: American Experimental Music in West Germany from the Zero Hour to Reunification* (Berkeley: University of California Press, 2006); Rachel Beckles Willson, *Ligeti, Kurtag, and Hungarian Music during the Cold War* (Cambridge: Cambridge University Press, 2007); Elizabeth Bergman Crist, *Music for the Common Man: Aaron Copland during the Depression and War* (New York: Oxford University Press, 2005); Carroll, *Music and Ideology in Cold War Europe*; Danielle Fosler-Lussier, *Music Divided: Bartók's Legacy in Cold War Europe* (Berkeley: University of California Press, 2007); David C. Paul, *Charles Ives in the Mirror: American Histories of an Iconic Composer* (Champaign: University of Illinois Press, 2013); and Lisa Jakelski, *Making New Music in Cold War Poland: The Warsaw Autumn Festival* (Oakland: University of California Press, 2016).

18. Alex Ross, *The Rest Is Noise: Listening to the Twentieth Century* (New York: Farrar, Straus & Giroux, 2007), of which the final third is by a considerable margin the freshest and most original part.

and the internecine warfare in the different camps. The information is well organized with the chief emphasis on music in America, and Taruskin's account is magnificently detailed. What he is unable to do, however, is give us any idea why anybody would want to write, or listen to, most of the music of the century that he treats at such length.[19]

I accept this assessment with gratitude, in all its aspects. The favorable comments, working here as a foil to set off what Rosen regards as my failure to accomplish the chief task of historians, actually relate to what I regard as legitimate historiography, while the failure is a failure of advocacy. Advocacy is not a historian's task, and a historian who indulges in it has become a propagandist. As one who regards Rosen's literary output—all of it—as Cold War propaganda, I am heartened that he perceives the distinction between our objectives and our methods the same way I do. But while I accept and appreciate his judgment, I dispute the facts as he presents them. For my account abounds in explanations of why many have wanted to write, perform, and listen to the music of the twentieth century, although it is presented without the obligatory endorsement Rosen correctly finds lacking.

It is that sense of obligatory endorsement that characterizes Cold War accounts of modernist music, and provides a counterpart to the obligatory rejection demanded of historians writing on the other side of that long-lasting geopolitical divide. This comes out most clearly when Rosen reaches my chapter devoted to Elliott Carter (and devoting a whole chapter to Carter—something other reviewers have viewed with surprise and occasional indignation—should leave no doubt as to the historical importance I ascribe to him). Carter is a composer Rosen has long and fervently championed both as a performer and as a critic. My account of Carter's career took specific note of Rosen's role in promoting him, and that insured a counterpunch:

> Taruskin finds himself goaded by the prestige Carter's music has recently gained to write forty pages on him that are detailed without ever being illuminating, unable to explain why some find the music so eloquent and fascinating. I know of no other distinguished scholar so anxious to display not only his talents but his limitations with such panache, as if they were stigmata.[20]

The last sally is witty, but it is contextualization itself that for Rosen counts as a limitation—as indeed, in some ways, it is. My whole purpose in writing those forty pages was to account for and interpret Carter's superlative prestige, dating as it did precisely from the European première of Carter's First Quartet, which took place in 1954 at the Rome festival of contemporary music that his old friend Nicolas Nabokov had organized on behalf of the Congress for Cultural Freedom, the most

---

19. Rosen, "From the Troubadours to Frank Sinatra," part 2.
20. Ibid.

prominent—and by now (thanks to its subsequently disclosed CIA connections) the most notorious—cultural organization on the Western side of the Cold War, which Nabokov then headed as secretary-general. I did little else but quote rapturous comments—from Stravinsky, William Glock, Joseph Kerman, Andrew Porter, Bayan Northcott, and Rosen himself, among others—testifying to their belief in Carter's eloquence and allure (an enthusiasm that in the case of that First Quartet, among other works, I fully share, although the *Oxford History* was not the proper place for me to say so). But I did not and do not acknowledge that such responses are wholly innocent, spontaneous, and unmediated reactions to the immanent qualities of "the music itself." They are certainly not disinterested. Critics, performers, and impresarios are participants in prestige machines both as dispensers and as recipients. Rosen's involvement with Carter in the network of such relationships came a little later than Nabokov's, but it was, similarly, both personal and professional, and included the receipt of emoluments in the form of stipends administered through the Fromm Foundation for Music and the rent-free use of the Carters' apartment for long periods of time.[21]

Thus they are not *schuldlos und nicht blutbefleckt,* and I did not instruct my readers to embrace them. The cardinal tasks of the historian, as I conceive them, are to maintain skepticism in the face of such claims and exhortations; if not to dispute taste, at least to interrogate and account for it; and above, all, to disenchant auras and demystify discourses. Those are indeed limitations, if one so chooses to describe them. They are the constraints and injunctions that preserve the special identity and the special mission of scholarship amid the manifold pressures that constantly threaten to divert or seduce it to other tasks.

Carter was as emblematic a figure on the one side of the Cold War divide as, say, Tikhon Nikolayevich Khrennikov was on the other. Both were well trained and highly competent makers; both produced works that defined a standard of orthodoxy—of exemplary values given a model realization—within their respective milieux; both were beneficiaries of organized prestige machines; both were insulated from negative critique; both were rewarded with every prize and perquisite of rank within the power of their respective milieux to bestow; and both enjoyed major careers and achieved true historical significance (and in Carter's case, as he approached his hundredth birthday, genuine if relatively minor media celebrity) without having any real audience for their work. That is one of the things that the Cold War made possible. Any account of such careers that does not acknowledge the role of publicity and propaganda in their maintenance is an example of that propaganda.

---

21. See Rachel S. Vandagriff, "An Old Story in a New World: Paul Fromm, the Fromm Music Foundation, and Elliott Carter," *Journal of Musicology* 35 (2018): 535–66.

All of this has always gone without saying when speaking of Soviet music and the Soviet musical establishment. But why should it be any less obvious on the other side? Merely because it's "our" side, and what is ours is transparent? And above all, why should it be kept from view? Because a political advantage is at stake? That asymmetry is a historiographical blemish. As long as it remains, the role of Cold War politics cannot and must not go without saying when speaking of Carter or Babbitt; or the political (and, at first, the Allied military) sponsorship of the Darmstadt *Ferienkurse;* or the role of politically connected philanthropic foundations in the maintenance of modern music in America; or the high subsidies set aside for the dissemination of avant-garde music on West German radio, where stations (in the cunning words of Björn Heile) "competed for prestige but not for resources," and which lasted only—and exactly—until reunification.[22]

But is it really so transparent or invisible? Do we not see more than we claim or say we see (or allow ourselves, having seen, to register and report)? Is it not plain as day that the same artists and spokespersons who habitually deride political contextualization habitually use the language of politics to describe artistic phenomena? Open practically any text on twentieth-century music, historical or analytical, practically at random, and you will see words like *progressive* or *conservative* or *radical* or *reactionary*—the same words you will hear in any political campaign (not to mention *revolutionary,* a word that also sees a lot of use in marketing). "Varèse," writes Arnold Whittall, "whose early contacts were with Strauss and Busoni, and whose style was grounded in Debussy and Stravinsky, was never as determinedly progressive as Ives or Satie."[23] "Some of Scriabin's devices," James M. Baker complains, "seem surprisingly conservative."[24] "Although they are cast in seemingly traditional moulds," Ethan Haimo reassures us, "the forms of [Schoenberg's] Wind Quintet are quite revolutionary."[25] (Love that "quite"!)

Such usages are not innocuous. They do sow confusion. When used to describe artistic styles and methods, they are not purged of their political associations, and the proof is the persistence of the wholly mistaken assumption that "progressive" artists are politically "progressive" as well—an assumption that has been much shaken over the last couple of decades by the gradual emergence (against much opposition from idealizers) of evidence as to the actual political sympathies of Stravinsky, Schoenberg, Webern, and many other modernists. But yet it persists,

---

22. Björn Heile, Review of *New Music, New Allies: American Experimental Music in West Germany from the Zero Hour to Reunification* by Amy Beal, *Music & Letters* 89 (2008): 686–687.

23. Arnold Whittall, *Musical Composition in the Twentieth Century* (Oxford: Oxford University Press, 1999), 268. The sentence comes from a chapter called "Radicals and Rituals."

24. James M. Baker, *The Music of Alexander Scriabin* (New Haven, CT: Yale University Press, 1986), 20.

25. Ethan Haimo, *Schoenberg's Serial Odyssey: The Evolution of His Twelve-Tone Method, 1914–1928* (Oxford: Clarendon Press, 1990), 108.

and adds to the complacency with which Cold War attitudes have withstood changes in the political weather, including the end of the Cold War. But without understanding why Stravinsky, Schoenberg, or Webern should have been led at various times to embrace the political right, including its most *blutbefleckte* strains, one can hardly hope to understand modernism as a cultural phenomenon. Or antimodernism, for that matter: when George Rochberg broke with modernism in the 1970s, he was attacked as a political reactionary as well as an artistic one, and the pitch neared hysteria. "His works could become cultural fodder for the New Right: Down with progressive thought! Down with progressive music!" ranted Andrew Porter.[26] "I used to wonder," John Rockwell has confessed, "how could highly politicized neo-conservative critics like Hilton Kramer and Samuel Lipman idolize modernism? Surely, I assumed, modernism had a built-in revolutionary component."[27] If such views look silly now, it is the scholars who have brought the hidden discourses of the Cold War into the light of day whom we have to thank.

Peter Schmelz has written of the "difficulties surrounding a topic as contentious as the Cold War, especially for those who still personally recall its tumultuous events."[28] Perhaps that is why most of the scholars who have thematized the Cold War in their work come from younger generations, for whom the Cold War is as closed a book as the Civil War or the Hundred Years War. But those of us who do remember the period remember it not only for its tumultuous events—I for one will never forget wandering aimlessly all day, a seventeen-year-old college sophomore, from movie theater to movie theater (and they were all full of wanderers like me, even at noon), on Thursday, October 25, 1962, when the Strategic Air Command was in the air in a state of full readiness for the only time in its history, when Soviet freighters bearing military hardware were approaching the quarantine line John F. Kennedy had declared around Cuba, and when millions like me were convinced it was the last day of their lives—but also, and perhaps more significantly, for the daily routines and conditions that made us all constantly aware of our helplessness and fragility. From first grade until high school, I was accustomed to "taking cover" under my classroom desk in instantaneous response to a barked command over the school public address system that might interrupt any lesson or activity. Various streets in my neighborhood bore signs warning that they would be closed "in the event of atomic attack." The magazine *Junior Scholastic,* distributed to American schoolchildren monthly, regularly showed us drawings of robotic com-

---

26. Andrew Porter, *Musical Events* (New York: Summit Books, 1987), 292.

27. John Rockwell, "Music View: Reactionary Musical Modernists," *New York Times,* 11 September 1988.

28. Peter Schmelz, "Introduction: Music in the Cold War," *Journal of Musicology* 26 (2009): 12 (the first of a pair of special issues, with contributions by Joy H. Calico, Laura Silverberg, Leslie A. Sprout, Stephen A. Crist, Robert Fallon, and Phil Ford; the present essay served as the opposite bookend, the afterword to the second special issue).

munist legions poised to strike at a word from their maniacal leaders. Everyday conversation was peppered with phrases like MAD (mutually assured destruction) and "nuke-speak." Popular culture flooded us with doomsday dramas: one week Rod Serling's *Twilight Zone* might show us neighbors killing neighbors over access to fallout shelters during a sneak attack; the next week we might see a fantasy of stopping time with the bomb-bearing rockets visible in the night sky, with no possibility of starting up again without bringing on the looming catastrophe.

I believe it is fair to say that the Cold War gave Americans at home a far greater scare than any of the actual wars our armies fought overseas. (And not even the Civil War, fought on American soil, threatened such massive civilian casualties.) How could anyone's psychic equilibrium remain undisturbed? (Mine was definitely unbalanced in my early college days: I could never take seriously plans or promises that had to do with anything that lay more than a few days in the future.) How could the artistic expressions of such psyches fail to reflect that disturbance? According to Robert Fallon, not even the sublimely unobservant Messiaen managed to escape.[29] And even Arnold Whittall recently conceded of Allen Forte, that most ardent upholder of the *Schuldlosigkeit* of atonal (and tonal) music, that "no doubt the extent to which he was intellectually formed by war and Cold War should no more be discounted than the extent to which some British analysts were formed by grammar schools" (even if, unsurprisingly, no follow-through was forthcoming).[30] No wonder it was an age of artistic extremes. Is there any point in pretending that the autonomous history of art, unaided, had brought art to such a pass?

Today's young scholars have no emotional investment in such a pretense. Somewhat alleviated fear enables a more dispassionate perspective, whether on the musical history of the Soviet bloc, which can be viewed now other than as a monolith, or on that of the postwar West, where politics took the form of frantic endeavors to put political engagement at bay. Louis Menand's insistence that when contemplating a picture by Jackson Pollock one does not "think about 'artistic free enterprise' or the C.I.A. or the cultural politics of *Partisan Review*" is an excellent example of that frantic endeavor. It is an attempt to control what viewers shall think, and it is a particularly odious defiance of historians and an attempt to counter their influence. Menand's further contention that, instead, "you think about how a painter could have taken all he had experienced across a creative threshold that no one had crossed before, and produced this particular thing," in no way

---

29. Robert Fallon, "Birds, Beasts, and Bombs in Messiaen's Cold War Mass," *Journal of Musicology* 26 (2009): 175–204.

30. Arnold Whittall, "Allen Forte in *Music Analysis*," *Music Analysis* 26 (2007): 10. The reference to grammar schools was an oblique concession to Dai Griffiths's "Genre: Grammar Schoolboy Music," *Critical Musicology Newsletter*, no. 3 (1995); reprinted in *Music, Culture and Society: A Reader*, ed. Derek B. Scott (Cambridge: Cambridge University Press, 2000), 143–45.

contradicts the historian's project.[31] It is just that he espouses, and advocates, an unaccountably (and inadmissibly) partial—and sanitized—version of the experience that impels, governs, and finds itself embodied in artistic creation.

With Pollock, surely, one is not dealing with someone who is *schuldlos und nicht blutbefleckt*. But the guilt and blood a critic like Menand will admit into a discussion of Pollock is presumably only guilt over booze and fornication, and the blood shed in a fatal car crash. Most musicologists won't admit even that much into a discussion of their favorite composers. But Pollock was an entirely knowing beneficiary of Cold War promotion, and so were John Cage, Morton Feldman, and any number of others of whom it is still conventional to say that they were so much better appreciated in Europe than at home. The role of Cold War policy in their histories is part of our history, and we must report it. That effort will spur our discipline toward an infusion of *neues Blut* and a new recognition of our proper *Schuldigkeiten*. It is and will remain for us *der rechte Fleck*.

POSTSCRIPT, 2018

Charles Rosen replied to this piece with his accustomed panache and in his accustomed venue, the *New York Review of Books,* in the issue of 7 April 2011 under the title "Music and the Cold War," and reprinted it the next year in what turned out to be his last book, *Freedom and the Arts,* as an addendum to his reprinted—very feisty—review of *The Oxford History of Western Music.*[32] Like me, my late colleague and frequent adversary was always ready and willing to engage. Both of us have taken criticism for excessive polemical zeal, but I was always grateful for his keenness, which even as it occasionally stung, more than compensated for whatever annoyance it may have caused with extra opportunities for the airing of views and (eventual) shedding of light. I miss his presence on the scene, which is duller without him, and hope that this final detailed rejoinder, to which he will not be able to respond, will be taken by those who do read it in a spirit of appreciation, as I intend it.

As I might have expected, Rosen read my argument about the effect of the Cold War on the reception of modernist art the way such arguments were often read when they were new. "Whatever success and prestige in music and painting American modernism has achieved," he said I said, "are mainly due to the efforts of promotion by the CIA and the US State Department in order to counter Soviet propaganda during the cold war years," and in almost immediate reiteration, "the

---

31. Louis Menand, "Unpopular Front: American Art and the Cold War," *New Yorker,* 17 October 2005, 178.

32. Charles Rosen, *Freedom and the Arts: Essays on Music and Literature* (Cambridge, MA: Harvard University Press, 2012), 240–47.

prestige of American modernism is basically due to the programs of the CIA and the American government."

But the claim is no longer new, and there is no longer any excuse for such distortion by exaggeration. Substitute "partly" for "mainly" and "basically," and substitute "Congress for Cultural Freedom" (or CCF, the visible and vocal patron) for "CIA" (one of its covert funders), and the claim becomes moderate, plausible, and in fact uncontroversial now that so much evidence has been adduced in so many sober publications, like the ones listed in note 17 above.[33] Thus Rosen's assertion that "there is no evidence at all that the CIA was interested in twelve-tone music or even simply in difficult and dissonant modernism," while literally and narrowly true, is an impertinence. The CIA was interested in abetting organizations, like the CCF, that could persuade Western European intellectuals that the *laissez-faire* policies toward the arts and sciences favored by the liberal democracies of the West were worthy of their endorsement, that the best evidence of creative freedom was diversity, and that tolerance of elitist art gave good evidence of disinterestedness on the part of those who might elsewhere be inclined to oppose or police it.[34]

Rosen adduces the fact that works by Samuel Barber, one of the most conservative American composers in Carter's age cohort, were also performed "at the very same festival in Rome at which Carter's First Quartet was introduced to a European public," as if that refuted the "taint" (echoing Schopenhauer's *Fleck*) of Cold War promotion. But Cold War promotion is just a fact, not a *Fleck*. (Rosen himself allows that "any success whatever in the arts is always due to some kind of promotion, whether the beneficiary be the Beatles or Jackson Pollock or Richard Taruskin.") And the fact that Barber was promoted too only proves the point about diversity. He objects to my use of the epithet "prestige machine," which to him implies wickedness. But what I actually meant by the phrase was only that organizations like the CCF were set up for the specific, dedicated, and morally neutral purpose of creating prestige as an aspect of what was known as "soft power," defined by Joseph Nye, who coined the term, as the way in which "one country gets other countries to want what it wants."[35]

With respect to Carter's First String Quartet, Rosen argues that its success, and the "superlative prestige" it brought its composer, were "not due principally to the

---

33. On the rhetorical ploy of substituting "CIA" for all the overtly political patronage the arts received during the Cold War, see R. Taruskin, "In from the Cold," a review of *Nicolas Nabokov: A Life in Freedom and Music* by Vincent Giroud, *Times Literary Supplement*, 3 August 2016, 3–5

34. The classic statement of purpose, once the CIA's role was exposed, was "I'm Glad the CIA Is 'Immoral,'" by Thomas W. Braden, the head of the agency's International Organizations Division, which appeared in the *Saturday Evening Post* in the issue of 20 May 1967 (pp. 10–14) and which may be accessed online at www.cambridgeclarion.org/press_cuttings/braden_20may1967.html.

35. Joseph S. Nye, Jr., *Bound to Lead: The Changing Nature of American Power* (New York: Basic Books, 1990), 166.

CIA-sponsored performance at the Rome 1954 festival of contemporary music but to admiration for the work and recognition of its quality." But again a prejudicial word (this time it is *principally*) is inserted into a true statement to make it appear false, and a specious pair of alternatives is advanced. There is no contradiction between my citation of the politically marked circumstances surrounding the quartet's performance and the admiration expressed in the review that William Glock published in *Encounter,* the CCF's chief English-language organ, which (as I made sure to mention) I fully share, and which started the quartet on its way toward wide exposure, and the composer toward preeminence among American modernist composers.[36] Against this Rosen quotes Anne C. Shreffler, who correctly records the fact that the quartet elicited "mixed reviews" after its Rome performance.[37] But Glock's review, both because of its venue and because of the stature of the reviewer, was the one that counted. (Rosen, or the *NYRB* editors, indirectly if inadvertently acknowledged this by illustrating Rosen's rebuttal to my piece with a photograph of Carter and Glock, for many years the controller of music for the BBC and, along with Rosen, one of Carter's most faithful and influential promoters.)

Martin Brody, whose article on Milton Babbitt's "Cold War music theory" got the ball rolling on these questions a quarter century ago, wrote a letter to the editor of the *New York Review* to clarify some of the points at issue in Rosen's quarrel with me. It was not printed at the time, but Prof. Brody sent me a copy that he has now given me permission to cite. He is an important witness, exceptionally well situated to comment. His vantage point was the American Academy in Rome, where he served in 2001 as composer in residence, and later as arts director. (Nicolas Nabokov had preceded him in the former position.) What follows is his description, based on what he described to me as "snooping around" the academy's (and other) archives in preparation for an eventual fully documented account, of the relevant soft-power network that surrounded the Rome festival at which Carter's quartet had its auspicious European première:

> For all of 1953–4, Nicolas Nabokov, Secretary-General of the Congress for Cultural Freedom and impresario of the Rome Festival, was also Resident Composer at the American Academy in Rome. Carter was also a Fellow of the Academy during the same year. After its re-opening shortly after the war, the American Academy in Rome became a hotbed of US cultural diplomacy, known as the third American Embassy, alongside the US embassies to Italy and the Holy See. The Academy's Director Laurance Roberts and his wife Isabel held court, with Nabokov often at their side, as premiere US cultural ambassadors in the Eternal City, then a site of intense anti-Communist soft power machinations. While mingling in this heady atmosphere,

---

36. William Glock, "Music Festival in Rome," *Encounter* 2, no. 6 (June 1954): 60–63.
37. Felix Meyer and Anne C. Shreffler, eds., *Elliott Carter: A Centennial Portrait in Letters and Documents* (Woodbridge, Suffolk: Boydell Press, 2008), 101.

and aided by his long time friend Nabokov, Carter wove his own tight set of professional networks—one that provided him with varied forms of encouragement and support for years to come.

Carter served as a trusted confidant to Secretary-General Nabokov, who . . . saw himself as a chameleon-like double agent (politics and art) and an old school humanist, whose musical tastes were colored as much by personal affinities as shifting compositional aesthetics or political expediency. His big gamble on the avant-garde in Rome was a one-off affair with messy results. But even as his strategies as a political operator and cultural impresario morphed repeatedly over the ensuing years, his loyalty to Carter and Stravinsky endured for the remainder of his life.

This is, of course, a condensed summary of a small part of a big story about the complex, volatile interplay of ideology, patronage, compositional theories and practices, musical reception, and (yes) propaganda involved in the 1954 Rome festival. In this context, Rosen's claim[s] . . . elide the question of how Carter's music might have received a significant lift from his relationship with Nabokov, et al., both during the crucial year in Rome and thereafter, and just at a time when the music was making unprecedented demands on its performers.[38]

It ought to have gone without saying, but apparently it needs to be said, that Carter's career could never have enjoyed such a rich boost from the Rome festival had his First Quartet not been the impressively excellent and moving composition that it was. To speak of its promotion or the composer's networking skills is in no way to diminish or preclude "recognition of its quality." As I used to tell my doctoral students, both with reference to the eminences about whom they were doing their research and writing and about their own impending careers, which was an even more pressing—if often tacit—concern, there are three indispensable components to any successful career: ability, ambition, and luck. These factors can be given all kinds of names. Ability subsumes aptitude, talent (genius if you wish), mastery, or call it what you will; and it can be attributed to works as well as their authors (as when Rosen invokes "quality"). Ambition, treated by the sentimental as a dirty secret, can go by such names as drive, strategy ("networking"), or industriousness, terms that have varying evaluative nuances, depending on the degree of squeamishness with which one entertains the idea that artists must make careers as well as art. Luck need not be dumb; it can be dressed up as opportunity, favorable or unfavorable environmental conditions, or "affordances." Spurious standards of musicological decorum, romantic heirlooms that I hope to see discarded one day, have long decreed that in the case of admired figures only the first category shall be deemed kosher for scholarly contemplation. But without the other two, ability would go for naught, as would the others without ability. Anyone who has

---

38. Martin Brody, undated and unpublished letter to the editor of the *New York Review of Books*, emailed to the author on 19 April 2011.

had their benefit will recognize that all three are needed, and all three need to be understood in their mutual relations.

The sin I committed in the *Oxford History*, in the eyes of Rosen and many others, was to give attention to them all in whatever proportion the case and its narrative needs seemed to demand—not only with respect to Carter but also to Schoenberg, Stravinsky, Shostakovich, Britten, and various other figures who may have been controversial in their day but who now are usually idealized in retrospect. The strongest narrative need in the case of Carter, who loomed so large at such a politically fraught juncture, pertained to the career rather than to its products, although the products were certainly not neglected. To resist idealization can register in the eyes of advocates as disrespect. I reject that assessment, to be sure, but I understand it. I offer no apology or reassurance to those who have found my approach unmannerly, but I appreciate that my efforts to resist sentimentality, being conscious and at times studied, may give offense, and I do not wonder that they have aroused anger.

Rosen is at his angriest on the subject of the Princeton PhD in composition. "Taruskin . . . oddly ascribes [it] to the cold war," he oddly writes, and warns that "Taruskin is surely too intelligent to claim seriously that Sputnik was an actual cause of the creation of the Ph.D. program, but he strategically places the phrase 'the year after Sputnik' in the hope that his readers will be stupid enough to believe it." I do take exception to the insinuation of bad faith, which is reinforced by yet another bout of prejudicial adverbs and adjectives when Rosen accuses me of peddling a "cut-rate version" of contextualization "which downgrades all serious studies by determining the ideology or significance of a work of music or art solely and simplemindedly by the ideology of the social class of the individual patrons who paid for the work." Reaching back into the vocabulary of the 1930s, he calls my version "vulgar Marxism," and offers this peroration:

> It is astonishing to see its reappearance on the stage of postmodernist theory. Such criticism is only a novel way of avoiding any serious engagement with a work or a style that one happens not to like, a way of indulging one's prejudices without admitting them, a way, in fact, of giving the impression of objectivity—exactly what I have charged Taruskin with in his writing on the twentieth century. Contextualization is an important tool of the historian, but it is never by itself a complete account of artistic success. Politics will inevitably influence some of our judgments, but to imply that all the favorable reactions quoted to Carter's First Quartet were due entirely to political propaganda is not only ungenerous, but historically irresponsible—and it does not explain why the prestige of Carter's work has endured for half a century.

Solely, simplemindedly, complete, all, entirely . . . well, enough said. I liken this mode of argumentation to a marital spat (But what about *x*? All you ever think about is *x!*). It never persuades, never moves opinion. Like a lot of today's political rhetoric, it merely plays to the "base." (And I must say, it always amuses me to see how inaccurately—and so confidently!—my critics infer my tastes from my coverage.)

But the story of the PhD program in composition is one that deserves to be gotten right. Rosen, who had a Princeton PhD (albeit not in music but in French literature), offered a corrective to my account. It contained some interesting information, as well as some misinformation. "A Ph.D. in musical composition," he wrote:

> was created for reasons that Taruskin either does not know or does not wish to know, but had nothing to do with international politics. In the 1950s, American universities were rated by the number of Ph.D.s on their faculties (although many prestigious professors did not then have a Ph.D., including the distinguished literary critic R. P. Blackmur, who did not even have a BA—he left Harvard in the middle of his undergraduate work, because, as he said, it interfered with his reading). [The two most distinguished musicologists on the Princeton faculty then, Oliver Strunk and Arthur Mendel, also did not have doctorates, and neither did Milton Babbitt, whose dissertation, notoriously, had been rejected.—R.T.] Nevertheless, a Ph.D. became necessary to a job applicant. Graduate students in musical composition were awarded only a Doctorate of Music [not so: the highest degree Princeton awarded composers then was the MFA, Master of Fine Arts—R.T.], while the prestigious Ph.D. was reserved for musicologists. This meant that when a post in a university music department for teaching harmony, counterpoint, and composition became open, it generally went to a young musicologist—a composer, as a mere D.Music, was shut out of the job market.

Yes indeed, parity of employment opportunity was the practical objective advanced by those who argued for the PhD in composition. At the conference "After the End of Music History," held at Princeton in 2012, Jeffrey Levenberg, then a graduate student in the music department there, presented some documents illustrating the history of the argument: memos from Arthur Mendel, serving as chair, detailing the disadvantages composers were suffering on the job market.[39] But that history went back much longer than Rosen, who dated it to the 1950s, seemed to realize. Michael P. Long, a musicologist now on the faculty of Indiana University but then teaching at SUNY Buffalo, serendipitously found there and later sent me a copy of a transcript recording a meeting of the Graduate Study Committee of the National Association of Schools of Music (the predecessor of all the current professional organizations of music scholars in America) that was held in December 1936, when graduate programs in music scholarship were only just being mooted, with Howard Hanson, the famous composer who then headed the Eastman School of Music at the University of Rochester, serving as chair, and such

---

39. Jeffrey Levenberg, "Bombs, Telescopes, Tunings, Timbres, and the Masses: The Cold War as Compositional Determinant," paper delivered at the session "PhD Music," 10 February 2012.

early luminaries of American musicology as Oliver Strunk (soon to join the Princeton faculty) and Otto Kinkeldey in attendance. As Prof. Long put it in his cover letter, the committee's deliberations laid "the programmatic foundation for academic music study (from language requirements to qualifying exams) as it is still configured at the post-baccalaureate level in most U.S. universities."[40]

The one issue that proved contentious, and which was left unresolved with a vote split down the middle, was precisely the question of whether it was appropriate to award the PhD, a research degree, for creative work. Thus the issue had been festering a long time by the time Milton Babbitt made his appeal at Tanglewood on its behalf in 1957, the year (as I say) of Sputnik. The argument in favor in 1936 was already the meal-ticket argument to which Rosen called attention: "Composers coming from our universities," one proponent asserted, "need a job in the university," and, consequently, needed the prestige degree. The argument against was the one at which Babbitt would rail in his Tanglewood talk: the incongruity between musical composition and standard definitions of "independent" or "scientific" research. "Our dean would not consider creative work as . . . graduate work," one member of the committee warned the others. To submit such a proposal would be futile. Howard Hanson tried to broker a compromise, prefiguring what actually became the case at Princeton starting in 1962. He suggested that along with the composition, the PhD candidate submit some actual research in the form of a "written thesis." It was Oliver Strunk, eventually of Princeton, who ironically enough found this unacceptable in 1936; and others piled on, one muttering that everyone would then be "calling himself a musicologist."

The question I sought to answer by invoking Sputnik was not what motivated Babbitt's appeal, but why it proved successful this time after two decades of inconclusive complaint and fruitless debate. Babbitt's new and specific contribution to the discussion was the scientistic turn—the claim that academic composition (by which he meant serial composition) had become so rationalized and methodical as to make it tantamount to research and, as such, eligible for recognition with a PhD without having to alter in scope or intent, or in any way dilute, the highest of all earned academic degrees. That proved to be a winning argument, and it was reflected in the degree requirements that Princeton eventually formulated, which did entail a written thesis, but not the kind that Hanson had had in mind. Rather, Princeton stipulated a rigorous formal analysis of the submitted composition (or, as it often transpired in practice, some other composition that presented related "issues"). Prof. Long calls the Babbitt argument "a scientific rehabilitation of Hanson's 1936 compromise." *My* argument, not at all anachronistic in the light of this evidence, was that the Cold War, with its science anxieties, created the intellectual atmosphere in which the argument for the PhD in composition would finally per-

---

40. Michael P. Long, email to the author, 31 March 2011.

suade that reluctant dean. *That* is the reason for insisting on historical contextualization. Without it, it is impossible to say why things happened when they did.

But this is elementary, and no longer has to be explicitly defended among music historians today. My dispute with Rosen was a reverberation of ancient generational politics, and it showed its age as well as ours. In his peroration Rosen spoke for his cohort, it seems to me, when he drew such a vivid contrast between his attitude toward the Cold War and mine. "Taruskin was admittedly psychologically troubled by the atmosphere of the cold war, much more so, I think, than most Americans." I will leave it to my readers, most of whom will be even younger than I, to assess the truth of that imputation. I think it scurrilous, calculated to discredit my argument as one founded on the "unbalanced psychic equilibrium" to which I had testified. But Rosen goes on from there in a fashion that, more than anything else, associates his memories of the time with the triumphalist mood that attended the end of the world war, which I was just too young to remember myself. "For me," he wrote, "the cold war years were a time of hope and looking forward. I got a Ph.D., made my first recordings and my New York debut, and obtained a two-year Fulbright fellowship to work in Paris. The 1950s were the time when I found stronger ties to modernism, which already interested me."

These words fit so snugly into the picture I was drawing—of "postwar" on the point of shading into Cold War—in the early pages of the fifth and last volume of my *Oxford History* that were I writing the book now I would surely have pounced on them for quoting, or even pressed them into service as an epigraph. Charles Rosen, in all that he said and did, in public at any rate, exemplified that optimistic, confident mood at its best and most fruitful. He was a walking object lesson, at times a deliberately enunciated lesson, in what a gifted person granted freedom of action in the arts could make of that liberty. He was jealously and splendidly protective of his and others' freedom, to the point where anyone suggesting that there were nevertheless constraints and limiting conditions could seem to be bent on imposing said constraints and conditions. To say this of him, and I say it in admiration, is an affirmative counterpart to the negative characterization (where I declared myself "one who regards Rosen's literary output—all of it—as Cold War propaganda") that by his own avowal incited my antagonist into action. The positive and negative aspects, and the evaluations that may be drawn from them, are equally pertinent and valid. We can cherish the one without losing sight of the other.

8

What Else?

On musical representation

It's not as though representation were a neglected field, even within musicology. What else do we talk about these days? Semiotics, hermeneutics, intertextuality, topical and discourse analysis have been musicology's growth industries for decades now, and all of them take representation for granted. Even musicologists, scholarship's diehard romantics, have accepted by now that language and art are artful, and that art is meaningful. It's rather a long time since I've seen the formerly obligatory scare quotes around the word *meaning* in musicological titles. A decisive moment for me was the appearance in 1994 of the essay collection *Theory, Analysis, and Meaning* [no scare quotes] *in Music*, edited by Anthony Pople. To see such inroads even within the world of music theory and analysis, formalism's last redoubt, meant the fight was over. Why belabor it now?

But what was the fight about? It was never really about the actuality or the possibility of musical representation. No one ever denied it, not even the usual suspects. When Stravinsky, through his ghostwriter, laid down the famous gauntlet we all know by heart—

Music is, by its very nature, essentially powerless to *express* anything at all[1]

Originally presented as keynote address at the conference "Music and Representation," Merton College, University of Oxford, 25 March 2010; published as "Afterword: What Else?" in *Representation in Western Music*, ed. Joshua S. Walden (Cambridge: Cambridge University Press, 2011), 287–309.

1. Igor Stravinsky, *An Autobiography* (1936; New York: W. W. Norton, 1962), 53. The original French: "la musique, par son essence, est impuissante à *exprimer* quoi que ce soit. " The ghostwriter was Walter Nouvel.

—he (or his ghostwriter) took pains to italicize the word *express,* and by doing so implied that the word had been carefully—artfully—chosen. He knew perfectly well that if he had written *represent* instead of *express,* the assertion would have been absurd on its face, and it would not have become a point of endless debate, no matter how commanding Stravinsky's authority. The argument is not between expression and its absence, but among the many available alternatives: *express, evoke, arouse,* and so on, in addition to *represent*. Among these alternatives, *represent* certainly makes the most modest claim.

But perhaps more importantly, it has been a debate about the place of representation in the scheme of things musical. That is what Hanslick, for one, debated in his famous treastise of 1854. He never denied the existence or the possibility of representation in music; he merely claimed that it was beside the aesthetic point, and that to insist on seeking out musical representations, or to claim that therein lay the value of music, was in a fundamental way to misunderstand the musical experience. Specifically, he claimed—beginning with the implicit claim of his title—that the representational side of music was not the source of *das musikalisch-Schöne*. Aesthetics was the study or elucidation of beauty, Hanslick insisted (against what was then the New-German tide), and representation made no necessary contribution to that.

The claim could easily be expanded into other realms or media, and was. What else could Walter Pater have meant when he wrote, all in italics, that "*All art constantly aspires to the condition of music*"? He wrote this almost immediately after conceding that "some of the most delightful music seems to be always approaching to figure, to pictorial definition," which shows that he admitted representation even in the case of music, and also that it was pleasurable and, to that extent, to be valued. But when it came to what really mattered, music had an edge: "While in all other kinds of art it is possible to distinguish the matter from the form, and the understanding can always make this distinction, yet it is the constant effort of art to obliterate it." He went on from there, in the nearly impenetrable syntax that figured ecstasy:

> That the mere matter of a poem, for instance, its subject, namely, its given incidents or situation—that the mere matter of a picture, the actual circumstances of an event, the actual topography of a landscape—should be nothing without the form, the spirit, of the handling, that this form, this mode of handling, should become an end in itself, should penetrate every part of the matter: this is what all art constantly strives after, and achieves in different degrees.[2]

Music was the medium, Pater assumed, that owed the least to all those "mere" things—matter, subject, incidents, situation, circumstances, topography—and

---

2. Walter Pater, *The Renaissance: Studies in Art and Poetry* (1873; London: Macmillan, 1922), 134–35.

most to the form and spirit of the handling. Music was preeminently the medium—quoting now from Susan Sontag, one of Pater's innumerable progeny—"that dissolves considerations of content into those of form."[3] That is from "Against Interpretation," Sontag's aestheticist manifesto of 1964, and Sontag was not speaking of music; she was speaking of the arts in general, which is why I take her remark as a paraphrase of Pater's. For if critics, over the near century between Pater's 1870s and Sontag's 1960s, could look forward to the day when content would disappear into form, this only shows how baldly the form/content dichotomy was drawn in all arts media, and how unequally the members were weighted.

But we musicians were always out in front of the aestheticist wave. We are the ones, after all, who coined the word *extramusical* to denote objects of musical representation. I have never seen the face in a portrait described as extrapainterly, or the plot of a novel described as extraliterary, but I have seen actual musical allusions of an intertextual kind—quotations like "Columbia, Gem of the Ocean" in Ives, or *Dies Irae* in the *Symphonie fantastique*, or references to "characteristic" idioms as in Mendelssohn's *Scottish* or *Italian* symphonies, or even Liszt's "Gypsy" scale—described as extramusical.[4] How can actual music be extramusical? My God, but we are squeamish.

The word *extramusical*, surprisingly enough, is not to be found in the *OED*; the Merriam-Webster Online Dictionary gives 1923 as the date of earliest use.[5] The date, right in the middle of the Pater-to-Sontag century, seems plausible; but Merriam-Webster's definition—"lying outside the province of music"—is clearly inadequate, unless Liszt's Gypsy scale can be so described.

So what *does* it mean, and why?

I was first drawn into debate over musical representation when Peter Kivy began issuing his books on musical aesthetics. Until then I was a proper little formalist and had been one ever since my senior year in college, when I first read Hanslick. Hanslick seemed so much more sophisticated than his antagonists; his appreciation of art was so refined. I proselytized for him when I began teaching music appreciation, making all the usual arguments: viz., that describing form was objective, while meaning was "merely" subjective, or that when you describe form you were describing the music, whereas when you described its meaning you were merely describing yourself, and how interesting do you think *you* are?

---

3. Susan Sontag, *Against Interpretation* (New York: Delta, 1967), 12.

4. Cf. James Hepokoski, "Beethoven Reception: The Symphonic Tradition," in *The Cambridge History of Nineteenth-Century Music*, ed. Jim Samson (Cambridge: Cambridge University Press, 2001), 430; or Sok-Hoon Tan, "The 'Gypsy' Style as Extramusical Reference: A Historical and Stylistic Reassessment of Liszt's Book I 'Swiss' of *Années de pèlerinage*" (Master's thesis, University of North Texas, 2008), available via http://digital.library.unt.edu/ark:/67531/metadc6046.

5. www.merriam-webster.com/dictionary/extramusical.

Kivy's first book, *The Corded Shell*, was an attempt to show that, *pace* Hanslick, expression in music was not only pertinent to its beauty, but constituted its virtual source. To cite one specific formulation, he claimed that since saying "How full of joy Haydn's 'Emperor Quartet' is!" counts as praise, it follows that "musical discourse treats the presence of expressive properties not only as relevant to the aesthetic value of music but, in effect, tantamount to it."[6] Kivy called his theory of expression the "contour and convention" theory, from which it was already evident that he saw expression in terms of representation. He claimed that the expressive content of music could be objectively determined, understanding objectivity as intersubjective consensus, amounting in practice (imaginary practice, that is, consisting of hypothetical polls of imaginary listeners) to an appeal to majority vote.

Reviewing Kivy's book, I tried to nail him with a counterexample.[7] Twice Kivy cites the opening measures of Mozart's G-minor symphony as a self-evident paradigm of sad music, for all that it is marked *Molto allegro*, which of course literally means "very happy." "No one," Kivy remarked, "has ever been tempted to characterize [those opening measures] as 'spritely' and 'good humored.'"[8] I was able to cite two dissenters. One was Schumann, refuting the characterization of G minor in Schubart's *Ideen zu einer Aesthetik der Tonkunst* (1806). "In G minor he finds discontent, discomfort, worried anxiety over an unsuccessful plan, ill-tempered chewing of the lips," he wrote. "Now compare this idea with Mozart's Symphony in G minor, full of Hellenic grace!"[9] But the other counterexample was the one I really thought conclusive. It came from a music appreciation primer, Sigmund Spaeth's *Great Symphonies: How to Recognize and Remember Them*, in which symphonic themes were fitted out with mnemonic texts. The opening of the G-minor, Spaeth assures us, is "a very happy tune, . . . full of laughter and fun."[10] And here are the words:

> With a laugh and a smile like a sunbeam,
> And a face that is glad, with a fun-beam,
> We can start on our way very gaily,
> Singing tunes from a symphony daily.

Proof positive, this (I thought), that musical affect was not immanent but attributed. I was therefore quite astonished to find Spaeth dismissed, in Kivy's sub-

---

6. Peter Kivy, *The Corded Shell: Reflections on Musical Expression* (Princeton, NJ: Princeton University Press, 1980), 121, 125, slightly adapted for the sake of syntax.
7. R. Taruskin, Review of *The Corded Shell* by Peter Kivy, *Musical Quarterly* 68 (1982): 287–93.
8. Kivy, *The Corded Shell*, 16.
9. Robert Schumann, *On Music and Musicians*, ed. Konrad Wolff, trans. Paul Rosenfeld (New York: W. W. Norton, 1969), 60.
10. Sigmund Spaeth, *Great Symphonies: How to Recognize and Remember Them* (Garden City, NY: Garden City Publishing Co., 1936), 39.

sequent book, *Sound Sentiment* (actually a reissue of *The Corded Shell* with some extra chapters to answer his critics), as a "merely subjective" outlier, and the principle of make-believe majority vote upheld without a qualm.[11] Now there's a complacent fellow, I thought. Would that I possessed his mental insulation.

II

But I have changed my mind. I now think that I was wrong to hold up Spaeth or Schumann against Kivy's characterization of Mozart's theme—not because (as Kivy suggests in his complacency) outliers are "seriously deficient in a basic human accomplishment,"[12] but because (like me at first) they did not properly appreciate the mechanisms through which musical representation works. Representation is constrained—readily and fruitfully constrained—by convention, just as language is constrained; and therefore the sadness in Mozart's theme, being the product of a long-standing signifying practice or device, relied on insider knowledge for its correct interpretation. No party to the representational tradition that governed Mozart's choice would have mistaken the "pathetic" message that this device was designed to send, and Spaeth's or Schumann's dissent merely showed that even by Schumann's time the device in question had atrophied through desuetude.

The device, of course, was the the *pianto*, or *Seufzer*, a slurred two-note scalar descent that was originally an imitation of a sigh or moan, rife in seventeenth-century Italian operas and cantatas whenever characters or singing personas had reason to weep. Its history has been traced through the nineteenth century (as Schumann might have known; as Wagner surely did), despite the weakening hold of convention, and into the twentieth.[13] The main eighteenth-century event in its history was the wholesale transfer of the device from vocal music into instrumental genres. This can be as easily illustrated in Bach as in Mozart—for example by comparing, say, the famous aria "Seufzer, Thränen, Kummer, Noth" from Bach's cantata BWV 21 (*Ich hätte viel Bekümmerniss*) (ex. 8.1a) with the F-minor prelude from Book II of the *Well-Tempered Clavier* (ex. 8.1b).

True, the *Seufzer* is most often identified with dissonant appoggiaturas or suspensions and their resolutions, whereas Mozart uses the descending slurred semi-

---

11. Peter Kivy, *Sound Sentiment: An Essay on the Musical Emotions, Including the Complete Text of "The Corded Shell"* (Philadelphia: Temple University Press, 1989), 204.

12. Kivy, *The Corded Shell*, 148.

13. The most sustained discussion I know is Raymond Monelle, *The Sense of Music: Semiotic Essays* (Princeton, NJ: Princeton University Press, 2000), 17, 66–73; see also Robert Hatten, *Interpreting Musical Gestures, Topics, and Tropes* (Bloomington: Indiana University Press, 2004), 140–42. Hatten reminds us that the two-note descending slur, while remaining an iconic sign, has alternative uses, e.g., "as the musical analogue to such ritualized social gestures as bows, nods, inflections of the wrist and hand, and other aristocratic social graces."

EXAMPLE 8.1A. Bach, Cantata BWV 21 (*Ich hätte viel Bekümmerniss*), Aria: "Seufzer, Thränen, Kummer, Noth," mm. 22–24.

EXAMPLE 8.1B. Bach, *Well-Tempered Clavier*, II, F-minor prelude, mm. 1–2.

tone as a pickup. But its pervasiveness as a motive, in conjunction with the tonality and the extra-dark scoring at the outset (like one of Mozart's late quintets with extra viola), makes its expressive—that is, representational—intent clear enough. It is the pervasiveness that makes what for me is the essential point—viz., that there is no sense trying to separate the representational role of the gesture from the constructive role of the motive, and therefore no earthly reason even to call the affect of the music an extroversive reference, let alone an extramusical one.

Pinning the proper label on the music may seem like an accomplishment, but what has actually been accomplished? The signified attribute, the "affect" if you will, is static. It pervades the music, and the ingenuity with which Mozart manipulates the signifier—turning the *Seufzer* over or around, embedding it in strettos, sneaking it into inconspicuous corners of the texture—all of that is fascinating to ferret out and describe, but we are no longer describing a representation when we describe that. The interesting stuff still seems to be formal, or at least syntactic, as

Kofi Agawu suggests when he complains that topics, to which he has devoted so much scholarly energy, "can provide clues to what is being 'discussed' in a piece of music [but] do not seem to be able to sustain an independent and self-regulating account of a piece; they point to the expressive domain, but they have no syntax." Thus when topic succeeds topic, as they do so prodigally in Haydn or Mozart, accounts quickly devolve into lists—again static, inert. No one, Agawu admits, has found a way to tell us "why," in the introduction to Mozart's *Prague* Symphony, "the singing style should come after the outbursts of sensibility, or why fanfare is used toward the conclusion of the period."[14]

Wye J. Allanbrook, the most accomplished topical analyst by far, echoed Agawu's verdict even more pessimistically. "We have not yet been able to contribute a topical syntax, in which principles for the combination of topics are laid out," she agrees, then adds, "I have some doubt that such a thing is possible."[15] Peter Kivy himself, in his second book, *Sound and Semblance: Reflections on Musical Representation*—after mounting a vigorous, not to say vehement case for the existence of "examples of music . . . that can properly be called pictorial or representational"— admits, in the book's very last paragraph, that he has not argued, let alone shown, "that music is a representational art, if by that one means an art essentially, primarily, or even *importantly* representational."[16]

Could the implied or threatened judgment of triviality be among the reasons why interpretive studies of instrumental music, once the topical analysts gave the green light, so quickly spun out of control into gross exaggeration and fantasy? Why messages read were so confidently taken for messages sent? Why topics were inevitably teased and tarted up into all-embracing narratives and allegories? Never was a burgeoning or resurgent field more quickly plagued with abuse, it seems, than the one Carolyn Abbate so memorably dubbed, and debunked, as "low hermeneutics."[17] The article in which she did this, "Music—Drastic or Gnostic?" was a reverberation of Sontag's "Against Interpretation," and replayed Sontag's tactic of equating a practice with its abuse. Sontag's essay would have been more accurately titled "Against Overinterpretation," and Abbate's should have been called "Music—Drastic and Gnostic," but in that case we would not be quoting them today. Even so, the abuses they detailed were plain as day and needed to be called out. Low hermeneutics has given us the Shostakovich Wars and Bach the Jacobin.

14. V. Kofi Agawu, *Playing with Signs: A Semiotic Interpretation of Classic Music* (Princeton, NJ: Princeton University Press, 1991), 20.

15. Wye J. Allanbrook, "Two Threads through the Labyrinth," in *Convention in Eighteenth- and Nineteenth-Century Music: Essays in Honor of Leonard G. Ratner,* ed. W. Allanbrook, J. Levy, and W. Mahrt (Stuyvestant, NY: Pendragon Press, 1992), 170.

16. Peter Kivy, *Sound and Semblance: Reflections on Musical Representation* (Princeton, NJ: Princeton University Press, 1984), 19, 216.

17. Carolyn Abbate, "Music—Drastic or Gnostic?" *Critical Inquiry* 20 (2004): 505–36, at 516.

It has reduced composer after composer to essentialist stereotypes—sexual, national, racial, gendered—and the narratives it has proposed have been the opposite of illuminating.

I'll instance Susan McClary's reading of the opening movement of Mozart's *Prague* Symphony because it seems a direct answer to Kofi Agawu's query, quoted above. McClary organizes what for Agawu is just a random sequence of topics into a political narrative:

> Although the introduction's military rhythms and instruments suggest absolutist power ... , it begins quite benevolently. But the constant intrusion of sentimental gestures eventually seems to provoke this power into revealing itself in its most oppressive form: it turns suddenly from radiant D major to malignant D minor, and while a pleading violin line seeks to rise, the brass and timpani repeatedly come in to thwart all movement. The introduction closes locked on a dominant pedal from which there appears to be no escape.[18]

But doesn't (practically) every slow introduction end with a dominant pedal, from which we have long since learned to expect imminent release? And do contrasts always imply dialectics? McClary's assumption that sensibility is Us and fanfare is Them presupposes a subject persona implicitly identified with the composer (and thus with the listener). That subject persona, "the protagonist of the movement," as McClary calls it, is given its main portrayal in the opening theme of the Allegro (ex. 8.2a). Observe the lengths to which McClary is prepared to go—or perhaps I should say the leniency she is prepared to show—in order to uphold the coherence of the narrative:

> Mozart does not show us how the protagonist of the movement's main part manages to pull out of that apparently hopeless situation. After a fermata, the new subject simply takes over—shaky at first, but without a trace of the events that might be posited somewhere in the gap between the fermata and the Allegro. Just as a film might fade on a prison scene, then move directly to a scene we understand to be situated some years later, so Mozart suggests "that was then, this is now." Yet what causes us to accept without much hesitation this fairly abrupt juxtaposition ... is the fact that however much the materials associated with that dominant pedal imply the impossibility of progress, the harmonic function itself stands in a cause/effect relationship with the tonic. Thus when the main part of the movement begins in D major ... , the new materials serve as the proper, even inevitable resolution of the old. No struggle, no Bastille, certainly no Reign of Terror. We just find ourselves relocated in the new order. (102, 104)

So an imagined French Revolution, or at least a bloodless coup, has occurred between the fermata and the Allegro—and all because dominant has resolved to

---

18. Susan McClary, *Conventional Wisdom: The Content of Musical Form* (Berkeley: University of California Press, 2000), 102; further citations will be made in the main text.

EXAMPLE 8.2A. Mozart, Symphony no. 38 in D (*Prague*), I, mm. 1–5, 130–36.

EXAMPLE 8.2B. Mozart, Symphony no. 38 in D (Prague), I, mm. 130-36.

tonic. The shape of the exposition, from quiet first theme to ebullient codetta (ex. 8.2b), is also read as a political allegory, this time of the perpetually ascendant bourgeoisie.

> Once past the introduction, the opening movement pursues two agendas—both crucial agendas in most areas of culture at the time: first, the self-generation of the self from relatively unformed beginnings to full maturation, and second, the demonstration that the persona thus fashioning itself also harbors deep inner feelings. Again, the critical distinction in German thought between aristocratic *Civilisation* and bourgeois *Kultur* demands this articulation of inside versus outside. . . . Mozart satisfies the external narrative of becoming by starting with an unusually insecure theme

EXAMPLE 8.2C. Mozart, *Il Re Pastore,* K208 (1775) Sinfonia, mm. 1–16.

that . . . even seems uncertain about which of its elements—melody or bass—constitutes its identity. Eventually, however, it develops into a triumphant closing theme that is every bit as powerful . . . as the materials in the militant introduction. (104–5)

But again a quite ordinary sequence of events is given a very particular reading, cast moreover not as the listener's interpretation but as the composer's strategy. A chance hearing on the radio of the overture to *Il re pastore,* K. 208, a two-act serenata by the nineteen-year-old Mozart to a libretto by Metastasio, composed eleven years before the *Prague* Symphony for performance at the palace of the Archbishop of Salzburg (ex. 8.2c), made me wonder whether McClary would read its drawn-out crescendo of an opening gesture, too, as the formation and maturation of the bourgeois subject. There really is nothing to stop her, or any of us, from imposing the narrative of our choice on any favorite piece of music if doing so inspires us or enhances our pleasure, but attributing the move to the composer is a particularly flagrant example of what I call the poietic fallacy, and what Abbate, long before me, called ventriloquism.[19] It is a bid for the composer's authority.

19. See Carolyn Abbate, "Ventriloquism," in *Meaning in the Visual Arts: Views from the Outside,* ed. Irving Lavin (Princeton, NJ: Institute for Advanced Study, 1995), 305–11.

EXAMPLE 8.3. Beethoven, *Fidelio,* Act II, no. 12 (Duet).

Let's call it an esthesic abuse. But abuses connected with representation occur on the poietic side as well. Berlioz once made bold to censure Beethoven for mimetic excess. In his essay "De l'imitation musicale" he complained that, when Rocco the jailer and the disguised Leonore move a big rock out of the way while digging a grave for Florestan in act 2 of Beethoven's *Fidelio,* Beethoven has the double basses and contrabassoon accompany the rolling rock with a clumsy phrase in sixteenth-notes that makes the audience titter (ex. 8.3). "This imitation," Berlioz fumed, "being in no way necessary either to the drama or to the effectiveness of the music, is really an end in itself for the composer: he imitates in order to imitate—and at once he falls into error, for there is in such imitation no poetry, no drama, no truth."[20]

I read these words with astonishment the first time, not because Berlioz was writing disparagingly about a composer he would have us revere, but because his words confirmed misgivings I had had (and have) about a composer we have been taught to revere even more worshipfully, namely J. S. Bach. In the 1970s and 80s I was active as a viola da gamba soloist. Like any working gambist, I looked forward

---

20. Hector Berlioz, "De l'imitation musicale," trans. Jacques Barzun; quoted in Berlioz, *Fantastic Symphony,* ed. Edward T. Cone (New York: W. W. Norton, 1971), 39.

every year at Easter time to participating in performances of Bach's passions, in each of which there is an aria with a juicy gamba obbligato. The one in the St. Matthew, "Komm, süßes Kreuz," is one of the pinnacles of the literature. I was always honored to be asked to play it, and always leapt at the chance, even though Passion gigs had their drawbacks. The chief one was sitting for an hour or so on stage with nothing to do except play along occasionally with the chorales to make sure you were still in tune, and gawk at the audience. After the solo, there was nothing at all to do but gawk. So I noticed something curious that always happened at the recitative, "Und siehe da, der Vorhang im Tempel zerriß," in which the evangelist tells of the violent earthquake that follows the death of Jesus (ex. 8.4). The virtuoso continuo part, which I always envied the cellist, is pure imitation or illustration of the most literal kind. And what I noticed was that the audiences I was gawking at invariably smiled, even chuckled at it, despite the terrible events it depicted and despite the solemnity of the moment in the context of the Good Friday Gospel narrative. In rehearsals, the musicians would always laugh aloud and shout teasing encouragement to the cellist. ("Stick a fork in him" is one I've never forgotten.)

This is obviously no place for a joke; but that, it struck me, is what Bach's imitation of the earthquake inevitably was. No matter how lofty the context or exalted the theme, such imitations rely on the mechanisms of humor: puns (plays on similarities of sound), wit (apt conjunctions of incongruous things), caricature (deliberate exaggerations that underscore a resemblance). When they are good, it is because the intractability of the medium has been adroitly circumvented. When they are not, it is because they call excessive attention to their own contrivance, as is so often the case with puns. Jean-Jacques Rousseau already knew this, complaining in his *Dictionnaire de musique* of 1768 that representationally inclined composers "have to follow the example of the inept painter who must label his figures: *this is a tree, this is a man, this is a horse.*"[21] "Of course music *can* represent," I thought (and wrote when I came to review Kivy's *Sound and Semblance*), "just as a man can breathe underwater. In both cases, however, special equipment is required, special constraints are imposed, and special allowances must be made. In neither case is the thing done especially well or naturally, nor can invidious comparisons be avoided: music with painting, man with fish."[22]

Did Bach actually think of musical mimesis in terms of jokes? At times, I think, he surely did, not to say that his intention necessarily redeems them. Consider the very popular cantata BWV 67 (*Halt im Gedächtnis Jesum Christ*) for the Sunday

---

21. Jean-Jacques Rousseau, *Dictionnaire de musique* (Paris, 1768), 452; translated by R. Taruskin in *Music in the Western World: A History in Documents*, ed. Piero Weiss and Richard Taruskin, 2nd ed. (Belmont, CA: Thomson/Schirmer, 2007), 244.

22. R. Taruskin, Review of *Sound and Sentiment* by Peter Kivy, *Journal of Music Theory* 29 (1985): 349.

EXAMPLE 8.4. Bach, St. Matthew Passion, no. 73 (recit.): "Und siehe da, der Vorhang im Tempel zerriß," mm. 1–10.

after Easter. One of its aria texts proclaims, "Mein Jesus ist erstanden," so of course the last word of the incipit, *risen*, is set to an ascending melodic line that is prefigured in the ritornello. The second time the tenor sings the incipit, Bach playfully accompanies it with six reiterations of the ascending motive. So far so virtuosic, and appropriately merry—indeed, inevitable (after all, the *ascendit/descendit* antithesis was depicted by Palestrina pretty much the same way in the Credo of every one of his 104 Masses). But in the second part of the aria Bach evidently got a little tired of the device and started to mock it by turning it around so as to make it do the opposite of what Christ is doing (ex. 8.5). I don't know whether making the viola the one going the wrong way was part of the joke, nor do I think Bach's congregation was supposed to notice and laugh. I'd guess it was just a little wink between Bach and the viola player (who may even have been Bach himself). But it certainly seems intentional: a comment on the artificiality of the device, and perhaps, even, a comment on its banality.

But with Handel, I feel certain that he not only knew that musical imitations were humorous, but he often intended his audience to find them funny and laugh, even when the ostensible subject was anything but merry. Take *Israel in Egypt*. Berlioz, who didn't know it (citing it by hearsay and inaccurately), singled it out for rebuke right after rebuking Beethoven for his lapse in *Fidelio*. "The same could be said of Handel," he wrote:

> If it be true—as is commonly said—that in his oratorio *Israel in Egypt* he tried to reproduce the flight of locusts, and this to the point of shaping accordingly the rhythmic figure of the vocal parts. Surely that is a regrettable imitation of a subject even more regrettable—unworthy of music in general and of the noble and elevated style of the oratorio.[23]

But the imitation of the locusts (not in flight but, as the text explicitly states, "on the ground") takes place not in the voices but in the orchestra, when the cellos, basses, and bassoons come in with a running bass line in sixteenth notes to join the violins, who had already been imitating flies in thirty-seconds. Nobody who hears this passage ever receives it with a straight face. Before this the audience had made merry over Handel's imitation of frogs in the first and second violins, who play overlapping leaps—yes, leapfrog. And yet, what Handel is imitating here is no benign menagerie but rather the Ten Plagues God visited on the Egyptians. Handel turns this harrowing biblical episode into one of the funniest twenty minutes in all of dramatic music, and a doughty classroom standby.

When I play it for my music history students I stop to examine Handel's portrayal of the darkness, which relies on chromatic harmony and murky timbres (bassoons doubling violins now instead of the basses), which gives us a chance to

---

23. Berlioz, "De l'imitation musicale," quoted in Berlioz, *Fantastic Symphony*, 39.

EXAMPLE 8.5. Bach, Cantata, BWV 67 (*Halt im Gedächtnis Jesum Christ*): Aria, "Mein Jesus ist erstanden," mm. 6–8, 35.

explore a more sophisticated, more indirect, and more serious sort of mimesis. But then comes "He SMOTE all the FIRST-born of EEE-GYPT," and we're all laughing again. Here is where I wheel around and ask the students, "Hey, what are you laughing at?" And we all realize that we've been had, that Handel has manipulated us into withholding empathy from the suffering Egyptians. That suppression is an essential part of the biblical account of the Exodus, and the scorn of the biblical Israelites and their religious descendants in Handel's audience for the ancient oppressor is what enables the success of Handel's strategy of turning an awful tale into a merry entertainment. This musically engineered separation of self and other plays also into the ideology of nationalism, on which Handel was very successfully trading. A great deal of English national pride (or anybody's) depends on a perception of separateness from other nations, and superiority to them.

But such chauvinism and self-interest is at considerable variance with the liberal ideas we propagate nowadays in institutions of higher learning, and when the political message of Handel's oratorio is broached, and juxtaposed with contemporary events unfolding in the Middle East, the students are apt to feel embarrassed at the way Handel's music has persuaded them to dissociate their reactions as listeners from their ethical sentiments. It's what we now call "cognitive dissonance," and it creates what we like to call "a teachable moment." What I am particularly intent on teaching by means of this example is the power of music—exactly through its representational aspects—to influence thought and behavior.

III

Minimize or deride them though we may, then, musical representations are potent—and (again *pace* Kivy) important. Nor have we even begun to take their measure, for mimesis hardly exhausts the possibilities of musical representation. Nor is musical representation exclusively or even primarily the business of the composer, even though all of the examples discussed so far have been examples of composers invoking or resorting to some form of mimesis. This is how musical representation is still usually conceived, in accordance with the poietic fallacy. If we wish to break the fallacy's hold, and open up the process of representation to a wider social agency, where shall we look to see it happening?

One area in which I see the esthesic side in effective balance—or, more actively, in effective dialectic—with the poietic is the discourse of musical nationalism. Certainly composers have represented themselves as nationalists, but just as often communities of listeners have made the decision as to what music shall represent them. One standard example of this is Weber's *Der Freischütz*, a work that is stylistically quite French, but which since its première as the initial offering in an officially designated National Theater has become an unshakable emblem of

Germanness in music (just ask Wagner).[24] Even more suggestive of the role of esthesis are the contests over the right to represent the nation in music that have taken place over the years, involving many national groups: Hungarians, Jews, Roma, and particularly (in terms of social contentiousness, length of debate, and breadth of attendant issues) Americans. Issues like these—that is, issues of social mediation and contention—are no longer new to musicology, but they still offer tremendous scope for innovative research, particularly as regards representation. Whom does what represent, for what purpose, and who gets to decide? Such questions, by no means confined to nationalism, are always political, because they involve the assertion and exercise of power and privilege. Whole repertories can be contested in this way, but also individual musical artifacts that work as social or political catalysts. Handel's manipulation of the audience's response to the plagues in *Israel in Egypt* already shows the political potential of musical representation within the realm of the poietic. Some recent examples of political contestation over musical meaning offer a glimpse of where esthesic ground might yet be broken.

A book by Eric Drott, which I had the pleasure of editing for my University of California Press series, *California Studies in Twentieth-Century Music*, gives a tantalizing preview of where such studies may go.[25] It illustrates interactions between a wide variety of musics and politics in France after May 1968, and the myriad ways in which musical genres mediated political expression, in part by solidifying or disrupting group identities. One chapter, on free jazz, describes the efforts of certain critics to tie free jazz to third-world politics and African-American political activism—that is, to turn free jazz into a representation of a particular, politically volatile ideology or faction. Another, on street politics, concerns appropriations of musical artifacts (chiefly *La Marseillaise* and the *Internationale*) both as a way of fashioning political identities and as a way of challenging them. Drott's work shows how the topic of representation in music might be refreshed and brought into dialogue with some of the most pressing of our recent musicological projects, completely bypassing the bad old questions that have dependably bedeviled discussions of musical representation—questions of immanence, of poetic (or poietic) intent, of mimesis. Rouget de Lisle, Eugène Pottier, and Pierre Degeyter do not figure at all in Drott's discussion, for they, the authors of the hymns in question, are of no account in this context. The intentions of men long dead are irrelevant to his story.

---

24. See Richard Wagner, "'Le Freischütz': Bericht nach Deutschland," *Abend-Zeitung*, 20 June 1841; reprinted in *Richard Wagner's Prose Works*, trans. William Ashton Ellis, vol. 7 (London: Kegan Paul, Trench, Trübner, 1898), 183–204.

25. Eric Drott, *Music and the Elusive Revolution: Cultural Politics and Political Culture in France, 1968–1981* (Berkeley: University of California Press, 2011).

But if work like his, which delivers musical representation out of the clutches of poets and composers, greatly enlarges the scope and weight of the concept, there remains an even broader, more encompassing sense in which we can speak of musical representation. Many have expressed an intuition that, even if we allow that music is a product of culture not nature, and add for good measure that music is alone among the arts in having no obvious natural model, nevertheless music *has* a nature in that there are things that music always accomplishes, irrespective of anyone's intention, whether composer, performer, listener, or mediator. Roger Sessions enunciated my favorite version of this in that dictum of his that I have been quoting for decades (and as I have already done in this very book), when he wrote that music's power to convey to us "the nature of our existence, as embodied in the movement that constitutes our innermost life" is "not the consciously formulated purpose of the composer" but rather "*the nature of the medium itself*" (his italics).[26]

Those are beautiful words, and I can't tell you exactly what they mean, any more than I can tell you exactly what Mozart's G-minor symphony means, but from the moment I first read them, my whole musical being responded with a great Yea (a response the consciously formulated purpose of Sessions the composer has never evoked in me)—and a great Yea, I suppose, is what we mean by an intuition, especially as my intellect rejects it (for which I offer a justification elsewhere in this book).[27] But one thing I *can* say about this intuition is that it casts music as inherently representational. By nature, or at least by inveterate and immemorial use, it is a conveyance. And if we agree (as I suggest in chapter 4) that Sessions is saying something similar to what W. H. Auden said when he called music "a virtual image of our experience of living as temporal, with its double aspect of recurrence and becoming," then Auden, too, casts music as inherently representational—or rather, and even stronger, he sees music as being *by nature* a representation.[28]

Another writer whose intuitions have inspired me is Wye Allanbrook, whose interest in topical analysis was prompted by her realization that "most music I know can't help but imitate some form of human motion—breath length, gesture, dance, as do the symphonies [of Haydn and Mozart] in a graceful mimeticism removed from all actual occasions but still bearing the marks of their social and affective provenance."[29] Unlike Sessions's insight or Auden's, Allanbrook's formulation, which recalls the primary insight from her book *Rhythmic Gesture in Mozart*, does not put my visceral reaction at odds with my intellectual response; for she is

26. Roger Sessions, *Questions about Music* (New York: W. W. Norton, 1971), 45.
27. See chapter 10 ("Essence *or* Context?").
28. W. H. Auden, "Music in Shakespeare: Its Dramatic Use in His Plays," *Encounter*, December 1957, 31–44, at 33.
29. Wye J. Allanbrook, "The Conundrum of the *Magic Flute*," paper read at the conference "After *The Magic Flute*," University of California at Berkeley, 6 March 2010, typescript, p. 7.

not attributing a nature to music, only showing how Mozart's instrumental music was indebted for its expressive effects to the conventions deployed in his operas. What she attributes to music, in other words, is not a representational nature but a representational purpose. In his operas, her book contended, Mozart's purpose was "to move an audience through representations of its own humanity." She located the source of these representations in the repertoire of ritualized movement called social dance.[30] Even within that book she pointedly extended the purview of this insight to cover the sort of textless instrumental music it is still conventional to call abstract.[31] In her late work she extended the purview still further, seeing social representation also in harmonically articulated musical form, whose closures are a virtual image (as Auden would say) of life's consummations as embodied in comic plots.[32] But surely we all knew this intuitively even before Allanbrook brought it to consciousness. While no one would call *Tristan und Isolde* a comedy, it is surely no tragedy either. What tells us that it is instead a drama of redemption is the world's most colossal harmonic close.

IV

This aspect of musical representation—its standing as in some sense inherent in the musical experience—has another side that is right now commanding a great deal of attention. That is the school of thought that sees the representation not in the music, which can itself have no agency (and which, as my conscience continues to insist, has no essential nature), but in our minds (which do have a nature insofar as they are a function of our natural brains), as we listen. According to this idea, music is intelligible to us—a condition that must precede all its other effects—because we can represent it mentally in a way that mediates its sounds and makes them meaningful. That intuition is obviously related to Chomskian theories of linguistic competence. Its most extensive elaboration as yet is Fred Lerdahl and Ray Jackendoff's *Generative Theory of Tonal Music*, which is directly beholden to Chomsky as well as to gestalt psychology.[33] But it is also reflected in the work of

---

30. Wye J. Allanbrook, *Rhythmic Gesture in Mozart* (Chicago: University of Chicago Press, 1983), 16.

31. As did Karol Berger, whose characterization of Tamino's magical flute music as the birth of "modern abstract music" (in *Bach's Cycle, Mozart's Arrow* [Berkeley: University of California Press, 2007], 286) provided the immediate context and pretext for the remark referenced in note 29.

32. See her last (posthumous) book, *The Secular Commedia: Comic Mimesis in Late Eighteenth-Century Music*, ed. Mary Ann Smart and Richard Taruskin (Berkeley: University of California Press, 2014).

33. Fred Lerdahl and Ray Jackendoff, *A Generative Theory of Tonal Music* (Cambridge, MA: MIT Press, 1983).

cognitive music theorists like Lawrence Zbikowski,[34] and that of some psychologists, some philosophers and anthropologists, and a few evolutionary biologists as well.

And now add one more ingredient. Roger Sessions's and Wye Allanbrook's compelling suggestions about music's *raison d'être* both rely on metaphors of movement. Such metaphors are common; indeed, they are customary, accounting for much of our ordinary musical vocabulary. Symphonies have movements. (Yes, in Italian *movimento*, the originating word, means tempo; but that merely restates the definition of time, going back to Aristotle, as the measure of motion.)[35] There are walking basses and running sixteenths. The tempo of the former is *andante*, and we will often find the latter in a *corrente*.

But we all experience music as motion in yet another way that is intimately tied up with the behavior of symphonic movements. When listening to what we conventionally call "tonal" music, by which we mean music in which form is articulated by harmony (and there was no such term as "tonal" before the existence of "atonal" music made necessary the contrivance of a retronym), we hear that harmonic articulation in terms of movement: specifically, in terms of departure and return. My vocabulary for describing this effect, as now inscribed in my *Oxford History*, was transformed by a conversation I had many years ago with a then-new colleague at Columbia University, the composer Dennis Riley (1943–99), when we were fellow assistant professors. Dennis had earned his PhD in composition at the University of Iowa, where one of his principal teachers was Donald Jenni (1937–2006). He told me about some of the teaching strategies he intended to take over

---

34. See, *inter alia*, Lawrence Zbikowski, *Conceptualizing Music: Cognitive Structure, Theory, and Analysis* (New York: Oxford University Press, 2002).

35. See Aristotle, *Physics*, book IV, part 12. Not every language calls the large divisions of an extended musical work "movements," and that can create problems of translation. In German, they are *Sätze*, an ambiguous term adapted from grammar (where it usually means "sentence") and applicable not only to what we call movements but also to lower divisions like expositions and developments, or even phrases. In Russian, the movements of a symphony are simply called *chasti*, "parts." I recall an argument I once had with the late Simon Karlinsky, who was a trained composer before he became a literary scholar, and who wrote extensively about Stravinsky. He complained about the Russian edition of Stravinsky's Symphony in Three Movements that translated the title using the Russian word *dvizheniya*, which refers, literally and generally, to any sort of movements, including physical ones. Simon wrote that the proper Russian should have been *Simfoniya v tryokh chastyakh*, "Symphony in Three Parts," rather than (as he put it) "Symphony in Three Motions" (see Karlinsky, "The Repatriation of Igor Stravinsky" [a review of *I. F. Stravinskii: Stat'i i materialy*, ed. L. S. Diachkova and B. M. Yarustovsky], *Slavic Review* 33 [1974]: 528–32, at 530). I agreed, but I had to disagree when he made a similar complaint about the Russian title of Stravinsky's Movements for Piano and Orchestra, which also used *dvizheniya*. It seemed utterly senseless to call that piece "Parts for Piano and Orchestra," as actual movement seemed an integral part of its concept (just ask George Balanchine). Stravinsky was evidently (to me obviously) playing on the double meaning of the word. I'm glad that English translates *movimento* with a cognate, for that preserves an intuition about music that I would hate to give up.

from Jenni's teaching, and one of these was the term "far out point" to denote the point from which the harmonic vagaries of the development section begin their turn toward the retransition. Jenni having studied at Stanford, the term was probably a variation on "point of furthest remove," a favorite expression of Leonard Ratner, whose contribution to the reconceptualization of eighteenth-century music has been sorely underacknowledged (so I take pleasure in acknowledging it here).[36] But Jenni's variant, "far out point," which in the *Oxford History* is turned into an acronym, FOP, has a terrific ring, and it has never left me since that casual conversation some four decades ago. I have striven ever since to get my students to conceptualize musical form in terms of a harmonic trajectory—that is, a virtual movement in the form of a round trip that coincides with what we actually call a movement.

Of course, thinking about harmony virtually moving over actual time invokes a concept of virtual space as well, and just as many writers resort to metaphors of space as to motion when discussing musical concepts. Fred Lerdahl recently published a treatise titled *Tonal Pitch Space*,[37] but he certainly did not originate the concept his titular phrase so neatly encapsulates. In an article published more than thirty years ago, Robert P. Morgan wrote, "Not only do listeners perceive changes in density and volume, they are conscious of different 'locations' within the available tonal range." And now recall that in the terminology of medieval music theory, particular pitches—for example, *C sol fa ut* (our "middle C")—were called just that: *loci*, i.e. places or locations. Morgan goes on to observe that the available tonal range, "understood as an abstract indication of the range of humanly perceptible pitches, is in fact commonly referred to by musicians as 'tonal space,' a designation that corresponds to our perception of music as moving through something—for example from a higher position to a lower one." Later he describes musical space as "a space of relationships" of a sort that exists "in all musical cultures," being "an accepted set of possible, or 'allowable,' musical relationships that exists prior to any given composition."[38] That is precisely what Lerdahl sets out to describe in his book.

Morgan claims that the space of relationships is purely conventional, but among the conventions he enumerates are a few that come close to being universals. "The concept of the octave, for example," he writes, "one of tonality's most basic assumptions, provides for the division of the total pitch range into a series of 'compartments,' each covering an equal segment of tonal space and defined by the appearance of the 'same' pitch in different registers."[39] But octave equivalency is not the

---

36. See, for example, Ratner's "Development" entry in the second edition of the *Harvard Dictionary of Music*, ed. Willi Apel (Cambridge, MA: Harvard University Press, 1969), 229–30, or his discussion of development in *Classic Music: Expression, Form, and Style* (New York: Schirmer Books, 1980), 225–27.
37. Fred Lerdahl, *Tonal Pitch Space* (New York: Oxford University Press, 2001).
38. Robert P. Morgan, "Musical Time/Musical Space," *Critical Inquiry* 6 (1980): 527–38, at 538.
39. Ibid., 530.

exclusive assumption of "tonality." There is no formalized theory of music (hence no theoretically formalized musical practice), to my knowledge, that does not assume it; and one team of researchers claimed to have observed or elicited recognition of octave equivalency in rhesus monkeys.[40] Morgan goes on to describe some features of tonal space that do correlate with tonality, such as a sense of relative distance from what he calls "a central pitch," involving such additional distinctions as that between diatonic and chromatic members of the total field. Summing up, he writes that "the uniqueness of any given composition is . . . primarily a function of the particular 'route' along which it moves temporally through this prescribed space," and hence, "any meaningful concept of musical space must incorporate, at some level, the factor of musical time; and equally, a meaningful concept of musical time must include that of musical space."[41]

Thus it is really a time/space continuum that Morgan describes. Both the temporal and spatial aspects of Morgan's concept, and the specific way in which they are necessarily interrelated as he stipulates, depend once again on the metaphor of motion, as he implies again when he imagines a musical composition moving through his postulated space according to its own particular route. Heinrich Schenker naturally appears in the vicinity of this remark, since Morgan is making music the agent, "mov[ing] through, and thereby defin[ing], its own musical space"[42] according to the dictates of the tones—*der Tonwille,* if you please, ranging through *der Tonraum.*[43]

IV

But what if we were to think of musical space somewhat differently: not as something through which music moves, but as something through which *we* move as we listen? In his first book of conversations with Robert Craft, Stravinsky makes a really striking comment along these lines: "We are located in time constantly in a tonal system work, but we may only 'go through' a polyphonic work, whether Jos-

---

40. Anthony A. Wright, Jacquelyne J. Rivera, Stewart H. Hulse, Melissa Shyan, and Julie J. Neiworth, "Music Perception and Octave Generalization in Rhesus Monkeys," *Journal of Experimental Psychology: General* 129 (2000): 291–307. It is true that musical modernists have occasionally denied octave equivalency by fiat—Charles Wuorinen, for example, in a long-ago, dimly remembered classroom discussion of his method of composing *Time's Encomium,* an electronic composition of 1969, or Jonathan Bernard in formulating a method for analyzing the works of Edgard Varèse ("A Theory of Pitch and Register for the Music of Edgard Varèse" [PhD diss., Yale University, 1977] and the book derived from it, *The Music of Edgard Varèse* [New Haven, CT: Yale University Press, 1987])—but such utopian and opportunistic "poietic" conceptualizations, unconstrained and uncorroborated by cognitive evidence from listeners, are of little relevance to a discussion of musical perception.

41. Morgan, "Musical Time/Musical Space," 530.

42. Ibid., 532.

43. *Der Tonwille* was actually the name of a periodical that Schenker singlehandedly authored and published in 1921–24 (ten issues in all).

quin's *Duke Hercules Mass* or a serially composed non-tonal-system work."⁴⁴ The two things that strike me most forcefully in this remark are, first, that Stravinsky is so comfortable with the assumption of a time/space continuum that he uses a space-word, *located,* to describe our perception of the temporal unfolding of music without any inkling that this usage could be seen as anomalous, or even as metaphorical. Second, as Stravinsky reports his experience, it is not the music that moves; rather, he moves (or we move) through the music. Musical space is registered, as it were, somatically, by our imagined physical location, and it affords our virtual bodies a field through which to move.

Add this intuition to those of Sessions and Allanbrook, Ratner and Jenni, and you have a very close approximation of my own sense of involvement in music—or, what I really wish to say, my own inner representation of it. The verbal formulation that comes closest to my own, and it was a delight to discover it, is that of Charles Nussbaum, a philosopher with a strong musical past (having started his career as a professional bassoonist), whose recent book *The Musical Representation* has given me some new and useful concepts to think with.⁴⁵

The main one, paradoxically enough, is *affordance.* I borrowed it a moment ago in saying that conceptualized or internally represented musical space *affords* our virtual bodies a field through which to move. What is paradoxical is that the term was coined by James Gibson, an ecological psychologist who made a career of disputing the necessity for internal representation. And yet Nussbaum makes a strong case for appropriating the term, despite that irony. Gibsonian affordances are defined as "properties of objects in the environment that offer action possibilities to the observer."⁴⁶ A chair, for example, has, according to Gibson, a "sit upon" affordance; a table has an "eat at" or a "write at" affordance depending on whether we are hungry or, say, need to work on a conference paper.

Nussbaum's application of affordance theory conceives of music as implicating our haptic and motor responses, but without actually initiating action. He calls this an "off-line" response. "To run commands off-line," he writes, "is to simulate actions imaginatively without engaging the relevant motor systems." And yet, he maintains, our internal representations of music "effect appropriate motor commands that [do] proceed outward to muscle effectors."⁴⁷ Our actual motor commands are both initiated and inhibited by our musical responses. They are not entirely killed, for many of us—perhaps all of us—do indeed respond to music by

---

44. Igor Stravinsky and Robert Craft, *Conversations with Igor Stravinsky* (Garden City, NY: Doubleday, 1959), 23.

45. Charles O. Nussbaum, *The Musical Representation* (Cambridge, MA: MIT Press, 2007).

46. Clint Heinze, *Modelling Intention Recognition for Intelligent Agent Systems* (Edinburgh, South Australia: DSTO Systems Sciences Laboratory, 2004), 31.

47. Nussbaum, *The Musical Representation,* 35.

moving our bodies while listening, even if we manage to inhibit our impulse to march or dance.

Talk of inhibition will bring the work of Leonard B. Meyer to a musicologist's mind, and Nussbaum classifies his theory of musical representation as being, like Meyer's, a "weak arousal theory." But the theories have significant differences, and one of the most convincing passages in Nussbaum's treatise invokes affordance theory to answer a question that gave Meyer trouble. "To a fleet quadruped," he writes, "a flat expanse appears runnable; to a hydrodynamic fish, a body of water appears swimmable." And to us music-minded humans, listening to music confronts us imaginatively with a similar "actionable" environment. This is the source not only of motor responses but of affective responses as well, which arise, Nussbaum claims, "out of an ongoing attempt to negotiate a musical virtual terrain, to act in accordance with its musical affordances, dealing with surprises, impediments, failures, and successes on the way, and requiring the constant reevaluation of strategy to which emotional response is keyed."[48]

This negotiation can be enjoyably—or at least effectively—replayed, and this is the way in which it differs from the familiar Meyerian "implication-realization" model of mental musical representation. Meyer's model was based on information theory. Meyer viewed musical expectations and their pleasurable fulfillment or affect-laden frustration as occurring in actual rather than virtual circumstances; and that is why pleasurable rehearing could be an effectual counterexample to his theory.[49] As Nussbaum observes, "we are not put into significant *informational* suspense with each subsequent hearing concerning what will happen next, even if we countenance musical 'nuance properties' [as Meyer proposed] that are registered in peripheral modular input systems but not centrally represented or retained in long-term memory." Like any reasonable person, Nussbaum agrees that "acquiring the same piece of information over and over again quickly palls. Indeed, any reaction, short of genuine reflex, to a novel event will be extinguished through repetition." Since our pleasure in rehearing music is not extinguished, it cannot derive from information acquisition. And yet, he reminds us,

> *doing* the same over and over again, even something as mundane as a challenging and varied daily exercise set, can maintain interest, because the interest lies in the doing. The powerful affective feelings that continue to attend the experience even of well-known recorded performances where nuances, even if some of them cannot be held in long-term memory in all their detail, remain exactly the same between hear-

---

48. Ibid., 214.
49. For his not very convincing rejoinder, see Leonard B. Meyer, "On Rehearing Music," *Journal of the American Musicological Society* 14 (1961): 257–67; reprinted in L. B. Meyer, *Music, the Arts, and Ideas*, 2nd ed. (Chicago: University of Chicago Press, 1994), 42–53.

ings, far more plausibly derive from simulated action *undertaken* and experience *undergone*. . . . They derive from *doing*, not from *discovering*.[50]

As I grasped Nussbaum's theory of actionable environments and affordances, my memory furnished a steady supply of corroborations, both from my own experience and from remarks and accounts I've read of other musicians. I was reminded of Scriabin's remark that his exploration of symmetrical tonal pitch space (to use Fred Lerdahl's term) was sparked by his wish to be able "to walk around a chord" (to use his term).[51] I was reminded of Wagner's conceptualization of harmony as a sea, which is nothing if not a Gibsonian affordance, it being to Wagner a navigable expanse. I even thought of Hanslick. What else could "tönend bewegte Formen" mean? Why else speak of *Bewegen*? Indeed, Hanslick identifies himself as a Gibsonian in the second chapter of his treatise, where he writes: "The concept of motion has up to now been conspicuously neglected in investigations of the nature and effects of music. It seems to us the most important and fruitful concept."[52]

But most spectacularly of all, I remembered Edgar Varèse, who was still a charismatic presence on the new music scene when I was a student. One saw him at concerts from afar, radiating a kind of electricity, not least by virtue of his electrified hair—thin kinky wires that seemed to be standing up or even taking a walk around his head in reaction to some sort of internal ionization. Once I saw him up close, the evening of 19 April 1965, less than seven months before his death, when he came up to Columbia to hear a concert at which his *Intégrales* was played by Charles Wuorinen and Harvey Sollberger's Group for Contemporary Music. He plunked himself down right in front of me, and I spent the whole evening staring at his broad round shoulders and magic hair from behind. He was already quite infirm and had to be helped in and out of his seat and supported when he walked. He sat slumped and motionless throughout the program, including the intermission. But when the last piece on the program, namely his, began to sound, he jolted—or was jolted—into an erect posture and began twitching in response to the music as if a current were passing through him. How I wished at that moment I could have joined him on his inner journey, but then I realized that I could do that and was in fact doing it, responding along with him to the wonderful music he had written and, though I would not learn the word for another forty-five years, its affordances.

The night I was privileged to observe him, Varèse was eighty-one. To me (I had just turned twenty), he was unimaginably old, though my perspective on that has undergone some change as I have racked up years. So let me end by recalling an

---

50. Nussbaum, *The Musical Representation*, 216–17.

51. Remark communicated to Georgiy Mikhailovich Rimsky-Korsakov, who then communicated it to Varvara Dernova, who recorded it in *Garmoniya Skryabina* (Leningrad: Muzïka, 1968), 352.

52. Eduard Hanslick, *On the Musically Beautiful*, trans. Geoffrey Payzant (Indianapolis: Hackett, 1986), 11.

even older lion in winter, Carl Ruggles. In 1970, when Ruggles was ninety-four, Michael Tilson Thomas (then twenty-six) performed and recorded Ruggles's largest work, *Sun-Treader*, with the Boston Symphony Orchestra, and then sought the composer out at the nursing home where he was living in obscurity. "I had been told that Mr. Ruggles was inclined to be suspicious of new people and retreat behind the curtain of his infirmities," Maestro Thomas recalled.

> So... I just walked into his room, said "Hello," set up a tape recorder, put some light earphones on his old and shriveled head, cranked the volume up as high as possible and started to play an air check of the performance of *Sun-Treader*. The first timpani stroke of the work hit the old man like a hammer. Suddenly he was sitting bolt upright, his eyes wild and open, like an eagle, his breath coming in fast, hoarse grunts and growls and guttural noise: "Fine." "Great!" "Damn, DAMN FINE WORK!" He kept it up right through the whole piece, sometimes singing or moaning along with the music until the end.

As the conductor left, he asked Ruggles whether he still thought about music:

> "Think about it every day—always. I'm composing, you know, right now—all the time. But my body, do you see? It is totally diseased, there's not a part of it that works right. So I'm sorry that I can't write anymore, can't finish what I've started—or start new. But in my spirit I am unvanquished. I can't write but I'm composing. Every day."
> I asked him if he could sing some of what he was composing.
> "First there are horns... " He began to sing, rasp, scream musical lines, all with his distinctive shapes, interjecting, "Here flutes! And strings—molto rubato, rubato!" And as we turned to go, he said:
> "Now don't go feeling sorry. I don't hang around *this* place, you know. Hell, each day I go out and make the universe anew—all over!"[53]

Runnable fields, swimmable water, a rangeable universe—that's music. Ruggles was out there with Wagner navigating the sea of harmony. We also negotiate that inner terrain and can at least tag along with the great navigators. Do we need a representation of the music to avail ourselves of its affordances? I can agree with Gibsonians that we don't need the kind of representation that Jonathan Bernard (arbitrarily denying octave equivalency) has provided of Varèse's space, or Allen Forte of Stravinsky's.[54] These static images are indeed redundant reproductions of our intuitions, because they try to capture an abstracted image devoid of space and movement. But, as Sessions first disclosed to me, there is an inner space which composers and listeners do inhabit, where they can move and meet. Music, in representing it, provides the meeting place. What else could be its purpose?

---

53. Liner note to *The Complete Music of Carl Ruggles*, Buffalo Philharmonic etc., conducted by Michael Tilson Thomas (CBS Masterworks M2 34591, 1980).

54. Bernard, *Music of Edgard Varèse*; Allen Forte, *The Harmonic Organization of "The Rite of Spring"* (New Haven, CT: Yale University Press, 1978).

9

Unanalyzable, Is It?

I

I'll begin with something I found by happy accident while looking for something else that I will be quoting later. In a 1978 issue of *Nineteenth-Century Music,* the University of California Press journal that had started publication only a year before, I came across a notice about the founding of the Society for Music Theory in America, which (as you may or may not know or remember, or care) started as a bolt from the American Musicological Society. "Word reaches us from the Mid-West," it began, "that Musicology and Theory have broken up." And it continued that way, as if describing a nasty divorce.

> One always feels it is a shame when things like this happen to such intelligent people. They had such a contribution to make. Did they seriously try to save the relationship? Did they go see anyone? Did they sit down calmly and try to talk their problems out? But part of the problem, of course, is that M. could never stand listening to T. talk.... There has been less and less communication between them in recent years, say friends who know and respect them both.... While there are some who have been urging them to patch things up right away, others argue that separation for a while might not be a bad thing. Both need to develop a bit more maturity, so the argument goes, before they are ready for a truly meaningful relationship.[1]

Are we ready now?

Originally presented as keynote address ("Is Anything Unanalyzable?") at EuroMAC 2014, Leuven, Belgium, 20 September 2014.

1. "Comment & Chronicle," *Nineteenth-Century Music* 2 (1978–79): 90–91.

That, by the way, and it was only a small excerpt, was by my old friend and late colleague Joseph Kerman, who also had his occasional differences with music theory. I'm quoting it partly in affectionate remembrance of Joe, but also because it is a propos today. I say Joe Kerman "*also* had his occasional differences with music theory" because I know very well why I am here today. You wanted to get a good look at "the presentday's most notorious theorist-basher."[2] That is what Arnold Whittall called me in a recent issue of the *Musical Times*. Many music theorists and analysts have complained about what Suzannah Clark calls my "rejection of analysis."[3] What is rather amazing is that Clark made this comment in the course of describing a very elaborate musical analysis of Schubert's Impromptu in E-flat, op. 90, no. 2, in the third volume of my *Oxford History of Western Music*—an analysis that she honors me by calling "one of the most illuminating technical discussions of Schubert's harmonic language available in modern scholarship."[4] So what could she possibly mean when she says that I reject analysis, or that I claim that "to analyze Schubert's music is superfluous," when she has just seen me do it, and even approved of what I was doing?

I think I know what got her goat. My discussion of the impromptu emphasized the key relationship on which the piece is built. The outer sections are in E-flat major, as the title of the piece declares, but the midsection is in the seemingly very distant key of B minor. My analysis concerned the nature of that relationship. The new key, which I call "the parallel minor of the flat submediant" of the original key, "is sustained," I write,

> as an alternate home tonality much longer than its counterparts in [earlier pieces by] Tomášek and Field. It is decorated with some fairly remote auxiliaries of its own—secondary dominants, Neapolitan sixths—that serve to promote its status as a stable region to the point where we can easily forget the instability of its traditional relationship to the original tonic. It is even given its own flat submediant, albeit in a context . . . that temporarily identifies the harmony as the "Neapolitan to the dominant of the original flat submediant." A mouthful like that is the equivalent of "third cousin on the mother's side twice removed." The relationship can be traced logically, and is therefore intelligible, but its distance, not the logic of its description, is what registers. The logic, while demonstrable, is beside the point. To insist on demonstrating it works against the intended effect.[5]

---

2. Arnold Whittall, "So Near Yet So Far" (review of *Audacious Euphony: Chromaticism and the Triad's Second Nature* by Richard Cohn), *Musical Times* 154, no. 1922 (Spring 2013): 111.

3. Suzannah Clark, "Rossini and Beethoven in the Reception of Schubert," in *The Invention of Beethoven and Rossini: Historiography, Analysis, Criticism*, ed. Nicholas Mathew and Benjamin Walton (Cambridge: Cambridge University Press, 2013), 102.

4. Ibid., 102–3.

5. R. Taruskin, *Oxford History of Western Music* (New York: Oxford University Press, 2005), 3:88–89.

Was that a rejection of analysis? No, it's an analysis. But it's a somewhat ironically distanced and critical analysis, which even as it recognizably performs the task normally expected of analysis, simultaneously transgresses what I have called the poietic fallacy by acknowledging the difference between what the analyst uncovers—that is to say, the composer's calculations—and what the listener perceives (and, in my opinion, values).[6] It raises the possibility that explaining music can sometimes have the effect of explaining a joke or a magic trick: even as the mechanism is clarified, the effect is dampened. In back of that is the notion that the interests of analysts and listeners do not always coincide. People who watch magic tricks think they want to know how it's done, but when they find out they are predictably disappointed. "Is that all?" is the usual reaction. The trick beguiles; the explanation disenchants or even disgusts with its prosaic simplicity. And of course it threatens to put the magician out of business, so magicians are especially ambivalent about explanations, if they are even ambivalent at all rather than altogether opposed. (And of course, magicians are standing in here for composers.)

Analysts, myself included, are like sorcerers' apprentices rather than spectators. We want to know the trade secrets more than we enjoy the mystification, or so we think, and so we are willing to risk sacrificing some of the pleasurable mystification for the sake of knowing. It seems to me that we can both analyze Schubert's composing practice and at the same time appreciate the perplexity that it is calculated to perpetrate, even if we are no longer exactly sharing in it. We as analysts can recognize the parallel minor of a flat submediant and mentally trace the process of its derivation, and at the same time exclaim, "Wow! Far out!" Does Suzie Clark really think otherwise? I really doubt it. She wanted, somehow, however, to put distance between her take on Schubert and mine. Why do you suppose that is? That is the question that has been on my mind, and that I want to impose on yours, and therefore I leapt at the chance given me by the organizers of this conference when they invited me to address you today.

You can see why this little story occurred to me as a suitable gambit to address a conference that has as its title "Analyzing the Unanalyzable," and why I chose to title my talk with a rhetorical question to which we all know that the answer must be a resounding "NO," and that is because analysis can always be rigged in such a way as to produce results. There is an old—a *very* old—joke about two Vermont farmers talking over the back fence between their adjoining properties. One (let's call him Clem) says to the other (let's call him Zeke), "Last night in town I heard this feller Norman Thomas give a lecture." "You mean the socialist?" says Zeke. "Yup," says Clem, "and you know what? He made a lot of sense."

---

6. See R. Taruskin "The Poietic Fallacy," *Musical Times* 145, no. 1886 (Spring 2004): 7–34.

"You a socialist now, Clem?"
"A-yup, guess so."
"You mean to tell me that if you had two barns you'd give me one?"
"A-yup."
"And if you had two tractors you'd give me one?"
"A-yup."
"And if you had two cows you'd give me one?"
"Wait a minute, Zeke. You know I've got two cows!"

I love to tell this joke to my seminars when we're talking about analysis, and here's how I adjust it:

"Last night in town I heard this feller Allen Forte give a lecture."
"You mean the pitch-class set analyst?"
"Yup, and you know what? He made a lot of sense."
"You a pc set analyst now, Clem?"
"A-yup, guess so. I can analyze anything now."
"You mean to tell me that you can analyze Pee-row Loo-nair?"
"A-yup."
"And you can analyze Le Sacruh doo prantom?"
"A-yup."
"And you can analyze the Ee-roica?"
"Wait a minute, Zeke. We know how to analyze the Ee-roica!"

It's because of my old—my *very* old—clash with Allen Forte—it took place more than thirty years ago!—that I am known as a theorist-basher.[7] What a bum rap! Anyone who knows my published work knows that I help myself enthusiastically to the work of many theorists; and Gretchen Horlacher, Pieter van den Toorn, Robert Gjerdingen, and Lawrence Zbikowski, to name only four theorists I have lavishly and recently praised in print, can testify that however disreputable some might think me, others know that I can be an ardent theorist-lover, and one who, as the saying goes, never kicks down. When I first engaged with Forte I was an assistant professor at Columbia University with, I think, two articles to my name (both on Russian opera, my dissertation topic). When I wrote my letter to *Music Analysis* in 1985 I was a newly tenured associate professor who had just been roundly bashed in the pages of that high-prestige journal by Paul Hindemith's successor as the Battell Professor of the Theory of Music at Yale University, for something I'd published in 1979 in the very low-prestige pages of *Current Musicology*,

---

7. Richard Taruskin, "Letter to the Editor," and Allen Forte, "Making Stravinsky Soup and Other Epistemusicological Pursuits: A Hymenopteran Response—Letter to the Editor in Reply to Richard Taruskin," *Music Analysis* 5 (1986): 313–37

the graduate student journal at my home institution.[8] That something was a review of Forte's book on *The Rite of Spring*. Jonathan Bernard, writing just last year, called my review a "guardedly favorable" appraisal.[9] Forte had been more discerning. He saw that there was a basic philosophical difference between us, and that my polite words conveyed a critique that, against his usual policy, he needed to answer. The fact that it is I who am remembered as the basher is, in my view, due to the outcome rather than to the tenor of the exchange, which I invite my critics to reread.

What was I bashing, in my at-first hesitant and diffident way? Not a theorist but a theory, and not just any theory but a method of analysis that was so widely practiced at the time as to be part of almost every musicology and music theory curriculum. By now, however, it has as far as I can see been pretty much discarded, even at Yale, its original headquarters and bastion. I am far from claiming sole credit for that. I was not the first to raise doubts about pc set analysis. The first important doubter, as I remember it, was William Benjamin, in a review of Forte's main exposition of his method, a manual titled *The Structure of Atonal Music*, which had appeared in 1973 and which by 1979 had become a major textbook for music analysis in every Anglophone graduate, and even undergraduate, program.[10] Later, many voices senior to mine, notably that of George Perle, were raised in opposition.[11] But if mine is the one that lives in infamy, it is because mine came, as Richard Hoffmann said when he opened the door to Arnold Schoenberg's house and beheld Ingolf Dahl, from "zomeone from ze ozzer camp."[12] My critique could be used as cannon fodder in the interminable, if utterly bogus, war between musicology and music theory. And because it was conducted (on my side, anyway) in very concrete and specific analytical terms rather than lofty theoretical generalizations, it proved efficacious.

I would couch the argument, from my much more mature—or at least more elderly—perspective of today, rather differently from the way I enunciated it in 1979. I would not now insist, as I did then, on the necessity of historical contextualization, or on the identification of the analyst's methods and terms with those of the composer, or at least terms contemporaneous with the composer. I had not yet become

---

8. See Richard Taruskin, Review of *The Harmonic Organization of "The Rite of Spring"* by Allen Forte, *Current Musicology*, no. 28 (1979): 114–29; and Allen Forte, "Pitch Class Analysis Today," *Music Analysis* 4 (1985): 29–58.

9. Jonathan Bernard, "Le Sacre Analyzed," in *Avatar of Modernity: "The Rite of Spring" Reconsidered*, ed. Hermann Danuser and Heidy Zimmermann (London: Boosey & Hawkes/Basel: Paul Sacher Stiftung, 2013), 287.

10. Allen Forte, *The Structure of Atonal Music* (New Haven, CT: Yale University Press, 1973); review of same by William E. Benjamin, *Perspectives of New Music* 13, no. 1 (Autumn–Winter, 1974): 170–90.

11. See George Perle, *The Listening Composer* (Berkeley: University of California Press, 1996), chapter 2 ("The Martian Musicologists"), 27–54.

12. See Robert Craft, "Assisting Stravinsky: On a Misunderstood Collaboration," *Atlantic Monthly* 250, no. 6 (December 1982): 65.

suspicious of what I have since called the poietic fallacy—that is, the exclusive preoccupation with the composer's input into the musical text. These aspects of my argument were the ones Forte found it easy to refute, or at least dismiss from view.

Not so easy to dismiss were two other points. The first was my query as to the epistemological status of pc sets and their relationship to the work analyzed, on the one hand, and to the activities of either the composer or the listener, on the other. The method seemed impertinent to both the poietic and the esthesic components of Jean Molino's once-famous *tripartition sémiologique*, as popularized within musicology by Jean-Jacques Nattiez.[13] Instead, pitch-class set analysis purported to describe what Molino called the *niveau neutre* (the neutral level) and Nattiez called "the trace," the part of the tripartition that seems to have fallen out of semiological practice as people realized that the act of description was already inherently esthesic. Hence, an analytical method that purported to inhabit the discarded realm of the thing-in-itself had to be discarded along with the fantasy that the thing itself was available for inspection and description.

Besides this reservation, or rather in consequence of it, I had gone on, as my second point, to challenge Forte to justify his method of segmentation (cutting up the surface), or even show that he had a method beyond the purely opportunistic aim of maximizing recurrences of pc sets, this being his primary (or, as I would say, his sole) criterion of coherence, hence of musical excellence. His analyses, my critique implied, were entirely circular—mere tautological confirmations of preconceived and (within the academy) mandatory judgments. They were arbitrarily constructed inventories devoid of explanatory content, and therefore unworthy of the designation "analysis." It would seem that the consensus among theorists by now upholds my judgment. And you're welcome.

That is how I earned my reputation as a theorist-basher. But if I have been a basher, it is only poor or subscholarly theory that I have bashed—and so should you, say I. What does it say about the field of music theory that to do so attracts personal opprobrium?

II

Leaving that question diplomatically unanswered, or rather leaving it to hang portentously in the air, I will submit a further, much more recent exhibit to show that even after the dust had settled on the matter of pc set analysis, resistance has continued to my efforts to explicate Stravinsky's creative evolution. Much of the resistance has superficially centered around what is perceived as my insistence on Stravinsky's identity as a Russian composer. That aspect of the resistance, I think,

---

13. See Jean-Jacques Nattiez, *Music and Discourse: Toward a Semiology of Music*, trans. Carolyn Abbate (Princeton, NJ: Princeton University Press, 1990), 10–16.

can be easily accounted for by observing the low level of prestige that Russian music has always enjoyed within the Western European or North American academy. To call him a Russian was to diminish Stravinsky in the eyes of many, including Stravinsky, who worked hard to deracinate himself. Many have leapt to his assistance. I actually devoted a paper to this strenuous uprooting effort and delivered it, weirdly enough, as the keynote address at a conference in honor of Rimsky-Korsakov's centennial, held in St. Petersburg in 2010 (yes, two years late, but that's Russia). I called it "Catching Up with Rimsky-Korsakov," and on a lark I submitted it afterwards to *Music Theory Spectrum,* the organ of the Society for Music Theory. I did not expect it to be accepted there, but much to my surprise, the new editor, Severine Neff (admittedly an old pal of mine from our days together as junior faculty at Columbia), not only took it but solicited responses from most of the individuals whose work I discussed in the piece.

I agree with Jonathan Bernard that "the results make for occasionally entertaining, occasionally depressing, but mostly thought-provoking reading," though I suspect that Prof. Bernard's entertaining is my depressing and vice versa, and that our provoked thoughts have little in common. His description of the piece will, I think, corroborate my point about the persistence of condescension toward Russian music and the need to protect Stravinsky from its taint. "The latest episode in the debate over the historical ramifications of the octatonic," he writes,

> has featured a typically polemical article by Taruskin in a journal where his prose is not usually encountered. [But it was not the first time I had published there.] "Catching Up with Rimsky-Korsakov," ... begins as an effort to elevate the status of that composer to something approximating what he enjoys in Russia (and practically nowhere else)—undertaken, it soon becomes clear, mainly in order to improve the plausibility of a continuity of compositional approach between Rimsky and his famous pupil—but then gets personal and ends by accusing theorists collectively of harboring "creationist" sympathies.[14]

Using the word *creationist* did get people's attention, all right, and Jonathan Bernard was not the only one to interpret it as a personal affront. When I read the paper at McGill University in Montreal, Jean-Jacques Nattiez, who had come from his own institution across town to hear it, admonished me from the floor: "You don't need that, Richard; you're better than that." To which I could only answer, "No, Jean-Jacques, actually I'm not better than that." I really meant it, and it introduces what I consider the more important aspect of the resistance my work on Stravinsky has provoked. Discussing this aspect will bring us back to the rubric "Analyzing the Unanalyzable," and will also facilitate a transition into the more

---

14. Bernard, "*Le Sacre* Analyzed," 295.

recent, post–World War II repertory the organizers of this year's EuroMAC conference have asked me to address.

Begging your indulgence, then, I'll quote one last time from Jonathan Bernard, who, when reporting my findings about the prevalence of actual quoted Russian folklore in Stravinsky's early work, could not keep a familiar indignation at bay. "Missing entirely from this account," he writes,

> is an acknowledgment that, wherever these tunes may have come from, even the readily identifiable ones have been transformed, collectively, into something else: an indisputable masterpiece of twentieth-century music that, however much of an episodically derived patchwork it may seem from an account of the compositional process, has been absorbed into musical history as an indestructible whole—for that is how the piece has made its impact on a world of audiences, performers, and critics, ranging from the casual concertgoer to the most distinguished of interpreters to the countless composers whose initial inspiration to enter that demanding profession has often turned out to be an early audition of *Le Sacre*.[15]

Well, excu-u-u-u-use me! But seriously, whence this remarkable defensiveness? Is Dr. Bernard defending Stravinsky against Russia or against me? Or is it something else that is making him nervous? What is it about my work that so threatens, in his eyes and in those of numerous others, to diminish Stravinsky and his musical achievement?

The thing that bothers him most, I think—as it has bothered others who have written in rebuttal, such as Pieter van den Toorn, Arnold Whittall, and Dmitri Tymoczko, to name a few[16]—is not so much that I am proposing to Russianize—or re-Russianize—Stravinsky as that I am implying that there can be definitive explanations for some aspects of his work. It is the same objection, ironically enough, that had previously greeted Pieter van den Toorn himself, when he began touting the octatonic collection, the collection of pitches (or more accurately, intervals) that can be represented as a scale of alternating tones and semitones, as being particularly relevant to Stravinsky's practice. All I did was add a bit of corroborative history to the thesis that van den Toorn had already arrived at by inference. Bringing Russia into the picture antagonized van den Toorn's opponents even more severely than he had initially antagonized them, and even made an antagonist out of van den Toorn for a while.

But the actual transgression, as one can see from van den Toorn's experience, was unrelated to Russia. It had to do, I think, with what antagonists saw as an arro-

---

15. Ibid., 294.
16. See van den Toorn, "Communication," *Journal of the American Musicological Society* (*JAMS*) 53 (2000): 445–48; Arnold Whittall, Review of *Stravinsky and the Russian Traditions*, *JAMS* 50 (1997): 519–29; Dmitri Tymoczko, "Stravinsky and the Otatonic: A Reconsideration," *Music Theory Spectrum* 24 (2002): 68–102.

gant foreclosing of the free play, the limitless speculation that had formerly reigned in Stravinsky studies, and still does in many areas of music analysis. Julian Horton, in his keynote speech at the 2014 Theory and Analysis Graduate Symposium (TAGS) of the Society for Music Analysis, illustrated the defensiveness to which I am calling attention by giving his address the title "In Defence of Musical Analysis" and claiming that I was out to make "theory subservient [sic; surely he meant subordinate] to history, since history is [according to me, he says] the source of verification for theoretical explanations." A couple of months later, in his President's Letter, his ex-officio editorial in the Society for Music Analysis's *Newsletter*, Prof. Horton followed up on that with an even more fundamental complaint, accusing me of infringing upon "the theorist's right to construct new readings without recourse to historical context."[17]

Bringing up the matter of rights and claiming victimization is a familiar and (if you'll pardon the oxymoron) transparent smokescreen, a plea for immunity from critique, and a tactic best discarded. No one has questioned the right of music theorists to do as they please; but I have called the validity of some of their methods and findings into question. Such interrogation calls not for a show of defensiveness but merely for a show of evidence that methods and findings are defensible, which is only to ask that those who reject one set of explanations or propose alternatives to it be willing to defend (not their right to life but) their rejection or their proposals. Surely the defense of free play can be distinguished—can it not?—from the defense of invalid methods and findings. To confuse—or rhetorically conflate—criticism and censorship is an old and dishonorable dodge.[18]

I'm sure that Julian Horton had no ignoble motive in defending his right to free play, but I will press the issue further by asking whether the play is really free. Is music-theoretical speculation really limitless and unconstrained? Or might it, at times, serve *a priori* agendas? Consider the verdict with which Arnold Whittall ends his review of my monograph *Stravinsky and the Russian Traditions*. Having cited a comment by Stephen Walsh, who found in Stravinsky's Symphony in Three Movements "a miraculous balancing act between the implied continuities of classical tonality and gesture and the architectural non-continuities with which Stravinsky had worked in his Russian period," Whittall writes in peroration:

> It may be that we get too little sense of that "miraculous balancing act" from Taruskin's ... narrative of the absorption of traditions, since their transformation—their role in a Stravinskianism that is multifarious, beyond allegiance to any single strain,

---

17. Julian Horton, "In Defence of Musical Analysis," *SMA Newsletter*, September 2014, 11–30, at 13; "President's Letter: EuroMAC Roundtable: Music Theory and Historicism," *SMA Newsletter*, December 2014, 4.

18. For a more detailed discussion of this point, see "Did Somebody Say Censorship?," chapter 2 in this volume.

national, cultural, or aesthetic—is not the topic that concerns him. With an impassioned advocacy embodying his principled commitment to the task in hand, Taruskin may appear to rush to judgment on issues fraught with the kind of tensions that tempt other musicologists to leave them endlessly open to alternative interpretations.[19]

Of course Whittall overstates my claim, although he does so very courteously. Nevertheless, the position he espouses is, in my view, subscholarly and therefore objectionable. If I claim what Whittall calls a privilege for my view of Stravinsky's style and methods, and of their patrimony, it is on the basis not of passionate advocacy or principled commitment, but rather of a massive presentation of hard-won evidence in support of my claims. In an earlier, joshing reply to Whittall's review I joked that "a book of nearly 1800 pages seems a mighty slow rush."[20] Today, before a distinguished audience of scholars, I want to get serious. Whittall offers no evidence to counter mine, nor does he advance any actual thesis of his own. He says he wants to keep things endlessly open, but in fact he is offering a limited model and a hackneyed one. He calls it "a Stravinskianism that is beyond allegiance to any single strain, national, cultural, or aesthetic." This, of course, is the view of Stravinsky on which Stravinsky himself insisted, beginning in 1920 with the much-quoted interview in which he disavowed the scenario of *Le sacre du printemps*; continued through the *Chroniques de ma vie*, in which he proclaimed his music to be free of all specific cultural or expressive baggage; through the *Poétique musicale*, with its scathing chapters both on Russian music and on the impurities of the *Gesammtkunstwerk*; and through the books of memoirs in part dictated to and in part ghostwritten by Robert Craft (as the *Chroniques* and *Poétique* had been ghostwritten before them)—debunking which has provided me with a career for four decades and counting.

I don't know whether Arnold Whittall's championship of this shopworn "Stravinskianism" was a matter of deference to the great composer's authority or whether it was motivated by an attractively egalitarian sense that everyone has a right to his own Stravinsky, but I do know that a viewpoint authoritatively asserted in the absence of evidence or proof is not a scholarly argument but political propaganda.

Such viewpoints are rife in the analytical literature, and they are often asserted with greater subtlety than Whittall's. Dmitri Tymoczko's attempt to refute the work of Pieter van den Toorn is an excellent case in point. His argument boiled down to the observation that the musical constructs and surfaces that van den Toorn has referred to the octatonic collection may be otherwise referred—say, to the melodic or harmonic minor, or to the whole-tone scale. All of this is perfectly true, but does anyone really buy the notion, after van den Toorn's voluminous demonstrations,

---

19. Whittall, Review of *Stravinsky and the Russian Traditions*, 529. The cited comment is from Stephen Walsh, *The Music of Stravinsky* (London: Routledge, 1988), 198.

20. R. Taruskin, "Catching Up with Rimsky-Korsakov," *Music Theory Spectrum* 33 (2011): 180.

that it is equally likely? Like Whittall, Tymoczko ignores the presence of evidence on one side of the debate—evidence that my work supplied and that van den Toorn, ironically enough, at first resisted—and the absence of evidence on the other. Evidence should not be regarded as optional, it seems to me, and yet it is so regarded by musicologists all the time, and not only by musicologists who identify themselves as theorists or analysts. In a fashion reminiscent of Tymoczko, who with ostensive modesty asks merely whether it is possible that Stravinsky had the harmonic minor in mind rather than the octatonic collection, one of my colleagues in Russian music history has asked, in a paper as yet unpublished and therefore not to be quoted directly, whether it is "conceivable" that Nikolai Miaskovsky (and by implication Shostakovich, Prokofieff, and Khachaturyan as well, the "Big Four" of Soviet music) altered their styles after their denunciation at the behest of Andrey Zhdanov in 1948 out of genuine aesthetic conviction rather than in response to political pressure.

There can be only one answer to such a question. Asked whether something is possible or conceivable, one can only say "yes." Anything is possible. And even more things are conceivable than are possible. But since the answer to the question is foreordained, both question and answer are devoid of informative content. To contrive hypothetical alternatives in no way constitutes a rebuttal. Only assertions that are testable—or, to put it Karl Popper's way, only an assertion that can in principle be disproved—can contribute to knowledge or understanding. To say that something is possible cannot be falsified, to use the insider's term, since we know that nothing is impossible a priori. Similarly, no sentence containing the word *may* can be refuted. No one possesses the omniscience it would require—which is to say, no one has the right—to say *it may not be*. So if the limitless proliferation of possibilities is your objective, you will confine yourself to hypotheticals and conditionals and never look for evidence. But however attractive the prospect of limitless possibility may be, it ultimately promises nothing but the waste of time and energy.

To analyze "inductively," without constraint, is to live in Dostoyevsky's world without God, where everything is permitted (and, it therefore follows, nothing matters).[21] Dostoyevsky did not think that a good place to be, and I agree with him. Many of the analyses we admire display laudable ingenuity; but the display of ingenuity is not—or at least in my view should not be—the purpose of analysis. Whether it should be the purpose of composition is something we can debate another day. In the realm of analysis, we want to achieve results that matter: that are not merely true (the way Forte's endless inventories, as he was wont—and content—to claim, revealed

---

21. Or, in Dmitry Karamazov's exact words, "Без бога-то и без будущей жизни? Ведь это, стало быть, теперь всё позволено, всё можно делать?" (You mean without God or the life to come? And that therefore everything is now permitted, that one could do anything?); Dostoyevsky, *The Brothers Karamazov*, part 4, book 11, chap. 4.

"demonstrable relations"), but also relevant, and that make a difference to the way we listen. The requirement of relevance requires a criterion of relevance, and the requirement of falsifiability requires a standard of proof. We want hypotheses, whether inferential or based on documentation, that can survive testing, not evade it.

III

You can see how these matters relate to our propaedeutic concerning "analyzability." As long as any possibility is regarded as being as good as any other possibility, nothing is unanalyzable. But in that utopia of endless options, nothing is purposeful either. What, after all, *should be* the purpose of analysis?

I would like to approach the answer to that ultimate question by way of some preliminary examples, which, in keeping with the conference program, I will draw from the repertory post-1945, a period that exactly coincides, as it happens, with my own lived experience.

My first example is utterly predictable: *Le marteau sans maître*. You must have smelled it coming, because for more than thirty years it was preeminently the unanalyzable piece. Attempts at analyzing it were few and far between because, thanks to Boulez's unopposable authority, analysis of *Le marteau* could not take place in the utopia of unconstrained prospects. Boulez had let it be known that the composition was serial; contradicting him was unthinkable, and in any case a conclusive negative proof is never possible—and so the only permissible question for analysis was *how* it was serial. As long as that question remained unanswered, the principles governing the choices that went into its composition remained arcane. That so many musicians played the piece, listened to it with enjoyment, or at least with great interest and respect, and paid it tribute in the absence of any knowledge of its justifying principles served to crystallize the problem that always attended the serial music of the midcentury avant-garde, a problem that has aroused the interest of cultural historians now that the period of its creation has been reconceptualized as postwar, or Cold War, or the age of anxiety, or the era of existentialism—all of them characterizations that put an emphasis on ideology.

For surely ideology and even mystique are in play when a composer as eminent as Stravinsky (whose music, while offensive to many when it was new, was never a puzzle to audiences, only to analysts) could in 1960 say of a piece whose technical basis was still a mystery that "in this new period of exploration the only significant work so far is still Boulez's *Le Marteau sans maître* (1954)."[22] But then Stravinsky,

---

22. Igor Stravinsky and Robert Craft, *Memories and Commentaries* (Garden City, NY: Doubleday, 1960), 118. Stravinsky heard Boulez conduct the work in Los Angeles, at a Monday Evening Concert, 11 March 1957; see Robert Craft, ed., *Stravinsky: Selected Correspondence*, vol. 2 (New York: Alfred A. Knopf, 1984), 350.

going through a period of insecurity as he felt his own way toward the serial method, often went out of his way to praise music that he did not understand technically, revealing and even admitting as much, as when he touted Elliott Carter's Double Concerto as a masterpiece while under the impression that it was not only serial, but even Darmstadt-serial, with a "rhythmic series" as well as a series governing pitch. "I cannot comment upon or add to the composer's own analysis," Stravinsky (or his ghostwriter) wrote, confining his commentary to the most general matters of shape and timbre; "but analysis," he added, in terms of quasi-religious abasement that have become famous, "as little explains a masterpiece or calls it into being as an ontological proof explains or causes the existence of God."[23] So what, again I ask, should in that case be the purpose of analysis? On our way to an answer we will circle back to Carter.

But first, back to *Le marteau*. It was the subject, or pretext, for the most acidulous words that Arnold Whittall has ever flung in my direction. I was not thinking of *Le marteau* in particular when I wrote the paragraph that Whittall chose to excoriate from my *Oxford History of Western Music*, but raising the matter in connection with *Le marteau* was fair enough. As transcribed and condensed by Whittall, I wrote:

> The paradox created by "total serialism" is this: once the algorhythms [sic!] governing a composition are known (or have been determined) it is possible to demonstrate the correctness of the score (that is, of its component notes) more decisively and objectively than is possible for any other kind of music [and I would suggest that this is one of the conditions that attended the inception of music analysis as a separate branch of musicology with its own societies and journals]; but in the act of listening to the composition, one has no way of knowing . . . that the notes one is hearing are the right notes, or (more precisely) that they are not wrong notes.[24]

Whittall derided my "fixation on audibility as it functioned in the tonal and modal past," as proof of my nostalgic incompetence as a listener and my intolerance (claiming that I wanted to see "emancipated dissonance . . . proscribed"). But I did not speak of audibility. It's a familiar dodge. Haven't we all heard the matter of "audibility" mocked? I'll bet some of us have done it ourselves. Some do it better than others. When Milton Babbitt was asked the question "But can you *hear* it?" he always said, "Of course you can hear it; what are you, deaf?" And as always, Babbitt, unlike Whittall, was not just indulging in invective. By making the questioner laugh, he was making the questioner realize that he did not really mean "hear" when he asked the question about hearing, but rather was broaching a serious

---

23. Igor Stravinsky and Robert Craft, *Dialogues and a Diary* (Garden City, NY: Doubleday, 1963), 48–49.

24. Taruskin, *Oxford History of Western Music* 5:36, as quoted in Arnold Whittall, *Serialism* (Cambridge: Cambridge University Press, 176.

matter that Whittall (and Stravinsky, in his eagerness to praise Boulez and Carter) evaded: that of conceptualization or mental representation on the basis of perception, something that is very close to what we all mean by "understanding" when we are speaking of music.

"So it is rather more constructive," Whittall continued, "to ask what listeners do actually hear, in a work where Boulez's thinking about serial principles reached its most sophisticated form."[25] I agree! And I even thought, on reading this, that Prof. Whittall might actually tell us what he heard. But no, he does not. What he tells us, alas, is only what Lev Koblyakov told us all, in an analytical tour de force that cracked the *Marteau* code at last. Koblyakov's analysis was his dissertation, written at the Hebrew University of Jerusalem between 1975 and 1977. It was published in preliminary summary the year in which the dissertation was completed, and set forth in full in a book published in 1990.[26] But this analysis, while very impressive because it was made without recourse to sketches or other "precompositional" material, and sensational enough to merit reporting in *Time* magazine,[27] was made, like all such analyses, by looking, not by listening.

What do actual listeners actually hear when they hear *Le marteau?* Whether or not they have read Koblyakov, or one of the expositions of "pitch-class set multiplication" that have appeared subsequent to his work, I think it is fair to say that they actually hear pretty much what Alex Ross reports hearing, which corresponds pretty much with what I hear in the piece, and which is quite enough to account for its exceptional popularity among the products of the early Darmstadt years. Ross writes, in his widely read (and by academic theorists widely disparaged) *The Rest Is Noise*, about "a glistening spiderweb of alto flute, viola, guitar, mallet percussion, bongos, maracas, claves, and other percussion. In the exotic instrumentation there are hints of Balinese, African, and Japanese music . . . This is ultramodern Orientalism that exploits world music at the highest remove and with the utmost refinement."[28]

Needless to say, it was never permissible to mention any of this in academic writing about *Le marteau*, except to the extent that Boulez permitted it. In his essay "Sprechen, Singen, Spielen" of 1972, which concerns the relationship between

---

25. Whittall, *Serialism*, 176.
26. See Lev Koblyakov, "P. Boulez's *Le marteau sans maître*: Analysis of Pitch Structure," *Zeitschrift für Musiktheorie*, 1977, no. 1, 24–39; Koblyakov, *Pierre Boulez: A World of Harmony* (Chur, Switz.: Harwood Academic Publishers, 1990). Besides Koblyakov himself, Whittall cites two sources that enlarge upon Koblyakov's work: Stephen Heinemann, "Pitch-Class Set Multiplication in Theory and Practice," *Music Theory Spectrum* 20 (1998): 72–96; and Ciro Scotto, "Reevaluating Complex Pitch-Class Set Multiplication and Its Relationship to Transpositional Combination in Boulez's *Le Marteau sans maître*," paper presented at Royal Holloway, London, 19 November 2005.
27. See Michael Walsh, "Boulez ex Machina," *Time* 118, no. 27 (28 December 1981): 104.
28. Alex Ross, *The Rest Is Noise* (New York: Farrar, Straus & Giroux, 2007), 398.

Le marteau and *Pierrot lunaire* (something it was not only permissible but mandatory to mention in connection with *Le marteau*), Boulez acknowledged that he "was influenced by non-European models in choosing this particular combination of instruments, the xylophone representing the African balafron [*sic; recte* balafon], the vibraphone the Balinese gender and the guitar recalling the Japanese koto." Then he adds, preemptively:

> In actual fact, however, neither the style nor the actual use of these instruments has any connection with these different musical civilizations. My aim was rather to enrich the European sound vocabulary by means of non-European listening habits, some of our traditional classical sound combinations having become so charged with "history" that we must open our windows wide in order to avoid being asphyxiated. This reaction of mine has nothing whatever to do with the clumsy appropriation of a "colonial" musical vocabulary as seen in the innumerable short-lived *rhapsodies malagaches* and *rhapsodies cambodgiennes* that appeared during the early years of the present century.[29]

In other words, the non-European sounds are there precisely so as *not* to bring any extraneous associations to mind (pay no attention to that belly dancer behind the curtain!), the way, say, the use of a string quartet, with all that unwanted historical baggage, might have done. We are thus bidden to follow the old alchemist's recipe for turning lead into gold (Ready? Melt and stir for three hours without thinking of the word *rhinoceros*).[30] As an example of obedience to Boulez's puritanical authority one could cite Paul Griffiths, from the revised edition of his study of music after World War II:

> Boulez has ... suggested that the vibraphone relates to the Balinese gamelan, the xylorimba to the music of black Africa, and the guitar to the Japanese koto, to which one might add that the ensemble, like that of [Stockhausen's] *Kreuzspiel*, is flavoured with the modern jazz of the period. *Le marteau* is thus a pioneering essay in the "music of the whole world" that Stockhausen was to take as an ideal—though it draws away from embracing exotic qualities of modality, rhythm, or ritual presentation: refusal is still what partly gives Boulez's music its energy, and this particular piece its quick temper.[31]

---

29. Pierre Boulez, *Orientations*, ed. Jean-Jacques Nattiez, trans. Martin Cooper (Cambridge, MA: Harvard University Press, 1986), 341. I wonder whether Boulez's final sally was prompted by an illustration in Vladimir Jankelevitch's venerable study of Ravel, which shows a *Rapsodie Cambodgienne* (1882) by Louis-Albert Bourgault-Ducoudray prominent among Ravel's "last scores" (Jankelevitch, *Ravel*, trans. Margaret Crosland [London: John Calder; New York: Grove Press, 1959], 123).

30. I've been citing this "recipe" for years, so I might as well reveal at last that I learned about it from a chance viewing on television, long ago, of the play *The Great Sebastians*, with its original stars, Alfred Lunt and Lynn Fontanne; see Howard Lindsay and Russel Crouse, *The Great Sebastians: A Melodramatic Comedy* (1957; New York: Dramatists Play Service, 1998), 50.

31. Paul Griffiths, *Modern Music and After: Directions since 1945* (Oxford: Oxford University Press, 1995), 82.

But I would say that Boulez's insistence that we cleanse our minds of the obvious associations his music evokes is an example of what, in a mellower phase, he acknowledged in response to a question from a member of the audience at the Edinburgh Festival in 1999. Asked why the music of the postwar avant-garde had not achieved a place in the concert repertoire after half a century, he did not answer in terms of Adornian *hauteur*, as he would certainly have done in earlier years when he insisted that serial music "demands the intelligent participation of the audience, which is 'making' the work at the same time as its author," and if they were not intelligent enough to participate as instructed, *tant pis!*[32]

That is what Boulez wrote in 1968, and it confirms the first maxim of modernism: *the customer is always wrong*. That principle was so firmly entrenched as to infect the discourse of music criticism no matter what the subject. Stanley Sadie, a writer on music who had no connection with, or interest in, modernism as such, nevertheless invoked modernist principles when he said of the *opera seria* (e. g. Handel's) and the "problems" attendant on its twentieth-century revival that "for the historically minded interpreter, there is no problem, or if there is, it belongs with the audience, whose responsibility it is to solve it for themselves (or to go away)."[33] Sadie calls this the "historical" position, but it is a position that, as any historian would have to acknowledge if forced to think about it explicitly, could never have occurred to Handel, or to anyone whose lifetime overlapped with his. It was the midcentury modernist position, born of undiagnosed romanticism, uncritically absorbed, accepted, internalized and (implicitly) universalized. Its source was not Handel's cohort but that of Boulez, inherited directly from Schoenberg.

But in 1999 Boulez allowed, in a phrase that made a lot of news at the time, that if his cohort's music had not achieved repertory status after half a century had passed, the reason may have been that "perhaps we did not take sufficiently into account the way music is perceived by the listener."[34] Usually this remark is interpreted as an admission that serial organization, Koblyakov's revelations notwithstanding, is cognitively opaque, a sore point about which Arnold Whittall remains intransigent to the point of impugning the competence of those who dare agree. Yet even Whittall gives evidence that as a listener he perceives *Le marteau* the way I am suggesting we all do, when he cites "the alto flute solo at the beginning of the third movement" as giving "a sense of the not-so-distant presence of one of Boulez's most admired precursors, Debussy."[35]

---

32. Pierre Boulez, "Where Are We Now?" (1968), in *Orientations*, 462.
33. Stanley Sadie, "No Squirming, Please," *Times Literary Supplement*, 14 May 1993, 21.
34. Stephen Johnson, "What Happened When the Wall Came Down?" *BBC Music Magazine*, September 2002, available at www.stephen-johnson.co.uk/publications/bbc-music-magazine.php.
35. Whittall, *Serialism*, 176.

This is a response to instrumental color. Can we admit here, among friends and without embarrassment, that it is the glamorous tone colors (and, I would definitely add, the quality of the rhythm with its suggestion, precisely, of ritual presentation) that so attract the ear to *Le marteau*? Joseph Straus was still trying to stigmatize such reactions when he wrote condescendingly that Stravinsky's well-advertised admiration for the work "certainly had more to do with the surface colors . . . than its serial structures, of which Stravinsky was entirely unaware."[36] So were we all—ergo, so was Joseph Straus—and I think Boulez knew that perfectly well when he fashioned the unmentionably seductive and, in that sense, pornographic sonic surface of his music, while at the same time elaborately covering his tracks so that the derivation of the pitch structure—or rather the pitch content, since the pitch successions on the surface were virtually unordered despite their derivation from an ordered succession (and so much for "serial structures")—would remain his personal secret, unavailable, whether to the listener's ear or to the analyst's eye, until a particularly determined analyst came along almost a quarter of a century later and earned a doctorate by finally uncovering those tracks. Don't tell me that the pitch structure of *Le marteau* is unimportant. It was important enough to hide away for twenty-five years.

Boulez was well repaid for his trouble. That double allure—an unmentionable sensuality combined with an inscrutable, riddling, and ostentatious intellectuality—has kept *Le marteau* alive for half a century as one of the Darmstadt evergreens: a piece that everyone involved with twentieth-century music—certainly everybody in this room—has heard and remembers, and in some fashion enjoys. (Griffiths was quite right to rank it alongside *Kreuzspiel*, the other easy-listening favorite from the period.) Boulez knew he had a winning combination, and wanted to keep it that way. When Lev Koblyakov presented his analytical findings to an audience at IRCAM that included the composer, he naturally sought confirmation. In a taxi afterward, in which he and Boulez were sitting alongside David Wessel, then the educational director at IRCAM and later my colleague at Berkeley from whom I heard the story, Koblyakov asked, "Well, Pierre? Was I right?" What do you think Boulez said? He said exactly what Stravinsky would have said if Pieter van den Toorn had asked him about octatonicism. He said, "Oh, my dear, it was so long ago!" You don't ask magicians how they do their tricks. Explanations are fatal.

Have they been fatal to *Le marteau*? Fred Lerdahl was surely right that Lev Koblyakov's discoveries have had little effect on how the piece is heard, nor, to my knowledge (and perhaps you will correct me) has any composer adopted or extended the method Boulez devised to organize its pitch content. Pitch-class set multiplication is not a technique taught in school, the way Stravinsky's equally idiosyncratic hexachordal rotations and "verticals" were adopted for a while by other

---

36. Joseph Straus, *Stravinsky's Late Music* (Cambridge: Cambridge University Press, 2001), 34.

composers such as Charles Wuorinen and Oliver Knussen after they had been deduced and described, and incorporated into curricula.[37] Lerdahl found that lack of impact on compositional practice "disturbing."[38] But I would venture to say that most people have not found the cognitive opacity of *Le marteau* to be an insuperable obstacle to enjoyment, even if, given the irrelevance to it of the serial structure even now that we know what it was, the enjoyment that we experience must be of a fairly superficial order (using the word *superficial* now in the most literal sense, viz., denoting confinement to the *superficies*, that magically beautiful, iridescent sounding surface, as it unfolds).

IV

If we agree that it has not affected the experience of listening to the piece in real time, what, then, is the status of Koblyakov's analysis? What did it accomplish? What does it tell us? Broadly speaking, analyses can serve two separable (but also combinable) purposes: they can tell us how the piece works, or they can tell us how the composer worked. In that sense, analysis is comparable to another activity that musicologists perform, that of genetic criticism, to give it its fancy name, or sketch studies, as they are commonly called by those who do them. Sketch studies underwent a crisis in the late 1970s, shortly after their high-water mark with the two Beethoven centenaries, the bicentennial of his birth in 1970 and the sesquicentennial of his death in 1977, which fostered a great wave of sketch studying, Beethoven being at once the paradigmatic great composer and also the composer who, thanks to his distinctive personal habits, left more sketches behind than any other musical giant. (I'm not referring to the habit of making sketches, which most everybody does, but to the habit of never throwing them away.) It used to be thought that sketch studies were like analysis in that they gave insight into the content and meaning of music, or (if we are formalists) at the very least into its structure.

In 1978, a young Beethoven scholar named Douglas Johnson, who had just completed a dissertation at UC Berkeley under Joseph Kerman, typical for the time, on one of Beethoven's sketchbooks,[39] published a fairly explosive article called "Beethoven Scholars and Beethoven's Sketches" (actually the introductory chapter to the dissertation), in which he challenged—in fact impugned—the then rarely questioned assumptions as to the value of information derived from sketches

---

37. See, for example, Charles Wuorinen, *Simple Composition* (New York: Longman, 1979), 105–7.

38. Fred Lerdahl, "Cognitive Constraints on Compositional Systems," *Contemporary Music Review* 6, no. 2 (1992): 97–121, at 97.

39. Douglas Porter Johnson, "Beethoven's Early Sketches in the 'Fischhof Miscellany,' Berlin Autograph 28" (PhD diss., University of California, 1978).

to the process of analysis.⁴⁰ Invoking the so-called intentional fallacy, named after a manifesto by W. K. Wimsatt and Monroe Beardsley that was one of the founding documents of what in the 1940s and 50s was known in America as New Criticism⁴¹—or rather refuting the arguments of another scholar who had claimed that the intentional fallacy did not apply to musical sketches⁴²—Johnson made a case for the irrelevance of sketch studies to analysis that has always reminded me of the rationale given by Caliph Omar for burning the library at Alexandria in 640 AD. To an underling who had asked for instructions, the Caliph is said to have written, "If those books are in agreement with the Quran, we have no need of them; and if these are opposed to the Quran, destroy them." So they burned the lot.⁴³ In a similar spirit, Douglas Johnson asserted that if the sketches confirm one's analysis of the finished score, they are superfluous, and if they contradict it, they are irrelevant, for using them "to enhance conceptually a relationship that the composer has ... weakened [or effaced] is to reverse the compositional process and substitute the sketches for the work—in short, to contradict [the composer's] intentions."⁴⁴

Johnson allowed that Beethoven's sketches remained valuable as biographical documents—for establishing chronology above all, but also for educing from that chronology a more refined "understanding of Beethoven's stylistic development," as he put it.⁴⁵ I can corroborate that value from my own study of Stravinsky's sketches, which helped me answer some very important questions. I was able to ascertain the presence of actual Russian folk melodies in *Le sacre du printemps* on the basis of the sketchbook. I was able to demonstrate from sketches the ways in which Stravinsky deliberately distorted the prosody of the texts he set in every language, including English, a language he spoke poorly, where his distortions had often been attributed to ineptitude. I was able to show on the basis of sketches what Pieter van den Toorn called Stravinsky's (and Rimsky-Korsakov's) "in-the-act awareness" of the octatonic collection as an *a priori* concept; and I was even able to corroborate a textual correction that I had proposed for the first of the *Pribaoutki* of 1914 on the basis of a sketch, which for me was the most important finding of all, since I believe that the most reliable mark of a valid analytical procedure is its usefulness for textual criticism. My first inkling that Forte's methods were useless came when I saw how many

---

40. Douglas Johnson, "Beethoven Scholars and Beethoven's Sketches," *19th-Century Music* 2 (1978–79): 3–17.

41. Wimsatt and Beardsley's essay was first published in the *Sewanee Review* 54 (1946): 468–88, and endlessly anthologized thereafter.

42. The article he sought to refute was Philip Gossett, "Beethoven's Sixth Symphony: Sketches for the First Movement," *JAMS* 27 (1974): 248–84, esp. 261–68.

43. Bar Hebraeus (Abu'l Faraj), *Historia Compendiosa Dynastiarum*, trans. Edward Pococke (Oxford: H. Hall, 1663), 114.

44. Johnson, "Beethoven Scholars and Beethoven's Sketches," 16.

45. Ibid., 13.

misprints he was uncritically analyzing. Arthur Berger and Pieter van den Toorn had preceded me in octatonicism, so to speak, but they could not prove their points to skeptics.[46] My sketch findings, which offered support to their inferences, obviously had a bearing on analysis, but I do not object to their being classified as biographical. I think biography is perfectly okay.

There were many, however, who did object to what they saw as Johnson's insult to sketch studies. I felt a strong sense of solidarity with him, because like me in my somewhat later debate with Forte, he committed his heresies at an early and potentially vulnerable stage of his career, and received, as I did, a great deal of curt and even abusive criticism from senior colleagues who regarded him as an upstart. Biography was considered a much lower order of musicological endeavor in those days than analysis, which, as Joseph Kerman observed at the time, was the closest thing to criticism musicology then had to offer.[47] By the time he wrote that, Kerman, who was a practicing critic as well as a musicologist, was widely known—by some revered, by some reviled—for advancing a drastically hierarchical view of musicology in which "each of the things we do—paleography, transcription, repertory studies, archival work, biography, bibliography, sociology, *Aufführungspraxis*, schools and influences, theory, style analysis, individual analysis—each of these things, which some scholar somewhere treats as an end in itself, is treated as a step on a ladder. Hopefully the top step affords a platform of insight into individual works of art"—that being Kerman's working definition of criticism (and, of course, as was widely pointed out, he seemed to regard himself as alone on that top step).[48] You can see from the fact that in the earlier discussion Kerman distinguished analysis from criticism rather than identifying the two with one another

---

46. R. Taruskin, "Russian Folk Melodies in The Rite of Spring," *JAMS* 33 (1980): 501–543; Taruskin, "Stravinsky's 'Rejoicing Discovery' and What It Meant: In Defense of His Notorious Text Setting," in *Stravinsky Retrospectives,* ed. Ethan Haimo and Paul Johnson (Lincoln: University of Nebraska Press, 1987), 162–205; Taruskin, "Chernomor to Kashchei: Harmonic Sorcery; or, Stravinsky's 'Angle,'" *JAMS* 38 (1985): 72–142; for "in-the-act awareness," see van den Toorn, *The Music of Igor Stravinsky* (New Haven, CT: Yale University Press, 1983), 463n5. The most dismissive resistance to van den Toorn's work came from Joseph N. Straus, whose doctoral dissertation it challenged; in an article derived from the dissertation, "Stravinsky's Tonal Axis," *Journal of Music Theory* 26 (1982): 261–90, he disparages a large and heterogeneous assortment of Stravinsky analysts under the rubric "The Tonal and Octatonic Fallacies." Straus's latest exposition of his view, unchanged in its essentials, is "Harmony and Voice Leading in the Music of Stravinsky," *Music Theory Spectrum* 36, no. 1 (Spring 2014): 1–33.

47. Joseph Kerman, "The State of Academic Music Criticism," a lecture given in 1978 and published in *On Criticizing Music: Five Philosophical Perspectives,* ed, Kingsley Price (Baltimore: Johns Hopkins University Press, 1981), 38–54, esp. 38–40. The relevant point emerges more forcefully from this version than from the better-known revision, published as "How We Got into Analysis, and How to Get Out," *Critical Inquiry* 7 (1980): 311–31.

48. Kerman, "A Profile for American Musicology," *JAMS* 18 (1965): 61–69; reprinted in Kerman, *Write All These Down* (Berkeley: University of California Press, 1994), 3–11, at 5.

that he was, and remained, ambivalent about the status of analysis, but even in the early formulation analysis was the highest rung but one, with biography much further down the ladder.

So that is why Johnson's assignment of the value of sketch studies to biography rather than analysis was regarded as an unacceptable demotion. But I do not regard it so. I even think that analysis, if it truly tells us how the composer worked, is in essence, and valuably, biographical; and if it purports to tell us how the piece works, it is apt to be a hollow and a futile, not to say a worthless, endeavor.

Again sketch studies can furnish an illuminating analogy. Sketch studies that purport to narrate the process through which a work takes shape operate under a very elaborate set of assumptions. To begin with, the work chosen for such a demonstration had better be worth the effort. Perhaps needless to say, that applies to works chosen for full-scale analytical treatment as well. If the work is chosen for its exemplary quality, that means that the end of the story is in view before the narrative is even begun, and so the story becomes a predictable (indeed predicted) story of consumption. I do not think one will find any study of the creative process of a masterwork by a master composer—and what other sort of work or author would be studied that way?—that does not follow this narrative archetype. And so genetic studies, like happy families, are all alike. I used to joke to my friends, back when sketch studies were rife, that I was waiting for the sketch study that would regard Beethoven's creative process as flawed. Only if such a study could be undertaken—and published, and taken seriously—could one really believe that the usual narrative really told the story of "an individual work of art" rather than a heroic myth or a bedtime story that ended with everyone, according to the inexorable formula, living happily ever after.

Is work-oriented analysis not liable to the same strictures? Its purpose, to quote Kerman once more, is "to discern and demonstrate the functional coherence of individual works of art, or, as is often said, their 'organic unity'"?[49] And do we not choose for these demonstrations works that we already regard as being functionally coherent? In *Analyse und Werturteil* (1970), Carl Dahlhaus made the distinction I am making here between analysis that seeks to reveal how the composer works and analysis that seeks to reveal how the music works, or (as I like to put it for the sake of the tautology thus exposed) how the work works. He put it a little differently, distinguishing between analysis that uncovers technique of composition and analysis that uncovers form.[50] Typically, Dahlhaus asserted no preference between them, but I have no hesitation in declaring my preference for the former. It seeks to describe real historical acts performed by real historical agents rather

---

49. Kerman, "The State of Academic Music Criticism," 39.
50. Carl Dahlhaus, *Analysis and Value Judgment*, trans. Siegmund Levarie (New York: Pendragon Press, 1983), 53.

than a fiction produced by a set of often unstated premises that only become "real" when historically contextualized. Only what is historically real can be said to be uncovered. The fictive is not uncovered but constructed. It has no reality beyond the historical conditions that give rise to its premises—and which can, of course, be uncovered by means of historical research. To conceive of form—or of harmonic functions, or of coherence based on the recurrence of pitch-class sets—as something "real" that analysis "uncovers" is to adopt an uncritical attitude toward premises scholars should be interrogating.

So I actually think that the biographical can plausibly outrank the analytical or the critical as a scholarly objective. And that is why Koblyakov's analysis of *Le marteau* has indubitable value. Its findings are indeed biographical in that it uncovers and describes something Pierre Boulez actually did, even if he later claimed to have forgotten it. What it describes, moreover, is a method that others can appropriate to their own purposes. If no one has actually done so, that is testimony to the fact that solving the riddle of how *Le marteau* got written did nothing to solve the aesthetic and cognitive problem that has attended it—the problem, as Lerdahl put it, of the "huge gap . . . between the compositional system and cognized result."[51] This formulation restates the gist of the argument developed in Lerdahl and Jackendoff's *Generative Grammar of Tonal Music*, in which the poietic aspect of Molino's tripartition is referred to a "compositional grammar" and the esthesic to a "listening grammar." One does not have to subscribe to Lerdahl's inescapably controversial "aesthetic claim" that "the best music arises from an alliance of a compositional grammar with the listening grammar"[52] to recognize, as I do, that Koblyakov's analysis of *Le marteau* at least has the merit of describing an actual compositional grammar, whereas a lot of analysis, especially (but not only) of music whose compositional grammar is dimly or imperfectly understood, describes neither a compositional nor a listening grammar, but some sort of utopian domain unattached to actual historical agents or artifacts. Obviously I am talking about Forte again, who devised his method precisely for music whose compositional grammar is arcane (it being the method one uses, to recall our Vermont farmers, when one has no method); but it also applies, I believe, to a great deal of formal or "structural" analysis of music partaking of well-established composing grammars that purports to dig beneath the listening surface for . . . what? Like the upshot of sketch studies, that "what," which is sometimes undefined, and sometimes predefined, tends to be suspiciously (and uninterestingly) uniform.

51. Lerdahl, "Cognitive Constraints," 97.
52. In his "Cognitive Constraints on Compositional Systems," in *Generative Processes in Music: The Psychology of Performance, Improvisation, and Composition*, ed. John Sloboda (Oxford: Oxford University Press, 1988) 231–59, at 256; reprinted in *Contemporary Music Review* 6, no. 2 (1992): 97–121, at 118.

Koblyakov's analysis of *Le marteau* actually helps elucidate the gap Lerdahl deplores, because it illustrates the way in which Boulez used his technique of so-called pitch-class set multiplication to derive a great stream of essentially unordered pitch material from a strictly ordered twelve-tone row whose order is thus paradoxically rendered irrelevant to the composition as heard, however relevant it may have been to the process of its making. The same may be said of Stravinsky's hexachordal permutations, which continually reshuffle, or re-order, or in effect "un-order" the ordered interval content of the tone row, while his so-called verticals, being the sums of all the pitches occupying the same order position in each of the reshuffled hexachords, retain nothing of the intervallic order. For a final anomaly, the verticals' invertibility (or more accurately their non-invertibility arising out of intervallic symmetry), which certainly is relevant to the composition as heard, is the automatic product of the procedure that gave rise to them, and therefore neither dependent on the original twelve-tone ordering nor in any way a compositional achievement. In either case, analysis could be said to elucidate the reasons for the music's cognitive opacity and expose the contradictions between the theoretical premises that underlay Lerdahl's "huge gap ... between the compositional system and cognized result." Does that mean that the analysis undermines the aesthetic integrity of the music, as Lerdahl might think (though never openly contends)? Or does it mean that aesthetic integrity is unrelated to compositional method, in which case why do we need or wish to analyze music to begin with? (Yes, like the magician's audience we're curious, but maybe it's just an idle curiosity.)

V

It goes without saying, but I'd better say it anyway, that the imputation of cognitive opacity has been leveled at fully ordered serial music as well, and far more often. Some, like M. J. Grant, have argued (in my opinion not unpersuasively) that the charge is beside the aesthetic (or perhaps I should say, more generally, the philosophical) point of the music, which actually depends on its cognitive opacity.[53] Michael Hicks went even further, invoking the ancient aura of the sublime. "If the beauty of musical art is meant to imitate the beauty of nature"—and that's a big if!— "then *incomprehensibility* is ... a necessary if not sufficient condition of beauty."[54] I wonder how many would find plausible such an appeal to nature, which, unlike music or any art, is made not by human hands, and is not addressed to its observers, who are incidental and irrelevant to its existence and purposes (as indeed we are

---

53. M. J. Grant, *Serial Music, Serial Aesthetics: Compositional Theory in Post-War Europe* (Cambridge: Cambridge University Press, 2001).

54. Michael Hicks, "Serialism and Comprehensibility: A Guide for the Teacher," *Journal of Aesthetic Education* 25, no. 4 (Winter 1991): 82.

often made to feel, if perhaps less often now than when I was a student, at concerts of new music). We may hold, with Arthur Mendel in a famous old screed, that "our delight in [a] work consists partly in being baffled by it, and perhaps there is no theoretical reason to believe that analysis cannot eventually remove our bafflement; but then it would at the same time have removed our delight."[55] Or we may regard the apprehension of music the way Wagner described Lohengrin, who "sought a woman who would believe in him: who would not ask who he was or whence he came, but would love him as he was because he was what he appeared to her to be, ... [one] to whom he would not have to explain or justify himself, but who would love him unconditionally."[56] As Leonard Meyer observed a quarter of a century ago in what for me has remained the greatest of all music theory keynote addresses, "Formalism in aesthetics is an almost perfect counterpart of such Romantic love" as Lohengrin sought, along with Stravinsky and Boulez.[57]

Others, possibly put off by the irrationality of such claims, have tried to deny the reality of the problem, proposing ways in which the aural comprehension of serial structure might be achieved either through sheer repeated exposure or by practiced strategy. My experience with such purported demonstrations of "aural analysis"—and I have always sought them out at conferences—has been disappointing. Sooner or later, and usually sooner, the scores come out, and looking takes the place of listening. Andrew Mead, who as a loyal explicator of Milton Babbitt's music and his very rationalistic theories must surely dissent from M. J. Grant's interpretation of "serial aesthetics," has proposed that the problem of cognition with respect to serial structure devolves into the simpler matter of perceiving aggregates, since the completion of aggregates is the basic structure-making fact of serial music. He portrays the matter, in his book on Babbitt, as being quite unproblematical: "Can we hear aggregates—and if so, how?" he asks. This is his fairly well-known answer:

> Given a collection of a large number of different pitch classes, each represented once, we *can* recognize—although we are not able vividly to determine what pitch classes we have not yet heard—whether or not any additional note represents a new pitch class. By interpreting the recurrence of a pitch class as a signal that we have crossed a boundary, we can parse a highly chromatic and differentiated musical surface into a discrete series of large bundles of pitch classes that we might call *perceptual aggregates*. Perceptual aggregates may or may not contain all twelve pitch classes, but

---

55. Arthur Mendel, "Evidence and Explanation," in *International Musicological Society: Report of the Eighth Congress, New York 1961*, ed. Jan LaRue, vol. 2 (Kassel: Bärenreiter, 1962), 3–18, at 15.

56. Richard Wagner, "A Communication to My Friends," quoted in Carl Dahlhaus, *Richard Wagner's Music Dramas*, trans. Mary Whittall (Berkeley: University of California Press, 1980), 40.

57. Leonard B. Meyer, "A Pride of Prejudices; or, Delight in Diversity," *Music Theory Spectrum* 13 (1991): 241–51, at 248. This was the keynote address to the Eleventh Annual Meeting of the Society for Music Theory, Baltimore, 1988.

because of their size this will not be a particularly vivid aspect of our hearing. Their pitch class content is not vivid, but our awareness of their boundaries will be.[58]

Will it now? Schoenberg never thought so. We all know his letter to Rudolf Kolisch in which he thanks his devoted former pupil, now his brother-in-law, for making a row analysis of his third quartet, but then he turns around and says,

> You must have gone to a great deal of trouble, and I don't think I'd have had the patience to do it. But do you think one's any better off for knowing it? My firm belief is that for a composer who doesn't yet quite know his way about with the use of series it may give some idea of how to set about it—a purely technical indication of the possibility of getting something out of the series. But this isn't where the aesthetic qualities reveal themselves, or, if so only incidentally. I can't utter too many warnings against overrating these analyses, since after all they only lead to what I have always been dead against: seeing how it is *done;* whereas I have always helped people to see: what it *is!* I have repeatedly tried to make Wiesengrund understand this, and also Berg and Webern. But they won't believe me.[59]

(Forgive me for quoting at such length, but I just had to get to the part about Wiesengrund.)

Now, Schoenberg doesn't actually say that a listener cannot deduce the row structure, only that it is not important that he do so. He is anticipating Lerdahl's distinction between the compositional grammar and the listening grammar, but differing from Lerdahl in his assumption that the listening grammar can function meaningfully when divorced from the compositional grammar. In Schoenberg's actual music it often can, most of us would agree, because his style maintained so many links with the older practice on which listening intuitions formed on tonal music are based. But in the music of the postwar era, or should I say the post–*Schoenberg est mort* era, it is no longer the case that older intuitions can offer an effective *entrée,* and that was very much by design. The features of Schoenberg's music that allow its parsing by the listening ear were precisely the ones Boulez ridiculed in that notorious essay, and the ones the composers of his generation consciously tried to root out of their music, much to the applause of theorists then and since. (For one enthusiastic instance, see the concluding historical discussion in Koblyakov's book on *Le marteau.*)[60] In Lerdahl's terms, Schoenberg's atonal and twelve-tone music retains a certain amount of elaborational structuring on top of the basic series organization, which is permutational. This replacement of the elaborational by the permutational is not an incidental consequence of the series

---

58. Andrew Mead, *An Introduction to the Music of Milton Babbitt* (Princeton, NJ: Princeton University Press, 1994), 12–13.

59. Letter of 27 July 1932, in Arnold Schoenberg, *Letters,* ed. Erwin Stein, trans. Eithne Wilkins and Ernst Kaiser (Berkeley: University of California Press, 1987), 164.

60. Koblyakov, *Pierre Boulez,* 105–24.

organization, but integral to its conception, since Schoenberg's own definition of twelve-tone technique—"Method of Composing with Twelve Tones Related Only to Each Other"—placed appropriate emphasis on the abolition of hierarchy. This, according to Lerdahl, was the crucial utopian decision, the one that, as an older (and wiser?) Boulez is said to have put it, "did not take sufficiently into account the way music is perceived by the listener."

Lerdahl has been subjected to a great deal of often heated criticism for misapplying the theory he and Jackendoff worked out for explaining the way listeners parse tonal music and rendering on its basis an impertinent invidious judgment on an unrelated repertoire.[61] Theory is never unbiased, perhaps, but experimental evidence tends to support the contention that the sort of parsing of aggregate boundaries that Andrew Mead assumes to be salient to an attentive listener is at the very least an extremely difficult task to perform, even under simplified laboratory conditions.[62] Of course, experimental evidence can also be biased or manipulated; but even without investigating the matter experimentally, or even if an empirical study should one day confirm Mead's proposal, one has to grant its utopian character once we get outside the music perception lab. Is there, to begin with, any twelve-tone piece beyond the very first one—Schoenberg's Waltz for Piano, op. 23, no. 5—in which aggregate succeeds identical aggregate discretely, so that pitch-class repetition actually signals boundaries between aggregates the way Mead describes? In the real world of music, rows succeed one another in varied permutations and transpositions, and coexist contrapuntally in time, so that pitch repetitions are rarely confined to boundary positions. Indeed, they can occur anywhere.

Awareness of this basic fact immediately tugged at Andrew Mead's conscience; he sought to allay it thus:

> In most twelve-tone music there are extensive examples of pitch class repetition within aggregates, so that it is necessary to distinguish those repetitions within from those between aggregates. Both Schoenberg and Babbitt distinguish among the different kinds of repetition articulated in different musical dimensions, and in both composers' music repetition has the effect even within aggregates of indicating

---

61. Fred Lerdahl and Ray Jackendoff, *A Generative Theory of Tonal Music* (Cambridge, MA: MIT Press, 1983); for an especially fiery rejoinder (in the first instance to Lerdahl's "Cognitive Constraints on Compositional Systems" [see note 38 above]), see James Boros, "A 'New Totality'?" *Perspectives of New Music* 33 (1995): 538–48.

62. In his book *Tonal Pitch Space* (New York: Oxford University Press, 2001), Lerdahl cites experimental work by Cheryl L. Bruner, Diana Deutsch, W. Jay Dowling and Dane L. Harwood, and Robert Francès. Asked about more recent work, Lerdahl mentioned Carol Krumhansl, *Cognitive Foundations of Musical Pitch* (New York: Oxford University Press, 1990), 241–53 and added, "I have not seen more recent empirical studies of these issues. Perhaps I am not up to date. More likely, psychologists ignore them because serial music is of little interest to younger generations" (email communication, 22 August 2014).

boundaries of some kind. While the potential for ambiguity is frequently employed to good effect, context generally makes clear the function of repetition in both their work.[63]

This bland assurance fails to assure me that I will know the difference between repetition within and repetition between when I hear it in real time, or that I will even be able to recognize ambiguities in the music or appreciate the good effect to which it is employed, nor can I guess exactly how context will clear it all up. Mead does not tell us. With these two paragraphs he is done with the—to him—uninteresting question of perception. I actually prefer M. J. Grant's or Michael Hicks's premises to Mead's, because theirs frankly acknowledge that the audience (within which they are willing to place themselves) has a real problem, even if they do not allow that the audience's problem creates any problems for the composer or the analyst.

VI

The ground has shifted a bit in the decades since Mead's book appeared. We are more apt than we used to be to question the status—intellectual, philosophical, aesthetic, call it what you will—of analytical findings that relate neither to a compositional grammar nor to a listening grammar. One of the signal early events in that shift was the widely commented-on review by Andrew Mead, a pupil and proponent of Babbitt, of a book, *The Music of Elliott Carter,* by David Schiff, who was a pupil and proponent of Carter, as well as the even more widely commented-on exchange of letters that followed. While allowing that Schiff's book "may serve as a general introduction to the composer and his music for the interested concertgoer," Mead complained of what he called the author's "lack of theoretical grounding." This lack was evident in Schiff's failure to bring the work of several well-known theorists of the day to bear on Carter's music, with the result that the discussion was focused too particularly on "the difference between Carter and his contemporaries" rather than on the "surprising ... degree to which they share concerns," as Schiff might have discovered were he "fully informed about theoretical developments which are now standard graduate school fare."[64] Schiff's failure to make use of Forte's *Structure of Atonal Music* as an analytical tool was a particular sore point. Schiff knew the book, mentioned it appropriately in relation to Carter's practice, noting correctly that "Carter uses the term 'chord' synonymously with Allen Forte's term 'pitch-class set': that is to say, a chord is a collection of pitches

---

63. Mead, *Introduction to the Music of Milton Babbitt*, 13.
64. Andrew W. Mead, Review of *The Music of Elliott Carter* by David Schiff, *Music Library Association Notes* 40 (1983–84): 544–47.

defined by the number of pitches and by their intervallic relation."[65] But because Schiff adduced Carter's own (now published, then inaccessible) catalogue of chords in an appendix and used Carter's numbering of them in his analyses, Mead complained that readers of Schiff's book will have to do as he did, and "work out a system of translation."[66]

Mead's review was a parochial and snooty performance, and as I've said, it elicited a backlash—but not from Schiff, who tells me that he has never read it.[67] The backlash came from an enraged Elliott Carter, who wrote a blistering letter to the editor of the journal in which the review had appeared. If Schiff had used Forte's methods or other techniques "widely accepted by American graduate students," Carter wrote, deriding a particularly galling phrase from the review, "the book would not have reflected my own thoughts about the music." Having thus asserted proprietorship over Schiff's analyses, he went on to complain that

> the reviewer neglects to point out what would be evident to anyone else, since my writings are generously quoted throughout the book, that the music is described in the composer's own terms, with all of what Mead considers their looseness, indefiniteness, and weak intellectual content. If Mead's strictures about the terminology used in the book have any justification they should be directed against me instead of Schiff who is dismissed so dogmatically by this reviewer.
>
> On the other hand, Schiff's survey could be considered valuable just because it does present the composer's views on his music—but such historical considerations do not concern set theorists as their many critics have pointed out.[68]

What chiefly drew attention at the time was Carter's implication that Schiff was acting as his mouthpiece, since in the foreword to his book Schiff had been at pains to acknowledge his personal relationship to Carter but also to insist that the book "is *my* perspective on Carter's music" and that it "should be read as an outsider's interpretation of the music," for which "the composer is in no way responsible." It is also of interest that in the same foreword Schiff anticipated the complaint that he did not set Carter's music in the context of other composers' work, writing that he avoided doing so "primarily because it tends to treat other composers superficially." He named a few other composers who might be mentioned "if Carter is to be compared" with others, but only those whose music made for unspecified "enlightening contrasts" with Carter's: Stefan Wolpe, Roberto Gerhard, and Witold Lutosławski.[69]

---

65. David Schiff, *The Music of Elliott Carter* (London: Eulenburg Books, 1983), 70n7.

66. Mead, Review of *The Music of Elliott Carter*, 545. See Elliott Carter, *Harmony Book*, ed. Nicholas Hopkins and John F. Link (New York: Carl Fischer, 2002).

67. Email communication, 20 August 2014.

68. "Communications," *MLA Notes* 41 (1984–85): 195.

69. Schiff, *Music of Elliott Carter*, ix–x.

These are the sort of pro forma disclaimers one is apt to find in any scholarly book, and yet the evident breach of decorum Carter's anger had induced was a potential embarrassment to Schiff, and Andrew Mead was quick to seize on it when answering Carter. The most interesting point he made in his rebuttal, however, was his defense of "an objectively verifiable formal theory of relations amongst unordered pitch-class collections" in preference to Carter's, or any other composer's, descriptions of his own or any other music. Mead was explicitly upholding abstraction as a virtue, or what earlier I called "that 'what,' which is sometimes undefined, and sometimes predefined," and which "tends to be suspiciously (and uninterestingly) uniform." In this case supremely predefined, it was responsible for what Mead had called the "surprising . . . degree to which" all of Carter's contemporaries "share concerns," or what Allen Forte, in rebutting my complaint that his analysis of *Le sacre du printemps* did not place it in a relevant context of common practice, called the "common practice shared by Stravinsky, Scriabin, Bartók, Webern, Berg, and Schoenberg, among others."[70]

A surprising degree? Who could be surprised by a finding that one's analytical method has guaranteed? This was precisely the pitfall of which the "many critics" to whom Carter made reference had warned. I think most of us have realized this by now, just as Andrew Mead himself has in all likelihood stopped touting "objectively verifiable formal theory" as the answer to all relevant questions. The wave of poststructuralism, though it went out of control and did some damage before receding, at least swept some of our more arrogant conceits away. Although it may have embarrassed David Schiff at the time, Carter's letter might have had the salutary effect of getting some—as I know, it got one, namely me—to nurture doubts as to the merits of universalism, and to acknowledge the need to understand the creations of God's creatures—that is, cultural artifacts—in their particularity, even if it took me longer to identify and oppose the poietic fallacy, which Carter's letter continued to espouse.

At any rate, I have now done what I set out to do—which was, in the spirit of the Judge's Song from Gilbert and Sullivan's *Trial by Jury*, to tell you how I came to be the theorist-basher you came to see. I would love to find that I have been beating dead horses before you today, but the latest issue of *Music Analysis*, the British journal, which carries a long and enthusiastic review of three recent universalist theories of tonality (or at least three theories the reviewer touts as universalist), suggests that there's life yet in the horses I've been thrashing.[71] In any case, I will

---

70. Forte, "Making Stravinsky Soup," 329.

71. Kenneth M. Smith, "The Transformational Energetics of the Tonal Universe: Cohn, Rings, and Tymoczko," *Music Analysis* 33 (2014): 214–56. As Steven Rings pointed out to me at the meeting where I read this paper, the reviewer quite misunderstood the point and purpose of his work; nevertheless, it is the reviewer's stance that interests me in the present context.

believe that I'm beating dead horses not because anyone will merely tell me so, in case you were about to. I want to be shown, as I attend the sessions and hear how analysts today go about the task for which the objectively verifiable malpractices of the past were devised, namely that of understanding what was previously a mystery, learning to analyze the unanalyzable.

10

Essence *or* Context?

On musical ontology

I

Never was I happier to receive an invitation than I was when, having established contact with the British philosopher Nick Zangwill, I found myself proposed as a keynoter for a conference in Vilnius convened under the title "Music: Essence and Context." My primary reason for rejoicing had nothing to do with the conference theme. It had to do with ancestral roots. My father's parents were born and grew up near the Lithuanian capital. My grandmother was born around 1884 in what was then known as Wilkomierz or Vilkomir, now Ukmergė, about 80 kilometers from where the conference took place. My grandfather was born, probably in the same year, in Dvinsk, now Daugavpils, not much farther away, even though it is now across the border in Latvia. It was in Dvinsk that my grandparents were married, and it was from there that they came to America in 1907 and 1908—first he, then she, after he had worked for a year and earned passage for the rest of the family, which by then included my father's older sister.

In my grandparents' time, of course, the border between today's Baltic republics was just a border between guberniyas, or administrative districts within the Russian empire. If you asked my grandparents where they were from, they would have just said "Russia," as I did when I knew them. If they were speaking their native Yiddish, they might have said they were Litvaks, as speakers of the northern Yiddish dialects were often called. When I was an exchange student at the Moscow

---

Originally presented as keynote address at conference "Essence and Context: A Conference Between Music and Philosophy," Lithuanian Academy of Music and Theater, Vilnius, 2 September 2016.

Conservatory in the early 1970s, I was unable to visit Daugavpils, in what was then the Latvian SSR, since like most of the territory of the Soviet Union it was off-limits to foreigners. So of course I leapt at the chance to come to Vilnius—you might even say in spite of the conference theme.

For ordinarily it might have been a deterrent. I alluded jokingly to the reason in the very act of leaping when I wrote to the organizers. "All right, I'll take context and the rest of you can have essence." I'm sure nobody was surprised to hear me say that. Relations between musicologists and philosophers who study music have not always been a model of harmony. It's been a rather dissonant counterpoint, in fact, when there has been polyphony at all rather than a case of simultaneous monodies, and the stated theme of the conference, though it used the conjunction *and*, named a binary more often cast in opposition than apposition. We musicologists often have the impression, moreover, that the difference between us and philosophers is that we read their work but they don't read ours. The bibliographies of many books I've read bear this out, as does a lot of anecdotal evidence, such as the story of how I first heard of Nick Zangwill—who, by the way, has an ancestry quite similar to mine. I first encountered his name in a live tweet sent out from a meeting of the Royal Musical Association's Music and Philosophy Study Group by a musicologist named Paul Harper-Scott, who was incensed at Nick's apparent lack of interest in the musicological literature, or in history, or in anything that smacked of "context," and especially at the nonchalance with which he asserted his lack of interest.

Meanwhile, we musicologists do try to keep abreast of current philosophical work, even if we have the annoying habit of contextualizing it historically. We do this precisely because we believe that situating anything in intellectual history effectively neutralizes its claim of universality—a claim that philosophers love to make, but which we regard as fatuously self-aggrandizing. It neither surprises nor deters us that the response from philosophers often amounts to euphemistic paraphrases of the title of an article by the literary scholar Rita Felski—"Context Stinks!"—that I used to assign to my pupils.[1] Whatever they think of our take on their work, we regard the work of contemporary philosophers—indeed, contemporary scholars of all stripes, insofar as their work intersects with ours—as contributions to reception and interpretation, and therefore part of the history of our shared subject.

There are four contemporary philosophers of music with whose work I have engaged in this way. In descending order, so to speak, of closeness of engagement, they are Lydia Goehr, Peter Kivy, and two who were in the room with me as I gave this talk: Jerrold Levinson and Nick Zangwill, the conference organizer and the man with whom I was sharing the stage (he being the session chair), and who, as I'd been warned, had been called out for his impatience with music historians.

1. Rita Felski, "'Context Stinks!'" *New Literary History* 42 (2011): 573–91.

With Lydia Goehr the engagement has been somewhat different from the rest. I don't know whether her fellow philosophers would agree, but to me her work, like Isaiah Berlin's, often resembles intellectual history rather than philosophy as such, precisely because it is so attentive to context. Her first and best known book, *The Imaginary Museum of Musical Works*, performs the sort of operation we musicologists like, historicizing the musical "work concept," as one tends to call it now (following her lead), and thus delimiting its sphere of applicability. Obviously, I think that is a salutary achievement. Indeed, so loudly have I touted her book that the publisher asked me for a foreword when it was reissued in a revised edition.[2] As to Peter Kivy, whose work was far more typical of Anglophone philosophical writing, I have reviewed two of his books (the first two), although I did so in musicological journals that philosophers do not usually read.[3] After the first review appeared, we became friends. The second review temporarily ended our friendship. I will come back to him.

With Levinson and Zangwill contact had been only in writing until we met in Vilnius. Prof. Levinson noticed my review of some Beethoven recordings in the long-defunct *Opus* magazine back in 1987,[4] was surprised to find references in it to names like Roman Ingarden and Nelson Goodman, and sent me a lovely garland of offprints. I made a grumpy response, and that was that for a while; but a decade later I read his *Music in the Moment*[5] with huge interest and wrote about it—or, to be more specific, about its formulation and reception, and that of the concatenationism it espouses—in the last volume of my *Oxford History of Western Music* (or, as I call it, The Ox).[6] Although, like so many works of its kind, Levinson's book sought (or presumed) to make points of general applicability, it looked to me, rather, like an especially pertinent and noteworthy sign of its own particular moment. That stance was then called postmodernism—a term that sounds as antiquated now as "New Musicology"—and like Goehr's work, I thought, it deserved historical contextualization in its own right. So that historicizing (read: relativizing) impulse may count as another indication of the difference between philo-

---

2. Lydia Goehr, *The Imaginary Museum of Musical Works: An Essay in the Philosophy of Music*, rev. ed. (New York: Oxford University Press, 2007).
3. Richard Taruskin, Review of *The Corded Shell: Reflections on Musical Expression* by Peter Kivy, *Musical Quarterly* 68 (1982): 287–93; Taruskin, Review of *Sound and Semblance: Reflections on Musical Representation* by Peter Kivy, *Journal of Music Theory* 29 (1985): 347–58.
4. Richard Taruskin, "Beethoven Symphonies—The New Antiquity," *Opus*, October 1987, 31–41, 43, 63; reprinted in Taruskin, *Text and Act: Essays on Music and Performance* (New York: Oxford University Press, 1995), 202–34.
5. Jerrold Levinson, *Music in the Moment* (Ithaca, NY: Cornell University Press, 1997).
6. Richard Taruskin, *Oxford History of Western Music* (New York: Oxford University Press, 2005), 5:511–13.

sophical and music-historical approaches, or reactions, to artistic and intellectual matters.

As to Nick Zangwill, imagine my surprise when only a few months after learning from Paul Harper-Scott's tweets that he was a particularly obnoxious specimen of insular music philosopher who had not read anything I had written (apparently Paul had asked him), I received, out of the blue, an email from him telling me that he had read—and not only read, but *liked*—the two pages in The Ox devoted to the man Nick called "my hero Hanslick." I had surprised him, he wrote, because, as he put it, "it is rare for him [that is, Hanslick] not to be summarily dismissed by musicologists." (I surprised him further by saying that that assumption surprised me.) He also wrote, most endearingly, that "anyone who dumps on Adorno is a friend of mine." Our mutual surprise was mutually gratifying. It led to an interesting correspondence and, I suppose, it led to my invitation to write and deliver this talk. Especially cheering was Nick's assurance that my treatment of Hanslick was "careful" and "fair." I hope that meant that he thought it was accurate, because I believe we owe it to one another to represent each other's viewpoints accurately whether or not we sympathize with them. There are many—far too many—who hold this most basic requirement to be impossible (and do so, in my opinion, so as to give themselves an alibi). So I will structure the serious part of this presentation as a gloss on the short passage from The Ox that, so to speak, built the bridge between at least one musicologist and one philosopher or aesthetician of music. It seemed an appropriate text on which to base my Vilnius sermon, because it bore directly on the conference theme, and because the position it sympathetically describes—that is, Hanslick's—is actually one with which I do not agree.

II. PLEASURE AND PAIN

Just to contextualize it (since context is my bag): the passage on Hanslick in The Ox comes at the very end of what I consider to be the key chapter of volume 3, *Music in the Nineteenth Century*. It comes right in the middle of that middle volume, and it is actually called "Midcentury." Its main subject is the *neudeutsche Schule* or "New German School," with close attention to its aesthetics, its Hegel-derived philosophy of history, and its universalism, with most of the musical illustrations drawn from the works of Liszt, especially the symphonic poems and the program symphonies. Immediately before the concluding section, on Hanslick, there are some acerbic quotations from Russian composers lampooning the German music of the day. And then this, under a subheading that introduces the catchphrase "Art for Art's Sake":

> As all these Russian quotes suggest, much of the opposition to the New German School came from outside the German-speaking lands, many foreign musicians sus-

pecting nationalistic designs behind the School's universalist pretensions. And yet the opposition's most famous single salvo came from the Austrian critic and music historian Eduard Hanslick (1825–1904), who in 1854 authored a tract called "On the Musically Beautiful" (*Vom musikalisch-Schönen*) that went through many editions (ten within the author's lifetime) and is still in print. It is difficult today to appreciate the polemical force of the title; but at the time, for a German critic to insist on beauty looked to many like virtual treason.[7]

So here is the first gloss. It seems that not only musicians but even aestheticians have forgotten this. In fact, it seems that Nick Zangwill might have forgotten this. In the course of the correspondence through which he and I established friendly relations, he sent me for comment the first draft of the introduction to his recent book, *Music and Aesthetic Reality: Formalism and the Limits of Description*, of which the working title then was *Elusive Music* (a phrase that continues to echo in the book's final sentence).[8] That introduction contains a discussion—under the heading "Beauty and Sublimity?"—of what Wagner called the *Schreckensfanfaren* at the beginning of the last movement in Beethoven's Ninth Symphony, the excruciatingly loud and dissonant bursts that precede the recitatives of the cellos and basses, and later the baritone, the first singer to enter. Nick takes sharp issue with the discussion of them I published in 1989 in an article called "Resisting the Ninth."[9] With apologies for quoting from the superseded draft, Nick's objections were as follows. Following Wagner (he thought), I had made the mistake of

> assigning some of the Ninth to the sublime rather than the beautiful. Hence Taruskin accepts the standard dichotomy [first enunciated by Edmund Burke one hundred years before Hanslick][10] whereby the beautiful and the sublime exclude each other. What is his reason? Surprisingly, Taruskin denies that pleasure is generated by listening to the discordant passages . . . of the Ninth Symphony. He says that many of the musical events "offend the ear," and "However much they move and thrill, they cannot be said to please the listener." This is implausible. [I'll let that go by for now.] These passages in fact give great pleasure, a kind of intense pleasure, a pleasure in "dissonance" and "shattering" sounds. It is just a different kind of pleasure from the pleasure we take in the Levinsonian [that is, Burkean] beauty of much Mozart. . . . But it is still pleasure. Would Taruskin deny that heavy metal fans feel pleasure when

---

7. Taruskin, *Oxford History of Western Music* 3:441–42.

8. Nick Zangwill, *Music and Aesthetic Reality: Formalism and the Limits of Description* (New York: Routledge, 2015).

9. Richard Taruskin, "Resisting the Ninth," *19th-Century Music* 12 (1988–89): 241–56; reprinted in Taruskin, *Text and Act*, 235–61.

10. Edmund Burke, *A Philosophical Enquiry into the Origin of Our Ideas of the Sublime and Beautiful*, in *Music and Aesthetics in the Eighteenth and Early-Nineteenth Centuries* (1757), ed. Peter le Huray and James Day (Cambridge: Cambridge University Press. 1981).

listening to Motörhead's "Ace of Spades"?[11] This is implausible. They love it—as they swing their heads up and down. . . . I am sure that Taruskin does not need reminding that some bodily pleasures can also be intense and overwhelming without ceasing to be pleasures. [Who, me?] Taruskin seems to have an over-simple view of the pleasures that we may take in musical beauty. Only that explains his severing beauty from the sublime.

All I can say in response to that is that if I am simplistic, then so are Burke and Kant, who committed the same severance, as did almost all nineteenth-century thinkers about aesthetics—all but Hanslick, in fact. Burke wrote, as explicitly as you please, that the sublime and the beautiful "are indeed ideas of a very different nature, one being founded on pain, the other on pleasure."[12] If everyone in Hanslick's time had disagreed with that, and agreed instead with Nick about the sublime and the beautiful, and about pleasure and pain as embodied and conveyed not only by nature (which provided most of the models for the sublime) but also by art, then Hanslick would not have had to write his book, and it would not have been at all controversial in its own day or subsequently. That is why even Hanslick must be contextualized, say I—and even Nick Zangwill needs to be contextualized, whether or not it gives him pleasure. I wrote back to Nick after reading his introduction and raised these points. "I think it wrong to equate beauty with pleasure," I told him,

> and then define pleasure so broadly that it includes the sublime. I take seriously Burke's distinction between beauty based on pleasure and sublimity based on pain, and so did Beethoven in the Ninth, when he has his baritone (words here by Beethoven, not Schiller) ask for something *angenehmerer* [more pleasant]. The beautiful for Beethoven and Burke (and Kant) is what is *angenehm*. Your more strenuous pleasures they would not have called pleasant.

There are so many other voices I might have quoted. There is Schumann: "People say, 'It pleased,' or 'It did not please'; as if there were nothing higher than to please people!"[13] There is Berlioz, weeping at a concert, who said to a neighbor who asked him why he did not leave: "Madame, do you think I am here to enjoy myself?"[14] The bland equation of beauty and pleasure, and the assimilation of the

---

11. Available online here for those who want to test it for pleasure: www.youtube.com/watch?v=1iwC2QljLn4.

12. Burke, *A Philosophical Enquiry*, 260–65.

13. Robert Schumann, *Gesammelte Schriften über Musik und Musiker*, vol. 4 (Leipzig: Georg Wigand, 1854), 278: "'Es hat gefallen' oder 'es hat nicht gefallen' sagen die Leute. Als ob es nichts Höheres gäbe, als den Leuten zu gefallen!"; translated by Piero Weiss in *Music in the Western World: A History in Documents*, ed. Piero Weiss and Richard Taruskin, 2nd ed. (Belmont, CA: Cengage Learning, 2007), 307.

14. Ernest Legouvé, *Soixante ans de souvenirs* (Paris: J. Hetzel, 1886), 321: "Est-ce que vous croyez que je suis ici pour mon plaisir?"

sublime to the beautiful as just another form of pleasure, is thus at least anachronistic or acontextual—which is fine if you think it's fine to decontextualize. I don't. I think the act of decontextualization entails a significant loss. When you deliberately adopt an ahistorical, essentialist viewpoint, it becomes impossible to make what seem to me necessary distinctions—as Nick himself demonstrated when revising his introduction.

In fact, he did me the honor of taking on board my points regarding Burke, whom he had not mentioned in the original version, and also regarding Beethoven's use of the word *angenehm*. Here is what he wrote in the published version of the book, somewhat condensed:

> We could frame a conception of sublimity, following Edmund Burke, where pleasure in the sublime is a mix of pleasure and pain [not in fact what he said], and this may fit *some* examples of sublimity in nature, for example, when we enjoy perceiving a powerful wave or a huge precipice. But . . . the question is: why think that anything threatening is in question when we listen to (literally) harmless music? The pleasure we take in discordant music, such as in passages of the 9th, . . . is just pleasure with no pain mixed into it.[15]

To which I can only reply, "Speak for yourself, sir." Burke would surely find Nick's blithe dismissal unacceptable, as do I. If you are in fact doing that, i.e., speaking for yourself, then you are merely taking yourself as the measure of all things. I will concede that Kant might have accepted Nick's argument, but as you may recall from the passages on music from the *Critique of Judgment*, Kant was incapable of hearing in music anything beyond a pretty tinkling.[16] Not somebody, he, whose musical judgments we should follow. Beethoven would have found Nick's lack of receptivity to his message utterly incomprehensible, as we know from his text. But here is how Nick accounted for that:

> In the last movement of the 9th Symphony, Beethoven has his tenor [sic] ask for something "angenehmerer," which might indeed be supposed to contrast with what went before. He is presumably asking for some Levinsonian [well, Burkean] beauty. But the implied contrast *might* not be with pleasure mixed with pain, as in a scary fairground ride, but with a less sweet kind of pleasure.[17]

---

15. Zangwill, *Music and Aesthetic Reality*, 6.

16. According to Immanuel Kant, then: "If . . . we estimate the worth of the fine arts by the culture they supply to the mind, and adopt for our standard the expansion of the faculties whose confluence, in judgement, is necessary for cognition, music, then, since it plays merely with sensations, has the lowest place among the fine arts—just as it has perhaps the highest among those valued at the same time for their agreeableness" (Kant, *Critique of Judgement*, trans. James Creed Meredith [Oxford: Oxford University Press, 2007], 158).

17. Zangwill, *Music and Aesthetic Reality*, 6 (italics added).

Or again, it might not. Here I am tempted to get gruff like John Maynard Keynes, who when accused of inconstancy is popularly reported to have said, "When my information changes, I alter my conclusions. What do you do, sir?"[18] I always used to tell my pupils that sentences containing words like *may* or *might* are not legitimate arguments, because they cannot be falsified. What do you tell your pupils, Prof. Zangwill? But let me quote the conclusion he drew from the discussion in question: "The issue about the sublime is not: what is our conception of it? But: which conception of the sublime do we need? . . . We certainly do not need to be bound by Burke's pleasure/pain conception of the sublime." And this enabled him to finish this section of the introduction the way he had finished it previously, by concluding that "we may take beauty to be the central aesthetic value in thinking about music, even in the case of Beethoven's 9th Symphony."[19] I would interpret such talk of what we "need" in a conception of the sublime—that is, Nick's definition of the purpose his conception of the sublime was meant to serve—in terms of that conclusion. The conception we need is the one that will lead us to the conclusion that we want. Is that not the very model of a circular path of reasoning?

Another thing I used to remind my pupils is that when rules get too easy, games become dull. Giving due weight to counterexamples is an important rule, and it is one that I have often seen philosophers flout. I said I'd come back to Peter Kivy, who liked to take polls of imaginary listeners to confirm his postulates about musical meaning, implying that such questions might be decided by an imagined majority vote. That's a difference from musicological practice right there. When we want to find out whether people actually agree with us, we ask actual people. And the reason is that actual people, as opposed to imaginary ones, will often surprise us. Polls of imaginary listeners, like North Korean elections, always come out the way they are supposed to. It was an imaginary poll that supported Kivy's assignment of immanent affect to the opening measures of Mozart's G Minor Symphony, no. 40; and when I reported results of an actual poll that did not conform, and which, I thought, supplied proof positive that musical affect, here and everywhere, was not immanent but attributed,[20] I was astonished to find, in Kivy's next book, my evidence quite casually dismissed. Sigmund Spaeth, an actual person who, unlike Kivy's imaginary ones, found the symphony's opening theme to be "a very happy tune, . . . full of laughter and fun,"[21] was, Kivy asserted, a "merely subjective" outlier, and no threat to the principle of (imaginary) consensus. That was truly

---

18. It may have been the later economist Paul Samuelson who, purportedly quoting Keynes, actually said it first. See Samuelson, "The Keynes Centenary: Sympathy from the Other," in *The Collected Scientific Papers of Paul Samuelson*, ed. Kate Crowley (Cambridge, MA: MIT Press, 1986), 275–76, at 275.

19. Zangwill, *Music and Aesthetic Reality*, 6.

20. See "What Else?," chapter 8 in this volume, p. 229–30.

21. Sigmund Spaeth, *Great Symphonies: How to Recognize and Remember Them* (Garden City, NY: Garden City Publishing Co., 1936), 39.

enviable mental insulation, I thought. Nick Zangwill never retreats that far into complacency, even if he also tends to rely a bit too much for my taste on introspection (which is to say, on the assumption of an immutable human nature that he reliably exemplifies). But here is how Kivy justifies his rejection of Spaeth's take on Mozart's theme:

> What we . . . do when confronted with an expressive characterization of a piece of music, is to go back to the music itself [and that is an expression we, too, will have to come back to] with that interpretation in mind, to see if we, too, can hear what the interpreter claims to hear. And if no consensus develops, surely we are arguing to the best explanation here, as in the case of . . . aberrant judgment[s] about wine, when we argue that that characterization is "merely subjective." What else, for example, could we say, or need we say, to Sigmund Spaeth?[22]

III. SOUND AND SENSE AND VALUE

Kivy's locution "the music itself" is one that we have probably all employed. Nick Zangwill certainly uses it, along with tautological variants like "music as music."[23] I have tried hard to wean myself from using such phrases, and I hope I have made all my pupils self-conscious enough to avoid them, because they reek of hidden assumptions about the very thing we are met here to investigate, namely the nature or essence of music—assuming that there is such a thing. I've even written about the term "the music itself" and reasons for avoiding it.[24] But in order to reframe the issue, let me resume the discussion of Hanslick from The Ox, which I interrupted after its first paragraph for what turned out to be a rather lengthy gloss:

> Unsurprisingly, Hanslick located the beautiful in music not in its freight of meaning, but in its sheer patterning ("arabesques") of sound. The object of derisive caricature from the beginning, his views are often misunderstood. Contrary to what his critics have alleged, he did not deny the emotional effects of music, nor did he deny its power to embody and convey poetic subject matter. What he did deny was the essentially musical nature of such a task (that is, its relevance to the true aims and tasks of music as an art), and hence the ultimate musical value of those effects and that embodiment.
>
> "The Representation of Feeling," reads the title of the crucial second chapter, "Is Not the Content of Music." Needless to say, everything hinges on how the word "content" is defined, and on whether it is to be distinguished from "form" (another pro-

---

22. Peter Kivy, *Sound Sentiment: An Essay on the Musical Emotions, Including the Complete Text of "The Corded Shell"* (Philadelphia: Temple University Press, 1989), 204.
23. E.g., *Music and Aesthetic Reality*, 1, 11 ("music itself"), 155 ("music as music").
24. Richard Taruskin, "A Myth of the Twentieth Century: *The Rite of Spring*, the Tradition of the New, and 'The Music Itself,'" *Modernism/Modernity* 2 (1995): 1–26; reprinted in Taruskin, *Defining Russia Musically* (Princeton: Princeton University Press, 1997), 360–88.

tean concept). The New German position [that is, the position of the *neudeutsche Schule*] cast feeling and form in opposition; the Hanslickian stance melded them. Hanslick's very definition of musical content (which became a famous and notoriously untranslatable slogan) was *tönend bewegte Form*—something like "form put in motion by sound" or "sounding form in motion."[25]

I can see why Nick Zangwill approved of my description of Hanslick and his theory, because these two paragraphs summarize, and do not attempt to refute, the formalist postulates from which Nick developed his own theory of what he calls aesthetic realism, including Hanslick's famous metaphorical definition of music, which gave rise to Nick's own original theory of Essential Metaphor. There is a winning passage in the preface to his recent book in which Nick describes his first reading of Hanslick: "I devoured the book in a frenzy, walking around the centre of [Los Angeles], punching the air, muttering 'Yes!', 'You are right!', 'Thank God someone is saying this!', 'You hit the nail on the head!'"[26]

I had a similar experience when I first read Mr. H. as a college undergraduate. He had been assigned to us by the professor in a class on nineteenth-century music, which was not considered canonical in those days (the early 1960s) but was taught as an elective supplement to the required music history sequence. And what our professor told us when assigning the book was: "You will be amazed at how much of Hanslick you will agree with." It was a disguised Svengali-like command. We were told to agree, and agree we did. Only much later did I come to question these positions. So it was not at all the case in those days that musicologists tended to dismiss Hanslick. I don't even think they (that is, we) do that even now, as a matter of consensus. But for now let us concentrate on the matter of musical content as Hanslick defines it, and the consequences that Nick Zangwill, among many others, has drawn from it. The starting point for him was Hanslick's assertion that the beauty of music, hence its value, "consists simply and solely of tones and their *artistic combination*."[27]

---

25. Taruskin, *Oxford History of Western Music* 3:441. The published translations of Hanslick's treatise all stumble over this phrase. Gustav Cohen (1891) finessed the issue of form altogether by translating the sentence in which the phrase occurs (with Hanslick's italics)—"Der Inhalt der Musik sind *tönend bewegte Formen*"—as "The essence of music is sound and motion." Geoffrey Payzant (1986) has "tonally moving forms," which, by rendering *tönend* with a false cognate, seems to invoke a particular style of music. Most recently, Lee Rothfarb and Christoph Landerer offer the overly literal "sonically moved forms," which conveys little to anyone who has not read their elaborate justification for it (*Eduard Hanslick's "On the Musically Beautiful": A New Translation* [New York: Oxford University Press, 2018], xl–xliii), although it is worth keeping in mind their admonition that the German *Ton* means more than the English *sound* (for which the German would be *Klang*), since *Ton* implies the fixed pitch by which musical tones differ from nonmusical sounds.

26. Zangwill, *Music and Aesthetic Reality*, xi.

27. Eduard Hanslick, *On the Musically Beautiful*, trans. Geoffrey Payzant (Indianapolis: Hackett, 1986), 28 (italics added), quoted frequently in Zangwill, *Music and Aesthetic Reality*, beginning on page 10.

Minus the "simply and solely," who would disagree? When I used to teach introductory music courses, first at Columbia and then at Berkeley, my first lecture was unabashedly Hanslickian. All the examples were drawn from speech rather than song, starting with my own lecturing voice, proceeding through poems of increasingly obvious "musicality." The culminating trio of examples were, first, Andrey Voznesensky's stentorian recording of *Goya*, perhaps the most alliterative and assonant poem ever written (which came through even to students who knew no Russian and who therefore heard it as music by default—or so I told them):

Ya – Goya!	I am Goya!
Glaznitsy voronok mne vykleval vorog sletaya na polye nagoye	Of the bare field, by the enemy's beak gouged till the craters of my eyes gape
Ya – gorye,	I am grief!
Ya – golos,	I am the tongue
Voyny, gorodov golovni na snegu sorok pervogo goda.	of war, the embers of cities on the snows of the year 1941.
Ya – golod.	I am hunger.
Ya – gorlo	I am the gullet
Poveshannoy baby, ch'yo telo, kak kolokol bilo nad ploshchad'yu golovoy...	of a woman hanged whose body like a bell tolled over a blank square.
Ya – Goya!	I am Goya!
O grozdi vozmezdiya!	O grapes of wrath!
Vzvil zalpom na Zapad ya pepel' nezvannogo gostya!	I have hurled westward the ashes of the uninvited guest!
I v memorial'noye nebo vbil krepkiye zvyozdy—	And hammered stars into the unforgetting sky—
kak gvozdy!	Like nails!
Ya – Goya![28]	I am Goya!

Next, a sublimely hokey rendition, recorded in 1915 by the actor Taylor Holmes (1878–1959), of Kipling's "Boots (Infantry Columns)," which manipulated musical parameters, rhythm and dynamics in particular, in an obvious way to achieve an emotional payoff:

We're foot—slog—slog—slog—sloggin' over Africa!
Foot—foot—foot—foot—sloggin' over Africa—
(Boots—boots—boots—boots—movin' up and down again!)
There's no discharge in the war! [etc.]

[28] Andrey Voznesensky, *Гойя* (1959), in Voznesensky, *Antiworlds and the Fifth Ace,* bilingual ed. (New York: Schocken, 1973); translation by Richard Wilbur. Both the original and the translation are aurally available at www.youtube.com/watch?v=JteoA15W1fU.

And finally, Ernst Toch's *Fuge aus der Geographie* (you know, *Rrrratibor!*, or, in English, *Trrrrinidad!*), which by then the students had no trouble seeing as having nothing to do with Trinidad the island, or the river Mississippi, or the lake Titicaca, but was "simply and solely," as Hanslick would have said, about the sound of words. It was music, not poetry, and Ernst Toch, who made it, was a composer, not a poet. My closing maxim was a virtual paraphrase of the line that Nick Zangwill prised out of Hanslick to serve as his motto: Whatever else it may be, I used to tell my students, music consists first of sounds that are manipulated artistically to produce patterns to which our minds (I didn't call them "organs of pure contemplation,"[29] but I might as well have done so at that stage) respond with pleasure of sometimes amazing intensity. And I'd say, "But of course you know that already," and hope that the final bell would ring on cue.

But what did they know? That those patterns were alone what made music valuable to them? They certainly did not know that, and I never tried to persuade them of that, because I did not believe that. Do you? "Tones and their artistic combination" was merely a default definition of music, at best a *sine qua non*, or a ground zero, but hardly the essence of "music qua music" or "music as music," or whatever other tautological phrase one might summon up, as every philosopher of music seems to need to do—and many musicologists as well, notably Joseph Kerman, my late friend and colleague, whose book *Contemplating Music* sought to redefine the field of musicology, and failed—precisely, in my opinion, because it continued to rely, and to founder, on the old tautologies.[30] To identify the aesthetic properties of music as "consist[ing] simply and solely of tones and their artistic combination" seems to me tantamount to asserting that writing has grammar before it has subject matter, and so when we discuss a poem or a novel we should talk simply and solely about grammar. Rather than pure, I would call that approach limited. In a bad mood I might call it impoverished. I suspect everyone here would agree with me in the case of literature; I know that Nick does. So why not music?

I wrote some of this back to Nick when he showed me his draft introduction, but unlike the points about the beautiful and the sublime, my objections on this score had no effect at all, and I suspect that Nick regarded my views the way Peter Kivy regarded my review of his second book: as coming from someone untrained in philosophy and therefore impossible to reply to within the terms of the discipline. But that would reinforce mental and disciplinary insulation and would again cause me to wonder whether philosophers actually seek isolation and promote it by way of pedagogy, whereas I have been at pains to discourage my pupils from seeking refuge from outsiders in professional discourse.

---

29. As translated by Gustav Cohen in 1891; see Eduard Hanslick, *The Beautiful in Music*, trans. G. Cohen (Indianapolis: Hackett, 1957), 11.

30. Joseph Kerman, *Contemplating Music: Challenges to Musicology* (Cambridge, MA: Harvard University Press, 1985), 32, 55, 163, 165, etc.

IV. REACHING THE ESSENCE (OF THE DISPUTE)

It would be a pity if we were to maintain our mutual isolation, because I am not asking rhetorical questions when I query such things as the identification of musical essences. I really want an answer—I want dialogue—because my difficulties with essence go further down than identification. I have a problem not only with the naming of this or that as the essence of music, but with the whole idea of essence as applied to music, or to any other product of culture. Realizing that in order to question the use of the word intelligently, or even intelligibly, I needed to know how it is defined by those who use it, I scoured Nick's recent book for a definition. *Essence*, alas, has no entry in its index, but "Essential Metaphor Thesis" has a whole chapter, so I went there. And I learned that the Hanslick-derived (or at least Hanslick-compatible) aesthetic properties of music that constitute its value, and which can only be described using metaphors, are nevertheless real, located "out there" (or perhaps I should say "in there"), and are therefore to be regarded as "mind-independent."

That was another term whose definition I needed to learn, so I pursued it in the index. And on its first occurrence Nick wrote, "These aesthetic properties are thought of as 'mind independent,' in some suitable sense—an issue that I will not explore in this book."[31] That's the sort of thing that makes you want to kill an author, but the murderous impulse found a peaceable outlet in a note that referred the reader to Nick's earlier book, *The Metaphysics of Beauty*. In the first flush of our bromance I had purchased that book, so I could follow the lead. It had nearly a whole chapter on mind-independence, so I was back in business. And this is what I read: "By mind-independence I shall mean that whether something possesses a property does not depend on whether we think it does."[32] The definition hardly surprised me. It was just what I might have guessed the term meant. But professional discourse is always full of snares and traps for the unwary, and I had to be sure. But now that I have a concrete formulation to test against my own intuitions, you must forgive the little boy in the crowd for saying bluntly what is on his mind.

Is it not paradoxical, in the most literal sense of the word, to describe a product of our minds (in this case music) as having mind-independent properties? Music owes its very existence to our minds. How then could it be independent of them? Nor is this the only time in Nick's work where what I regard as a basic category distinction—that between nature and culture—is rather blithely disregarded, as it is rather commonly, I have found, in works of analytical philosophy. And well might it be. Such a category confusion is ensured—all but mandated, in fact—by the resolutely ahistorical methods that philosophers insist upon when dealing

---

31. Zangwill, *Music and Aesthetic Reality*, 15.
32. Nick Zangwill, *The Metaphysics of Beauty* (Ithaca, NY: Cornell University Press, 2001), 177.

with what to me are inescapably historical manifestations, delimited by the historical circumstances in which they arise. An excellent case in point is Hanslick's very treatise, which, I believe (and showed, I think, in The Ox), could only have been written when in fact it *was* written, in the 1850s, because it took the environment in which Hanslick was then living (an environment disagreeably dominated by Wagner) to provoke it.

There was a footnote in Nick's draft introduction that anticipated this very objection:

> Sometimes, I suspect that a concept/object confusion is being made by writers who step from a claim about the historical context for the idea of absolute music [that is, music whose aesthetic properties are not compromised by the admixture of words] to a claim about absolute music itself. The emergence of the concepts of evolution or the big bang was historically specific but they apply to things far beyond those historically restricted limits; in fact they refer to events before human beings evolved.

So even if Hanslick was historical, this meant, the truths he uncovered were not. I went ahead and made the anticipated objection anyway in my correspondence with Nick, questioning the propriety of putting Hanslick in the company of biologists and cosmologists. To say that the values Hanslick identified were timeless values despite the fact that their identification had to await Hanslick is not very convincing, I thought. Evolutionary and cosmological theorists deal with God's creations, which existed before us and will outlast us. (And that is why I have no problem regarding the ontological status of mountains and galaxies as mind-independent.) We discover whatever it is that we know about them. But music is the creation of God's creatures. We are its makers, not its discoverers. It did not and could not exist before human beings evolved, and it will not outlast us. We assert rather than discover its values.

Not only that, but it flouts the history of musical thought and practice to say that formal properties are anterior to representational ones, or that the propositional content of music is necessarily secondary to its aesthetic properties, however these are defined. Until the end of the eighteenth century there was not a person on earth who would have agreed with Hanslick or with Zangwill (or with me when I am in the mood) in valuing instrumental music above vocal. By the end of the nineteenth century there were many people who did. The changing preference depended on changes in historically contingent cultural attitudes, not on the discovery or the correct identification of the nature of music. So I would call out the linking of Hanslick with Darwin or the Big Banger, whoever she or he may have been, as another category error.

Nick took that footnote out of the published text, but the published book continues to lump nature and culture in a way that continues to perplex me, and to cloud the issue, and I wonder how widespread is the habit among philosophers to devalue or minimize the distinction.[33] A particularly vivid example of its potential for doing harm comes in the chapter of Nick's book in which he meets head-on the claims of "New Musicology" from the formalist perspective. Inevitably, Susan McClary's writings on Beethoven's Ninth are exhibit A. To his great credit, Nick does not quote her most inflammatory comment, namely that the recapitulation in the first movement embodies "the throttling, murderous rage of a rapist incapable of attaining release," which appeared only in a newsletter of very limited circulation and was already toned down for publication in her first book of essays.[34] He then loses credit by telling us about it in a Ciceronian footnote: "I discuss these passages not her infamous reference to rape in an earlier version."[35]

Nevertheless, what remains—ascriptions to the music of violence, explosive rage, and "the contradictory impulses that have organized patriarchal culture since the Enlightenment"—suffices to provide the necessary grist for philosophical ridicule.

> At first sight, this seems like a ludicrous delusion, like finding expressions of patriarchal values in clouds or rock formations. Perhaps the cumulonimbus cloud is masculine or male or violent whereas the cirrus cloud is feminine or female or peaceful? Or perhaps thinking that is sexist and we should really think the opposite? Why is saying something similar about patterns of sounds any less ridiculous? Nevertheless, McClary has found sympathetic ears among musicologists. Why is this? Partly, no doubt, because of fashions in the humanities and wider political trends.

Having just quoted an author out of context in his presence, and having done so at a conference that is actually devoted (or half-devoted) to context, I hasten to adduce Nick's next sentences in mitigation: "And yet, I confess that I find that there is a residual remainder that is somewhat compelling in her descriptions. . . . I urge

---

33. At least one philosopher, Roger Scruton, insists on the distinction at least as adamantly as I do, writing recently that philosophy "should be intent on distinguishing the human world from the order of nature, and the concepts through which we understand appearances from those used in explaining them," adding that "for this reason . . . I believe aesthetics to be central to philosophy, being the branch of philosophy that deals directly with our most studied attempts to create and discern what is truly meaningful" (Roger Scruton and Timothy Williamson, "But Is It Science?" *Times Literary Supplement*, 3 November 2017, 16–18, at 16). To boil down the rest of Scruton's long argument in terms relevant to the present discussion, natural science looks for essence, humanities (i.e., the study of human artifacts) looks for meaning.

34. Susan McClary, "Comment: Getting Down Off the Beanstalk—The Presence of a Woman's Voice in Janika Vandervelde's *Genesis II*," *Minnesota Composers Forum Newsletter*, January 1987, 7; McClary, *Feminine Endings: Music, Gender, and Sexuality* (Minneapolis: University of Minnesota Press, 1991), 128.

35. Zangwill, *Music and Aesthetic Reality*, 134. The allusion is to Cicero's famous use of apophasis in the First Oration against Cateline: "*I pass over* older instances, such as how Caius Servilius Ahala with his own hand slew Spurius Maelius when plotting a revolution in the state" (trans. C. D. Yonge [London, 1856]).

the reader to listen to the passage with McClary in hand. There is something right about her descriptions of the music itself."[36]

The solution to the problem, of course, is to be sought in metaphor. The rapist's rage, we are assured, is not inherent in the music, but invoking it gives us a way of describing our reaction and justifying our evaluation. The violence and rage exist not in "the music itself" but only in McClary's persuasive description of it. Such things can only exist in descriptions, not in the thing itself; and yet it is an important part of Nick's theory that it must be where it is, for metaphor is the only avenue along which music can be evaluatively described. And this is because (quoting now a very important thesis statement) "the essence of music and of our musical experience lies in the aesthetic properties of sound and does not lie in emotion or meaning" (so far this is boilerplate Hanslick), but to this Zangwill adds that this view of music itself "is accompanied by a view of linguistic descriptions of music, which denies literal sense to the bulk of our linguistic descriptions of music."[37]

"Paradigm aesthetic properties"—those properties, that is, that are actually inherent and real—are only two: "beauty and ugliness." Other properties are admitted to "the music itself" in a secondary capacity, as designating ways of being beautiful or ugly. One list of them includes "elegance, plaintiveness, forcefulness, [and] delicacy."[38] Descriptions of rage and violence, then, are admissible into a discussion of Beethoven's Ninth so long as we take it as read that we are not really talking about rage and violence but about loud and dissonant sounds. To put it in terms relevant to our conference propaedeutic, "The aesthetic description of music is *essentially* nonliteral."[39]

So it would appear that masculine rage does potentially have a place in a description of Beethoven's Ninth—and that it might even have a place in a description of a cumulonimbus cloud, so long as the description is suitably metaphorical and offered as such. And that is because both clouds, which God makes, and musical patterns, which we make, have a mind-independent essence that supports metaphorical descriptions. The category error that I persist in diagnosing in the aesthetic realist position would seem to remain in place. Meteorology has room for a McClary after all. Moreover, the way the thesis is framed in the sentence I have quoted—"the aesthetic description of music is *essentially* nonliteral"—makes its truth depend on the definition of *aesthetic*, for there are other ways of describing music, including some other, nonaesthetic and literal, ones that are legitimate with respect to the aesthetic realist theory (for example, description in terms of composing technique, as in music analysis). But if the identification of music's

---

36. Zangwill, *Music and Aesthetic Reality*, 129.
37. Ibid., 16.
38. Ibid., 15.
39. Ibid., 20 (italics original).

essence depends on the meaning of the word *aesthetic,* then "essence" is actually being ascribed to a definition. Is that allowed? Really?

V. TIME AND SPACE

And there is yet another problem I've been having with this theory, which, as I learn from Nick, is an "ineffabilist" position. It involves the theory's definition of metaphor, which appears to me to be fraught with inconsistencies. I was very surprised to find "plaintiveness" listed above among the secondary aesthetic properties, along with forcefulness, elegance, and delicacy. The word simply means "sadness," which is something I regard as quite effable. How is that to be squared with the *echt*-Hanslickian assertion that "the essence of music and of our musical experience lies in the aesthetic properties of sound and does not lie in emotion or meaning"? But that is the less important or damaging horn of the dilemma. Nick lists all kinds of concepts and attributes that might be carelessly regarded as literal when applied to music but which are properly to be viewed as metaphors, and yet his definition of aesthetic realism, explicitly provided for uninitiated readers like me, and one of the most important passages in the book, is as follows (I will give the whole paragraph, so as to provide sufficient context):

> "Realism" is a word familiar to philosophers, but others may not be familiar with it. By "realism" about musical experience, I mean a view that foregrounds the *aesthetic properties* of music and our experience of these properties: musical experience is an awareness of an array of sounds and of the aesthetic properties that they determine. Our experience is directed onto the sound structure and its aesthetic properties. This is the *content* of musical experience. Anything else, such as other mental states caused by such musical experience, is not part of *the intrinsic nature* of musical experience. They are a distraction from *the music itself.* Our basic or primary musical experience is of the music—of the sounds and their aesthetic properties.[40]

I take it that there are no metaphors in this passage. Here we are talking, as realists, about the real thing. And yet a metaphor lurks withal, demanding justification in this context. That metaphor, I hope you have noticed, is "structure." The word properly denotes complex entities, that is, wholes consisting of parts that define the whole in their mutual relations. I maintain the word is, and can only be, a metaphor when applied to temporal unfoldings, and the dictionary supports me. My trusty desk dictionary, the 1950 edition of the *American College Dictionary,* which has been on my desk for a very long time, gives these meanings:

1. A mode of building, construction, or organization; arrangement of parts, elements, or constituents.

---

40. Ibid., 14 (italics added).

2. Something built or constructed: a building, bridge, dam, framework, etc.
3. A complex system considered from the point of view of the whole rather than of any single part: *the structure of modern science.*
4. Anything composed of parts arranged together in some way; an organization.
5. *Biol.* mode of organization; construction and arrangement of tissues, parts, or organs.
6. *Geol.*
    a) the attitude of a bed or stratum, or of beds or strata of sedimentary rocks, as indicated by the dip and strike.
    b) coarser features of rocks as contrasted with their texture.
7. The manner in which atoms in a molecule are joined to each other, especially in organic chemistry where it is represented by a diagram of the molecular arrangement.[41]

Particularly telling is the seventh definition, because as we all know—all us musicologists, at any rate—what is called the structure of a musical composition is often—in fact, usually—represented for purposes of discussion by abstracted diagrams, i.e., visually, which is to say atemporally. So if the word is to function as a musical descriptor at all, it must be in a metaphorical sense that puts space in place of time. I am sure that Jerrold Levinson will recognize this covert appeal to metaphor, because he has written a whole book whose purpose is exposing it. It is the book I have already mentioned, *Music in the Moment,* which endeavors to debunk "the notion," as the author puts it on the first page of the preface, "often only implicit in the writing of many music commentators and theoreticians, that keeping music's form—in particular, large-scale *structural* relationships, or spatialized representations of a musical composition's shape—before the mind is somehow central to, even *essential* for, basic musical understanding."[42] Prof. Levinson defines musical understanding entirely in terms of the perception and cognition of immediate short-range connections between consecutive musical events, without any need for metaphorical visual aids or analogies.

As you can guess, I am sympathetic to Levinson's revision of Zangwill's aesthetic realism, even if I think he, too, overstates his case. For one thing, trained musicians do consciously learn, as part of their training, to listen over longer spans than Prof. Levinson deems natural, and I believe that nonprofessionals can also profitably learn to extend the compass of their hearing. But we can leave that point moot, because I think I can show that we all do hear long-range relationships

---

41. *American College Dictionary,* ed. Clarence L. Barnhart (New York: Random House, 1950), 1200.
42. Levinson, *Music in the Moment,* ix (italics added)

when the composer wants us to, as our listening experience (and my "our" here is meant to include Prof. Levinson) will confirm.

There is a half-hearted chapter later in *Music in the Moment* in which the author somewhat grudgingly allows that thematic recalls between movements are available to alert nonprofessional listeners' perception, and that they might even enhance aesthetic pleasure. As an example, he cites the brief and understated reminiscence, near the end of the second movement in Schumann's Piano Concerto, of the first movement's main theme. He had previously called attention to vague thematic resemblances or allusions among the various movements of Brahms's Third Symphony, Ravel's String Quartet, and pieces by Bach and Haydn. He tries hard to minimize the significance of such relationships to the listener:

> When conscious recognition of connection between a current bit and some earlier component of the piece saliently occurs, what exactly is the content of such a recognition?
>
> The answer, I think, is that such content is of an almost completely nonspecific sort. That is, the content is on the order of: "This bit, or something like it, occurred earlier." ... Not only is it the rule for such recognition in even experienced listeners to be in this sense nonspecific, rather than specific, but they need be no more than that in order to heighten a listener's sense of a piece's unity, or to provide the ancillary pleasure of detecting construction.[43]

But I think he is underestimating both the listener's imaginative engagement and the composer's ability, when he wishes, to enlist it. Think of another Schumann piece, the Piano Quintet in E-flat Major, op. 44, in which (as discussed in detail in chapter 4) the opening theme from the first movement comes back as an unanticipated countersubject to provide the blazing climax to the big fugue in the finale.[44] It is no subtle allusion, but a calculated emotional thrill, and it enlists another metaphor: the metaphor of return, which puts the quintet in a line of artworks and legends that, as noted in that prior chapter, includes *The Odyssey,* the parable of the Prodigal Son, and the Book of Revelation. Is it possible to miss the return and still enjoy the moment? Of course it is, but I still think we are meant to notice it and that most of us do, and that when we do our enjoyment is greatly enhanced. And there is an even more vivid example from Schubert, to whose First Piano Trio Prof. Levinson makes a very pertinent reference,[45] but whose Second Piano Trio contains an even more spectacular, because twofold and very impressively sustained, full quotation of the slow movement's main dead-march theme at the climax of the finale. I feel quite sure that that thrilling moment is the reason

---

43. Ibid., 64–65.
44. See chapter 4, "Is There a Baby in the Bathwater?" pp. 118–19.
45. Levinson, *Music in the Moment,* 27.

why, of the two trios, the second was the one that was published (as opus 100) during Schubert's lifetime.

I'll bet that Prof. Levinson has heard it, and that it gave him goose bumps. Goose bumps surely beat the "ancillary," rather smug and cerebral "pleasure of detecting construction," no? But despite these occasional exaggerations or oversights I think Prof. Levinson is entirely correct to place the musical emphasis where he puts it (and where it belongs): that is, on the temporal unfolding and its real-time effect on the listener. To place the emphasis on the temporal is to emphasize the actual performance over the idealized work, and the actual performance is what actual listeners to music actually attend to. Hanslick knew that. That's what the *Bewegung* in *tönend bewegte Formen* is all about. In the second chapter of his treatise, he wrote that "the concept of motion has up to now been conspicuously neglected in investigations of the nature and effects of music, [but] it seems to us the most important and fruitful concept."[46] And he knew that it was a metaphor. Honoring Christ over John the Baptist, I prefer Hanslick's version, which chooses motion-in-time as the primary metaphor, to Zangwill's, which chooses atemporal structure. But even Hanslick, I think, was too intent on locating the essence of music in the work rather than the performance, which is to substitute a less appropriate for a more appropriate metaphor.

VI. IN CONCLUSION

So although I am gratified—and grateful—that Nick Zangwill credits me with fairness to his hero, for me he is not "the great Hanslick." I think he has been too readily followed and believed. I do not see that he has been rejected, the way Nick has claimed. For a very long time he was one of musicology's gurus, and although there have been noisy and occasionally exaggerated defections, he is still a powerful presence on our scene. So let me resume and conclude my little passage from The Ox, which I have now twice interrupted for lengthy glosses. Earlier in the chapter I had referred to a pronouncement by the Russian composer and critic Alexander Serov, who despite his nationality was a major spokesman of the *neudeutsche Schule*. Writing in 1859 in the *Neue Zeitschrift für Musik,* which under the editorship of Franz Brendel had become the *Schule*'s official organ, Serov poached some terminology from economics so that he could grandly proclaim: "Das Criterium des musikalischen Gesetzes liegt nicht in den Ohren des Consumenten, es liegt in der Kunstidee des Producenten" (The basis of musical law lies not in the ear of the consumer but in the artistic inspiration [literally, the "art-idea"] of the producer).[47] That

---

46. Hanslick, *On the Musically Beautiful,* 11.

47. Quoted from Vladimir Vasilievich Stasov, "Ein Wort der Gegenwart gegen zwei Phrasen der Zukunftgilde," *Niederrheinische Musik-Zeitung,* 1859; reprinted and translated in Stasov, *Izbrannïye sochineniya v tryokh tomakh* (Moscow: Iskusstvo, 1952), 1:40.

maxim was, in the first place, a defense of Wagner and *das Kunstwerk der Zukunft*, and of course Hanslick wasn't buying:

> Although his antagonists tried to brand him a reactionary, and while he himself (like any contender in a war of ideas) tried to portray his ideas as age-old verities, Hanslick's ideas were in fact new. By asserting that there were timeless musical values that took precedence over the *Kunstidee des Producenten* and the *Ohren des Consumenten* alike, Hanslick and his followers introduced a new faction to what was fast becoming a struggle over the right to inherit and define the elite literate tradition of European music. To the extreme romantic view that privileged the producer, and the old aristocratic view that privileged the consumer, was now added a "Classical" or classicizing view that privileged Art itself and its so-called inviolable laws [or what some of us call its "essence"] over the designs or wishes of its ephemeral practitioners and patrons. The real privilege, of course, was enjoyed by whoever could successfully claim the right to assert the law [or define the essence]. These were the true stakes of the game. It is arguable that Hanslick, one of whose biographers proclaimed him the "Dalai Lama of music",[48] emerged the big winner.

> And that is because more than any other nineteenth-century academic, Hanslick was a forerunner of today's musicology. [I wrote that around 1998 or so, and stand by it still; and it has been corroborated by recent research.][49] His side, in other words, was the one that got to tell the story of nineteenth-century music in the twentieth century. Indeed, a more revealing and less tendentious name for his tendency would be *academic* rather than "classical," since the academy has been its main home and breeding ground. It is the very opposite of an accident that Hanslick, its chief early formulator, was hired two years after the publication of his famous treatise by the University of Vienna as an adjunct lecturer, later as a full-time professor.

> He spent forty years at the university, lecturing on what we would now call music appreciation. He was the first musician ever to occupy a German university chair; hence he was the first academic musicologist in the modern sense of the word. His formalist esthetic is the one that has underwritten the concept of classical music ever since his time. His neo-Kantian "art for art's sake" views have been the (sometimes tacit) mainstay not only of music appreciation but of practically all university music study until at least the middle of the twentieth century. [And if it has lost its dominance at the cutting edge of the discipline, it is only since the 1980s.]

---

48. This was a careless error, which I am glad to have the opportunity herewith to correct. Actually it was Hanslick who called his own teacher, Václav Tomášek (1774–1850), by this impressive name. I was misremembering this sentence from Eric Sams's article on Hanslick in the first (1980) edition of the *New Grove Dictionary of Music and Musicians:* "His own phrase for Tomášek in Prague, 'the dalai lama of music,' might well describe his own eminence not only in Vienna but throughout the German-speaking world, and beyond."

49. See Kevin Karnes, *Music, Criticism, and the Challenge of History: Shaping Modern Musical Thought in Late Nineteenth-Century Vienna* (New York: Oxford University Press, 2008), esp. part 1: "Eduard Hanslick and the Challenge of *Musikwissenschaft*."

By presuming to draw a hard and fast distinction between what was "musical" and what was not in the work of his contemporaries; by insisting that the musical must be identified with the beautiful (rather than the spiritual or the expressive or the sublime or the true); and by so effectively propagating his views in the teeth of formidable opposition, Hanslick set the terms of an unsettleable (perhaps misconceived) debate that continues into our own time. Its terms would probably have been altogether unintelligible to musicians of the early nineteenth century and before; so in this sense, too, the middle of the nineteenth century marks the beginning of the musical world we have inherited and inhabit today.[50]

Hanslick, then, has my nomination as the great musical essentializer. But I reject essentialism in this as in all humanistic domains. My vote is for the ephemeral practitioner as I put it in The Ox (although within the confines of The Ox I was not voting). So my hero is not the great Hanslick but the great Meyer—that is, Leonard B. Meyer (1918–2007), whom Prof. Levinson frequently invokes, but whom Nick Zangwill ignores in both of the books of his that I have read. Meyer's most famous book was his first, *Emotion and Meaning in Music*, which proposed a behaviorist model for musical expression that relied entirely on tracking response to the temporal unfolding.[51] Meyer was way in advance of, say, Carolyn Abbate and all the others, including me, who have tried to put the emphasis back on music as a performance rather than a text—which of course means music as a practice rather than a thing. The fashionable jargon for this now is "musicking," after a book by Christopher Small that claimed to be original and revolutionary but was really just a tepid rehash of Meyer.[52]

Meyer's last major essay was called "A Universe of Universals." It appeared in 1998, the same year as Small's book, when Meyer was eighty years old. In what for him was a typically and deceptively disarming gambit, he wrote, "My premise is simple: one cannot comprehend and explain the variability of human cultures unless one has some sense of the constancies involved in their shaping."[53] But readers who at this point thought that this was to be yet another essay in musical essentialism were in for a surprise. The real thesis statement came a little later:

> To explain why human beings in some actual cultural-historical context think, respond, and choose as they do, it is necessary to distinguish those facets of human behavior that are learned and variable from those that are innate and universal. But it is a mistake—albeit a common one—to conceptualize the problem as a search for

---

50. Taruskin, *Oxford History of Western Music* 3:441–42.

51. Leonard B. Meyer, *Emotion and Meaning in Music* (Chicago: University of Chicago Press, 1956).

52. See Christopher Small, *Musicking: The Meanings of Performing and Listening* (Middletown, CT: Wesleyan University Press, 1998); cf. Carolyn Abbate, "Music—Drastic or Gnostic?" *Critical Inquiry* 30 (2004): 505–36.

53. Leonard B. Meyer, "A Universe of Universals," *Journal of Musicology* 16 (1998): 3–25, at 3.

"musical" universals. *There are none.* There are only the acoustical universals of the physical world and the bio-psychological universals of the human world. Acoustical stimuli affect the perception, cognition, and hence practice of music only through the constraining action of the bio-psychological ones.[54]

The particulars are not especially pertinent to this discussion, though as a witness to the dramatic swerve from universalism to particularism in musicology that Meyer's work stimulated and reflects, I found them thrilling. What matter to us here are the places where Meyer looked for his universals—not the nature of music, but the nature of sound and the nature of human cognition. In short, he looked for nature in nature rather than in culture, where he looked for culture. Makes sense to me.

It was this swerve—the practical turn, you might call it—that threatened (and I would say doomed) Hanslick's ascendency among musicologists, although the process is far from complete. Many students of musical aesthetics, who might once have been essentialists like Hanslick or Zangwill, have been converted to a behaviorist model. An excellent example would be Karol Berger, a musicologist who has branched out into general aesthetics, and who uses Hanslick's chief antagonist—the dread mage of Bayreuth himself—to explain the nature of musical expression in terms of stimulus and response, which of course presupposes terms of temporal unfolding. It also presupposes that beauty is no longer regarded as the essence of music, and the reasons for that are much older than Hanslick. They go back to Gotthold Ephraim Lessing, another name that is absent from Nick Zangwill's indices, for reasons I can well imagine, but also from Prof. Levinson's, who could have used him. As a temporal art, in Lessing's view, music is dynamic rather than static, and beauty is at all times to be equated with stasis.[55] Dynamic unfoldings have tendencies that kindle expectations, which is to say, desires. So, Karol Berger writes:

> What I actually experience when I experience the tonal tendency of a sound is the dynamics of my own desire, its arousal, its satisfaction, its frustration. It is my own desire for the leading tone to move up, the satisfaction of my own desire when it so moves, the frustration thereof when it refuses to budge or when it moves elsewhere, that I feel. . . . Thus, the precondition of my being able to hear an imaginary pattern of lines of directed motion in a tonal work is that I first experience the desires, satisfactions, and frustrations of this sort. In tonal music, the direct experience of the dynamics of my own desire precedes any recognition of the represented object, of lines of directed motion, and is the necessary precondition of such a recognition. I must first experience the desire that the leading tone move up, before I can recognize the representation of an imaginary ascending line when it so moves.

---

54. Ibid., 5–6 (italics original).
55. See Gotthold Ephraim Lessing, *Laokoön; oder, Über die Grenzen der Malerei und Poesie* (1765).

And therefore, Berger concludes,

> It follows that tonal music, like a visual medium, may represent an imaginary object different from myself, an imaginary world, albeit a highly abstract one, consisting of lines of directed motion. But, unlike a visual medium, tonal music also makes me experience directly the dynamics of my own desiring, my own inner world, and it is this latter experience that is the more primordial one, since any representation depends on it. While visual media allow us to grasp, represent, and explore an outer, visual world, music makes it possible for me to grasp, experience, and explore an inner world of desiring. While visual media show us objects we might want without making us aware of what it would feel like to want anything, music makes us aware of how it feels to want something without showing us the objects we want. In a brief formula, visual media are the instruments of knowing the object of desire but not the desire itself, tonal music is the instrument of knowing the desire but not its object.[56]

So like Hanslick and Zangwill, Berger sees (or hears) music as acting on a deeper plane than that of representation. Like Hanslick but unlike Zangwill, he sees music as being always in motion. Unlike both Hanslick and Zangwill, but like Meyer, he sees the motion as directed in a fashion that enlists emotion through desire. And he locates the aesthetic essence, if we continue to insist upon identifying one, not in the stimulus but in the response, not in the intentional object but in the attending subject. Although the perceptions that Berger describes here are local, moment-to-moment perceptions, his theory, unlike Levinson's, does not rule out longer-range awareness and responses.

To me this offers a superior model. It seems to correspond to terrestrial music, that is, to music as we practice it here on earth—at least terrestrial classical music, the only kind to which I've given thought that I would dare present at a meeting like this. I don't see any reason why, in the absence of musical universals, a philosophy of music needs to pretend to universal relevance. A well-specified context will do, and must do.

---

56. Karol Berger, *A Theory of Art* (New York: Oxford University Press, 1999), 33–34.

11

But Aren't They All Invented?

On tradition

I

My interest in tradition is intense, long-standing, and above all, overdetermined. Questions about its nature (if indeed it has a nature), its mechanism, and its ethical and practical effects were among the points of intersection between the two quite disparate fields that for a long time defined my activity as a musician and a scholar. In the early part of my career, up to my move from New York City to California in 1987, I divided my time between performing early music as a choral conductor and viola da gamba player and studying and writing about Russian music of the nineteenth and twentieth centuries. That unlikely combination is what got me interested in the philosophical and cultural issues surrounding what was known only a few decades ago as *authenticity* in musical performance, which billed itself in those days as the revival of lost musical traditions. My close contact with the works and, in particular, the words of Igor Stravinsky, and with the discourse of neoclassicism in the 1920s, furnished my entrée into the problematics of that term—that "baleful term," as Joseph Kerman once called it, which "resonates with unearned good vibrations."[1]

My thinking about authenticity, behind which lurked a lot of thinking about tradition, embroiled me in heavy debate, once I'd noticed the abundant and then-surprising parallels between the discourse of authentic performance practice as enunciated in the 1960s and 70s and what Stravinsky (together with the many other

---

Originally presented as keynote address ("But Aren't All Traditions Invented?") at Orpheus Institute doctoral conference, "Traditions/Transitions," Ghent, 22 February 2017.

1. Joseph Kerman, *Contemplating Music: Challenges to Musicology* (Cambridge, MA: Harvard University Press, 1985), 192.

modernists lurking behind him) was saying and writing in the 1920s and 30s. That was one of the ways in which my early-music and Russian-music interests intersected around the issue of tradition. Another pathway was opened up by my study of Russian opera in the nineteenth century (the topic of my doctoral research), which of course brought up the issue of nationalism—another discourse that laid a heavy emphasis on the recovery of traditions.

It was of course as a student of nationalism that I first happened on the work of Eric Hobsbawm. His *Nations and Nationalism since 1780* is one of the indispensable works on which all subsequent scholarship in that field has to some extent depended. It was based on a set of lectures that Hobsbawm delivered by invitation at the Queen's University of Belfast in 1985. Four years later, momentous events in Europe rendered it out of date, and Hobsbawm, undaunted and agile at the age of seventy-five, revised his last chapter as well as his general conclusions.[2] As anyone knows who knows him, Hobsbawm was a Marxist historian; and so for him nationalism was a vexed issue. As a historian he of course had to acknowledge that nationalism was (as I put it when writing on the subject for the *New Grove Dictionary of Music and Musicians*) "a major factor in European cultural ideology by the end of the 18th century, and ... arguably the dominant factor in geopolitics since the end of the 19th."[3] But as a Marxist he could not have been happy to acknowledge that fact, since nationalism, to a Marxist, was one of the most pernicious of all false consciousnesses. Of course, that only quickened Hobsbawm's interest in it, as it did mine. I don't count myself a Marxist, but I have my own reasons for being wary of nationalism, it never (for one thing) having been particularly good for the Jews, even when the Jews themselves took it on board—but that, as they say, is another story. My suspicion of nationalism is not only a matter of social identification with a particular class of frequent victims. Many liberal pluralists revile nationalism. Karl Popper was especially harsh. For him, "Nationalism is a criminal conceit or a mixture of cowardice and stupidity."[4] Popper's brand of hostility toward nationalism is easily transferred to its main conduit, tradition.

In any case, Hobsbawm's wariness of nationalism was a gift to us, because it made him an especially critical historian of it. The finest fruit of his skepticism was the famous collection of essays *The Invention of Tradition*, which Hobsbawm co-

---

2. Eric Hobsbawm, *Nations and Nationalism since 1780: Programme, Myth, Reality*, 2nd ed. (Cambridge: Cambridge University Press, 1992).

3. R. Taruskin, "Nationalism," available at www.oxfordmusiconline.com/subscriber/article/grove/music/50846.

4. Quoted from Popper's interview in Herlinde Koelbl, *Jüdische Portraits: Photographien und Interviews* (Frankfurt am Main: S. Fischer, 1989), 191: "Ich halte jede Form des Nationalismus für einen verbrecherischen Dünkel oder für eine Mischung von Feigheit und Dummheit. Feigheit, weil der Nationalist die Unterstützung der Menge braucht: Er wagt nicht, allein zu stehen. Dummheit, weil er sich und seinesgleichen für besser halt als andere."

edited with the Africanist Terence Ranger.[5] The 1980s were the heyday of social constructionism in the humanities, and 1983 was a banner year, because it saw the publication not only of the Hobsbawm-Ranger book, but also of Benedict Anderson's transformative study of nationalism, with its very suggestive (and, as it has turned out, potentially misleading) title *Imagined Communities,* also the work of a self-described Marxist scholar.[6] Musicology lost little time getting on this bandwagon. Matthew Gelbart's *The Invention of "Folk Music" and "Art Music"*[7] is one noteworthy example, which I proudly single out, as a good academic nationalist, because it originated as a Berkeley dissertation. By naming Ossian, an imagined, invented poet, in its subtitle, the book signaled its allegiance to the new, shall we say, tradition of tradition-debunking.

One of the most useful debunking tropes is oxymoron, and "invented tradition" is a choice example. Our casual notion of tradition, like our casual notion of a folk song, is of something primordial—and "primordial," which literally means existing from the beginning of time, is casually equivalent to eternal. The coinage "invented tradition" comes out of the debate between so-called primordialists and circumstantialists among historians of nationalism, that is, between those who consider nations to be determined by ethnicities, which are biological and prehistoric, and those who consider nations to be pragmatic, instrumental constructs created by politicians to advance particular social and political agendas. In the 1980s, circumstantialists were winning. (The tide may be turning back now.) So the phrase "invented tradition" quickly became a slogan. It was widely deployed by people who had not read the Hobsbawm-Ranger book to unmask and counter the whole concept of tradition as a political force assumed to be conservative, if not reactionary. It is true that tradition is often invoked in defense of horrible practices—think of slavery or female genital mutilation. Their proponents seek sanctuary by co-opting the arguments of relativistic postmodernist anthropologists like James Clifford and their followers in the humanities, like Gary Tomlinson in musicology or Stephen Greenblatt in comparative literature. Greenblatt awoke to the quandary and owned up in a passage I once quoted with admiration in a debate with Tomlinson: At a world conference on human rights held at the United Nations in 1993, he reported, "it was the most brutally oppressive governments that invoked 'history' and 'difference,' claiming that concepts of fairness and justice should be

---

5. Eric Hobsbawm and Terence Ranger, ed., *The Invention of Tradition* (Cambridge: Cambridge University Press, 1983).

6. Benedict Anderson, *Imagined Communities: Reflections on the Origin and Spread of Nationalism* (London: Verso, 1983).

7. Matthew Gelbart, *The Invention of "Folk Music" and "Art Music": Emerging Categories from Ossian to Wagner* (Cambridge: Cambridge University Press, 2011).

measured against regional particularities and various historical, cultural, and religious differences. These are the 'progressive' arguments of torturers."[8]

The notion, or slogan, of invented tradition takes away the sanctuary. It is an effective tool of propaganda for advancing progressive arguments against those of torturers—or colonialists, or monarchists, or bigots as the case may be. That is how most of the authors of the essays in the Hobsbawm-Ranger collection deployed it. They described various ritualized aspects of life in the non-English parts of the British Isles, as well as areas under British rule in India and Africa, often aspects that native populations thought of as important components of their self-definition as peoples. The historians gleefully exposed them as having been imposed on indigenous populations by their English rulers, by means of a ruse that disguised novelty as revival. The idea of a manufactured past, concocted to gain acceptance for an existing social or political structure and assure its maintenance in the future, problematized the concept of authenticity, which depends for its authority on a demonstrable conformity with an original or prototype. It was precisely the reality of the prototype that the notion of invented tradition attacked. You can see why it migrated so easily from its native disciplines, history and anthropology, into musicology.

II

One of the curious aspects of the theory of invented tradition was the fact that, despite its being the invention of a pair of distinguished historians, it took so little cognizance of its own history. It was not in fact a new idea, although Hobsbawm and Ranger did tout it as such. It had an important precursor in Nietzsche, who in his famous essay "Vom *Nutzen und Nachteil der Historie* für das Leben" (On the Advantage and Disadvantage of History for Life) wrote of the attempt "to give oneself a past from which one would like to be descended in opposition to the past from which one is descended."[9] I quoted that almost thirty years ago in the essay "Tradition and Authority," my own response to Hobsbawm and Ranger, which I prepared for the international conference "Performing Mozart's Music" at Lincoln Center in the big Mozart bicentennial year 1991.[10] What I did not know then was that there was an even older, more relevant precedent to the new discourse of invented tradition, by Jean-Jacques Rousseau, whose name, I find upon checking,

---

8. Stephen Greenblatt, "Kindly Visions," *New Yorker*, 11 October 1993, 120; cf. R. Taruskin, "Others: A Mythology and a Demurrer," in Taruskin, *Defining Russia Musically: Historical and Hermeneutical Essays* (Princeton, NJ: Princeton University Press, 1996), xxix.

9. Friedrich Nietzsche, *On the Advantage and Disadvantage of History for Life*, trans. Peter Preuss (Indianapolis: Hackett, 1980), 22.

10. R. Taruskin, "Tradition and Authority," *Early Music* 20 (1992): 11–25; reprinted in Taruskin, *Text and Act: Essays on Music and Performance* (New York: Oxford University Press, 1995), 173–97.

and much to my surprise, is not even to be found in the index to Hobsbawm and Ranger's book.

That precedent, *Considérations sur le gouvernement de Pologne,* was Rousseau's last political tract. An important document in the history of nationalism, one might think; but I just checked the index of Hobsbawm's *Nations and Nationalism* and found that it isn't mentioned there either. Its obscurity can be explained. Rousseau wrote it in 1771–72, but did not publish it. It did not see the light of day until the state whose sovereignty it was intended to bolster had already been partitioned and obliterated, so its prescriptions were never implemented or much discussed. And yet it sheds a great deal of light on modern nationalism, because it carefully, and presciently, distinguished between the concepts of state (a legal entity) and nation (already viewed by Rousseau as an imagined community). Charged with the task of bolstering the state, Rousseau saw his mission as entailing first of all the task of creating the nation—or as he put it, of "establishing the republic in the Poles' own hearts, so that it will live on in them despite anything your oppressors may do.... See to it," Rousseau exhorted the nervous Polish patriots who had solicited his advice, "that every Pole is incapable of becoming a Russian, and I answer for it that Russia will never subjugate Poland."[11]

In this prescription, with its shift in emphasis from the Enlightenment's celebration of human universality to the commendation and cultivation of human difference, Rousseau had planted one of the earliest seeds of modern Romantic nationalism. And like many radical thinkers, in our field as well as his, Rousseau cloaked his innovations in a pretended revival of ancient ways:

> *National* institutions: That is what gives form to the genius, the character, the tastes, and the customs of a people, what causes it to be itself rather than some other people; founded upon habits of mind impossible to uproot ... There is no such thing nowadays as Frenchmen, Germans, Spaniards, or even Englishmen—only Europeans. All have the same tastes, the same passions, the same customs, and for good reason: Not one of them has ever been formed *nationally,* by distinctive legislation.... Give a *different* bent to the passions of the Poles; in doing so, you will shape their minds and hearts in a national pattern that will set them apart from other peoples, that will keep them from being absorbed by other peoples, or finding contentment among them, or allying themselves with them.... Where love of fatherland prevails, even a bad legislation would produce good citizens. And nothing except good citizens will ever make the state powerful and prosperous. (11–12; emphasis added)

To achieve this love of fatherland, Rousseau prescribes, more than two centuries *avant la lettre,* the very thing that, following Hobsbawm and Ranger, we now call invented traditions:

---

11. Jean-Jacques Rousseau, *The Government of Poland,* trans. Willmoore Kendall (Indianapolis: Bobbs-Merril, 1972), 10–11. (Further references to this source will be made in the main text.)

You must maintain or revive (as the case may be) your ancient customs and introduce suitable new ones that will also be purely Polish. Let these new customs be neither here nor there as far as good and bad are concerned; ... they would still afford this advantage: they would endear Poland to its citizens and develop in them an instinctive distaste for mingling with the peoples of other countries. I deem it all to the good, for example, that the Poles have a distinctive mode of dress; you must take care to preserve this asset. ... See to it that your king, your senators, everyone in public life, never wear anything but distinctively Polish clothing, and that no Pole shall dare to present himself at court dressed like a Frenchman. ... You must create games, festivities, and ceremonials, all peculiar to your court to such an extent that one will encounter nothing like them in any other. (14)

The instilling of national pride in the citizenry must begin with "the games they play as children, through institutions that, though a superficial man would deem them pointless, develop habits that abide and attachments that nothing can dissolve" (4)—all of which will replicate in plural that sentiment of unique being—in a word, of authenticity—that Rousseau had celebrated in his *Confessions,* when he insisted that "I know men" and therefore "venture to believe that I am not made like any of those who are in existence. If I am not better, at least I am different"— and therefore noteworthy and valuable.[12] The big "I" of Romanticism begot the big "we" of nationalism. Rousseau left no doubt that the big we, on one level a distinguishing sentiment of being, is on another level an all-encompassing one. He passes over this contrast, but within it lurked a contradiction that greatly complicates the idea of tradition, whether invented or not.

I say "invented or not," but what is the actual difference between the invented and the not? Strange to say, no one has ever defined it, or (it seems) even tried to define it, not even Hobsbawm and Ranger, who occasionally refer quite casually to something they call "custom," though without much of a definition beyond its very casualness, as when Hobsbawm writes that "'custom' cannot afford to be invariant, because even in 'traditional' societies, life is not so."[13] This implies that tradition is something articulated and purposeful and resistant to change, while custom is an unreflective and therefore accommodating practice; or, as the ethnomusicologist Sumitra Ranganathan puts it in an effort to understand the distinction, Hobsbawm and Ranger "demarcate tradition as an utterance, and custom as a largely uncritical doing."[14]

Rousseau's prescriptions for Poland certainly meet Hobsbawm and Ranger's definition of the invented kind, as set out on page one of Hobsbawm's introductory

12. *The Confessions of Jean-Jacques Rousseau* (New York: Random House [Modern Library], n.d.), 1.
13. Hobsbawm and Ranger (ed.), *Invention of Tradition,* 3.
14. Sumitra Ranganathan, "Dwelling in My Voice: Tradition as Musical Judgment and Aesthetic Sense in North Indian Classical Dhrupad" (PhD diss., University of California at Berkeley, 2015), 16.

chapter. "Invented tradition," he writes there, "is taken to mean a set of practices, normally governed by overtly or tacitly accepted rules and of a ritual or symbolic nature, which seek to inculcate certain values and norms of behavior by repetition, which automatically implies continuity with the past." Rousseau's proposals add some crucial points that the actual discussions in Hobsbawm and Ranger will validate. His "Polish" traditions have a determinate historical origin, and like all invented traditions they are, crucially, "top-down" in that a legislative elite (or, if we take Rousseau to be the inventor, a single despot) is their creator and the population at large will be their followers, their bearers and practitioners. Their symbolism and their ritualism serve a specific and explicitly defined social and political agenda, namely the preservation and maintenance of social cohesion and political independence. And their relationship to the actual Polish past is altogether—and quite nonchalantly—factitious.

Hobsbawm is likewise nonchalant. Tacitly alluding to Nietzsche, he writes that invented traditions "normally attempt to establish continuity with a *suitable* historic past."[15] That is what makes them invented. What makes them traditions is the intention that the body of proposed invented lore be infinitely replicated, that it have transmitters and receivers: in fine, that it be communicated through time and in perpetuity. Ultimately, like the inventors of tradition we can read about in Hobsbawm and Ranger, Rousseau looked forward to the day when the determinate historical origin of the invented tradition will be forgotten and it will become, simply, tradition. Once it has become immemorial, it does not matter how old or recent a tradition actually is. When its origin and purpose have been forgotten, it becomes an unreflective practice by default (Ranganathan calls it "the cocoon of continuity"),[16] which begins to suggest that the difference between an invented tradition and the other kind (which I am still reluctant to name) is not so very categorical after all—and that is precisely why I am loath to give it a name. Hobsbawm has the same difficulty. Not until the other end of the book, in the very last paragraph of the concluding essay, does Hobsbawm for the very first time attempt to define the alternative to an invented tradition, previously identified as "custom." He invokes, as if it were entirely unproblematical, "the relation between 'invention' and 'spontaneous generation,' [between] planning and growth." Invented traditions, or what he occasionally qualifies as "consciously invented" traditions, he now stipulates, "have significant social and political functions, and would neither come into existence nor establish themselves if they could not acquire them."[17]

---

15. Hobsbawm and Ranger (ed.), *Invention of Tradition*, 1 (italics added).

16. Ranganathan, "Dwelling in My Voice," 8.

17. Eric Hobsbawm, "Mass-Producing Traditions: Europe, 1870–1914," in Hobsbawm and Ranger (ed.), *Invention of Tradition*, 307; for "conscious invention" see page 263, the opening page of the final chapter.

As you can see, the distinction between invented traditions and the other kind, call it custom or whatever you like, is inadequately developed by its main theorist. In view of the enormous currency the term has acquired and the equally enormous influence the eponymous book has exerted, this seems odd, and a bit disturbing. The concept of invented tradition has become traditional among us, but traditional in the negative or pejorative sense that Hobsbawm and Ranger clearly wished to oppose, along with many in our own field who have lodged similar complaints against what my late friend and colleague Philip Brett, when defining traditions of performance practice, called "assimilating works unthinkingly to our mode of performing and perceiving."[18] I would suggest that we may have been unthinking in our haste to endorse Hobsbawm and Ranger's notion without giving it a proper test to see how far the distinction holds up between invented tradition and what we normally mean by tradition *tout simple*. If it turns out that it doesn't hold up, then the whole notion of invented tradition will be exposed as a so-called genetic fallacy—i.e., a mistaking of origin for essence—which comes down in turn to a fallacy of irrelevance (taking as crucial something that turns out not to matter, in this case how the thing got started). So, in the consciousness-raising spirit that Hobsbawm and Ranger's work itself exemplifies, I propose administering some tests of the formulation on which we have been relying now for a generation.

III

To recall Hobsbawm's formulation: with respect to tradition, "invention" is to be contrasted with "spontaneous generation," and "planning" is to be distinguished from "growth." What could he possibly have meant by "spontaneous generation," with its whiff of mechanics or (worse) biology, its connotation of randomness and inevitability, and its implicit denial of agency? One is used to speaking of spontaneous combustion in the case of hay or straw, or other flammable substances like coal or (I just learned from Google) pistachio nuts; but though an external stimulant to ignition may be lacking, what is called spontaneous combustion is not in fact spontaneous. Its causes are determinable and it is therefore predictable and preventable. So what we are calling spontaneous is more correctly called endogenous, occurring from an internal rather than external cause. Applied to culture, talk of spontaneity is more than an innocent mistake of diction. It is a rhetorical transgression. When applied to endogenous combustion *spontaneous* is a metaphor, not a description, and so it must be when applied to the generation of traditions, like the word *organic*, which used to be used a lot by anthropologists (as well

---

18. Philip Brett, "Text, Context, and the Early Music Editor," in *Authenticity and Early Music*, ed. Nicholas Kenyon (Oxford: Oxford University Press, 1988), 114.

as musicologists) until its metaphorical nature was commonly understood and accepted. To continue using it now would be an act of deception.

The fact that we do not remember the reason for something, or its purpose, does not mean that it had no purpose or reason to exist, any more than the fact that a tradition has become immemorial means that it had no origin. All traditions, I would therefore contend, had origin and purpose, and were brought about not spontaneously but through human agency, implying choice and volition. I would also suggest that any tradition that serves a purpose has had to be planned, that is, premeditated (if not by the first person to perform the act or say the saying, then at least by the first person to replicate it, thus making it traditional). And all traditions that meet the definition of the term must have undergone growth, including the ones that Hobsbawm and Ranger, and of course Rousseau, would have called invented ones. Rousseau certainly looked forward to the spread of his set of Polish traditions to the point where they stopped being invented ones, so far as anyone would be able to determine. Is the difference between invented traditions and "real" ones simply a matter of how much we remember about them? Does a tradition become an invented one when we learn how it got started? Am I contending that all traditions are in effect invented traditions, and that "real" traditions are only invented traditions that have not yet been exposed as such? Does that mean that we don't need the Hobsbawm-Ranger expression that has become so habitual in the humanities and social sciences? Or is something there that is still worth saving?

Here is one possible testing question: Even if we admit that all traditions serve a purpose, can there be other purposes besides the sort of ulterior purpose that the Hobsbawm-Ranger notion ascribes to invented traditions? Hobsbawm defines such purposes (or functions, to use his word) as social and political. Can there be other ones? And here is another question: Part of the definition of invented tradition (and here I am relying more on Rousseau's explicit remarks than on Hobsbawm and Ranger's implications) is that they are imposed. Are there other ways of getting started? And how do we distinguish them? What are their mechanisms?

Casting about for a homely example, and one that in some minimal way entails music, I thought of my own practice every year when Hanukkah rolls around. I am what is known as a secular Jew. For the sake of my father's mother, who was born in what was then Russia to a Hasidic family, and who was what is known as a *frummer yid,* a pious or observant Jew, I received a rudimentary religious education as a child, and was *bar mitzvah* shortly after my thirteenth birthday, in accordance with the *mitzvah,* that is the commandment, that Jewish boys assume the role of adults within the religious community (that is, become eligible for inclusion in a prayer quorum or *minyan*) at that age and that they demonstrate their competence by reading from scripture during a service. I had to learn to sing the so-called tropes for the Torah and the Prophets, and of course I learned to do it by example, in an oral tradition transmitted to me by the sexton of the local synagogue where I grew up. But that is not the tradition I want to tell you about. I have long since forgotten those tropes, because once past bar mitzvah, I forsook the religious practices in which I had been minimally trained. I still identify myself as a Jew and feel kinship with other Jews, knowing that even if I didn't I would be so identified by others. But that, too, is another story.

The story I want to tell concerns the one traditional Jewish religious practice I have kept up to this very day, albeit with interruptions, and that is the lighting of the Hanukkah candles and reciting (which is to say, singing) the blessings over them. I was taught to do this the traditional way, that is by my father, and I still sing the tunes as he taught me to do, and still pronounce the Hebrew words the way he did, which is the way he had been taught by his Russian-born father, who pronounced the language the Ashkenazi way, as all the Jews of eastern Europe did, which is very far from the way Israeli Jews now pronounce it. The Israeli way has become standard now throughout the world and my way is now a very quaint way indeed, and my adherence to it marks me as someone whose Jewish development was, shall we say, arrested. Indeed, for decades I neglected even this one tiny religious observance, and only resumed it at a time I am sure you could easily guess: I started doing Hanukkah (and, for a while, Passover too—that is, the other Jewish holiday that is celebrated in the home rather than the synagogue) when I had children of my own.

I taught them the blessings my father taught me, and we still recite them together every year—even now, when my children are grown and my daughter lives thousands of miles away. She comes "home for Christmas" (having been brought up in a mixed household), hence for Hanukkah too whenever the two holidays are close enough in date (and last December they actually happened to coincide). The fact that my children, who were not bar or bat mitzvah (since they did not have a grandparent who needed to be appeased) and who never had any Jewish religious upbringing beyond the two holidays, still want to observe this one reveals something that everyone knows and values about tradition and its purpose. It maintains that sense of kinship which I mentioned earlier, both within the family and within the larger Jewish community, with which my children still identify, if only to this infinitesimal extent. Sociologists in the German tradition call this *Gemeinschaft*, and I will come back to that. To that extent my children and I are still communicants in a community (or, as I count them, two communities), and communication (that is, transmission and reception) over time is indeed the most general purpose that all traditions can be said to serve.

This purpose or function is the one I most consciously value in the Hanukkah observance, and it accounts, in a seeming paradox, for the one conscious and deliberate change that I have on my own initiative made in the manner of our observance—which is an important point to emphasize, because if you remember my essay "Tradition and Authority," one of its most salient points is that tradition, far from a time capsule, is, in reality, and inherently, an engine of change.[19] The Hanukkah blessings, sung while the menorah or candelabra is being lit, are three in number. The first blesses the Lord for commanding us to light the Hanukkah lights; the second blesses Him for the miracle that the ceremony commemorates; and the third, which is recited not only at Hanukkah but at many other religious and commemorative occasions as well, blesses the Lord *shehecheyanu, v'kiy'manu, v'higianu laz'man hazeh*, "who has granted us life, sustained us, and enabled us to reach this occasion." I especially like this last blessing, because it is actually about *Gemeinschaft*, the sense of familial and cultural community or what we sometimes call "togetherness" in America. And because I like it, I sing it with my children on all eight nights of Hanukkah, although the official tradition is that this third blessing, unlike the other two, which are Hanukkah-specific, is to be sung only on the first of the eight nights.

So: I invented a tradition. Or rather, I contributed to the continual process of reinvention that lasting traditions undergo. As far as my children are concerned—unless they happen to read this paper—the tradition they have learned is the immemorial Jewish tradition, which, should they decide to do so, they might hand on to their children. It's a top-down tradition in that when I invented it I had a certain amount of authority with my kids, which in this case they were in no position to question. It served to inculcate a particular value that I wished to impart to them. Thus my own practice, while motivated by loyalty to an immemorial Jewish tradition, was contaminated endogenously by desiderata of my own. Quite possibly my children, if they hand it on to the next generation of Taruskins, will modify it further, out of preferences that I cannot foresee. Ethnomusicologists, while they often used to deplore this process as compromising the "authenticity" of artifacts maintained in oral tradition, have long recognized it nevertheless as normal and inevitable. The younger anthropologists of the 1980s and 90s, the contemporaries and counterparts to what we used to call "new musicologists," began to accept the inevitability of change without prejudice and to measure the authenticity of traditions and their artifacts in terms of the subjective experience of participants rather than those of "hard" historical evidence.

IV

One of my earliest inklings of the inexorability of change within a traditional practice came when I was taking an undergraduate survey at Columbia that, in those days of pre-postcolonial innocence, was called "Oriental Civilizations" (an elective companion course to the required core-curriculum survey of "Western" institu-

---

19. R. Taruskin, "Tradition and Authority," *Early Music* 20 (1992), 311–26; reprinted in Taruskin, *Text and Act*, 173–98.

tions that went—and I think still goes at Columbia—by the name "Contemporary Civilization"). It was team-taught by historians of India, China, and Japan. The Japanese specialist who lectured during the final third of the semester was Herschel F. Webb (1924–83), then an assistant professor, who told us a story about the German harpsichordist and musicologist Eta Harich-Schneider (1897–1986), who had lived in Japan during the Second World War and had studied Japanese language and history at Columbia in the late 1940s and early 50s in preparation for writing her once-standard *History of Japanese Music*.[20]

Harich-Schneider's specialty was the imperial court music, known as *gagaku*. She had been assured by her informants that the *gagaku* repertory had been maintained rigorously unchanged over a period of 1,300 years, yet she noticed small discrepancies between the performances she was witnessing in the field and the old part-books she was studying. In one case, one of her informants conceded that he himself had introduced one such modification, which he minimized as a slight and necessary improvement (not a change, you see, but an *improvement*). From this, Harich-Schneider proceeded to a hypothesis, much disputed by Japanese musicians, that such tiny "improvements," multiplied over a period exceeding a millennium, guaranteed that twentieth-century *gagaku*, especially since it had been revived in the nineteenth century after a period of neglect, bore very limited resemblance to the music as originally performed. When it came to writing up her findings, she strove hard to maintain a diplomatic tone. "It is impossible to decide," as she put it in one early article,

> how far and according to what points of view the court music was remolded when, after the Meiji restoration [of 1868], the remains of the old cult and the deteriorated feudal arts were refurbished for reasons of Imperial prestige. I can confirm, however, that the performance of certain court-music numbers still follows the directions given in earlier sources and that the partbooks in present use do not show divergences from earlier ones. On the other hand, the strange willingness of the court musicians to adapt their music to the trends of the time—at the moment [i.e., during the postwar occupation], American taste—strongly suggests the existence of such a tendency in earlier periods, particularly those in which the Imperial musicians were under less strict control. Thus, the theory of a strictly secluded court music, unchanged and immune to the ravages of time, is difficult to judge: it seems to be authentic in parts and a shrewdly and skillfully staged myth in other parts.[21]

The musicians of the *gagaku* orchestra, in Harich-Schneider's account, seemed to have an attitude somewhat like mine with regard to Hanukkah blessings. In her *History*, she put it this way:

20. Eta Harich-Schneider, *A History of Japanese Music* (London: Oxford University Press, 1973).
21. Eta Harich-Schneider, "The Present Condition of Japanese Court Music," *Musical Quarterly* 39 (1953): 49–74, at 50.

Between 1873 and 1895 the notion of an immutable *gagaku*, unchanged since Nara times [i.e., the eighth century CE], was fabricated and became established. This theory was accepted with enthusiasm—almost as an article of faith. No such claim is found in earlier sources which limit themselves to a justified pride in the great antiquity of this music, and recount its natural development, decay, or resurgence.[22]

The musicians she describes, in short, were practicing an invented (or reinvented) tradition, and I ask again, is there any other kind? As F. Allan Hanson says, "all culture is invented, and is rendered in no way inauthentic for that fact."[23] And who is F. Allan Hanson? He is the anthropologist from the University of Kansas who in the early 1990s found himself in trouble for an article in which he had reported, first, that many aspects of Maori mythology had been invented by people like him (that is, Western anthropologists) in their efforts to amalgamate bits of collected lore into a continuous narrative, but second, that this Western invention had been accepted by many Maori and was therefore to be regarded as authentic.[24] The Maori did not especially appreciate being told this. A reporter for the *New Zealand Herald* quoted a local anthropologist as saying that "the American Indians don't like anthropologists sitting in the tepees any more—and neither do we."[25] The postmodern take, as it was called then, only seemed to compound the colonialist insult. The big white brother now presumed to judge not only whether indigenous belief was factually true, but also whether it was genuine, that is, truly believed by those who professed it. Or as the anthropologist James Clifford put it with explicit reference to Hobsbawm and Ranger's theories, "There was residual imperialism in the outside expert's claim to distinguish between invented tradition and organic custom, between conscious fabrication and the constant recombination or bricolage of any society in transition"—as all societies are at all times. As a result, "Definitions of 'traditional' authenticity became sites of struggle."[26]

I could attest to that much, having said some very similar things about the performance practice of European art music. I had expressed skepticism as to whether

---

22. Harich-Schneider, *History of Japanese Music*, 550; quoted in James Siddons, "On the Nature of Melody in Asia and Medieval Europe" (PhD diss., North Texas State University, 1983), 41.

23. F. Allan Hanson, "Empirical Anthropology, Postmodernism, and the Invention of Tradition," in *Present Is Past: Some Uses of Tradition in Native Societies*, ed. Marie Mauze (Lanham, MD: University Press of America, 1997), 199.

24. See F. Allan Hanson, "The Making of the Maori: Culture Invention and Its Logic," *American Anthropologist* 91, no. 4 (December 1989): 890–902.

25. Wendy Nissen, "Academics Stand Up for Maoritanga," *New Zealand Herald*, 1 March 1990; quoted in Hanson, "Empirical Anthropology," 199.

26. James Clifford, "Traditional Futures," in *Questions of Tradition*, ed. Mark Salber Phillips and Gordon Schochet (Toronto: University of Toronto Press, 2004), 156. The chief "question" to which this very stimulating book is addressed is similar to my question: to cite the title of Phillips's introductory essay, "What Is Tradition When It Is Not 'Invented'?"

those who claimed to revive broken historical traditions were truly doing that. Their style of performance, I argued, was not a revival but an invention. But I had agreed with Hanson, whose work I did not yet know, that this fact—the fact that so-called historical performance practice was actually new, and that historical research, carried on by musicologists as well as adventurous performers, to the extent that it figured into the process of its formulation, was one of the means of inventing it—did not in any way lessen its authenticity. What so-called historically informed performers were doing was authentic precisely as an expression of contemporary taste. Not that anyone thanked me for saying so, any more than the Maori thanked Allan Hanson. I was guilty of the same double transgression: I had impugned the factual truth of what (on the analogy of Hellenic vs. Hellenistic) I called "authentistic" performance practice, and I had also presumed to say that the convictions motivating authentistic performers, while not historically veridical in accordance with their claim, were nevertheless valid as motivators and were producing valuable and beautiful modern performances of a new kind that was in that sense truly modern rather than a perpetuation of a previous style that was once modern but was now old and often stale. It was because it was invented rather than "truly" traditional that the authentistic style was able to become a tradition of example and emulation in its own right, and therefore authentic in a manner that required no ironic scare quotes.

Allan Hanson noticed the first piece I published in the *New York Times*.[27] Having spotted these parallels, he wrote to me about them, putting me onto a whole anthropological and sociological literature on which I began drawing heavily in my own papers, starting with "Tradition and Authority," which quotes his work. My position, which counts I suppose as an early application of the "invented tradition" idea to Western music, is quite widely accepted now and no longer so controversial—and no longer so firmly associated with me, which especially pleases me to be able to say. The old claim—that historically informed performance practice as recovered in the twentieth century chimed with the actual performance practice of the eighteenth and earlier centuries, and that the nineteenth-century performance style in which most twentieth-century performers were trained was just a blip, a deviation, a hiatus, or a vagary, which might be bracketed and forgotten—is, by and large, no longer believed. We now accept, I think, that the twentieth-century style was no recovery, and that nineteenth-century performance practice evolved out of eighteenth-century practice the way traditional practices always evolve. We no longer see the progression of performance style for canonical repertory from the eighteenth century to the twentieth as a kind of A-B-A, with the twentieth a resumption of the eighteenth, but rather as A-B-C, with time moving in only one direction, the

---

27. Richard Taruskin, "The Spin Doctors of Early Music," *New York Times*, 29 July 1990, Arts and Leisure, 1; reprinted (under its intended title, "The Modern Sound of Early Music") in Taruskin, *Text and Act*, 164–72.

only way it actually can move. If there is a break, it comes between B and C, not between A and B.

One result of this realization, or this metamorphosis of belief (or growth of tradition), has been quite constructive. Consider the reassessment of Vladimir Horowitz in the *New Grove Dictionary of Music and Musicians*. The first edition of the *New Grove*, which came out in 1980, had treated Horowitz very harshly, judging his performances, from the standpoint of then-reigning modernist taste, to have been a distortion and misrepresentation of the music he played. The last sentence of the article, by Michael Steinberg, was haughty and insulting: "Horowitz," he wrote, "illustrates that an astounding instrumental gift carries no guarantee about musical understanding."[28] I wrote a piece for the *New York Times* in which I held that sentence up to tough scrutiny, though I tried to fall short of haughty or insulting, and received a nice note from Harold C. Schonberg, formerly the *Times*'s chief music critic and a Horowitz biographer, expressing his hearty agreement with my defense of the great pianist.[29] I was very gratified to get this letter, because Schonberg was, I thought, a true connoisseur of Romantic piano playing and his agreement was, as they say, praise from Sir Hubert.

Who do you think was engaged, seven years later, to write the article on Horowitz for the second edition of the *New Grove*, published in 2001? Yes, it was Schonberg. I have no idea whether my *New York Times* piece had anything to do with it, but here is how the new article ended:

> [Horowitz] was never regarded as an expert in Beethoven and the Classical composers. Yet his 1932 recording of the Haydn E-flat Sonata (no. 52) has style, grace, bracing rhythm, incredible articulation and complete responsiveness to the lyricism as well as the music's architecture.
>
> A future revisionist period may pay more attention to Horowitz's performances of Mozart, which many have derided as unstylistic. Towards the end of his life Horowitz returned to Mozart, a composer he carefully studied. He had memorized everything that Mozart ever wrote about performing practice, and tried to put those precepts into effect. His recordings of several sonatas, a few shorter pieces and the A major Concerto K488 were not generally well received. In recent years, however, it has come to be realized that Mozart style is not academic literalism. Rather (as Mozart himself explained in his letters) it demands freedom, a sensuous sound, a degree of rubato and faster tempos than musicians of the 20th century are generally willing to adopt. It could well be that Horowitz's flexible and expressive approach to Mozart will eventually be recognized as in some sense more authentic than the work

---

28. Michael Steinberg, "Horowitz, Vladimir," in *The New Grove Dictionary of Music and Musicians*, ed. Stanley Sadie (London: Macmillan, 1980), 8:723.

29. See R. Taruskin, "Why Do They All Hate Horowitz?" *New York Times*, 28 November 1993; reprinted, with an update that refers to and quotes Schonberg's letter, in Taruskin, *The Danger of Music and Other Anti-Utopian Essays* (Berkeley: University of California Press, 2009), 30–36.

of so many late 20th-century "authenticists." In any case, the position of Vladimir Horowitz as one of the supreme pianists in history cannot be challenged. (11:740)

The last sentence was overly optimistic. Horowitz is still challenged, but now it is the challengers who must beware. I don't necessarily agree with everything that Schonberg said about Horowitz and historical verisimilitude. But I do approve the general sense he conveyed, that Horowitz's style of playing, precisely because it reflected his training in early twentieth-century Russia, participated in a tradition that included Mozart, and that this made Horowitz—far from "a master of distortion and exaggeration," as Virgil Thomson, perhaps the paradigmatic modernist critic, called him[30]—one of the tradition's authentic transmitters. Realizing this has freed today's pianists to adopt a more flexible, unapologetically eclectic approach to canonical repertory, which to my mind can only make their performances more authentic, interpreting the word now the way moral philosophers use it, rather than the way it was used by academic musicians in the middle of the twentieth century.

A few years ago, in December 2014, I received another strong impression that tradition, in this postmodernist sense, has reasserted itself, when I was honored by an afternoon of presentations and discussion at the Conservatorium van Amsterdam called "Catching Up with Richard Taruskin." Among the offerings was a chamber orchestra playing some seventeenth-century Dutch music, and I was asked to comment on the performance in the light of my publications on performance practice. I said that the Low Countries had always been at the forefront of early-music research and performance, and that whatever was being done in Amsterdam had to be regarded as "cutting edge" for the movement, and that if the performance had been given ten or twenty years earlier, it would have been a lot weirder than the one we had just heard. I had already said something similar in "Tradition and Authority," when I called attention to a certain normalization in the style of historical performers. "Why do we hear so much less self-conscious downbeat bashing than we used to, so much less distracting *messa di voce*?" I asked, so that I could answer, with some irony but also a pleasant sense of satisfaction:

> It's not because the performers are reading better treatises, . . . or because their hardware is improving. . . . It's because they are not just chaining themselves to the documents. They are listening to and competing with one another, starting younger and with more experienced teachers, thinking of themselves increasingly as normal rather than as deviant or alienated members of musical society. In short, the movement has spawned a viable oral tradition. Around that authentic modern product I admire so much a hardy social practice has been growing up that obeys its own dictates, has its own momentum, is becoming more and more eclectic, contaminated, suggestible.[31]

---

30. Quoted from Bernard Holland, "Vladimir Horowitz, Titan of the Piano, Dies" (obituary), *New York Times*, 6 November 1989.
31. R. Taruskin, "Tradition and Authority," in *Text and Act*, 194.

It was behaving, that is, the way all traditions behave. Note the phrase "oral tradition." We all tended to use that qualifier a quarter of a century ago, when it was a newer idea that oral practices survive in literate cultures. But it is a pleonasm: performing traditions are oral by definition, in a wider sense that goes beyond the mouth to encompass all transmission by example, including the use of hand and ear (so that "aural" might actually describe them better). Traditions are based on listening, imitating, and trying first to match, and then to do better. Rote learning and conditioning are their essence, fly though it does in the face of all modernist theorizing (such as José Ortega y Gasset's insistence that art be "full clarity, high noon of the intellect").[32] Such a manner of cultural transmission can easily be derided as "unthinking," and we have seen that it *is* derided that way, though perhaps decreasingly (and perhaps unthinkingly). Such derision is no more constructive than the traditionally anti-intellectualist defense of tradition against rational investigation of its premises or history. If we agree with Mark Salber Phillips that "a simple opposition between 'genuine' and 'invented' traditions is unworkable," we need to replace opposition with dialectics.[33] The "unthinking" aspect of traditional practice works in a dialectical relationship with conscious thought, as innovation works in a dialectical relationship with repetition. That dialectic has become, increasingly, a lively topic for observation and analysis.[34]

V

Two very recent articles that have come serendipitously to my attention show this dialectic with exceptional clarity, because they concern artifacts once considered absolutely antithetical to the idea of tradition: compositions by Pierre Boulez and Karlheinz Stockhausen, the two most representative figures of the mid-twentieth-century European avant-garde, perhaps the most ardently and explicitly antitraditionalist faction in the whole history of music.

---

32. José Ortega y Gasset, *The Dehumanization of Art and Other Essays on Art, Culture, and Literature,* trans. Helene Weyl (Princeton, NJ: Princeton University Press, 1968), 27.

33. Mark Salber Phillips, "What Is Tradition When It Is Not 'Invented'? A Historiographical Introduction," in Phillips and Schochet (eds.), *Questions of Tradition,* 6.

34. The accommodation within traditions of what had once been disruptive is something we have all observed. The paradigmatic instance in music history is Stravinsky's *Sacre du printemps,* which after a stormy first-night rejection became hugely influential on composers and eventually a basic constituent of the performing repertoire as well. Or compare the account, by the opera director Mary Zimmerman, of the reception of her once-controversial staging of Bellini's *La sonnambula:* "The second time we did it [in 2014], it was kind of loved. That's not an uncommon switch in the world of opera. The idea of the traditional holds sway until there's the new traditional and the radical always feels outlier until through time it's shaped into the traditional" (quoted in Zachary Woolfe, "Fourth Time's the Charm?" *New York Times,* Arts and Leisure, 29 January 2017, 10).

Their antitraditionalism was, in a rather hackneyed paradox, itself traditional in the sense that it was inherited from the already two-centuries-old posture of romanticism. Boulez's old battle cry, "There is no such thing as tradition!"—shouted at early music practitioners, among others (who did not need to be told)[35]—was a late reverberation from a big bang, detonated, again in a seeming paradox, by the same Rousseau whose prescriptions for inventing Polish national traditions have figured so prominently in this discussion. Rousseau, in his *Confessions*, was perhaps the first to equate personal authenticity or integrity with originality. I've already quoted it: "If I am not better, at least I am different." A work of art was supposed to be able to say that too, especially if the author was one of those who felt the strong need to reject the disastrous history that had led Europe to its so-called zero hour.

In a wide-ranging essay called "Musicology and Performance," Daniel Leech-Wilkinson zeroes in on Boulez as one of those composer-performers whose preaching and practice can be directly juxtaposed and compared. You might remember Leech-Wilkinson as one of musicology's great consciousness-raisers, especially in his seminal work with a very Hobsbawmian title, *The Modern Invention of Medieval Music*.[36] His article on Boulez is a further application of his wonderful knack of discerning the ideological biases informing musical performances. As a preliminary example of the sort of analysis he performs, he compares various recordings of Schoenberg's *Pierrot lunaire*, and finds that they describe exactly the same trajectory as the early music performances that I have traced over a comparable span of time:

> To take just one song as emblematic, in no. 7 [*Der kranke Mond*] for flute and voice we hear in Boulez's 1961 recording (and also in Schoenberg's [from 1940]) rather straight flute tone with relatively little dynamic change or dynamic articulation, considering the markings in the score. At the opposite extreme, in Boulez's 1997 recording we find much greater dynamic fluctuation within notes and more flexible timing: it is more conventionally musical, with the desiderata of continuity and shape overseeing all the details. Between these, in terms of expressive style, come both [Jane] Manning versions, the 1967 [with the unconducted Vesuvius Ensemble] less and the 1977 [with the Nash Ensemble under Simon Rattle] somewhat more expressive in a manner that Boulez by 1997 has simply taken further (as has everybody else, of course). I think what this amounts to is a consistent pattern of change, in which modernist performers deliberately removed themselves from current style before turning back ever more enthusiastically to meet up with it again.[37]

---

35. P. Boulez, "The Vestal Virgin and the Fire-stealer: Memory, Creation, and Authenticity," *Early Music* 18 (1990): 335; quoted with commentary in Taruskin, *Text and Act*, 192.

36. Daniel Leech-Wilkinson, *The Modern Invention of Medieval Music: Scholarship, Ideology, Performance* (Cambridge: Cambridge University Press, 2007).

37. Daniel Leech-Wilkinson, "Musicology and Performance," in *Music's Intellectual History*, ed. Zdravko Blažeković and Barbara Dobbs Mackenzie (New York: Répertoire International de Littérature Musicale, 2009), 796.

The crucial words in this account, of course, are "of course," as when Leech-Wilkinson notes that Boulez's increasing expressivity is to be found in "everybody else, of course." The change he notes in the performance of avant-garde repertoire matches the change I have noted along with him in early-music performance. Both have bent toward the "conventionally musical," as he puts it. "Mainstream performance style," he continues, "in gradually accommodating 'historically informed' performance, was also accommodating modernism, bringing itself, by developing a style that was both clean *and* expressive, within the increasingly conservative modernist pale. It is at least a three-way process that allowed the avant garde, the HIPsters and the mainstream to converge towards something they could all live with."[38]

But what does he—or we—mean by "musical," as when Leech-Wilkinson uses that word to distinguish Boulez's 1997 recording of *Pierrot* from his earlier ones in the extract above? The term is famously elusive, but Leech-Wilkinson clarifies it with an apt pleonasm: *conventionally musical*. The adjective already implies the adverb. And to call a performance "conventionally musical" is already to invoke what Leech-Wilkinson calls "expressive style," which for him is the default style. Both of these terms, as well as *natural* when applied to music-making, have crucially to do with the role of tradition in musical culture and beyond. To perform "naturally" or "musically," I would suggest, means to adhere to what are traditionally considered good standards in a manner that appears effortless and intuitive. What that really means, I would further suggest, is an easy and ingratiating adherence to conventional or default norms—ingratiating because it matches the expectations of listeners who have been brought up musically in a manner similar to the way in which the performer has been formed. Upbringing, formation—these are the functions performed by tradition. Similarly, to perform expressively is to vary tempo and loudness in ways that we have all learned as part of our acculturation to associate with emotionally significant behavior, especially speech behavior. To be acculturated is to learn by example, which is to say that all these standards and norms are transmitted and inculcated by tradition; and in that sense musicality and expressive performance are inherently conservative, because they seek, and promote, *Gemeinschaft*—community, social solidarity.

So if one of the cardinal traits of "modernism," as an attitude, is opposition to tradition and the communitarian conservatism it is thought to embody, and if one of the characteristics of modernist behavior is the defiance or rejection of conventional norms, we might expect self-avowed modernists to oppose "musicality" with the same sort of disdain that Mahler is said to have voiced toward tradition when he called it "mere *Schlamperei* (sloppiness)."[39] And sure enough, enough

---

38. Ibid.

39. For the Mahler phrase, in many variants, see Henry Louis de la Grange, *Gustav Mahler*, vol. 3: *Vienna: Triumph and Disillusion, 1904–1907* (Oxford: Oxford University Press, 1999), 4.

modernists have gone on record mocking musicality—"that blissful state of cretinism," in Paul Zukofsky's much-quoted phrase[40]—to cement the relationship between notions of musicality and those of tradition. So what Daniel Leech-Wilkinson is noticing in performances of and by Pierre Boulez is the resurgence of tradition, supervening on modernist resistance to it. His report brought back to mind some eloquent words I read many years ago in a review by Richard Franko Goldman of Elliott Carter's Cello Sonata, the earliest work in which Carter employed his signature device of tempo modulation (more familiarly called by a misnomer, "metrical modulation," that Goldman coined in this very article). The critic, who found the work not only intellectually impressive but also emotionally moving, tried to explain Carter's creative evolution in a fashion that, in light of the tendencies that we are all observing now, strikes me as prescient. "Among artists," Goldman wrote,

> aware of the smothering nature of today's mass audience, the temptation unquestionably exists, as strongly as ever before in history, to exploit cleverness as a defense or refuge, by emphasizing the separation of creativeness from mass-mindedness. The composer of so-called intellectual tendencies is perhaps more apt even than other artists to succumb to this temptation, but it is, of course, possible to resist. The solution of puzzles is seldom more than a personal satisfaction, without communicable value. It is a retreat that is a typical manifestation of the artist's spiritual isolation. One may be sure that any composer whose music shows thought has at times explored the abstractions of disembodied sound, in the remotest detachment from expressiveness or even from considerations of utility. But he comes back, if he is a composer, to apply whatever gains he has made in this flight, to the more prosaic, but also more human, problem of performable music sufficiently within a tradition to be understood.[41]

This sharp *aperçu* by a now-forgotten but most unusual writer on music shows a profound understanding, it seems to me, both of the modernist antipathy to tradition and of the discontent that tradition may assuage. It anticipates by nearly half a century the widespread phenomena that we are now witnessing in performance as well as composition, and a tendency that has eventually claimed even the most resistant, if Boulez can be taken as the gold standard of modernist intransigence.[42] What has brought it about?

---

40. Paul Zukofsky: "The Performer: Revitalization or Stagnation?" *Perspectives of New Music* vol. 3, no. 2 (Spring-Summer 1965): 172–73.

41. Richard Franko Goldman, "Current Chronicle," *Musical Quarterly* 37 (1951): 84–85.

42. And he was that even in 1951. In the very next issue of the *Musical Quarterly*, Mr. Goldman was back with a brief, very unfriendly review of David Tudor's première performance of Pierre Boulez's "much-heralded" Piano Sonata no. 2 at a League of Composers concert in New York—actually (according to the review) the first performance in New York of any Boulez composition. "This piece is a curiosity of the type that advanced or non-commercial groups are under moral obligation to present," the reviewer stipulated, not without irony, "since no work of Boulez has been heard here, and since no recitalist is likely

Who knows? But Leech-Wilkinson senses, as strongly as I have sensed it, that this adjustment of musical behavior is symptomatic of something big. "There are all sorts of reasons one might propose for that change of direction," he writes: "economic, social, even political." And he detects it in composing as well as performing, in theory as well as composition, and in musicology as well as theory. After a peak around 1960, when, as he puts it, "composers led the way in their composing, their writing about their composing, and their performances of their compositions, all making a coherent modernist whole that deeply influenced everyone else and reshaped a generation's way of thinking about how to study atonal music," the same sort of regression toward traditional values (or "community values") that Goldman observed in Carter in 1951 can by the 1980s be observed in everyone: "What's happened since . . . the mid 1970s (Stockhausen's formula pieces such as *Mantra* and *Inori*, Boulez's harmonic elaboration in *Rituel* and subsequent pieces), and for theorists from around 1980, is a move towards more attractive sounds, more humane commentary, more immediately appealing scores, and criticism grounded more in literary than in musical theory."[43]

I particularly like Leech-Wilkinson's application of this model to musicology, and in the first instance to music analysis, which had been his own early specialty:

> Many of the most influential analysts were first and foremost concerned with modern music, then diversified. David Lewin wrote on Schoenberg in the 1960s, moving out to Brahms and Wagner later; Allen Forte wrote on atonal music in the 1950s, moving into Mozart, Mahler and Liszt in the 1980s; Edward T. Cone, who was older, moved into Stravinsky and the Second Viennese School in the 1960s and then out again later; Arnold Whittall moved into contemporary music in the 1960s and then diversified into Wagner especially from the early 1980s; and one could go on: the pattern is strikingly consistent.[44]

---

to invite the disappearance of his audience by performing it. 'Advanced' (or 'sophisticated') modern-music audiences are supposed to be made of stronger stuff; but this is by no means always true. In this respect, the pale Stravinskian echo seems to have accomplished its debilitating work. The first performance of the Boulez Sonata proved nothing: its effect was strikingly flat. Perhaps it is, after all, paper music; or perhaps, as has been suggested, the performance was not what Boulez envisioned. What meets the eye should, in music, eventually meet the ear, but it would be untruthful to say that such a union occurred, except perhaps as a negative impression of a series of uninteresting ideas worked out with the help of an IBM computing device" ("Current Chronicle," *Musical Quarterly* 37 [1951]: 254). The somewhat cryptic reference to "the pale Stravinskian echo" seems to imply that the neoclassical vogue was still ascendant in New York at the time of this performance; but equally sarcastic is the reference at the end to a computer by IBM (that is, the International Business Machines Corporation, whose acronym was then synonymous with advanced technology). The reviewer may not have been fully aware of the degree to which he was actually correct in diagnosing the composer's dependence in this work on the use of algorithms as a way of avoiding traditional compositional choices. Here, too, he turned out to be prescient.

43. Leech-Wilkinson, "Musicology and Performance," 799.
44. Ibid.

We could extend the pattern into historical musicology as well, which is far less inclined than it used to be toward extolling the uniqueness of individual compositions through analysis, and is interested once again in grouping them, but no longer just sorting them by style. We are interested in the larger historical factors that condition style change and its transmission, and whenever we look at transmission we are looking at tradition.

VI

And that brings me to an even more recent text, one that actually came my way after I had begun drafting this essay: an exceptionally interesting article in what is, as I write, the current issue of the *Journal of the Royal Musical Association* called "Interpretation and Performance Practice in Realizing Stockhausen's *Studie II*."[45] This work, you may recall, was the first electronic composition to be published as a notated score. The existence of the score was supposed to make the piece both autographic and reproducible; but instead it raised the familiar ontological problems that have always attended notated and reproducible music, the chief one being whether to identify the work with the score or with the sound. The author calls this "the ontological problem surrounding this and other similar pieces of electronic music," but when the composition was created there were no other electronic pieces to which it applied. Electronic composition, in which the sound preceded and even obviated the need for the score, was supposed to have transcended the ontological problem. But as the author found out, the making of the score revived many old dilemmas. The two media, sound and score, turned out to be no more identical in the case of an electronic composition than in the case of conventional (which is to say traditional) vocal or instrumental pieces. The article is a record of the author's attempt to follow what appeared to be a simple and explicit recipe, and all the unexpected questions that intruded on the process.

Said author, Sean Williams, whose designated position on the faculty of the University of Kent is that of lecturer in audio electronics, set out to make a sonically improved version of Stockhausen's old electronic composition, composed (as you will recall) out of nothing but sine tones generated by an oscillator, thinking that all he would have to do would be to do as the publisher advertised and realize the specifications in the printed score as to the frequency, amplitude, and duration of all the sounds in the piece, denoted with complete quantitative precision. At the outset he admits, very discerningly, that even to conceive of the project implied an assumption that may have differed from that of the composer: namely, that the score, rather than the recorded realization that Stockhausen produced in 1954, is

---

45. Sean Williams, "Interpretation and Performance Practice in Realizing Stockhausen's *Studie II*," *Journal of the Royal Musical Association* 141 (2016): 445–81.

the primary embodiment of the work, even though it came afterwards and was not published until 1956. "If *Studie II* is identified as the recording," he writes, "then the new realization may be of only academic interest" (using the term *academic* in the ironic way that academics normally resent). "However," he continues, "if *Studie II* is identified as the score, then it should be possible to add something in its interpretation, even if there seems at first to be very little, if any, room for interpretation of such a specific score." In the end he decides not to decide, preferring to regard the work as "a combination of the recording and the score, possibly together with other elements including sketches, commentaries, interviews and further related archival material," which will allow "a case for the authenticity of the new realization" to be "built slowly, with critical reflection at every step."[46]

As in his title, the author is speaking the language here of performance practice, which is by definition something mediated by tradition. The whole motivating principle behind the development of electronic music in its earliest phases, coinciding with the so-called zero hour, was the elimination of that sort of mediation. The author quotes scripture in this regard: Hans Heinz Stuckenschmidt, writing in the maiden issue of *Die Reihe* about the aesthetics of electronic music, had insisted that the term *electronic music* be applied not to music performed on instruments like the trautonium or the *ondes Martenot* (he might have mentioned the theremin as well), but rather to "music conceived purely for the electronic sound generator . . . which for its realization does not require, indeed excludes, human interpreters."[47] The author's experience, and the whole eventual thrust of the article in which he reports it, is that this familiar promise of liberation was hopelessly utopian.

The first inkling that the real world was more complicated than utopia came when trying to decide whether it would be in keeping with the composer's intention to realize the algorithms (or, as he puts it, the "compositional ideas") that governed the composition with even greater precision than the technology of the 1950s allowed. In a new guise, this was exactly the old performance-practice question of "original" versus "modern" instruments. Williams decided that "any such differences in stability or timbre would be less significant than the advantage gained by producing accurate frequency values," even if the increased precision went "far beyond what the human ear can differentiate." As long as "the technology afforded this level of accuracy," he writes, "I felt it was consistent with the idea of fidelity to the composer to use it." This decision put him in the camp of "modern instruments." He actually compares his decision to the decision to perform Bach's Goldberg Variations on a grand piano, on the assumption that Bach would have

---

46. Ibid., 446–47.

47. Hans Heinz Stuckenschmidt, "The Third Stage: Some Observations on the Aesthetics of Electronic Music," *Die Reihe* 1 (1958): 11–13; quoted ibid., 447.

done so if he could. He of course acknowledges that doing that "may elicit reactions ranging from high praise to accusations of infidelity."[48]

That range of reactions is in fact a barometer of attitudes about tradition. Those who use the modern instrument will often claim, as our Stockhausen restorer is claiming here, that they are acting in accordance with the composer's implied intention. But can the composer's intention really be extrapolated? That's an old, old question, and one that can never be fully put to rest (or to the test); and Williams quickly came up against a problem that analysts of serial or other kinds of algorithmic compositions encounter all the time. In his words, "Engaging with the score at this [very close] level has enabled me to identify a number of mistakes made by Stockhausen himself" in applying his algorithms.[49] There is a sizable literature regarding similar discoveries in many composers' works, from Schoenberg and Stravinsky on down.[50] Are they to be corrected on the basis of the algorithm, thus implying that the algorithm is tantamount to the composer's intention? Or are we to assume instead that deviations from an apparent plan "are indicative of a level of interpretation on the part of the realizer—in this case, the composer himself," and therefore evidence of a specific intention that supervenes upon the general one—an intention that may not be intelligible to the analyst but which is nevertheless not up for review?[51] At least some deviations in *Studie II* could be rationalized as "an interpretative choice made on aesthetic grounds." An example of that sort of interpretative choice is the very last sound in the piece, which is much longer in the recording than in the score, and fades out, thus conforming to traditional notions of what an ending should sound like. "After realizing the final sound according to the score, and being disappointed by it," Williams reports, "I deferred to the master recording and allowed this final sound to decay naturally[!] into silence after that point, rather than stopping it abruptly, thus relying on the authenticity of the composer's own interpretation."[52]

We have already discussed the use of the word *naturally* in musical contexts. As to Williams's use of the word *authenticity*, it seems to be an example of the frequent interchangeability of that word with *authority*, a usage that I have been opposing for many years. Not that I am opposed to consulting appropriate authorities. Williams did just that when he consulted Gottfried Michael Koenig, the long-surviving technician who worked with Stockhausen on realizing the *Studie* at the Westdeutscher Rundfunk sixty years earlier, for guidance on the matter of the

48. Williams, "Interpretation and Performance Practice," 453, 459–60.

49. Ibid., 473.

50. Cf. Ethan Haimo, "Editing Schoenberg's Twelve-Tone Music," *Journal of the Arnold Schoenberg Institute* 8 (1984): 141–55; Joseph Straus, "Stravinsky's Serial 'Mistakes,'" *Journal of Musicology* 18 (1999): 231–71.

51. Williams, "Interpretation and Performance Practice," 473.

52. Ibid., 474.

troublesome deviations. Koenig's suggestions were what one might have expected from a member of Stockhausen's generation. He counseled that they be left uncorrected. "The exact values generated by the serial process are unimportant," he maintained; "there is no real sense of a mistake in the same sense of a mistake in a tonal or harmonic system." Here he was invoking what Milton Babbitt called the "low redundancy" of serial music (although Babbitt regarded low redundancy as a reason to insist on absolute fidelity to the algorithm rather than the fallible composer, it being the only thing that stands between serial music and utter meaninglessness). For Koenig, contrariwise, "the important factor is not the exact value as such, but the striving for achieving an exact value within a defined system. In this way, according to Koenig, any error or deviation from the system is not important as long as the system is being followed in good faith."[53]

And of course good faith can only be assumed. I am reminded of Stravinsky's retort to Ernest Ansermet, who was complaining, as so many have done, that serial music was "contrary to the laws of hearing," and that serial simultaneities were fortuitous and therefore meaningless as harmony. "You know that I pay attention to harmony," Stravinsky protested, arguing on behalf of his fortuities not that they were comprehensible to man but that "they must justify themselves before God!"[54]

Sean Williams made another decision on his own initiative—namely, not to take advantage of digital technology to eliminate the audible clicks, unspecified in the score (or, as he puts it, "neither specified nor prohibited by the score"), that the use of splicing blocks and razor blades, the primitive manual equipment of the 1950s, had introduced into the actual sounds of the recording of Stockhausen's *Studie*. Here he was making an assumption about the composer's intention (or what earlier writers on performance practice would have called his "low-level intentions").[55] On this view, one should accept aspects of Stockhausen's sound-world that the composer took for granted and therefore never questioned. As Sean Williams puts it, "I made the decision . . . so that the fundamental sound material of the piece could be as close as possible in character to that created by Stockhausen."[56]

That statement might well have been signed Christopher Hogwood or Nikolaus Harnoncourt. But one could argue that it contradicted Williams's other decision—the decision to realize the algorithms with greater precision than Stockhausen or his technicians were able to achieve. The one decision privileged the idea of the piece, the other privileged the sound; the one prioritized the score, the other the

---

53. Ibid.

54. Ernest Ansermet and Jean-Claude Piguet, *Entretiens sur la musique* (Neuchâtel, Switz.: À la Baconnière, 1963); quoted in Vera Stravinsky and Robert Craft, *Stravinsky in Pictures and Documents* (New York: Simon & Schuster, 1978), 248.

55. Cf. Randall R. Dipert, "The Composer's Intentions: An Examination of Their Relevance for Performance," *Musical Quarterly* 66 (1980): 205–18.

56. Williams, "Interpretation and Performance Practice," 454.

recording. Both decisions were justified by appealing to the composer's presumed intention. Williams, a very subtle thinker, recognized this difficulty. Citing another work of Stockhausen's, *Mikrophonie I*, he reports that "the intrinsic noisy clicks of the ... filter used [in that piece] were initially found to be infuriating, but were later deemed an essential part of the instrument's sound and the sound of the piece itself." Stockhausen had himself spoken of "integrat[ing] the family of noises into the composition," leading Williams to reflect that "this is an area where the affordances of the processes and tools used had a significant impact on the nature of the sound of the music that was produced, acting as an interpretative agency."[57] This, too, is an idea that is (or was) rife in the discourse of early music. Hans Redlich called it *musealer Klangmaterialismus*,[58] and disapproved of it precisely in the name of tradition, or perhaps I should say traditionalism.

So we have seen signs both of traditionalism and of antitraditionalism in Sean Williams's restoration (or re-creation) practice. Finally, in accordance with his motivating premise, he was bound to side with the traditionalists, writing that his aim, as he came to define it over the course of his labors, was to "produc[e] a version as faithful to the score as possible but with much improved clarity and definition."[59] In short, he took the composer at his word that the score, not the recording, contained all the essential information. It specified the sound source, the frequencies, the durations, and the amplitudes; as long as these specifications were observed (and as we have seen, Williams observed them even more scrupulously than Stockhausen himself was able to do), the criterion of fidelity and (if that is how you define it) authenticity is met. Finally, he elects the Bösendorfer over the harpsichord, recognizing that musical artifacts change over time along with their environment and its affordances. That environment consists not only of changing technological potentialities but also of changing subjective (or intersubjective) preferences—i.e., tastes. That sort of change over the *longue durée* is exactly what anthropologists like Allan Hanson think of as tradition.

And I think it is what Williams meant when writing that his version of *Studie II* "represents an improvement" over Stockhausen's, because "ontologically, ... I favored the compositional idea over both the score and the master recording."[60] On the face of it, that statement is a tautology that leaves undefined the ontological status of the "compositional idea." What is it, if it is not to be identified with either score or recording? What gives access to it? How is it to be realized? Williams reports that "at different stages of my own realization I have relied on the primacy

---

57. Quotations in this paragraph are from ibid., 458–59; the one from the composer is in Stockhausen, *Texte zur Musik*, ed. Dieter Schnebel, vol. 2 (Cologne: M. DuMont Schauberg, 1975), 22.

58. Hans Redlich, *Claudio Monteverdi: Life and Works* (London: Oxford University Press, 1952), 164.

59. Williams, "Interpretation and Performance Practice," 461.

60. Ibid., 475.

of the score, the master recording, the performance practice, subsequent commentary, ethnographic research and my own aesthetic judgment."[61] Thus it stands at a certain distance from the work of which it is a realization. Williams finally calls his product "an interpretation of *Studie II*," using a term that in its contingency usually describes performances rather than compositions. And when it comes to defining the work "itself," Williams retreats to a stance that may remind us of Roman Ingarden and his very complex answer to the question of what constitutes a musical work and defines its identity. "For me at least," Williams writes, "this work . . . is exclusively defined neither by the score nor by the tape, but exists in a more distributed manner."[62] Ingarden would have called it therefore an intentional object, since as an entity it is located only in the apprehender's mind.[63]

How did it get there? Since elements of discourse—subsequent commentary, ethnographic research, and performance practice—are among the defining elements the author lists, one must conclude that in order to conceive of the work at all (that is, conceive of it as a work rather than as a recording or a score), one must see it within a tradition. Williams agrees. After producing his realization, he concludes (*using the T-word*) that a technician capable of carrying out a valid realization needs "a kind of cultural knowledge similar to that needed by an instrumentalist working from a traditional musical score." That knowledge, consisting of "all kinds of attitudes relating to practice, quality, judgment and motivation," is what tradition transmits and preserves. Indeed, that is what a tradition is for. "In this way," Williams writes, "we can consider the electronic music of the 1950s and 1960s not as an entirely new paradigm, but as a continuation of traditional instrumental musical practice." Utopia bites the dust again. At best, he writes, "we can put forward the date of any paradigm shift, as heralded by Stuckenschmidt [you remember—the dream of total elimination of humans], at least to the introduction of computers and other automated systems in the late 1960s."[64]

But let's ask Paul Lansky about that, or David Wessel, or one of the many others who found that the most satisfying application of computer technology to music was in so-called "live" electronics, the use of computers to modify or otherwise cooperate in real-time, human music-making. And when Paul Lansky retired from the Princeton faculty in 2008, he surprised everyone by retiring from the world of automated systems as well. An interview with him in the *New York Times*, under the headline "A Computer-Man Unplugs," struck some readers as charming and others as alarming for bringing word that "Mr. Lansky," one of the giants of the

---

61. Ibid., 480.
62. Ibid.
63. See Roman Ingarden, *The Work of Music and the Problem of Its Identity*, trans. Adam Czerniawski (Berkeley: University of California Press, 1986).
64. Williams, "Interpretation and Performance Practice," 479.

medium, "has abandoned the art form that made his name and has turned to more traditional composition." The T-word again! And Mr. Lansky's own comments corroborated the nexus between the T-word and the solace of human community. "I hate to say this, but I think I'm done," he said. "Here I am, 64, and I find myself at what feels like the beginning of a career. I'm interested in writing for real people at this point."[65] *Gemeinschaft.* Perhaps we should not have been surprised.

Every composer's authority, even Stockhausen's, is contingent on, or mediated by, the social contract. *Gesang der Jünglinge,* Stockhausen's most famous electronic composition, was originally composed in five stereophonic channels, later mixed down to four channels for most performances, and later still mixed down to two channels for commercial release as an LP disk by Deutsche Grammophon. Which version is definitive? According to Sean Williams, Stockhausen decided that "by dint of so many performances in four instead of the originally intended five channels, that version had become the absolute and final version."[66] On this basis Williams concludes that in the case of *Studie II,* which has also been widely performed, Stockhausen "would have continued to regard the tape version, not the score, as the master expression" of his electronic works. But Williams nevertheless overrode what he acknowledges to be Stockhausen's preference in realizing the "compositional idea," which is transmitted by a source that, as he finally recognized, possesses greater authority than the composer. That source is tradition.

VII

Needless to say, this is not a settled argument. There may not be much controversy at the moment about definitive versions of Stockhausen tape compositions, but there is plenty where the warhorses of the classical repertory are concerned, and where there is, arguably, a great deal more at stake. As I was writing this piece, the big Chaikovsky piano concerto was back in the news. As happens every now and then, a young pianist had discovered the earliest version of the piece (the so-called Boston version, because that is where the 1875 première took place, with Hans von Bülow as soloist). The most noticeable difference between it and the familiar, or standard, version comes right at the beginning, or right after the beginning, when the soloist enters not with the crashing chords in three registers that have become the concerto's signature effect, but with decorous rolled chords in a narrower range. The young pianist in question, Kirill Gerstein, having recorded it in 2015, made a big noise about it, at first in an article called "The Real Tchaikovsky" in the *New York Review of Books,* and a couple of years later in a *New York Times* interview that ran with the title "Listen to Tchaikovsky, Stripped Down to His Inten-

---

65. Quoted in Daniel J. Wakin, "A Computer-Man Unplugs," *New York Times,* 3 August 2008.
66. Williams, "Interpretation and Performance Practice," 480.

tions." Both articles were equipped with online versions that made parallel audio excerpts available.⁶⁷

The relevance of this issue to the one I have been pondering here is clear enough; but Gerstein foregrounds or—should I say?—forces the issue by labeling the familiar version the "traditional" one, and wielding the label as a stigma. The traditional version is very easily stigmatized from one well-established (I might even say traditional) point of view, because the famous crashing chords were contributed to the concerto, so to speak, not by Chaikovsky but by one of its leading performers, the pianist Alexander Siloti (1863–1945), a pupil of Liszt, with whom Chaikovsky consulted during the winter of 1888–89 when he decided to revise the work for a new edition. The crash-bang effect can thus be described (and a textual critic actually would describe it, in a purely technical sense sans opprobrium) as a contamination—something that occurs in all traditions in the course of normal transmission.

Heavily hyping what he calls the "new" opening of the concerto, even though it was the earlier one, Gerstein answers a question ("How did the usual edition come about?") posed by David Allen, his interlocutor for the *New York Times,* with a raft of moral innuendos:

> There's a tragedy, especially in Russian culture, of geniuses surrounded by less talented well-wishers. Tchaikovsky was one of those, where certain people in his circle—in this case Alexander Siloti, his student and an uncle [actually a cousin] of Rachmaninoff—thought they knew better. Siloti had been in Europe and studied with Liszt. His tendency toward the superficially brilliant, and some of the traits of 19th-century pianism that are less noble than the tradition generally is in its best manifestations, resulted in these posthumous editorial changes.
>
> Some people like to eat organic food—that's Tchaikovsky's version—and some people like to eat everything with sprinkles of MSG. That's fine, as long as you know that what you're sprinkling is monosodium glutamate. So if one wants to play Tchaikovsky-Siloti, do that. I think it's better to do what the composer himself wrote.

That's pressing a lot of buttons: superficiality vs. nobility, genius vs. mediocrity, adulteration vs. whole foods, you name it. One of Gerstein's points is actually a lie, which might as well be disposed of first. The edition with Siloti's crash-bang was not posthumous. It appeared in 1889; Chaikovsky approved it and conducted from it before his death in 1893.⁶⁸ It was reissued with further modifications in 1894, but

---

67. Kirill Gerstein, "The Real Tchaikovsky," 9 March 2015, is at www.nybooks.com/daily/2015/03/09/real-tchaikovsky; David Allen, "Listen to Tchaikovsky, Stripped Down to His Intentions," 1 February 2017, is at www.nytimes.com/2017/02/01/arts/music/listen-to-kirill-gerstein-tchaikovsky-stripped-down-to-his-intentions.html.

68. See Jeremy Norris, *The Russian Piano Concerto,* vol. 1: *The Nineteenth Century* (Bloomington: Indiana University Press, 1994), 122–23.

the crash-bang was not added behind Chaikovsky's back, as Gerstein implies. (Nor, by the way, was Gerstein's the first recording of the Boston version, despite his claims; Jerome Lowenthal recorded it in 1993 for the Chaikovsky centennial,[69] and there may well be others; the score was republished many years ago in the Soviet academic edition of the composer's complete works, edited by Alexander Goldenweiser.) But these fibs do not have any bearing on the status of the standard version as canonical, because (despite whatever scholars may wish or say) it is tradition, not scholarly fiat, that canonizes. The flamboyant opening is too firmly a component of the concerto's tradition to be dislodged either by hype or by research, it seems to me, especially when the hype is so obviously self-serving, of a piece with the sort of political propaganda we hear every day, in which opportunistic arguments dress themselves up as high principle. One can just as easily find aesthetic arguments in support of the contaminated version. Michael Steinberg, so fastidious in his condemnation of Horowitz, declared himself "totally in favor of the 1889 version. The effect is splendid, it is even exciting to watch, and it makes much more of Tchaikovsky's bold idea of having the first solo entrance be an accompaniment—but what an accompaniment!"[70]

Persuasive or not, Steinberg's argument is a more honest one than Gerstein's. It is concerned not with the assertion or display of superior standards but with actual effect in performance (*Wirkung*, the Germans would say), the thing that audiences actually witness, and with the relationship between effect and reception. That is why it is the winning argument. Musicology is coming around. Do you remember Carolyn Abbate's manifesto, "Music—Drastic or Gnostic?"?[71] It is a call to stop studying works and start studying performances—not "performance practice," but actual performances.

At stake is a social issue rather than an aesthetic one, leading us back to the fundamental question on which I framed the whole second half of *The Oxford History of Western Music*: does art exist in history or in society? The modernist answer (and this includes the old "authenticist" answer) was that it exists in history, and there are no audiences. Robert Craft's remark, that Schoenberg's *Pelleas und Melisande*, "by reason of its superior construction . . . is destined to become a war horse," has always struck me as naive, indeed Parsifalianly innocent, because it so utterly mistakes the source of popular approval.[72] And Schoenberg's own widely quoted boast, "I venture to credit myself with having written truly new music which, being based on tradition, is destined to become tradition," remains

69. Arabesque Recordings Z6611, with Sergiu Comissiona and the London Symphony Orchestra.
70. Michael Steinberg, *The Concerto: A Listener's Guide* (New York: Oxford University Press, 1978), 478.
71. Carolyn Abbate, "Music—Drastic or Gnostic?" *Critical Inquiry* 30 (2004): 505–36.
72. Notes to *The Works of Arnold Schoenberg*, vol. 2 (Columbia Records M2S 694 [1963]).

debatable as a prediction, no matter how widely his compositions have been imitated or his methods adopted.[73] Despite his assertion and Craft's, I think most would agree that Schoenberg's tone poems (*Verklärte Nacht* apart) have not joined the catalogue of warhorses, whereas those of Richard Strauss, against which Craft was surely if tacitly (and invidiously) measuring Schoenberg's, will remain there as long as there is one. Is that tantamount to saying that Strauss's work (plus Schoenberg's one warhorse), rather than the rest of Schoenberg's output, is traditional within our musical culture (or, to be maximally safe, within the musical culture of the now-completed twentieth century)?

It is if we define tradition the way I have already defined it—as that which expresses or promotes *Gemeinschaft:* community, or community values. Those values are expressed and experienced in the act of thronging together to witness a euphoria-inducing event, such as hearing a thrilling performance of *Ein Heldenleben,* or seeing Van Cliburn crash-banging his way through the Siloti-contaminated Chaikovsky Piano Concerto no. 1. Having experienced that euphoria, one wants to experience it again; so back to the throng, and the pianist had better be using the crash-bang edition or the ritual will not have its desired community-nurturing force. This is one of the answers to the bothersome old question about the evident value of rehearing familiar musical compositions.[74] It is a necessary, and often overlooked, component of the canonization process, which is too often assumed to be an "invented tradition" according to the old top-down or "legislative" model that by now, I hope, will seem inadequate.[75]

VIII

One has to resort to German to make this point, because German sociology, beginning with the famous eponymous treatise of 1887 by Ferdinand Tönnies, has

---

73. Arnold Schoenberg, "National Music" (1931), in Schoenberg, *Style and Idea,* ed. Leonard Stein, trans. Leo Black (Berkeley: University of California Press, 1984), 174.

74. See Leonard B. Meyer, "On Rehearing Music," *Journal of the American Musicological Society* 14 (1961): 257–67; reprinted in Meyer, *Music, the Arts, and Ideas: Patterns and Predictions in Twentieth-Century Culture* (Chicago: University of Chicago Press, 1967), 42–53, for a provocative posing of the question and some generally unsatisfactory answers.

75. For an especially crude application to the musical canon, already quoted in chapter 1 of this book, that will now, I hope, seem altogether unsustainable, see Robert Walser, "Eruptions: Heavy Metal Appropriations of Classical Virtuosity," *Popular Music* 11 (1992): 263–308, at 265: "Classical music is the sort of thing Eric Hobsbawm calls an 'invented tradition,' whereby present interests construct a cohesive past to establish or legitimize present-day institutions or social relations. The hodgepodge of the classical canon—aristocratic and bourgeois music; academic, sacred and secular; music for public concerts, private soirees and dancing—achieves its coherence through its function as the most prestigious musical culture of the twentieth century."

canonized a distinction between two words, *Gemeinschaft* and *Gesellschaft*, either of which could be translated as either "community" or "society" in English.[76] The usual translation of Tönnies's title into English is *Community and Society* or (in its most recent translation) *Community and Civil Society*. *Gemeinschaft* denotes a personal or subjective affinity, together with the practices and attitudes that maintain it; *Gesellschaft* refers to institutional or legal structures that define our interactions with one another, not out of a sense of spontaneous personal predilection but rather out of a rational calculation of costs and benefits. In their initial formulation these terms were not supposed to be value-laden; but Tönnies's pessimistic assertion that *Gemeinschaft* was natural to man and *Gesellschaft* "mechanical" and unstable assured endless controversy over values. *Gemeinschaft* is often allied with authenticity, organicism, and other qualities that radiate warmth and romantic good vibrations, while *Gesellschaft* is cool: impersonal, objective, remote, "classical." Tradition promotes *Gemeinschaft*; legislation promotes *Gesellschaft*. Hobsbawmian "invented tradition," it seems to me, might be better called legislation posing as tradition, *Gesellschaft* passing itself off as *Gemeinschaft*.

But before giving ourselves over to good vibrations, let's remember the political debate over these terms that has been going on for more than a century, ever since their coinage as a dichotomy. In his review of Tönnies's book as early as 1889,[77] Émile Durkheim already reproached his German colleague for portraying the transformation of *Gemeinschaft* into *Gesellschaft* as a degeneration rather than as progress: from mere consanguinity to a rationalized complexity based on commerce, contracts, and the division of labor (compare Freud: "Where id was, there ego shall be").[78] Durkheim's view implied that liberal democracy was the product of the very progression that Tönnies regarded with foreboding. *Gesellschaft*, in this optimist view, was the guarantor of judicious civic liberalism, whereas organic *Gemeinschaft* was atavistic, irrational—what Bismarck had in mind when he exhorted the Germans to think with their blood, a pronouncement for which Hit-

---

76. Ferdinand Tönnies, *Gemeinschaft und Gesellschaft* (Leipzig, 1887); translated by Jose Harris and Margaret Hollis as *Community and Civil Society* (Cambridge: Cambridge University Press, 2001).

77. In the *Revue philosophique* 27 (1889): 416–22; see "An Exchange between Durkheim and Tönnies on the Nature of Social Relations, with an Introduction by Joan Aldous," *American Journal of Sociology* 77 (1972): 1191–1200.

78. Or in Freud's less jargonish German, "Wo Es war, soll Ich werden" (Where It was, there I shall be): Sigmund Freud, *Neue Folge der Vorlesungen zur Einführung in die Psychoanalyse* (New Series of Introductory Lectures on Psychoanalysis) (Vienna: Internationaler Psychoanalytischer Verlag, 1933), 191; translated by James Strachey as *New Introductory Lectures on Psych-Analysis*, vol. 22 of *The Standard Edition of the Complete Psychological Works of Sigmund Freud* (New York: W. W. Norton, 1964), 100.

ler usually and wrongly gets credit.[79] In his very last book, published when he was ninety, our doughty Eric Hobsbawm mapped these terms onto our current political scene and its debates, associating *Gesellschaft* with globalization and *Gemeinschaft* with identity politics.[80] The values associated with tradition fluctuate in their appeal directly with those associated with *Gemeinschaft*.

And that brings us face to face with today's headlines. As contending forces, *Gemeinschaft* and *Gesellschaft* are in the air in America, at least among the more intellectual political pundits. Resurgent *Gemeinschaft*, it seems, the revolt of identity politics against globalization, brought us Donald Trump (and brought the British Brexit). On the day of Trump's inauguration, David Brooks, a moderate conservative with a reputation for erudition, published a little primer on the subject in the *New York Times*. "All across the world," he wrote,

> we have masses of voters who live in a world of gemeinschaft: where relationships are personal, organic and fused by particular affections. These people define their loyalty to community, faith and nation in personal, in-the-gut sort of ways.
>
> But we have a leadership class and an experience of globalization that is from the world of gesellschaft: where systems are impersonal, rule based, abstract, indirect and formal.
>
> Many people in Europe love their particular country with a vestigial affection that is like family—England, Holland or France. But meritocratic elites of Europe gave them an abstract intellectual construct called the European Union.
>
> Many Americans think their families and their neighborhoods are being denuded by the impersonal forces of globalization, finance and technology. All the Republican establishment could offer was abstract paeans to the free market. All the Democrats could offer was Hillary Clinton, the ultimate cautious, remote, calculating gesellschaft thinker.
>
> It was the right moment for Trump, the ultimate gemeinschaft man.[81]

So what do we think of tradition now? One can see the reasons for Hobsbawm's suspicions, and the motives for his attempt to impugn what he saw as the invented ones. But if Brooks is right, the "real" ones are even worse. And if I am right, then the "real" ones are only the means through which the manipulators whom Hobsbawm impugned as inventors work their nefarious ways. Was the increasingly traditional "humanism" of Pierre Boulez's late performances only a sign of backsliding toward Brexit? I can imagine a resurrected Adorno saying so. Is Kirill Gerstein's advocacy of the nontraditional version of Chaikovsky's Piano Concerto no. 1 a secret blow against Trump, which we can abet by buying his records?

---

79. See Walker Connor, *Ethnonationalism: The Quest for Understanding* (Princeton, NJ: Princeton University Press, 1993).
80. Eric Hobsbawm, *Globalisation, Democracy, and Terrorism* (Boston: Little, Brown, 2007).
81. David Brooks, "The Internal Invasion," *New York Times*, 20 January 2017.

Well no, I am not saying any of that. The purposes (or functions, as Hobsbawm would prefer to say) that traditions serve are what deserve our scrutiny. Ends are what we must judge rather than means, which serve ends good, bad, and indifferent. To answer the question I posed at the outset: Tradition, being a social and cultural instrument, does not have a nature, hence no inherent predilections. It does what we need or want it to do. Our needs and wants are what we need to evaluate before we take a stand about the traditions to which they give rise.

12

Which Way Is Up?

On the sociology of taste

I enjoy listening to classical music, but even more I enjoy telling people I enjoy listening to classical music.
—STEPHEN COLBERT, ON *LATE NIGHT*, 15 JUNE 2017

I. THE ELEPHANT IN THE ROOM

It's always flattering to be asked to keynote a conference. Or was, until this time. Seeing as I have not actually written anything for publication about the middlebrow phenomenon—unlike Joan Rubin, our other keynoter, who literally wrote the book on it[1]—I must be taken to exemplify it somehow, or, to put it as favorably as possible, to be exemplary of it. The invitation reminded me of the old Harvard story about Roman Jakobson, the Slavic linguist, who, when someone proposed naming Vladimir Nabokov to a chair in comparative literature, is said to have said, "Gentlemen, even if one allows that he is an important writer, are we next to invite an elephant to be Professor of Zoology?"[2] So thank you very much, but it is, forgive me, an equivocal honor to be elected your Middlebrow in Chief, or perhaps your elephant in the room.

We could—and probably will—spend the whole conference trying to decide just what "middlebrow" is or means. But whatever it is or means, I don't think one has ever claimed the title for oneself. It is always something attributed, and never in praise. Sometimes it just means "philistine," as in the very first sentence of Tom Perrin's *The Aesthetics of Middlebrow Fiction*, whose subtitle identifies it as a study

---

Originally presented (in part) as keynote address at the conference "Music and the Middlebrow," University of Notre Dame's London Global Gateway, 22 June 2017.

1. Joan Shelley Rubin, *The Making of Middlebrow Culture* (Chapel Hill, NC: University of North Carolina Press, 1992).

2. Brian Boyd, *Vladimir Nabokov: The American Years* (Princeton, NJ: Princeton University Press, 1993), 303.

of "popular US novels, modernism, and form, 1945–75." These are the opening paragraphs:

> Here are Craig Price and Susan Strong, characters from Robert Ruark's forgotten middlebrow epic *Poor No More* (1959), on modernist icon William Faulkner:
>> "I can't read him, him and that Makalpawhichawaymultnomah County. Posturing bore. Writes in loops. You can take Mr. James Joyce and Miss Stein and . . . "
>> "Watch it. There ain't enough room in there for both of them."
>
> Ruark's protagonist, Price, is someone who might, in 1959, have been called a middlebrow reader. "He prefers," Ruark tells us, "Marjorie Kinnan Rawlings," author of the hugely popular, sentimental, yet critically acclaimed novel *The Yearling* (1939), to the highbrow Françoise Sagan, "and believes William Faulkner to be unreadable."[3]

And I, it has often been alleged, prefer Benjamin Britten, the author of the hugely popular, sentimental, yet critically acclaimed opera *Peter Grimes* (1945), to the highbrow Arnold Schoenberg, and believe Elliott Carter to be unlistenable.

But note that for Tom Perrin, writing in 2015, *middlebrow* still denotes a genre, even an "aesthetic category." He applies the term to works and authors. The fact that, like many who now populate postmodernist English departments, he seeks to rehabilitate the middlebrow does not mitigate what I see as his misapplication of the term. His view of the middlebrow hardly differs from that of persistent (and by now belated) highbrow detractors, less likely to be academics, such as Tom McCarthy, a British novelist, who continues to deplore "the naive or uncritical realism dominating contemporary middlebrow fiction," for which he blames "the doctrine of authenticity peddled on creative writing classes the world over."[4] Despite the traditional slinging of the muddy word *peddle* to besmirch a hackneyed institutional target, his definition of middlebrow is essentialist, not transactional. Both Toms—the one deliberately, the other by default—ignore the mediating structures that gave meaning to the term. They both see the middlebrow as a baked-in ingredient, to be approved or disapproved at the discretion of the critic. Whether approving or disapproving, their evaluations are equally regressive.

As applied to music, the middlebrow, conceived immanently, as a particular genre or style, is roughly tantamount to what Adorno, our exemplary squeamish highbrow, called *die gemäßigte Moderne*. Christopher Chowrimootoo has drawn precisely this parallel in his programmatic statement "Reviving the Middlebrow, or: Deconstructing Modernism from the Inside," which appeared in the round table "Modernism and Its Others," published by the *Journal of the Royal Musical*

---

3. Tom Perrin, *The Aesthetics of Middlebrow Fiction* (New York: Palgrave Macmillan, 2015), 1.
4. Tom McCarthy, *Typewriters, Bombs, Jellyfish: Essays* (New York: New York Review Books, 2017), 60.

Association (*JRMA*) in 2014.⁵ The appropriateness of this equation is something I mean to question today; but one point in its favor is the apparent lack, to my knowledge at least, of any composers who have proudly, or even humbly, aligned themselves with *die gemäßigte Moderne*. The phrase is opprobrious, and so is "middlebrow." Can they be rid of opprobrium, as some writers now wish, and become neutral designators like "baroque," which was also once a slur?

Somewhat less degrading, though still patronizing, is the idea that middlebrow culture is a striving one, that it is upwardly mobile, presumably toward highbrow-hood. It was this concept that originally spawned the term, as in the 23 December 1925 issue of *Punch* (often cited, not quite accurately, as its earliest occurrence in print), where it was reported that "the B.B.C. claim to have discovered a new type, the 'middlebrow,' . . . consist[ing] of people who are hoping that some day they will get used to the stuff they ought to like."⁶ An industry was by then developing to help them; and this aspirational side of middlebrow culture, to which my title alludes, was the most controversial aspect of the whole enterprise. It combined high-minded "genteel" rhetoric with the crasser language of marketing. The oxymoronic combination produced a very distinctive sort of bombast. Here is a musical example. Try and guess who wrote it:

> If one collected all the music in the world written by men who were not Germans, put it together, and multiplied it by ten, the product would not equal in value the music written by Germans alone. In the Music Hall facing the lake on Michigan Avenue in Chicago, the committee placed on the façade the names of what they considered to be the five greatest composers in all history. They are Bach, Mozart, Beethoven, Wagner, Schubert—all Germans. And the first names on a substitute list would also be Germans.⁷

Except for the part about Chicago, you might have guessed it was by Joseph Goebbels or Heinrich Schenker or Arnold Schoenberg or some other strange bedfellow in chauvinism. But, obviously, the author was American, which, far from a surprise, only demonstrates the immoderation of traditional Anglophone Germanocentrism when it comes to classical music—something against which many of us are struggling within the musicological profession in the face of still-vocifer-

---

5. Laura Tunbridge, ed., "Round Table: Modernism and Its Others," *Journal of the Royal Musical Association* 139 (2014): 187–93.

6. "Charivaria," *Punch*, 23 December 1925, 673; quoted in Laurie Hanquinet and Mike Savage, eds., *Routledge International Handbook of the Sociology of Art and Culture* (Abingdon, UK: Routledge, 2016), 352. The online site Middlebrow Network cites a slightly earlier, noncommittal occurrence: "Ireland's musical destiny, in spite of what the highbrows or the middlebrows may say, is intimately bound up with the festivals" (*Freemen's Journal*, 3 May 1924); see www.middlebrow-network.com/DefiningtheMiddlebrow.aspx.

7. William Lyon Phelps, *Music* (New York: E. P. Dutton, 1930), 20.

ous if weakening resistance. The example just quoted does not come from musicology, of course, but from music appreciation: the delivery system that implemented the melioristic objectives of middlebrow musical evangelism. It was a spinoff from the Great Books movement about which Prof. Rubin and others have written. And the author of the passage was somebody about whom Prof. Rubin has written at length: William Lyon Phelps, the Lampson Professor of English Literature at Yale University, who liked to be called Billy.

Phelps was a Browning specialist, an enthusiastic and much-beloved classroom popularizer who went on to a career in radio broadcasting. The passage comes from a little book, hardly more than a pamphlet, simply called *Music*, published in 1930 by E. P. Dutton in a series of inspirational tracts by Phelps that included previous items titled *Happiness, Love,* and *Memory*. It reads like a radio lecture (which it may well have been), starting right off with a whiff of the contemporaneous Yale classroom, unless it was the locker room: "Music," the first sentence proclaims, "is essentially the manly art." (You know why: women can't compose.) And the author continues in the mode of another set of Billys, the ones named Sunday or Graham:

> I have in mind an American family at dinner—father, mother, sons and daughters—discussing the Beethoven Symphony concert as eagerly as women now discuss clothes, and men discuss athletic sport. Why do average, healthy, respectable American men and boys hate good music? Perhaps you will say they don't. Unfortunately they do. The majority of respectable men are bored by classical music, and will not go to a symphony concert unless there is some famous soloist.
>
> Why do they hate good music? The answer is simple. It is because they do not listen.
>
> I was once myself in that condition of ignorance and darkness. With no one to teach me, with no explanatory books, with no musical education, I became a passionate, discriminating lover of the best music.
>
> Today I had far rather hear good music than hear anything else on earth. No music is too elevated for me. The stiffer the programme, the better it is.[8]

You won't be surprised to learn that the author of these words became the special *bête noire* of another Yale man, Dwight Macdonald, a writer who is probably best remembered now for his tireless crusade against middlebrow culture, or what he called Midcult. His enmity toward Billy Phelps went back to his undergraduate days, when (as I learned from Prof. Rubin's book) he wrote (but was dissuaded from publishing) a column called "The Romantic Lecturers of Yale" for the *Yale Record*, the undergraduate newspaper of which he was then the editor, calling Phelps's style of lecturing "ridiculous and distasteful" owing to the constant "injection of the teacher's personality into every . . . word uttered on the platform." And then, as Prof. Rubin relates it, he "charg[ed] that instructors such as

8. Ibid., 4–5.

Phelps appealed to 'precisely that element of the class who have no business to be in college.'"[9]

There you have *in nuce* the project of Macdonald's life: to keep the precious products of high culture out of the hands of those who have no business knowing them. The whole point of his most famous essay, "Masscult and Midcult,"[10] is prefigured in this fledgling piece. Helping the aspiring masses toward access to "the best that has been thought and said," in the words of Matthew Arnold (often thought of as the middlebrow's progenitor), does not elevate the masses.[11] Rather, it degrades through dilution the quality of the cultural goods to which plebeian access has been gained. Phelps was not bringing his Yale men up to the level of Shakespeare (to name the subject of the course that provoked Macdonald's irascibility); rather, he was bringing Shakespeare down to them.

The idea that there were people who had no business hearing about Shakespeare, and that telling them about Shakespeare was injurious to Shakespeare—that is the idea over which the fur has flown at least since 1927, the year the young Macdonald inveighed against the venerable Phelps. Does it remind you, as it does me, of phrases like "Keep your cotton-pickin' hands off [whatever]," or of our more recent fraught debates over same-sex marriage and its alleged threat to the institution of holy matrimony?

II. FAMILY VALUES

How new an idea *was* that in 1927? Is it fair to enlist Matthew Arnold as a middlebrow prototype? The program of the conference for which this essay was first drafted included papers that related to the nineteenth and even eighteenth centuries. I've seen the term applied to much earlier figures and phenomena. One application that really startled me came from Timothy Taylor's very recent study *Music and Capitalism*. He was glossing a passage from my *Oxford History of Western Music* (or, more familiarly, The Ox). The chapter in question was titled "Middle and Low," but I wasn't talking about brows. I was talking about rhetorical styles, classically defined by Cicero as

---

9. Rubin, *The Making of Middlebrow Culture*, 342–43n32.

10. In Macdonald, *Against the American Grain: Essays on the Effects of Mass Culture* (New York: Random House, 1962), 3–71.

11. The famous catchphrase comes from the preface, added in 1875, to Matthew Arnold, *Culture and Anarchy: An Essay in Political and Social Criticism* (first published in 1869), where culture is defined, nothing if not aspirationally, as "a pursuit of our total perfection by means of getting to know, on all the matters which most concern us, the best which has been thought and said in the world, and, through this knowledge, turning a stream of fresh and free thought upon our stock notions and habits, which we now follow staunchly but mechanically, vainly imagining that there is a virtue in following them staunchly which makes up for the mischief of following them mechanically" (M. Arnold, *Culture and Anarchy*, Oxford World Classics [Oxford: Oxford University Press, 2009], 5).

gravis, mediocris, and *attenuatus* (weighty, middling, and plain), and thence restated through the ages, always as a high-middle-and-low trio, which Tinctoris, writing in the late fifteenth century, had been the first to apply to musical genres: *magnus* for the Mass, *mediocris* for the Latin-texted motet, and *parvus* for the vernacular song or chanson. Entirely off the scale were the textless chanson arrangements called *carmina* that made up the contents of the *Glogauer Liederbuch,* the earliest surviving set of partbooks (hence the forerunner of all later publications of instrumental chamber music), and its immediate successors, the early publications of Ottaviano Petrucci, the Venetian printer who introduced movable type to the production of sheet music. I noted that we now often use the expression "absolute music" to characterize instrumental pieces without text or utilitarian function, but then I cautioned that

> the modern concept of "absolute music" is not completely or even accurately defined if we do not emphasize the supreme value placed on it as an art-experience since the nineteenth century. By contrast, the fifteenth-century forerunner, compared with a cyclic Mass or a motet or even with a texted courtly song, was of all genres the lowest and the lightest, mere fluff. And yet the leisured clerical senior citizens who sat around amusing themselves with the *Glogauer Liederbuch* in the last decades of the fifteenth century could nevertheless be described as the earliest literate "music lovers" in the modern, esthetic sense.
>
> It was the spread of that kind of music-loving that supported the earliest music business—written music as a commodity possessing monetary exchange value. It is no accident that the very earliest printed publication containing polyphonic music [Petrucci's *Harmonice musices odhecaton* of 1501] was largely given over to textless chanson arrangements.[12]

"It is no accident that" was, of course, a parody of Marxist rhetoric, so it is no wonder that Tim Taylor pricked up his ears. But here is how he paraphrased my text:

> The commodification of music as a published good began at the end of the fifteenth century with the invention of movable type for music by the Italian printer Ottaviano Petrucci, who petitioned the Venetian government to protect his invention in 1498. Petrucci published his first collection in 1501, a collection not of religious music but of mainly textless arrangements of chansons aimed at a *middlebrow* audience. This collection of "fluff," concludes the musicologist Richard Taruskin, was important to the future of making music from scores in the West. It is less a question of the nature of the music, however, than of the fact that it was published and disseminated, which created new markets, new musical forms, genres, and techniques, and new composer-entrepreneurs—all subject to the vagaries of the new capitalist market.[13]

---

12. R. Taruskin, *The Oxford History of Western Music,* rev. ed., vol. 1: *Music from the Earliest Notations to the Sixteenth Century* (New York: Oxford University Press, 2010), 542. See also chapter 4 above, "Is There a Baby in the Bathwater?"

13. Timothy Taylor, *Music and Capitalism: A History of the Present* (Chicago: University of Chicago Press, 2015), 22 (italics added).

Taylor calls attention to the way the capitalist order creates new markets, new genres, new techniques, and new composer-entrepreneurs (the last category quite unsupported by the example he borrowed from me, which dealt with clerics and printers), but to me the striking locution here is "middlebrow audience," which, as Taylor invokes it, seems already to exist, whereas if anything is created by commodification (besides the commodity itself), it is the consumer. So basic is this relationship that it seems to have escaped the author's notice.

The actual buyers of Petrucci's *Odhecaton* were a class of wealthy or aristocratic bibliophiles making a status purchase. Calling them a middlebrow audience is a real solecism. I don't know whether to call it a misnomer or an anachronism, but it exemplifies the crudest possible construal of "middlebrow," the one that merely equates it with commercial consumption. To see the sort of romanticism that equates commerce with aesthetic degradation passing itself off as a Marxist analysis is remarkable. But it has a long tradition, one that includes Dwight Macdonald and Clement Greenberg on its way to Tim Taylor. It goes back not to Marx but to aristocratic derision of "trade." According to this haughty tradition, helping consumers gain access to the sacred precincts of art is original sin.

We can gain another angle on this confusion by going back for a moment to Billy Phelps (fig. 12.1), whose picture, as it happens, graces books by both of your keynote speakers. That it appears in Prof. Rubin's history of middlebrow culture is no surprise; but it may surprise you that the very same picture—and it's a delightful one (wouldn't we all have liked to have an office like that?)—appears in The Ox as well, in volume 4, chapter 5, a chapter largely devoted to yet another Yale man named Charles Ives, class of 1898. I first encountered the picture in *Charles Ives: The Ideas behind the Music*, the first of the two books that J. Peter Burkholder derived from his University of Chicago dissertation, "The Evolution of Charles Ives's Music: Aesthetics, Quotation, Technique" (1983). There, the photo is printed big enough and clearly enough that you can tell that Phelps is holding a book of Browning's poems (edited by himself).[14]

Phelps, who taught Ives English literature, was one of only four mentor-figures Burkholder chose to illustrate his book, the others being George Ives, Charles's venerated and much-idealized bandmaster father; Horatio Parker, his principal composition teacher; and John Cornelius Griggs, the New Haven organist and choirmaster who was the young Ives's professional role model. Phelps, as you see, was the single nonmusician among these most powerful influences. Burkholder commented that, unlike Ives's other mentors, Phelps "ha[d] received no attention from Ives scholars despite his apparent importance in shaping Ives's literary

---

14. J. Peter Burkholder, *Charles Ives: The Ideas behind the Music* (New Haven, CT: Yale University Press, 1985), 73.

FIGURE 12.1. William Lyon Phelps, Images of Yale individuals, ca. 1750–2001 (inclusive). Manuscripts & Archives, Yale University.

interests," particularly his preoccupation with Emerson.[15] I took these words to heart, especially since by the time I read Burkholder I already knew Phelps's book on music, and immediately suspected that the shaping may have gone beyond the literary. When it came time to write about Ives in The Ox, I went straight back to Phelps, and from Phelps straight back to Matthew Arnold.

It shouldn't be surprising that Charles Ives got a lot more out of Billy Phelps than Dwight Macdonald did—or at least that he valued what he got from him a lot more. The reasons probably had in part to do with the difference between the Phelps Macdonald knew—the local Mr. Chips, a Yale celebrity on the cusp of national fame, beloved for his eccentricities—and the Phelps Ives knew three decades earlier, a young instructor only a decade or so older than his undergraduates, who was regarded by his senior colleagues as a somewhat disreputable innovator because he included contemporary fiction in his course curricula.[16] Already, however, Phelps was known for the traits that would render him disreputable in the eyes of Dwight Macdonald. He was friendly, enthusiastic, and unpretentious. As one of Ives's classmates recalled, "Billy Phelps . . . attended all our reunions and was probably the most popular professor in our day."[17]

That begins to suggest another reason why Ives appreciated him. As Burkholder, who read Ives's college transcript, points out, "Ives was a sorry student, but his grades for his three classes with Phelps are generally higher than for any of his other classes except those with Parker."[18] That can mean either (or both) of two things: either Ives worked harder for Phelps than for his other professors, and/or Phelps was an easier grader than the others. Either way, one begins to suspect that Charles Ives belonged "precisely," as Dwight Macdonald would have said, to "that element of the class who have no business to be in college," and that that is why he appreciated Phelps's easygoing ways. You get a sense of teacher and pupil at the other end of their lifelong relationship when one reads Phelps's review of *Essays before a Sonata*, the book Ives self-published as a companion to his *Concord Sonata*, consisting of chapters on the subjects of its four movements, all of them figures whose works Ives had studied with Phelps in a survey of American literature during his senior year at Yale.[19] Here in their entirety are the two sentences in Phelps's review describing Ives's *Essays*, as they appeared in the *Yale Alumni Weekly* (issue of 17 December 1920), as part of a roundup of books by Yale men published that year (Sinclair Lewis's *Main Street* among them):

---

15. Ibid., 74.
16. Rubin, *The Making of Middlebrow Culture*, 182.
17. Vivian Perlis, *Charles Ives Remembered: An Oral History* (New Haven, CT: Yale University Press, 1974), 21; quoted in Burkholder, *Charles Ives: The Ideas behind the Music*, 136n47.
18. Burkholder, *Charles Ives: The Ideas behind the Music*, 136n48.
19. Charles E. Ives, *Essays before a Sonata* (New York: Knickerbocker Press, 1920).

This is a brilliant and provocative book, full of challenging ideas, and marked by chronic cerebration. I enjoyed every page of it, and I heartily recommend it to those who have minds, and wish to use them.[20]

Do you think he actually read it? As Frank R. Rossiter, a historian of American culture who was the first (even before Burkholder) to put Ives and Phelps in conjunction, noted drily, Phelps remembered, in the lead-up to his perfunctory description, to mention that Joseph Twichell, Ives's father-in-law, was a member of the Yale Corporation, but forgot to say what Ives's book was about.[21]

The review of Ives's *Essays* is very similar to the capsule reviews that Prof. Rubin quotes from Phelps's broadcasts, where he exemplified what Dwight Macdonald would later excoriate under the rubric of "appreciation"—and that, of course, brings music back to mind. Prof. Rubin bolsters Phelps's musical credentials by noting his collaboration—on a weekly program called *The Swift Hour*, sponsored by the giant meatpacking company—with Sigmund Romberg, the operetta composer, and also his regular appearances as an intermission commentator for the broadcasts of Toscanini's NBC Symphony, about which Adorno and his epigone Joseph Horowitz have so loved to exercise themselves.[22] Here is Prof. Rubin's summary of Phelps's middlebrow pitch. Read it and seethe:

> To appreciate culture . . . was to understand that it was good for you, to pay homage to experts who guarded the heritage of Western civilization, to acknowledge aesthetic judgments and standards, to make a limited commitment of time and energy to the improvement of personality, to grace your home with the voice of refinement—and then to move on to activities more central to twentieth-century American life.[23]

This middlebrow credo, with its emphasis on conformity to conventional social values (or what Prof. Rubin calls "genteel manners and moralism"),[24] corresponds to the principles according to which Charles Ives lived his life—and according to which he created his works of art, as historians of American culture like Rossiter and Robert M. Crunden were the first to point out in contributions, vigorously resisted (as I can bear witness), to the Charles Ives Centennial Festival-Conference in 1974.[25] What

---

20. Quoted in Burkholder, *Charles Ives: The Ideas behind the Music*, 137n59.
21. Frank R. Rossiter, *Charles Ives and His America* (New York: Liveright, 1975), 185.
22. Theodor W. Adorno, "Analytical Study of the NBC 'Music Appreciation Hour'" (1938–40), *Musical Quarterly* 78 (1994): 325–77; Joseph Horowitz, *Understanding Toscanini: How He Became an American Culture-God and Helped Create a New Audience for Old Music* (New York: Alfred A. Knopf, 1987).
23. Rubin, *The Making of Middlebrow Culture*, 290.
24. Ibid., 293.
25. See Robert M. Crunden, "Charles Ives's Place in American Culture," and Frank R. Rossiter, "Charles Ives: Good American and Isolated Artist," in *An Ives Celebration: Papers and Panels of the Charles Ives Centennial Festival-Conference*, ed. H. Wiley Hitchcock and Vivian Perlis (Urbana: University of Illinois Press, 1977), 4–15, 16–28.

provoked opposition was the incompatibility of this view with the image of Ives as precocious modernist that had underwritten the Ives boom that generated all the centennial hoopla to begin with. Middlebrow culture, at least the kind that Billy Phelps purveyed, was as a rule explicitly antimodernist. As Phelps put it in *Appreciation*, another in the same E. P. Dutton series of little instructional tracts that included *Music*, "Our modern writers" too often offer "pictures of slime ... of little value because there is no suggestion that there ought to be, as of course there is, a higher level of character and environment."[26]

The very same assumption pervades the writings of Charles Ives, especially the book Phelps called "brilliant and provocative." In the epilogue to *Essays before a Sonata*, Ives declared that good music, whether his own or anyone's, had to display "wholesomeness, manliness, humility and deep spiritual, possibly religious feeling," values that were "missing and not made up for" in the works of Ives's modernist contemporaries, like Debussy, Ravel, Strauss, Stravinsky, and even Wagner—depraved sensualists all. The "once transcendent" and "luxuriant" harmonies that had thrilled him in the music of Wagner and his epigones "were becoming slimy," Ives wrote, as if poaching Phelps's very word.[27] Ives mentions four composers whose music preserved the values he sought to emulate in his own, two of whom were still alive at the time of his writing—and if you do not know who these two were you will never guess that they were Vincent d'Indy and Edward Elgar. Elgar! Dwight Macdonald, who generally steered well clear of music, named only two composers in "Masscult and Midcult," his call to arms. One was Stravinsky, in a list of "classic masters" of the "avant-garde" (Macdonald evidently oblivious of the oxymoron) along with Picasso, Joyce, Eliot, and Frank Lloyd Wright, the definers of what was unassailably kosher for a highbrow diet.[28] The other was Elgar, in a list of utterly outmoded "academicists," too dowdy even for Midcult.[29]

III. CLASS MOBILITY

Now here is where confusion sets in. The classic definition of American "brows" was made by Russell Lynes, a magazine editor who wrote several essays and books that earned him a reputation as an "arbiter of taste," to quote the headline of his *New York Times* obituary in 1991.[30] They included what you might call pop ethnographies of "Snobs" and "Tastemakers," to cite the titles of two of his books. Bear

---

26. William Lyon Phelps, *Appreciation* (New York: E. P. Dutton, 1932), 33; quoted in Rubin, *The Making of Middlebrow Culture*, 282.
27. Ives, *Essays before a Sonata*, 85, 84.
28. Macdonald, "Masscult and Midcult," 20.
29. Ibid., 50.
30. Richard Severo, "Russell Lynes, 80, an Editor and Arbiter of Taste," *New York Times*, 16 September 1991.

in mind, though, that Lynes disavowed the role of arbiter. He was not interested, he said, in telling people what to like, only in observing what they in fact did like (or said they did). "I'm not a critic," he told an interviewer. "The public thinks of a critic as someone who's against everything, and I'm not. I'm amused by a lot of things."[31] What seemed above all to amuse him, as Prof. Rubin writes, was the "siege mentality of the avant-garde," as expressed by Cassandras of culture like Virginia Woolf and Clement Greenberg, who had sounded the early alarms against the encroachment of the middlebrow.[32]

His original intervention—"Highbrow, Lowbrow, Middlebrow," which appeared in *Harper's*, the magazine he edited, in February 1949—was casual, anecdotal, and, yes, amusing, but also, in its detachment, acutely observant. By making clear that debate about taste was not purely aesthetic but also had a strong social component (something that we now take as axiomatic), Lynes succeeded in relativizing the aesthetic issues, thus working by indirection against the highbrow project, rather than explicitly opposing it. In this he reminds me of another writer I admire, Fred Lerdahl, a composer and music theorist who has used the empirical work of psychologists and linguists to challenge the high aesthetic value that has been placed on serial music, and who, when accused of telling people how to listen (or even "enslaving the listener"), has countered, with what his opponents decry as false modesty, that he seeks, rather, "to find out how they [do] listen."[33]

Lynes had a real insight. Here is his opening paragraph to "Highbrow, Lowbrow, Middlebrow," which, since he was not just a journalist but an actual editor of journalists, wastes no time proclaiming the "lede":

> The old structure of the upper class, the middle class, and the lower class is on the wane. It isn't wealth or family that makes prestige these days. It's high thinking.[34]

So brow replaces class—which of course means that brow is a euphemism. It's still all about (newly sorted) class. And since sociologists had long been subdividing the nebulous and protean middle class, Lynes did the same, breaking the middlebrow into an upper and a lower. Like the middle class, moreover, the middlebrow was where all the social action was. Where the highbrow and the lowbrow

---

31. Ibid.
32. Rubin, *The Making of Middlebrow Culture*, xiii; cf. Virginia Woolf, "Middlebrow" (a letter written but not sent to the *New Statesman*), in Woolf, *The Death of the Moth, and Other Essays* (New York: Harcourt, Brace, 1942), 180–84; and Clement Greenberg, "The State of American Writing," *Partisan Review* 15 (1948): 876–83.
33. James Boros, "A New Totality?" *Perspectives of New Music* 33 (1995): 546 (for "enslaving the listener"); Fred Lerdahl, "Tonality and Paranoia: A Reply to Boros," *Perspectives of New Music* 34 (1996): 246.
34. Russell Lynes, "Highbrow, Lowbrow, Middlebrow," *Harper's*, February 1949; reprinted in the *Wilson Quarterly* 1, no. 1 (Autumn 1976): 146–60, at 146.

were stable, even static, the middlebrow was aspiring and mobile, and was distinguished by active efforts to disseminate and acquire quote-unquote "culture," and so Lynes drew his distinction between upper and lower middlebrow accordingly. The upper middlebrow was the knowing contingent that disseminated and purveyed (hence the real class traitors in the eyes of the Woolfs, the Greenbergs, and the Macdonalds); the lower middlebrow was the hungry consuming contingent that the poet and social activist Margaret Widdemer had originally identified with the term *middlebrow:* the "men and women, fairly civilized, fairly literate, who support the critics and lecturers and publishers by purchasing their wares," the "majority reader" to which the uppers catered.[35]

Margaret Widdemer, by the way, was married to Robert Haven Schauffler, the author of that middlebrow masterpiece *Beethoven: The Man Who Freed Music*.[36] So Prof. Phelps and Mr. Schauffler and those other critics and lecturers who spread their preaching, and the merchants who packaged it, constituted the upper middlebrow; those who read them or tuned in to their broadcasts were the lower. The highbrow consisted of the patron class and the artists they patronized. They had not the slightest interest in spreading the word and wouldn't be caught dead listening to the likes of Phelps, who represented for them the type responsible for "the decay of culture in mass society," in the words of Hannah Arendt, the author of the most impassioned, and at the same time the most snobbish, of all the many putdowns I have read by now of middlebrow culture. The real enemy, she warned, is

> not the Tin Pan Alley composers [but] a special kind of intellectual, often well-read and well-informed, whose sole function is to organize, disseminate and change cultural objects in order to make them palatable to those who want to be entertained or—and this is worse—to be "educated," that is, to acquire as cheaply as possible some kind of cultural knowledge to improve their social status.[37]

As for the lowbrow, they'd never heard of Billy Phelps or Hannah Arendt, and posed no threat to either.

This four-part breakdown was the Lynes line, and it has informed pretty much all subsequent work on middlebrow culture and its mechanisms. Charles Ives (an insurance man by profession, lest we forget) would on this account be classified as lower middlebrow, and his actual tastes confirm the assignment. And then there is

---

35. Margaret Widdemer, "Message and Middlebrow," *Saturday Review of Literature*, 18 February 1933, 433–34; quoted in Rubin, *The Making of Middlebrow Culture*, xii.

36. Robert Haven Schauffler, *Beethoven: The Man Who Freed Music* (New York: Doubleday, Doran, 1929).

37. Hannah Arendt, "Society and Culture," in *Culture for the Millions? Mass Media in Modern Society*, ed. Norman Jacobs (Boston: Beacon Press, 1964), 49; quoted in Ian Wellens, *Music on the Frontline: Nicolas Nabokov's Struggle against Communism and Middlebrow Culture* (Aldershot, UK: Ashgate, 2002), 101.

his music, which presumably should have embodied those tastes (as in fact they did, if you asked Ives himself). But no: here is the once-celebrated chart that Lynes, in collaboration with an editor at *Life* magazine, concocted a couple of months after his piece appeared in *Harper's*, to summarize his scheme and enable curious readers to locate themselves within it (fig. 12.2).[38] We could spend the rest of the day on this breakdown of tastes in clothes, furniture, "useful objects," entertainment, salads, drinks, reading, sculpture, records, games, and causes. But we are here to talk about music, so let's go right to the column on records, and in the top spot, the highbrow level, we find "Bach and before, Ives and after."

No surprise, really: Bach-and-before, Ives-and-after is just what the BBC used to call the "third programme," consisting of the esoteric stuff that was older or newer than what one was likely to hear at concerts attended by large paying (that is, middlebrow) audiences. The drawing shows albums of Monteverdi, Couperin, J. S. Bach, Bartók, and Schoenberg (the last two being composers Ives surely detested) alongside his work. But I doubt whether anyone is surprised to find Ives among the highbrow selections. The surprise was learning, if you had not known it already, that Ives liked Phelps and Elgar. He was a timely highbrow choice in 1949. He was just emerging from obscurity. Two years earlier his Third Symphony was performed for the first time, thirty-seven years after it was written, and had won the Pulitzer Prize. The year before, in 1948, Columbia Records finally issued John Kirkpatrick's recording of the *Concord* Sonata, which had been pronounced "the greatest music composed by an American" a decade earlier, but which had remained inaccessible to most listeners.[39] Inaccessibility, of course, was a highbrow *sine qua non*. And whatever content or substance Ives sought to express in his music, the manner of expression—what in The Ox I call a maximalist style, and for a long time the only thing that anyone noticed about Ives—was seemingly calculated to offend middlebrow taste. The Ivesian substance may have been romantic and uplifting, but the manner was taken as modernist in the extreme: what Greenberg or Macdonald would have called avant-garde.

Going down the Lynes line under "recordings" we find, in the upper middlebrow slot, "symphonies, concertos, opera," and the albums are of Brahms, Sibelius, and Chopin, representing symphonies and concertos, and for operas there is *Parsifal* and *Kiss Me, Kate*: popularizable stuff you might order from a record club or hear on "mainstream" classical radio. One might quibble about the need to popularize *Kiss Me, Kate*, or the possibility of popularizing *Parsifal*, but the interesting

---

38. "High Brow, Low Brow, Middlebrow: These are Basic Categories of a New U.S. Social Structure, and the High Brows Have the Whip Hand," *Life*, 11 April 1949, 99–102 (including Winthrop Sargeant, "In Defense of the High-Brow").

39. Lawrence Gilman, "Music: A Masterpiece of American Music Heard Here for the First Time," *New York Herald-Tribune*, 21 January 1939, 9.

EVERYDAY TASTES FROM HIGH-BROW TO

	CLOTHES	FURNITURE	USEFUL OBJECTS	ENTERTAINMENT	SALADS
HIGH-BROW	**TOWN** Fuzzy Harris tweed suit, no hat / **COUNTRY** Fuzzy Harris tweed suit, no hat	Eames chair, Kurt Versen lamp	Decanter and ash tray from chemical supply company	Ballet	Greens, olive oil, wine vinegar, ground salt, ground pepper, garlic, unwashed salad bowl
UPPER MIDDLE-BROW	**TOWN** Brooks suit, regimental tie, felt hat / **COUNTRY** Quiet tweed jacket, knitted tie	Empire chair, converted sculpture lamp	Silver cigaret box with wedding ushers' signatures	Theater	Same as high-brow but with tomatoes, avocado, Roquefort cheese added
LOWER MIDDLE-BROW	**TOWN** Splashy necktie, double-breasted suit / **COUNTRY** Sport shirt, colored slacks	Grand Rapids Chippendale chair, bridge lamp	His and Hers towels	Musical extravaganza films	Quartered iceberg lettuce and store dressing
LOW-BROW	**TOWN** Loafer jacket, woven shoes / **COUNTRY** Old Army clothes	Mail order overstuffed chair, fringed lamp	Balsam-stuffed pillow	Western movies	Coleslaw

On April 11, 1949, *Life popularized Lynes's analysis, adding a chart (reproduced above, with minor changes) and an essay by Winthrop*

FIGURE 12.2. Russell Lynes's chart of brows (*Life* magazine, 1949).

OW-BROW ARE CLASSIFIED ON CHART

DRINKS	READING	SCULPTURE	RECORDS	GAMES	CAUSES
A glass of "adequate little" red wine	"Little magazines," criticism of criticism, avant garde literature	Calder	Bach and before, Ives and after	Go	Art
A very dry Martini with lemon peel	Solid nonfiction, the better novels, quality magazines	Maillol	Symphonies, concertos, operas	The Game	Planned parenthood
Bourbon and ginger ale	Book club selections mass circulation magazines	Front yard sculpture	Light opera, popular favorites	Bridge	P. T. A.
Beer	Pulps, comic books	Parlor sculpture	Jukebox	Craps	The Lodge

Chart reprinted from Life *courtesy Time Inc.*

Sargeant defending the "faddish," fussy highbrows who, he argued, saved America from total inundation by "cultural sewage."

item here is Sibelius, now that James Hepokoski has "place[d] the Fifth Symphony squarely within the general culture of European musical 'modernism.'"[40] It used to be the Fourth Symphony "that fanatics cite[d] when they wish[ed] to establish Sibelius's 'modernist' credentials"; now almost any of his works will do.[41] But Sibelius is the least of it. I'm sure most of us have read, or at least seen or heard tell of J. P. E. Harper-Scott's *Edward Elgar, Modernist*, cited by Chris Chowrimootoo as the paradigmatic musical example of what has been long established in literary studies as the "expansionist" interpretation of modernism, which finds "exclusivity and esotericism" in formerly despised quarters "as a pretext to broaden" the scope of the modernist canon, "to rescue marginalized composers and redeem them as viable."[42] Harper-Scott has since been back with a similar expansionist treatment of Walton.[43] I think it is clear that in this usage *modernist* is just an honorific, conferred by an increasingly besieged and jumpy elitist faction that consists nowadays mainly of musicologists and composers cloistered within university music departments.

But it is paradoxical, is it not, that the response to the siege should take the form of infiltration in both directions. To put it as paradoxically as possible, exclusivity is safeguarded by inclusion, as in the case of Sibelius and Elgar. Promoted to modernist status, they can join Ives, who never really belonged there either. Or is this merely the blurring of categories that happens whenever you get up close to something? Or whenever there is a stone in the path to kick away? As one who doesn't believe in cultural paradoxes, but who has written that what appear to be paradoxes "are not contradictions given in the material, but contradictions created by confusion in the mind of the apprehender,"[44] and in the first instance by the inadequacy of categories, I recognize the symptoms here of deconstruction, in exactly the sense that Chris Chowrimootoo had in mind in the title of that programmatic statement to which I have already referred: "Reviving the Middlebrow, or: Deconstructing Modernism from the Inside." Indeed. Where else can deconstruction take place, other than from the inside? You remember the old slogan, "Texts always

---

40. James Hepokoski, *Sibelius: Symphony No. 5*, Cambridge Music Handbooks (Cambridge: Cambridge University Press, 1993), publisher's descriptive blurb on back cover.

41. Alex Ross, "Prospero's Songs," *New Yorker*, 12 January 1998, 74–77, at 74; online at www.newyorker.com/magazine/1998/01/12/prosperos-songs.

42. Christopher Chowrimootoo, "'Britten Minor': Constructing the Modernist Canon," *Twentieth-Century Music* 13 (2016): 261–90, at 262; cf. J. P. E. Harper-Scott, *Edward Elgar, Modernist* (Cambridge: Cambridge University Press, 2009).

43. J. P. E. Harper-Scott, *The Quilting Points of Musical Modernism: Revolution, Reaction, and William Walton* (Cambridge: Cambridge University Press, 2012).

44. R. Taruskin, "Speed Bumps" (review of Jim Samson, ed., *The Cambridge History of Nineteenth-Century Music*, and Nicholas Cook and Anthony Pople, ed., *The Cambridge History of Twentieth-Century Music*"), *19th-Century Music* 29 (2004–5): 185–207, at 197.

WHICH WAY IS UP? 357

FIGURE 12.3. Russell Lynes's chart of brows (*Harper's* magazine, 1949).

already deconstruct themselves."[45] We don't have to lift a finger. Meanings can only slip and slide under scrutiny, and both "middlebrow" and "modernism," now getting far more than their fair share of scrutiny, are slipping and sliding away.

The ever-perceptive Russell Lynes was well aware of this sort of slippage. His original *Harper's* essay had a chart of examples like the one he later produced for *Life*, but diachronic, illustrating changes in taste and taste-categories (only three at this point) over time, rather than providing a grid for analyzing the current spectrum of taste (fig. 12.3). Like everything Lynes produced, it is funny. What James McNeill Whistler called his "Arrangement in Gray and Black, No. 1" topped the highbrow chart in the 1870s–1890s. By the 1910s it had become a middlebrow cynosure, under a new title ("Portrait of the Artist's Mother") that referred to its subject rather than to its formal properties, thus illustrating the devolution Clement Greenberg warned of in his highbrow manifesto "Avant-Garde and Kitsch":

> The avant-garde poet or artist sought to maintain the high level of his art by both narrowing and raising it to the expression of an absolute in which all relativities and contradictions would be either resolved or beside the point. "Art for art's sake" and

45. Or, more formally: "'Writing' . . . is the structure that would . . . deconstruct all texts, being . . . the always already differentiated structure of deconstruction" (Gayatri Chakravorty Spivak, "Translator's Preface," in Jacques Derrida, *Of Grammatology* [1977] [Baltimore: Johns Hopkins University Press, 2016], lxxxi).

FIGURE 12.4. Mother's Day commemorative postage stamp, 1934.

"pure poetry" appear, and subject matter or content becomes something to be avoided like a plague.[46]

By the time we get to what was the present at the time of Lynes's writing, "Whistler's Mother" had been absorbed into the popular culture as a wholly utilitarian artifact of greeting cards and Mother's Day stamps (fig. 12.4), more no-brow than lowbrow.

When he reprinted his article in 1976, Lynes reflected that what happened to "Whistler's Mother" was only an especially dramatic instance of a general drift. "As I look back at the chart [i.e., the one shown in fig. 12.2], which a *Life* editor and I concocted over innumerable cups of coffee years ago," he wrote, "it strikes me, as it must you, that what was highbrow then [in 1949, twenty-seven years previously] has become distinctly upper middlebrow today . . . , and what was upper has become lower."[47] Clement Greenberg would have taken this as confirmation of his worst fears, later echoed by Dwight Macdonald. The original 1949 version of Lynes's essay quoted something Greenberg had written a year earlier:

> It must be obvious to anyone that the volume and social weight of middlebrow culture, borne along as it has been by the great recent increase in the American middle

---

46. Clement Greenberg, "Avant-Garde and Kitsch," *Partisan Review* 6, no. 5 (1939): 34–49, at 36.
47. Lynes, "Highbrow, Lowbrow, Middlebrow," *Wilson Quarterly* reprint, 160.

class, have multiplied at least tenfold in the past three decades. This culture presents a more serious threat to the genuine article than the old-time pulp dime novel ... ever has or will. Unlike the latter, which has its social limits clearly marked out for it, middlebrow culture attacks distinctions as such and insinuates itself everywhere, devaluating the precious, infecting the healthy, corrupting the honest, and stultifying the wise.[48]

That is indeed the siege mentality, and it is still with us—or with those, at any rate, who fear the loss of distinction, like my friend and occasional sparring partner Karol Berger, writing about something distinct from yet obviously related to our present concern, namely canons and repertories, as differentiated by Joseph Kerman in a famous article of yore:[49]

The distinction between the canon and the repertoire may seem, but is not, a merely terminological quibble. Both a canon and a repertoire represent selections of examples drawn from the archive, but they are two distinct kinds of selection, made by different kinds of people, with different objectives in mind.... The specific terms do not matter all that much. What matters is that there is a genuine distinction here, which needs to be reflected in distinct terms.[50]

What matters is that there is a distinction. On one level—the purely psychological level that resists the "blooming, buzzing confusion" of unmediated reality[51]— one can only agree. But on another level, the social, I feel obliged to fight the insistence, recalling the words of Allan Bloom, whose *Closing of the American Mind* was the *reductio ad absurdum* of the Greenbergian paranoia, and who lamented the abandonment by American youth of classical music, which had once been "the only recognizable class distinction between educated and uneducated in America."[52]

But Lynes took note of the opposite tendency as well, as Greenberg and Berger did not. As of the 1910s–1920s, in the pre-*Life* diachronic chart (fig. 12.3), the lowbrow entry is a popular silent film by D. W. Griffith, *The Crossroads of Life* (1908),

---

48. Clement Greenberg, contribution to "The State of American Writing, 1948: A Symposium," *Partisan Review* (August 1948); reprinted in in Greenberg, *Arrogant Purpose, 1945–1949*, vol. 2 of *Collected Essays and Criticism* (Chicago: University of Chicago Press, 1988), 257 (as quoted by Lynes in 1949, but with the last thirteen words restored from the original text).

49. Joseph Kerman, "A Few Canonic Variations," *Critical Inquiry* 10 (1983): 107–25; reprinted in Kerman, *Write All These Down* (Berkeley: University of California Press, 1994), 33–50.

50. Karol Berger, "Five Canonic Theses: An Attempt at a Conceptual Clarification," original English-language typescript text (by kind courtesy of the author) of an essay published in German translation as "Fünf Thesen zum Kanon: Versuch einer konzeptuellen Klärung," in *Der Kanon der Musik: Theorie und Geschichte—Ein Handbuch,* ed. Klaus Pietschmann and Melanie Wald-Fuhrmann (Munich: edition text+kritik 2011), 65–71.

51. The famous phrase is William James's, in *Principles of Psychology* (New York: Henry Holt, 1890), 488.

52. Allan Bloom, *The Closing of the American Mind* (New York: Simon & Schuster, 1987), 322.

about (so IMDb informs me) the fall and redemption of a minister's daughter who seeks a career on the stage.[53] By the 1940s, silent films had become museum pieces—literally so: I went to MoMA in New York to see the kind of movie one would have seen in nickelodeons half a century earlier. And so Lynes puts *The Crossroads of Life* in his last highbrow slot, representing the present (i.e., the 1940s–1950s)—the most radical jump of any item on the chart. A whimsical touch, but it underscores an important point. All writers, be they descriptive like Lynes or prescriptive like Greenberg or Woolf, agree that the highbrow is tolerant of the lowbrow even as it strives to exorcise the middle. The lowbrow presents no comparable threat of corruption, nor does it compete with the highbrow, as Bourdieu would say, for social space.[54] For Lynes the lowbrow was "the highbrow's friend," because

> the highbrow enjoys and respects the lowbrow's art—jazz, for instance [remember, this was pre-bebop]—which he is likely to call a spontaneous expression of folk culture. The lowbrow is not interested, as the middlebrow is, in preëmpting any of the highbrow's function. In fact, he is almost completely oblivious of the highbrow unless he happens to be taken up by him.[55]

And thus Virginia Woolf:

> Highbrows, for some reason or other, are wholly incapable of dealing successfully with what is called real life. That is why ... they honour so wholeheartedly and depend so completely upon those who are called lowbrows. By a lowbrow is meant of course a man or a woman of thoroughbred vitality who rides his body in pursuit of a living at a gallop across life. That is why I honour and respect lowbrows—and I have never known a highbrow who did not. In so far as I am a highbrow ... I love lowbrows; I study them; I always sit next the conductor in an omnibus and try to get him to tell me what it is like—being a conductor. ... All that lowbrows do is of surpassing interest and wonder to me, because, in so far as I am a highbrow, I cannot do things myself.[56]

Only Macdonald among Anglophone writers seems wholly intransigent on this score. For him there was only one brow. What others indulged as lowbrow he denounced as Masscult, the most degraded of taste categories, and the middlebrow was the pernicious, pretentious dilution he called Midcult. He made no allowances, at least in what he wrote. But wait . . . .

---

53. www.imdb.com/title/tt0000638/plotsummary=.

54. See Pierre Bourdieu, *Distinction: A Social Critique of the Judgement of Taste,* trans. Richard Nice (Cambridge, MA: Harvard University Press, 1984), 60.

55. Lynes, "Highbrow, Lowbrow, Middlebrow," *Wilson Quarterly* reprint, 151.

56. Virginia Woolf, "Middlebrow," 182. The definition of *lowbrow* parodies that of the *highbrow* on page 180: "a man or woman of thoroughbred intelligence who rides his mind at a gallop across country in pursuit of an idea."

IV. DECONSTRUCTION OVER TIME

Was there ever a musical writer as militantly highbrow as Macdonald? None but Joseph Kerman comes to mind. His *Opera as Drama*—derived from a series of critical essays he had written in the late 1940s and early 1950s, when he was a very young man, for the *Hudson Review*, one of the many "little magazines" devoted to high culture in midcentury America—is the only musicological book (or perhaps I should say, the only book by a certified, sheepskin-carrying musicologist) that seems to exemplify in all its purity the highbrow or snob position defined by Richard Peterson, the leading American sociologist of brows, as "moralistic contempt for and distancing from all cultural manifestations that do not fit with what is taken to be proper."[57] Kerman's book has been compared with F. R. Leavis's *The Great Tradition* as an exercise in winnowing.[58] Its ten chapters comprise what John Updike (thinking of Vladimir Nabokov's literary judgments) called a "willful little pantheon" of exemplary works.[59] Its tone is suitably irritable and prim, in keeping with the class anxiety to which snobbery gives outward expression. As Peterson writes, to a thoroughbred highbrow "even the 'serious' study of popular culture by academics is a threat to 'standards,' because, within the received perspective, it is seen as lending legitimacy to that which is vulgar, and it thus threatens the sanctity of the status boundaries distinguishing between what is fine and what is common."[60] *Opera as Drama* starts right off with a warning that "flabby relativism is certainly the danger," and with foreboding: "it is hard to think that all our operatic activity can proceed much longer without standards."[61]

Indeed, in his salad days Joe Kerman expressed an extreme of intransigence that even *Opera as Drama* failed fully to reflect. He spent the academic year 1957–58 in New York on a fellowship and sent back a season's worth of occasional reviews to the *San Francisco Chronicle* (where Alfred Frankenstein, to whom Joe in those days looked up as a mentor, was the long-serving chief critic of both art and music). Reviewing a Callas performance with the highest praise he could muster ("it seems as though the composer himself were singing"), he had only this to say about the opera she was singing that night: "*Lucia* is a vile piece."[62] About the same composer's *Anna Bolena* he wrote, "Your correspondent went in the same spirit that animated Henry VIII's subjects at a state execution: There was going to be a

---

57. Richard A. Peterson, "Understanding Audience Segmentation: From Elite and Mass to Omnivore and Univore," *Poetics* 21 (1992): 243–58, at 245.

58. David Schiff, "Riffing the Canon," *Music Library Association Notes* 64 (2007–8): 216–17.

59. John Updike, Introduction to Vladimir Nabokov, *Lectures on Literature*, ed. Fredson Bowers (New York: Harcourt Brace Jovanovich, 1980), xxiii.

60. Peterson, "Understanding Audience Segmentation," 245.

61. Joseph Kerman, *Opera as Drama* (New York: Alfred A. Knopf, 1956), 6.

62. Joseph Kerman, "Callas Is One Singer Who Is Emotionally Equal to the Job," *San Francisco Chronicle*, 2 March 1958, 36.

violent, low entertainment and he wasn't going to miss a minute of it." And then, "Next to 'Anna Bolena' the score of 'Lucia' appears refined and inventive, and the plot of 'Lucia' seems a model of Racinian sobriety."[63] Like Dwight Macdonald, Kerman is a delight to quote no matter how you feel about what he is saying.

My favorite nugget of hard Kermanian diktat, and closest of all to the hard line that Peterson describes, comes from his contribution to a "critical symposium" edited by William Arrowsmith (the founding editor of *Hudson Review*) and Roger Shattuck, titled *The Craft and Context of Translation*. Kerman's assignment, naturally, was "Translation for Music," and he does a conscientious if somewhat grudging job of weighing all the pros and cons and closely analyzing the singing translation, by W. H. Auden and Chester Kallman, of Tamino's aria, "Dies Bildnis ist bezaubernd schön," from Mozart's *Magic Flute*. But his heart is not in it because, as he blurts out in the last paragraph, "arguments in favor of 'opera in English'" are mostly "vulgarian."[64] Well, yes. That's what the word means. Surely Joe knew that the retranslated Latin Bible was called the Vulgate, and why. I am sure he would, if pressed, have defended Saint Jerome's project of making God's word more common (that is, accessible)—or maybe (I never asked him) he thought St. Jerome the first vulgarian. In any case, Schikaneder's words were entitled to no such assistance. "Without reasonable rewards in artistic satisfaction, no species of mediative work is likely to flourish, whatever its abstract virtues or vices," Joe wrote. "Difficulty, unattainability—that is really less of a problem."[65] In fact it is no problem at all, if you are interested in maintaining the sanctity of the status boundaries. Even when produced by the likes of Auden, translating an opera libretto is an act of middlebrow betrayal.

But as ever, things, given time, deconstruct themselves. By now it is obvious that the highbrow judgments expressed by a Joseph Kerman were no less conventional than the middlebrow sentiments expressed by a Billy Phelps. In fact, they were usually the same judgments, differing only in valence. What Phelps would proclaim positively and enthusiastically on behalf of what he liked, Kerman would proclaim negatively and invidiously against what he detested, but the objects promoted and quashed were likely to be the same, and beneath their differing styles the two writers were engaged in similar projects of exhortation. Phelps loves and Kerman reviles in perfect complementation; at bottom their tastes were one, and so were their purposes. Kerman's efforts to transmit his values to his readers, though acerbically expressed, are highbrow in style but resolutely upper-middle-

---

63. Joseph Kerman, "'Anna Bolena'—Out-of-the-Way Opera in Concert Form," *San Francisco Chronicle*, 3 November 1957, 24.

64. Joseph Kerman, "Translation for Music," in *The Craft and Context of Translation*, ed. William Arrowsmith and Roger Shattuck (Garden City, NY: Anchor Books [Doubleday], 1964), 164.

65. Ibid.

brow in function. His polemics are addressed not to fellow academics, where they would have been taken quite amiss, but to "anyone ... who buys an opera season ticket," as he says in the first section of the introduction to *Opera as Drama*.[66] It is a strong-medicine version of music appreciation addressed, like all such enterprises, to consumers.

The key chapter of *Opera as Drama* is the fifth, on *Otello*. Together with *Falstaff*, approved of but not discussed at length, *Otello* was the one delegate from the vast wasteland of post-Monteverdian Italian opera to gain admission into Kerman's tight little canon. It earned its exemption from the omnibus curse upon its kind, or rather Verdi did, by dint of a gradual triumph over the "demands of the tradition in which Verdi wrote"—a victory made possible by Verdi's having eventually come round to Kerman's dissatisfaction with "the depraved state of opera" in his day, and in particular "the abysmal lack of integration of lyricism into a sensible dramatic plan.... He gained this knowledge painfully," Kerman writes, "and only at the end of his career."[67] Then comes the famous comparison between the murder scenes in Verdi's *Otello* and Rossini's, designed to exemplify the two great advances Verdi made over the work of his predecessors, including his own former self. "First," Kerman writes, "Verdi had to learn to be merciless with the singers"; and "second," he had to "re-complicate the form" of his vocal numbers, in the first place by pitilessly curtailing or dropping the *cabaletta*, "one of the worst lyric conventions of early nineteenth-century opera," thus to regain the "subtle interrelation of one sentiment and the next, and a sense of flux between them," such as one found in the "composite arias of Mozart and Beethoven."[68]

Thus, while Kerman is at pains to disavow the hackneyed "charge of Wagnerism,"[69] his account of Verdi's self-emancipation from the shackles of outmoded convention exactly corresponds, in its joint hostility to singerly virtuosity and rounded musical form, to Wagner's complaints and prescriptions in *Opera and Drama*, the book on whose title Kerman's own title depended. Since he attributes Verdi's victory to his unprecedented (for an Italian composer) solution to the problem of "action and the musical continuity," as defined in the title to an earlier chapter of his book, Kerman sees Verdi as the sole Italian heir to the breakthroughs achieved by German composers in their instrumental music a hundred years before. The supremacy of German music, and the universality of its values, both of them articles of upper-middlebrow Billy-Phelps faith, are thus affirmed.

When the University of California Press reissued *Opera as Drama* in 1988, in a revised edition by an author who was exactly twice as old as he had been at the

---

66. Kerman, *Opera as Drama*, 6.
67. Ibid., 143.
68. Ibid., 146.
69. Ibid., 149.

time of the original publication, its intransigence—its "hectic," as Kerman put it—was conspicuously reduced, to the point where Kerman felt obliged, in a preface to the new edition, to make some apology. "Running through *Opera as Drama*," he now wrote,

> there was an excited polemic about the urgency of maintaining artistic standards, the ill effects of the standard opera repertory, true and false values in art, and so on. To opera lovers of an argumentative turn of mind, this too proved interesting, if one may judge from their equally excited responses pro or con. But not everybody enjoys an argument, and not everybody appreciated the book's provocative tone.[70]

No doubt readers were relieved to find that "shabby little shocker"—surely the most famous string of words ever strung by a musicologist—remained in place.[71] (Google records 3,220 echoes of it online.) The other Puccini putdown—"it is consistently, throughout, of café-music banality"—reappears too, verbatim, at both ends of the book (applied first to *Tosca* and then to *Turandot*, evidently the result of sloppy editing when assembling the first edition from various *Hudson Review* pieces and missed again on revision).[72] Kerman attributed "the deletion of many of the spot judgments in the original *Opera as Drama*—judgments about composers, operas, scenes, and individual operatic numbers" to "the climate of today's criticism, which is so much more hospitable to interpretation than to evaluation." These *péchés de jeunesse*, as the author judged them to be in his maturity, included "an unduly shrill attack on the operas of Gian-Carlo Menotti and a gratuitous wisecrack about Benjamin Britten."[73] But what made the former undue and the latter gratuitous was the fact that settled opinion had rendered Kerman's judgments obsolete. Nobody gets worked up any more about the more-than-half-forgotten Menotti, and Britten has become so firmly canonical that feigning pity that too much was being expected of him, as was the commonplace jibe in 1956, would only reflect badly on the feigner.

But of course time has also vindicated Puccini and Strauss, Kerman's *bêtes noires*; and if you are asking me, I would say that Kerman's attitude that music in an opera is guilty until proven innocent should have gone out with the Mighty Kuchka. The book is valued now, I think, as a period piece, and still admired as writing for its passionate integrity—that is, for its solid upper-middlebrow virtues. That is why I cannot fathom Kerman's decision to add a discussion of *Idomeneo* to the Mozart chapter. True, that opera has joined the repertory in a way that no one could have predicted in 1956, but admitting it to the Kermanian canon sorely compromises the

---

70. Joseph Kerman, *Opera as Drama*, new and rev. ed. (Berkeley: University of California Press, 1988), ix–x.
71. Ibid., 205.
72. Ibid., 15, 206.
73. Ibid., x.

author's basic thesis, that opera lost its dramatic way after Purcell and did not recover it till Mozart met up with da Ponte. Now we read, "most of us would rather have notes by Mozart than drama by anyone else," and "what gives 'Idomeneo' a certain haunting power as drama," despite its problems, "is its basic subject matter."[74]

To grant subject matter such a privilege would have horrified Clement Greenberg, and I dare say it would have dismayed the younger Kerman as well, for it is tantamount to revoking his patented anathema on what he called opera's "dark ages." It was on its subject matter that the *opera seria* (of which *Idomeneo* was a latter-day and wholly typical example) had staked its claim to seriousness. Kerman's whole enterprise was devoted to contesting and rejecting that claim. So, flabby or firm, the revised *Opera as Drama* gave evidence that by the 1980s relativism, which Kerman had defined and vehemently opposed in 1956 as "the tacit assumption that everything is all right in its own terms," was irrevocably on the rise. (Sociologists, as I will show in conclusion, have empirically corroborated this impression.)

Observing this trend in 1990 (in a Mozart bicentennial piece for the *New York Times*), I blamed "musicology, always a great omnivore," for bringing about this somewhat unexpected and (to me) disappointing change in Kerman's tone.[75] And indeed, both the modifications themselves and the reference to the changed critical climate ("so much more hospitable to interpretation than to evaluation") indicated to me that Kerman had after all turned away from consumers and toward his colleagues (the ones who, partly at his instigation, were now avid for interpretation as well as fact-gathering) as his primary audience. Kerman was now more narrowly an academic writer than he had been in his early days (when, as I know from knowing him, he saw figures like Virgil Thomson, Donald Francis Tovey, B. H. Haggin, Michel Calvocoressi, and above all the PhD-less R. P. Blackmur, whom he had known at Princeton, as his role models)—which meant, paradoxically enough, that with the softening of the hectic or hectoring tone, the lessened intransigence, and the more accommodating purview he had become not less but more of a highbrow. As always, though, the paradox is only seeming. The upper middlebrow, as defined by Russell Lynes, is not just a stance or a status, but a function. To the extent that Kerman renounced exhortation in favor of exegesis, he renounced the function that made his book an upper-middlebrow classic. For if the middlebrow has any definition at all, it is defined by its relentlessly upward thrust. *Empor, empor!* Without that inexorable restless push, it's just highbrows placidly chewing the fat.

74. Ibid., 83.
75. R. Taruskin, "Why Mozart Has Become an Icon for Today," *New York Times*, 9 September 1990, Arts and Leisure; reprinted (as "An Icon for Our Time") in Taruskin, *Text and Act: Essays on Music and Performance* (New York: Oxford University Press, 1995), 263–72, at 268.

V. THE BIG OTHER

So now I am ready to re-pose the question I broached at the beginning: why am I the elephant in this room? It goes back, I strongly suspect, to that *JRMA* roundtable, "Modernism and Its Others." I could not have read it with keener interest, or perhaps I should say, with greater curiosity. Musical modernism, whether defined in terms of aesthetic ideas or in terms of styles and techniques, had been one of the focal points of my research and writing since the beginning of my academic career, and of my listening and thinking since long before that. It had intersected with all my objects of inquiry, from Stravinsky, in wholly obvious ways, to historical performance practice, in ways that were at first far from obvious. I had been particularly interested in its genealogy, that is to say its location in intellectual history and in relation to social and political ideas and environments. That sensitized me to the possibility of alternative viewpoints and discourses, something that had not been seriously entertained in the academy during the period of my education. So I knew that a discussion of modernism and its "others" would intersect with discussions and debates to which I had been a party. I expected resonance and stimulation.

What I did not quite expect was the degree to which I would be interpellated. Five of the six contributions invoked my writings in varying degrees of skepticism or hostility. Even the friendliest contributor, Peter Franklin, who intended only a compliment, referred to my "bracing historical hatchet-work"—not so far, when all is said and done, from a hatchet-job.[76] Clearly, to the *JRMA* symposiasts I was one of modernism's others, and in terms of frequency of mention I was perhaps the Big Other. Did I really deserve that honor?

Obviously the answer to that question had to come from Chris Chowrimootoo, whose contribution to the *JRMA* symposium made explicit the association between the two ideas, middlebrow and modernism. Modernism's "red thread," as Chris put it, its defining or unifying characteristic, is "an investment in distinction and hierarchy," and in particular an insistence on the reality of that categorical Great Divide between high and popular culture on which "modernist discourse has thrived."[77] There is plenty of corroboration for this assertion in the work of

---

76. Peter Franklin, "Modernismus and the Philistines," *JRMA* 139 (2014): 186.

77. Christopher Chowrimootoo, "Reviving the Middlebrow, or: Deconstructing Modernism from the Inside," *JRMA* 139 (2014): 187–93, at 188; further pages references to this source will be made in the main text. The catchphrase "Great Divide" comes from the title of Andreas Huyssen's essay collection *After the Great Divide: Modernism, Mass Culture, Postmodernism* (Bloomington: Indiana University Press, 1986); from the way his phrase has been appropriated, one would not guess that Huyssen's stated purpose was to "challenge the belief in the necessary separation of high art from mass culture, politics, and the everyday" (x).

sociologists and literary historians.⁷⁸ One can quote illustrative slogans galore from modernist luminaries. My personal favorite is from Schoenberg's 1924 letter to his patron, Prince Max Egon zu Fürstenberg, thanking him for remaining true to that halcyon time before the then-recent Great War "when a prince stood as a protector before an artist, showing the rabble that art, a matter for princes, is beyond the judgment of common people."⁷⁹ Chris chose another Schoenbergian gem, from the foreword to "Three Satires for Mixed Chorus," op. 28, written a year later: "The middle road is the only one that does not lead to Rome."⁸⁰

Quoting that one was especially a propos, given Chris's purpose, which was to uphold the middlebrow as a bridge between avant-garde and kitsch (to add Clement Greenberg's catchphrase to the mix) and thus restore wholeness to our riven culture. That view of the thing strikes me as idealized. It bears only a scant resemblance to what I take to be the middlebrow properly—that is, functionally—defined by those who coined the term just as Schoenberg was casting his aspersions on the middle road, but unbeknownst to him. In any case, I do not identify myself with it, or with the terms of the Great Divide, even though that is how Chris characterized me, listing me among "modernism's staunchest opponents," and perhaps (since mine is the only name to be found in the footnote that follows that epithet) the staunchest one of all (189). Fiddlesticks to that. It is not modernism that I oppose, but the valorizing discourse that attaches it spuriously to the discourse of brows. That is how I arrived at the title of this talk. We have forgotten which way is up.

As a historian, moreover, I oppose the effort Chris might appear to be endorsing—he attributes it to the music scholar Brigid Cohen (and the earlier work of the film scholar Miriam Hansen from which Cohen's is avowedly derivative),⁸¹ but it has been around far longer than they have been—to expand the definition of modernism to the point where it loses the spurious attachment that I oppose. Hansen, writing about the early Hollywood film industry, entered a plea for "understanding modernism as a much wider, more diverse phenomenon" than had become customary, "eluding any single-logic genealogy that runs, say, from Cubism to Abstract Expressionism, from T. S. Eliot, Ezra Pound, James Joyce, and

---

78. See, inter alia, Martha Woodmansee, *The Author, Art, and the Market: Rereading the History of Aesthetics* (New York: Columbia University Press, 1994); and Lawrence Rainey, *Institutions of Modernism: Literary Elites and Public Culture* (New Haven, CT: Yale University Press, 1999).

79. Letter written April 1924, in Arnold Schoenberg, *Letters,* ed. Erwin Stein, trans. Eithne Wilkins and Ernst Kaiser (London: Faber & Faber, 1964), 108.

80. Quoted from Joseph Auner, ed., *A Schoenberg Reader* (New Haven, CT: Yale University Press, 2003), 186.

81. He cites Brigid Cohen, *Stefan Wolpe and the Avant-Garde Diaspora* (Cambridge: Cambridge University Press, 2017), and Miriam Bratu Hansen, "The Mass Production of the Senses: Classical Cinema as Vernacular Modernism," *Modernism/Modernity* 6, no. 2 (April 1999): 59–77.

Franz Kafka to Samuel Beckett and Alain Robbe-Grillet, from Arnold Schönberg to Karlheinz Stockhausen."[82]

Making obeisance to the maiden editorial from *Modernism/Modernity*, the journal in which her article appeared (and where I serve quite passively on the editorial board, I should probably disclose); to Peter Bürger's *Theory of the Avant-Garde*;[83] and, of course, to Andreas Huyssen,[84] she elaborated that plea into a program. "In addition to opening up the modernist canon," she wanted to see more studies that

> assume a notion of modernism that is "more than a repertory of artistic styles" [that being the quote from the maiden editorial], more than sets of ideas pursued by groups of artists and intellectuals. Rather, modernism encompasses a whole range of cultural and artistic practices that register, respond to, and reflect upon processes of modernization and the experience of modernity including a paradigmatic transformation of the conditions under which art is produced, transmitted, and consumed. In other words, just as modernist aesthetics are not reducible to the category of style, they tend to blur the boundaries of the institution of art in its traditional, eighteenth- and nineteenth-century incarnation that turns on the ideal of aesthetic autonomy and the distinction of "high" vs. "low," of autonomous art vs. popular and mass culture.[85]

If I may roughly but, I hope, serviceably apply Hansen's plea to our habitual discourse, she is in effect telling Schoenberg that contemporary art unprotected by a prince from the rabble is also modern art, and should be studied alongside the protected art without prejudice. Fair enough. Study away. But do not lose the distinction between what is modern and what is modernist. The elitism that informs the discourse about the protected art informed the art as well; and it also informed the descriptors by which that art was identified. We are not absolved from taking the social and political import of terms into account, however we may now wish to reject them. To loose the term *modernism* from its moorings in intellectual history—that is, from the specific environments that spawned it and the talk that surrounded it— is to give its agents an alibi. Chris recognized the danger when he wrote that modernism is not just a historiographical problem but also a historical one. Unless we understand it historically, we do not understand it at all, and the same caveat applies to the middlebrow. So I would turn Chris's friendly critique of my work back upon him. Using a word—*arguably*—that I would prohibit if I could, since its sole purpose is to give the user what politicians call "deniability," he says that my alleged opposition to modernism has "arguably helped to reinforce its terms and oppositions, even making them seem more unassailable than they really are" (189). But if we are talking terms and oppositions, how does "reviving the middlebrow" not revive ideas of high

---

82. Hansen, "Mass Production of the Senses," 59–60.
83. Peter Bürger, *Theory of the Avant-Garde* (Manchester: Manchester University Press, 1984).
84. Huyssen, *After the Great Divide*.
85. Hansen, "Mass Production of the Senses," 59–60.

and low as well? I think alternative terms are indeed required if we are to think freshly, and in fact they have already been proposed. I'll get to them.

As I have noted, Chris's version of middlebrow is congruent with a newly valorized or rehabilitated *gemäßigte Moderne*. In his *JRMA* manifesto he juxtaposes Adorno's vituperations in *Philosophie der neuen Musik* against what Adorno calls the "new conformists," those who "with undaunted pretensions to modernity and seriousness, conform with calculated idiocy to mass culture,"[86] with the views of J. B. Priestley, the man to whom Virginia Woolf was furiously rejoining in what is usually taken as the foundation text of middlebrow-ology. "According to J. B. Priestley," Chris wrote, "middlebrows were those who avoided the herd mentality of both high and low, who 'snap their fingers at fashions, who only ask that a thing should have character and art, should be enthralling, and do not give a fig whether it is popular or unpopular [. . . or] belongs to a certain category'" (190).[87]

Bully for them, but Priestley never actually used the term *middlebrow* to describe his finger-snappers and fig-withholders. His *tertium quid* to supplement highbrow and lowbrow was "broadbrow," which has a very different connotation. The broad encompasses both of the others rather than coming, as Virginia Woolf would later snort, "betwixt and between."[88] According to Chris, "most commentators agreed" that "the middlebrow's cultural impulses . . . gave rise to a decidedly eclectic or ambivalent style, whose characteristic feature was its ability to confuse the categories of modernist criticism" (190–91). That strikes me as a fantasy. While many would be glad to be called broadminded, hence (possibly) broadbrow, the category of middlebrow, I would still insist, is one that none would willingly apply to themselves. There is no such thing, I therefore suggest, as "middlebrow style," if we take "style" to mean a poietic practice. And if one takes seriously, as I do, the import of Russell Lynes's breakdown of upper and lower middlebrow as denoting the two sides of a transaction, then one could never say of the middlebrow, as defined by him and chronicled by Prof. Rubin, that it was eclectic or indifferent to categories. The appeal remained quite frankly a highbrow appeal, which is precisely why it so antagonized highbrows.

VI. THE ACTUAL PITCH

To demonstrate this point, I will recall a hideously hilarious late-night TV ad I used to see in, I guess, the late 1970s. The product was a set of 10 LP disks containing an

---

86. T. W. Adorno, *The Philosophy of New Music*, trans. R. Hullot-Kentor (Minneapolis: University of Minnesota Press, 2006), 9.

87. Quoting J. B. Priestley, "High, Low, Broad," in Priestley, *Open House: A Book of Essays* (London: Heinemann, 1927). The article originally appeared in *Saturday Review* the year before, and that is where Virginia Woolf read it; see Ina Habermann, *Myth, Memory, and the Middlebrow: Priestley, du Maurier, and the Symbolic Form of Englishness* (London: Palgrave Macmillan, 2010), 33.

88. Woolf, "Middlebrow," 180.

FIGURE 12.5. John Williams in *Dial M for Murder* (1954).

assortment of recycled recordings from various back-catalogues; the pitchman was the fellow shown in figure 12.5: a natty, avuncular, Oxford-accented British-American actor named John Williams (1903–83), who had played the moustache-combing Inspector Hubbard in *Dial M for Murder* and the title character's father in *Sabrina*, both movies made in 1954, so he would have been remembered by most viewers at the time from their childhood or youth. The slogan he pitched was inspired: "All the classical music your family will ever need."[89]

Why would you need it? For social betterment, obviously, as Hannah Arendt would have appreciated, sneering. Upper-middlebrow pundits and publicists, whether Great Books advocates like Mortimer Adler or Clifton Fadiman, or radio commentators like Alexander Woolcott or our friend Billy Phelps (or Clifton Fadiman again), or actual salesmen like Harry Scherman, the founder of the Book of the Month Club (or yet again Clifton Fadiman), or creators of outlines and digests like Will Durant, always saw themselves in a line of descent from Matthew Arnold or Walter Pater as purveyors of the highest and best, of pure aesthetics, of sweetness and light, of the hard, gemlike flame. They came in Pater's footsteps, proposing frankly to give nothing but the highest quality to your moments as they passed and, as if incidentally, to elevate your social standing.[90]

Recall Billy Phelps preaching the gospel of good music. Nothing eclectic or indifferent about it. "No music is too elevated for me," he pontificated. "The stiffer the programme, the better it is"—and when he got finished with you, you'd be better, too. That was the promise of Music Appreciation, and in particular, of the division of the Book of the Month Club devoted to the dissemination of classical music

---

89. Online I found a corroborating witness to the date: a column ("Needless to Say") by Alan Rich in *New York* magazine, 16 February 1976, 72, devoted to taking umbrage at the slogan's utilitarianism.

90. To the already-cited catchphrases from Arnold I have added a few from Pater's "The School of Giorgione," in his collection *The Renaissance*, ed. Adam Phillips (Oxford: Oxford University Press, 1986), 95–96.

FIGURE 12.6. Thomas Scherman, Denver Symphony Orchestra.

on long-playing disks. When you ordered records from the Book of the Month Club, you didn't just get the 12-inch record you ordered; they also sent you an auxiliary disk (usually 10 inches across) on their own Music Appreciation label (custom-produced by arrangement with RCA Victor), containing a musically illustrated lecture. In a few of these the lecturer was Leonard Bernstein, not yet at the pinnacle of his fame. More often, the lecturer was Thomas Scherman (1917–79; fig 12.6), the son of Harry Scherman, the Book of the Month Club founder himself. (And when you heard his lisping voice on the record you knew that he had to be the founder's son to get the job.) Quite often the author of the text that Thomas Scherman read was Howard Shanet (1918–2006; fig. 12.7), a man I knew well, who conducted the student orchestra at Columbia University in my undergraduate days (so I played cello right under his nose) and who was later my colleague there for many years.

FIGURE 12.7. Howard Shanet, courtesy of the estate of Howard Shanet.

Let me regale you now with snatches from two Music Appreciation Records lectures to support my contention that the message they delivered was indeed a highbrow message. Dwight Macdonald, I believe, would have approved of every word, even if he would have put it a lot more elegantly, and with humor in place of the middlebrow solemnity. What he would not have approved of was the mission of outreach. The only difference between highbrow taste and upper-middlebrow taste, this shows, is that highbrows kept it to themselves, and middlebrows wanted to spread it around—or rather, wanted to spread it among those who highbrows thought (to recall Macdonald's complaint about Billy Phelps) "ha[d] no business" knowing it.

The two exegeses from which I will quote concern Stravinsky's *Le sacre du printemps* and Chaikovsky's First Piano Concerto, respectively (fig. 12.8a–b). You may be surprised that *Le sacre* was part of the Music Appreciation Records program at all, since middlebrow culture, always characterized by its opponents as "bland, undemanding, and *easy*," was supposed to be antimodernist.[91] But Music Appreciation Records tout *Le sacre* precisely for its modernism, and praise it not only, or even primarily, on the basis of its specific aesthetic value, but in terms of its revolutionary character (as evidenced by the usual grossly exaggerated description of its first-night reception)[92] and its subsequent influence on the history of musical style. The demonstration may be crude: to make the point the lecture juxtaposes *Le sacre*, from 1913, with the namby-pambiest piece from 1912 the writers could find. But that only underscores the point that the terms invoked are precisely the terms—the eminently historicist terms—of conventional modernist critique. "The first performance of Stravinsky's ballet, *Le sacre du printemps*, or *The Rite of Spring*," it begins:

> was undoubtedly the most celebrated première of this century. Nothing like this work had ever been heard before. The conservative Paris audience had been hearing and enjoying music such as this elegy by Saint-Saëns written in 1912 [here an excerpt is heard from C. Saint-Saëns, *Élégie pour violon et piano*, op. 160]. Imagine their reaction when, the following year, they listened to a passage like *this* from *Le sacre du printemps*: [sound clip of the "Glorification de l'Élue," beginning with the 11/4 bar of pounding chords; it continues as underscoring to accompany the following description]. It was very nearly a national scandal. A spectacular riot broke out two minutes after the piece had begun. In the audience, fists flew everywhere. The stage was pelted with all sorts of missiles. The performance was completed, but the theater was promptly closed by the police. Stravinsky made his escape through a window in the rear.
>
> *Sacre*, as it is usually called, is really the beginning of modern music as we know it. In this piece, Stravinsky introduced, or developed, techniques that have become standard methods of the greater part of contemporary music. The furious public and critical reaction at first given to *Sacre* is the usual lot of such groundbreaking works.[93]

---

91. Wellens, *Music on the Frontline*, 101.

92. For the actual details of that legendary première, which came nowhere near to being a riot, see R. Taruskin, "Resisting *The Rite*," in Taruskin, *Russian Music at Home and Abroad* (Oakland: University of California Press, 2016), 396–409.

93. RCA Victor MARH 2085 (1960), Stravinsky, *The Rite of Spring*, Musical Program Notes directed by Thomas Scherman.

FIGURE 12.8A AND 12.8B. Music Appreciation Records: Stravinsky, *Le Sacre du printemps*; and Tchaikovsky, Piano Concerto no. 1.

The Chaikovsky concerto, by contrast, is exactly the kind of piece one would expect an enterprise like the Book of the Month Club to be touting. But you probably would not expect marketers to approach the wares they hawk quite so severely as my old friend and colleague Howard Shanet did in the script he wrote for Thomas Scherman to read. The passage concerning the development section in the concerto's first movement begins by citing a typically self-deprecating comment from the composer's correspondence about the need to resort at this point to calculation rather than spontaneous inspiration and employ constructive techniques one learned at school.

Such "artificialities," as Chaikovsky calls them, occur most often in the middle part of a movement, the so-called development section. After he has presented the beautiful

FIGURE 12.8B. *(Continued)*

themes that his genius seems to provide so easily, he sometimes gives the impression of a nervous and self-conscious man who wishes he were finished, but continues to work desperately because he knows that it is expected of him.

One illustration from the piano concerto should suffice. Chaikovsky has just presented, at some length, no less than four excellent themes, and he now seems prepared to pay special attention to two of them: this exquisite one [the continuation of the second theme from the movement's exposition] and this very usable folk tune [*sic:* actually the exposition's first theme, in Lombard rhythm]. Now that they have been introduced, we can almost hear him asking himself, "What *does* one do with them?" And, incredible though it may seem, the best answer that can be devised by that fertile musical mind is to pile fragments of the two themes mechanically on top of each other, step by step. Oh, it's true, I suppose, that a sort of artificial excitement is created by gradually getting louder, getting faster, adding more instruments, and adding more notes. But this kind of routine development is, to Chaikovsky's glorious creativity, what a neat stack of lumber is to the Taj Mahal. [Here the passage is played, and continues as underscoring when the speaker comes back to say:] And so on for measures and measures.

That is all on the negative side.[94]

We've all heard Chaikovsky put down in this snobbish way, but not lately by music appreciation lecturers. You wouldn't hear that in a preconcert talk today. (I'm thinking of Robert Greenberg, who is the mainstay of San Francisco Performances and has recorded innumerable videos for The Great Courses, Inc. He praises everything with equal fervor and fine impartiality.) And that gives a foretaste of the difference between what I would call authentic upper-middlebrow discourse and the promotional lectures concertgoers hear today, betokening the general change in patterns of consumption and dissemination that I will describe in conclusion. In the case of the Music Appreciation Records lectures that we have just sampled, it is clear that they were selling not the pieces but the discourse. They illustrate what T. S. Eliot so authoritatively called the function of criticism, "the elucidation of works of art and the *correction of taste.*"[95] The author of the lecture, *pace* J. B. Priestley, does not ask only that the thing be enthralling; he wants you to love Chaikovsky in a discriminating way, distinguishing what is good from what is not. He is educating you in a version of snob taste. But why should this surprise us? It is, after all, the wish of the lower-middlebrow consumer to become upper, and eventually high. Like the middle class, the middlebrow is the socially and culturally mobile stratum. It wants to be uplifted, in every sense of the word.

Whether because music is supposedly abstract and not to be promoted on the basis of its conceptual or propositional "content," or because of the participation of academics like Howard Shanet (who as a conductor was heavily involved with contemporary music), the middlebrow promotion of classical music seems to have been far less antimodernist than its literary counterpart. But if you are thinking that *Le sacre du printemps* was after all an easy sell by 1960, what with the sensational legend of its first night, its folkish tunes, and its vivid scenario, and that its promotion did not really amount to a modernist pitch, recall that curious article by Ben Earle, "Taste, Power, and Trying to Understand Op. 36," which appeared a little over a dozen years ago in *Music & Letters.*[96]

---

94. RCA Victor MARH 2252 (1958), Tchaikovsky, Piano Concerto No. 1 in B-flat Minor; Eileen Flissler, piano; Thomas Scherman conducting the Music Appreciation Symphony Orchestra; analysis written by Howard Shanet.

95. T. S. Eliot, "The Function of Criticism" (1923), in *Selected Prose of T. S. Eliot,* ed. Frank Kermode (New York: Harcourt Brace Jovanovich/Farrar, Straus & Giroux, 1975), 69 (italics added).

96. Ben Earle, "Taste, Power, and Trying to Understand Op. 36: British Attempts to Popularize Schoenberg," *Music & Letters* 84 (2003): 608–43.

The subtitle, "British Attempts to Popularize Schoenberg," reveals whose op. 36 was the one in question. Schoenberg's op. 36 was the famously rebarbative Violin Concerto. There was nothing forgiving about *its* modernism. You couldn't say of it what Nicola Humble said of *The Feminine Middlebrow Novel*, in a passage that Chris Chowrimootoo singled out to quote, that it offered "narrative excitement without guilt, and intellectual stimulation without undue effort" (191). To get stimulation from Schoenberg required enormous effort; yet middlebrow promoters were undeterred. That so many made, and continue to make, the effort to popularize Schoenberg may illustrate what Chris has called the "ever-expanding boundaries" of the middlebrow (192). But there was a limit. As Ben Earle has shown, the effort was in vain. Trying to expand the outreach enterprise may have been commendable, the way that the philosopher Gary Gutting suggests in his answer to Virginia Woolf's "snobocratic" critique. For him, the middlebrow "refer[s] to those who ... employ the opportunities of a democratic society to reach a level of culture they were not born to."[97] For my part I would suggest that Gutting has grabbed the wrong end of the stick, and that the true opportunists were not the ones reaching for the rope (the lower middlebrow) but the ones dangling it (the upper). Yet whether altruistic or opportunistic, the effort to bring the quintessentially snobocratic Schoenberg, in direct contravention of his evident wishes, to the rabble might seem misguided in precisely the way that once so troubled Lionel Trilling.

Trilling's celebrated confession, "On the Teaching of Modern Literature," was published in 1961, the year I entered as a freshman the university where he taught, and where everybody was talking about it when I arrived on campus. In it, he described a predicament. Coming to the job of teaching literature to undergraduates as a self-identified member of the church of Matthew Arnold, the church of Sweetness and Light, Trilling was stricken by the thought that the works he was administering to his wards in a survey of modern literature communicated pitilessly and even hideously subversive messages, which deviated horribly from the Arnoldian straight and narrow. The worst of it was that, as Trilling discovered,

> almost none of the students have been taken aback by what they have read: they have wholly contained the attack. . . . I asked them to look into the Abyss, and, both dutifully and gladly, they have looked into the Abyss, and the Abyss has greeted them with the grave courtesy of all objects of serious study, saying: "Interesting, am I not? And exciting, if you consider how deep I am and what dread beasts lie at my bottom. Have it well in mind that a knowledge of me contributes materially to your being whole, or well-rounded men" [that, of course, being the widely touted educational ideal of Columbia's famous "general education" or great-books curriculum].[98]

---

97. Gary Gutting, *What Philosophy Can Do* (New York: W. W. Norton, 2015), 205.

98. Lionel Trilling, "On the Teaching of Modern Literature," in Trilling, *The Moral Obligation to Be Intelligent: Selected Essays*, ed. Leon Wieseltier (New York: Farrar Straus Giroux, 2000), 398–99.

Trilling's disappointment in his pupils' complacent response, and what seemed the inescapably numbing, sanitizing, and denaturing effect of disseminating modern literature in the ameliorative atmosphere of a college classroom, did not imply that the enterprise had been undertaken in bad faith. But Ben Earle's critique of comparable British efforts on behalf of Schoenberg did make that claim, and that is what so arrested my attention when I encountered his article, for I agreed with him. His essay, in effect, was calling a bluff, and he named the bluffers: Donald Mitchell, Anthony Payne, Arnold Whittall, Oliver Neighbour, Jonathan Dunsby, Malcolm (or Calum) MacDonald, right down to Ivan Hewett, writing past the start of the twenty-first century. Earle's claim was that these writers did not really believe their own affirmation that, as MacDonald put it, Schoenberg's serial music would eventually become as intelligible as any other music "on the basis of the simple experience of listening for enjoyment," so that listeners need do nothing more than gain familiarity with the music by dint of "repeated listening to sympathetic performances," that they should be "listening in no special way, but bringing to Schoenberg's music the same kind of response as one brings to any music whatever."[99]

A thrice-familiar pitch, this: the last phrase quoted is actually a near-plagiarism of something Roger Sessions wrote in 1944, echoed most recently, perhaps, in Allen Shawn's *Arnold Schoenberg's Journey*.[100] And it goes straight back from there to the granddaddy of all musical middlebrow pitchmen, Billy Phelps himself, who exhorted his readers that

> all one needs to become a passionate, intelligent, discriminating lover of the greatest music, is normal hearing and a strong will. If one is deaf, or lacking in determination and perseverance, then one cannot become a lover of music. But if one can and will listen, that is all that is necessary. Music will do the rest. But one must listen, listen as if it were one's only means of salvation.[101]

The evangelist rhetoric on behalf of Schoenberg was hardly less intense. The extension of middlebrow proselytizing to the hard modernist core is the connection between our two subjects that finally accounts for my presence here. What motivated that nexus? Why not let sleeping dogs lie, and leave Schoenberg to his

---

99. Malcolm MacDonald, *Schoenberg*, The Master Musicians (London: Oxford University Press, 1976); quoted in Earle, "Taste, Power, and Trying to Understand Op. 36," 618.

100. Roger Sessions, "Schoenberg in the United States" (1944), in *Roger Sessions on Music: Collected Essays*, ed. Edward T. Cone (Princeton, NJ: Princeton University Press, 1979), 353–70, at 362 ("He must listen to Schoenberg's music in exactly the same spirit as he listens to any music whatever, and bring to it the same kind of response"); Allen Shawn, *Arnold Schoenberg's Journey* (New York: Farrar Straus Giroux, 2002). For a critique of the latter, see R. Taruskin, "The Poietic Fallacy," *Musical Times* 145, no. 1886(Spring 2004): 7–34; reprinted in Taruskin, *The Danger of Music and Other Anti-Utopian Essays* (Berkeleys: University of California Press, 2010), 301–29.

101. Phelps, *Music*, 14–15.

princes? What made it so necessary to preach him in questionable faith to the masses?[102] Pondering answers to these questions gave me the first glimmerings of what became my title.

VII. ROTATING THE AXIS

The most discerning account of the discourse that so exalted Schoenberg, and all that can be seen to derive from him, was given by Peter Franklin in his remarkable first book, *The Idea of Music*, which elaborates a particular set of "idiosyncratic notions about artistic progress," adapted from the general discourse of German idealism, beginning with Schopenhauer and culminating in a book we've all struggled with, Adorno's *Philosophie der neuen Musik*.[103] Peter's struggle with it was exceptionally fruitful. I think he found there the key to the relationship between the lateral axis of progress—from right to left, let us say, with the left strongly valorized—and the vertical axes with which we are primarily concerned: the high-to-low axes of social classes, of brows, and by extension, of artistic and aesthetic values.

In a very short but exceptionally trenchant analysis of Adorno's text that constitutes his own fourth chapter, Franklin casts the valuable part of the book (that is, the essay about Schoenberg, which in its very title—"Schoenberg and Progress"— attaches him to that lateral axis) as a single overarching dialectic, in which the thesis was the great breakthrough that made possible Schoenberg's atonal works up to *Erwartung*. These works had at last succeeded in solving the problem set by the *neudeutsche Schule* in the middle of the nineteenth century, of letting the content of a musical work determine its form. Schoenberg not only solved this problem, but did so at a previously unimaginable level of emotional intensity, so that,

---

102. The effort continues to this day, albeit by writers who by now are just going through the motions: e.g., Bayan Northcott, "Who's Afraid of Serialism?" *BBC Music*, April 2018, 48–51. Northcott goes to really astonishing lengths to smooth over the rough edges: "On publishing his first 12-tone scores in 1923, [Schoenberg] summoned his pupils, and explained the discovery which he thought would 'ensure the supremacy of German music for the next 100 years.' This was probably not an outburst of cultural chauvinism but rather a way of saying that the new method would enable German composers once more to do what they had always done best: compose large-scale symphonies, concertos, string quartets and operas." (Like Webern's?) Mark Berry does an even more strenuous dance around the "fateful declaration," seizing upon the groundless allegation, put about by Schoenberg's grandson E. Randol Schoenberg, that the remark had been invented by Josef Rufer, the pupil who first reported it (see "The Most Famous Thing He Never Said," *Journal of the Arnold Schoenberg Institute* 5 [2003]: 27–30)—or if Schoenberg did say it, it may "have had a touch of irony to it," or if not irony, then perhaps defensiveness, "as if to say: 'I am as German as they are, more German.' For in 1921 neither Germany nor Austria appeared to have any prospect of 'supremacy' other than of the cultural variety" (Mark Berry, *Arnold Schoenberg* [London: Reaktion Books, 2019], 102–3). Who ever suggested otherwise?

103. Peter Franklin, *The Idea of Music: Schoenberg and Others* (London: Macmillan, 1985); the quoted phrase is on page xiii.

in *Erwartung*, the "registration of traumatic shock becomes . . . the technical structural law of music."[104]

To this the twelve-tone method of systemizing pitch content, and all its subsequent refinements, was the antithesis. In the name of aesthetic autonomy it eliminated content, leaving only form. It was a tragic renunciation, as Adorno recognized, defeating the artistic success of the earlier phase for the sake of what Adorno rationalized as truth, a value greater than the embodiment and expression of subjective emotion. Adorno puts it, as usual, in terms that attribute agency to styles and ideas, and by giving human agency short shrift, gives human agents an alibi: "For the sake of its blind unique law," he wrote, "this technique denies itself expression."[105] But Peter Franklin is not deceived. It was Schoenberg, not the technique, who did the denying. His twelve-tone turn left his music emptied of the humane content that had been his greatest achievement.

Unflinchingly, Franklin understands Adorno's description of the twelve-tone technique as "harsh and squarely-hitting criticisms."[106] Schoenberg agreed. He thought Adorno's book an attack on him that would "give many of my enemies a handle."[107] Whatever we make of it now, Schoenberg's surrender to formalism, combined with the cognitive opacity that has prevented the music from becoming intelligible to naive listeners (i.e., those equipped with no more than "normal hearing and a strong will"), is what has made Schoenberg's later music so singularly unpromising a prospect for popularization, as Ben Earle so copiously attests. Why, then, the persistence in this hopeless endeavor, even up to the present? What is the great value this music possesses despite everything, that it attracts so many proselytizers, if not proselytes? Adorno's synthesis provides the answer. It attaches Schoenberg's creative journey to the discourse one associates (though Adorno never names him) with José Ortega y Gasset and named after Ortega's famous essay "The Dehumanization of Art."[108]

On a hunch, I looked up Ortega's name in the indexes of Stefan Müller-Doohm's huge biography of Adorno, and also the huge anthology of Adorno's musical essays edited by Richard Leppert[109]—and (as I expected) did not find it even once. If I

---

104. Theodore W. Adorno, *Philosophy of Modern Music*, trans. Anne G. Mitchell and Wesley V. Blomster (London: Continuum, 2006), 42; quoted ibid., 66.
105. Adorno, *Philosophy of Modern Music*, 104; quoted in Franklin, *The Idea of Music*, 69.
106. Franklin, *The Idea of Music*, 69.
107. Schoenberg to Josef Rufer, 5 December 1949; quoted in Hans Heinz Stuckenschmidt, *Arnold Schoenberg: His Life, World, and Work* (New York: Schirmer Books, 1978), 508.
108. José Ortega y Gasset, "La deshumanización del arte" (1925), in *The Dehumanization of Art and Other Essays on Art, Culture, and Literature*, trans. Helene Weyl (Princeton, NJ: Princeton University Press, 1968), 3–56.
109. Stefan Müller-Doohm, *Adorno: A Biography* (Cambridge: Polity Press, 2004); T. W. Adorno, *Essays on Music*, ed. Richard Leppert, trans. Susan H. Gillespie (Berkeley: University of California Press, 2002).

were Harold Bloom, that would be all the evidence I needed[110]—and there would be even better evidence in the fact that when Adorno does speak of dehumanization, it is in the context of barbarism and Stravinsky. But I will cautiously refrain from positively asserting a connection between Adorno's synthesis and Ortega's conception of "dehumanization," which of course carried as strong a positive valence for Ortega as it did a negative one for Adorno. Yet despite that extreme divergence in evaluation, it is clear that Adorno and Ortega would have defined the word similarly. For both, dehumanization connoted aesthetic purity at a high cost in terms of accessibility. For Ortega the compensating payoff to the artist is in what Pierre Bourdieu would have called cultural capital.[111] For Adorno the payoff is in fact much greater, because it consists of moral authority. As the one musical artist to face up to the impossibility of, in Adorno's words, "overcom[ing], through his own individual resources, the contradictions of enchained art within an enchained society," Schoenberg's artistic failure was his moral triumph, as Peter Franklin recognizes when he writes, "To see Schoenberg as a tragically, even heroically necessary failure may prove paradoxically to grant him that very place of importance in the history of Western music that he clearly believed himself to occupy," and which set him apart from all others, even the other members of his own faction.[112]

Once again I am reminded of that telling anecdote in Adorno's little book on Berg, his teacher, in which he recalled having to "console" Berg over the fantastic success of *Wozzeck* at its Berlin première.[113] *Wozzeck* has remained a middlebrow favorite; Joseph Kerman devoted a whole chapter to it in *Opera as Drama*. Adorno reassured Berg that nobody had really understood him, repeating the assurance in his *Introduction to the Sociology of Music*, where he rationalized the defiling taint of success by reminding the reader that, however vividly *Wozzeck* conveyed its social message, and however dramatically effective were its scenes of sex and violence, in the end "neither the details nor their structural connection were fully understood," and that redeemed the work.[114] Nevertheless, Adorno did feel that the opera's accessibility had compromised it, at least by comparison with the epitome of uncompromising truth that Berg's teacher had by then achieved. In *Philosophie der neuen Musik*, he asserted explicitly, with reference now to *Lulu*, in a sentence

---

110. See his old classic of *Wirkungsgeschichte*, *The Anxiety of Influence: A Theory of Poetry* (New York: Oxford University Press, 1973), and the weird criteria of proof therein proposed.

111. Bourdieu, *Distinction*.

112. Franklin, *The Idea of Music*, 74.

113. Theodor W. Adorno, *Alban Berg: Master of the Smallest Link*, trans. Juliane Brand and Christopher Hailey (Cambridge: Cambridge University Press, 1991), 10. See chapter 4 above ("Is There a Baby in the Bathwater?") for the quotation.

114. Theodor W. Adorno, *Introduction to the Sociology of Music*, trans. E. B. Ashton (New York: Seabury Press, 1976), 74.

that Peter Franklin plucked from Adorno's text to represent the quintessence of his argument, that "Schoenberg's inhuman coldness is superior to Berg's magnanimous warmth."[115] This sentence is indeed key, not only to Adorno's argument, or Franklin's, but to mine as well.

Before proceeding, I'd better step back and remind you that I am not endorsing the discourse I am now describing. I do not think it is correct; nor do I think it successful even to the extent that Peter Franklin allows when he writes that Adorno's powerful synthesis "revitalizes our almost lost belief in the importance of the artist in Western cultural experience."[116] I would prefer to move the word *almost* in that sentence so that it credits Adorno, more pessimistically, with *almost* revitalizing our by now irrevocably lost belief in the importance of the artist. But Adorno's bald and, be it said, crude value judgment uses a word—*überlegend*, which the translator renders as "superior"—that indicates a vertical location or direction, namely *über*, that is, "above," or more simply, "up." Literally, the word means "overlying," and by invoking categories of high and low it rotates the lateral axis of progress by ninety degrees so that it merges with the vertical axis of classes, brows, tastes, or, in this case, moral value. Left is now above. More advanced technique is now to be equated with enhanced moral standing. That way is now up. And so it is with the politicized critical vocabulary we use today, in which *progressive* is given a default aesthetic privilege and *conservative* is stigmatized. The privilege is routinely abused in the defensive literature decrying the "backlash against modernist music" in which I am frequently said to be engaged.

The phrase just quoted, about the perceived and chided backlash, is Björn Heile's, in a self-pitying article, "Darmstadt as Other," that graced the maiden volume of the journal *Twentieth-Century Music*. Heile distinguished what he called the "anti-modernist onslaught" peculiar to Anglophone musicology from "the critique of modernism," which "plays an important, and indeed necessary, role in the critical discourses of many countries" on the European continent. But even among the onslaughterers Heile makes distinctions, disdaining even to consider the cognitive issues raised by Fred Lerdahl (and me) because he adjudges them to have issued from a "conservative" perspective.[117] But neither he nor anyone else has ever attempted to meet or rebut what they are content thus to stigmatize. The use of the stigmatizing word grants the user an alibi permitting denunciation rather than engagement.

---

115. Adorno, *Philosophy of Modern Music*, 109; quoted in Franklin, *The Idea of Music*, 70. The whole original sentence: "Das Unversöhnte am späten Schönberg—das sich nicht bloss auf die Intransigenz bezieht, sondern eben auch auf die Antagonismen in der Musik selber—ist der zu frühen Versöhnung Bergs überlegen, die unmenschliche Kälte der grossherzigen Wärme" (Adorno, *Philosophie der neuen Musik* [Frankfurt am Main: Suhrkamp, 1978], 105).

116. Franklin, *The Idea of Music*, 74.

117. Björn Heile, "Darmstadt as Other: British and American Responses to Musical Modernism," *Twentieth-Century Music* 1 (2004): 161–62.

An abuse, then—not only of diction but also of what I call the poietic fallacy. Ruling out all perspectives but that of the composers of the music takes the discussion out of the realm of aesthetics and into that of ethics. Adorno made sure of that. The superiority that he ascribed to Schoenberg's twelve-tone music, and that conventional critical parlance now ascribes to all "progressive" music, was not an artistic or aesthetic superiority. As Peter Franklin made clear, Adorno explicitly ruled that out. It was, rather, a moral superiority that grants such music its insurmountable privilege. So when I spoke of proselytizing, I was not using figurative language. The discourse that has promoted musical modernism has become an essentially religious discourse.

Nothing new in that. A religious, ethical impulse undergirds all art promotion that sees art consumption as a means of self-improvement. That especially includes middlebrow promotion, going all the way back to Matthew Arnold himself. With Adorno's version these spurious pieties may be said to have reached their maximal phase. In his peroration, Adorno widened his purview beyond the single case of Schoenberg, proclaiming that authentic New Music, in its very sacrifice of aesthetic quality, has "taken upon itself all the darkness and guilt of the world."[118] *Agnus Dei, qui tollis peccata mundi.* Do you think Adorno was unaware of that reverberation? Are we? The privilege, asserted in strongest terms, is essentially unrelated to what the music sounds like. (And that may be why Adorno eventually had cold feet and retreated: in a memorial article he published in 1953 he claimed that "many of [Schoenberg's] large twelve-tone pieces, especially those composed in America," were in fact "convincingly successful.")[119]

But it is the strong, religiose version that continues to surround Schoenberg in the promotional or middlebrow literature that Ben Earle has sampled. His introductory specimen, given pride of place because it was the most recent one at the time of his writing, was Ivan Hewett's exhortation in the London Proms Guide for 2001, urging that year's Union Jack–wavers that "we should love [Schoenberg's] music" because "his time is now," and this because his "refusal to compromise . . . offers [us] a moral as well as a musical beacon."[120] Similar appeals have been made on behalf of Elliott Carter, whose biography is often cast in a lives-of-the-saints mode, with its desert retreat and subsequent transfiguration.[121] Nor is there any-

---

118. Adorno, *Philosophy of Modern Music*, 133; quoted in Franklin, *The Idea of Music*, 72.

119. T. W. Adorno, "Arnold Schoenberg, 1874–1951," in Adorno, *Prisms*, trans. Rodney Livingstone (Stanford: Stanford University Press, 1999), 167; quoted in Earle, "Taste, Power, and Trying to Understand Op. 36," 635.

120. Quoted in Earle, "Taste, Power, and Trying to Understand Op. 36," 610.

121. One typical version: "By going to the desert, Carter left his routine patterns of living in order to discover a new kind of time. Friends refer to this time in the desert as a 'conversion,' for a new composer emerged with the First Quartet, uncompromising and visionary" (David Schiff, *The Music of Elliott Carter,* 2nd ed. [Ithaca, NY: Cornell University Press, 1998], 55).

thing inherently modernist about this discourse. It is, rather, inherently middlebrow. It is how Charles O'Connell, a paid huckster for the Victor Talking Machine Company, touted César Franck (and also how Charles Ives wrote about Franck, in whom he saw a role model as an organist-composer).[122] It was how William Lyon Phelps touted Beethoven's Ninth.[123] And most recently, it is how Julian Johnson touted classical music taken as a whole, in a latter-day middlebrow exhortation to which I have already registered strong objection.[124]

VIII. SHUTTING DOWN DEBATE

I had a bit of sober academic fun debunking these religious appeals in *The Oxford History of Western Music,* as regarded both César Franck and Elliott Carter.[125] Nobody paid much notice in the case of Franck, but there was a furious reaction to the discussion of Carter, especially because the Carter chapter was paired with one on Britten to illustrate what I was calling "the essential question of modern art," namely, "whether artists lived in history or in society."[126] Pretty much everyone with a stake in the question assumed I was coming down heavily on the side of society, and therefore on the side of Britten. That is how I gained my middlebrow and antimodernist spurs. You may remember the most garish phase of that backlash, which was initiated by Charles Rosen's review of The Ox and carried forward in a rather lopsided exchange between me, writing in the *Journal of Musicology* with a circulation in the low hundreds, and Rosen, writing in the *New York Review of Books*.[127]

The most recent comment as of this writing, and a particularly pertinent one, came from Seth Brodsky, deriding my "positively operatic two-chapter 'standoff'

---

122. See Charles O'Connell, *The Victor Book of the Symphony* (New York: Simon & Schuster, 1941), 235; Charles Ives, *Essays before a Sonata* (1920), epilogue, part 2 (Fairfield, IA: 1st World Library Literary Society, 2004), 89–90.

123. "When we see the Sistine Madonna, or read Hamlet, we admire the extraordinary power of Rafael, of Shakespeare. But when we hear the Ninth Symphony, we are truly listening to the voice of God. Beethoven was more passive than active, the channel through which flowed the Divine Will" (William Lyon Phelps, "Browning, Schopenhauer, and Music," *North American Review* 206, no. 743 [Oct. 1917]: 622–27, at 624).

124. Julian Johnson, *Who Needs Classical Music? Cultural Choice and Musical Value* (New York: Oxford University Press, 2002); R. Taruskin, "The Musical Mystique," *New Republic,* 22 October 2007, 34–45; reprinted in Taruskin, *The Danger of Music,* 330–53.

125. Taruskin, *Oxford History of Western Music* (rev. ed.), vol. 3: *Music in the Nineteenth Century,* 781–82; vol. 5: *Music in the Late Twentieth Century,* 280–81.

126. Taruskin, *Oxford History of Western Music* 5:221.

127. Charles Rosen, "From the Troubadours to Frank Sinatra," part 2, *New York Review of Books,* 9 March 2006, 44–49; R. Taruskin, "Afterword: Nicht Blutbefleckt?" *Journal of Musicology* 26 (2009): 274–84; Rosen, "Music and the Cold War," *New York Review of Books,* 7 April 2011, 40–42. My side of the exchange is now chapter 7 of this book.

between Britten and Elliott Carter." My opera, Brodsky thinks, is set in the "boxing ring" where modernists engage, "an Oedipal arena in which allegedly bigger fighters went to town battling their proverbial fathers—and each other—while Britten himself was sidelined, persistently assessed as not strong enough, deep enough, negative enough, 'man enough.'" Having already summoned Harold Bloom to the judgment seat, Seth immediately doubled down by calling my pairing of Britten and Carter a "strong misreading" of the usual trope: "staged at the 'mid-twentieth-century divide,'" he writes, "it throws Britten in the ring, bets on him, and wins."[128]

Brodsky's use of the word *operatic* is a beautiful example of what the Shakespeare scholar Jonas Barish, in a book famous among literary historians, called the antitheatrical prejudice.[129] The word is meant to distinguish my viewpoint from "subtler approaches such as [Heather] Wiebe's and Philip Rupprecht's, each of which transforms the arena into something less partisan and more complex."[130] Well, fiddlesticks again. I think anyone who reads my chapters carefully—or perhaps I mean naively, in the strict philosophical sense—will see that I treat both one-sided positions on the question of history vs. society with skepticism. But who ever reads such a text without preconceptions? To treat Carter and Britten as figures of comparable weight or significance is already to grant an unjustified privilege to Britten in the eyes of those who have internalized the discourse that assigns not only an aesthetic but also a moral advantage to Carter. The moral privilege is the only one I sought to revoke. But for many readers that move was intolerable enough, and made me a synecdoche for the imagined conspiracy about which you can read in essays, reviews, and whole books by Gianmario Borio, Ian Pace, Christopher Fox, and J. P. E. Harper-Scott, to name but four, three of whom put their paranoia on display in connection with that *JRMA* symposium in which Chris Chowrimootoo published the essay that seems to have jump-started the whole red-hot Music and the Middlebrow topic.

That colloquy got off to a discouraging start with Borio's phobic reaction to what he chose, rather tardily, to call "postmodernism" (even while whining at the use of the term *modernism*, since "the '-ism' suffix tends to place the concept in a negative light").[131] He offered a litany of complaints at the unfairness of a historiography that concerned itself with individual agency and motivation rather than assigning the determining force of history to "the dynamic of the cultural sphere itself, which makes selections on the basis of shared criteria, identifies and discusses the problems that occur, determines the paradigmatic value of certain works and rejects

---

128. Seth Brodsky, "Remembering, Repeating, Passacaglia: Weak Britten," *Acta Musicologica* 88 (2016): 166.
129. Jonas Barish, *The Antitheatrical Prejudice* (Berkeley: University of California Press, 1981).
130. Brodsky, "Remembering," 166.
131. Gianmario Borio, "Musical Communication and the Process of Modernity," *JRMA* 139 (2014): 178.

other solutions"—and all quite impersonally, as "inscribed in the [historical] process."¹³² How unfair of postmodernists to render "an ethical judgment that admits of no reply," when what is called for when talking about art is obviously and only "an aesthetic rather than an ideological judgment."¹³³ Adorno has long since rendered that distinction quaint, and yet, believe it or not, Borio called Adorno as a witness in support of his self-pity. Perhaps he has never read him.

I can't help taking a certain naughty amusement in the aggrieved tone that writers like Borio and Björn Heile now adopt. There is no bigger cliché in American politics right now than the spectacle of those accustomed to privilege claiming the status of victim and railing against the "political correctness" that has revoked their advantages. I toyed with the idea of adding to the *JRMA* discussion a tuppence of my own on the vainness of such complaints, at first by putting out a feeler to Peter Franklin, who had begun his contribution to the symposium in a manner very much to my liking, by asking, "How modern *is* modernism?"¹³⁴ Peter referred my inquiry to Laura Tunbridge, the journal's editor, who informed me of the existence of a student blog she had set up to accommodate commentary, and invited me to post therein. That did not strike me as a very good idea; I had seen the effect of intrusion by professors on student forums in the past. So I refrained, and eventually the impulse to reply died down.

But then the student blog suffered just the sort of invasion I had hoped to avoid, by a pair of professors who obviously intended to shut it down by force of intimidation, and succeeded in doing so. They were familiar names to me, because both of them had played conspicuous roles in the paranoid response to my treatment of late twentieth-century music in The Ox, and so I fancy that the many references to my writings within the symposium must have played a part in luring them out of their lairs. Their bullying tactics were time-honored, and tediously familiar to anyone who has read Dai Griffiths's breezy sketch "On Grammar Schoolboy Music" or my own more ponderous "Poietic Fallacy."¹³⁵

Ian Pace, the first to join in, complained that only musicologists, rather than performers and composers, had been invited to the party—talkers, not doers, according to the old cliché. Then he appointed himself gatekeeper, listing "sixteen post-1945 compositions" and stipulating that only such musicologists as could apply their ideas to these, or to "another group of equally contrasting pieces," should be allowed to participate in the discussion. Jun Zubillaga-Pow, originally from Singapore and a student of the new music scene there, and one of the few

---

132. Ibid., 180.
133. Ibid., 178, 179.
134. Peter Franklin, "Modernismus and the Philistines," *JRMA* 139 (2014): 183.
135. Dai Griffiths, "Genre: Grammar Schoolboy Music," *Critical Musicology Newsletter* 3 (July 1995); reprinted as "On Grammar Schoolboy Music," in *Music Culture, and Society: A Reader*, ed. Derek B. Scott (Oxford: Oxford University Press, 2000), 143–45.

hardy souls to stand up to the faculty intruders, pointed out from his extra-European perspective that Pace's list was not all that contrasting; but to me the ploy brought back ancient memories of Milton Babbitt's similarly motivated attempt (later published) to cow a roomful of musicologists that included twenty-four-year-old me by quoting a paragraph on twelve-tone music by a cultural historian, then adding: "This authoritative crescendo of howlers I shall leave ungilded as one—if by no means the only—appropriate commentary, but I do suggest as an exercise for the reader that he detect such a howler for each half dozen or so words of this excerpt or otherwise regard himself as unequipped to continue the reading of this paper."[136]

Christopher Fox, besides joining Pace in decreeing that Adorno must be quoted in the original German (which is why I made sure to provide a gloss above on Adorno's use of the word *überlegen*), was even more intransigent than his precursor in denying the student bloggers the right to speak. His advice: shut up and listen to the music (and "what it has to say") and stop "continuing such an ill-informed debate."[137] This sort of intervention, too, has a long tradition among British composers. It brought back some slightly less ancient memories to me, of Hugh Wood's aggressively anti-intellectualist review of recent books on Elgar (including Harper-Scott's *Edward Elgar, Modernist*, which especially offended his sense of exclusivity). Culturally contextualized studies, Wood warned from across the great subdisciplinary divide, are not "genuine musicology, inhabiting its proper province," a judgment that chimed with another peremptory verdict by Ian Pace, condemning "the use of context as a substitute for musical engagement."[138] Indeed, Wood wrote, even performing a technical analysis, if it does not conform to what a British composer would have said about his own music, "gives the whole proceeding [forgive me for quoting this] a rabbinical air."[139] Such displays of highbrow snobbery and Britannic bigotry give the middlebrow a right good name.

Or would, if I could really say that the middlebrow was our safe haven from intolerance, or if I really believed what Chris Chowrimootoo has written, that the

---

136. Milton Babbitt, "Contemporary Music Composition and Music Theory as Contemporary Intellectual History," in *Perspectives in Musicology*, ed. Barry S. Brook, Edward O. D. Downes, and Sherman van Solkema (New York: W. W. Norton, 1972), 155. The "excerpt" in question was from Morse Peckham, *Man's Rage for Chaos: Biology, Behavior, and the Arts* (Philadelphia: Chilton Books, 1965), 234, and, though a propos of nothing, it was indeed a salad of howlers.

137. For the interventions of Pace and Fox, as well as those by the graduate students for whom the blog had been set up, see www.rma.ac.uk/students/?p=1585 (last accessed 8 June 2017; apparently no longer active as of 4 June 2018).

138. Hugh Wood, "The Hopes and Glories of Edward Elgar," *Times Literary Supplement*, 19 March 2008; Ian Pace, Review of *Luigi Dallapiccola and Musical Modernism in Fascist Italy* by Ben Earle, *Music and Letters* 98 (2017): 155.

139. Wood, "Hopes and Glories."

all-accommodating middlebrow offered infinite "shades of grey" to offset the "black and white of modernism."[140] But all the brows, in the traditional account, have their affinities and their aversions: high loves low and hates middle; middle loves high and hates low; low just doesn't care. Nor, within the duplex Lynesian middlebrow, are the two levels necessarily engaged in a cooperative endeavor; each could as easily be seen as exploiting the other. Nor have I even presented the best evidence I know of the vector ambiguity that my title invokes, the story that gave this talk its initial push into being.

IX. LOOKING UP AND/OR DOWN

As the organizers can confirm, whenever anyone asked me what I intended to say at the middlebrow conference, I would ask them whether they had ever heard of Anatole Broyard, always hoping that the answer would be no, and that I would be able to tell there, to listeners who did not know it, the tale I am about to narrate here. The answer usually *was* no, and that is what encouraged me to accept the invitation to assume the role of Jakobsonian elephant at the conference.

Anatole Broyard was a New Orleans–born book reviewer for the *New York Times,* whom I especially enjoyed reading both for his insights and for his witty, elegant style, cool and at times perhaps a bit gracefully cruel. He died in 1990, but that was not the end of his literary career, nor of his news value. It was posthumously revealed that he was of mixed-race ancestry, but had never publicly acknowledged the African-American component. This gave rise to some controversy, which in turn stimulated interest in his literary legacy and led to the publication of two posthumous books, both of them memoirs. One was about his final illness; the other, a book called *Kafka Was the Rage,* concerned life in Greenwich Village, New York's bohemian colony, in the immediate postwar years, when Broyard was a newcomer to the city. Its chapters were self-contained, exquisitely wrought stories, one of which, touching on music, so captured my imagination that I had an impulse to assemble an anthology just so I could include this item in it and bring it to a wider musically interested readership.[141]

Its cast of characters included the poet Delmore Schwartz, Clement Greenberg, and, the real star of the story, Dwight Macdonald, Mr. Masscult-and-Midcult himself. It begins with the three of them sitting with the author around a table in a Greenwich Village bar. Broyard had just published a piece on jazz, and the others thought him therefore "an aficionado of the primitive." Learning that he occasionally visited dance halls in Spanish Harlem, they begged him to take them there.

---

140. Chowrimootoo, "Reviving the Middlebrow," 191.
141. The story is chapter 14 in Anatole Broyard, *Kafka Was the Rage: A Greenwich Village Memoir* (New York: Vintage Books, 1993), 110–21; all quotations are from these pages.

"For all their intellectual sophistication," Broyard wrote, "Village writers were suckers. They were awed by action and passion.... They wanted to see Spanish Harlem. They wanted to visit the primitive, see it in the flesh." For his part he was glad to take them, not only because their awe flattered him, but also because

> it was Latin American music that I loved most. I don't know why, because much of it was terrible. The arrangements were full of churning horn sections and awkward staccatos and the singers, who were almost always male, sang through their noses in a high pinched tenor. Yet I loved it.... I suppose it was the rhythm section, the drums, that appealed to me. I had always felt that life was a rhythmical process.

Not the most bracing observation, I know. But it tells us why he was so eager to take his trio of suckers to the *baile*.

> It was my secret conviction that Delmore and the other writer-intellectuals had very little sense of rhythm.... There was not much syncopation in their writing.... I liked it better when writers danced. Even Hemingway, another clumsy man [like Delmore], knew how to dance, and I can imagine even Gertrude Stein and Alice B. Toklas dancing. Writers used to get more out of simply being.

So they arrive at the Park Plaza, the dance hall, and Broyard offers to find his companions dance partners.

> Delmore, who never hesitated to play the crazy, impulsive poet, had a blank look on his face. Clem was sliding his eyes around—not like an art critic, but a tourist. Only Dwight, who was a permanent revolutionary, wanted to dance and appeared to be at home in the Park Plaza. I found him a girl named Dinamita, which appealed to his political tastes, and he gyrated away with her. He didn't know what he was doing, but it didn't matter, because he had rhythm, and also an air of conviction, as if there was nothing in human behavior that was alien to him. Tall, thin, white-haired even then, with glasses and a goatee, he was every inch an intellectual—yet he was something more too. He wasn't standing outside of culture looking in. He was in the thick of it. He felt its rhythm.... When Dwight came back, he announced that Dinamita had drums in her belly.

That is the first part of the story. The rest concerns Broyard's pursuit of another Park Plaza girl. "Her name, of course, was Carmen," he writes, and "she was the best female dancer in the place." He was attracted partly by her exoticism; in fact, precociously using language that later became *de rigueur*, he writes that "she was more authentically *other* than any woman I had ever known." Nevertheless:

> I thought I knew something about Carmen. I thought that she too had drums in her belly, that her life was a strong rhythm. I believed I could learn from her, that I could warm my hands over her flames. It was unlikely, though, because I had nothing to offer her. Those cruel slanting eyes of hers passed right over me. I was so pale to her as to be invisible.

But one night she surprised him by demanding that he dance with her, and then leave with her. In a taxi, on the way to the hotel room where they would spend the night, she surprised him again.

> I hate that music, Carmen said, leaning back in the cab. She spoke English almost without an accent, except that she bit off her words.
> You hate it? I said. What kind of music do you like?
> Classical music, she said. André Kostelanetz, Morton Gould. Then she crooned the entire lyrics to Nat King Cole's "Lush Life." She wasn't what I had thought . . .

Forgive me for skipping over the sex scene. It is torrid enough, and imaginatively rendered; but what I just quoted is the real climax of the story, because after their little discussion of music, Broyard found Carmen uninteresting. After describing their lovemaking, he admits that while he found the dancing exciting, and her sexual interest in him flattering, once in bed "I never got into the spirit of the thing. I remained detached and, as a result, the business went on for quite a while." She, however, was beside herself with pleasure:

> ¡Hombre, she said, fenómeno!
> After that I couldn't get rid of her. She would call me up and plead with me on the phone. I'll wash you; I'll powder you. I'll light your cigarettes and bring you a glass of whiskey. She had an interminable list of the things she would do, and none of them interested me. What I had wanted was to cross over into her world, and what she wanted was to enter mine.

So the story ends with a display of male ego that nowadays might require an apology; but on the matter of taste and brows it's very informative—and not entirely what I, at least, would have expected. The big surprise is Carmen's middlebrow aspiration, made pathetic by her naiveté. I shouldn't take for granted the familiarity of the names she mentioned when declaring her preference for "classical music," although they were household names in the 1940s. André Kostelanetz (1901–80), who was born Abram Naumovich Kostelyanets in St. Petersburg, along with the Venetian-born Annunzio Paolo Mantovani (1905–80), who worked in Britain, and George Melachrino (1909–65; born Miltiades, but in London), were among the main purveyors of what was sometimes called "pops," or light music, or dinner music, or semiclassical music: the repertoire now most prominently associated with André Rieu and his Johann Strauss Orchestra.

If you know this sort of music, you know that it is the sort that brings out the Dwight Macdonald even in lower middlebrows, because, as we all know, "every man is a king so long as he has someone to look down on."[142] When George Martin suggested adding strings to the orchestration of "Yesterday" on the Beatles album

---

142. That is the campaign slogan of Berzelius ("Buzz") Windrip, the neofascist presidential candidate, in Sinclair Lewis's novel *It Can't Happen Here* (1935) (New York: Signet Reprint Edition, 2016), 157.

Help! in 1965, Paul McCartney resisted, saying, "I don't want Mantovani."[143] Nat King Cole's recording of Billy Strayhorn's "Lush Life" does sound like Mantovani,[144] and that is what elevated it in Carmen's ears. Morton Gould (1913–96), a composer as well as an orchestra leader, had a more serious reputation, but was best known for pieces with cutely adapted titles like "Pavanne" or *Latin American Symphonette,* which tended to justify the claims, if not the indignation, of those who saw the middlebrow as dilution and nothing more.[145] His closest counterpart, perhaps, was Leroy Anderson, the author of what were often called "novelty pieces" for the Boston Pops Orchestra.

Carmen's preference for this corny, gooey stuff enabled her to look down on the other habitués of the Park Plaza dance hall, and it forced Anatole Broyard to look down on her, whereas previously he had been looking up. And so had Dwight Macdonald, who within the story never experiences Broyard's disillusion, and never condescends either. The way he is contrasted with Delmore Schwartz and Clement Greenberg in Broyard's telling is to me very appealing. He was not in the dance hall solely as a voyeur or a tourist. He wanted some sort of sublime experience, and found it. His attitude toward the lowbrow can be contrasted with Virginia Woolf's in her little classic of snobbery. When she says "I love lowbrows; I study them; I always sit next the conductor in an omnibus and try to get him to tell me what it is like—being a conductor," it simply drips with condescension, like that famous saying of Jerome K. Jerome, the professional snob who wrote the essay collection *Idle Thoughts of an Idle Fellow* (1886). I'm sure you know it: "I like work; it fascinates me. I can sit and look at it for hours."[146] But what Jerome and Woolf looked down on, in a curious way Dwight Macdonald looked up to. He was actually, and (as Broyard saw it) unpretentiously, looking up to the lowbrow—which corroborates my own long-standing impression of Macdonald, whose writings even at their snootiest displayed intellectual honesty and, above all, the gift of humor.

X. SWALLOWING UP THE BROWS

But if you can look up to the lowbrow, what does "up" even mean? Not only can low appear high; high can just as easily appear low, especially when attached to spurious morality. One of the contributors to the *JRMA*'s student blog, Amanda Hsieh, wrote about the possibility of exchanging the rigidly hierarchical romanti-

---

143. *The Beatles Anthology* (San Francisco: Chronicle Books, 2000), 175.

144. On YouTube at www.youtube.com/watch?v=fCrCiMJOmWk.

145. *Latin American Symphonette* was Gould's Symphonette no. 4, on YouTube at www.youtube.com/watch?v=fBl8dsEllPo; "Pavanne" comes from his *American Symphonette,* on YouTube at www.youtube.com/watch?v=HRbslD5nz-8.

146. J. K. Jerome, *Three Men in a Boat* (1889), chapter 15 (https://en.wikiquote.org/wiki/Jerome_K._Jerome).

cism (as she called it, after Peter Franklin) that still weighs musicology down, for a more eclectic set of values "that could contribute to diverse ways of hearing." She called that bid "my generation's metaphorical slap in the face to the sense of righteousness that has been claimed for and by the High Modernists"—and it brought down upon her a bit of high righteous fury from Ian Pace, again waxing huffy over the question of who had the right to speak (in this case, "for a whole generation"), and over the poor breeding shown by the use of "metaphors implying domestic violence."

Allow me to point out, first, what most of us know: that the metaphor of a slap in the face (or *soufflet*) comes down to us not from domestic violence but from the rituals of dueling, and that it connotes not physical injury but rather a rebuff, or a snub, or an insult, or a simple rejection—that is, exactly what Amanda Hsieh evidently intended to convey. And secondly I would point out that the rejection to which she alluded is widely recognized by sociologists as applying, in contemporary culture, not only to High Modernism, however that is defined, but to the whole question of brows as we have been pondering it. For a quarter of a century now, Richard A. Peterson of Vanderbilt University, the leading American sociologist of taste—the American Bourdieu, as I would be tempted to call him did he not usually disagree with Bourdieu—has been documenting and analyzing a change in consumption habits and preference patterns that he first reported in an article of 1992, which bore the title "Understanding Audience Segmentation: From Elite and Mass to Omnivore and Univore."[147]

The old brow model, which in Peterson's description is "the view of cultural stratification that places a discriminating and exclusive elite on the top and an undiscriminating mass on the bottom," and which, to use plainer language, "counterpoised 'snob' and 'slob,'" has, he writes, been superseded (243–44). Peterson reports a survey undertaken by one of his graduate students and himself, which identified practically no respondent who answered to the old highbrow profile, which is to say exhibited the "moralistic contempt for and distancing from all cultural manifestations that do not exactly fit with what is taken to be proper," to which reference has already been made above (245). The absence of a clearly delineated highbrow category leaves "those in the middle of the status hierarchy" without a clear model for emulation. The highest-status groups in Peterson's survey by education and occupation—those with university degrees and in the professions—did not turn out in force for the traditional snob genres. Thirty percent declared a preference for classical music, and a mere 6 percent selected opera as their favorite genre; but—and this is the significant fact—almost none "fit the model of the aesthetically exclusive snob" (248). With only statistically negligible exceptions,

---

147. Richard A. Peterson, "Understanding Audience Segmentation: From Elite and Mass to Omnivore and Univore," *Poetics* 21 (1992): 243–58; page references will be indicated in the main text.

all professed enjoyment of lower forms, and "9% of this top status group say they like country and western music best—the music with the lowest prestige of all!" (248).

None of this could possibly come as a surprise to anyone who, like me, had been teaching music to university students for fifty years. Richard Peterson was among the sociologists who first observed and reported in the journals the transformation that my generation of music professors witnessed in the classroom: that, beginning in the 1960s, students entering college were no longer expected to change their musical consumption habits to reflect their new social status. Whereas formerly college students normally eschewed the "top forty" in favor of one or two—never all three!—of the then higher-status genres (classical, jazz, or coffeehouse "folk"), starting in the mid-sixties and correlated (it couldn't be a coincidence) with the so-called British invasion, students retained their enthusiasm for the music they had enjoyed previously, and remained faithful to it for life, even if they added higher-status tastes to their previously acquired ones.

This change seriously compromised the *raison d'être* of the sometimes (as at Columbia) required music appreciation courses that American colleges offered or imposed on their students to facilitate the maturation process. The culture wars of the 1980s and 90s strengthened the pattern by adding a political component to it. The correlation between socioeconomic status and cultural consumption became so fluid that Peterson found himself casting about for genres that remained "distinctive of the lower class," and found he had to go beyond music, speculating that "activities such as professional wrestling and betting on the numbers" *might* still qualify as class markers (252). I found this hilarious, because I happened to remember that watching professional wrestling on TV was the favorite leisure pursuit of the elderly Arturo Toscanini.[148]

But if there was no genre (at least no musical genre) that was exclusively the preference of the lower class, Peterson's survey did uncover an important difference between the lower class and those that had formerly populated the highbrow and middlebrow categories as defined between the 1920s and the 1950s. Where the formerly highbrow and middlebrow were now eclectic and unpredictable in their professions of taste, the lowbrow held firm and was usually partial to a single genre. For that reason, Peterson now proposed a new breakdown: omnivore vs. univore, with the latter corresponding to the older lowbrow and the former designating all the rest. Clearly, it no longer designated much.

Nevertheless, the eclectic model has certainly influenced patterns of commercial production and dissemination. Just last week, as I write, the *New York Times* pub-

---

148. See, for example, Erich Leinsdorf's memoir in Harvey Sachs, ed., *Arturo Toscanini from 1915 to 1946, Art in the Shadow of Politics: Homage to the Maestro on the 30th Anniversary of His Death* (Turin: Edizioni di Torino, 1987), 129.

lished an article commemorating the twentieth anniversary of the best-selling Nonesuch recording of Gorecki's Third Symphony (*Symphony of Sorrowful Songs*) and the frenzy of crossovers and—what shall I say?—*Mischlings* that Gorecki's fabulous success both contributed to and intensified.[149] One of the interviewees was Peter Gelb, who in the nineties headed Sony Classical Records, and who was responsible for some of the most cynical attempts to exploit the new eclecticism (e.g. Yo-Yo Ma's classical/country bluegrass crossover album, *Appalachian Journey*).[150] Can you blame me for wondering, when Gelb was appointed general manager of the Metropolitan Opera, when the Andrew Lloyd Webber festival was coming?

That hasn't happened—yet; and I didn't really expect it would, since the Met has always been, and will probably always be, the last house in the world to try anything new. But I will tell you that I cannot stand the sound of Lord Lloyd Webber's music, so maybe—joke's on you—I am the highbrow in the room today after all. If so, I am a much-chastened highbrow. I willingly entertain a possibility that Richard Peterson, in 1992, only raised reluctantly, that the changes in consumption that he began documenting a quarter century ago "mean that the U.S. is becoming a more egalitarian society" (252). Not a more equal society, mind you; greed is still an issue worth marching and struggling over. But we are a society that is getting less likely to accord greed the moral and aesthetic camouflage that the arts once extended to it. That is undoubtedly social progress, even if it is creating an economic crisis for the kind of music to which I have devoted my life.

Peterson attributes this desertion, this *trahison des clercs,* to a lowered perceived social advantage in highbrow taste. "A number of social processes at work over the past century," he writes, "make exclusion increasingly difficult. Rising levels of living, broader education, and presentation of the arts via the media have made elite aesthetic taste more accessible to wider segments of the population, devaluing the arts as markers of exclusion."[151]

This would account for the revulsion evident in the writings we've been sampling, by such as Clement Greenberg or Hannah Arendt, that, as we have seen, react to middlebrow efforts to popularize high art the way the Family Research Council reacts to gay weddings. Spread implies devaluation. And while I too regret the devaluation of what I value, and while I too see that the spread has led to lessened commitment and, of course, the loss of social capital,[152] I cannot join the gram-

---

149. William Robin, "The Success of a Somber Symphony," *New York Times,* 11 June 2017, Arts and Leisure, 11.

150. Sony Masterworks SK66782 (2000).

151. Richard A. Peterson and Roger M. Kern, "Changing Highbrow Taste: From Snob to Omnivore," *American Sociological Review* 61 (1996): 900–907, at 905.

152. See Richard A. Peterson, "The Rise and Fall of Highbrow Snobbery as a Status Marker," *Poetics* 25 (1997): 75–92.

mar schoolboys in righteous revanchist wrath. I remember too well the debate between George Steiner, the proudest of latter-day highbrows, and Joseph Brodsky, the ex-Soviet poet, on the subject of art and democracy. Steiner recapitulated the indictment he had made in his now-notorious essay of 1981, "The Archives of Eden," in which he took the highbrow/middlebrow model to its logical extreme, projecting it on a vast historical and geographical canvas. There are places in this essay that it is hard to believe were written by an actual American intellectual rather than by a character escaped from a novel by Ayn Rand; for example:

> Ninety-nine per cent of humanity conducts lives either of severe deprivation—physical, emotional, cerebral—or contributes nothing to the sum of insight, of beauty, of moral trial in our civil condition. It is a Socrates, a Mozart, a Gauss or a Galileo who, in some degree, compensate for man. It is they who, on fragile occasion, redeem the cruel, imbecile mess which we dignify with the name of history.[153]

Never have indefinite articles done more spectacularly pretentious work (*a* Socrates, *a* Mozart). This is truly the lunatic fringe of elitism. Steiner goes on from there to note that the relationship between European and American culture is precisely that which, in my interpretation, obtains between the highbrow and the middlebrow: "The dominant apparatus of American high culture," he writes, in that pompously imprecise diction of his, "is *that of custody*" and (I'll add) dissemination (281; emphasis emphatically his). Europe creates the masterpieces; America builds the museums and creates the means of diffusing the masterpieces of Europe through "a totally superficial and mendacious populist ideal of general education" (294). How could it be otherwise, Steiner asks, when "the correlations between extreme creativity . . . and political justice are, to a significant degree at least, negative" (300). And finding himself this far out on a limb, he goes all the way, saw in hand, to the eugenic extreme:

> it may well be that the ethnic-demographic elements in the successive waves of American settlement are "Darwinian negative," that they embody the brilliant survival of an anti-historical species, where "anti-historianism" would entail an abdication from those adaptive mechanisms of tragic intellectuality, of ideological "caring" (Kierkegaard's, Heidegger's word *Sorge*) which are indispensable to cultural creation of the first rank. Those who abandoned the various infernos of social discrimination and tyrannical rule in Europe were not, perhaps, the bold and shaping spirits, but very ordinary human beings who could "no longer take it." (284)

---

153. George Steiner, "The Archives of Eden," *Salmagundi*, no. 50/51 (Fall 1980–Winter 1981): 57–89; reprinted in Steiner, *No Passion Spent* (New Haven, CT: Yale University Press, 1996), 266–303, at 274 (further page references will be made in the main text).

Shades of Nordau's *Degeneration!* America, by attracting the tired, the poor, the huddled masses, the wretched refuse, the homeless, the tempest-tost, became the land created by, of, and for a bunch of artistically impotent losers.[154]

To which the immigrant Joseph Brodsky, who had decided he could no longer take what the Soviet Union was handing out, replied, "Yes, but liberty is the greatest masterpiece."[155] Brodsky's recognition and acceptance of a precious home truth—that the attribution of moral value to the aesthetic is a sham, despite all that it has done to engender and sustain the middlebrow—consoles me. (And vindicates my grandparents and their generation, who, I have always believed, showed a formidable degree of courage in forsaking the hostile Russian Empire for America and its risky promises.) And that is why I do not deplore what Richard Peterson called "the emergence of the omnivore" to supplant all brows but the least pretentious of them.

Despite his initial cautious reluctance to see the new taste breakdown as evidence of broad social changes, Peterson did speculate in 1992 about possible reasons for it. The demographics that Steiner abhorred, and the spread of multiculturalism (though the word was not yet in wide circulation at the time of his writing), were of course factors. (In a slightly later study, Peterson speaks of omnivorousness as arising when "the ethnocentrism central to snobbish elitism is replaced by cultural relativism.")[156] The point that speaks most forcefully to me is the one he places first and asserts most plainly: "The fundamental humanist belief in the moral superiority of fine culture," he proposes, "was sharply contradicted by the realities of the two World Wars" (255). I have no sociological data to back that up, but it certainly accords with my own perceptions and convictions.

I am led back to George Steiner, and to a place I have often visited in my writings: the interview with a *New York Times* reporter in which he confessed himself unable "to explain those who sing Schubert in the evening and torture in the morning.... I'm going to the end of my life haunted more and more by the question 'Why did the humanities not humanize?' I don't have an answer."[157] This pathetic admission of one who has never been able to shake his humanist illusions in the light of the "realities" to which Peterson called attention has been haunting me now for almost twenty years. I quoted it in a 2007 article (which Peter Franklin was kind enough to compliment in the *JRMA* symposium), where I followed it with a little homily of my own: Steiner's question—"Why did the humanities not

---

154. Americans will recognize here the allusions (all the way down to its idiosyncratic spellings) to "The New Colossus," the poem by Emma Lazarus (1849–87) that celebrated the dedication of the Statue of Liberty and is now immortalized inside the pedestal on a plaque.

155. Quoted in James Wood, *The Broken Estate: Essays on Literature and Belief* (New York: Picador, 1999), 172.

156. Peterson and Kern, "Changing Highbrow Taste," 904.

157. Peter Applebome, "A Humanist and Elitist? Perhaps," *New York Times*, 18 April 1998.

humanize?"—was the wrong question, I wrote. "It is all too obvious by now that teaching people that their love of Schubert makes them better people teaches them nothing but vainglory, and inspires attitudes that are the very opposite of humane."[158] I even allowed Steiner's question and a condensed echo of my comment into The Ox, where it meant somewhat compromising a stance—that of the detached reporter—which I otherwise tried very hard there to maintain.[159]

It seems to me by now a truism that the Nazis put paid to our assumptions about the inherent morality of the fine arts. But I still get backtalk. The easiest evasion is to seek the insulation of tautology. Anna Goldsworthy, writing in the Australian journal *The Monthly*, allowed that "singing Schubert is clearly not enough to cure genocidal impulses. But is it possible to make a more modest claim on the music's behalf? If we properly engage with it, surely it offers an experience of empathy."[160]

Properly is the amulet word this time. We listen properly, the Nazi's didn't. For the third time, fiddlesticks. More tortuous is the evasion by Gary Gutting, the philosopher I have already quoted in reference to Virginia Woolf's "snobocratic" critique of the middlebrow. He willfully misreads my objection to the question "Why did the humanities not humanize?"

> Taruskin assumes we are telling people that their ability to love Schubert's extraordinary music is a result of their already being morally superior persons. Rather, I would say, our love of Schubert opens us to experiences that can help us move to a higher moral level.... Profound moral transformation is a result of loving Schubert's music, not its cause.[161]

But this gets it totally backwards, Steiner as well as me. Steiner knew which was the cart and which the horse. What does it mean to "humanize," if not that loving Schubert makes us better, or that it "opens us to experiences that . . . move us to a higher level"? That was the claim Steiner made, the very claim I reject. Love of Schubert, I think the Nazis have sufficiently proved (by not being "moved . . . to profound moral transformation" with the rest of us), is unrelated to our moral character. And I think George Steiner has sufficiently proved that love of Schubert offers no antidote to smug conceit.

---

158. R. Taruskin "The Musical Mystique," in Taruskin, *The Danger of Music*, 344.

159. Taruskin, *Oxford History of Western Music* 3:783, where Steiner's question is placed in the context of the "[Matthew] Arnoldian art-religion."

160. Anna Goldsworthy, "The Lost Art of Listening: Has Classical Music Become Irrelevant?" *The Monthly*, October 2015, www.themonthly.com.au/issue/2015/october/1443621600/anna-goldsworthy/lost-art-listening.

161. Gutting, *What Philosophy Can Do*, 217.

Without a moral claim, what is left of our brows? Just taste, which, to remind you, Bourdieu defined as "manifested preference."[162] The definition is important: it shows why *de gustibus non est disputandum* gets it wrong. We incessantly declare and dispute, in pursuit of social capital or (as it used to be called) social advantage, the very thing that the proverb tells us is beyond dispute. In an important sense, then, our tastes are not even tastes unless we are disputing them. As long as there was perceived social advantage in a taste for high art, and as long as its pursuit mandated the negation and avoidance of the low, the middlebrow could thrive—but, much more vitally, so could high art itself in countries, like the United States, without a tradition of aristocratic patronage. The middlebrow was part of the support system that sustained the art that could not pay its way, of which classical music was perhaps the archetype. The middlebrow's much-deplored, easily derided commercial enterprises gave classical music a purchase it now seems to be losing irreversibly.

The evidence is all around us. One of many death knells now sounding in the daily press was an article by Michael Cooper, the classical music reporter for the *New York Times* (which, by the way, now runs classical music reviews only twice a week). It appeared on 15 November 2016 under the headline "It's Official: Many Orchestras Are Now Charities," and documented a decisive shift in the balance from ticket sales to subsidies from individual donors in the budgets of American symphony orchestras: a reversion, you might say, to aristocratic patronage, and testimony to the death of the middlebrow. How long can individual donors take up the slack? More pointedly, how much longer will they wish to do so?

Sociologists working in the wake of Richard Peterson confirm his status as our Cassandra. They are showing that today's "highly educated youngsters are less inclined toward highbrow culture than their older counterparts." They "do not pursue an elitist lifestyle, despite the fact that they meet the intellectual prerequisites traditionally assumed to lead to such a lifestyle."[163] These findings, which I quote from the work of a Dutch sociologist, are something I can confirm anecdotally by observing my own now-grownup children, who (as far as I can judge) do not even practice what sociologists call "symbolic exclusion," the most elementary form of taste assertion.[164]

Why am I watching all of this with such equanimity? Is it a variety of Reinhold Niebuhr's Serenity Prayer (that is, knowing what it is that is beyond your control, and accepting it)? Or am I after all what Ian Pace and Paul Harper-Scott have

---

162. Bourdieu, *Distinction*, 56.

163. Koen van Eijek, "Richard A. Peterson and the Culture of Consumption," *Poetics* 28 (2000): 207–24, at 209.

164. See Bethany Bryson, "'Anything but Heavy Metal': Symbolic Exclusion and Musical Dislikes," *American Sociological Review* 61 (1996): 884–900.

accused me of being—an agent of the neoliberal conspiracy? Or could it possibly be a touch of the fatalism Sergey Diaghilev once expressed in a toast he tendered in the revolutionary year 1905:

> We are witnesses of the greatest moment of summing up in history, in the name of a new and unknown culture, which will be created by us, and which will also sweep us away. That is why, without fear or misgiving, I raise my glass to ruined walls of the beautiful palaces, as well as to the new commandments of a new aesthetic. The only wish that I . . . can express, is that the forthcoming struggle should not damage the amenities of life, and that the death should be as beautiful and as illuminating as the resurrection.[165]

No, nothing as grand as that. I think it is simply that I realize, with Joseph Brodsky, that there can after all be more important things than what may matter most to me.

---

165. Quoted in Arnold Haskell (in collaboration with Walter Nouvel), *Diaghileff: His Artistic and Private Life* (New York: Simon & Schuster, 1935), 137.

13

A Walking Translation?

On musicology east and west

I

So, who do you suppose might have written this:

> A musical work possesses true being (i.e., becomes a fact) only when it is reproduced by someone and perceived by someone. It is indisputable that "fact" implies both a certain state of mind on the part of the perceiver and a definite creative consciousness at the moment of conception, realization, and configuration of the art work in question.[1]

No, not Husserl or Heidegger or Ingarden, although whoever wrote it is obviously to be classed, knowingly or not, among the phenomenologists. But there is a whiff here as well of social transaction and cognitive psychology, and an insistence on agency, which gives it a rather modern ring as a musicological pronouncement. It's the kind of thing that "new musicologists" in America were saying in the 1980s and 90s, especially when arguing with musical philologists or music analysts. It's the kind of thing that *I* might have said back then, even if I wouldn't have used words like "true being" or "creative consciousness." So it may be a bit of a surprise to learn that these words come from a book that was published in Petrograd—

Originally presented as keynote address at the conference "Found in Translation," University of Chicago, 15 April 2016.

1. A. V. Finagin, "Sistematika muzïkal'no-teoreticheskikh znaniy," in *De Musica: Sbornik statey*, ed. Igor Glebov (Petrograd: Petrogradskaya gosudarstvennaya akademicheskaya filarmoniya, 1923), 185; quoted in Tatyana Bukina, *Muzïkal'naya nauka v Rossii 1920–2000-kh godov: Ocherki kul'turnoy istorii* (St. Petersburg: Izdatel'stvo RKhGA, 2010), 45–46.

already you know from that name not only where it was published but also when—in 1923 (that is, slightly before the work of Heidegger or Ingarden that it might seem to recall). The book, an anthology of essays, was called *De Musica;* it was edited by Igor Glebov, who in those days reserved his actual given name, Boris Asafiev, for his compositions rather than his musicological publications; and the author of the essay in question was a man who is not as well remembered today as his *chef* Asafiev, but who is well worth rediscovering: Alexey Vasil'yevich Finagin (1890–1942), a remarkable scholar who at the time was the *uchyonïy sekretar'* (executive secretary), under Asafiev, of the Russian Institute for the History of the Arts (Rossiyskiy institut istorii iskusstv, or RIII).

I had been reading about Finagin and his relationship to his *chef* in the dissertation, completed in 2015, of my pupil Olga Panteleeva, who came to us at Berkeley after graduating from the masters program at the University of Utrecht, where she had studied with Karl Kügle, and before that from the St. Petersburg Conservatory, where she was the pupil of Olga Manulkina and Lyudmila Kovnatskaya. As I put it in a memoir I was asked to contribute to Mila Kovnatskaya's festschrift, through Olga Panteleeva our musicological families had joined—and, in a larger sense, in her the traditions of Russian, western European, and Anglo-American musicology had all been cross-bred.[2]

She was, and is, very conscious of her unique status—the first Russian musicologist (non-*émigré*, though I guess we'll see) to go through an American graduate program and qualify as a PhD. That consciousness, plus the fact that at Berkeley she had to go through an intensive introductory course required of all our graduate students in the history of musicology and its many issues and debates, impelled her to attempt, in her dissertation and in her subsequent work as well, to supplement the existing literature on the history of musicology with a study focused on Russia.[3] She was particularly interested in observing and interpreting the cross-over from prerevolutionary, fairly casual, music history instruction at the St. Petersburg Conservatory, where the subject was taught by the venerable Liberio (or, in Russian, Liveriy) Sacchetti (1852–1916), the son of an Italian flautist who was hired to play in the orchestra of the St. Petersburg Imperial Theaters, to the professionalized musicology of the early Soviet period, as preeminently exemplified by Asafiev and the institute that he and Finagin administered.

2. R. Taruskin, "Насколько я помню . . ." (As far as I remember . . .), trans. Anastasia Spiridonova and Vladimir Khavrov, in *Liber amicorum Lyudmile Kovnatskoy,* ed. Olga Manulkina, Lidia Ader, and Nin Drozdetskaya (St. Petersburg: BiblioRossika), 536–39.

3. Olga Panteleeva, "Formation of Russian Musicology from Sacchetti to Asafyev, 1885–1931" (PhD diss., University of California, Berkeley, 2015). Early spin-offs include "St Petersburg Conservatory and the Beginnings of Russian Musicology," in *Rimsky-Korsakov and His World,* ed. Marina Frolova-Walker (Princeton, NJ: Princeton University Press, 2018), 223–48; and "How Soviet Musicology Became Marxist," *Slavonic and East European Review* 97 (2019): 73–109.

The transition she traced looked surprisingly similar to that traced by Kevin Karnes in a recent book that described the disciplinary trajectory from Eduard Hanslick to Guido Adler.[4] Russian musicology fought the same battles on its way to professionalization between idealists and positivists. The Russian world, though isolated and seemingly marginal in the eyes of Western observers who could not penetrate the barrier of language and alphabet, was aware of the international philosophical and institutional currents that attended the establishment of musicology as an academic discipline, first in Germany, thence throughout the Western world, and responsive to them.

The musicological culture wars were fought under various banners and rubrics. Their later Russian phases have been traced by Tatyana Bukina in a recent monograph, *Musical Scholarship in Russia, 1920–2000*,[5] a book I read with keen interest as I began preparing this essay. Bukina writes not as a dispassionate chronicler but as an advocate of the kind of musicology that was established at the RIII, which she calls sociocultural, the kind exemplified by the quotation from Finagin that furnished this discussion with its starting point, in which the emphasis is placed not on musical texts as such but on the *muzïkal'no-khudozhestvennïy fakt*, the "art-musical fact" as Finagin defined it, which Bukina characterizes as "the unique moment of the projection and reception of music in a concrete situation, accentuating the contextuality (both cultural and social) of any artistic event."[6]

As I say, this—minus the romantic insistence on uniqueness—is quite close to what I take to be good musicological practice in today's intellectual climate, when musicology and ethnomusicology are converging and music is often treated as a verb rather than a noun,[7] and I am happy to acknowledge an intellectual kinship with some of the musicological ideas of the early Soviet period, described by Panteleeva and Bukina, that provided the soil in which, for example, Asafiev's *intonatsiya* theory was rooted.[8] That is what I have been "finding in translation"—to invoke, albeit in a somewhat roundabout or figurative way, the designated theme this conference has been convened to address. The translation that interests me is the way in which the preoccupations and inclinations that many of us share have been variously inflected by the Russian and, well, non-Russian (not to say

---

4. Kevin Karnes, *Music, Criticism, and the Challenge of History: Shaping Modern Musical Thought in Late Nineteenth-Century Vienna* (New York: Oxford University Press, 2008).

5. Bukina, *Muzïkal'naya nauka v Rossii 1920–2000-kh godov*.

6. " ... уникальный момент звучания и восприятия музыки в конкретной ситуации, акцентирующий контекстуальность (в том числе культурную и социальную) любого художественного события" (ibid., 45).

7. Cf. Chistopher Small, *Musicking: The Meanings of Performing and Listening* (Middletown, CT: Wesleyan University Press, 1998).

8. Explicated for Anglophone readers in Malcolm H. Brown, "The Soviet Russian Concepts of 'Intonazia' and 'Musical Imagery,'" *Musical Quarterly* 60 (1974): 557–567.

"Western") environments in which we here have all been socialized into our habitus, as *bon père* Bourdieu might say.

Not that I was at all surprised to discover, or rediscover, that intellectual kinship. I have long been aware that many of the positions and principles to which I have tended as my work has evolved are congruent with certain varieties of Russian, and more specifically Soviet, thinking about music. Indeed, if I had not noticed this congruence myself, I would have been informed of it by those who have commented on my work, often in a critical or even hostile vein. I have long been aware that, to put it crudely and somewhat caricaturally, the end of the Cold War had an interesting effect on musicology, whereby the Russian and the non-Russian *habitūs* underwent opposing transformations, as if they were two pendulums swinging in opposite directions.

Were we to caricature the Anglo-American and Soviet brands at their extremes, they would exemplify "formalism" and "vulgar sociologism" respectively. That is to say, the Anglo-American would be wholly preoccupied with deducing methods of composition—or, more narrowly, principles of organization—from the evidence of musical texts, interested in nothing but how they were made, while the Soviet would be fixated on constructing a thinly yet rigidly causal nexus between the social situation of a musical practice and its products. (For a good parody of that kind of vulgar sociologism you can read the seventh chapter of Virgil Thomson's delightful old book *The State of Music*, called "Why Composers Write How: The Economic Determinism of Musical Style.")[9] From the Western perspective, the second of these stances would be described as political or ideological, the first as objective and therefore unaffected by politics. From the opposite (that is, economic-determinist) perspective, the Western stance would be dismissed as empty and sterile, the Soviet as revealing the true content of the music and explaining both its *raison d'être* and its effect.

And with the passing of the Cold War, as if by a wave of a magic wand, all of a sudden we Westerners were interested in social and political issues and post-Soviet Russians were interested in poetics and pure or immanent analysis. There is a grain of truth in this simplified narrative, and even a (smaller) grain of truth in the easy explanation for it, namely that each side was now free to revel in what had formerly been stigmatized or forbidden. Chronology could seemingly be adduced in support. "New musicology" got its start in the West at just about the same time as the start of "*glasnost*' and *perestroika*" in the tottering Soviet Union. My very public debate with Allen Forte over his supremely formalistic analytical method, often described in retrospect as a turning point in our disciplinary history, took place during the first year of Gorbachev's tenure as the last Soviet *gensek*.[10]

---

9. Virgil Thomson, *The State of Music* (New York: William Morrow, 1939), 86–137.
10. Letter to the Editor from Richard Taruskin, and Letter to the Editor in Reply to Richard Taruskin from Allen Forte, *Music Analysis* 5 (1986): 313–37.

At the same time, modernism, *bête noire* of new musicologist and old commissar alike, began gaining ground in Russia, the late ascendency of Edison Denisov being the prime symptom. Denisov had been in 1979 the ringleader of the so-called *khrennikovskaya semyorka*, the "Khrennikov Seven," a group of renegade composers so characterized and excoriated by Tikhon Khrennikov in the *otchotnïy doklad* or keynote report that he gave ex officio as general secretary of the Union of Soviet Composers at the union's sixth congress. In the mid-eighties, timed almost exactly with the advent of Gorbachev, Denisov was elected to the union's board of seven secretaries working alongside Khrennikov. And in 1990 he became the titular head of the revived ASM, or Assotsiatsiya sovremennoy muzïki (Association for Contemporary Music), a promotional agency for modernist music organized in the last year of Soviet rule not in opposition to the union but as an arm of it. This was real musical *perestroika*. It was taking place right alongside the attempted political perestroika that was meant to preserve the Soviet regime but instead destroyed it. And it was taking place alongside the opposite swing of the pendulum in western Europe, where the older generation of avant-gardists was mellowing alarmingly.

Here the corresponding symptom might be György Ligeti and his Horn Trio of 1982, which looms now in retrospect as another watershed, introducing a phase not only in Ligeti's output but in many outputs, to which the weirdly anomalous label "non-atonal" has been attached.[11] Ligeti explained what he was doing by, characteristically, denying that it was a retreat, but nevertheless acknowledging, in an interview with Claude Samuel, that "the avant-garde, to which I am said to belong, has become academic."[12] He said that at the beginning of the 1980s. By the end of the nineties, even Pierre Boulez, asked by an interviewer why performances of the music of the midcentury avant-garde had become infrequent, did not answer with fulminations against the stupidity of audiences, the way everyone loved to hear him do again and again, but with the admission that "perhaps we did not take sufficiently into account the way music is perceived by the listener."[13]

That interview with Boulez was published under the headline "What Happened When the Wall Came Down?" It was one of the journalistic clichés of the period to correlate the fall of the Western avant-garde with the fall of Soviet totalitarianism, or, conversely, with the rise of neoliberalism. And here, too, I have firsthand experience to report, since (although I regard myself at best as an equivocal repre-

---

11. Cf. Mike Searby, "Ligeti's 'Third Way': 'Non-Atonal' Elements in the Horn Trio," *Tempo*, no. 216 (April 2001): 17–22.

12. Claude Samuel, "Entretien avec György Ligeti" (1981), trans. Terence Kilmartin, in *Ligeti in Conversation* (London: Eulenburg Books, 1983), 123.

13. Stephen Johnson, "What Happened When the Wall Came Down?" *BBC Music Magazine*, September 2002, available at www.stephen-johnson.co.uk/publications/what-happened-when-the-wall-came-down.

sentative of "new musicology," and I am sure that most quondam new musicologists would agree), my work has been attacked in the West as "neoliberal" even as it has been attacked in the post-Soviet East as tainted with "vulgar sociologism."[14] Being attacked from both sides is always reassuring; it gives one a sense of stability. And of course nostalgics hankering after the old order, whether Soviet or avant-garde, always attempt to deny that the end of the Cold War had anything to do with the arts, or with scholarship, or *a fortiori* with arts scholarship.

But still, could all of this have been a coincidence? No, not a coincidence, though it is all too easy to oversimplify the story by exaggerating the correlation or deducing from it a spurious causality. Here is where I found Bukina's survey to be especially of use. It reminded me that formalism and vulgar sociologism—or, to put it positively, immanent analytical approaches and sociocultural ones—had been in a dialectical relationship throughout the history of Soviet and post-Soviet musicology, just as they had always been in the West, where I was up close to it and didn't need reminding. And there has always been a significant body of work on both sides that combined or synthesized the approaches, so that they don't have to be regarded as rigidly antithetical. That, then, is what I have found in translation—that is, what I have been rethinking of late: that the styles of musicology as practiced east and west are not in an antagonistic or inflexibly reciprocal relationship, but in a complex counterpoint in which both traditions have responded to internal and external pressures in ways that can be fruitfully compared. Here I'll sketch a few.

II

As already indicated, Bukina's book is not just a survey but in significant measure a polemic as well. She wants to reinstate sociocultural music scholarship—the kind pioneered by Asafiev and Finagin—against what she convincingly shows to have been the main current in recent Russian musicology. (A comparably against-the-grain project *chez nous*, in the mirror relationship already observed, might be

---

14. See J. P. E. Harper-Scott, *The Quilting Points of Musical Modernism* (Cambridge: Cambridge University Press, 2012), chapter 1 ("Modernism As We Know It, Ideology, and the Quilting Point"), in which I am accused of xenophobia; for vulgar sociologism, see Levon Hakobian's tirade, referenced in note 57 below. Alexander Belonenko, ranting from a Soviet-nostalgic, chauvinistic perspective, goes startlingly far into paranoiac territory: "Such costly, unprofitable publications [as the six-volume hardbound edition of *The Oxford History of Western Music*] cannot materialize fortuitously, in the interests of publishers or the academy alone. Such massive works appear, as a rule, by order of the government. And in the given instance we are dealing with propaganda literature. The reason for the appearance of Taruskin's work, or more precisely its commissioning, is clear enough. It lies in the new historical situation, when the USA has felt itself to be the sole master of the world, a new Rome, and when the new Carthage, the Soviet Union, has fallen" (A. S. Belonenko, "Proshloye i budushcheye klassicheskoy muzïki evropeyskoy traditsii. Zametki po povodu monografii *The Oxford History of Western Music*: Part 1," *Vestnik Sankt-Peterburgskogo Universiteta*, seriya 15, no. 3 [2015]: 160–218, at 214–15).

identified with the books by music theorists that appeared in the 1990s in reaction to the rise of "new musicology," such as Pieter van den Toorn's *Music, Politics, and the Academy* of 1996). Bukina's first task was to explain why the Asafiev-Finagin method, which had served so well to put Soviet musicology on a secure, and (in Russia) unprecedented, professional footing, lost its dominant position. Her explanation is provocative for the light it sheds on what has become one of the main debates among historians in the wake of the Soviet collapse: namely, the question whether the Soviet regime actually exercised the sort of control we in the West tend casually to assume that it did over aspects of its citizens' lives and activities—that is to say, the question of "totalitarianism."

No political regime is omnipotent, although some have wished to be. The extent to which the attempt to exercise total control succeeds or fails is the issue that scholars now so zealously debate. The key figure in the case of the Soviet regime has been Sheila Fitzpatrick, who has argued vigorously that the complexity of modern society and the inertia of institutions have effectively foiled all attempts at total control, and that the ways in which individual citizens have protected their interests by gaming the system is the area that will best repay historical investigation.[15] This approach has been implemented in the musical sphere most effectively in Russia by Leonid Maksimenkov, and in this country by Kiril Tomoff in his history of the Union of Soviet Composers.[16]

Bukina makes the provocative suggestion that sociocultural musicology began losing ground long before the end of the Soviet regime; in fact, it began to lose ground exactly when it became *de rigueur* in Soviet scholarship. As early as Anatoliy Lunacharsky, the first People's Commissar of Enlightenment (whose capacious bailiwick took in education and culture), the Soviet regime adopted an instrumental view of the humanistic disciplines, whereby the sociological study of the arts could function as what Bukina calls "a lever of cultural policy and a conduit of ideological discourse into the field of music."[17] I'm quoting her for the sake of the apt metaphors, not because the idea is particularly newsworthy. We all know that publication in Soviet times had to serve what the regime regarded as a positive or beneficent social (i.e., propagandistic) purpose.

Some writers found this a burden, others (the lucky ones) a pleasure. One who surely found it a pleasure—and I say this on the basis of having read a lot of his work, both scholarly and journalistic—was Georgiy Nikitich Khubov (1902–81), a

---

15. The programmatic statement of this position is Sheila Fitzpatrick, "New Perspectives on Stalinism," *Russian Review* 45 (1986): 357–73. It had been preceded, of course, by similar revisionary treatments of Nazism, beginning with Hugh Trevor-Roper's in *The Last Days of Hitler* (1947).

16. Leonid Maksimenkov, *Sumbur vmesto muzïki: Stalinskaya kul'turnaya revolyutsiya 1936–1938* (Moscow: Yuridicheskaya kniga, 1997); Kirill Tomoff, *Creative Union: The Professional Organization of Soviet Composers 1939–1953* (Ithaca, NY: Cornell University Press, 2006).

17. Bukina, *Muzïkal'naya nauka*, 61.

particularly *partiynïy*, or Party-minded, critic and scholar, who was an especially influential presence in Soviet musicography in the 1930s, when he was simultaneously the deputy editor (*zamestitel' glavnogo redaktora*) of *Sovetskaya muzïka*, the official organ of the just-organized Union of Soviet Composers; the editor responsible for the music articles in the *Bol'shaya sovetskaya èntsiklopediya;* and a *dotsent* (associate professor, more or less) at the Moscow Conservatory, where in 1935 he initiated courses in the history of Soviet music.

One of the first books I purchased during my year as an exchange student at the Moscow Conservatory in 1971–72 was Khubov's monograph on Borodin, published in 1933 to commemorate the composer's centenary (hence already almost forty years old when I read it), for which I plunked down thirty kopecks at the *bukinisticheskiy* counter at Dom Knigi, the big store on Prospekt Kalinina (now Novïy Arbat). I carried it around with me for a couple of weeks, and have the bus tickets (used as bookmarks) to prove it. I found it fascinating reading, not for what it taught me about Borodin, but for what it taught me about the Soviet musical historiography of its period. I have never cited it in my scholarly work—to do so would have been very bad form in the American academy of those days, when "metamusicology" was not a recognized subfield of the discipline—but today I want to describe it in some detail.

It was, the author asserted, only a first step toward a complete scholarly assessment of Borodin's work, a project that, he admitted, would "obviously materialize as the result of collective labor." His aim was to lay the cornerstone, which meant "showing in its general features the *klassovaya sushchnost'* [the "class essence"] of his quantitatively modest but, in terms of its artistic significance, enormous body of work."[18] That was the gist of the book's preface ("Ot avtora"). In the introduction that follows, that class essence is identified with the "enlightened liberal" layer of the contemporary Russian bourgeoisie, and Borodin's musical work is viewed as an adjunct to his scientific profession: "Borodin," Khubov asserted, "directly and in full consciousness carried out all his musical endeavors in conjunction with his primary civic-scientific activities" (*osnovnoy obshchestvenno-nauchnoy deyatel'nosti*), so that his musical works became "in essence, a national epic of Russian liberalism in the reformist era" (*v sushchnosti—national'naya èpopeya rossiyskogo liberalizm poreformennoy epokhi*) (3, 5).

That is the book's thesis. The rest is the demonstration and justification. The method is that of the funnel, beginning at the wide end with a first chapter called "'Prosvetiteli' i 'kuchka'" (Educators of the people, and the kuchka), referring to the two overlapping social groups to which Borodin belonged. There are two epigraphs— the first from Engels, to the effect that economic conditions are always the decisive influence on history, the second from Lenin, on the difference between a *prosvetitel'*

---

18. "Ot avtora," in Georgiy Khubov, *A. P. Borodin* (Moscow: Ogiz/Muzgiz, 1933), 2. Further references to this book will be made in the main text.

and a *narodnik* (an enlightener and a populist): "The enlightener believes in a given societal development, for he has not noticed its inherent contradictions; the populist fights a given societal development, for he has already noticed these contradictions." And, just to show you how wide that wide lip of the funnel was, here is the opening sentence from the body of the book: "If at the very beginning of the nineteenth century obvious signs of capitalist development were already beginning to appear, setting the course for upper-class Russia, the middle of the century marked the decisive turning point for the unruly and contradictory development of economic relations in old Russia" (7). The first chapter is entirely about that economic development, illustrated with tables detailing imports and exports, and many more quotations from Engels and Lenin, from the liberal historian Konstantin Kavelin (1818–85), and even from Tsar Alexander II—but then, in the first narrowing of the funnel, the *moguchaya kuchka* is introduced within the context of economic development and political reform, and we begin to hear from Vladimir Stasov alongside Engels and Lenin, and from an article from *Proletarskiy muzïkant* (the organ of the recently dissolved RAPM, the Russian Association of Proletarian Musicians) by the musicologist Anatoliy Aleksandrovich Groman-Solovtsov (1898–1965), called "The Class Roots of Kuchkism in the Light of Lenin's Views on Social Development in Russia" (*Klassovïye korni kuchkizma v svete leninskikh vzglyadov na obshchestvennoye razvitiye Rossii*).

From here on the funnel narrows quickly and radically, into a far more familiar sort of life-and-works narrative. But that narrative now serves an illustrative function in support of the theses stated in the introduction. Compared with the sociocultural music scholarship of the 1920s, Khubov's brand shows a great narrowing of purview in conformity with a well-established historical framework, supported by an even narrower range of authorities, all of which could be viewed either as an ideological constraint on the range of investigation and interpretation, or as a trustworthy guide that ensures an accurate analysis of the data, leading to reliable conclusions. Khubov obviously regarded it the more optimistic way, typical of Marxist critics, and not only in Marxist states. His descriptions of Borodin's works remind me at times of Ernest Gellner's variant of the old "black cat in a dark room" metaphor: "There is an old East European joke," Gellner once wrote,

> concerning the differences between science, philosophy, and Marxism. What is science? It is trying to catch a very small black cat in a very large, entirely dark room. What is philosophy? It is trying to catch a very small black cat in a very large, entirely dark room, when it is not there. What is Marxism? It is trying to catch a very small black cat in a very large, entirely dark room when it is not there, and pretending that one has caught it and knows all about it.[19]

19. Ernest Gellner, Review of *The Frankfurt School* by Rolf Wiggershaus and *Intellectuals in Exile* by Klaus-Dieter Krohn, *Times Literary Supplement*, 23 September 1994, 3–5, at 3.

Gellner was telling this joke at the expense of the Frankfurt School, so of course I found it irresistible. But it applies as well, I think, to Khubov's pages on Borodin's *In Central Asia,* in which the author performs an exemplary Marxist *razoblacheniye* or "unmasking," reading with utter confidence between the lines and against the grain so that the piece can illustrate his theses. The "reformist era," Khubov's term for Borodin's era, is called that after the liberal reforms of Alexander II, particularly the abolition of serfdom. But Alexander II was not just the tsar-emancipator. He was also preeminently the tsar-imperialist. It was under Alexander II that what Russians still call Central Asia was conquered and annexed to the Russian Empire. Borodin composed *In Central Asia* in 1880 to accompany one of a series of *tableaux vivants,* "living pictures from Russian history, of a patriotic character" (*zhivïye kartinï iz russkoy istorii, patrioticheskogo kharaktera*), which is why he called the piece a *simfonicheskaya kartina,* a symphonic picture. These tableaux were to be mounted as part of a celebration of the quarter century of Alexander II's reign, in explicit celebration of his imperialist triumphs. "However," Khubov interjects, "analysis of this work ... shows the profound contradictoriness of the inner fissure that was taking place in Borodin's creative development in this period of 'crisis' for Russian liberalism. Undoubtedly, Borodin was bound by the terms of the commission in composing this music, but those terms admitted various treatments, various ways of presenting the required theme" (104).

The program that Borodin provided with the music describes the appearance in the distance of a native caravan crossing the endless Central Asian steppe and its approach under Russian military guard. "Trustingly and fearlessly," Borodin writes in an epigraph, "it completes its long journey, protected by Russian military might." Anyone reading this will probably remember that the music consists, at the beginning, of a long-drawn-out note conveying the endlessness of the desert, then a motive in steady eighth-note motion conveying the motion of the caravan, and two themes, one in Russian style, played first by the clarinet and then by the horn, and one in *vostochnïy* or oriental style, played (inevitably) by the English horn, the orchestra's snake-charmer. At the climax, the two themes are montaged in counterpoint, and then everything dies away, leaving that long-drawn-out note, still conveying an endless expanse and an endless duration, to resume the representation of the impassive steppe.

Lest there be any doubt as to what all of this was designed to convey, Borodin actually wrote about performances of his symphonic picture abroad to his friend, the jurist and amateur cellist Ivan Ivanovich Gavrushkevich (1813–ca. 1899), remarking somewhat incredulously that "despite the unpopularity of the work's program (—it's all about the success of Russian arms in Central Asia!—) this music gets encored practically everywhere, and sometimes ... it gets repeated at the next concert b*y popular demand.*"[20] Khubov himself calls attention to certain repeated words in the program, particularly *mirnïy,* "peaceful" or "peaceable." "Russian arms," he writes, "are the bringer of peace and national prosperity—that, in essence, is the gist of the program as commissioned, wherein one easily sees a distinct enunciation of the nationalist-patriotic tendency of Russian imperialist policy in the East" (105). And yet, to the extent that the music sustains a sweet, harmonious mood, abetted by the neatly harmonized contrapuntal union of the Russian and the oriental themes, Borodin reveals his *"liberal optimism"* (Khubov's italics), by which he means Borodin's unwillingness to face, let alone portray, "the social contradictions of a dark reality," to which, by attempting to hide them, he only calls attention. "What is impossible in reality Borodin attempts to make possible in his art," Khubov writes,

> since from a truly realistic point of view this composition, with its juxtaposition of "Russian" and "oriental" themes, can in no way, whether by virtue of their character or by virtue of their development, correspond to "the success of Russian arms." ... This contradiction between his assignment and its fulfillment is very typical of Borodin, who has run up against the concrete thematics of contemporary reality. He not only did not see or wish to reveal the contradictions in Russian imperialist policy, but tried *symbolically* to combine (in a "peaceful harmony of interests") what was impossible." (108; italics original)

Black cat, at last I have you, Khubov might have said. Not only has he performed a *razoblacheniye* of Borodin's hidden contradictory and critical message in what is outwardly a celebration of Russian imperialism; he has also managed to portray Borodin as having performed a *razoblacheniye* of his own, a critical exposure of Russian imperialism. For make no mistake: "Borodin," Khubov assures us, "of course, inwardly understood" everything that Khubov has pointed out, and "having understood, found himself at a crossroads when it came to realizing the assignment that stood before him." His solution was neither to go the way of what Khubov calls *ura-patriotichnost'* (gung-ho patriotism, I guess we'd say)—which is why, Khubov suggests, Borodin's symphonic picture was received better in western Europe than at home; nor did he go the way of "revolutionary-democratic" exposure of political contradictions ("the way Musorgsky might have done," Khubov adds). Rather, "Borodin remained a liberal; and he chose *the middle way,* attempting to embody the assigned program in the style of a vaguely reconciliatory, romantically nationalist epic" (109).

My favorite part of this discussion is the gratuitous reference to Musorgsky and the revolutionary-democratic solution he might have achieved to the problem that

---

20. Letter of 6 May 1886, in *Pis'ma A. P. Borodina,* ed. S. A. Dianin, vol. 4 (Moscow-Leningrad: Muzgiz, 1950), 192.

Borodin's passive liberalism kept him from attempting. Surely Khubov knew that Musorgsky had also made a contribution to the planned twenty-fifth-anniversary celebration of Alexander II's reign. That contribution, a symphonic march called "Vzyatiye Karsa," or "The Taking of Kars," commemorated the last major operation of the Crimean War, Alexander's signal triumph in the first year of his reign. It, too, juxtaposes Russian and "oriental" themes, but does so in a more conventional way than Borodin's contrapuntal montage. In Musorgsky's march, the oriental theme, full of banal augmented seconds, provides the Trio before the triumphant Russian da capo, and the whole piece could not be more obviously *ura-patriotichnïy*. The view of Musorgsky as revolutionary democrat, which Khubov takes for granted, was pure Soviet fiction.

And what first seduced me into sociocultural musicology, the brand with which I suppose I am now identified, was my realization that the Soviet cliché about Musorgsky completely misread, indeed turned upside down, his *klassovaya sushchnost'* (his "class essence"), which was that of a dispossessed aristocrat, impoverished by Alexander II's reforms, of all social groups in the Russia of the *poreformennaya èpokha* among the most embittered and reactionary. Substantiating this point through a tandem of historical investigation and immanent analysis was perhaps the chief task of my book on Musorgsky,[21] and that tandem approach has been my method ever since. I emphasize this point because I have adopted what many have regarded as an approved Soviet method precisely so as to refute a Soviet orthodoxy.

III

Such a contentious path was no longer open to Soviet scholarship in the 1930s. Reliance on preconceived dogmatic truths, whether adhered to sincerely by committed Marxists like Khubov or submitted to as the price of publication, eventually discredited the sociocultural method in Soviet musicology, even as its orthodoxies were ever more stringently enforced. One of the most interesting chapters in Bukina's book describes precisely this process of enforcement and its consequences. The chapter is called "On the Path toward Socialist Realism: Investigations of Musical Culture during the Stalinist Period" (*Na puti k sotsialisticheskomy realizmu: Issledovaniya muzïkal'noy kul'turï v stalinskuyu èpokhu*). What it purports to demonstrate is that, once the theory of socialist realism had been enunciated—and this took place in 1934, the year after the publication of Khubov's book on Borodin—its principles were applied not only to artistic literature, but also to scholarship, and to historiography in particular, since historiography was most clearly identified with narrative and its attendant techniques.

---

21. R. Taruskin, *Musorgsky: Eight Essays and an Epilogue* (Princeton, NJ: Princeton University Press, 1993).

Again there is an obvious east-west "translation," a piquant correspondence between Bukina's account of Soviet musicology and some well-known recent Western theorizing on scholarly method. We are all familiar by now with Hayden White's literary analyses of historical writing, in which he demonstrates the kinship between fictional and historiographical narratives and comes close—at any rate closer than I am willing to allow—to finding no essential difference between the two modes.[22] One of the reasons for my resistance to what I regard as White's complacency is probably my awareness of what Bukina has observed about Soviet historiography in the age of socialist realism, when historical narratives were required to conform to certain approved literary models (that is to say, model narratives), to the extent that, as she writes (paraphrasing the émigré historian Evgeniy Dobrenko in his book *The Political Economy of Socialist Realism*), "the discourse of history was transformed into a purely aesthetic, literary project."[23]

The principles of historiography were now demarcated the same way as were those of fiction and drama, according to the classic originary definition of socialist realism, given by Andrey Zhdanov himself in a speech to the inaugural congress of the Union of Soviet Writers. Delivered on 17 August 1934, it was titled "Soviet Literature—the Richest in Ideas and the Most Advanced Literature in the World" (*Sovetskaya literatura—samaya ideynaya, samaya peredovaya literatura v mire*), and the relevant passage was this:

> Comrade Stalin has called our writers engineers of human souls. What does that mean? What obligations does that title impose upon you?
>
> In the first place, it means knowing life so as to be able to depict it truthfully in works of art, depict it not in a scholastic, dead manner, not simply as "objective reality," but to depict reality in its revolutionary development.
>
> And at the same time, truthfulness and historical concreteness in artistic depictions must be combined with the task of ideologically transforming and educating the toiling people in the spirit of socialism. Such a method of artistic literature and literary criticism we call the method of socialist realism.[24]

---

22. See Hayden White, *The Content of the Form: Narrative Discourse and Historical Representation* (Baltimore: Johns Hopkins Press, 1990); also White, *Tropics of Discourse: Essays in Cultural Criticism* (Baltimore: Johns Hopkins Press, 1986), chap. 1.

23. Bukina, *Muzïkal'naya nauka*, 67.

24. "Товарищ Сталин назвал наших писателей инженерами человеческих душ. Что это значит? Какие обязанности накладывает на вас это звание?

"Это значит, во-первых, знать жизнь, чтобы уметь ее правдиво изобразить в художественных произведениях, изобразить не схоластически, не мертво, не просто как «объективную реальность», а изобразить действительность в ее революционном развитии.

"При этом правдивость и историческая конкретность художественного изображения должны сочетаться с задачей идейной переделки и воспитания трудящихся людей в духе социализма. Такой метод художественной литературы и литературной критики есть то, что мы называем методом социалистического реализма." Translation adapted from www.marxists.org/subject/art/lit_crit/sovietwritercongress/zdhanov.htm.

According to this method, literary works were to be judged by their effects. Applied to history, the method demanded that historical development be portrayed as progressive, i.e., that it show movement toward socialist or more narrowly Soviet goals; but also, and increasingly, that such narratives enhance national pride (assuredly a non-Marxist criterion).

As a crisp example of how these standards were transmitted and maintained, Bukina focuses on one of the most prominent historians of Russian music of the period, Tamara Nikolayevna Livanova (1909–86), whose particularly successful socialization into the profession as then practiced had made her a notorious figure in the history of Soviet scholarship. Livanova's source-critical study of 1938, *Essays and Materials Concerning the History of Russian Musical Culture* (*Ocherki i materialï po istorii russkoy muzïkal'noy kul'turï*), a pioneering study of Russian music in the eighteenth century,

> provoked at the end of the 1930s a stormy polemic in the art-scholarly press. What called forth particular critical complaint was the author's "excessive exaggeration" [the pleonasm is original: *chrezmernoye preuvelicheniye*] of the role played by the church and by western European influences in the formative period of our country's musical tradition and the corresponding "underestimation" of its popular [*narodnïye*] sources. With abundant citations from Engels and Chernïshevsky, the musicologist Ivan Ivanovich Martïnov [1908–74, father of the composer Vladimir Martïnov], utterly in the spirit of Stalinist "historical" logic, demonstrated that "Livanova's scholarly outlook is anti-historical and anti-people in its very essence." A little over a decade after this episode, in 1950, by then made wise [*umudrennaya*] by experience, T. N. Livanova pressed similar charges (albeit in terms not quite as categorical) against B. V. Asafiev's monograph, *Glinka*, in which the author, in her opinion, "does not always remind the reader with sufficient clarity that at no time and nowhere did Glinka ever waver in his originality."[25]

"So Livanova was a *bitaya!*" exclaimed a friend to whom I had sent a draft of this essay for comment. *Bitaya,* the feminine past participle of the verb "to beat," used here as a substantive, means "one beaten down." According to the Leninist principle of *kto kogo* ("who [will do it] to whom," originally intended to encapsulate the inescapable class struggle, but colloquially something closer to "dog eat dog"), those beaten today will become tomorrow's beaters; and that certainly applied to the dreaded Livanova.

Bukina credits this process of socialization with the gradual "eradication" of sociocultural musicology, even as it was being ostensibly promoted and refined, because it became increasingly obvious that historians were under pressure to fic-

---

25. Bukina, *Muzïkal'naya nauka,* 70. The citations are from I. I. Martïnov, "Iskazhennaya istoriya: O knige T. Livanovoy" (Distorted History: On a Book by T. Livanova), *Sovetskaya muzïka,* 1939, no. 5: 83; and T. N. Livanova, "B. V. Asaf'yev i russkaya glinkiana," in *M. I. Glinka: Sbornik materialov i statey,* ed. T. N. Livanova (Moscow-Leningrad: Muzgiz, 1950), 370.

tionalize (read: lie)—or, to use the euphemism she borrows from Dobrenko, to turn historical reportage and interpretation into an elaborate process of "representation and de-realization" (*reprezentatsiya/derealizatsiya*).[26]

I found it interesting to compare her characterization with the more detailed, and perhaps more sympathetic, account of Stalin-era music historiography in the work of a non-Russian scholar, Jiří Smrž, a Czech-born Canadian historian, whose recent monograph *Symphonic Stalinism: Claiming Russian Musical Classics for the New Soviet Listener, 1932–1953*, its subtitle notwithstanding, concerns the work of professional musicologists writing monographs and, in particular, textbooks for use in musical schools and conservatories—instruments, in other words, for exactly the process of transmission and socialization that Bukina criticizes.[27]

Smrž wrote consciously as what I call a Fitzpatrician, with the avowed intention of countering the old totalitarian model of Sovietology. What his book reveals is the ingenuity with which those professional musicologists responded to the demand that they find a way of narrating the history of Russian music and critiquing its artifacts in accordance with the newly imposed but vaguely delineated doctrine of *sotsrealizm*. He recognizes that the vagueness of the doctrine, hence of the demand, was deliberate and necessary. It enabled the Party to avail itself of the professionals' expertise by leaving the details of the proverbially difficult application of realist ideas to music in professional hands. Following the Fitzpatrician line, the author touts this as evidence of the musicians' autonomous agency. But at the same time, he acknowledges that the cultural bureaucrats acting in the name of the Party retained the prerogative of redefining goals at will, with the consequence that "Soviet composers could be found perennially lacking in accomplishment, and Soviet critics perennially lacking vigilance."[28]

In Smrž's analysis, Soviet musicologists faced three tasks, involving, respectively, technical analysis, composers' biographies, and the general narrative of Russian musical history, with particular attention to the nexus between realism and national identity. In technical analysis, the task was to find musical analogues of the socialist-realist desiderata that had been formulated for literature (e.g., *konkretnost'*, *obraznost'* or "imagery," *dialektichnost'*, and, hardest of all, *tvorcheskoye soznaniye*, "creative consciousness"). Biographies were constructed in conformity with the outlines of the Soviet *Bildungsroman* as described by Katerina Clark and others,[29]

---

26. For eradication (*uprazdneniye*), see Bukina, *Muzïkal'naya nauka*, 71; for *reprezentatsiya/derealizatsiya*, see ibid., 9.

27. Jiří Smrž, *Symphonic Stalinism: Claiming Russian Musical Classics for the New Soviet Listener, 1932–1953*, with a foreword by Thomas Lahusen and Peter H. Solomon Jr. (Berlin: LIT Verlag, 2011); reviewed by R. Taruskin in the *Russian Review* 71, no. 3 (July): 510–11.

28. Smrž, *Symphonic Stalinism*, 21.

29. See Katerina Clark, *The Soviet Novel: History as Ritual* (Bloomington: Indiana University Press, 2000).

with father figures (chiefly Glinka and—inevitably—Vissarion Belinsky, the civic-minded literary critic of the 1840s) showing younger composers the path from spontaneity to full consciousness.

To illustrate the impact of *sotsrealizm* on the general narrative, Smrž compares the two standard textbooks on the history of Russian music that were in use in conservatories and music schools during the period that he surveys, the first edited by Mikhaíl Samoilovich Pekelis (1899–1979) and published in 1940, the other single-handedly authored by Yury Vsevolodovich Keldïsh (1907–95) and published in 1947. The nativism and xenophobia of Keldïsh's version, the one scholars of my generation are likely to have read, corresponds neatly and chillingly with the official mood of the early Cold War and the nearing anticosmopolitan campaign.

It is quite true that the methods and arguments that Smrž recounts were developed within the field of musicology rather than imposed upon it, and I agree that it took considerable inventiveness to come up with them. But to recognize these virtues does not in itself constitute an answer to Bukina's misgivings (or mine, come to that). Does it look better or worse for the scholars to give them full credit for the lies they told? In the case of Keldïsh, particularly, one has to wonder about his own *tvorcheskoye soznaniye* and its impact on his morale when savoring the nationalistic excesses of his historical account, considering that he was an old RAPMist, i.e., a former member of the left-wing Russian Association of Proletarian Musicians in the first postrevolutionary decade-and-a-half, whose Marxist orthodoxy was perforce inimical to *velikoderzhavnïy shovinizm* ("great-power chauvinism"), as Stalin had called it, let alone the *ura-patriotichnost'* of the incipient Cold War years. How could such a man's consciousness not have been painfully divided?

But that is not the only way in which I have to wonder whether Smrž's account supports the "post-totalitarian" paradigm as persuasively as he seems to think it does. He convincingly portrays socialist-realist doctrine as fluid, mutable, susceptible to revision, whereas the "totalitarian" viewpoint (or rather, I should say, the caricature of the totalitarian viewpoint that is adduced by post-totalitarians so as to knock it down) asserts Soviet doctrine as utterly rigid and monolithic. But one can reject the caricature without resorting to a normalizing countercaricature. Mutability is precisely what one would expect of an epiphenomenon reflecting changes in policy to which the arts then had to conform.

In any case, not one of the examples of revision in Smrž's book had its origin in a musicological initiative. The musicologists are portrayed throughout in a reactive posture, forced by changes in the official line to modify their approach—always resourcefully, always inventively, deftly—and come up with new "original" solutions. The dynamic remains at all times predictably top-down.

So if we rely only on Smrž's account, I don't think we have real evidence of professional autonomy or evidence of real agency in the evolution of Russian musicology during this most stringent period in Soviet history. In this, Smrž's account seems to me even more pessimistic than Bukina's. Like hers, it shows sociocultural music historiography in a state of decline, even degeneration. Professional autonomy means little if it only means the freedom to find new ways of conforming to prescriptions.

IV

Unlike Smrž's, Bukina's account does illustrate a way out for musicologists who wanted to protect the autonomy of their professional practice. One could avoid the risks of sociocultural studies, which intersected dangerously with official ideology, by moving musicology, or at least its cutting edge (if that is a correct translation of *vedushchiy diskurs*) out of institutes like RIII and into conservatories, where it could become a more purely (or "essentially") professional and technical branch of instruction and learning, focused on transhistorical issues and values, most of them concerned with what literary people (but also, famously, Stravinsky) call poetics.

Citing (who else but) Bourdieu, Bukina postulates this move as a necessary one for the maintenance of any artistic field—"securing its existence, investing it with intrinsic value and lending it a sacralized [that is, inviolate] status."[30] Of course, she is talking about what we would call "music theory" as opposed to "musicology." And again I am struck by the similarity between the disciplinary debates that took place in Russia and the ones here, although they were not precisely synchronized, in part because the sources of the pressures on the discipline differed, as did the historical conditions that brought the pressures to bear, hence the differing motivations for the similar movement toward autonomous music theory in two distinct geographical domains.

We are used to saying that the pressure in Soviet Russia was political, whereas in the so-called West it was "purely" professional (or, more indirectly, economic), but that is obviously a reductive oversimplification. Any disciplinary pressure has an economic component, because it affects employment and career prospects. And if you read the writings of American music theorists, especially the composer-theorists among them, you cannot miss the political subtexts (as many writers have been lately pointing out, including me). So as I turn now to figures like Lev Mazel' and Yury Kholopov, Americans might think of Milton Babbitt or Kofi Agawu, and our British delegates might think of Arnold Whittall or Jonathan Dunsby. Bukina's observation, that "the solidity [*nezïblemost'*] of the artistic field [that is, its firm definition or delimitation] becomes a guarantor of the music scholar's own identity, enhancing his authority, lending weight to his analyses and

---

30. Bukina, *Muzïkal'naya nauka*, 123–24 (citing Bourdieu, "La genèse historique de l'esthétique pure," *Cahiers du Musée national d'art moderne*, no. 27 [Spring 1989]: 95–106).

FIGURE 13.1. "A lesson in the analysis of musical form," *Sovetskaya muzïka*, 1937, no. 6, p. 84.

'sanctifying' the results of his research," penetrates to the heart of the debate, both as it was conducted in Russia and as we have known it.[31]

It was precisely when it became clear that practitioners of sociocultural musicology did not have a free hand in defining their goals and methods (which means, defining their identity) that theoretical musicology was able to challenge the dominant position of sociocultural studies in Russia. Theirs, unlike the maneuvers described by Jiří Smrž, was a true musicological initiative in that it was uncalled for by political authority. Pride of place in this phase of the story goes to Lev Abramovich Mazel' (1907–2000), who taught music theory at the Moscow Conservatory from 1931 to 1967 and whose name comes first in every list of Soviet *muzteoretiki*, whether Bukina's or Zhdanov's. He is the obvious counterpart on the Soviet scene to Milton Babbitt, not because he composed serial music or approved of it, but because his name is proverbially synonymous with the "scientific"—or, as we now often say with a touch of irony, the "scientistic"—approach to art. Like Babbitt, Mazel' was a trained mathematician in addition to being a music scholar.

31. Bukina, *Muzïkal'naya nauka*, 124.

That is perhaps a coincidence, but it is not at all a coincidence that both in Mazel's case and in Babbitt's, science was seen as a refuge, a safe haven from politics.[32]

He was at first regarded by the Soviet musical establishment with admiration. *Sovetskaya muzïka*, the official organ of the Union of Soviet Composers, had a regular feature called "Druzheskiye sharzhi" (Friendly caricatures), in one of which we see Mazel' in his Conservatory classroom, taking his pupils through "a lesson in the analysis of musical form" (fig. 13.1). To complete the effect, the cartoonist should have had him wearing a lab coat, but the idea that his classroom was a lab emerges clearly enough from the equipment the students are using. The caption reads,

Юнцы прилежным скопом,	Yuntsï prilezhnïm skopom,
прильнули к микроскопам,	pril'nuli k mikroskopam,
не видя в поле зрения	ne vidya v pole zreniya
ни музыки, ни пенья.	ni muzïki, ni pen'ya.
На то и дан анализ,	Na to i dan analiz,
чтобы юнцы старались!	chtobï yuntsï staralis'!

—["the kids, diligently working as a group, / have taken up their microscopes, / blinkered / from music and from song. / Analysis is only there / to make the kids work hard!"]

And if I were doing the caricature, I would have put a passage from Chopin's Fantasia in F minor, op. 49, on the blackboard, because Mazel's most celebrated publication was his first book, a volume of 183 pages devoted exclusively to an exhaustive analysis of that one work of Chopin. It was written in 1934, the very year that socialist realism was first promulgated as an official method, and published in 1937.[33]

I call the book exhaustive, but *le mot juste*—Mazel's own word—would be *tselostnïy*, which in connection with his analytical method has been variously rendered in English as "holistic" or "integrated" or "integral," occasionally as "complex" or "many-sided."[34] Though less literal as a translation, I would suggest that what Mazel' (and Victor Tsukkerman, the other luminary among *tselostnïye* analysts) meant by the word was "eclectic," if we can divest that word of the negative vibes with which modernist dogmas have saddled it. The idea was that the *proizvedeniye*, the work itself (and it was always specific works that such analysts

---

32. The whole discussion that follows of Mazel's thought and practice should be read with Martin Brody's seminal article "'Music for the Masses': Milton Babbitt's Cold War Music Theory" (*Musical Quarterly* 77 [1993]: 161–92) in mind.

33. Lev Abramovich Mazel', *Fantaziya f-moll Shopena: Opït analiza* (Moscow: Muzgiz, 1937).

34. See Daniil Zavlunov, "The 'Tselostnïy Analiz' (Holistic Analysis) of Zuckerman and Mazel," *Music Theory Online* 20, no. 1 (September 2014), www.mtosmt.org/issues/mto.14.20.3/mto.14.20.3.zavlunov.html.

addressed, not their composers), should prompt the choice (or invention) of an approach, so that analysis would not be merely the application of a preconceived method or theory, such as the theory of "modal rhythm" (which despite its name is a theory of symmetrical pitch organization) advanced by Boleslav Yavorsky (Tsukkerman's teacher), which was a very ingenious way of understanding post-Wagnerian harmony, but which had been aggressively advanced as a new "revolutionary" universal, saddling practitioners with unnecessary difficulties when it came to analyzing ordinary major-minor tonality. In the words of Yury Kholopov, "Having witnessed the end of functional tonality, Yavorsky was wrong to turn around and say his new system accounted for this defunct tonality."[35] *Tselostnïy analiz* promised a more flexible, less dogmatic *ad hoc* approach that could encompass both older and newer principles of tonal organization, each on (what the analyst determined to be) its own terms. That was the sense in which it aspired to be truly holistic.

But the term sanctioned a different, more expansive claim as well, namely that *tselostnïy analiz* integrated all aspects of a given composition—structure, content, and historical context—into one comprehensive view. This it never did. It is quite obvious that the primary interest of holistic analysts, like that of pretty much all music analysts who identify themselves as such, was structure. That, more or less, was tantamount to what Mazel' and Tsukkerman meant by a *proizvedeniye*. It meant the score, the actual object produced by the composer, certainly not something "reproduced by someone and perceived by someone" at a given moment, to recall the definition of a work by Finagin, the exemplary sociocultural musicologist, with which this discussion began. Mazel's testamentary work, published as he approached his eightieth birthday, was a textbook expressly intended to supersede the classic conservatory textbook he had coauthored with Tsukkerman. The earlier book was called *Analiz muzïkal'nïkh proizvedeniy* (The Analysis of Musical Works). Its replacement was called *Stroyeniye muzïkal'nïkh proizvedeniy* (The Structure of Musical Works).[36]

The changed title did not represent a change of heart, although it may have reflected a difference in temperament between the coauthors. In a conversation with a former pupil, Liana Genina, Mazel' said that he and Tsukkerman "study the same subject, music, but we relate to it the way a poet and a scientist might respectively relate to the moon: Victor Abramovich extols its beauty, its brilliance, the

---

35. Yu. Kholopov, L. Kirillina, T. Kiuregian, G. Lyzhov, R. Pospelova, and V. Tsenova, *Muzïkal'no-teoreticheskie sistemy* (Moscow: Kompozitor, 2006), 381; paraphrased in Philip A. Ewell, "Rethinking Octatonicism: Views from Stravinsky's Homeland," *Music Theory Online* 18, no. 4 (December 2012), par. 2.16, www.mtosmt.org/issues/mto.12.18.4/mto.12.18.4.ewell.html.

36. Lev Abramovich Mazel' and Victor Abramovich Tsukkerman, *Analiz muzïkal'nïkh proizvedeniy* (Moscow: Muzïka, 1967); Lev Abramovich Mazel', *Stroyeniye muzïkal'nïkh proizvedeniy* (Moscow: Muzïka, 1986).

inspiration it gives to lovers; whereas I try to find out how and from what it is made."[37] Poetics, as opposed to poetry.

Yet if Mazel' was eclectic in method, he nevertheless had his biases, and they were the familiar biases of romantic aesthetics, which holds sacred the organic metaphor and its insistence that there is always a higher unity behind the diversity of the surface, and that the analyst's *a priori* goal is to uncover it. (In his later writings, Mazel' even coined the term *muzïkal'noye otkrïtiye*—musical discovery or disclosure—to identify the result of a good analysis, which is to say, making available to experience or cognition that which was previously hidden.)

His method of establishing that unity differed considerably from the one now usually instilled in Anglophone music analysts. Unlike Heinrich Schenker, whose methods have dominated Anglophone analysis since the 1940s, Mazel' did not see elaboration in terms of diminution, nor did he practice reduction. The end product of his analyses did not consist of a detemporalized visual display like a Schenker graph. He was always interested in temporality, in narration, in describing the moment-to-moment unfolding of music, and in this he was closer to Ernst Kurth or Schoenberg than to Schenker. That narrative *razbor*, or analytical commentary, was always the heart of a *tselostnïy analiz,* whether by Mazel' or by Tsukkerman. (Out of the 183 pages in Mazel's monograph on the Chopin Fantasie, for example, the *razbor* occupies more than 100.) And the rest, the part given over to content and context, never contains the discovery, only background information of a conventional kind—the "encyclopedia facts."

This was even true of the legendary *chef d'oeuvre* of *tselostnïy analiz,* Tsukkerman's 500-page tome that explicates Glinka's seven-minute-long orchestral showpiece, *Kamarinskaya*.[38] The book was touted as the exemplary instance of integration, in which analytical, historical, and cultural investigations would all intersect in a single blinding flash of *illuminatio*. I approached this book with the keenest interest and the highest expectations when I was making my own study of *Kamarinskaya*. I had a similar aim—namely, to integrate an analysis within a historical discussion[39]—and I was very disappointed, because the historical and cultural component of Tsukkerman's book was subject to all the constraints that had hobbled sociocultural history since the promulgation of socialist realism, including the xenophobic requirement that Russian music be represented as entirely autochthonous. Accordingly, Tsukkerman had to maintain a direct influence from Rus-

---

37. Quoted in Liana Genina, "Poslesloviye" (Afterword), following L. A. Mazel', "Tselostnïy analiz—zhanr preimushchestvenno ustnïy i uchebnïy," *Muzïkal'naya akademiya,* no. 4 (2000): 135.

38. Victor Abramovich Tsukkerman, *"Kamarinskaya" Glinki i eyo traditsii v russkoy muzïke* (Moscow: Muzgiz, 1957).

39. Richard Taruskin, "How the Acorn Took Root: A Tale of Russia," *19th-Century Music* 6 (1982–83): 189–212; reprinted in Taruskin, *Defining Russia Musically* (Princeton, NJ: Princeton University Press, 1997), 113–51.

sian folklore on the composition of this orchestral fantasia on the themes of two Russian folk songs, and entirely ignore (so as not to have to deny) the obvious influence on the work of German instrumental music, especially Beethoven's, about which Tsukkerman was a world-class expert. Here, more than anywhere else, it was obvious that music analysis, to the extent that it could retreat from sociocultural concerns, was able to find a safe space where investigations could be undertaken with far less risk of bureaucratic interference or ideological reprisal. To reincorporate the sociocultural was to reintroduce political constraints, hence reintroduce obligatory falsehoods. As another of my Russian friends—a member of my own generation who earned her *kandidat* degree at the Leningrad Conservatory with a dissertation, later published, on the eighteenth-century Russian composer Dmitry Bortnyansky—put it to me, "There was a wish to avoid history, especially of Russian music, so as to tell fewer lies, and to lay low in theory or in Western music (the older the better), or in folklore."[40]

V

Did the practitioners of *tselostnïy analiz* see what they were doing the way my friends and I saw it? I was always convinced that they had to know exactly what they were doing, because I knew them for the brilliant and erudite musicians that their pupils (who never spoke of them except in reverent whispers) always described. And now there is documentary corroboration in Mazel's tiny, last, posthumously published article, called "*Tselostnïy analiz*—A Predominantly Oral and Pedagogical Genre," written when the author was past ninety, more than sixty years after the publication of his Chopin monograph.[41] Half resigned rumination, half exposé, it is one of the most deeply moving documents I have ever found in the pages of a musicological journal.

It opens with a reminder: "In scholarship, particular interest in *tselostnïy analiz* was aroused here in the 1930s, when it was insistently demanded of music theory that it address not only the form but also the content and the expressively meaningful side of music" (133). And that triple approach was precisely the claim that the method advanced on its own behalf. But now, in his valedictory essay, Mazel' seemed to retract the famous claim:

---

40. Marina Ritzarev, email to author, 24 June 2018. Now living in Israel, Ritzarev (née Marina Grigoryevna Rïtsareva) has established herself as the preeminent specialist in Russian art music of the eighteenth century. Her dissertation was published as *Kompozitor D. Bortnyanskiy* (Leningrad: Muzïka, 1979), and her most comprehensive and authoritative study is *Eighteenth-Century Russian Music* (Abingdon, UK: Ashgate/Routledge, 2006).

41. L. A. Mazel', "Tselostnïy analiz—zhanr preimushchestvenno ustnïy i uchebnïy," *Muzïkal'naya akaemiya*, no. 4 (2000). In the following discussion, page references will be given in the main text).

A scientific [or scholarly; *nauchnïy*] analysis does not necessarily presuppose either full comprehensiveness or exhaustive detail. It must merely be sufficiently comprehensive and detailed to achieve the aim of the analysis, the task the author has proposed. [Such analyses] are bent on revealing something new, something hitherto unknown about a work, its properties, its internal and external connections, sometimes even seeing the work as a whole from an unaccustomed point of view. From such an analysis one expects not that it be all-embracing but that it be novel and purposeful (the latter demand sometimes entering into contradiction with an oversimplified notion of *tselostnost'*). (133)

So *tselostnïy analiz* was not necessarily *tselostnïy* after all. What Mazel' was really after was not *tselostnïy* but *tselenapravlennïy* [i.e., purposeful] *analiz*. Amen to that! After six decades, Mazel' was not only ready to admit that much, but also ready to specify what he was prepared, and actually inclined, to jettison from the definition and the practice. The content and expressivity of the music, he now strongly implied, were included in the original definition mostly as camouflage. "Every scholarly or pedagogical discipline must rest upon clearly delineated ideas and terms," he stipulated. Accordingly, "*Tselostnïy analiz* was understood from its beginnings to disclose the content of a work together with its form. But what is the content of a musical work?" (134).

Now he asks! The answer, pent up for so many decades, was explosive. Stand back. "For a long time," he began,

> we mouthed official clichés like "the reflection of social reality." (I also used them frequently.) These clichés have long since fallen away [except among Adorno's western epigones—R.T.], but a serious definition or even a clarification of the idea of "content" (which is, after all, an actual historical term in general use) in relation to instrumental, nonprogrammatic works of European music of the seventeenth to the twentieth centuries has been lacking. (Allow me to observe in this connection that when scholarship questions itself, so to speak, it usually advances.)
>
> The idea of "musical imagery" [Asafiev's term, one of the foundations of socialist realism as applied to music] will hardly help us out here, for it is vague and poorly understood. It might be better, in my view, to use the German word *Gestalt*, one of whose meanings envisages something approximating inner structure and which has already entered into our scholarly practice (for example, the German term *Gestaltpsychologie* is usually translated as "Gestal'tpsikhologiya" [and in English we say "Gestalt psychology"]).
>
> Our everyday understanding of musical content as the emotional shape or character of a work is naive and inadequate. Other construals are possible (I have sometimes used the definition "the artistic problems solved in the work," which touches somehow on the work's "function" [*naznacheniye*; and here it sounds as though Mazel' had been reading Carl Dahlhaus]), but they, too, it seems, are unsatisfactory. Yury Kholopov was probably right when he asserted that "the mysterious [*zavetnaya*] final task of music theory turns out to lie in the realm of philosophy." (134)

Which to me sounds like a dismissal: Get thee to philosophy! And even more like a dismissal is a passing remark a little earlier in the essay, when Mazel' writes, "In a *tselostnïy analiz* one can dispense (or nearly dispense) with interpretation" (134).[42] This effectively cuts out half of what one normally means by a scholarly investigation, which is the joint product of observation and inference (*nablyudeniye* and *vïvod*). Can one draw an inference without construal (*istolkovaniye*)? Obviously not—not even if one is merely describing or deducing form, and Mazel' was obviously aware of that. So I will hazard my own *istolkovaniye* here, and suggest that Mazel' was speaking in code, a process in which Soviet writers—and readers—were schooled to the point of expertise. What Mazel' actually meant to convey with his seemingly absurd aphorism was that *tselostnïy analiz* created a space where the kind of *tolkovaniye* that got you into trouble, or that compromised scholarly standards, could be avoided. So much for content.

Mazel' was aware that he was making a momentous concession. The first sentences of this poignant last testament (or what the Russians would call a *zavet*) make ironic reference to a maxim attributed to Aristotle. "Enthusiasts of *tselostnïy analiz* will perhaps greet this thesis with objections," Mazel' allows; "and yet, 'while Plato is my friend, dearer yet is truth'" (132).[43] What he was now admitting, of course, was what had to be denied at all costs during more stringent times, when the kind of delimitation of the field that Mazel' now openly proposed would have been denounced with what was surely among Soviet epithets the most baleful one of all, *formalizm*.

Sure enough, together with practically the whole musicological fraternity, Mazel' was among those tarred with that dread brush in 1948. After the *soveshchaniya*, the hearings at the headquarters of the Central Committee of the Communist Party where Zhdanov read his bill of indictment and the accused mounted the rostrum to offer their thanks, *Sovetskaya muzïka* published another cartoon showing Mazel's face, but this one was in a group titled *Nedruzheskiye sharzhi*— "Unfriendly caricatures"—and it shows Mazel', along with Tsukkerman, and Igor Fyodorovich Boelza, and Daniyel' Vladimirovich Zhitomirsky, and Semyon Isaakovich Shlifshteyn, and Izraíl' Vladimirovich Nest'yev, and Alexander Naumovich Dolzhansky, among others, worshiping an idol who looks more than a little like Igor Fyodorovich Stravinsky (fig. 13.2). "Slaves to a robot," the legend reads, and the rhyming part of the caption goes like this:

---

42. "В целостном анализе можно обходиться без (или почти без) толкований."
43. "*Platon mne drug, no istina dorozhe*"; quoting a famous Latin paraphrase (attributed by some to Roger Bacon) of a line from Aristotle's Nichomachean Ethics: *Nam Plato dicit: "Amicus est Socrates, magister meus, sed magis est amica veritas."*

FIGURE 13.2. "Slaves to a robot," *Sovetskaya muzika*, 1948, no. 2, p. 152.

Погибла лира	Pogibla lira
в тисках кумира.	v tiskakh kumira.
И все же он	I vsyo zhe on
превознесён	prevoznesyon.
Забыв о чести,	Zabïv o chesti,
в припадке лести	v pripadke lesti
разбили лбы	razbili lbï
его рабы.	yego rabï.

—[the lyre is out of action / in the clutches of an idol. / And still he is / extolled. / Forgetting honor, / in a fit of flattery, / its slaves / bow down.]

I included the patronymics in the list of names so as to make obvious what was already obvious to Soviet readers in 1948, namely that with the exception of Igor Boelza, who descended from Polish nobility (which was not much better), everyone named in the caption was Jewish. When applied to musicologists, the antiformalist campaign intersected with the anticosmopolitan campaign, for Jews were disproportionately represented in the ranks of science and scholarship in Soviet Russia, as they were everywhere in Europe and America.

It was not easy to live down the taint of formalism if one's profession was studying and describing form; so that preoccupation had to be minimized if not altogether concealed. The discourse of *tselostnïy analiz* was one way of doing that, and the effort went much further into the language and practice of the discipline. We have seen the word *analiz* (analysis) used as a euphemism for *stroyeniye* (structure) in the titles of textbooks, to avoid the association of "structure" with "form." As Yury Kholopov has further attested, the time-honored conservatory course "Analysis of Musical Forms" (*analiz muzïkal'nïkh form*) had to be changed post-*zhdanovshchina* to "Analysis of Musical Works" (*analiz muzïkal'nïkh proizvedeniy*).[44]

VI

By the 1960s the ideological atmosphere had relaxed sufficiently so that music theorists did not have to pretend to encompass sociocultural issues in their analyses; but as the pretense lost its necessity as a ploy, and the delimitation of music theory to formal and structural matters became overt, it also became an issue for discussion. A debate arose between historians and theorists that began to resemble the turf wars of the West.

One of its early rounds was an essay, "In Defense of Historical Scholarship," that appeared in *Sovetskaya muzïka* in June 1967, and reappeared the next year as the preface to a book with a title that has a weird ring for any but Soviet musicologists: *Studies*

---

44. Yu. Kholopov, "Teoriya muzïki," in E. Dolinskaya, L. Nikitina et al., *Istoriya sovremennoy otechestvennoy muzïki*, vol. 3 (Moscow: Muzïka, 2001), 576; quoted in Bukina, *Muzïkal'naya nauka*, 172n284.

in Foreign Music (*Etyudï o zarubezhnoy muzïke*)⁴⁵—a title that reflects the romantic nationalistic history of Russian music and music scholarship, which has led to the bifurcated organization of Soviet (and now post-Soviet) musicology departments, segregated into *kafedrï* of *russkaya muzïka* and *zarubezhnaya muzïka*, a situation designed to perpetuate the mythology of autochthony that had led to so much historiographical distortion, which led in turn to the discrediting of historical musicology and the rise of analysis (*tselostnïy* or not) as a separate discipline in Russia.

The author was Valentina Dzhozefovna Konen (1909–91), one of the most famous Soviet musicologists—indeed, I think it is fair to say the foremost Soviet musicologist specializing in "foreign music"—but one whose career took shape, to an unusual degree, outside the institutional structure of Soviet musicology. This was not by her choice. She was born in Baku into the family of a Russian revolutionary who had to leave Russia for political reasons. (Her surname is a variant of Kunin, one of her father's pseudonyms; by birth it was Roberson or Roberman, depending on the source of information.) From the age of one year she was brought up outside of Russia, at first in Bessarabia (then part of Romania), then in western Europe, and finally in the United States.

Here I have to get personal. Valentina Konen lived in Brooklyn, New York, from 1921 to 1931, that is, from the age of twelve to the age of twenty-two. And during that time, one of her closest friends was my (future) mother, who was three years younger than Val (the name I always knew her by from my mother's stories). They met in the studio of their common piano teacher in Brooklyn, whose name was Lillian Wolf, and later they both studied piano at the Institute of Musical Art (now the Juilliard School of Music).

In 1931 her father decided to take the family back to Soviet Russia, at first back to Baku, to help build communism, as the slogan went. After a time studying at the local petroleum institute, Val Konen decided on musicology and enrolled at the Moscow Conservatory. She also worked as a music critic and as the Moscow correspondent of the *Musical Courier*, an American magazine. But here the story takes an untoward turn, when, like so many other returning émigrés, her father was arrested and executed.

My mother never saw Val Konen again after 1931, but I looked her up during my first visit to the USSR in 1966, and got to know her and her husband, Yevgeniy Lvovich Feynberg, an eminent nuclear physicist and an Akademik (i.e., a member of the Soviet Academy of Sciences along with Asafiev) during my year as an exchange student in 1971–72. I won't say any more about my personal relationship

---

45. Valentina Dzhozefovna Konen, "V zashchitu istoricheskoy nauki," *Sovetskaya muzïka*, 1967, no. 6: 18–23; V. D. Konen, "Ot avtora," in Konen, *Etyudï o zarubezhnoy muzïki* (Moscow: Muzïka, 1968), 3–13 (translated into German as "Zur Verteidigung der historischen Musikwissenschaft," *Kunst und Literatur* 16 [1968]: 199–207).

FIGURE 13.3. Valentina Dzhozefovna Konen (1909–91).

with her, except to note that my having found her was a tremendous thing for my mother. Val sent some pictures through me, one of which my mother kept framed on her wall until her death, and it is now on my piano (fig. 13.3).

I had to tell all of this not only in the name of hackneyed "full disclosure," but also as a way of explaining the fact about Val Konen with which I introduced her—that is, her extra-institutional career. The fact—or rather the three facts—that she had lived in America, that she was Jewish, and that her father had been an "enemy of the people" made serious problems for her throughout her career. When her father was executed in 1940, she was expelled from the graduate program in musicology at the Moscow Conservatory without a degree. She was readmitted in 1944 and, on the basis of her knowledge of the United States (by then an ally of the USSR in World War II), wrote a dissertation, defended in 1947, on American music (published in 1961 as the first book on American music by a Soviet author).[46] But in 1948, because her book was a serious scholarly study rather than an attack on American music, she was accused of *prekloneniye* (or worse, *nizkopoklonstvo*) *pered zapadom* ("kowtowing to the West") and fired from her job as a docent at the Gnesin Institute in Moscow. One of her chief persecutors, in a manner that links up neatly, and chillingly, with earlier phases of the present discussion, was Tatyana Livanova, Konen's exact but better-connected contemporary, who had served as her supervisor for the aborted *kandidat* degree (with a dissertation, "Predposïlki klassicheskoy simfonii," on the stylistic harbingers of the classical symphony).

From 1951 to 1953 Konen taught at the only institution that would hire her, the Ural Conservatory in Sverdlovsk (the former and future Yekaterinburg), about seven hundred miles east of Moscow. It was a de facto exile. She came back to Moscow after Stalin's death, and was eventually, in the late 1960s, invited to give lectures to graduate students at the Moscow Conservatory, but she was never a regular faculty member there. Instead, she worked at the later incarnations of Institut istorii iskusstv, the old RIII. On the basis of her published work and her network of personal relationships, she managed to become a very prominent figure, widely regarded both as the true heir to the mantle of Roman Il'yich Gruber, the longtime head of foreign music at the Moscow Conservatory, and as the worthiest Moscow counterpart to Mikhaíl Semyonovich Druskin, the legendary Leningrad Conservatory professor who kept a corner of St. Petersburg alive for the benefit, and to the lasting gratitude, of his pupils. He and Konen divided the subject of *zarubezhnaya muzïka* between them when it came to writing the conservatory textbook on the subject, Konen covering the late eighteenth and early nineteenth centuries and Druskin the rest of the nineteenth. Konen's half went through seven editions.[47] You could call it the Russian *Grout*.

At the time of her intervention in *Sovetskaya muzïka,* Konen was *starshiy nauchnïy sotrudnik,* or senior research fellow, at the III. As such, she was writing from outside the pedagogical establishment and offering a critique of its curricula and the consequent state of Soviet musical scholarship. She recalled the glory days of early Soviet musicology, starting with the figures cited at the beginning of this

---

46. V. D. Konen, *Puti amerikanskoy muzïki: Ocherki po istorii muzïkal'noy kulturï SShA* (The Paths of American Music: Chapters in the History of the Musical Culture of the USA), 2nd. rev. ed. (Moscow: Muzïka, 1965).

47. *Istoriya zarubezhnoy muzïki* (Moscow: Muzgiz, 1958), vol. 3: From 1789 to the mid-nineteenth century (V. Konen); vol. 4: Second half of the nineteenth century (M. Druskin).

essay. She lamented the loss of historical perspective in Soviet musicology since that time. "Even in music history textbooks," she complained, "books designed to set a standard for historical thinking, one finds pages where rather than a broad general evaluation of a composer's work one finds only a technical dissection of separate elements of his musical style."[48] While "a fluent mastery of analysis according to the latest methods is just as necessary as general artistic erudition as a prerequisite for functioning professionally," only "a synthesis of both aspects of scholarly preparation will allow one to avoid dilettantism" (19).

Musicologists, she acknowledged, needed more technical training in the craft of composition and analysis than their counterparts in other art-historical disciplines; and therefore, she conceded, the fact that Soviet musicologists were trained in conservatories rather than universities gave them an advantage over their counterparts elsewhere. But she warned that "there is a negative complement to this positive phenomenon, namely the lack of a true university-level humanistic culture" (19). She listed eight specific tasks for which she thought Soviet musicologists were inadequately trained. They seem to be in ascending order of importance, so I will cite the last two as representing Konen's essential claim. What musicologists cannot do but must be able to do, she asserted, culminated in these skills:

- To determine the dependency of creative activity in music on the broad social and cultural features of a period
- To support one's conclusions on the basis not only of technical musical analysis, but also on the observed developmental patterns [she writes *zakonï razvitiya*, which translates literally as "laws of development"] of a particular artistic tradition, a given style, genre, formal or expressive device. (19).

One can easily imagine how Lev Mazel' might have responded to this, and of course so could Konen. So she added a somewhat defensive or preemptive footnote:

I deliberately refrain from analyzing now the reasons for such a situation as I am describing. This is a complicated matter [*slozhnïy vopros*] and would demand an investigation of its own. My proposals in this area might call forth a polemic, which would distract us from the main problem at hand. It seems to me more important to limit discussion at this point to the specification of the relevant issue. (20n)

Indeed, all of Konen's real fighting words are relegated to footnotes. Having written that there has been an especial dearth of serious books on *zarubezhnaya muzïka*, she seeks the sanctuary of a footnote to add this: "I underscore the importance of such works not only because it happens to be my specialty. To work out the problems of Russian music's past also demands deep knowledgeability about

---

48. V. D. Konen, "V zashchitu istoricheskoy nauki," 18. Further citations will be given in the main text.

the processes that were taking place in western Europe in the preclassical and classical periods" (22n).

There was a time when this sentence could have drawn a sentence, for *nizkopoklonstvo*. By the 1960s, penalties were professional rather than political, and there were many who never forgave Konen for saying this, and much else, in this coolly incendiary piece. Starting in the 1960s, when they were no longer so severely policed by political authorities, scholarly disciplines began to show what you might call autonomous divisions and rivalries, and music theorists were moved to defend what they regarded by then as hard-won turf—just as they did here. What had once been a political refuge had become a protected specialist preserve.

But by then historical musicology had also undergone a depoliticizing transformation, as would have been apparent if I had quoted the less polemical parts of Konen's essay. Her brand of musicology was not nearly as sociocultural as was the musicology practiced by the patriarchs of the RIII, or her own student work up to her doctoral dissertation, that pioneering study of American music, which contained only one chapter on "professional composerly music" (*professional'noye kompozitorskoye tvorchestvo*), devoted to Edward MacDowell and his frustrated career, the rest being devoted to popular genres and their social settings and tasks.[49]

By the time she wrote her defense of historical scholarship, Konen, more than any other Soviet musicologist, resembled the Western, that is German or Anglo-American, musicologist of the 1960s and 70s, interested above all in source studies and style criticism. Her crowning book, in my opinion, was *Teatr i simfoniya*, published in 1968, which means she was working on it when she made her polemical intervention. It anticipates some of the groundbreaking work of Daniel Heartz, Elaine Sisman, and other familiar scholars of eighteenth-century music in exploring the interrelationship of dramatic and instrumental genres. If her work had been translated in time, and if Soviet scholarship had not been so isolated from Western scholarship, and in consequence so subject in the West to not-wholly-unjustified suspicion, hers would have been a big name here as well as there. That a woman could be such a weighty presence in Soviet musicology, the more so as she had had such a checkered and politically troubled career, speaks eloquently on behalf of her qualities as a scholar. Perhaps her fortunate marriage has to be factored into the equation.

But that sort of status and authority breeds resentment on its own account, and so it will not surprise anyone familiar with the disciplinary debates in our own neck of the musicological woods that it festered and grew until, more than twenty

---

49. A chapter breakdown (taken from the revised edition): (1) New England choral hymnody; (2) the sources of Negro music; (3) spirituals; (4) minstrels; (5) the birth of theatrical jazz, George Gershwin; (6) the role of Latin American culture in the development of jazz; (7) the paths of development of jazz in the USA; (8) protest songs; (9) the MacDowell chapter; (10) the problem of a national school.

years later, it exploded into the open—by coincidence or not, precisely at the time when *glasnost'* became the order of the day in the run-up to the Soviet collapse. It was a spectacular example of what happens when the lid comes off a pressure cooker.

VII

The protagonist of this phase was one whose name has already figured in this account: Yury Nikolayevich Kholopov (1932–2003), a younger scholar, which added a dollop of generational warfare to the polemical stew. Kholopov, the mainstay of the music theory faculty at the Moscow Conservatory, was an outstanding specialist and a prolific author. His field was twentieth-century harmony, which he studied analytically and inferentially rather than historically, armed (as I can personally attest) with an amazing knowledge of repertoire from all periods and places, and an astounding memory. An outspoken and unabashed formalist (not that he would have applied such a tainted word to himself), Kholopov saw no need to camouflage his position for the sake of protecting it. By the time of his death he (along with his sister, Valentina Nikolayevna, who—as if by agreement to divide the world of music between them—studied rhythm) had achieved virtual preeminence among Russian music scholars, especially in terms of international recognition; and yet, at the time of his debate with Konen et al., he was still fighting under something of a handicap in that, until the era of *glasnost'*, his generation and his musicological faction lacked equal access to the press, which, like all public media in the Soviet Union, remained subject to centralized control. Surely it was the frustration he had been suffering that accounts for the evident lowering of the tone of debate once he had joined in. Where Konen had been lofty and maintained a façade of magnanimity, Kholopov was all sarcasm and indignation.

He had a right to it. *Sovetskaya muzïka* had followed up on Konen's "Defense of Historical Scholarship" with a "round table" of musicological heavy-hitters—Boris Mikhailovich Yarustovsky, Mazel', Druskin, Keldïsh, Elena Semyonovna Berland-Chernaya, Nest'yev, Konen herself, and Elena Andreyevna Grosheva, the journal's editor—at which, to quote the beginning of Keldïsh's contribution, "everyone here shares [Konen's] attitude and warmly welcomes it," so that the twenty-two double-column pages the journal devoted to the discussion make pretty dull reading.[50]

One might have expected Lev Mazel' to offer some defense of his beat, but he was still obliged to camouflage his position. He offered a veiled reminder, cast in what Russians call Aesopian language, of some of the factors Konen had elaborately avoided addressing—that is to say, the politically fraught reasons why music

---

50. Boris Yarustovsky, Lev Mazel' et al., "Istoriya i sovremennost'," *Sovetskaya muzïka*, 1968, no. 3: 2–23 (quoted words of Keldïsh on page 9).

analysis had arisen as a separate subject in the first place. The "natural aspiration to base music-historical inferences on data drawn from the analysis of the music itself," he said, was "at root a healthy one, but has sometimes been taken to absurd lengths." And yet, he reminded his colleagues, "we have to recall that in the late twenties and early thirties"—that is, the period immediately preceding the organization of creative unions and the imposition of socialist realist standards—

> lecture courses in music history were mainly devoted to general observations and no time was set aside for studying the literature itself. That is when mistaken notions of "music history babble" arose and it became fashionable to contrast theorists as "doers" with historians as "talkers." In the thirties the analysis of individual works worked its way into a leading position in our scholarship and our pedagogy.

Mazel' was plainly assuming that his listeners and eventual readers would remember why. Thanks to the introduction of analysis into the curriculum, Mazel' concluded, "the deficiencies typical of the twenties were to a large extent overcome; but at the same time some corresponding minuses evolved."[51]

Kholopov was in no mood to maintain this conciliatory tone. He was furious. In the meantime *Sovetskaya muzïka* had convened yet another round table, in 1977 (as if marking the tenth anniversary of Konen's original intervention), to which he was invited, as Mazel's de facto successor, to submit a response, which he did. It was rejected at the time, and when it finally appeared in 1988, Year One of *glasnost'*, it bore a note from the author declaring that he had been the victim of censorship: "This article, written in 1977–78, was intended as the author's contribution to the journal *Sovetskaya muzïka*'s 'round table' 'Musicology as a social, humanistic science', . . . but its printing was not permitted."[52]

It is prefaced with an epigraph drawn from Konen's contribution to that 1977 symposium, which restated the position she had advanced in 1967: "History cannot rest on technical analysis alone. It must have the benefit of a wide-ranging intellectual synthesis, it must possess a broad humanistic horizon, [and] an associative turn of thought." Kholopov left no doubt, however, that it was the original 1967 piece to which he was irately responding. His wrath was not entirely misplaced: surely he was not alone in finding the title of Konen's very aggressive intervention somewhat paradoxical. "'In defense of historical scholarship?' Pardon me,

---

51. Ibid., 5.

52. Yury Kholopov, "Teoreticheskoye muzïkoznaniye kak gumanitarnaya nauka, problema analyza muzïki," *Sovetskaya muzïka*, 1988, no. 9: 73–79; no. 10: 87–93. The note is printed as a footnote in no. 9, p. 73. (The remaining quotes from this piece are from no. 9, p. 74.) At the end of the second installment, the editors objected to Kholopov's characterization, saying that the refusal to print the piece in 1977 had been the normal result of in-house negative referee reports rather than censorship. They did not mention it, but Kholopov's response exceeded the length of the original round table in its entirety.

but 'defense' against what? Against whom? Might it be against the successes of 'young' theorists in the absence of any such successes by 'young' historians?"

He objects heatedly to the binary oppositions on which Konen and the other panelists had relied: "technicians" vs. "humanists," "historians" vs. "theorists." He makes very heavy weather of the word *alone* in the epigraph from Konen— "History cannot rest on technical analysis alone"—and performs a neat little *razoblacheniye*: "With regard to musical analysis, theorists are, so to speak, 'sub-historians' [*nedoistoriki*; cf. *nedorosl'* (a minor child), *nedouchka* (an educational dropout), etc.]; historians do everything that theorists do, but in addition they add a certain humanistic layer, they bring in the intellectual culture that technician-theorists cannot possibly have." His mockery hits bottom with a sly allusion to an old and unprintable joke about Lenin that our Russian guests will probably recognize: "Get it?" he taunts: "The historian does the same thing as the theorist, but does it on a high intellectual level: does it broadly, eruditely, humanistically."[53] Finally he lets V. D. Konen have it with both barrels, in a passage suppurating with italics, boldface, and caps:

> I will formulate now in one word what is never stated outright in [Konen's] article, but what the author's every point portends. What is humanistic musicology according to V. D. Konen? *Leaving out the music, that's what.* **Humanistic means extramusical.** What is lacking for me in every remark the author makes about what is humanistic? **THERE'S NO MUSIC.**[54]

Caps plus boldface is something I have never seen, before or since, in a Russian scholarly journal (or a non-Russian one, come to that).

It is familiar, though. Depressingly familiar. When I first read it, I was just two years past my "notorious exchange" with Allen Forte in the pages of the British journal *Music Analysis*.[55] That exchange marked a point of polarization between musicology, informally so-called, and music theory, one that I never intended (since I was fully trained in music analysis and have always been a practitioner and a contributor to that discipline, if not an uncritical one).

I have told you of my personal relationship with Valentina Konen. Well, I had one with Yury Kholopov, too. I met him at a national meeting of the American Musicological Society in New Orleans in 1987, and got to know him several years later (it must have been around 1994 or 1995) when he extended another American

---

53. All right, the old joke: an aged Party member recalls an early Party conference, during which he found himself in the men's room in the stall next to the one in which Lenin was sitting: "What I was doing, he too was doing—but how he did it: so simply, so humanely, so profoundly!"

54. "Чего мне не хватает во всех рассуждениях автора о гуманитарном? **МУЗЫКИ НЕТ.**"

55. Letter to the Editor from Richard Taruskin and Letter to the Editor in Reply to Richard Taruskin from Allen Forte, *Music Analysis* 5 (1986): 313–37; the characterization is from Arnold Whittall, "Allen Forte in *Music Analysis*," *Music Analysis* 26 (2007): 3–13, at 6.

visit in order to come out to California for the express purpose of reading my Stravinsky monograph, which was then in press and available for perusal only *chez moi* or at the offices of the University of California Press. (See what email has done for us since?) I felt honored by the intensity of his interest in my work. We had long, fervid discussions of my analyses in that book, which Yury Nikolayevich basically approved, and at times actually liked, because I had all unawares been working, as he put it, "in the tradition of Yavorsky," whose work I had not yet read (but only read about).

I found Yury Nikolayevich an utterly delightful companion, and as things warmed up between us I told him about my mother's friendship with Valentina Konen, my own acquaintance with her, and asked him why he had responded to her so bitterly. He didn't really answer me, just assured me that he had great respect for her withal. But I understood. We were all in the grip of what I have subsequently called the "Great Either/Or," something to which Yury Nikolayevich himself had drawn exasperated attention in his reply to Konen.[56]

VIII

I have been trying ever since to surmount the Great Either/Or, both in my own work and in the influence I have sought to exert, first on my own pupils, and, through my writings, on the discipline at large. What I have been trying to restore to musicology, without letting go of the other, is precisely the sociocultural dimension that political conditions on *both* sides of the Cold War had militated against—although in the one case (the "Western") the minimizing of the sociocultural dimension was an orthodoxy and in the other (the Soviet) it was a resistance to orthodoxy which affected not only the work of music theorists but also that of their antagonists like Konen, who had had to soft-pedal the sociocultural dimension after suffering what amounted to Stalinist persecution.

Because I was putting it back, my work has occasionally been described—not only by phobic post-Soviet formalists like Levon Hakobian, who dismisses my work the old-fashioned way as "vulgar sociologism,"[57] or by rabid political opponents like Shostakovich "revisionists," but also by some of its most knowledgeable readers—as having submitted to Soviet orthodoxy.

In his final, perorative paragraph, for example, Jiří Smrž, the best informed of the lot, wrote that "much like the integral analysis of the Stalin era [his translation of *tselostnïy analiz*], many Western scholars [I only wish there were many!] (includ-

---

56. On the Great Either/Or, see chapter 1 above ("The History of What?").

57. L. B. Bayakhunova, "Levon Akopyan: 'Mï mnogim obyazanï zapadnïm ispolnitelyam, muzïkovedam, kritikam'" http://infoculture.rsl.ru/donArch/home/KVM_archive/articles/2011/03/2011-03_r_kvm-s9.pdf.

ing one of the leading authorities in North America on Russian music, Richard Taruskin) no longer view musical compositions as closed autonomous entities and approach them instead as a complex interplay of cultural historical factors."[58] And Anne Shreffler, in a very shrewd comparison between Carl Dahlhaus and his East German counterpart Georg Knepler, actually came close to putting me down as a disciple of the latter, whom I did actually meet once (in Moscow, at a meeting of the UNESCO-sponsored International Music Council in the fall of 1971) and whose writing I had, long ago, actually praised in print (being one of the very few Western music historians who even knew his name in those days).[59] Summarizing Knepler's significance, she wrote: "The scholarly project that Knepler and his colleagues opened up (and ultimately did not finish) resonates strongly with many current concerns, even though there was, as far as I can tell, little or no direct influence of East German and Soviet Marxist musicology on the North American scene (with the possible exception of Richard Taruskin's work)."[60]

I took strong umbrage at this at the time, and even dashed off an angry email to Anne, which I later had to patch up. Having lived something like a Soviet student's life for ten months, and having seen up close the conditions that my own relatives and their friends were facing, including a number of what in those days were known as *otkazniki* ("refuseniks" in "English"), I came back from my year on the academic exchange with a view of the Soviet Union that, as I liked to put it then, was somewhat to the right of Ronald Reagan's. And yet that same student year contained experiences that I have described in my own writing that did have a strong impact on my musicological thinking, including a performance of Shostakovich's *Leningrad* Symphony that educated me in the social value that music can have, precisely because of the constraints imposed by the totalitarian institutions whose authority, as I had been taught up to then, had vitiated the music's aesthetic value.[61]

One of the things that educated me was first-hand knowledge that those who subscribed to Soviet ideas on music, including the most orthodox ones, were at the very least my intellectual and musicianly equals. So I am willing to describe myself at this point as a walking translation of Eastern ideas into a Western musicological

---

58. Smrž, *Symphonic Stalinism*, 165.

59. "To the Editor," *Current Musicology* 19 (1975): 33–40, at 33. This was a rebuttal to a paper by Hans Helms called "Charles Edward Ives: Ideal American or Social Critic," *Current Musicology* 17 (1973): 37–44.

60. Anne C. Shreffler, "Berlin Walls: Dahlhaus, Knepler, and Ideologies of Music History," *Journal of Musicology* 20 (2003): 498–525, at 523.

61. R. Taruskin, "Double Trouble," *New Republic*, 24 December 2001, 26–34; reprinted with an update as "When Serious Music Mattered," in *A Shostakovich Casebook*, ed. Malcolm H. Brown (Bloomington: Indiana University Press, 2005), 360–84, and in R. Taruskin, *On Russian Music* (Berkeley: University of California Press, 2009), 299–321.

context, and—now that my work has at least a few Russian readers—of Western ideas into an Eastern context. It is one more Either/Or to surmount, and I am always in favor of that.

But there is still work to do. Sociocultural musicology has yet to make a decisive post-Soviet comeback. It is what Tatyana Bukina is still agitating for, as she looks longingly on "new musicology"[62]—the term we used in the 1990s to describe some big changes in purview that were then taking place, particularly in American musical scholarship. The term is old now, partly because the new musicology quickly took a wrong turn, away from the sociocultural into naive hermeneutics, which caused it to age with stunning rapidity. We are still feeling our way back to what both Soviet musicology and German musicology were doing in the 1920s, before both were tainted with totalitarianism: not as the next exclusive purview, which would only spawn at best a new Either/Or, at worst a new totalitarianism, but as one more string in our bow. There cannot be too many.

---

62. Bukina, *Muzïkal'naya nauka*, 120.

INDEX

"9/11" (terrorist attack), 168–70, 176

Abbate, Carolyn, 6n12, 303; "Music—Drastic or Gnostic?" 178, 232, 335
Abel, Carl Friedrich, 83
Abraham, Gerald, 79–80
Abraham Lincoln Brigade, 60
absolute music, 25, 33, 108, 115–17, 295
abstraction, 134, 280
Adams, John, 61–62, 126–27, 169, 172, 176; *On the Transmigration of Souls*, 126
Adès, Thomas, 65
Adler, Guido, 105, 182, 186, 402; "Umfang, Methode und Ziel der Musikwissenschaft," 210
Adler, Mortimer, 370
Adorno, Theodor Wiesengrund, 19–23, 35, 70n72, 107, 142–45, 152–53, 156, 159–60, 176, 191, 201, 338, 341, 349, 369, 386; *Alban Berg: Master of the Smallest Link*, 143, 381; *Introduction to the Sociology of Music*, 143; "Neue Musik, Interpretation, Publikum," 145; *Philosophie der neuen Musik*, 379–83; "What National Socialism Has Done to the Arts," 144
aesthetic autonomy, 17–19, 25, 33, 70, 99–146, 153, 177; as bulwark against totalitarianism, 159
affect, 231
affordance(s), 11, 14, 78–80, 221, 248–51

Agawu, V. Kofi, 232, 416
agency/agents, 36–37, 40, 77, 124, 138, 177, 400
agitprop, 60
Albrechtsberger, Johann Georg, 97
Alexander II, Tsar, 408–11
Allanbrook, Wye J., 90, 232, 248; *Rhythmic Gesture in Mozart*, 243–44
alla turca topic, 91
Allen, David, 334
Al-Qaeda, 70
American Musicological Society, 252
Amerikanismus, 191
analysis, musical, 25–27, 252–81; and "audibility," 264–65; and induction, 262; and textual criticism, 205; purpose of, 263, 269, 272–73; *tselostnïy* (holistic), 418–23, 434
Anderson, Benedict, *Imagined Communities*, 308
Ansermet, Ernest, 330
Antheil, George, 191
anti-Semitism (*see also* Jews), 132, 425
antitheatrical prejudice, 385
Apel, Willi, 183, 186
Apocalypse, 119
apophasis, 296n35
Arendt, Hannah, 352, 370, 394
Argyll, Duchess of, 65
Aristotle, 109, 245
Arnold, Matthew, 344, 348, 370, 383, 397n159

Arrowsmith, William, 362
ars subtilior, 183
Asafiev, Boris Vladimirovich, 401, 405; *Glinka,* 413; *intonatsiya* theory, 402
Ashcroft, John, 171
Ashkenazy, Vladimir Davidovich, 51–52
Assotsiatsiya sovremennoy muziki (ASM), 404
asymptote, 10
Attaingnant, Pierre, 36
Auden, W. H., 119–20, 172, 243–44, 362
Austin, J. L., 12
"authenticity" in musical performance, 306, 316, 319–20; and authority, 329; and difference, 195
avant-garde, 181–82; "fall" of, 404
Avison, Charles, 92

Babbitt, Milton, 15, 127, 208–11, 223–24, 264, 416–17; and low redundancy, 330; "Past and Present Concepts of the Nature and Limits of Music," 209n6; "Who Cares If You Listen?" 209
Bach, Johann Sebastian, 194, 200; *Kunst der Fuge, Die,* 203; "Mein Jesus ist erstanden" (Cantata BWV 67, *Halt im Gedächtnis Jesum Christ*), 237, 239–40; *Musikalisches Opfer, Das,* 182, 203; Prelude in F minor (*Well-Tempered Clavier,* Book II), 230–31; St. John Passion, 42, 44–45, 71, 131–33, 176; St. Matthew Passion, 42–43, 131, 236–38; "Seufzer, Thränen, Kummer, Noth" (Cantata BWV 21, *Ich hatte viel Bekümmernis*), 230–31
BACH cipher, 197
Bacon, Francis, 30–31, 35
Baker, James M., 215
Balakirev, Miliy Alexeyevich, 184
Balanchine, George, 245n35
Balkin, Jack, 41
Barab, Seymour, 82
barbarism, refined, 131, 133
Barber, Samuel, 219
Barenboim, Daniel, 53n27, 170
Barish, Jonas, 385
Bartók, Béla, 39
Baumgarten, Alexander: *Aesthetica,* 100
Beardsley, Monroe, 270
Beatles, 390–91
Beethoven, Ludwig van, 35, 103–4, 144–45, 198; as standard of perfection, 151; *Fidelio,* 236; Fifth Symphony, 39; *glorreiche Augenblick, Der,* 53–55; *Missa solemnis,* 152; Ninth Symphony, 152, 384; "Schreckensfanfaren" in, 286–89; Violin Sonata No. 9, "Kreutzer," 144
Becker, Howard: *Art Worlds,* 39–40
Beckett, Samuel, 4
Bellini, Vincenzo: *La sonnambula,* 322
Belonenko, Alexander Sergeyevich, 405n14
Benjamin, William, 256
Berdyayev, Nikolai Alexandrovich, 3
Berg, Alban, 140, 143, 199, 381–82; *Wozzeck,* 143, 381
Berger, Arthur, 271
Berger, Karol, 106, 131, 133, 162n37, 304–5, 359
Berland-Chernaya, Elena Semyonovna, 431
Berlin, Irving: "I'm an Indian," 65
Berlin, Isaiah, 3–4, 136, 284; "Two Concepts of Liberty," 133–34, 143
Berlioz, Hector, 198, 287; "De l'imitation," 236, 239; *Symphonie fantastique,* 228
Bernard, Jonathan, 251, 256, 258–59
Bernstein, Leonard, 66, 371
Berry, Mark, 379n102
Beyoncé, 153
Bill of Rights, 16
Bilson, Malcolm, 131, 195
binarisms, 37–38, 137
Binkley, Thomas, 189, 192
Bismarck, Otto von, 337
Blachly, Alexander, 68n69
Blackmur, Richard P., 223, 365
Blake, David, 14–15
Blake, William: "Little Black Boy," 66–67
Bloom, Allan, 359
Bloom, Harold, 381, 385
Bodanzky, Artur, 53n27
Boelza, Igor Fyodorovich, 423–25
Böhm, Karl, 145
Bonds, Mark Evan, 36, 87n50
Book of the Month Club, 370–71
Boretz, Benjamin, 210n10
Borio, Gianmario, 385–86
Borodin, Alexander Porfir'yevich, 184; *In Central Asia,* 409–11
Boros, James, 277n61, 351n33
Boston Symphony Orchestra, 61, 136, 168, 171–74
Bostridge, Ian, 130
Boulanger, Lili, 14
Boulanger, Nadia, 14
Boulez, Pierre, 182, 193n32, 322–26, 404; on chromaticism, 181; *Rituel,* 326; *Marteau sans Maître, Le,* 183, 263–69; Sonata No. 2, 325–26n42

INDEX 439

Bourdieu, Pierre, 33, 123, 392, 398, 403, 416
Bourgault-Ducoudray, Louis-Albert, 266n29
Braden, Thomas W., 219n34
Brahms, Johannes, 161, 191–92: Cello Sonata No. 2 in F, op. 99, 198; Symphony No. 1 in C minor, 198; Symphony No. 3 in F, 300; Variations on a Theme by Haydn, 198
Brand, Max, 191
Brendel, Franz, 121–23, 182, 198
Brett, Philip, 313
Brexit, 338
Brinkmann, Reinhold, 62
Britten, Benjamin, 45, 222, 341, 364, 384–85
Brody, Martin, 208–9, 220–21
Brodsky, Joseph, 395–96, 399
Brodsky, Seth, 19, 384–85
Brook, Barry S., 164
Brooks, Mel: *The Producers*, 52
Brown, Curtis, 173
Brown, Malcolm H., 402n8
Broyard, Anatole, 388–91
Bubner, Rüdiger, 18
Bukina, Tatyana Vadimovna, 402m 405–6, 411–14, 416, 436
Bürger, Peter, 368
Burke, Edmund, 98, 286–89
Burkholder, J. Peter, 105–6, 346, 348–49
Burney, Charles, 75, 84, 91
Busbey, Fred, 59
Busnoys, Antoine, 110; *Quant j'ay au cuer,* 114; *Victimae paschali laudes,* 67–69, 71, 131
Bychkov, Semyon Mayevich, 53n27

cabaletta, 363
Caccini, Giulio, 182
Cage, John, 218
Calico, Joy H., 216n28
Calvocoressi, Michel Dimitri, 365
Cambridge History of Nineteenth-Century Music, 136–39, 156
Cambridge History of Twentieth-Century Music, 136, 140–41, 156
canon, 31, 139
carmina, 110–17, 345
Carter, Elliott, 11, 13, 57n38, 124–25, 213–15, 219–22, 279–80, 325–26, 341, 383–85; Cello Sonata, 325; First String Quartet, 124, 213–14, 219–22
Castle, Terry, 70n74
censorship, 2, 15–16, 23–24, 41–71, 134, 136, 176

Central Intelligence Agency (CIA), 214, 217–18
Chadwick, Tim, 158
Chailley, Jacques, 31
Chalmers, David J., 3–5
Chaikovsky, Pyotr Ilyich, 184; *Ouverture solennelle 1812,* 55–56; Piano Concerto No. 1, 333–36, 338, 374–76
chanson, Parisian, 26
Chansonbearbeitungen see carmina
Cheney, Dick, 175
Chernyshevsky, Nikolai Gavrilovich, 2, 413
children's songs, 184–85
Chodowiecki, Daniel: "Aufklärung" (copperplate engraving), 73–74
Chomsky, Noam, 177, 244
Chopin, Fryderyk Franciszek: Fantasia in F minor, op. 49, 418
Chowrimootoo, Christopher, 341, 356, 366–69, 377, 387–88
Christo, 70
Cicero, 296, 344–35
circular reasoning, 289
Clark, Katerina, 414
Clark, Suzannah, 253–54
classical music, and class distinction, 359
Clemens non Papa, Jacobus, 182
Clifford, James, 308, 318
Clinton, Bill, 172
Cocteau, Jean, 140, 142, 148
cognitive concerns, 382, 400
Cohen, Brigid, 367
Cohen, Gustav, 291n23
Colbert, Stephen, 185, 340
Cold War, 24, 38, 58, 118, 124–26, 137, 156, 208–25, 263, 403, 405, 415
Cole, Nat King, 390–91
Communist Manifesto, 60
Communist Party of the USA, 60
Cone, Edward T., 326
Congress for Cultural Freedom (CCF), 124, 213–14, 219–21
Conrad, Joseph, 119
contextualization, 213–15, 222, 224, 283–85, 287; *vs.* universalism, 305
contour and convention, 229
contrafactum, 69
Conversations with Igor Stravinsky (Stravinsky and Craft), 247–48
Cook, Nicholas, 136
Cooper, Anthony Ashley *see* Shaftesbury
Cooper, Michael, 398

Copland, Aaron, 80, 211; *Lincoln Portrait, A*, 59–61; *Second Hurricane, The*, 65–66
Cordier, Baude: *Par le deffaut*, 187
Craft, Robert, 46–48, 183, 186–88, 194, 202, 261, 335–36
Crequillon, Thomas, 182
Crist, Stephen A., 216n28
criticism, function of (Eliot), 376
Crocker, Richard L., 185
crossover, 394
Crunden, Robert M., 349
Cuban missile crisis, 216
Cultural and Scientific Conference for World Peace, 59
Current Musicology, 5
Currie, James, 19, 177
custom, 311
Cuyler, Louise, 186

Dahl, Ingolf, 256
Dahlhaus, Carl, 26–28, 137, 156, 422, 435; *Foundations of Music History*, 37
Dallapiccola, Luigi, 119
Danger of Music, The (Taruskin), 9n18
Danto, Arthur, 171
Danuser, Hermann, 140–41
Davison, Archibald T., 186
Death of Klinghoffer (Sellars-Adams-Goodman), 24, 61–62, 168–76
deconstruction, 90, 356–57
defamiliarization, 194
Degeyter, Pierre, 242
dehumanization, 380–81
Denby, Edwin, 66
Denisov, Edison Vasil'yevich, 202, 404
Des Prez, Josquin, 110, 182, 187; *La Bernardina*, 115; *Missa Hercules Dux Ferrariae*, 247–48
developing variations, 198
Dewey, John, 16
Diaghilev, Sergey Pavlovich, 154, 399
Dies, Albert Christoph, 80
Dies Irae, 228
discourse, 34–36, 138
disinterestedness, 87, 103, 124
disenchantment, 25–26
Dobrenko, Evgeny Ivanovich, 412
Dolan, Therese, 162n37
Dollimore, Jonathan, 171
Dolzhansky, Alexander Naumovich, 243–25
Domaine musical, 182
Dostoyevsky, Fyodor Mikhailovich, 262; *Brothers Karamazov*, 3

Douglas, Helen Gahagan, 60
Douglas, Melvyn, 59–60
Drachler, Jacob, 46, 135
Drobinsky, Mark, 202
Drott, Eric, 242
Druskin, Mikhaíl Semyonovich, 431
Dunsby, Jonathan, 378, 416
Durant, Will, 370
Durkheim, Émile, 337

Earle, Ben, 376–78
"Early music," 128, 180; *vs.* "alte Musik," 189–90
Eisenhower, Dwight David, 59
Eisler, Hanns, 58–59
electronic music, 328
Elgar, Edward, 350, 353
Eliot, T. S., 130, 376
Elston, Arnold, 197
Encounter, 124, 220
Engels, Friedrich, 407–8, 413
Enlightenment, 17, 72–77, 83–85, 118
entertainment (as distinct from art), 123, 130, 161
Epstein, Jacob, 65
Epstein, Mikhail, 2
essentialism, 27–28
Eszterházy, Nikolaus, Prince, 77
Eszterházy, Nikolaus II, Prince, 78
ethnomusicology, 6, 25, 402
Evenings on the Roof, 47
Expositions and Developments (Stravinsky and Craft), 200
Extramusical, 118, 228

Fadiman, Clifton, 370
fallibilism, 4, 12
Fallon, Robert, 216n28
Faulkner, William, 341
Feldman, Morton, 218
Felski, Rita, 283
Ferienkurse für neue Musik (Darmstadt), 126, 215
Ferneyhough, Brian, 185
Feynberg, Yevgeniy L'vovich, 426
Field, John, 253
Finagin, Alexey Vasil'yevich, 401–2, 405, 419
Fink, Robert, 173
Finscher, Ludwig, 196n38
Fischer, David Hackett, 37–38
Fitzpatrick, Sheila, 406
Ford, Phil, 216n28
"foreign music" (*zarubezhnaya muzïka*), 426
form, harmonically articulated, 244–26
form/content dichotomy, 227–28, 422

formalism, 118–19, 403, 405, 423, 425
Forster, E. M., 149
Forte, Allen, 204, 217, 251, 255–57, 262, 273, 280, 326, 403
Foss, Lukas, 45, 48
Foucault, Michel, 11, 177
Fox, Christopher, 124, 385, 387
Franck, César, 384
Frankenstein, Alfred, 361
Frankfurt School, 40, 151, 409
Franklin, Peter, 366, 379–83, 386, 392, 396
Freud, Sigmund, 337
Fried, Michael, 18
Frolova-Walker, Marina, 11n20, 13, 58n40
Fromm Foundation for Music, 214
Fukuyama, Francis, 88
Fürstenberg, Max Egon, Prince zu, 367
Furtwängler, Wilhelm, 53n27

Gabrieli, Andrea, 188
Gabrieli, Giovanni: *In ecclesiis*, 188
gagaku, 317–18
Gavrushkevich, Ivan Ivanovich, 409
Gay, Peter, 86
Geiringer, Karl, 86n42
Gelatt, Roland, 209n5
Gelb, Peter, 394
Gelbart, Matthew, 308
Gellner, Ernest, 408–9
gemäßigte Moderne, 369
Gemeinschaft, 315, 324, 333, 336–38; vs. *Gesellschaft*, 337–38
Generative Theory of Tonal Music, A (Lerdahl and Jackendoff), 244, 273
Genina, Liana, 419
Genzinger, Marianne von, 85–86
Gerhard, Roberto, 279
Gershwin, George: *Porgy and Bess*, 67
Gerstein, Kirill, 333–35, 338
Gestalt, 422
Gesualdo, Carlo, 181, 183, 188, 194
Ghiselin, Johannes, 110; *La Alfonsina*, 115–16
Ghizeghem, Hayne van: *De tous biens playne*, 110
Gibson, James, 78n18, 248
Gibson, Mel, 41
Gilbert, W. S., 62–64
Giuliani, Rudolph W., 165
Gjerdingen, Robert, 254
Glebov, Igor *see* Asafiev
Glikman, Isaak Davidovich, 57
Glinka, Mikhail Ivanovich: *A Life for the Tsar*, 48–50

Glock, William, 124, 214, 220
Glogauer Liederbuch, 111–16, 345
Godwin's Law, 17
Goebbels, Joseph, 172, 342
Goehr, Lydia, 19, 108–9, 116, 283–84; *The Imaginary Museum of Musical Works*, 108–9, 284
Goehring, Edmund, 119n31
Goethe, Johann Wolfgang von, 81
Goldenweiser, Alexander Alexandrovich, 335
Goldman, Richard Franko, 325–26
Goldsworthy, Anna, 397
Gombert, Nicolas, 182
Goodman, Alice, 61
Gorbachev, Mikhail Sergeyevich, 403–4
Górecki, Henryk: Third Symphony, 394
Gorodetsky, Sergey Mitrofanovich, 49, 54
Gossett, Philip, 21–23, 151
Gould, Morton, 390–91
Gozzi, Carlo, 13–14
Grant, M. J., 274–75, 278
Great Courses, The, 376
Great Either/Or, The, 37–38, 434
Great Sebastians, The (Lindsay and Crouse), 266n30
Green, Martyn, 64
Greenberg, Clement, 346, 351, 358–59, 365, 367, 388–89, 391, 394; "Avant-Garde and Kitsch," 357–58
Greenberg, Robert, 377
Greenblatt, Stephen, 18, 308–9
Grétry, André Ernest Modeste, 76
Griesinger, Georg August, 77, 96–97, 108
Griffith, D. W., 359–60
Griffiths, Dai, 217n30, 386
Griffiths, Paul, 130, 140–41; on *Le Marteau sans maître*, 266
Griggs, John Cornelius, 346
Groman-Solovtsov, Anatoliy Alexandrovich, 408
Group for Contemporary Music, 183, 250
Grout, Donald Jay, 75, 105
Groys, Boris, 18
Gubaidulina, Sofiya Asgatovna, 202
Gutman, Natalia Grigor'yevna, 202
Gutting, Gary, 377, 397
Guy Fawkes Day, 63

Haggin, B. H., 365
Haimo, Ethan, 215
Hakobian, Levon Oganesovich, 405n14, 434
Handel, George Frideric, 84, 267; viewed by Stravinsky, 200; viewed by *Wiener Schule*, 199. WORKS: *Israel in Egypt*, 239, 241

Hanslick, Eduard, 25, 28, 182, 228, 250, 285–87, 290–95, 297–98, 301–5, 402; on representation, 227; *tönend bewegte Formen* defined, 291
Hansen, Miriam Bratu, 367–68
Hanson, F. Allan, 318, 331
Hanson, Howard, 223–24
Hanukkah, 314–16
Hardy, Thomas, 119
Harich-Schneider, Eta, 317–18
Harmonice musices odhecaton, 116
harmony, sea of (Wagner), 250–51
Harnoncourt, Nikolaus, 330
Harper-Scott, J. P. E., 19, 283, 285, 385, 398; *Edward Elgar, Modernist,* 356, 387; *Quilting Points of Musical Modernism, The,* 405n14
Harrison, Frank Llewellyn, 6–7
Hartmann, Karl Amadeus, 141
Haydn, Franz Joseph, 17, 72–98, 108, 121; on genius, 97; and patronage, 85–86, 103. WORKS: *Armida,* 76; Baryton trios, 77; *Creation,* 73–74, 78, "Representation of Chaos" in, 98; "Emperor" Quartet, 229; *Harmonie-Messe,* 86; Piano Trio in G, Hob. XV:25, 91; Quartets, op. 33, 76, 84; Sonata No. 52 in E-flat, 320; *Seasons, The,* 78; *Stabat Mater,* 76; Symphony No. 92 in G, "Oxford," 90; Symphony No. 103 in E-flat, "Drumroll," 81; *Tageszeiten* symphonies, 98
Heartz, Daniel, 79n21, 430; "Approaching a History of 18th-Century Music," 197
Hegel, Georg Wilhelm Friedrich, 160
Heidegger, Martin, 400–1
Heile, Björn, 215, 382, 386
Heine, Heinrich, 1–2
Hempel, Carl, 210
Henderson, W. J., 56
Hensher, Philip, 65
hermeneutics, 6, 226, 232–33, 436
Hepokoski, James, 356
Herzen, Alexander Ivanovich, 2
Heston, Charlton
Hewett, Ivan, 378, 383
Hicks, Michael, 274, 278
Hindemith, Paul, 183, 191
Historical Anthology of Music (HAM), 186–88
historically-informed performance movement (HIP), 128–29, 324
historiography, 30–40, 148; and advocacy, 24; and fiction, 24; neo-Hegelian, 33; and socialist realism, 411–16

Hitler, Adolf, 17, 52, 140
Hobsbawm, Eric, 28, 31, 307–9, 311–14, 338
Hoffmann, E. T. A., 87, 102–4, 107, 122, 129
Hoffmann, Richard, 256
Hogwood, Christopher, 330
Holland, Bernard, 158
Holmes, Taylor, 292
Hood, Mantle, 6
Horlacher, Gretchen, 254
Horowitz, Joseph, 349
Horowitz, Vladimir, 320–21
horses, dead, 280–81
Horton, Julian, 260
Hsieh, Amanda, 391–92
Hulme, T. E., 192
Humble, Nicola, 377
Hunter, George, 189
Hurrian hymn, 185
Husserl, Edmund, 400
Huyssen, Andreas, 366n77, 368

ideology, 21–23
imitative textures, 206–7
Indy, Vincent d', 350
Ingarden, Roman, 332, 400–1
intelligentsia, 3
intentional fallacy, 270
Internationale, L', 242
International Music Council, 163
intonatsiya, 402
Invention of Tradition (Hobsbawm and Ranger), 28, 307–12, 318
Ippolitov-Ivanov, Mikhaíl Mikhaílovich, 154
Isaac, Henricus, 110, 114–15; Benedictus (*Missa Quant j'ay au cuer*), 114, 116; *Choralis Constantinus,* 186
intertextuality, 226
Ives, Charles, 120, 130, 215, 228, 346, 348–50, 352–53, 385; *Concord* Sonata, 353; *Essays before a Sonata,* 348–49
Ives, George, 346

Jackson, William, 83
Jakobson, Roman, 123, 340
Jameson, Frederic, 149
Jankélévitch, Vladimir, 266n29
Jannequin, Clément, 36
Japart, Jean, 110
J'ay pris amours, 110–14, 116
Jenni, Donald, 245–46, 248
Jerome, Jerome K., 391

Jewish identity, 314–16
Jews, 41, 46–48, 68 (*see also* Anti-Semitism)
Johnson, Douglas, 269–72
Johnson, Julian, 384
Jones, Sterling, 189
Journal of the Royal Musical Association, 366
journalism (as distinct from scholarship), 148
Joyce, James, 341
Julius, Anthony, 160–63, 166–67
Junior Scholastic, 216
Juszkiewicz, Anton, 184

Kabalevsky, Dmitry Borisovich, 58
Kaczynski, Theodore, 168
kalendarnïye pesni, 184–85
Kallman, Chester, 362
Kant, Emmanuel, 25, 72–75, 79, 87, 125, 133, 142, 287–90; "An Answer to the Question 'What Is Enlightenment?,'" 72–74, 118; *Critique of Judgment*, 96, 101–2, 106–7, 158–59, 288
Karajan, Herbert von, 145, 158
Karlinsky, Simon, 245n35
Karnes, Kevin, 402
Kateb, George, 175
Kavelin, Konstantin Dmitriyevich, 408
Keldïsh, Yury Vsevolodovich, 415, 431
Kempe, Rudolf, 53n27
Kenner und Liebhaber, 81–83
Kerman, Joseph, 23, 148, 214, 253, 269, 271–72, 306, 361–65; and Whiggishness, 160; *Contemplating Music*, 6–7, 293; *Opera as Drama*, 361–65; "Profile for American Musicology, A," 7n17, 156n17; "Translation for Music," 362
Keynes, John Maynard, 289
Khachaturian, Aram Ilyich, 58, 262
Kholopov, Yury Nikolayevich, 416, 419, 425, 431–34
Khrennikov, Tikhon Nikolayevich, 13, 404
Khrennikovskaya semyorka (The Khrennikov Seven), 404
Khrushchev, Nikita Sergeyevich, 50
Khubov, Georgiy Nikitich, 406–11; *A. P. Borodin*, 407–11
Kielberth, Joseph, 53n27
Kinderman, William, 54
Kilmer, Anne Draffkorn, 185
Kinkeldey, Otto, 224
Kipling, Rudyard: "Boots (Infantry Columns)," 292–93
Kirkpatrick, John, 353
Kissin, Yevgeny Igor'yevich, 31

kitsch, 123, 161
Kittel, Bruno, 70
Kivy, Peter, 228–30, 241, 283–84, 289–90, 293; *Corded Shell, The*, 229–30; *Sound and Semblance*, 232, 237
Klangmaterialismus, 195, 199–201, 331
Klein, Naomi, 177
Knepler, Georg, 38, 164, 435
knowledge, defined, 4
Knussen, Oliver, 269
Koblyakov, Lev, 265, 267–69, 273–74, 276
Kodály, Zoltán: *Psalmus Hungaricus*, 39
Koenig, Gottfried Michael, 329–30
Konen, Valentina Dzhozefovna, 425–34; *Puti amerikanskoy muzïki*, 430; *Teatr i simfoniya*, 430; "V zashchitu istoricheskoy nauki," 425–26, 428–30
Kostelanetz, André, 390
Koussevitzky, Serge Alexandrovich, 60
Kovnatskaya, Lyudmila Grigor'yevna, 401
Kramer, Hilton, 216
Kramer, Lawrence, 6n12, 162n37
Krasner, Louis, 141
Krenek, Ernst: *Jonny spielt auf*, 191
Kristol, William, 175
Kügle, Karl, 401
Kurth, Ernst, 420

Lachenmann, Helmut, 185
Lamar, Kendrick, 127
Lampell, Millard, 60
Landerer, Christoph, 291n25
Lang Lang, 158
Lang, Paul Henry, 156, 194
Lansky, Paul, 332–33
La Rue, Pierre de, 182
Lawson, Dominic, 158
Lazarevich, Gordana, 5
Lazarus, Emma, 396n154
Leavis, F. R., 361
Leech-Wilkinson, Daniel, 28, 323–26
Lenin, Vladimir Ilyich, 2, 407–8
Leppert, Richard, 19, 20n41, 380
Lerdahl, Fred, 244, 246, 250, 268, 273–74, 276–77, 351, 382
Lessem, Alan, 94n67
Lessing, Gotthold Ephraim, 304
Levenberg, Jeffrey, 223
Levinson, Jerrold, 283–84, 305; *Music in the Moment*, 284, 299–301
Levinson, Sanford, 41

Lewin, David, 326
Libman, Lillian, 46, 135
Ligeti, György, 125; *Artikulation*, 125; Horn Trio, 404
Lincoln, Abraham, 59–60
Lipman, Samuel, 216
Lippman, Edward A., 5–9
Listenius, Nikolaus, 109, 115–16
Lister, Rodney, 124
Liszt, Franz, 285, 334; "Gypsy scale" in, 228
Literacy, 32–33, 117
Livanova, Tamara Nikolayevna, 413
Lockwood, Lewis, 53–54
Loge Olympique de Paris, 78
Logical positivism, 209–11
Lomax, Alan, 164
London Review of Books, 168
Long, Michael P., 223–24
Lowe, Melanie, 90–91, 93
Lowenthal, Jerome, 335
Lowinsky, Edward, 151–52, 156
Lunacharsky, Anatoliy Vasil'yevich, 406
Lutosławski, Witold, 279
Lvov, Alexey Fyodorovich: *Bozhe, tsarya khrani!* 55
Lynes, Russell, 350–55, 357–60, 365, 369

Ma, Yo-Yo, 202, 394
Maazel, Lorin, 53n27
McCain, John, 62
McCarthy, Tom, 341
McCartney, Paul, 391
McClary, Susan, 19, 90, 162n37; on Beethoven's Ninth Symphony, 296–97; on Mozart's "Prague" Symphony, 233–35
Macdonald, Dwight, 343–44, 346, 348, 350, 358, 360, 372–73, 388–89
MacDonald, Malcolm, 378
MacDowell, Edward, 430
Mackerras, Charles, 64
Macque, Giovanni de: *Seconda Stravaganza*, 187
Madonna, 153
magic tricks, 254
Mahler, Gustav, 324
Manet, Edouard: *Olympia*, 162
Mann, Thomas, 104; *Betrachtungen eines Unpolitischen*, 104–5n12
Manning, Jane, 323
Mantovani, Annunzio Paolo, 390–91
Manulkina, Olga Borisovna, 401
Maori, 318

Marcuse, Herbert, 165
Marissen, Michael, 42, 44–45
Marseillaise, La, 242
Martin, George, 390
Martin, Peter, 39n11
Martin, Steve, 147
Martini, Johannes, 110; *La Martinella*, 115
Martino, Donald, 62
Martïnov, Ivan Ivanovich, 413
Martïnov, Vladimir Ivanovich, 413
Marx, Karl, 152–53
Marxism, 408
Masterpieces of Music before 1750 (Parrish and Ohl), 188
Mathew, Nicholas, 54
Matteo da Perugia: *Le greygnour bien*, 183
Mazel', Lev Abramovich, 416–20, 421–25, 429, 431–32
Mazzetti, Remo Jr., 69
Mead, Andrew, 275–78; on David Schiff, *The Music of Elliott Carter*, 278–80
meaning, 34–35, 119–21, 178, 226
mediation, 138, 153, 178, 242
Melachrino, George, 390
Melchior, Lauritz, 53n27
Mendel, Arthur, 223, 275
Mendelssohn, Felix, 198, 228
Mendelssohn, Moses: *Briefe über die Empfindungen*, 100
Menotti, Gian-Carlo, 364
Menuhin, Yehudi, 163–64
Merkel, Angela, 166
Messiaen, Olivier, 217
metanarrative, 33
metaphors, 118–20, 245–46, 294–97, 298–301
Meyer, Ernst Hermann, 7n15
Meyer, Leonard B., 122, 249, 275, 303–4; "On Rehearing Music," 249n49, 336n74; "Universe of Universals, A," 303–4
Meyerhold, Vsevolod Emil'yevich, 13–14
middlebrow, 340–47, 349–60; and antimodernism, 350; as aspiration, 342, 349, 351–52, 369–76; vs. broadbrow, 369; as critical function, 365; as genre, 341–42; as style, 369; as transaction, 351–52, 369–76
Mikado, The (Gilbert and Sullivan), 63–64
Mikhailov, Mikhaíl Larionovich, 1–2
Mill, John Stuart, 133, 136
mimesis, conventions of, 243–44
mind-independence, 294–95
Minin, Kuzma, 49

Miró, Joan, 125
Mitchell, Donald, 378
Mitchinson, Paul, 208
modernism, 404; and aesthetic autonomy, 122–28; "expansionist" interpretation of, 356, 367–68; first maxim of, 267; *vs.* modernity, 368; and performance, 128–29; and transgression, 161–63
"Modernism and Its Others" (JRMA roundtable), 366–67, 385–86
Moldenhauer, Hans and Rosaleen, 141
Molière, 91
Molino, Jean, 157, 257
Monday Evening Concerts, 182
Monteux, Pierre, 129
Monteverdi, Claudio, 119, 183, 188, 194; *Orfeo*, 195n36; *seconda prattica*, 182
morality, art and, 29
Morgan, Robert P., 246–47
Morley, Thomas: *Christes Crosse*, 183
Morton, Lawrence, 182
Morzin, Karl Joseph, Count, 78
Motörhead: "Ace of Spades," 287
Mouton, Jean, 182
movement, metaphors of, 245–46
movements (divisions of musical works), 245n35
Mozart, Wolfgang Amadé, 77, 82–83, 103, 243–44; florid embellishment in, 131. WORKS: Fugue in C minor for two pianos, K426, 193; *Idomeneo*, 166, 364–65; Piano Concerto No. 17 in G, K453, 90; Piano Concerto No. 23 in A, K488, 320; *Re pastore, Il*, 235; *Requiem*, 70–71, 176; Symphony No. 38 in D, "Prague," 232–35; Symphony No. 39 in E-flat, 103; Symphony No. 40 in G minor, 229–30, 243, 289; *Zauberflöte, Die*, 362
"Muddle Instead of Music" (Zaslavsky), 56
Müller-Doohm, Stefan, 380
music, condition of (Pater), 18, 101–2, 159, 227
music, nature of, 243
musica poetica, 109
Music-Appreciation Records, 371–76
music business, incipient, 116–17
"music drama" defined, 120
"music itself, the," 290–91, 293, 298
"musicality," 323
music theory, 25–26; *vs.* musicology, 431–34
musical space, 246–51, 298–300
musical structure, 298–301
"musicking," 303, 402
musicology, Romantic heritage of, 155–57

Musicology (Palisca, Hood, Harrison), 6–7
Musorgsky, Modest Petrovich, 150, 410–11; *Boris Godunov*, 56, 150, 153–55, versions of, 150–51; *Taking of Kars, The*, 411
Mussolini, Benito, 65
Myaskovsky, Nikolai Yakovlevich, 58, 262

Nabokov, Nicolas, 213, 220–21
Nabokov, Vladimir, 340, 361
National Association of Schools of Music, 223
National Council of American-Soviet Friendship, 60
nationalism, 241–42, 307–8, 310–11
Nattiez, Jean-Jacques, 157–58, 257, 258
nature *vs.* culture, 294–95, 303–4
Nazis, 140, 144–45, 397
NBC Symphony, 349
Neff, Severine, 258
Neighbour, Oliver, 378
Nekrasov, Nikolai Alekseyevich, 2
neoclassicism, 124, 140, 142, 306
neoliberalism, 404–5
Nest'yev, Izraíl Valdimirovich, 423–25
neudeutsche Schule, 182, 285, 301–2, 379
Neuenfels, Hans, 166
neue Sachlichkeit, 191
Neusiedler, Hans: *Der Juden Tanz*, 187n16
Newlin, Dika, 190; *Bruckner, Mahler, Schoenberg*, 156–57
"new musicology," 6, 35–36, 296, 316, 400, 403, 405, 436
New Oxford History of Music, 79–80
Niebuhr, Reinhold, 398
Nietzsche, Friedrich, 120, 312; "Vom Nutzen und Nachteil der Historie für das Leben," 309
Nixon, Richard M., 59
Nono, Luigi, 161, 182
Nordau, Max: *Degeneration*, 396
Northcott, Bayan, 47–48, 214, 379n102
Norton, Mildred, 47
Nussbaum, Charles, 248–50
Nye, Joseph, 219

Obrecht, Jacob, 110
Ockeghem, Johannes, 182
Ockl, Karl, 98
O'Connell, Charles, 384
octatonic collection, 205, 259, 261–62, 270–71
octave equivalency, 246–47
Odyssey, 119
Oestreich, James, 9

Ofili, Chris, 166
omnivory, 392–94, 396
ondes Martenot, 328
ontology, 27–28, 331–32
opera, birth of, 182
Orgelbewegung, 201
Ortega y Gasset, José, 322, 380–81
Orwell, George, 172
Ossian, 308
Oxford History of Western Music, 9, 10–15, 30–40, 44n6, 105, 123, 132–33, 147–48, 177–78, 180, 203, 212–14, 218, 222, 225, 245–46, 253, 264, 284–86, 290–91, 295, 301–3, 335, 344–46, 348, 353, 384, 397, 405n14

Pace, Ian, 19, 177, 203–5, 385–87, 392, 398
Paddison, Max, 19
Paine, Thomas: *The Age of Reason,* 75
Palestrina, Giovanni Pierluigi da, 239
Palisca, Claude V., 6
Panteleeva, Olga, 401–2
paranoid reading, 15, 405n14
Parker, Horatio, 346
Parrish, Carl: *Treasury of Early Music,* 187
partbooks, 111, 116
Partisan Review, 217
Passmore, Walter, 63
Pater, Walter, 159, 370; on musical representation, 227
Patou, Jean, 65
patronage, 128, 398
Payne, Anthony, 378
Payzant, Geoffrey, 291n25
Peckham, Morse, 387n136
Pederson, Sanna, 108n22
Pekarsky, Mark Ilyich, 202
Pekelis, Mikhaíl Samoilovich, 415
perestroika, 403–4
performance practice, 128–31, 321
Perle, George, 256
Perrin, Tom, 340–41
Peterson, Richard A., 361, 392–94, 396, 398
Petrucci, Ottaviano, 116, 345–46
Pfitzner, Hans, 104, 140–41; *Palestrina,* 123
Phelps, William Lyon, 343–44, 346–50, 353, 362–63, 370, 378, 385
phenomenology, 400
Phillips, Mark Salber, 322
pianto, 230–31
Pinker, Steven, 89n55
Pinturicchio, 119
Piovesan, Alessandro, 188

pitch-class set analysis, 255–57
pitch-class set multiplication, 265
Plato, 182
pleasure and pain, 285–90
Pleyel, Ignace, 81n31
Podolski, Michel, 187n16
poietic fallacy, 45, 124, 157–58, 166, 173, 177–78, 203, 241, 254, 257, 383, 403
"political correctness," 386
political manipulation through music, 242
Pollock, Jackson, 217–18
Pople, Anthony, 136, 226
Popper, Karl, 4; on nationalism, 307
Popular Front, 60
Porter, Andrew, 214, 216
Porter, Cole: "You're the Top," 64–65
Porter, Fairfield, 71
Pottier, Eugène, 242
Pound, Ezra, 129, 142, 192
Powder Her Face (Adès and Hensher), 65
Pozharsky, Dmitry Mikhailovich, 49
Prest, Julia, 76
prestige, 123
Priestley, J. B., 369, 376
Princeton University, PhD in composition, 209–10, 222–24
Pritchard, Matthew, 101n4
prodigal son, 119
progress, 3–5
Prokofieff, Serge, 119, 262; *Cantata for the Twentieth Anniversary of October,* 50n21; *Love for Three Oranges, The,* 13–14; Seventh Symphony, 57–58; *Zdravitsa,* 49–52, 55, 133
protyazhnïye pesni, 184–85
pseudohistory, 181
Puccini, Giacomo, 364
Puffett, Kathryn, 203, 206
Pulitzer Prize, 126–27
Punch, 342
Putin, Vladimir Vladimirovich, 51

Rachmaninoff, Sergei Vasilievich, 334
Rainey, Lawrence, 367n78
Ramm, Andrea von, 189
Ranganathan, Sumitra, 311–32
Ranger, Terence, 28, 308
Ratner, Leonard, 246, 248
Rattle, Simon, 323
Ravel, Maurice: String Quartet, 300
Rawlings, Marjorie Kinnan, 341
reception history, 35
Redlich, Hans, 195, 331

Reese, Gustave: *Music in the Middle Ages,* 188
reflective morality, 16
Reid, Ellen, 127n51
Reihe, Die, 328
Rembrandt van Rijn, 199
representation, 25, 226–51; conventions of, 230–31; and mechanisms of humor, 237–41; mental, 244–51
Richardson, John, 74
Richter, Franz Xaver, 83
Richter, Sviatoslav Teofilovich: on Prokofieff's *Zdravitsa,* 52
Riethmüller, Albrecht, 17–18, 99
Rieu, André, 390
Riley, Dennis, 245
Rimbault, Edward Francis, 88
Rimsky-Korsakov, Nikolai Andreyevich, 184, 258
Rings, Steven, 25–26, 280n71
Rinkenberg, Martin, 111
Ritzarev (Rītsareva), Marina (Grigor'yevna), 421
Roberts, Laurance, 220
Robinson, Earl: *The Lonesome Train,* 60
Rochberg, George, 216
Rochlitz, Friedrich, 54
Rockwell, John, 51–52, 133n67, 216
Roerich, Nikolai Konstantinovich, 184
Rogers, Nigel, 189
Rore, Cipriano de, 181
Rosen, Charles, 10, 25, 44n6, 105, 131–33, 149n4, 203, 212–14, 218–23, 225, 384
Ross, Alex, 169, 212; on *Le Marteau sans maître,* 265
Rossini, Gioachino: *Guillaume Tell,* 49
Rossiter, Frank R., 349
Rothfarb, Lee, 291n25
Rouget de Lisle, Claude Joseph, 242
Rousseau, Jean-Jacques, 126, 309–12, 323; *Confessions,* 311; *Considérations sur le gouvernement de Pologne,* 310–12; *Dictionnaire de musique,* 237
Ruark, Robert, 341
Rubin, Joan Shelley, 340, 343, 346, 349, 351
Ruggles, Carl, 251; *Sun-Treader,* 251
Rumph, Stephen, 54
Rupprecht, Philip, 385
Russkaya assotsiatsiya proletarskikh muzikantov (RAPM), 408

Saatchi, Charles, 165
Sacchetti, Liberio, 401
Sadie, Stanley, 267
Sagan, Françoise, 341

Saint-Saëns, Camille, 202; *Élégie pour violon et piano, op. 160,* 373
Salomon, J. P., 78, 81, 103
Samosud, Samuil Abramovich, 58n40
Sams, Eric, 302n48
Samson, Jim, 136–39
Samuel, Claude, 404
Samuelson, Paul, 289n18
Satie, Erik, 215
Schauffler, Robert H., 352
Schenker, Heinrich, 211, 247, 342, 420
Schering, Arnold, 187
Scherman, Harry, 370–71
Scherman, Thomas, 371, 373–76
Scherzinger, Martin, 173–76
Schiff, David: *The Music of Elliott Carter,* 278–80
Schiller, Friedrich, 152
Schmelz, Peter J., 216
Schmidt, Thomas, 19
Schoenberg, Arnold, 122–23, 139–40, 141, 142, 145, 159, 160, 180, 211, 215, 222, 341, 342, 376–78, 420; conducts Mahler, 193; criticized by Nazis, 62; on analysis, 276; on Handel vs. Bach, 199n47; humor, his sense of, 202–5; misprints in, 205–6; and textual criticism, 329; use of xylophone, 202. WRITINGS: "Brahms the Progressive," 198; "Composition with Twelve Tones" (1947), 204; "Method of Composing with Twelve Tones Related Only to Each Other," 277; "National Music," 195–96; *Style and Idea,* 190; "Today's Manner of Performing Classical Music," 190–91; "Verhältnis zum Text, Das," 204n67. WORKS: arrangement of J. S. Bach, "St. Anne" Prelude and Fugue, 192, 201; arrangements of J. S. Bach chorale preludes, 200; *Begleitungsmusik zu einer Lichtspielszene,* 202; Cello Concerto after Monn, 201–2; *Drei Satiren für gemischten Chor,* 367; *Pelleas und Melisande,* 335; *Pierrot lunaire,* 323–24, "Der Mondfleck" from, 203–5, 207; Quartet Concerto after Handel, 199, 201; Septet-Suite, op. 29, 186; Suite, op. 25, 197; Variations for Orchestra, op. 31, 197; *Verklärte Nacht,* 336; Violin Concerto, op. 36, 376–77; Waltz, op. 23, no. 5, 277
Schoenberg, E. Randol, 379n102
Schonberg, Harold, 320–21
Schopenhauer, Artur, 104–7, 119–20, 123, 137, 211
Schroeder, David P., 74, 76–77, 81–82, 84–85, 88–89
Schubart, Christian: *Ideen zu einer Ästhetik der Tonkunst,* 229

Schubert, Franz: Impromptu in E-flat, op. 90, no. 2, 253–54; Piano Trio No. 2 in E-flat, op. 100, 300–301
Schuller, Gunther, 130
Schumann, Robert, 229, 287; *Dichterliebe*, 130; Piano Concerto, 300; Piano Quintet in E-flat, op. 44, 118–21, 300
Schütz, Heinrich, 183, 188, 194
Schwartz, Delmore, 388–89, 391
Scriabin, Alexander Nikolayevich, 215, 250
Scruton, Roger, 89n56, 296n33
Searle, Humphrey, 196
Seeger, Ruth Crawford, 14
Sellars, Peter, 61
semiotics, 35, 226
Sennfl, Ludwig, 115
Serial music, and aural cognition, 274
Serling, Rod: *The Twilight Zone*, 217
Sermisy, Claudin de, 36
Serov, Alexander Nikolayevich, 301–2
Serra, Richard: *Tilted Arc*, 165, 167–68, 171, 174
Sessions, Roger, 107, 119, 243, 248, 251, 378
Setiya, Kieran, 1
Seufzer see pianto
Shaftesbury, Third Earl of (Anthony Ashley Cooper), 87
Shanet, Howard, 371–72, 374–76
Shaw, Robert, 45
Shawn, Allen, 378
Shebalin, Vissarion Yakovlevich, 55
Sheffer, Harry, 3–4
Shlifshteyn, Semyon Isaakovich, 423–25
Shnitke, Alfred Garriyevich, 202
shocker, shabby little, 364
Shostakovich, Dmitry Dmitrievich, 34, 58, 121, 163, 222, 262; debates about, 117–18, 232. WORKS: *Fall of Berlin, The*, 51; *Lady Macbeth of the Mtsensk District, The*, 56–57; Symphony No. 7, "Leningrad," 435
Shreffler, Anne, 141, 435
Sibelius, Jean, 356
Siloti, Alexander Ilyich, 224
Silverberg, Laura, 216n28
Simpson, Alan K., 59
Sisman, Elaine, 77n17, 98, 430
situational ethics, 16, 176
sketch studies, 150–51, 269
Slonimsky, Nicolas: *Lexicon of Musical Invective*, 56n34
Small, Christopher, 303, 402n7
Smart, Mary Ann, 162n37

Smith, Adam, 92–97
Smrž, Jiří, 414–17, 434
socialist realism, 411–16
Society for Music Theory, 252
sociology of taste, 34, 340–99
soft power, 219
Solie, Ruth, 90–91
Sollberger, Harvey, 183
Solzhenitsyn, Alexander Isayevich, 163
Sontag, Susan: "Against Interpretation," 228, 232
Spaeth, Sigmund, 229–30, 289–90
space, musical, 246–51, 298–300
Spano, Robert, 168–69
Sprout, Leslie A., 216n28
Sputnik, 224
Staël, Madame de (Anne Louise Germaine de Staël-Holstein), 74, 98
Stafford, Barbara, 18
Stalin, Iosif Vissarionovich, 5, 49–52
Stasov, Vladimir Vasil'yevich, 408
Stein, Erwin, 197
Stein, Gertrude, 341
Stein, Leonard, 190, 206
Steinberg, Michael, 320, 335
Steiner, George, 139, 146, 396–97; "Archives of Eden, The," 395; *In Bluebeard's Castle*, 139
Sterne, Laurence, 87
Sternfeld, Frederick W., 79
Stockhausen, Karlheinz, 70, 162, 182, 322; and 9/11, 176. WORKS: *Gesang der Jünglinge*, 333; *Inori*, 326; *Klavierstück XI*, 125–26; *Kreuzspiel*, 266, 268; *Mantra*, 326; *Mikrophonie I*, 331; *Studie II*, 327–33; *Zeitmasse*, 183
Stone, Oliver, 62
Straus, Joseph N., 268, 271n46; "Stravinsky's Serial 'Mistakes,'" 207n66
Strauss, Leo, 17
Strauss, Richard, 336, 364
Stravinsky, Igor Fyodorovich, 25, 192, 214, 222, 306, 330, 423; on Carter's Double Concerto, 264; and early music, 184–90; on expression, 226–27; and ghostwriters, 261; hexachord rotation technique, 274; and historiography, 134, 137; on *Le Marteau sans maître*, 263; plays Mozart, 193; as a Russian, 257–61; on Soviet music, 163; and textual criticism, 329; and twelve-tone music, 211. WRITINGS: *Poétique musicale*, 129, 186, 190, 193. WORKS: *Cantata on Old English Texts*, 46–48, 71, 134–36, 162, 182, 186; *Canticum sacrum ad honorem Sancti Marci Nominis*,

188, 194; *Firebird*, 184; *In Memoriam Dylan Thomas*, 182; Mass, 182, 187–88; *Movements for Piano and Orchestra*, 193–94, 245n35; *Orpheus*, 188; *Pribaoutki*, 205, sketches for, 270; *Pulcinella*, 200; *Sacre du printemps, Le*, 129, 161, 184–85, 261, 322n34, 373–74, sketches for, 270; Symphony in Three Movements, 245n35, 260
Stravinsky, Soulima, 193
Strayhorn, Billy, 391
Strunk, Oliver, 223–24
Stuckenschmidt, Hans Heinz, 328, 332
Studio der frühen Musik, 189, 192
style criticism, 105
sublime, 98, 286–89
Subotnik, Rose Rosengard, 20–23, 151–53
Sullivan, Arthur, 62
Suñol, Gregory, Dom, 188
Sutcliffe, Tom, 172
Swed, Mark, 169–71
symbolic exclusion, 398

Tansman, Alexandre, 47
taste, defined by Bourdieu, 398
Tate, Allen, 2
Taylor, Timothy, 344–46
Tchaikovsky *see* Chaikovsky
tenor tacet, 114; and rise of pervasive imitation, 206–7
Text and Act (Taruskin), 9n18
Thatcher, Margaret, 59
Theremin, 328
Thomas, Michael Tilson, 251
Thomson, Virgil, 69, 321, 365; *Five Songs from William Blake*, 66–67; *State of Music, The*, 403
Tinctoris, Johannes, 345
Toch, Ernst: *Fuge aus der Geographie*, 293
Tolstoy, Lev Nikolayevich, 2, 123
Tomášek, Václav Jan Křtitel, 253, 302n48
Tomlinson, Gary, 6n12, 177, 308
Tommasini, Anthony, 170
Tomoff, Kiril, 406
Tönnies, Ferdinand, 337
topical analysis, 226
Toscanini, Arturo, 192–94, 349, 393
totalitarianism, 406
Tovey, Donald Francis, 365
tradition, 28, 306–39
transgression, 160–68, 170; easing of, 178–79
trautonium, 328

Tregear, Peter, 172
Treitler, Leo, 89–90
Trial by Jury (Gilbert and Sullivan), 280
Triest, Johann Karl Friedrich, 87n49
Trilling, Lionel, 377–78
tripartition sémiotique, 157–58, 257, 273
Trollope, Anthony, 39–40
Trump, Donald J., 338
"truthiness," 185
tselostnïy analiz (holistic analysis), 418–23, 434
Tsukkerman, Victor Abramovich, 418–21, 423–25; *"Kamarinskaya" Glinki i eyo traditsii v russkoy muzïki*, 420–21
Tudor, David, 325n42
Tunbridge, Laura, 386
Twelve-tone technique, 134, 188, 210–11, 380; moral superiority of, according to Adorno, 383
Tymoczko, Dmitri, 205, 261–62

Union of Soviet Composers, 128
universalism, 303–5; German, 196–98, 363
Updike, John, 361

value judgments, 35
Vandagriff, Rachel, 11n21, 214n21
Van den Toorn, Pieter, 26, 46n14, 135n72, 211–12, 254, 259, 261–62, 270–71, 406
Van der Merwe, Peter, 127–28, 149, 184–85
Vanhal, Johann Baptist, 84
Varèse, Edgar, 247n40, 250; *Intégrales*, 250
Verein für musikalische privataufführungen, 210
verbunkos, 91
Verdi, Giuseppe: *Ballo in maschera, Un*, 151; *Otello*, 363
verisimilitude, 185
versions, problem of, 150–51
Victimae paschali laudes (Easter sequence), 67–68
Vilner Gaon, 196
vitalism, 192, 194
Völker, Franz, 53n27
Voznesensky, Andrey Andreyevich: *Goya*, 292
"vulgar sociologism," 403, 405, 434
Vulgate, 362

Wagner, Richard, 161, 182, 242, 250, 286, 304; and absolute music, 108; and *Gefühlsverständnis*, 82; in Israel, 170; and "music drama," 120. WORKS: *Lohengrin*, 52–53, 275, *Tristan und Isolde*, 120, 244

Wagner, Wieland, 53n27
Waldorf Conference *see* Cultural and Scientific Conference for World Peace
Walser, Robert, 20n40, 31–32, 160n30, 336n75
Walsh, Stephen, 48, 186, 260
Walton, William, 356
Watkins, Glenn, 181–82, 189
Webb, Herschel F., 317
Webber, Andrew Lloyd, 394
Weber, Carl Maria von: *Freischütz, Der,* 241–42
Weber, William, 80n24
Webern, Anton, 182, 186; canons in, 207; complete works, recorded by Robert Craft, 183; nationalism of, 196–97; political leanings of, 140–41. WORKS: arrangement of J. S. Bach, six-part ricercar from *Das Musikalisches Opfer,* 181, 198–99; arrangement of Schubert, *Deutsche Tänze, D820, 193;* String Quartet, op. 28, 197; *Weg zur neuen Musik, Der, 198, 207*
Weill, Kurt, 191
Weiss, Piero, 94
Wellens, Ian, 373n91
Werckmeister, Andreas, 75
Wessel, David, 268, 332
Wheelock, Gretchen A., 87n50
Whistler, James McNeill, 99, 357–58
"Whistler's Mother," 358
White, Hayden, 12, 412
Whittall, Arnold, 215, 217, 253, 260–61, 264–65, 326, 416; on *Le Marteau sans maître,* 267
Widdemer, Margaret, 352
Wiebe, Heather, 385
Wiegand, David, 61n47, 169

"Wiener Schule, die," 180–84, 194–95
Wieseltier, Leon, 9
Williams, John, 370
Williams, Sean, 327–33
Wimsatt, W. K., 270
Windgassen, Wolfgang, 53n27
Wipo of Burgunday, 67
Wolff, Christoph, 131
Wolpe, Stefan, 279
Wood, Hugh, 387
Woodmansee, Martha, 367n78
Woolf, Virginia, 351, 360, 377, 397
work-concept, 108–9, 116
Worringer, Wilhelm, 192
Wuorinen, Charles, 127, 183, 247n40, 269

Yarustovsky, Boris Mikhailovich, 431
Yates, Peter, 192
Yavorsky, Boleslav Leopol'dovich, 419
Yeats, William Butler, 119
Young, Alexander, 46

Zangwill, Nick, 28, 282–91, 294–98, 304–5
Zaslaw, Neal, 131
Zbikowski, Lawrence, 245, 254
Zeitopern, 191
Zhdanov, Andrey Alexandrovich, 57–58, 262, 412
zhdanovshchina, 57, 126, 423
Zhitomirsky, Daniyel' Vladimirovich, 423–25
Zhukovsky, Vasiliy Andreyevich, 49, 55–56
Zimmerman, Mary, 322n34
Zubillaga-Pow, Jun, 386–87
Zukofsky, Paul, 325
Zweckmäßigkeit ohne Zweck, 103, 107

Founded in 1893,
UNIVERSITY OF CALIFORNIA PRESS
publishes bold, progressive books and journals
on topics in the arts, humanities, social sciences,
and natural sciences—with a focus on social
justice issues—that inspire thought and action
among readers worldwide.

The UC PRESS FOUNDATION
raises funds to uphold the press's vital role
as an independent, nonprofit publisher, and
receives philanthropic support from a wide
range of individuals and institutions—and from
committed readers like you. To learn more, visit
ucpress.edu/supportus.

www.ingramcontent.com/pod-product-compliance
Lightning Source LLC
Chambersburg PA
CBHW031410230426
43668CB00007B/259